Everyman's book of English Verse

Everyman's
book of
English Verse

Edited by
John Wain

J M Dent & Sons Ltd
London, Melbourne and Toronto

First published 1981
Introduction and selection © J M Dent & Sons Ltd, 1981

This book is set in VIP Sabon by
D. P. Media Limited, Hitchin, Hertfordshire

Printed in Great Britain by
Richard Clay (The Chaucer Press) Ltd, Bungay, Suffolk for
J M Dent & Sons Ltd
Aldine House, Welbeck Street, London

British Library Cataloguing in Publication Data

Everyman's book of English verse.
  1. English poetry
  I. Wain, John
  821'.008   PR1174

  ISBN 0-460-04369-2

Introduction

. . . let us realize that great talent is the complement of a great soul; a great gift cannot be grafted upon a spirit that is not great in generosity.

William Soutar, *Journal*, March 1935

'It is a happy thing that there is no royal road to poetry. The world should know by now that one cannot reach Parnassus except by flying thither. Yet from time to time more men go up and either perish in its gullies fluttering *excelsior* flags or else come down again with full folios and blank countenances.' So wrote, in his Journal for 1864, Gerard Manley Hopkins, one of the finest of English poets and one of the most neglected in his lifetime. Certainly Hopkins was of their company who flew to Parnassus. He invented a new idiom, both linguistically and rhythmically separate from the manner of the admired poets of his day, and yet its newness seems to us, looking back, to be no restless itch for novelty but a profound rediscovery of ancient powers latent in English speech; just as his strenuous inventiveness seems to us true to the energy and seriousness of the Victorian age, and the delicate accuracy of his observation of natural things true to its spirit of expanding scientific inquiry. In fact, as usually happens with men of genius, it is Hopkins – in his own day seeming so painfully isolated and idiosyncratic – who in retrospect appears to be treading so harmoniously with the *Zeitgeist*, the Spirit of the Age, that he makes everyone else appear out of step.

Let us, then, in settling to enjoy a feast of English poetry, give up at the outset any notion of a formula, a set of rules to which poetry must conform, a definition even. Poetry is a vehicle for the human imagination, in its deepest workings, as that imagination has expressed itself in language. It makes use of conventions because a *con-vention*, a 'coming together', is a useful assembly-point for reader and writer. But once we have assembled and been identified, we have a right to choose the direction of our departure, and for the major poet that direction will always be towards his individual vision. Poetry is a traditional art, but its most sacred tradition is to be original.

1

One of the recurrent questions, wherever poetry is discussed or for that matter practised, is that of the poet's relationship to the world, and to the currents that sweep through the world.

Every age has its over-arching preoccupations: questions, problems, opportunities, which have been ripening in the seed-bed of history and now suddenly will wait no longer. At the end of the Middle Ages the nodal point was the breakdown of the feudal system and its replacement by money and trade. At the beginning of the modern epoch it was expansion, the outward thrust of the European nations into what they regarded as unclaimed territories, with all the results in terms of jealousy among themselves and hostility from the original inhabitants. The scientific revolution of the seventeenth century altered the pattern of men's thinking; it took two hundred years for that revolution to work itself down into a technology that altered every detail of life, so that the nineteenth century saw the upsurge of industrialism with its tension between labour and capital, between the primary producers and the developers, which has led to the political unrest of the twentieth. Standing off at a certain distance, we can see these movements in large outline, and some critics have proceeded on the assumption that the most interesting literature is that in which the patterns are most directly reflected. In its pure form this doctrine is probably too simple-minded to grasp the complexities of any art; people do not spend *all* their time thinking about the dominant issues of their epoch; they fall in love and beget children and laugh and grieve and suffer and die, in much the same ways in one historical period as in another. All the same, it is true that the large issues, the general backdrop against which life is seen, affect everyone's thinking and feeling in subtle ways. Even falling in love is somewhat different in a feudal age from what it is in an age of unrestricted movement between social classes and of easy contraception; even mourning the dead is different in a society that assumes an after-life as compared with one that does not. When we realize this we are in a position to enjoy one of the subtlest pleasures of literature, the appreciation of historical flavour; all wine is made from grapes but each has its own bouquet, and so does each period of art. Poetry is particularly successful in conveying this bouquet because it is adapted to subtle shades of meaning, but to get this pleasure we must read carefully, and in particular remember that words change their meaning in slight and subtle ways. The best companion to a reading of English poetry – in some ways the *only* companion – is the *Oxford English Dictionary*, I mean the big one in which each word is given its biography.

Meanwhile one can, with due caution, give qualified assent to the proposition that poetry, like most other things, has more power when it is going with the general thrust of the world. The *Zeitgeist* undoubtedly does exist and speaks through the arts as it speaks through everything else, from philosophy to cooking, from entertainment to agriculture. Thus, Professor W. W. Robson begins his essay, 'The Romantic Poets':

> Even after a century or so of being canonized, embalmed, and petrified in textbooks as the 'Romantic Movement,' the great outburst of English poetry at the end of the eighteenth century has still not ceased to put out vibrations of its power. For the last time, perhaps, in the history of English literature our poetry felt itself moving *with* the forces that move the world; and the

excitement of this far-off moment can still be felt in the rhythms, the imagery, the mythological creation of the great romantic poets.

(*Critical Essays*, 1966, p. 115)

Even with the safeguarding 'perhaps', one wonders whether the conjecture about 'the last time' is not unnecessarily pessimistic; surely the turmoil of the 1920s and 1930s finds total expression in all Yeats's poetry from *The Tower* onwards, while the anguished and self-questioning 1940s, when men stopped their ears against the howl of war only to hear the silence ringing inside their own heads, is reflected in Eliot's *Four Quartets*. (But perhaps an Irish poet and an American-born British subject do not fit into Mr Robson's notion of 'our poetry'.) Setting these matters aside, we must all recognize the justice of that remark about the great Romantic poets, that their work owes its energy and immediacy, in some ways, to the fact that it is 'moving *with* the forces that move the world'. But what ways?

The answer, clearly, is nothing to do with public acceptance or large, shared general attitudes. Moving with the forces that move the world did nothing to endear the Romantic poets to the world as represented by literary opinion or the book trade. If the sense of a supporting public, the confidence that one is talking to people who are listening, gives strength to a writer (and by general consent, it does), then these great poets must have been nourished from some other source. Blake, the first and in some ways the largest of the Romantic visionaries, produced his life's work in an atmosphere of total neglect. Keats suffered so much critical derision that he was popularly supposed to have been killed by it. Wordsworth finally triumphed over recalcitrant reviewers and an indifferent public, but then he was long-lived and very tough; during most of his life, he had to endure an atmosphere of hostility, misrepresentation and sheer insolence that would be unbelievable if we did not already know it to be the portion of so many major artists. As for Shelley, he of the pure lyric voice and the keenly questing intellect, on the day he was drowned in the Gulf of Spezzia there were no more than fifty people in the world who knew that he wrote poetry; his reputation was that of a political trouble-maker and headlong wife-deserter. To such a *rapport* with the world does one come if one 'moves with the forces that move it'. Only Byron became a best-seller, and the reasons are clear enough, for Byron with his simple poster-colours and broad, vigorous general effects brought Romanticism to a mass public; in the exhausted years that followed the Napoleonic Wars he stalked across Europe, scattering the seeds of a new hope and a new vision in simple, easily assimilated granules.

To think of Byron is of course to think of that other but cognate question, the relationship of the man to the hour. Is it the right hour that calls out the great man, or does the great man step forward and claim the passing hour for his own? Personally I agree with the view that the available stock of human genius stays roughly the same, and issues in achievement according to the prevailing conditions. I do not, that is, believe that men of genius arise one after another by a kind of divine accident, independent of what is happening around them. The reason why post-Renaissance Europe has had no poet as great as Shakespeare is probably that since Shakespeare's day the conditions for so gigantic an achievement in poetry have not been there. The supreme moments of art always occur when some individual is gifted enough, and lucky enough, to catch the social and historical atmosphere on some kind of rising thermal.

For instance, why is Pope's *Dunciad* so totally a masterpiece? Partly, of course, because Pope was a fine poet, with an exquisite sensibility working to shape the powerful emotional and moral impulses that beat through his frail, crippled body. But it is also clear that *The Dunciad* was composed at its own special moment. Literature, which previously had been a vocation rather than a means of making money, was suddenly ripe for commercial exploitation. In earlier times many writers, like many doctors or lawyers or clergyman, may have been mercenary in their outlook; but this mercenary spirit could not, or not directly, flow through their professional lives as writers. But now came new roads, new communications, great strides in the printing and manufacture of books, and finally the stage-coach, which could carry new books and periodicals to every corner of the country in a few days. At last the writer was face to face with a paying public, and a new type came into existence – the hack writer who produces for the market-place and whose values are those of the market-place. *The Dunciad* is accordingly erected on three pillars. The first is personal: Pope is counter-attacking enemies who have tried to take away his reputation. The second is the European literary tradition whose values and standards Pope continually evokes, as after ten years spent in translating Homer he had a right to do. The third is the new adversary, Grub Street and the penny-a-liner. A few years earlier, this balance would have been impossible; a few years later, it would have lost its novelty. A great poem was written because the right man was in the right place at the right time. Which is not to say that if Pope had not written *The Dunciad* someone else would have written it. That moment in social and literary history would have found its way into literature one way or another, but not necessarily in a major statement; what Pope contributed was his unique individuality. *The Dunciad* is a great and representative eighteenth-century work, but the fact of its being 'representative' does not make it resemble *Gulliver's Travels* or *Rasselas* or 'Holy Willie's Prayer'. The personality and gift of the individual artist is still centrally important.

To convey the spirit of an age, to dramatize its deepest issues and channel its energies, is nearly always a shared task. With the possible exception of Shakespeare, one cannot think of an English writer whose gifts and perceptions are wide-ranging enough to embody all the energies of his time. That part of the earlier eighteenth century that is not expressed in Pope is probably there in Swift or in Fielding. To take another example, if we go back four hundred years from *The Dunciad* we find an epoch, the hungry and disaster-haunted fourteenth century, in which two great English poets divide the territory between them almost as if by mutual agreement. On one side, it was, however precarious, an old, well-matured civilization; the literate men of that time could look back over three centuries of high mediaeval poetry and philosophy; in Italy, the first tremors of the Renaissance were making themselves felt within Chaucer's lifetime, but in England the fourteenth century represents the moment of poise as an incoming wave hangs before breaking. Chaucer's work, with its formal beauty, its tolerance and irony, its high courtesy of tone (broken only when the proletarian characters set about each other with pelting abuse), represents that face of the late Middle Ages; it is, for all its occasional flights of religious piety, a celebration of the values of this world; its presiding hero is the brave and gentle knight who

> never yet no vileynie ne seyd
> In al his lyf, unto no manere wight.

Langland, on the other hand, though he is a master of realistic observation, is a penitential religious visionary; the driving force of his great poem is the fear of God and the vision of blessedness. There are many debates in Chaucer's poetry, but none of them is anything like, or is intended to be anything like, the debate between Love, Peace, Justice and 'Book', as they discuss what can be the meaning of the strange light that shines on hell-mouth. (It is here, on pages 57–61.) The urgency of Langland's poetry, its haunting moral earnestness, together with the breadth of his visionary imagination, make him the only English poet to come anywhere near Dante on Dante's own ground. Chaucer, as we can see from his many references, was acquainted with Dante's work and admired it; but it was Langland – much further from Dante's urbane and lettered world, perhaps indeed never having heard of him – who had the temperamental affinity.

2

Thinking of the Middle Ages reminds one that it has been a tradition, since at any rate the seventeenth century, to place the beginning of English poetry, the *fons et origo*, at the point where mediaeval English becomes intelligible to the modern reader with no prior study, just the odd looking-up and some patience; which means, effectively, with Chaucer. Certainly Chaucer was widely influential on succeeding poets; for several generations it was usual to employ his metres and his range of subject-matter. His honorific title of 'Father of English Poetry' is therefore no oddity. On the other hand Chaucer was far from being an innovator; he is, as we have already noted, backward-looking, a late and fine flower of the long mediaeval tradition. That his example prolonged this tradition for at least another hundred years merely indicates the vitality and freshness with which he handled it. By temperament he was the kind of artist who prefers to breathe new life into well-established, even well-worn, forms rather than invent new. If against the background of fourteenth-century English poetry he appears innovative, that is because the tradition he inherits and passes on is not on the whole an English tradition. The other important poets of fourteenth-century England – William Langland, and the anonymous authors of *Pearl* and *Sir Gawain and the Green Knight* – appear more conservative than Chaucer because their line of descent is straight from Anglo-Saxon. *Gawain* was written in the North-West, a region sparsely populated and less open to cosmopolitan influences than Chaucer's London, while Langland appears to have hailed from the Herefordshire border country. Both these poets use a loosened version of the Anglo-Saxon alliterative metre, whose main procedure was to break the line into two halves with a distinct caesura or hinge in the middle, and alliterate forcibly at four points (two in each half) or three (one in one half and two in the other). By the fourteenth century, the alliterative metre had lost its early strictness, the lines had lengthened and sounded more rhetorical, and the result was a metre admirably suited to serious poetry, possibly the only form of English verse to rival the stateliness of the classical hexameter, that Homeric metre which Coleridge both described and exemplified in two brilliant lines:

> Strongly it bears us along in swelling and limitless billows,
> Nothing before and nothing behind but the sky and the ocean.

In the hands of Langland, the mediaeval alliterative metre is a wonderful instrument. And other poets, whose names have not come down to us, were equally alive to its possibilities.

But strong and full of potentiality as this verse is, it represents the last utterance before a long silence. A new music was in the air, a new measure was dancing its way over the Channel from France. Alliterative verse can be sombre, intricate, grave, tender, urgent; it cannot be epigrammatic or lyrical – at any rate as lyricism was to be interpreted in the next five centuries. People in the later fourteenth century seem to have made the assumption that a North-country poet would naturally write in alliterative verse (Northerners are always more tenacious of tradition, slower to adopt new habits) while a poet from the South, more open to new influences, would rhyme. 'Trusteth wel,' says Chaucer's parson,

> But trusteth wel, I am a Southren man,
> I kan nat geeste 'rum, ram, ruf' by lettre,

though, half inclined as the pious man is to think of poetry as an invitation to hedonism and worldliness, he is fair-minded enough to add at once,

> Ne, God woot, rym holde I but litel bettre.

Perhaps Chaucer's real innovation in English poetry, the respect in which he really *is* the father of what came after, is that he is the first poet – or at any rate the first successful, widely-read poet – to use as his staple rhythm the ten-syllable iambic line, that steady but infinitely variable beat that has been ever since his day the habitual measure of the English poet when he deals with serious subjects: whether we think of

> Tomorrow, and tomorrow, and tomorrow

or   Of man's first disobedience, and the fruit

or   The curfew tolls the knell of parting day

or   Season of mists and mellow fruitfulness

or   The woods decay, the woods decay and fall.

With all honour to the Earl of Surrey, who in the hope of finding an English equivalent for the Virgilian hexameter took to writing those ten-syllable lines without rhyme and thus gave us that 'blank verse' which is the medium of Shakespeare's plays and of *Paradise Lost* – with all honour to him, it remains Chaucer who first widely accustomed the ears of English-speakers to the iambic pentameter and thus created the rhythmic expectations that underlay our poetry for six hundred years and still underlie it, despite the curious twentieth-century pretence that poetry ought to sound like conversation. (Conversation, as a matter of fact, often does find itself using the iambic pentameter.) This being so, it is amusing that the first line of the General Prologue to the *Canterbury Tales*, the single line of Chaucer that is most often quoted and is known to virtually every literate English person, is also the most frequently misquoted in its rhythm: most people say

> Whăn thăt Ăprílle wíth hĭs shoúrĕs sótĕ,

making a trisyllable of 'Aprille', whereas in fact it should be

> Whắn thăt Áprĭlle wíth hĭs shoúrĕs sótĕ,

starting on a heavy syllable, inverting the first iambic foot, and ignoring the redundant 'e' in 'Aprille'; thus demonstrating at the very outset that monotony, the enemy of the iambic line, is an enemy easily enough defeated.

We can see, with hindsight, that the ten-syllable, five-stress line was going to sweep all before it. In the fourteenth century that could not have been so obvious; a reader, or writer, of poetry put his money where his tastes and habits had become preferences, and two hundred years later the matter was still not entirely settled. The sixteenth century saw many interesting metrical experiments, virtually all of them derived from Latin practice, as was natural in an age when every educated person read that language and when the humanists had urged the claims of classical Latin, even more than Greek, as the basis for a whole new European civilization. Edmund Spenser, in his youth in touch with humanistic circles and a friend of the fertile and inventive critic Gabriel Harvey, was an ambitious experimenter with metre and diction, but none of his work is more completely successful, more triumphant on its own terms, than the exquisite short poem 'Iambicum Trimetrum' which will be found on page 114. Here as elsewhere, the search was evidently for a line that should be longer than ten syllables while not sagging or sprawling.

Many poets have found that ten syllables give too little elbow-room, especially in meditative verse or lofty narrative; but the French alexandrine of twelve syllables does not really work in English – it breaks up too easily into two sixes, and begins to sound jog-trot – and the fourteener sounds merely thumping, like a rabbit signalling with its hind feet.

While remaining basically faithful to the ten-syllable iambic, English poetry has returned often to the quest for a viable long line; Arthur Hugh Clough, in Victorian times, made the important break-through of discovering that the Latin hexameter, when written as nearly as possible in English, is actually a conversational metre, giving familiar and ironic effects rather than epic; and in our own century Robert Bridges composed his stately *Testament of Beauty* (1930) in a twelve-syllable iambic deliberately loosened. More recently still, W. H. Auden showed a willingness to learn from alliterative verse, and in later years, was drawn more and more to Latin-based metres. So the poet's search goes on, a search for freedom within the shaping and directing framework of art, which guides and concentrates. To have no art at all, to observe no conventions, may yield a short-term advantage in immediacy, but it will never sustain ambitious work; for, as Robert Frost remarked, 'Writing poetry without metre is like playing tennis without a net.'

3

And this selection? It is an act of homage, an utterance of thanksgiving for the richness and beauty of English poetry, a tribute from an English writer to the great tradition that buoys him up. I have felt free to depart from what seems to be the standard anthological diagram: the most celebrated gems are here, the universally known standards round which any selection must be built, and so is a mass of lesser-known verse (in many cases, I think with perhaps foolish pride, virtually *un*known), including the anonymous, the scurrilous, the randy and the rollicking.

I have also given due weight to the fact that certain important developments in poetry have been introduced first by the English in the guise of jokes and games, and later made a more solemn second appearance in continental European literature where they were expounded *au grand sérieux* and given names ending in -ism. The Victorian nonsense poets, for example, anticipated many of the procedures of Surrealism; Edward Lear, with his dream-imagery and his devastating use of irrational but powerful associative jumps, seems to me an important modern poet – which doesn't mean that one has to read him with a relentlessly straight face.

Other differences from the standard anthologies will be obvious enough. I have not shrunk from taking bits out of long poems. A long poem, by definition, has features that cannot be represented in an anthology – narrative sweep, amplitude, effects that enforce themselves by repetition – but the greatest long poems have short passages of supreme beauty and memorability to which one returns again and again to get that particular flavour, so that in the end these short passages take on identity in one's mind as separate poems, and I have tried to give a sampling of these. In the same spirit, I have included a few of the greatest speeches from Shakespeare's plays. Shakespeare is, out of sight, our best poet, and his best work is in the plays. To represent him, as anthologists generally (and understandably) do, by his non-dramatic work only is to show him as a fine poet among fine poets, but not as the colossus he actually is. Of course no selection can represent Shakespeare as a dramatist – and I recollect, suddenly, that W. H. Auden and Norman Holmes Pearson, in their five-volume *Poets of the English Language*, solved the problem of Shakespeare by simply printing *Antony and Cleopatra* in its entirety – but the high moments of a Shakespeare play, even when shorn of their supporting dramatic framework, are so obviously the best things in English poetry that I am simply not going to send this book to the printer without them.

But perhaps the most glaring difference between this anthology and its respected predecessors is that instead of beginning with the sixteenth century, or at the earliest with Chaucer, we begin with a sampling of Anglo-Saxon verse. Since Anglo-Saxon is unintelligible to a modern person who has not formally set out to learn it, this involves the use of translations. To push back the frontier so far might seem extreme or even perverse; after all, the Anglo-Saxons displaced the Ancient Britons, who already had a poetic tradition in their own Celtic tongue; why not translate some of that, if our aim is to represent all the poetry that has been written in this land? The answer is that the living tradition of Celtic poetry is still there on our western flank, as a visit to any *Eisteddfod* will show; we are concerned here with the English tradition, which was fully developed already in the ninth century and gave us masterpiece after masterpiece. The achievement of the Anglo-Saxons is slowly coming to be valued at its true worth; they had certainly a finer civilization than that of the Normans who in an unlucky hour ousted them by a combination of luck and aggressiveness; the Anglo-Saxon poet was as fine a craftsman, and as clearly uttered the innermost thoughts of his people, as the Anglo-Saxon goldsmith or stone-mason. If we begin the story of English poetry with Chaucer, that gives a history of six centuries; in fact, we had six centuries of achievement before Chaucer was born.

If I seem to you too dogmatic in my assertion of the claims of Anglo-Saxon, blame my education in the Oxford of thirty-five years ago. My tutor, C. S. Lewis, was firmly convinced that Anglo-Saxon poetry was the essential key to what followed. He saw in it a melancholy, a yearning, a turning away from *nuance* and irony in favour of emphasis and gravity, that appeared to him characteristic of the English poetic mind whenever that mind is serious rather than playful. To him, anyone who had not made acquaintance with this Englishness at the very beginning of our tradition would go endlessly wrong in trying to account for it later.

'This mere Englishness,' he says (in *Rehabilitations*, 1939) 'is usually called Romanticism by those who do not know Anglo-Saxon. They are fond of tracing it to the French Revolution or even to the Celtic strain in our blood. They bring far-fetched explanations why the English wrote melancholy poems about ruins in the eighteenth century, not knowing that they had begun to do so in the eighth.'

And in another essay in the same book Lewis returns to the theme: 'The tap-root, Anglo-Saxon, can never be abandoned. The man who does not know it remains all his life a child among real English students.' (Does that mean that most university English departments nowadays are largely staffed by men and women who must always remain children in the presence of real scholars of English? Be careful. The answer may be Yes.)

One of Lewis's reasons for insisting that we go back and start from Anglo-Saxon was that, 'There we find the speech-rhythms that we use every day made the basis of metre.' This is surely so. It is perhaps not too much of a simplification to say that all poetry is a blend of the speaking voice and the singing voice, with the proportions weighted now on one side, now on the other. When the new measures arrived from France, the singing voice became dominant in that great lyrical outburst which takes us from the anonymous mediaeval lyricists through Campion and Peele to Ben Jonson. What Anglo-Saxon verse does so well is to make poetry out of the speaking voice, out of the natural sound of English voices talking to one another: not casually, but gravely and strongly.

Gavin Bone, whose interesting essays in translation appeared posthumously in the mid-1940s, gives an impartial view of the matter, a scholar's view and a practitioner's:

> After all, we have, as some writers tell us, the same fundamental language as the Anglo-Saxons, though theirs was apparently so different from ours. We have the same bold accents, landing with extraordinary fury on fixed points; but we have not now the same pure lingering sonorous vowels for the accents to fall upon. We have lost a number of the thick or splashy consonants, and we have added a number of little words nowadays, that patter along contentedly and get in the way or do their best to ensure that majesty and naturalness shall never in future join together in poetry. Long sonorous vowels and clashing consonants give the original alliterative effect, but we must never forget that this effect cannot be captured in modern English.
>
> (*Anglo-Saxon Poetry*, 1943, p. 13)

Perhaps not; Bone is very firm in his opinion, nor is he alone in it; Mr Richard Hamer, an Oxford don of a later generation than Bone's, whose parallel-text translations of short and medium-length Anglo-Saxon poems (in *A Choice of Anglo-Saxon Verse*, 1970) are so effective and helpful, also gives it as his belief that 'an attempt to produce verse similar in form to the Old English is doomed to failure as the structure of the language is now fundamentally different'.

One hesitates, always, to disagree with a professional; but this seems to me one of those matters in which a layman has the right to an opinion. Of course Anglo-Saxon (or, as for polemical reasons it is called at Oxford, Old English) was an inflected language, and of course the case-endings gradually disappeared as the language ceased to be spoken in its classic form, their work being taken over by prepositions and auxiliary verbs; so that, as Mr Hamer himself says, 'the verse gradually evolved to longer and more flowing lines to be found at their best in fourteenth-century poems such as *Sir Gawain and the Green Knight* and *Piers Plowman*'. That tightness and solidity can never come back, but nevertheless English still falls on the ear as a succession of light and heavy syllables, and it still lends itself very naturally to alliteration; a pair of lines like Shakespeare's

> When to the sessions of sweet silent thought
> I summon up remembrance of things past,

though it is written to an iambic rhythm, still comes down strongly on *sessions* and *things past*, still alliterates naturally, linking the lines together with the echoing s's and th's. If we unpick the iambic measure, and group the lines with four heavy syllables, two in each half, the result is – not, indeed, classic Anglo-Saxon metre, but a recognizable descendant of it, without being as flowing and free as the line of *Piers Plowman* or *Gawain*; thus:

> When to the sessions / of sweet thought-silence
> of things past / I summon remembrance.

Above all, any modern version must give the reader some notion of what Anglo-Saxon poetry *sounded* like; and surely it would not be wise to brush aside Lewis's view that the 'speech-rhythms' we find in Anglo-Saxon are the ones 'we use every day'. Rhymed verse, such as Bone himself – disastrously, I must think – employed for *Beowulf*, or iambic blank verse like Mr Hamer's, simply give no impression of the original, and if we are not doing that, there is no point in merely carrying over the paraphrasable content. That, essentially, is the argument in favour of Ezra Pound's translation of 'The Seafarer', which appeared in about 1912 and has afforded amusement for scholars ever since; it is, indeed, full of gross blunders, but it has rhythmic vitality and it *sounds* like an Anglo-Saxon poem; anyone who had read and responded to it was to that extent already prepared for the impact of G. M. Hopkins, whose poems, written in the last thirty years of the nineteenth century, were at last published in 1918 and showed, once and for all, what could be done even in modern English to bring out the music of the speaking voice:

> Now no matter, child, the name:
> Sorrow's springs are the same.
> Nor mouth had, no nor mind, expressed
> What heart heard of, ghost guessed:
> It is the blight man was born for,
> It is Margaret you mourn for.

And Hopkins had studied Anglo-Saxon as he had studied Latin and Greek. Nor does the influence show any sign of dying out. John Heath-Stubbs, writing almost a century after Hopkins and half a century after Pound's 'Seafarer', has made admirable use of alliterative verse in the narrative section of his long poem *Artorius*.

Holding these views, I had no choice but to begin this selection of English poetry with some pages of translated Anglo-Saxon. These pages do not aim at anything like a fair representation of the range of that poetry. The Anglo-Saxons went in for long poems, and there is nothing here from *Beowulf* or *Exodus*; but then neither are there any of the Riddles, many of them brilliant short poems with a surprisingly modern ring. My choice has, in this area, been guided solely by personal preference: the essential thing, it seemed to me, was to have, at the beginning of the book, an unmistakable Anglo-Saxon presence.

After we leave Anglo-Saxon and get into mediaeval English, which is reasonably accessible to the modern reader who has goodwill and only needs help with obsolete words, my policy has been to leave the text mainly as it stands and offer help marginally, rather than attempt an adaptation which would inevitably turn the poetry into something else. Nevill Coghill's adroit and scholarly modern translations of Chaucer, originally undertaken for the radio, are deservedly successful, yet even he cannot help making Chaucer into something else; and for the purposes of a book like this we need Chaucer as he is, not as he would be if a modern Englishman had written his poems for him. *Piers Plowman*, too, is widely known in modern translation, but I have preferred to use the text of the Everyman edition in which Carl Schmidt, himself a poet, has very sensitively worked over Langland's verse, offering essential help but tampering as little as possible.

This leads on to the next consideration: the modernization of spelling and punctuation in language otherwise familiar. Sharp-eyed readers will soon notice an element of inconsistency here. Broadly speaking, mediaeval English has been altered as little as possible: no amount of modernization would make it seem anything but mediaeval, and this is part of its charm and interest. Hard words have been glossed in the margin, the obsolete þ has been replaced by modern 'th', but the mediaeval flavour has been left intact. When modern English arrives and the poems begin to be intelligible at sight, spelling and punctuation have in general been brought into line with modern practice. After about 1645 the need for this diminishes, and by the later years of the seventeenth century unmodernized texts should, in my opinion, no longer cause the reader any difficulty.

It seems to me, in brief, that the modern reader's need for a re-spelt and re-punctuated text is at its greatest in the case of the major Elizabethan writers, Shakespeare in particular. There are two reasons for this. The first is that modernization of Shakespeare's spelling is in itself a deeply-rooted tradition. His work has always been part of the mainstream of English life, always read by people of all kinds; it has been of actual, immediate interest, never merely antiquarian, and each succeeding generation has printed Shakespeare according to the conventions of its own day. This is so strongly rooted that there seems, to most people, something odd and even offensive about an 'original-spelling' version of Shakespeare; he belongs to 'us', the generality of readers, not to 'them', the professors and researchers, however grateful we are to these same professors and researchers for sorting out the dreadful tangles which abound in Shakespeare's texts in their untreated form. Even scholarly editions, like the Arden and the New Cambridge, which set out to serve the needs of the student, still present the text in modern spelling, as if to do anything else would be somehow an offence against nature.

If, therefore, we follow this tradition and present Shakespeare in modern spelling, then Marlowe and Donne and Ben Jonson are going to look very strange and somewhat quaint if they appear beside him 'tricked in antique ruff and bonnet'. (Spenser, whose deliberately archaic language is part of the special atmosphere of *The Faerie Queene*, is of course another matter.)

Shakespeare, then, is the prime mover in dictating this policy of modernization; but there is also my second reason, which is this. The vagaries of spelling, the sheer riot of individual preference, are a sixteenth-century phenomenon. An Elizabethan gentleman did not consider that there was a right and a wrong way of spelling a word: he simply spelt everything as he thought best. Printers, too, plumped out or thinned their lines to fit the shape of the page by using more or fewer letters at will; so that sixteenth-century books abound in fantastic spelling such as 'with' spelt 'wyththe', purely to take up more room. This genial go-as-you-please approach to spelling I personally would enjoy and I regret its demise; but it could not stand up to modern pressures, especially since we read more quickly if we read with the eye and not the ear, and modern people (for some reason) always want to read quickly.

The Civil War, with its vast requirements of propaganda and counter-propaganda, turned the English into a nation of pamphleteers and the printing-press into a weapon. Apprentices had to be trained quickly; there was no time for a lad to indulge in his own lexicographical vagaries. Spelling norms were imposed, not by anyone's decree but by the demands of practice.

The divide, in our book, runs neatly between Shakespeare and Milton. Though Milton was born in the lifetime of Shakespeare, he lived into a totally changed England. Also, where Shakespeare (we may reasonably surmise) would be primarily concerned with how his lines *sounded* rather than looked, Milton as a scholar poet, with a keen sense of etymology, would have his own strong views on spelling. The spelling of *Paradise Lost* evidently conforms to a system and is often an essential key as to how the poem should be read. Blind though he was, Milton would keep his amanuenses in line on such matters. It seemed reasonable to give the extracts from *Paradise Lost* (1667) in Milton's own spelling, and to extend this principle back to include the author's earlier poems gathered in the exquisite volume of 1645. Shakespeare and his contemporaries, then, are modernized. Milton is unmodernized. And from about 1645 onward, the matter recedes into the background in any case.

Still on the subject of those features of this book that might come to some readers as a surprise, I should mention that two of the most familiar poems in English appear in these pages in a somewhat less than familiar form. They are Thomas Gray's 'Elegy Written in a Country Churchyard' and S. T. Coleridge's *The Ancient Mariner*.

In the case of Gray's poem, I have been for many years convinced that the poet's first thoughts were better than his later ones. The earliest version of the 'Elegy' is found in the manuscript now preserved at Eton, where Gray went to school; this manuscript belonged to William Mason, Gray's close friend and literary executor, and in a written note Mason described it as the 'Original copy of the Elegy in a Country Churchyard'. The date when this great poem was first written has never been established despite much scholarly investigation; Mason, who had the best chance of knowing, thought it was 'begun, if not concluded' about 1742, though it did not see print till 1751. All we can know is that at one stage the poem in its first form, that in which it appears in this book, seemed to Gray good enough, and complete enough, to be copied out and (presumably) given to Mason. It is simpler and more direct than the later, and standard, version; it consists of the first eighteen stanzas of the poem as generally printed, followed by four stanzas which Gray later removed, keeping a few images and a few turns of phrase which he built into the much more elaborate and sententious structure. Essentially, in this early form, the 'Elegy' consists of a meditation on the village dead, who after so many years of arduous and necessary work have taken their humble joys and sorrows with them into the ground; and then four stanzas in which the personality of the poet himself makes an oblique and hesitant appearance. The result seems to me quite perfect, embodying all those qualities that have made a classic of the longer version, while avoiding the touches of pomposity and artificiality. The late Wyndham Ketton-Cremer, who had an eye and ear for all that is finest in eighteenth-century literature and art, gave it as his opinion that this first version was 'a perfect artistic whole, completely harmonious in form and content alike'; and I rejoice to concur with this uncommon reader. Nor is there anything daringly innovative in printing the 'Elegy' in its earlier form; Mason printed this version in his edition of Gray's poems in 1775, and there must always have been readers who preferred it.

To turn to *The Ancient Mariner*: Coleridge of course wrote this poem as part of his memorable collaboration with Wordsworth in *Lyrical Ballads* (1798). The aim of the two poets was to start from opposite points and meet in middle ground, that ground being the sense of wonder and a reverence for the strange miracle of life. As Coleridge remembered it later, in his *Biographia Literaria*:

... it was agreed that my endeavours should be directed to persons and characters supernatural, or at least romantic; yet so as to transfer from our inward nature a human interest and a semblance of truth sufficient to procure for these shadows of imagination that willing suspension of disbelief for the moment, which constitutes poetic faith. Mr Wordsworth, on the other hand, was to propose himself as his object, to give the charm of novelty to things of every day, and to excite a feeling analogous to the supernatural, by awakening the mind's attention from the lethargy of custom, and directing it to the loveliness and the wonders of the world before us.

In this aim the poets were completely successful; their book is one of the most fortunate examples of literary collaboration – perhaps, in English, *the* most fortunate. To achieve it, they adopted contrasting literary strategies. Both were writing ballads, but they were writing different kinds of ballad. When, in the later eighteenth century, folk art of every kind began to attract the attention of critics and scholars, and the collectors went out into the field, traditional ballads were copied down in huge numbers and given to the public in such collections as Bishop Percy's *Reliques of Ancient English Poetry*. What the public enjoyed about such ballads was their quaintness, their air of primitive antiquity, their 'romantic' flavour; Percy, in fact, prettified his ballads here and there to bring them more in line with his picturesque notion of the Middle Ages. (The real Middle Ages were not romantic enough for the age that built ruins and grottos to give mysterious beauty to a landscape.) That generation of readers enjoyed the archaic language of the ballads, and their taste was reflected in concoctions like Chatterton's 'Rowley' poems (a series of poems, actually of considerable imaginative power, which the luckless youth passed off as the newly-discovered work of a mediaeval writer named Rowley).

To this tradition does *The Ancient Mariner*, in its first version of 1798, belong. Mediaeval romance abounds in giants and monsters, the miraculous and the mysterious, and as Coleridge's aim was to 'body forth the forms of things unknown', he naturally used the kind of language made familiar by collections such as Percy's.

Wordsworth, for his part, was writing in the tradition of the street ballad and the chapbook. He used, for his everyday narratives, the familiar, popular style in which the ballad had actually survived, with no help from the official literary culture. It is this difference in aim that accounts for the endearingly absurd mediaeval paraphernalia of Coleridge's ballad, the amateurish attempts at mediaeval English, the tushery and gadzookery. He revised the poem continually for the rest of his life; there were altered versions in 1800, 1805, 1817, and finally in the posthumous *Collected Poems* of 1834. But by far the most important of these re-writings is that of 1800, done for the second edition of *Lyrical Ballads* and usually reprinted since. Here, the language is modernized and the mediaeval trappings largely thrown aside.

Not only this. Coleridge in the crucial revision, that between 1798 and 1800, made a change in the actual story-line of the poem. The 1800 and subsequent versions offer a different account of what happened when the ship, crewed by the dead men and aided by the miraculous breeze, enters the harbour at the end of its voyage. The Mariner, with the curse still heavy upon him, is fixed in dread of the corpses who cluster on the deck and pierce him with their unforgiving 'stony eyes'. This is reinforced by the famous dread-simile of the man walking the lonely road and not daring to turn his head. Then comes the healing breeze, and soon the Mariner is overcome with joy at the sight of the familiar harbour, the lighthouse, the hill, the kirk. There follows a wonderful visionary description of the dark-red shadows that rise from the moon-white, unrippled water of the harbour. Everything is bathed in a 'red and smoky light', so that the Mariner's own flesh looks red to him; then, with a fresh access of horror, he sees that the bodies have gathered before the mast and each one is holding up its stiff right arm:

> And each right arm burnt like a torch,
>   A torch that's borne upright.
> Their stony eye-balls glitter'd on
>   In the red and smoky light.

The Mariner prays – from which we gather that the curse is beginning to be lifted from him – and once more the poem tells us that the sea was bathed in white light and that the red shadows emerged from this whiteness; the repetition has the effect of a dream, in which a wave of peace is succeeded by a wave of agitation; when he next turns to look on deck, he sees that the corpses are lying prostrate, and that an angel stands beside each one. The power of the curse is broken; the angels, who have (one gathers) motivated the bodies of the seamen to bring the vessel home safely and give the Mariner another chance at life so that he can begin his penance, now appear in their own forms, as a sign that he has gained a measure of forgiveness. This moment passes, the angels disappear, and the corpses once more stand upright, but the vision has been vouchsafed and the Mariner is ready for penance. The next thing he hears is the plash of the oars as the pilot-boat comes out to take him off, and

>   it was a joy
> The dead men could not blast.

They have lost their power over him.

This passage seems to me magnificent; in keeping with the central vision of the poem, mysterious as a dream is mysterious, but speaking to the mind as forcefully; while in its hypnotic visual quality it links Coleridge the poet with the great visionary painters of the Romantic era, with Fuseli and Blake and Palmer. Now turn to the later version (it is not given here, but it is the version usually anthologized and usually given in selections of Coleridge's poetry). This likewise begins with dread of the dead men and with the famous simile; but when the ship enters the calm white light, the red shadows appear only once – we do not go from white light to red and then back to white and to red again; the unforgettable scene with its 'red and smoky light' and the stony eyeballs of the dead men is brought before our eyes much less strongly; and the dead men holding up their torch-like right arms, and the Mariner seeing his own flesh as having a red hue, are both left out. Since Coleridge thus (in my opinion) weakened the poem at a crucial point, the balance was effectively tipped in favour of using the earlier version, archaisms and all.

4

It is impossible to love the soul of Poetry without loving her body, and every reader who has ever felt deeply the strength and beauty of this supreme form of literary art, and responded joyously, has been willing – more than willing, eager and prompt – to pay attention to matters of form. It is a pity, I suppose, that we mostly make acquaintance with the devices used by poets, the shapes and sizes of poem, the patterns of rhyme and metre, in books written by grammarians and analysers and cataloguers generally, for whom all such matters come under the heading of 'Prosody', a horrible word if ever there was one. But of course forms like the ode and the sonnet, the couplet, the various stanza forms, blank verse, *terza rima*, the *canzone*, the villanelle and the sestina, were not invented by grammarians and pedagogues; they were invented by poets, who found them invaluable sources of aid and stimulus. A verse form is not a hindrance, nor a meaningless obligation that poets impose on themselves; it is a launching-pad, or a frame for the picture, or a vessel for wine to be poured into, whichever metaphor you prefer. A form imparts character to the matter that is expressed through it. When some anonymous genius invented the limerick (was it Edward Lear? no one seems to be sure) he guided comic (and unrespectable) verse into a channel it has run in ever since. The forms, as much as individual works, have their existence and their destiny, they appear to die and then come to life again, they are echoed from one poet to another, sometimes across a gap of centuries. One of Yeats's finest poems is the long and moving elegy to his patron's son, killed in the First World War, 'In Memory of Major Robert Gregory'. It has an unusual stanza form, very beautiful and dignified and, one would have said, very Yeatsian; it sounds like the kind of form Yeats would have invented for his own special requirements, especially as he went on to use it again later in a poem with an entirely different flavour, the visionary 'Byzantium'. But if we look back some two and a half centuries we shall find that metre and rhyme-scheme used, also in a lament for a dead friend who was a pattern of many skills and virtues, in Abraham Cowley's 'On the Death of Mr William Hervey'. Cowley is a poet who nowadays has few readers; he had a tremendous reputation in his own day and for a while afterwards, but we have it on the authority of Pope ('who now reads Cowley?') that he was already dropping out of sight before the middle of the eighteenth century; he continued for a few more decades to be a 'name', and Dr Johnson's celebrated critique of 'Metaphysical Poetry' is in fact a digression in his *Life of Cowley*, anchored to him rather than to Donne or Vaughan or Marvell where a modern critic would have sited it. The elegy on Hervey in fact recalls us to a sense of Cowley's stature; it is stately, grave, moving, and the measured organ music of the stanza form he uses here, and which to the best of my knowledge was his own invention, shows a wonderful sense of rhythm and cadence.

Poets are fascinated by form because form is a condition of life as well as of art. When molecules come together to form a living body they do so in forms; an acorn does not grow into a beech-tree, nor a sparrow's egg hatch into a newt. All artists, and poets among the rest, have a deep instinct to shape their words and thoughts into form, whether or not their conscious minds register what they are doing in detail. Did Matthew Arnold, one wonders, plan, or just instinctively come up with, that circular movement that brings the end of 'The Scholar-Gipsy' round again to the beginning? The poem begins with the image of the shepherd, preparing for departure, untying the light portable sheep-cotes used in the farming of that day. It ends with the Syrian trader, reluctantly moving deeper and deeper into the unknown world as the bustling Greeks take over the centres of trading civilization, landing on the inhospitable coast of Britain, and on the beach untying his bundles. Both are emblems of that retreat from the noisy, restless, uprooting forces of 'progress' of which the Scholar-Gipsy himself (who 'came to Oxford and his friends not more') is the great central symbol; what links them is not merely this notional relationship but the small, telling physical detail, the image of untying. Arnold may, of course, have blue-printed this effect from the beginning; but it is the kind of thing that poets usually do by instinct.

'But surely all that preoccupation with form belongs to the past? Surely it went out of the window when poetry became "modern"? Does any poet now use the traditional forms, any more than any composer writes preludes like Bach's or symphonies like Beethoven's?' The question, which usually comes up in some such form when poetry (or any art) is discussed in a modern context, needs to be answered at a level below the superficial. Modern composers don't, it is true, try to reproduce what Bach and Beethoven have already done perfectly; but they take a creative interest in form nevertheless, and contain their music in a shape which usually bears some relation to a shape they have met elsewhere, either in the European musical tradition or in Eastern or African music, or in jazz. They range over the vast field of music that is available to them in performance or on record, until they find something that helps them with what they want to say, as Yeats ranged over the centuries of poetry till he found that stanza-form of Cowley's.

Free verse, too, is a form; it has produced memorable poems, in which we feel ourselves to be listening to the actual voice of someone speaking from the centre of a human situation, and it has established its own tradition. There are times when an experience demands to be presented in its raw immediacy, as a flickering news-film from a hand-held camera can be moving in a way denied to a carefully studied painting that is framed and hung on the wall. The one has the immediacy of life, the other has the distilled power of art: and it is legitimate that some artists should aim at the raw, unframed immediacy (though it would be naïve to suppose that their work costs them any less effort, or goes through fewer stages of revision, than the work of artists who aim at the final, meditated statement).

On the other hand, the poet who tries to do without the traditional aids of form and procedure is playing a dangerous game. If he is to lift his work above the level of day-to-day comment, of journalism, advertising, entertainment or even the give-and-take of conversation, he must do it by a special intensity: and he must have a superb, even arrogant confidence that this intensity, *by itself*, will make his work as meaningful and memorable as poetry needs to be. When this strategy succeeds, it does so very well. Eliot's free verse is highly charged with intelligence and emotion. (Though it is interesting, when one looks through his work from end to end, to find how often Eliot employed strict forms of metre and rhyme.) So is the early verse of Ezra Pound, though there are vast stretches of boredom in the later Cantos. D. H. Lawrence is perhaps the best example of a poet who used a totally free verse, aiming at conversational immediacy; and while Lawrence can be stunningly effective in the single poem, the effect of reading him in bulk is ultimately stupefying, like being pinned in a corner by a brilliant talker. By contrast, a poet like Yeats can be read in bulk without any sense of weariness, not only because of the power of his vision, but because the artistry of his verse is beguiling and uplifting; and what is true of Yeats is true, at their varying levels, of Auden, Dylan Thomas, Graves, Empson, Larkin, Peter Levi or Seamus Heaney.

The great merit of free verse is that it can sound spontaneous, and it would be foolish to undervalue spontaneity as an important literary virtue. (Or rather, to be more precise, the *appearance* of spontaneity, since there is no external means of telling whether a piece of writing was in fact produced spontaneously or laboured over.) Ever since the late eighteenth century, sincerity and spontaneity (seen as opposed to conventionality and artifice) have been highly valued, as when Wordsworth called poetry 'the spontaneous overflow of powerful feelings'. What we are seeing in our century is partly a natural development of this tradition; anything that sounds like rhetoric and lofty style is avoided, very much as modern television actors try to sound and look like ordinary people in ordinary situations, where the old tragedians never tried to sound ordinary. All this is legitimate, and interesting work can come out of it, though it can never be enough by itself, can never satisfy the hunger of the spirit when confronted with the supreme demands of life at a point of crisis. Jackson Pollock produced some interesting paintings by riding a bicycle over the canvas, but when we really need sustenance, when we want art to come to the rescue of life or to celebrate those moments when life seems a miracle, we are more likely to turn to Rembrandt or Titian or Monet.

At its feebler end, what we are witnessing nowadays is the cult of spontaneity in decline, at the point where its noble ideals are lost in deliquescence. This is especially true when the cult of spontaneity meets that of egalitarianism, producing the strange notion that art not only is not, but *ought* not to be, the product of unusual gifts and unusual dedication. Nobody imagines that a first-division football match would be just as interesting if the real players retired to the dressing-room while twenty-two spectators, selected at random, kicked the ball about, taking no notice of the referee. Yet when a similar doctrine is applied to the arts, it can find adherents. Ordinary human feeling, powered by no exceptional gift and backed by no resources of knowledge or application, is felt to be enough to make a poet. What is sad about this notion is not that it exists and is widely held (experience, after all, shows that there is no opinion, however foolish, that is not held by someone, and usually by quite a lot of someones), but that it spoils budding talent. Many young poets who might have developed interestingly have remained mediocre because they have been told that the way to write poetry is to scribble down anything that comes into their head, and then refuse to revise or refine it; and that anyone who doesn't like the result is (blessed, thought-economizing word) 'élitist'.

Am I exaggerating? Unfortunately, no. Take for example a book published just as I write this, a collection of work by five feminist poets; I will not give its name because I do not want to hand it a free advertisement, but I assure you it exists and that I have it. In the preface, jointly expressing the views of all the contributors, we read: 'Standards are irrelevant to us, a bogey . . . We should be suspicious of the élitism implied in them.'

To be fair, it is true that the authors go on to say 'we already have standards, we revise our own poems, we criticise each other's work, we think we might not be "good" enough . . . It's liberalism to pretend we don't.'

So perhaps, in spite of the defensive quotation marks round 'good', there is hope after all, and those of us who do believe in objective standards can still take our bearings from Chaucer's line,

> The lyf so short, the craft so long to lerne.

The thrust towards populism, the uneasy suspicion that what everyone can't do no one ought to do, is of course partly political. But it is also, I think, an episode in literary history; it illustrates a swing of the pendulum. Thirty years ago, orthodox opinion held that poetry, if it had any pretensions to being 'modern' and up-to-date, should be difficult to understand. How many minor poets of the 1930s and 1940s found it gleefully easy to obey *that* directive, if no other! This appetite for difficulty was partly itself the product of a reaction; the great poets of the nineteenth century, certainly those such as Tennyson and Victor Hugo who commanded a large public, tended to express themselves with a certain noble obviousness. The French Symbolistes, who first put it across that one didn't need to understand what a poem was *about* in order to enjoy it ('de la musique avant toute chose', etc. etc.) were followed in English by the school presided over by Pound and Eliot, and the most powerful shove in the direction of hermetic obscurity of expression was given by the enormous popularity of *The Waste Land* and such critical pronouncements as Eliot's essay 'The Metaphysical Poets' (1920), in which he gives it as his opinion that the modern world is so complex that to make poetry out of it requires complex thought-processes on the part of both writer and reader.

This movement has now followed all previous -isms and theories, from neo-classicism to Symbolism, into the inevitable grave. Not that one would dispute for a moment that poetry sometimes needs to express itself with a subtlety, and a complexity, that most of us will find difficult. But there are, it seems to me, two kinds of difficulty in poetry. There is the poem that is difficult to construe from one line to the next, where the obscurity is in the actual phrasing, where the utterance is cryptic in the short term though perhaps the ideas in it are not difficult once one has straightened them out. (Poems of this kind are not necessarily pretentious and bad; as someone said, 'What is the use of a present that isn't wrapped up?') Then there is the poem whose sense, from one phrase to the next, is perfectly clear; the difficulty is one of interpretation. To this category many (most, even?) of the finest poems in any language belong, since 'the truth is rarely pure and never simple'. As an instant example, take Christina Rossetti's 'Goblin Market'. This poem, which is highly charged with imagination and highly individual, is perfectly 'clear' – until one stands back from it and attempts an interpretation of what it 'means'. I must confess straight away that although I greatly admire the poem, I cannot explain it. Quite evidently it is an allegory; but the allegory slips away when one tries to interpret it on a one-to-one basis of correspondences, as one can do with *Piers Plowman*, or *A Pilgrim's Progress*, or a modern allegory like *Animal Farm*. I take it to be saying something about female sexuality and the loss, and perhaps recovery, of innocence; but what? Yet its difficulty does not strike me as being due to any muddle in the poet's mind, but to my own impercipience; or perhaps to the complexity of human experience itself.

Do not, therefore, talk to me of 'difficult' poetry as if it were an invention of our own century. There are other kinds of difficulty than that of the crossword puzzle.

5

Now that the chips are down and I have made my selection, I stand off and look at it with feelings of exaltation and awe: not, obviously, at anything I have done by merely making a selection, but at the richness, power and beauty of the material itself. Perhaps the most satisfying thing of all is the awareness, that breaks over me as I read through it, of how faithfully these poets have reflected, down through the centuries, the character and moods of the English people, their thoughts and impulses and ideals and disillusions. It is so complete, so honest and rich, this self-portrait of a nation through the medium of its poetry. Here we see the inhabitants of this island, from the cross-gartered Anglo-Saxons to our gadget-ridden generation, as they actually have been and are: stubborn, kindly, individual; deeply imaginative, each one with a headful of dreams and impossible longings, yet also practical, empirical, inventive; gossipy, political, fond of buying and selling; humorous and melancholy either by turns or simultaneously; pleasure-loving, fond of food and drink, curious about sex, yet also profoundly religious, so that in these pages we see, in continual alternation, the body chasing after its delights and the soul humbly offering itself to God. And perhaps in the end the two can be reconciled, for 'I am come that they may have life, and have it more abundantly.'

In saying that the poets have succeeded so conspicuously in rendering the English mentality I am not forgetting the great success of other literary forms such as fiction and the theatre. But the novel is a newcomer, with a history of only two hundred and fifty years; it is as if this book should begin on about page 300. The theatre, too, has limitations; in Jacobean times it was a vehicle for great poetry, and indeed our greatest poet was not only a playwright but an actor, manager, shareholder, a man of the theatre to his fingertips; yet, since that blaze died down, the theatre has not been quite a central means of expression for the English imagination. If one compares English literature with, say, French, in which the drama is a central backbone running all the way through, one sees that the English genius is not really in the theatre; it is lyrical and reflective rather than dramatic; we tend to have our plays written for us by Irishmen, by Goldsmith and Wilde and Shaw and Synge and O'Casey and Samuel Beckett and Brendan Behan. Yeats, too, the greatest poet the English-speaking people have had in the last hundred years, is essentially a dramatic writer, though perhaps less so in his formal compositions for the stage than in the inherently dramatic nature of everything he wrote.

Why this pre-eminence of poetry? Can we assign any reason for the fact that it is the poets who have spoken, and continue to speak, so clearly and truthfully for the life of our people, to catch every mood and every thought? One possible answer lies in the nature of the imagination itself. To most of us, whether we are using the word formally or in some casual context, 'Imagination' is the power to escape from the cell of one's own personality; it is that part of our mind which voyages outside us, and when it voyages it goes towards other people, catching their vibrations and steering by their flashes of light.

All art does this, of course, but poetry is such a pure art, so little burdened with discourse, so little welded into a tight structure of plot or thesis, that the poet works very close to the central core of life, very close to dream and intuition and impulse, which is also the reason why poets go mad or have mental breakdowns more than other kinds of writer; their work is hazardous, like that of certain kinds of scientific worker who are exposed to radiation:

> We Poets in our youth begin in gladness;
> But thereof come in the end despondency and madness.

The impulse to write a poem, as poet after poet has testified, comes not from the directing intelligence but from something deeper, more mysterious, which the intellect can thwart but cannot command; which is why, if we did not have the metaphor of the Muse, we would have to have something just like it. Consider for instance, the testimony of T. S. Eliot:

> What you start from is nothing so definite as an emotion, in any ordinary sense; it is still more certainly not an idea; it is – to adapt two lines of Beddoes to a different meaning – a
>
> *bodiless childful of life in the gloom*
> *Crying with frog voice 'what shall I be?'*
>
> I agree with Gottfried Benn, and I would go a little further. In a poem which is neither didactic nor narrative, and not animated by any other social purpose, the poet may be concerned, solely with expressing in verse – using all his resources of words, with their history, their connotations, their music – this obscure impulse. He does not know what he has to say until he has said it; and in the effort to say it he is not concerned with making other people understand anything. He is not concerned, at this stage, with other people at all: only with finding the right words or, anyhow, the least wrong words. He is not concerned whether anybody else will ever listen to them or not, or whether anybody else will ever understand them if he does. He is oppressed by a burden which he must bring to birth in order to obtain relief. Or, to change the figure of speech, he is haunted by a demon, a demon against which he feels powerless, because in its first manifestation it has no face, no name, nothing; and the words, the poem he makes, are a kind of form of exorcism of this demon. In other words again, he is going to all that trouble, not in order to communicate with anyone, but to gain relief from acute discomfort; and when the words are finally arranged in the right way – or in what he comes to accept as the best arrangement he can find – he may experience a moment of exhaustion, of appeasement, of absolution, and of something very near annihilation, which is in itself indescribable. And then he can say to the poem: 'Go away! Find a place for yourself in a book – and don't expect *me* to take any further interest in you.'
>
> (*Of Poetry and Poets*, 1957, p. 98)

In that mood of 'something very near annihilation', what is annihilated is the defining and restricting outline of the poet's own personality, the frontiers that mark him off from humanity generally. The impulse that is thrusting towards expression, driving him mad with its demand to be embodied and set free, is the divinely-implanted lust to be at one with other living beings and with life itself. And perhaps here we come in sight of a solution to that puzzle arising from Professor Robson's words, 'moving with the forces that move the world', because to be united with other living beings involves a flowing in the same direction: not at a vogue level of day-to-day chatter and ephemeral fashion, but at a deep level; in Blake's wonderful metaphor, the sunflower 'counts the steps of the sun', and the sun is always shining at a changed angle so that the flower turns its eager face.

It is Blake, too, who will give us our closing metaphor. All of us who are alive try to be more and more alive, not to let experience flow over us as if we were cold stones on a river-bed being slowly smoothed but not modified: we want to participate, to enter fully into the abundance of life, to respond to the beauty of the earth, the cyclical drama of the seasons, the living tapestry of history, the complexity of human beings and of the natural world. Though we fall short of it every day, fall short through habit and fatigue and frustration and the limitations of our own intelligence, this remains our aim, and in pursuing it we have two great allies. One is our relationships; we are never more fully ourselves than when we forget our own nature in the joy and absorption of exploring another person's; the other is the arts, the complex of devices by which man has pushed to the limit his exploration of the world he has been given to live in, and his own role in it. Poetry, among these arts, occupies a queenly position. Since so much of our exploration of life is through words and images, the vivid freshness that poetry brings to us, its continual shock of recognition, keys up our responses and moves us nearer to a fruitful relationship with life. It can rescue us from dailiness and show us the miracle of existence through washed eyes.

That is its role in our more fortunate hours, when we are granted the energy and positiveness to reach out for fullness of experience and not flinch from the price it can often exact. But for everyone there are phases of lassitude, discouragement, disillusion, self-condemnation. And to these hours, also, poetry can minister. The poet's vision can be a challenge to action, an incitement to the stirring of the bones; but it can also be the solace of the times when we know we have failed, those times when the benison of the poet falls on us as a healing fantasy, a rescuing wish-fulfilment in a world that so often leaves us beaten and robbed, 'the lost traveller's dream under the hill'.

1981   John Wain

This anthology is for Eirian

Anglo-Saxon

1   ## Cædmon's Hymn
[7th Century]

Praise we the Lord
of Heaven's kingdom,
God's might and His wisdom.
Father of glory,
Lord everlasting,
wonders has He made.
First He built
for the children of earth
heaven as their roof:
guardian of mankind,
He created this world, our home,
the Lord everlasting,
Almighty God.

Trans. Sally Purcell

2   ## Deor

Among snake-patterned swords Weland tasted sorrow
noble in mind he knew misery
yearning and loss he lived alongside
winter-cold wandering: woe he found
when Nithhad cramped him with well-contrived
fetters for his sinews, the finer man.
That passed. So may this of mine.

To Beadohild the death of her brother even
was not so pitiful as her own plight
when beyond doubt she was driven
to know herself with child: never cheerfully
could she abide the thought of that birth-bringing.
That passed. So may this of mine.

We have heard how Meathhild's heart-grief
Geat's wife, grew beyond measuring:
love's sorrow stole from her all sleep.
That passed. So may this of mine.

Theodoric held down through thirty winters
the town of the Mearings: many marked it.
That passed. So may this of mine.

We know the evil name of Eormanric
he of wolf's mind, who worked his will
on Gothic ground. That was a grim king.
Many a man endured misery
inured to woe, hoping always
that his dominion might be dashed down.
That passed. So may this of mine.

The rueful man robbed of joy's rites
abides in darkness: doom, he decides,
wills that his end be woe forever.
But let him think all through this world
wise God chooses to bring unceasing change:
to many a man he shows mercy
assured success: and to some, sorrow.
That passed. So may this of mine.

I will speak now of my own state:
honoured beforetime as bard of the Heodenings,
dear to my lord. They called me Deor.
For many winters it was well with me
in my lord's loyalty, until lately
Heorrenda skilful in song was steaded
with the land my lord allotted me.
That passed. So may this of mine.

Trans. J.W.

3   *The Ruin*

A Fragment

Curious is this stonework! The Fates destroyed it;
The torn buildings falter: moulders the work of giants.
The roofs are tipped down, the turrets turn over,
The barred gate is broken, white lies on mortar
The frost, and open stands the arching, cumber of lumber
Eaten under with age. Earth has the Lord-Builders;
The dust holds them while a thousand
Generations are ended.
Lichen-gray, pink shining, this wall lasts out
Empire and empire again, stands long under storms
Steep, deep, – only to fall!
The foundations with clamps were marvellously fitted together
By some brave man. . . .
Bright were the palaces, baths were set in the palaces,
Gables high assembled, there was the press of people,

Many a hall to sup the mead, so rich with joys for men,
Till time when Fate the strong rescinded that!
    For then they shrank as pestilence came,
Pest took their strong pride. As for their towers,
Their prime fortress was waste foundations,
And men who could restore it in a multitude fell down.
So these courts stand lonesome still – red vaulting, and that roof
With its curved frame that sheds tiles – drop, stop, drop –
Where many a warrior once, glad-heart, gold-bright,
Well-fed, wine-protected, in display of armour,
Could look on treasure, on silver, on subtle skill-knit gems,
On wealth, on worth, on coloured coats, on pearls,
On a bright city in a broad kingdom!
    Stone courtyards stood there, and a stream threw hot
Its wide repulse of water; a wall went round about
Where the baths sit, with bosom bright,
Hot in the midst – facilitable enough!

                    [. . .]

They let hot streams lapse over blocks of grey,
Circle-tanks . . . hot . . .
Where the baths were . . . It is an admirable thing!

                                    Trans. Gavin Bone

4   *The Dream of the Cross*

            I would tell a marvellous vision
            that I dreamed at dead of night,
            when speech-gifted men were sleeping.
            I thought I saw the wondrous tree
            moving on high and wrapped in light,
            the most shining cross. All that glowing sign was
            streaming with gold; gems were set
            beautiful at its foot,
            five
            were on the cross-beam.
            All the angels of the Lord beheld it,
            they who were created fair;
            it was no evil-doer's gallows.
            And the holy spirits looked on it,
            men of earth looked on it.
            And all the great creation looked on it.
            Glorious was the cross of victory, and
            I
            stained with sin
            and wounded with iniquities.

I
saw the tree of glory
shine, adorned with banners of joy
and decked with gold; the jewels
fittingly covered the cross of the Lord.
Still I could see through the gold
its unhappy former conflict, when it began
to bleed on its right-hand side. I was filled with grief;
I was frightened
before so lovely a vision. I saw that moving beacon
change its appearance and colour; now it was wet with blood,
now adorned with treasure.

(*The cross speaks*: –)
'That was long ago – I still remember it –
when I was hewn down at the edge of the forest,
and separated from my trunk. There strange enemies laid hands on me,
there they made me a show to be stared at, made me bear the bodies
   of criminals;
men bore me on their shoulders, and set me on a hill,
and there my enemies rooted me right
firmly. I saw the Lord of mankind
in his great courage hasten to climb upon me.
I dared not disobey the Master's word
by bending or breaking, though I saw
the surface of the earth shake; I could have
beaten down all his enemies, but I stood firm.

They stripped the young Hero that was God Almighty,
He mounted the high cross,
courageous, a vision to many, that he might redeem mankind.
I trembled as that Man embraced me; yet I dared not bend earthwards
nor fall to the ground; I had to stand firm.
I the Cross was raised; aloft I held the powerful King,
the Lord of Heaven;
I dared not bow down.
They pierced me with dark nails; on me can be seen the scars,
open malicious wounds; I dared not harm one of them.
They mocked us both together. I was all flowing with blood
pouring from that Man's side, when he had sent his spirit on before.
On that hill I endured many
cruel fated torments; I saw the God of hosts
stretched in torture; darkness
covered with a cloud the Lord's body,
bright radiance. A shadow came forth,
dark below the cloud. All creation wept,
bewailed the King's fall; Christ Cradled on the Cross.
Yet there came eager ones from afar
to the Lord King; all this I saw.

I grieved, yet I bowed down to these men's hands
humbly, with a great effort. There they took Almighty God,
lifted him from that grievous torment; the warriors left me
standing covered in blood. I was all wounded by the nails.

They laid him down weary of limb, they stood by his head;
there they beheld the Lord of heaven, and he rested there a while
exhausted after that great struggle. The men began to build him a tomb
in the sight of his murderer; they carved it of shining stone
and there they laid the lord of victory. They began to sing the dirge for
   him,
sad-hearted, at eventide, then they returned
sorrowful from that great King; he remained there alone.
Yet I stood there dripping with blood a good while
until the voice of the warriors died away.
The corpse,
the soul's fair dwelling, grew stiff and cold. Then men cut me down
to earth — that was a fateful fall.
They buried me in a deep hole. Yet there the Lord's thanes,
his friends, found me out; they raised me from the earth,
decked me with gold and silver.

Now you may hear, my dear one,
that I suffered the pain of evils
and sore grief. Now is come the time
when far and wide men worship me
on earth and all the great creation,
praying to me — a symbol. On me God's Man
suffered a while: therefore now I tower
glorious under heaven, and have power to heal
whoever within him feels awe before me.
Long ago I was a cruel punishment
most hateful to men, before I opened the true way of life
to those who know to live.

The Ruler of heaven honoured me
above the trees of the wood
just as he honoured his mother Mary
above all woman kind.
Now I bid you, my dear one,
to relate this vision to men:
that for mankind's many sins
for Adam's deed of old
Almighty God suffered
Died and Rose
Through the cross
Of glory.'

Trans. Sally Purcell

5

The Seafarer

My purpose is to tell my own true tale,
to find words for my wanderings, how I in work-days
endured harsh times. Bitter troubles
in my heart's hold I have had to bear:
felt care clutch at my keel often.
The waves' chaos has many times caught me
in the ship's prow as she in peril
drove on to rocks. Ravenous cold
grasped my feet, fettered in frost's
cold chains: but the churning cares
were hot to my heart, and inmost hunger
stabbed at my tired mind.
                              Amid soft safety
the man in the land's lap will never learn
how I suffered storm-season and ice-cold sea
far from the soothing of friendly siblings.
Icicles hung from me. Hail came showering.
I heard no sound but the sea's smash,
the freezing swell. Sometimes the swan's voice
gave me a gladness: the gannet's language
or curlew's cry were my only carolling:
I knew no mead-hall, only the mew's call.

On stone cliffs the storms came crashing,
their only answer the icy-feathered
tern's whistle, and the wild shriek
of the horn-beaked eagle. No kin of my hearth
was near to comfort my needy spirit.
Ah, little he knows, who has lived
safe from such hell-journeys, in land's shelter
pouring wine, proud, how on sea-paths
I, weary, have watched and waited.

Night came down in darkness, north-snow driving,
frost gripped the earth, hail hit the ground
hardest of corn. Yet my heart cries out,
my heart that rules me, that the rearing waves,
salt water's tumult, I should try for myself.
Without cease my spirit spurs me:
hunger of mind keeps me homeless,
seeking far places and foreign people.

Yet there is none above ground so great-hearted,
so ready with gifts, so reckless with youth,
so lion-brave, by his lord so loved,
as to tempt the sea-tracks and never tremble
at what harms the Most High may send him.

That man has no mind for fine rings or harp-music,
worldly wishes, or the joy of women:
his thought is of naught but the wave's thrashing.

The woods are in blossom, towns grow brighter,
the fields fairer, earth's pulse faster,
and it all serves only to stir the striving
mind to movement, in him who means
to venture far across the flood-ways.
Likewise the cuckoo, with unlucky voice,
welcomes summer but warns of sorrow
bitter in breast's hold.
                Blissful he knows not,
the secure man, what some must suffer
on homeless roads who roam the farthest.
Even now my soul strays from my breast's stowage,
my spirit flies over the flood-fields,
wide-wandering in the whale's kingdom,
in earth's far reaches – then to me returns
greedy and hankering. The helpless heart
is called by the winging bird to the whale's way,
the immense waters. But the Almighty's
delights draw me more than this death-in-life,
brief loan of breath. I have no belief
that the good things of earth can be eternal.

Three things threaten every man's thoughts,
keep him in doubt till his doom's day:
illness, age or the sword's edge:
for every wayfarer, one of them waits.
For that reason, the rightest repute
for any hero, the highest hearsay,
is the love of the living. Before he leaves
this earth, he should earn, in spite of enemies,
the fair fame of fighting the devil,
that the sons of men should commend him
and his bright blazon be among the blessed
for a life without limit, eternity's largeness,
great among the graced.
                Days grow shorter,
earth's pride palls, lordship is poorer.
No kings come now, nor conquering Caesars,
no gold-givers like those who are gone:
those among whom were the mightiest marvels
and who lived in their fame as a fearless fellowship.
Those dauntless are departed, their glory dimmed:
weaker men walk the earth now, and wield power:
their having is a heaviness.

Fame is hushed,
the world's dignity withers up and drivels
as comes to every man now over middle-earth:
age presses on him, his face grows pale,
white-haired, he sorrows for his henchmen,
sons of greatness given to the ground.
His garment of flesh, as life goes from it,
loses sweetness, relish and suffering-shock,
neither his hand nor his brain can hold a burden.
And though for his born brother he will bury
treasure in the tomb, strew the grave with gold,
various riches, to rig fair his voyage,
yet if the departed soul was sin-darkened
no gold will keep off the grimness of God,
though he had deftly deceived those he dwelt among.

Great is the Maker's awe, it moves the earth,
which He fastened on a firm anchorage:
the reaches of land and the sky's rim.
A fool has no God-fear; unready death finds him,
but heaven's grace homes in to the humble-hearted:
the Father fixes such minds on a foundation of faith.
A man must rule himself with a strong heart, and steadily,
his word be trusted, his ways clean.
Every man must have dealings meetly
with friend and with foe, . . . disaster . . .
though he shall be tested with hell's own fires . . .*
and the friend he has found shall in the flames
of a pyre be powdered: Fate is more powerful,
the All-Mover mightier than a man's wishes!

Now let our hearts think where is their true home
and take counsel how we can come there,
and labour also that we may be allowed
to be in the abode of blessedness,
the right place for life, in God's love's realm,
amid heaven's hopes.
Now thank we the Holy One
that he, the world's Prince, put a price on us:
for all time, the Lord eternal.

AMEN

Trans. J.W.

* The manuscript is defective at this point.

6   *The Whale*

To explain the nature of fishes in craft of verse –
And first, the Great Whale. A grim purpose is his;
Mariners often find him against their will
Floating on eternal ocean.
His name is Fastitocolon,
His coat is like rough stone,
Like a huge sea-knot of wrack, ringed with sand-dunes,
That floats by the shore.
    Now when wave-borne men trust their eyes for an island,
And moor their high-beaked ships to the fraudy shore,
Tether their sea-horses at the brink of ocean
And roam up the island to explore:
While the keels lie at the tide-mark
The tired sailors make their camp,
They wake a fire on the island,
Happy are the men, and tired – glad to encamp.
But he is crafty and treacherous; when he feels
The travellers properly planted and set
Taking the pretty weather –
                                        Instantly down
Darts the oceanic animal,
And locks drowning in the hall of death
Both ships and souls!

Trans. Gavin Bone

Mediaeval Lyrics, Anonymous

7   *Sing cuccu nu! Sing cuccu!*
                     Sing cuccu! Sing cuccu nu!

Sumer is icumen in,
    Lhudè sing cuccu;
Groweth sed and bloweth med
    And springth the wodè nu.
        Sing cuccu!
Awè bleteth after lomb,
    Lhouth after calvè cu;   *Loweth*
Bulluc sterteth, buckè verteth;   *breaks wind*
    Murie sing cuccu.
        Cuccu, cuccu,
Wel singès thu, cuccu,
Ne swik thu naver nu.   *cease*

8 *Inordinate Love*

I shall say what inordinat love is:
The furiositè and wodness of minde,   *madness*
A instinguible brenning fawting blis,   *burning*
A gret hungre, insaciat to finde,
A dowcet ille, a ivell swetness blinde,   *dulcet*
A right wonderfulle, sugred, swete errour,
Withoute labour rest, contrary to kinde,   *nature*
Or withoute quiete to have huge labour.

9   This endris night   *other*
           I saw a sight,
               A star as bright as day;
               And ever among
               A maiden song
                  'Lullay, by-by, lullay.'

           That lovely lady sat and song
               And to her child can say:
           'My son, my broder, my fader dere,
               Why liest thou thus in hay?
               My swetè brid,   *child*
               Thus it is be-tid,
                  Though thou be King verrày;
               But nevertheles
               I will not ces
                  To sing "By-by, lullay".'

           The child then spak in his talking
               And to his moder said:
           'I be kidde for Heven-King   *proclaimed*
               In crib though I be laid.
               For aungeles bright
               Don to me light –
                  Thou knowest it is no nay –
               And of that sight
               Thou mayst be light   *glad*
                  To sing "By-by, lullay".'

           'Now sweet son, sin thou art King,   *since*
               Why art thou laid in stall?
           Why n'ere ordainèd thy bedding
               In some gret kingès hall?
               Me thinkth it is right
               That king or knight
                  Shuld ly in good aray;

And then among
　　It were no wrong
　　　　To sing "By-by, lullay".'

'Mary, moder, I am thy child,
　　Though I be laid in stall;
Lordes and dukes shal worship me,
　　And so shall kingès all.
　　　　Ye shall well see
　　　　That kingès three
　　　　　　Shal come the twelfthè day.
　　　　For this behest
　　　　Give me thy brest,
　　　　　　And sing "By-by, lullay".'

'Now tell me, sweet son, I thee pray –
　　Thou art me leve and dere –
How shuld I kepe thee to thy pay   *liking*
　　And make thee glad of chere?
　　　　For all thy will
　　　　I wold fulfill,
　　　　　　Thou wotst full well in fay;   *truth*
　　　　And for all this
　　　　I will thee kis
　　　　　　And sing "By-by, lullay".'

'My dere moder, when time it be,
　　Thou take me up on loft,   *aloft*
And set me right upon thy knee
　　And handel me full soft;
　　　　And in thy arm
　　　　Thou hill me warm   *cover up*
　　　　　　And kepe me night and day;
　　　　If I wepe
　　　　And may not slepe,
　　　　　　Then sing "By-by, lullay".'

'Now, sweet son, sin it is so,
　　That all thing is at thy will,
I pray thee grauntè me a bon,   *favour*
　　If it be both right and skill: *reasonable*
　　　　That child or man
　　　　That wil or can
　　　　　　Be mery upon my day,
　　　　To blis hem bring,
　　　　And I shal sing
　　　　　　"Lullay, by-by, lullay".'

10   *Lully, lulley, lully, lulley;*
    The faucon hath born my mak away.   *mate*

He bare him up, he bare him down,
He bare him into an orchard brown.

In that orchard there was an hall,
That was hanged with purpel and pall.

And in that hall there was a bed;
It was hanged with gold so red.

And in that bed there lieth a knight,
His woundès bleeding day and night.

By that bedes side there kneeleth a may,   *maid*
And she weepeth both night and day.

And by that bedes side there standeth a ston,
'Corpus Christi' writen ther-on.

11   *Draw me nere, draw me nere,*   *nearer*
    Draw me nere, the joly juggelère.

Here-beside dwelleth a rich barons doughter;
She wold have no man that for her love had sought her,
    So nice she was;
She wold have no man that was made of mold,
But if he had a mouth of gold to kiss her when she wold,
    So dangerous she was.   *haughty, conscious of power*

Therof herd a joly juggeler that laid was on the green,
And at this ladys wordes y-wis he had grete teen –   *indeed; fury*
    An-angred he was.
He juggeled to him a well good steede of an old hors-bone,
A sadel and a bridel both, and set himself theron –
    A juggler he was.

He priked and pransed both before that ladys gate;   *rode*
She wend he had been an angel was com for her sake –   *supposed*
    A prikker he was;
He priked and pransed before that ladys bowr;
She wend he had been an angel comen from heven-towr –
    A pranser he was.

Four and twenty knightes led him into the hall,
And as many squires his hors to the stall
    And gave him mete;

They gave him otes and also hay;
He was an old shrew and held his hed away,   *rascal*
  He wold not ete.

The day began to passe, the night began to com;
To bedde was brought the faire gentilwomàn
  And the juggler alsò.
The night began to passe, the day began to spring;
All the birdes of her bowr they began to sing,
  And the cukoo alsò.

'Wher be ye, my mery maidens, that ye cum not me to?
The joly windows of my bowr look that you undo,
  That I may see;
For I have in myn armes a duk or els an erle.'
But when she looked him upon, he was a blere-eyed cherle.
  'Alas!', said she.

She led him to an hill, and hanged shuld he be;
He juggeled himself to a mele-poke, the dust fell in her ee;   *meal-bag*
  Begiled she was.
God and our Lady and swete Saint Johàn
Send every giglot of this town such another lemmàn   *strumpet; lover*
  Even as he was.

12   I have been a foster long and many day;   *forester*
          My lockès been hore.
       I shall hang up my horn by the grene wode spray;
          Foster will I be no more.

       All the whiles that I may my bowe bende
          Shall I weddè no wife.
       I shall bigge me a bowr at the wodès ende,
          There to lede my life.

13   The cricket and the greshope wenten hem to fight,   *grasshopper*
      With helme and haburjone all redy dight;
      The flee bare the baner as a doughty knight;
      The cherubud trumped with all his might.   *beetle*

      The hare sete upon the hill and chappind her shone, *fastened; shoes*
      And swere by the knappes which were ther-upon   *buttons*
      That she would not rise ne gon
      Till she see twenty houndes and a won.

The milner sete upon the hill,   *miller*
And all the hennes of the town drew him till.
The milner said: 'Shew, henne, shew!
I may not shake my bagge for you.'

14   Tutivillus, the devil of hell,
            He writeth her names, sooth to tell,   *their*
                Ad missam garulantes.

            Bet were be at home for ay
            Than here to serve the devil to pay,
                Sic vana famulantes.

            These women that sitteth the church about,
            They beeth al of the deviles rout,   *liking*
                Divina impedientes.

            But they be stil, he wil hem quell,
            With kene crokes draw hem to hell,   *sharp crooks*
                Ad puteum multum flentes.

            For His love that you dere bought
            Hold you stil and jangel nought,
                Sed prece deponentes.

            The blis of heven then may ye win.
            God bring us al to His in
                'Amen, amen' dicentes!

15   Januar: By this fire I warme my handes,
            Februar: And with my spade I delfe my landes.
            Marche: Here I sette my thinge to springe,
            Aprile: And here I heer the fowlès singe.
            Maii: I am as light as birde in bow,   *merry*
            Junii: And I weede my corne well ynow.
            Julii: With my sithe my mede I mowe,
            Auguste: And here I shere my corne full lowe.
            September: With my flail I erne my bred,
            October: And here I sowe my whete so red.
            November: At Martinesmasse I kille my swine,
            December: And at Cristesmasse I drinke red wine.

16   *Singe we alle and say we thus:*
        'Gramercy, myn owèn purs!'

When I have in myn purs ynow,
I may have bothe hors and plow,
And alsò frendes ynow,
    Through the vertu of myn purs.

When myn purs ginneth to slak,
And ther is nought in my pak,
They wil sayn: 'Go, fare wel, Jak!
    Thou shalt none more drinke with us.'

Thus is al myn good y-lorn
And myn purs al to-torn;
I may play me with an horn
    In the stede al of myn purs.   *Instead*

Fare wel hors, and fare wel cow;
Fare wel cart, and far wel plow.
As I played me with a bow
    I said: 'God, what is al this?'

17   Lenten is come with love to towne,
        With blosmen and with briddès rowne,   *birdsong*
            That al this blissè bringeth:
        Dayèsèyès in thes dales,
        Notès swete of nightègales –
            Ech fowl song singeth.
        The threstelcok him threteth o,   *threatens without ceasing*
        Away is herè winter wo,
            When wodèrovè springeth.   *woodruff*
        Thes fowlès singeth ferly fele,   *strangely many*
        And wliteth on here winnè wele,
            That al the wodè ringeth.

        The rosè raileth hirè rode,   *shows; redness*
        The levès on the lightè wode   *bright*
            Waxen al with wille.
        The moonè mandeth hirè blee,
        The lillie is lofsom to see,
            The fenil and the fille.   *thyme*
        Wowès thesè wildè drakès;
        Milès murgeth herè makès,   *gladden their mates*
            As strem that striketh stille.   *runs silently*
        Mody meneth, so doth mo –
        Ich'ot ich am one of tho
            For love that likès ille.

The moonė mandeth hirė light;   *sheds*
So doth the seemly sunnė bright,
   When briddės singeth breme.   *gloriously*
Dewės donketh the downes;
Deerės with here dernė rownes,
   Domės for to deme;
Wormės woweth under cloude;   *underground*
Wimmen waxeth wonder proude –
   So wel it wil hem seme.
If me shal wantė wille of on,
This winnė wele I wil forgon,
   And wight in wode be fleme.

18   Whenne mine eynen misteth
        And mine eren sisseth
        And my nose coldeth
        And my tunge foldeth   *fails*
        And my rude slaketh   *colour fades*
        And mine lippes blaketh
        And my mouth grenneth   *gapes*
        And my spotel renneth   *spittle runs*
        And myn her riseth   *hair*
        And myn herte griseth
        And mine handen bivieth   *tremble*
        And mine feet stivieth   *stiffen*
        Al to late, al to late,
        Whenne the bere is at the gate!
        Thenne I shal flit
        From bedde to flore,
        From flore to here,   *hair (? shroud)*
        From here to bere,
        From bere to pit,
        And the pit fordit.   *will shut*
        Thenne lith myn hous uppe myn nese: *lies*
        Of al this world ne give ich a pese!   *pea*

19   Where beeth they biforen us weren,
        Houndės ladden and havekės beren,   *led; hawks*
         And hadden feeld and wode?
        The richė levedies in here bour,   *ladies*
        That werėden gold in here tressour,   *head-dress*
         With here brightė rode,   *complexion*

Eten and drunken and maden hem glad;
Here lif was al with gamen y-lad;   *led*
  Men knelèden hem biforen.
They beren hem wel swithè heye,   *very proudly*
And in a twinkling of an eye
  Here soulès weren forloren.   *lost*

Where is that lawing and that song,   *laughing*
That trailing and that proudè yong,   *gait*
  Tho havekes and tho houndes?   *Those*
Al that joy is went away;
That wele is comen to waylaway,   *happiness; wailing*
  To manye hardè stoundes.   *times*

Here paradis hy nomen here,   *they took*
And now they lien in helle y-fere;   *together*
  That fire it brennès evere.
Long is ay and long is o,   *always; ever*
Long is way and long is wo;   *misery*
  Thennes ne cometh they nevere.

Dreghy here, man, then, if thou wilt,   *Endure*
A litel pine that me thee bit;   *may*
  Withdraw thine eises ofte.   *comforts*
Thegh thy pinè be unrede,
And thou thenke on thy mede,   *reward*
  It shal thee thinken softe.

If that feend, that foulè thing,
Through wikkè roun, through fals egging,   *bad advice*
  Nethere thee haveth y-cast,   *down*
Up! and be good chaunpioun;
Stand, ne fall na more adown
  For a litel blast.

Thou tak the roodè to thy staf,   *cross as*
And thenk on Him that there-on yaf   *gave*
  His lif that was so leef.   *dear*
He it yaf for thee; thou yeeld it Him;
Ayein His fo that staf thou nim,   *Against; take*
  And wrek Him of that theef.   *avenge; on*

Maiden moder, hevene-queen,
Thou might and canst and owest to been
  Oure sheeld ayein the fende.
Help us sinnè for to fleen,
That we moten thy Sone y-seen   *may*
  In joye withouten ende.

20
> *Deo gracias, Anglia,*
> *Redde pro victoria.*

Our King went forth to Normandy
With grace and might of chivalry;
Ther God for him wrought mervelusly;
Wherfore England may call and cry
    'Deo gracias'.

He sette a sege, the sooth for to say,
To Harflu town with ryal aray;
That town he wan and made afray
That Fraunce shal rewe til domèsday:
    Deo gracias.

Then went our King with alle his host
Thorough Fraunce, for all the Frenshè bost;
He spared no drede of lest ne most
Til he come to Agincourt cost:
    Deo gracias.

Then, forsooth, that knight comely
In Agincourt feeld he faught manly.
Thorough grace of God most mighty
He had both the feeld and the victory:
    Deo gracias.

There dukes and erles, lord and baròne
Were take and slain, and that wel sone;
And sume were ledde into Lundòne
With joy and merth and gret renone:
    Deo gracias.

Now gracious God He save our King,
His peple, and alle his wel-willing;
Yef him good life and good ending,
That we with merth mowe savely sing
    'Deo gracias'.

21
> I sing of a maiden
>   That is makèles;   *without compare*
> King of alle kingès
>   To her son she ches.   *chose*
> He cam also stillè
>   Ther His moder was,
> As dew in Aprìlle
>   That falleth on the gras.

He cam also stillè
  To His moderes bowr,
As dew in Aprìlle
  That falleth on the flowr.
He cam also stillè
  Ther His moder lay,
As dew in Aprìlle
  That falleth on the spray.
Moder and maiden
  Was never none but she;
Wel may swich a lady
  Godès moder be.

22

I have a yong suster
  Fer beyonden see,
Many be the drouryes   *keepsakes*
  That she sentè me.

She sentè me the cherye
  Withouten any stone,
And so she did the dove
  Withouten any bone.

She sentè me the brere   *briar*
  Withouten any rind;
She bad me love my lemman
  Withoutè longing,

How shuld any cherye
  Be withoutè stone?
And how shuld any dove
  Been withoutè bone?

How shuld any brere
  Been withoutè rind?
How shuld I love myn lemman
  Withoutè longing?

When the cherye was a flowr
  Then hadde it non stone.
When the dovè was an ey   *egg*
  Then hadde it non bone.

When the brerè was onbred   *not germinated*
  Then hadde it non rind.
When the maiden hath that she loveth
  She is without longing.

23

I have a gentil cok   *fine*
  Croweth me day;
He doth me risen erly
  My matins for to say.

I have a gentil cok,
  Comen he is of gret;   *a great family*
His comb is of red corèl,
  His tail is of jet.

I have a gentil cok,
  Comen he is of kinde;   *noble blood*
His comb is of red corèl,
  His tail is of inde.   *indigo*

His leggès been of asur,
  So gentil and so smale;
His sporès arn of silver white   *spurs*
  Into the wortèwale.   *down to the root*

His eynen arn of cristal
  Loken al in aumber;   *set*
And every night he percheth him
  In myn ladyes chaumber.

24

Bring us in good ale, and bring us in good ale;
For our blessèd Lady sake bring us in good ale!

Bring us in no browne bred, for that is made of brane,
Nor bring us in no white bred, for therein is no gane,
  But bring us in good ale!

Bring us in no befe, for there is many bones,
But bring us in good ale, for that goth downe at ones,
  And bring us in good ale!

Bring us in no bacon, for that is passing fate,
But bring us in good ale, and gife us enough of that;
  And bring us in good ale!

Bring us in no mutton, for that is often lene,
Nor bring us in no tripes, for they be seldom clene,
  But bring us in good ale!

Bring us in no egges, for there are many schelles,
But bring us in good ale, and gife us nothing elles;
  And bring us in good ale!

Bring us in no butter, for therein are many heres,
Nor bring us in no pigges flesch, for that will makes us bores,
     But bring us in good ale!

Bring us in no podinges, for therein is all Godes good,
Nor bring us in no venesen, for that is not for our blod;
     But bring us in good ale!

Bring us in no capons flesch, for that is ofte dere,
Nor bring us in no dokes flesch, for they slober in the mere, *ducks*
     But bring us in good ale!

25   *To a Nun*

                  after the 15th Century Welsh

     Please God, forsake your water and dry bread
     And fling the bitter cress you eat aside.
     Put by your rosary. In Mary's name
     Leave chanting creeds to mildewing monks in Rome.
     Spring is at work in woodlands bright with sun;
     Springtime's not made for living like a nun.
     Your faith, my fairest lady, your religion
     Show but a single face of love's medallion.
     Slip on this ring and this green gown, these laces;
     The wood is furnitured with resting-places.
     Hide in the birch-tree's shade – upon your knees
     Murmur the mass of cuckoos, litanies
     Of spring's green foliage. There's no sacrilege
     If we find heaven here against the hedge.
     Remember Ovid's book and Ovid's truth:
     There's such a thing as having too much faith.
     Let us discover the shapes, the earthly signs
     Of our true selves, our souls, among the vines.
     For surely God and all his saints above,
     High in their other heaven, pardon love.

                              Trans. John Ormond

26   From *Pearl*

Perle, plesaunte to prynces paye
To clanly clos in golde so clere: *set flawlessly*
Oute of oryent, I hardyly saye,
Ne proved I never her precios pere.
So rounde, so reken in uche araye,   *radiant; every setting*
So smal, so smothe her sydes were,
Quere-so-ever I jugged gemmes gaye,   *wherever; judged*
I sette hyr sengeley in synglere.   *never found her equal*
Allas! I leste hyr in on erbere;   *lost; a garden*
Thurgh gresse to grounde hit fro me yot.   *grass; went*
I dewyne, fordolked of luf-daungere
                    pine away; wounded by the power of love
Of that pryvy perle wythouten spot.

Sythen in that spote hit fro me sprange,   *since; place*
Ofte haf I wayted, wyschande that wele,
That wont was whyle devoyde my wrange   *drive away my sorrow*
And heven my happe and al my hele.
That dos bot thrych my hert thrange,
My breste in bale bot bolne and bele.
Yet thoght me never so swete a sange
As stylle stounde let to me stele.
For sothe ther fleten to me fele,
To thenke hir color so clad in clot.
O moul, thou marres a myry juele,
My privy perle wythouten spotte.

That spot of spyses mot nedes sprede,
Ther such ryches to rot is runne:
Blomes blayke and blwe and rede   *yellow*
Ther schynes ful schyr agayn the sunne.   *brightly*
Flor and fryte may not be fede   *flower; cannot fade*
Ther hit doun drof in moldes dunne;
For uch gresse mot grow of graynes dede –
No whete were elles to wones wonne.   *barn; brought*
Of goud uche goude is ay bygonne:
So semly a sede moght fayly not,
That spryngande spyces up ne sponne
Of that precios perle wythouten spotte.   *from*

To that spot that I in speche expoun   *I describe*
I entred in that erber grene,   *into; garden*
In Auguste in a hygh seysoun,
Quen corne is corven wyth crokes kene.   *cut*
On huyle ther perle hit trendeled doun
Schadowed this wortes ful schyre and schene –

Gilofre, gyngure and gromylyoun,   *gillyflower; gromwell*
And pyonys powdered ay bytwene.   *peonies scattered*
Yif hit was semly on to sene,
A fayr reflayr yet fro hit flot.
Ther wonys that worthyly, I wot and wene,
My precious perle wythouten spot.

Bifore that spot my honde I spenned   *clasped*
For care ful colde that to me caght;
A devely dele in my hert denned,
Thagh resoun sette myselven saght.
I playned my perle that ther was spenned   *mourned; imprisoned*
Wyth fyrce skylles that faste faght;
Thagh kynde of Kryst me comfort kenned,
My wreched wylle in wo ay wraghte.
I felle upon that floury flaght,   *turf*
Suche odour to my hernes schot;   *rushed; head*
I slode upon a slepyng-slaghte
On that precios perle wythouten spot.

27   From *Sir Gawain and the Green Knight*

Thus laykes this lorde by lynde-wodes eves,
And Gawayn the god mon in gay bed lyges,   *lies*
Lurkkes quyl the daylyght lemed on the wowes,
Under covertour ful clere, cortyned aboute.   *canopy*
And as in slomeryng he slode, sleyly he herde
A littel dyn at his dor, and derfly upon;
And he heves up his hed out of the clothes,   *lifts*
A corner of the cortyn he caght up a lyttel,   *raised*
And waytes warly thiderwarde quat hit be myght.
Hit was the ladi, loflyest to beholde,   *loveliest*
That drow the dor after hit ful dernly and stylle,   *drew; silently*
And bowed towarde the bed; and the burne schamed,
                                         moved; was embarrassed
And layde hym doun lystyly and let as he slepte.   *artfully; pretended*
And ho stepped stilly and stel to his bedde,   *softly; stole*
Kest up the cortyn and creped withinne,
And set hir ful softly on the bed-syde
And lenged there selly longe, to loke quen he wakened. *stayed; very*
The lede lay lurked a ful longe quyle,   *low*
Compast in his concience to quat that cace myght
Meve other amount, to mervayle hym thoght.
Bot yet he sayde in hymself: 'More semly hit were
To aspye wyth my spelle in space quat ho wolde.'

Then he wakenede and wroth and to-hir-warde torned,   *stretched himself*
And unlouked his yye-lyddes and let as hym wondered,
And sayned hym, as bi his sawe the saver to worthe,
  with hande.
  Wyth chynne and cheke ful swete,
  Both quit and red in blande,   *together*
  Ful lufly con ho lete,
  With lyppes smal laghande.   *laughing*

William Langland

From *The Vision Concerning Piers Plowman*

28   [1]
[The fair field full of folk]

In a somer seson, whan softe was the sonne,   *mild; sun*
I shoop me into shroudes as I a sheep were,
In habite as an heremite unholy of werkes,
Wente wide in this world wondres to here.   *hear*
Ac on a May morwenynge on Malverne hilles   *But; morning*
Me bifel a ferly, of Fairye me thoghte.   *marvel*
I was wery forwandred and wente me to reste
Under a brood bank by a bourne syde;
And as I lay and lenede and loked on the watres,   *leaned (over)*
I slombred into a slepyng, it sweyed so murye.
 Thanne gan I meten a merveillous swevene –   *dream (v. & n.)*
That I was in a wildernesse, wiste I nevere where.
          uninhabited place; knew
A[c] as I biheeld into the eest an heigh to the sonne,   *east; high*
I seigh a tour on a toft trieliche ymaked,   *knoll; choicely*
A deep dale bynethe, a dongeon therinne,   *valley; dungeon*
With depe diches and derke and dredfulle of sighte.   *dark*
A fair feeld ful of folk fond I ther bitwene –   *field; found*
Of alle manere of men, the meene and the riche,   *kinds; humble*
Werchynge and wandrynge as the world asketh.   *Working; requires*
 Somme putten hem to the plough, pleiden ful selde,   *themselves; seldom*
In settynge and sowynge swonken ful harde,   *planting; toiled*
And wonnen that thise wastours with glotonye destruyeth.
          obtained that which

29   [2]

Yet I courbed on my knees and cried hire of grace,
Still further; bent; favour
And seide, 'Mercy, madame, for Marie love of hevene,   *love of Mary in*
That bar that blisful barn that boughte us on the Rode –
bore; blessed child; Cross
Kenne me by som craft to knowe the false.'   *skill; recognize*
'Loke upon thi left half, and lo where he stondeth –   *hand; see*
Bothe Fals and Favel, and hire feeres manye!'   *Deceit; their companions*
I loked on my left half as the Lady me taughte,   *instructed*
And was war of a womman wonderliche yclothed –   *aware; marvellously*
Purfiled with pelure, the pureste on erthe,   *Trimmed; fur; finest*
Ycorouned with a coroune, the Kyng hath noon bettre.   *Crown(ed)*
Fetisliche hire fyngres were fretted with gold wyr,
Gracefully; adorned; wire
And thereon rede rubies as rede as any gleede,   *red; glowing coal*
And diamaundes of derrest pris and double manere saphires,
highest value
Orientals and ewages envenymes to destroye.
Hire robe was ful riche, of reed scarlet engreyned,   *fast-dyed*
With ribanes of reed gold and of riche stones.   *bands*
Hire array me ravysshed, swich richesse saugh I nevere.
I hadde wonder what she was and whos wif she were.   *whose; might be*
'What is this womman,' quod I, 'so worthili atired?'   *nobly dressed*
'That is Mede the mayde,' quod she, 'hath noyed me ful ofte,
(who) has harmed
And ylakked my lemman that Leautee is hoten,   *disparaged; lover; called*
And bilowen h[ym] to lordes that lawes han to kepe.   *told lies about;*
administer
In the Popes paleis she is pryvee as myselve,   *palace; intimate*
But soothnesse wolde noght so – for she is a bastard,   *truth (fulness)*
For Fals was hire fader that hath a fikel tonge,   *treacherous*
And nevere sooth seide sithen he com to erthe;   *truth; since; came*
And Mede is manered after hym, right as [asketh kynde]:
takes after; nature requires
Qualis pater, talis filius. Bona arbor bonum fructum facit.

30   [3]
[The light that shone over hell; the harrowing]

What for feere of this ferly and of the false Jewes,   *wonder*
I drow me in that derknesse to *descendit ad inferna*,   *withdrew myself*
And there I saugh soothly, *secundum scripturas*,
Out of the west coste, a wenche, as me thoughte,   *region; woman*
Cam walkynge in the wey; to helleward she loked.   *toward hell*

Mercy highte that mayde, a meke thyng with alle,   *was named*
A ful benigne burde, and buxom of speche.   *kindly lady; courteous*
    Hir suster, as it semed, cam softely walkynge   *quietly*
Evene out of the est, and westward she lokede –   *Directly; east*
A ful comely creature [and a clene], Truthe she highte;
For the vertue that hire folwede, afered was she nevere.
                                                       Because of; power
    Whan thise maydenes mette, Mercy and Truthe,
Either asked oother of this grete wonder –   *Each; about*
Of the dyn and of the derknesse, and how the day rowed, *daylight dawned*
And which a light and a leme lay bifore helle.   *glow*
'Ich have ferly of this fare, in feith,' seide Truthe,   *wonder at; event*
'And am wendynge to wite what this wonder meneth.'
    'Have no merveille,' quod Mercy, 'murthe it bitokneth.
                                                joy; signifies, portends
A maiden that highte Marie, and moder withouten felyng *(sexual) contact*
Of any kynde creature, conceyved thorugh speche   *natural creature*
And grace of the Holy Goost; weex greet with childe;   *grew*
Withouten wem into this world she broghte hym;   *stain*
And that my tale be trewe, I take God to witnesse.
    'Sith this barn was ybore ben thritti wynter passed,
Which deide and deeth tholed this day aboute mydday –   *suffered*
And that is cause of this clips that closeth now the sonne,
                                                    eclipse; encloses
In menynge that man shal fro merknesse be drawe   *sign; darkness*
The while this light and this leme shal Lucifer ablende.   *glow; blind*
For patriarkes and prophetes han preched herof often –
That man shal man save thorugh a maydenes helpe,
And that was tynt thorugh tree, tree shal it wynne,   *that (which); lost*
And that Deeth down broghte, deeth shal releve.'   *raise up, restore*
    'That thow tellest,' quod Truthe, 'is but a tale of waltrot! *absurdity*
For Adam and Eve and Abraham with othere
Patriarkes and prophetes that in peyne liggen,
Leve thow nevere that yon light hem alofte brynge, *shall bring them above*
Ne have hem out of helle – hold thi tonge, Mercy!
It is but trufle that thow tellest – I, Truthe, woot the sothe.   *nonsense*
For that is ones in helle, out cometh it nevere;
Job the prophete patriark repreveth thi sawes: *disproves; words*
Quia in inferno nulla est redempcio.'
    Thanne Mercy ful myldely mouthed thise wordes: *uttered*
'Thorugh experience,' quod he[o], 'I hope thei shul be saved.   *she*
For venym fordooth venym – and that I preve by reson.   *destroys*
For of alle venymes foulest is the scorpion;
May no medicyne [am]e[nd]e the place ther he styngeth,   *heal*
Til he be deed and do therto – the yvel he destruyeth,   *placed upon it*
The firste venymouste, thorugh vertu of hymselve.   *poison; power*
So shal this deeth fordo – I dar my lif legge –   *destroy; wager*
Al that deeth dide first thorugh the develes entisyng;   *tempting*
And right as thorugh [gilours] gile [bigiled was man], *(a) deceiver's guile*

So shal grace that al bigan make a good ende
[And bigile the gilour – and that is good] sleighte: *stratagem*
Ars ut artem falleret.'
    'Now suffre we!' seide Truthe, 'I se, as me thynketh,   *let's be quiet*
Out of the nyppe of the north, noght ful fer hennes,
                                        cold region; from here
Rightwisnesse come rennynge; reste we the while,   *Justice*
For he[o] woot moore than we – he[o] was er we bothe.'
    'That is sooth,' seide Mercy, 'and I se here by sowthe   *(the) south*
Where cometh Pees pleyinge, in pacience yclothed.
Love hath coveited hire longe – leve I noon oother   *desired*
But [Love] sente hire som lettre, what this light bymeneth   *means*
That overhoveth helle thus; she us shal telle.'   *hovers over*
    Whan Pees in pacience yclothed approched ner hem tweyne,
                                    near the two of them
Rightwisnesse hire reverenced for hir riche clothyng,   *saluted courteously*
And preide Pees to telle hire to what place she wolde   *wished to go*
And in hire gaye garnements whom she grete thoughte?   *intended to greet*
    'My wil is to wende,' quod she, 'and welcome hem alle
That many day myghte I noght se for merknesse of synne –
                                    because of the darkness
Adam and Eve and othere mo in helle,   *more*
Moyses and many mo; Merce shul [synge],
And I shal daunce therto – do thow so, suster!
For Jesus justede wel, joye bigynneth dawe: *Because; to dawn*
Ad vesperum demorabitur fletus, et ad matutinum leticia.
    'Love, that is my lemman, swiche lettres me sente   *beloved*
That Mercy, my suster, and I mankynde sholde save,
And that God hath forgyven and graunted me, Pees, and Mercy
                                    'freely assigned to'
To be mannes meynpernour for everemoore after.   *surety*
Lo, here the patente!' quod Pees, '*In pace in idipsum*,   *authority*
And that this dede shal dure, *dormiam et requiescam.*'
                                document; be always valid
    'What, ravestow?' quod Rightwisnesse; 'or thow art right dronke!
                                Are you mad? dead drunk
Levestow that yond light unlouke myghte helle   *unlock*
And save mannes soule? Suster, wene it nevere!   *think, suppose*
At the bigynnyng God gaf the doom hymselve –   *gave; judgment*
That Adam and Eve and alle that hem suwede   *followed, came after*
Sholden deye downrighte, and dwelle in peyne after   *entirely, utterly*
If that thei touchede a tree and of the fruyt eten.   *one; ate*
Adam afterward, ayeins his defence,   *prohibition*
Freet of that fruyt, and forsook, as it were,   *Ate*
The love of Oure Lord and his loore bothe   *teaching*
And folwede that the fend taughte and his felawes wille   *i.e. Eve's*
Ayeins reson – I, Rightwisnesse, recorde thus with Truthe   *declare*
That hir peyne be perpetuel and no preiere hem helpe.

Forthi lat hem chewe as thei chosen, and chide we noght, sustres,   *quarrel*
For it is botelees bale, the byte that thei eten.'   *incurable evil; mouthful*
   'And I shall preie,' quod Pees, 'hir peyne moot have ende,
And wo into wele mowe wenden at the laste.   *happiness; turn*
For hadde thei wist of no wo, wele hadde thei noght knowen;
For no wight woot what wele is, that nevere wo suffrede,
Ne what is hoot hunger, that hadde nevere defaute.   *?hot/called; lack*
If no nyght ne weere, no man, as I leve,
Sholde wite witterly what day is to meene.   *properly; means*
Sholde nevere right riche man that lyveth in reste and ese   *a very rich*
Wite what wo is, ne were the deeth of kynde.   *natural death, mortality*
So God that bigan al of his goode wille
Bicam man of a mayde mankynde to save,
And suffrede to be sold, to se the sorwe of deying,
The which unknytteth alle care, and comsynge is of reste.
    unknits; the commencement
For til *modicum* mete with us, I may it wel avowe,   *'a little'*
Woot no wight, as I wene, what is ynogh to mene.
   'Forthi God, of his goodnesse, the first gome Adam,   *man*
Sette hym in solace and in sovereyn murthe;   *content; supreme joy*
And siththe he suffred hym synne, sorwe to feele –   *allowed (to)*
To wite what wele was, kyndeliche to knowe it.   *directly; i.e. suffering*
And after, God auntrede hymself and took Adames kynde
    ventured; nature
To wite what he hath suffred in thre sondry places,
Bothe in hevene and in erthe – and now til helle he thenketh,
    to; i.e. to go
To wite what alle wo is, that woot of alle joye.
   'So it shal fare by this folk: hir folie and hir synne
Shal lere hem what langour is, and lisse withouten ende.   *teach; pain; joy*
Woot no wight what werre is ther that pees regneth,   *war*
Ne what is witterly wele til "weylawey" hym teche.'   *misery ('alas!')*

   Thanne was ther a wight with two brode eighen;   *wide*
Book highte that beaupeere, a bold man of speche.   *i.e. 'Bible'; elder*
'By Goddes body!' quod this Book, 'I wol bere witnesse
That tho this barn was ybore, ther blased a sterre   *when; star*
That alle the wise of this world in o wit acordeden –   *one judgment agreed*
That swich a barn was ybore in Bethleem the citee
That mannes soule sholde save and synne destroye.
   'And alle the elements,' quod the Book, 'herof beren witnesse.
That he was God that al wroghte the wolkne first shewed: *heaven(s)*
Tho that weren in hevene token *stella comata*   *a comet*
And tendeden hire as a torche to reverencen his burthe;   *kindled*
The light folwede the Lord into the lowe erthe.
The water witnesseth that he was God, for he wente on it;
Peter the Apostel parceyved his gate,   *going*
And as he wente on the water wel hym knew, and seide,   *recognized*
"Iube me venire ad te super aquas."

And lo! how the sonne gan louke hire light in hirselve   *lock up*
Whan she seigh hym suffre, that sonne and see made.   *sea*
The erthe for hevynesse that he wolde suffre   *grief*
Quaked as quyk thyng and al biquasshed the roche.   *a live; shattered*
  'Lo! helle myghte nat holde, but opnede tho God tholede,
                                                  when; suffered
And leet out Symondes sones to seen hym hange on roode.   *Simeon's*
And now shal Lucifer leve it, though hym looth thynke.
                                              believe; seem hateful
For *Gigas* the geaunt with a gyn engyned
To breke and to bete adoun that ben ayeins Jesus.   *(those) who*
And I, Book, wole be brent, but Jesus rise to lyve   *burnt; unless*
In alle myghtes of man, and his moder gladie,   *powers; cheer*
And conforte al his kyn and out of care brynge,
And al the Jewene joye unjoynen and unlouken;   *Jews'; dissolve*
And but thei reverencen his roode and his resurexion,
And bileve on a newe lawe, be lost, lif and soule!'   *(they shall) be*
  'Suffre we!' seide Truthe, 'I herc and scc bothe   *Let us be quiet*
A spirit speketh to helle and biddeth unspere the yates: *bid unbar; gates*
"*Attolite portas.*"
A vois loude in that light to Lucifer crieth,
"Prynces of this place, unpynneth and unlouketh!   *undo; unlock*
For here cometh with crowne that kyng is of glorie." '   *(he) who*
  Thanne sikede Sathan, and seide to helle,   *sighed*
'Swich a light, ayeins oure leve, Lazar it fette;   *leave/belief; fetched*
Care and combraunce is comen to us alle!   *confusion*
If this kyng come in, mankynde wole he fecche,
And lede it ther Lazar is, and lightliche me bynde.   *easily*
Patriarkes and prophetes han parled herof longe –   *spoken*
That swich a lord and a light shal lede hem alle hennes.'   *from here*
  'Listneth!' quod Lucifer, 'for I this lord knowe;
Bothe this lord and this light, is longe ago I knew hym.
May no deeth this lord dere, ne no develes queyntise,   *harm; cunning*
And where he wole, is his wey – ac ware hym of the perils! *let him beware*
If he reve me of my right, he robbeth me by maistrie;
                                              deprive; sheer force
For by right and by reson the renkes that ben herc   *people*
Body and soule beth myne, bothe goode and ille.
For hymself seide, that sire is of hevene,   *lord*
That if Adam ete the appul, alle sholde deye,
And dwelle [in deol] with us develes – this thretynge he made.
                                              pain; threat
And [sithen] he that Soothnesse is seide thise wordes,   *since*
And I sithen iseised sevene [thousand] wynter,
I leeve that lawe nyl noght lete hym the leeste.'
  'That is sooth,' seide Satan, 'but I me soore drede;
For thow gete hem with gile, and his gardyn breke,   *got; broke (into)*
And in semblaunce of a serpent sete on the appultre,   *sat*
And eggedest hem to ete, Eve by hirselve,   *urged*

And toldest hire a tale – of treson were the wordes;   *treachery, deceit*
And so thou haddest hem out and hider at the laste.
It is noght graithly geten, ther gile is the roote!'   *duly obtained*
  'For God wol noght be bigiled,' quod Gobelyn, 'ne byjaped.   *fooled*
We have no trewe title to hem, for thorugh treson were thei dampned.'
     valid claim

  'Certes, I drede me,' quod the Devel, 'lest Truthe wol hem fecche.
Thise thritty wynter, as I wene, he wente aboute and preched.
I have assailled hym with synne, and som tyme I asked   *once*
Wheither he were God or Goddes sone – he gaf me short answere;
And thus hath he trolled forth thise two and thritty wynter.   *wandered*
And whan I seigh it was so, slepynge I wente   *in (her) sleep*
To warne Pilates wif what done man was Jesus;   *'make of'*
For Jewes hateden hym and han doon hym to dethe.
I wolde have lengthed his lif – for I leved, if he deide,   *prolonged*
That his soule wolde suffre no synne in his sighte;
For the body, while it on bones yede, aboute was evere   *walked alive*
To save men from synne if hemself wolde.   *(they) themselves*
And now I se wher a soule cometh [silynge hiderward]   *gliding*
With glorie and with gret light – God it is, I woot wel!
I rede we fle,' quod he, 'faste alle hennes –
For us were bettre noght be than biden his sighte.   *await, endure*
For thi lesynges, Lucifer, lost is al oure praye.   *lies; prey*
First thorugh the we fellen fro hevene so heighe;
For we leved thi lesynges, we lopen out alle with thee;   *believed; fled*
And now for thi laste lesynge, ylorn we have Adam,   *lost*
And al oure lordshipe, I leve, a londe and a watre: *on*
Nunc princeps huius mundi eicietur foras.'
  Eft the light bad unlouke and Lucifer answerde,   *Again; unlock*
'*Quis est iste?*
What lord artow?' quod Lucifer. The light soone seide,   *are you*
'*Rex glorie*,
The lord of myght and of mayn and alle manere vertues –
     strength; powers
Dominus virtutum.
Dukes of this dymme place, anoon undo thise yates,   *at once; gates*
That Crist may come in, the Kynges sone of Hevene!'
  And with that breeth helle brak, with Belialles barres –   *burst open*
For any wye or warde, wide open the yates.
  Patriarkes and prophetes, *populus in tenebris*,
Songen Seint Johanes song, '*Ecce Agnus Dei!*'   *Behold the Lamb of God*
Lucifer loke ne myghte, so light hym ablente.   *blinded*
  And tho that Oure Lord lovede, into his light he laughte,
     those; caught up
And seide to Sathan, 'Lo! here my soule to amendes   *in satisfaction*
For alle synfulle soules, to save tho that ben worthi.
Myne thei ben and of me – I may the bet hem cleyme. *better, more validly*
Although reson recorde, and right of myselve,
     declare; my own (principle of) justice

That if thei ete the appul, alle sholde deye,
I bihighte hem noght here helle for evere.   *promised*
For the dede that thei dide, thi deceite it made;   *caused it*
With gile thow hem gete, ageyn alle reson.   *got; against*
For in my paleis, Paradis, in persone of an addre,   *form; serpent*
Falsliche thow fettest there thyng that I lovede.   *brought away from*
   'Thus ylik a lusard with a lady visage,   *serpent; woman's face*
Thefliche thow me robbedest; the Olde Lawe graunteth   *Like a thief*
That gilours be bigiled – and that is good reson:
Dentem pro dente et oculum pro oculo.
Ergo soule shal soule quyte and synne to synne wende,
                                                  Therefore; pay for
And al that man hath mysdo, I, man, wole amende it.   *done wrong*
Membre for membre [was amendes by the Olde Lawe],   *satisfaction*
And lif for lif also – and by that lawe I clayme
Adam and al his issue at my wille herafter.
And that deeth in hem fordide, my deeth shal releve,   *destroyed; restore*
And bothe quyke and quyte that queynt was thorugh synne;
And that grace gile destruye, good feith it asketh.
                                            should destroy; requires
So leve it noght, Lucifer, ayein the lawe I fecche hem, *believe; against*
But by right and by reson raunsone here my liges: *ransom; subjects*
Non veni solvere legem sed adimplere.
   'Thow fettest myne in my place ayeins alle reson –
Falsliche and felonliche; good feith me it taughte,   *felonously*
To recovere hem thorugh raunsoun, and by no reson ellis,
                                                  no other method
So that with gile thow gete, thorugh grace it is ywonne.   *that (which)*
Thow, Lucifer, in liknesse of a luther addere   *treacherous, evil*
Getest bi gile tho that God lovede;   *Got; those*
And I, in liknesse of a leode, that Lord am of hevene,   *human being*
Graciousliche thi gile have quyt – go gile ayein gile!
                                           let guile go against g.
And as Adam and alle thorugh a tree deyden,   *one*
Adam and alle thorugh a tree shal turne to lyve;
And gile is bigiled, and in his gile fallen:
Et cecidit in foveam quam fecit.
Now bigynneth thi gile ageyn thee to turne
And my grace to growe ay gretter and widder.   *ever; wider*
The bitternesse that thow hast browe, now brouke it thiselve;
                                         brewed; enjoy ('brook')
That art doctour of deeth, drynk that thow madest!   *(You) who*
   'For I that am lord of lif, love is my drynke,
And for that drynke today, I deide upon erthe. *because of/for the sake of*
I faught so, me thursteth yet, for mannes soule sake;   *fought; I thirst*
May no drynke me moiste, ne my thurst slake,
Til the vendage falle in the vale of Josaphat,   *vintage take place*
That I drynke right ripe must, *resureccio mortuorum.*
And thanne shal I come as a kyng, crouned, with aungeles,
And have out of helle alle mennes soules.

'Fendes and fendekynes bifore me shul stande   *'fiendlings', minor devils*
And be at my biddyng wheresoevere [be] me liketh.
Ac to be merciable to man thanne, my kynde it asketh,   *merciful; nature*
For we beth bretheren of blood, but noght in baptisme alle.
                                             by blood; baptism
Ac alle that beth myne hole bretheren, in blood and in baptisme,   *entire*
Shul noght be dampned to the deeth that is withouten ende:
Tibi soli peccavi &c.
  'It is noght used on erthe to hangen a feloun   *customary*
Ofter than ones, though he were a tretour.   *once; traitor*
And if the kyng of that kyngdom come in that tyme   *came*
There the feloun thole sholde deeth oother juwise,   *suffer; judgment*
Lawe wolde he yeve hym lif, and he loked on hym.   *should grant; if*
And I that am kyng of kynges shal come swich a tyme
There doom to the deeth dampneth alle wikked;   *(final) judgment*
And if lawe wole I loke on hem, it lith in my grace   *lies*
Wheither thei deye or deye noght for that thei diden ille.
Be it any thyng abought, the boldnesse of hir synnes,   *redeemed*
I may do mercy thorugh rightwisnesse, and alle my wordes trewe.
And though Holy Writ wole that I be wroke of hem that diden ille –
                                             avenged upon
Nullum malum impunitum &c –
Thei shul be clensed clerliche and [clene] wasshen of hir synnes   *clearly*
In my prisone Purgatorie, til *parce* it hote.
And my mercy shal be shewed to manye of my bretheren;
For blood may suffre blood bothe hungry and acale,
Ac blood may noght se blood blede, but hym rewe.'
  Audivi archana verba que non licet homini loqui.
  'Ac my rightwisnesse and right shal rulen al helle,   *'strict justice'*
And mercy al mankynde bifore me in hevene.   sc. *shall rule*
For I were an unkynde kyng but I my kyn helpe –   *unless*
And nameliche at swich a nede ther nedes help bihoveth:
Non intres in iudicium cum servo tuo.
  'Thus by lawe,' quod Oure Lord, 'lede I wole fro hennes
Tho [leodes] that I lov[e] and leved in my comynge.   *people; believed*
And for thi lesynge, Lucifer, that thow leighe til Eve,   *lie; told to*
Thow shalt abyen it bittre!' – and bond hym with cheynes.
                                             pay dearly for
  Astroth and al the route hidden hem in hernes;   *crew; corners*
They dorste noght loke on Oure Lord, the [lothli]este of hem alle,
                                             most fearsome
But leten hym lede forth what hym liked and lete what hym liste.
                                             leave; wished
  Manye hundred of aungeles harpeden and songen,
'*Culpat caro, purgat caro, regnant Deus Dei caro.*'

Geoffrey Chaucer

31   *Balade*

Hyd, Absolon, thy gilte tresses clere;
Ester, ley thou thy meknesse al adoun;
Hyd, Jonathas, al thy frendly manere;
Penalopee, and Marcia Catoun,
Make of your wyfhod no comparisoun;
Hyde ye your beautes, Isoude and Eleyne.
My lady cometh, that al this may disteyne.   *outshine*

Thy faire body, lat hit nat appere,
Lavyne; and thou, Lucresse of Rome toun,
And Polixene, that boghten love so dere,
And Cleopatre, with al thy passioun,
Hyde ye your trouthe of love and your renoun;
And thou, Tisbe, that hast of love swich peyne.
My lady cometh, that al this may disteyne.

Hero, Dido, Laudomia, alle yfere,
And Phyllis, hanging for thy Demophoun,
And Canace, espyed by thy chere,   *face*
Ysiphile, betrayed with Jasoun,
Maketh of your trouthe neyther boost ne soun;
Nor Ypermistre or Adriane, ye tweyne.
My lady cometh, that al this may disteyne.

32   *Merciles Beautee*

A Triple Roundel

I

Your yen two wol slee me sodenly;
I may the beaute of hem not sustene,
So woundeth hit throughout my herte kene.

And but your word wol helen hastily
My hertes wounde, whyl that hit is grene,
    Your yen two wol slee me sodenly;
    I may the beaute of hem not sustene.

Upon my trouthe I sey yow feithfully,
That ye ben of my lyf and deeth the quene;
For with my deeth the trouthe shal be sene.
    Your yen two wol slee me sodenly;
    I may the beaute of hem not sustene,
    So woundeth hit throughout my herte kene.

II

So hath your beaute fro your herte chaced
Pitee, that me ne availeth not to pleyne;
For Daunger halt your mercy in his cheyne.

lordship; aloofness

Giltles my deeth thus han ye me purchaced;
I sey you sooth, me nedeth not to feyne.
  So hath your beaute fro your herte chaced
  Pitee, that me ne availeth not to pleyne.

Allas! that nature hath in you compassed
So greet beaute, that no man may atteyne
To mercy, though he sterve for the peyne.
  So hath your beaute fro your hert chaced
  Pitee, that me ne availeth not to pleyne;
  For Daunger halt your mercy in his cheyne.

die

III

Sin I fro Love escaped am so fat,
I never thenk to ben in his prison lene;
Sin I am free, I counte him not a bene.

He may answere, and seye this and that;
I do no fors, I speke right as I mene.
  Sin I fro Love escaped am so fat,
  I never thenk to ben in his prison lene.

Love hath my name ystrike out of his sclat,
And he is strike out of my bokes clene
For evermo; ther is non other mene.
  Sin I fro Love escaped am so fat,
  I never thenk to ben in his prison lene.
  Sin I am free, I counte him not a bene.

33   From *Troilus and Criseyde*

This Troilus, with blisse of that supprysed,
Put al in goddes hond, as he that mente
No-thing but wel; and, sodeynly avysed,
He hir in armes faste to him hente.
And Pandarus, with a ful good entente,
Leyde him to slepe, and seyde, 'if ye ben wyse,
Swowneth not now, lest more folk aryse.'

overcome

seized

What mighte or may the sely larke seye,   *innocent*
Whan that the sparhauk hath it in his foot?
I can no more, but of thise ilke tweye,
To whom this tale sucre be or soot,   *sweet*
Though that I tarie a yeer, som-tyme I moot,
After myn auctor, tellen hir gladnesse,
As wel as I have told hir hevinesse.

Criseyde, which that felte hir thus y-take,
As writen clerkes in hir bokes olde,
Right as an aspes leef she gan to quake,   *aspen*
Whan she him felte hir in his armes folde.
But Troilus, al hool of cares colde,   *unwounded*
Gan thanken tho the blisful goddes sevene;
Thus sondry peynes bringen folk to hevene.

This Troilus in armes gan hir streyne,
And seyde, 'O swete, as ever mote I goon,
Now be ye caught, now is ther but we tweyne;
Now yeldeth yow, for other boot is noon.'   *help*
To that Criseyde answerde thus anoon,
'Ne hadde I er now, my swete herte dere,
Ben yolde, y-wis, I were now not here!'   *yielded*

O! sooth is seyd, that heled for to be
As of a fevre or othere greet syknesse,
Men moste drinke, as men may often see,
Ful bittre drink; and for to han gladnesse,
Men drinken often peyne and greet distresse;
I mene it here, as for this aventure,
That thourgh a peyne hath founden al his cure.

And now swetnesse semeth more swete,
That bitternesse assayed was biforn;
For out of wo in blisse now they flete.   *float*
Non swich they felten, sith they were born;
Now is this bet, than bothe two be lorn!   *forlorn*
For love of god, take every womman hede
To werken thus, if it comth to the nede.

Criseyde, al quit from every drede and tene, *trouble*
As she that juste cause hadde him to triste, *trust*
Made him swich feste, it joye was to sene,
Whan she his trouthe and clene entente wiste.
And as aboute a tree, with many a twiste,
Bitrent and wryth the sote wode-binde, *twined around*
Gan eche of hem in armes other winde.

And as the newe abaysshed nightingale,   *cast down*
That stinteth first whan she biginneth singe,
Whan that she hereth any herde tale,   *herdsman's counting*
Or in the hegges any wight steringe,   *stirring*
And after siker dooth hir voys out-ringe;
Right so Criseyde, whan hir drede stente,
Opned hir herte, and tolde him hir entente.

And right as he that seeth his deeth y-shapen,
And deye moot, in ought that he may gesse,
And sodeynly rescous doth him escapen,
And from his deeth is brought in sikernesse,   *safety*
For al this world, in swich present gladnesse
Was Troilus, and hath his lady swete;
With worse hap god lat us never mete!

His armes smale, hir streyghte bak and softe,
Hir sydes longe, fleshly, smothe, and whyte
He gan to stroke, and good thrift bad ful ofte
Hir snowish throte, hir brestes rounde and lyte;
Thus in this hevene he gan him to delyte,
And ther-with-al a thousand tyme hir kiste;
That, what to done, for joye unnethe he wiste.   *hardly*

Than seyde he thus, 'O, Love, O, Charitee,
Thy moder eek, Citherea the swete,
After thy-self next heried be she,   *worshipped*
Venus mene I, the wel-willy planete;   *well-wishing*
And next that, Imenëus, I thee grete;
                        Hymenaeus, God of marriage
For never man was to yow goddes holde   *beholden*
As I, which ye han brought fro cares colde.

Benigne Love, thou holy bond of thinges,
Who-so wol grace, and list thee nought honouren,
Lo, his desyr wol flee with-outen winges.
For, noldestow of bountee hem socouren
That serven best and most alwey labouren,
Yet were al lost, that dar I wel seyn, certes,
But-if thy grace passed our desertes.

And for thou me, that coude leest deserve
Of hem that nombred been un-to thy grace,
Hast holpen, ther I lykly was to sterve,
And me bistowed in so heygh a place
That thilke boundes may no blisse pace,   *surpass*
I can no more, but laude and reverence
Be to thy bounte and thyn excellence!'

And therwith-al Criseyde anoon he kiste,
Of which, certeyn, she felte no disese.
And thus seyde he, 'now wolde god I wiste,
Myn herte swete, how I yow mighte plese!
What man,' quod he, 'was ever thus at ese
As I, on whiche the faireste and the beste
That ever I say, deyneth hir herte reste.

Here may men seen that mercy passeth right;
The experience of that is felt in me,
That am unworthy to so swete a wight.
But herte myn, of your benignitee,
So thenketh, though that I unworthy be,
Yet mot I nede amenden in som wyse,
Right thourgh the vertu of your heyghe servyse.

And for the love of god, my lady dere,
Sin god hath wrought me for I shal yow serve,
As thus I mene, that ye wol be my stere,   *helmsman*
To do me live, if that yow liste, or sterve,
So techeth me how that I may deserve
Your thank, so that I, thurgh myn ignoraunce,
Ne do no-thing that yow be displesaunce.

For certes, fresshe wommanliche wyf,
This dar I seye, that trouthe and diligence,
That shal ye finden in me al my lyf,
Ne I wol not, certeyn, breken your defence;
And if I do, present or in absence,
For love of god, lat slee me with the dede,
If that it lyke un-to your womanhede.'

'Y-wis,' quod she, 'myn owne hertes list,   *desire*
My ground of ese, and al myn herte dere,
Graunt mercy, for on that is al my trist;
But late us falle awey fro this matere;
For it suffyseth, this that seyd is here.
And at o word, with-outen repentaunce,
Wel-come, my knight, my pees, my suffisaunce!'

Of hir delyt, or joyes oon the leste
Were impossible to my wit to seye;
But juggeth, ye that han ben at the feste
Of swich gladnesse, if that hem liste pleye!
I can no more, but thus thise ilke tweye
That night, be-twixen dreed and sikernesse,
Felten in love the grete worthinesse.

O blisful night, of hem so longe y-sought,
How blithe un-to hem bothe two thou were!
Why ne hadde I swich on with my soule y-bought,
Ye, or the leeste joye that was there?
A-wey, thou foule daunger and thou fere,
And lat hem in this hevene blisse dwelle,
That is so heygh, that al ne can I telle!

From *Canterbury Tales*

34

[1]

From *The Prologue*

A good WIF was ther of biside BATHE,	*from near Bath*
But she was somdel deef, and that was scathe.	*a pity*
Of clooth-makyng she hadde swich an haunt,	*skill*
She passed hem of Ypres and of Gaunt.	*surpassed; Ghent*
In al the parisshe wif ne was ther noon	
That to the offrynge bifore hire sholde goon;	
And if ther dide, certeyn so wrooth was she,	*certainly*
That she was out of alle charitee.	
Hir coverchiefs ful fyne weren of ground;	
I dorste swere they weyeden ten pound	
That on a Sonday weren upon hir heed.	
Hir hosen weren of fyn scarlet reed,	*stockings*
Ful streite yteyd, and shoes ful moyste and newe.	
Boold was hir face, and fair, and reed of hewe.	
She was a worthy womman al hir lyve:	
Housbondes at chirche dore she hadde fyve,	
Withouten oother compaignye in youthe, –	*besides*
But therof nedeth nat to speke as nowthe.	*at present*
And thries hadde she been at Jerusalem;	
She hadde passed many a straunge strem;	*foreign river*
At Rome she hadde been, and at Boloigne,	
In Galice at Seint-Jame, and at Coloigne.	
She koude muchel of wandrynge by the weye.	*knew a lot*
Gat-tothed was she, soothly for to seye.	*gap-toothed*
Upon an amblere esily she sat,	*ambling horse*
Ywympled wel, and on hir heed an hat	
As brood as is a bokeler or a targe;	*buckler; shield*
A foot-mantel aboute hir hipes large,	*outer skirt*
And on hir feet a paire of spores sharpe.	
In felaweshipe wel koude she laughe and carpe.	*talk*
Of remedies of love she knew per chaunce,	
For she koude of that art the olde daunce.	

35   [2]

From *The Miller's Tale*

Fair was this yonge wyf, and therwithal
As any wezele hir body gent and smal.   *graceful*
A ceynt she werede, barred al of silk,   *girdle*
A barmclooth eek as whit as morne milk   *apron*
Upon hir lendes, ful of many a goore.   *loins*
Whit was hir smok, and broyden al bifoore   *embroidered*
And eek bihynde, on hir coler aboute,
Of col-blak silk, withinne and eek withoute.
The tapes of hir white voluper   *cap*
Were of the same suyte of hir coler;   *matched her collar*
Hir filet brood of silk, and set ful hye.
And sikerly she hadde a likerous ye;   *certainly; wanton eye*
Ful smale ypulled were hire browes two,
And tho were bent and blake as any sloo.   *they; sloe*
She was ful moore blisful on to see
Than is the newe pere-jonette tree,   *young pear tree*
And softer than the wolle is of a wether.   *wool*
And by hir girdel heeng a purs of lether,
Tasseled with silk, and perled with latoun.   *brass knobs*
In al this world, to seken up and doun,
There nys no man so wys that koude thenche   *imagine*
So gay a popelote or swich a wenche.   *poppet; such*
Ful brighter was the shynyng of hir hewe
Than in the Tour the noble yforged newe.
But of hir song, it was as loude and yerne   *as for; eager*
As any swalwe sittynge on a berne.   *swallow; barn*
Therto she koude skippe and make game,   *frolic*
As any kyde or calf folwynge his dame.   *its*
Hir mouth was sweete as bragot or the meeth,
                                          drink of ale; mead
Or hoord of apples leyd in hey or heeth. *honey; store; heather*
Wynsynge she was, as is a joly colt,   *frisky*
Long as a mast, and upright as a bolt.
A brooch she baar upon hir lowe coler,
As brood as is the boos of a bokeler.   *boss; shield*
Hir shoes were laced on hir legges hye.
She was a prymerole, a piggesnye,   *primrose*
For any lord to leggen in his bedde,   *lay*
Or yet for any good yeman to wedde.

36   [3]

From *The Pardoner's Tale*

But, sires, o word forgat I in my tale:
I have relikes and pardoun in my male,   *bag*
As faire as any man in Engelond,   *excellent*
Whiche were me yeven by the popes hond.
If any of yow wole, of devocion,
Offren, and han myn absolucion,
Com forth anon, and kneleth heere adoun,
And mekely receyveth my pardoun;
Or elles taketh pardoun as ye wende,
Al newe and fressh at every miles ende,
So that ye offren, alwey newe and newe,   *again and again*
Nobles or pens, whiche that be goode and trewe.
It is an honour to everich that is heer   *everyone*
That ye mowe have a suffisant pardoneer   *competent*
T'assoille yow, in contree as ye ryde,
For aventures whiche that may bityde.   *because of accidents*
Paraventure ther may fallen oon or two
Doun of his hors, and breke his nekke atwo.   *in two*
Looke which a seuretee is it to yow alle
That I am in youre felaweshipe yfalle,   *come by chance*
That may assoille yow, bothe moore and lasse,   *high and low*
Whan that the soule shal fro the body passe.
I rede that oure Hoost heere shal bigynne,   *advise*
For he is moost envoluped in synne.   *enveloped*
Com forth, sire Hoost, and offre first anon,
And thou shalt kisse the relikes everychon,
Ye, for a grote! Unbokele anon thy purs.'
'Nay, nay!' quod he, 'thanne have I Cristes curs! *may I have*
Lat be,' quod he, 'it shal nat be, so theech!
Thou woldest make me kisse thyn olde breech,
And swere it were a relyk of a seint,
Though it were with thy fundement depeint!   *stained*
But, by the croys which that Seint Eleyne fond,   *found*
I wolde I hadde thy coillons in myn hond   *testicles*
In stide of relikes or of seintuarie.   *holy things*
Lat kutte hem of, I wol thee helpe hem carie;
They shul be shryned in an hogges toord!'   *enshrined*
This Pardoner answerde nat a word;
So wrooth he was, no word ne wolde he seye.
'Now,' quod oure Hoost, 'I wol no lenger pleye
With thee, ne with noon oother angry man.'
But right anon the worthy Knyght bigan,
Whan that he saugh that al the peple lough,   *laughed*
'Namoore of this, for it is right ynough!   *quite*
Sire Pardoner, be glad and myrie of cheere;   *cheerful*

And ye, sire Hoost, that been to me so deere,
I prey yow that ye kisse the Pardoner.
And Pardoner, I prey thee, drawe thee neer,   *nearer*
And, as we diden, lat us laughe and pleye.'   *did (before)*
Anon they kiste, and ryden forth hir weye.

Thomas Hoccleve

37   O maister deere and fader reverent!
            My maister Chaucer, flowr of eloquence,
          Mirour of fructuous entendèment,   *understanding*
            O universal fader in scïènce!
            Allas that thou thyn excellent prudènce
              In thy bed mortal mightest nought bequethè!
              What ailèd deth? allas! why wolde he slee thee?

          O deth! thou didest nought harme singulèr,
            In slaughter of him; but al this land it smerteth.
          But nathèless, yet hast thou no powèr
            His namè slee; his high vertù asterteth   *escapes*
            Unslain fro thee, which ay us lifly herteth   *heartens*
              With bookès of his òrnat ènditing,
              That is to al this land enlumining.

          Hast thou not eek my maister Gower slain,
            Whos vertu I am insufficient
          For to descrive? I wot wel in certàin
            For to sleen al this world thou hast y-ment;
            But sin our Lord Crist was obedient
              To thee, in faith I can no ferther seye:
              His creäturès mosten thee obeye.

King James I of Scotland

38   From *The Kingis Quair*

          Now was there maid fast by the towris wall   *close*
            A gardin faire, and in the corneris set
          An herber grene, with wandis long and small   *arbour; stakes*
            Railit about; and so with treïs set   *enclosed*
            Was all the place, and hawthorn hegis knet,   *hedges; dense*
          That lif was none walking there forby
          That might within scarse any wight aspy.

So thik the bowis and the levès grene
　Beshadit all the aleyes that there were;
And middis every herber might be sene
　The sharpè grenè swetè jenepere,　　　　　　　*juniper*
　Growing so fair with branchis here and there
That, as it seemit to a lif without,
The bowis spred the herber all about.

And on the smallè grenè twistis sat　　　　　　　*twigs*
　The litil swetè nightingale, and song
So loud and clere the ympnis consecrat　　　　　*hymns*
　Of Lufis use, now soft, now loud among,
　That all the gardin and the wallis rong
Right of thair song and of the copill next　　　　*verse*
Of thair swete armony – and lo the text:

'Worshippe, ye that loveris bene, this May,
　For of your bliss the kalendis ar begunne,　　　*first days*
And sing with us "Away, winter, away!
　Cum, somer, cum, the swete sesòun and sunne!"
　Awake, for shame! that have your hevenis wunne,
　　　　　　　　　　　　　　　　　supreme happiness
And amorously lift up your hedis all;
Thank Luve that list you to his mercy call.'　　*is pleased to*

Quhen thay this song had sung a litil thrawe,　　*time*
　Thay stent a quhile, and therwith unafraid,　*ceased; awhile*
As I beheld and kest myn eyne a-lawe,　　　　*cast; down*
　From bough to bough thay hippit and they plaid,　*hopped*
　And freshly in thair birdis kind arraid
Thair fetheris new, and fret thame in the sunne,　*preened*
And thankit Lufe that had thair makis wunne.　　*mates*

Robert Henryson

39　　　　　From *The Testament of Cresseid*

I mend the fyre and beikit me about,　　　　*warmed*
Than tuik ane drink my spreitis to comfort
And armit me weill fra the cauld thairout.
To cut the winter nicht and make it schort
I tuik ane Quair and left all uther sport,
Writtin be worthie Chaucer glorious
Of fair Creisseid, and worthie Troylus.

And thair I fand efter that Diomeid
Ressavit had that Lady bricht of hew,
How Troilus neir out of wit abraid,
And weipit soir with visage paill of hew,
For quhilk wanhope his teiris can renew
Quhill Esperus rejoisit him agane.
Thus quhyle in Joy he levit, quhyle in pane.

Of hir behest he had greit comforting
Traisting to Troy that scho suld mak retour,
Quhilk he desyrit maist of eirdly thing
For quhy scho was his only Paramour,
Bot quhen he saw passit baith day and hour
Of hir ganecome, than sorrow can oppres
His wofull hart in cair and hevines.

Of his distres me neidis nocht reheirs,
For worthie Chauceir in the samin buik
In gudelie termis, and in Joly veirs
Compylit hes his cairis, quha will luik.
To brek my sleip ane uther quair I tuik,
In quhilk I fand the fatall destenie
Of fair Cresseid, that endit wretchitlie.

Quha wait gif all that Chauceir wrait was trew.
Nor I wait nocht gif this narratioun
Be authoreist or fenyeit of the new
Be sum Poeit, throw his Inventioun
Maid to report the Lamentatioun
And wofull end of this lustie Creisseid,
And quhat distres scho thoillit, and quhat deid.

Quhen Diomeid had all his appetyte,
And mair fulfillit of this fair Ladie
Upon ane uther he set his haill delyte
And send to hir ane Lybell of repudie
And hir excludit fra his companie.
Than desolait scho walkit up and doun,
And sum men sayis into the Court commoun.

O fair Cresseid the flour and A *per se*
Of Troy and Grece, how was thow fortunait?
To change in filth all thy Feminitie
And be with fleschelie lust sa maculait
And go amang the Greikis air and lait
Sa giglotlike takand thy foull plesance.
I have pietie thow suld fall sic mischance.

Yit nevertheles quhat ever men deme or say,
In scornefull langage of thy brukkilnes,
I sall excuse als far furth as I may
Thy womanheid, thy wisdome and fairnes
The quhilk Fortoun hes put to sic distres
As hir pleisit, and nathing throw the gilt
Of the, throw wickit langage to be spilt.

This fair Lady in this wyse destitute
Of all comfort, and consolatioun,
Richt privelie but fellowschip on fute
Disagysit passit far out of the toun
Ane myle or twa, unto ane Mansioun
Beildit full gay, quhair hir Father Calchas
Quhilk than amang the Greikis dwelland was.

William Dunbar

40   *To the City of London*

London, thou art of townes A *per se*.
  Soveraign of cities, semeliest in sight,
Of high renoun, riches, and royaltie;
  Of lordis, barons, and many goodly knyght;
  Of most delectable lusty ladies bright;
Of famous prelatis in habitis clericall;
  Of merchauntis full of substaunce and myght:
London, thou art the flour of Cities all.

Gladdith anon, thou lusty Troy Novaunt,
  Citie that some tyme cleped was New Troy,
In all the erth, imperiall as thou stant,
  Pryncesse of townes, of pleasure, and of joy,
  A richer restith under no Christen roy;
For manly power, with craftis naturall,
  Fourmeth none fairer sith the flode of Noy:
London, thou art the flour of Cities all.

Gemme of all joy, jasper of jocunditie,
  Most myghty carbuncle of vertue and valour;
Strong Troy in vigour and in strenuytie;   *strength*
  Of royall cities rose and geraflour;   *gillyflower*
  Empresse of townes, exalt in honour;
In beawtie beryng the crone imperiall;
  Swete paradise precelling in pleasure:
London, thou art the flour of Cities all.

Above all ryvers thy Ryver hath renowne,
  Whose beryall stremys, pleasaunt and preclare,   *famous*
Under thy lusty wallys renneth down,
  Where many a swanne doth swymme with wyngis fare;
  Where many a barge doth saile, and row with are,
Where many a ship doth rest with toppe-royall.
  O! towne of townes, patrone and not-compare:
London, thou art the flour of Cities all.

Upon thy lusty Brigge of pylers white
  Been merchauntis full royall to behold;
Upon thy stretis goth many a semely knyght
  In velvet gownes and cheynes of fyne gold.
  By Julyus Cesar thy Tour founded of old
May be the hous of Mars victoryall,
  Whos artillary with tonge may not be told:
London, thou art the flour of Cities all.

Strong be thy wallis that about the standis;
  Wise by the people that within the dwellis;
Fresh is thy ryver with his lusty strandis;
  Blith be thy chirches, wele sownyng be thy bellis;
  Riche be thy merchauntis in substaunce that excellis;
Fair be thy wives, right lovesom, white and small;
  Clere be thy virgyns, lusty under kellis: *coifs*
London, thou art the flour of Cities all.

Thy famous Maire, by pryncely governaunce,
  With swerd of justice the rulith prudently.
No Lord of Parys, Venyce, or Floraunce
  In dignytie or honoure goeth to hym nye.
  He is exampler, loode-ster, and guye;   *guide*
Principall patrone and roose orygynalle,
  Above all Maires as maister moost worthy:
London, thou art the flour of Cities all.

41   *Lament for the Makaris*   *poets*

  I that in heill wes and gladnes,
  Am trublit now with gret seiknes,
  And feblit with infermite;
    Timor mortis conturbat me.

  Our plesance heir is all vane glory,
  This fals warld is bot transitory,
  The flesche is brukle, the Fend is sle;   *brittle*
    Timor mortis conturbat me.

The stait of man dois change and vary,
Now sound, now seik, now blith, now sary,   *sorry*
Now dansand mery, now like to dee;
   Timor mortis conturbat me.

No stait in erd heir standis sickir;   *sure*
As with the wynd wavis the wickir,   *willow*
Wavis this warldis vanite;
   Timor mortis conturbat me.

On to the ded gois all Estatis,
Princis, Prelotis, and Potestatis,
Baith riche and pur of al degre;
   Timor mortis conturbat me.

He takis the knychtis in to feild,
Anarmit under helme and scheild;
Victour he is at all mellie;
   Timor mortis conturbat me.

That strang unmercifull tyrand
Takis, on the moderis breist sowkand,   *sucking*
The bab full of benignite;
   Timor mortis conturbat me.

He takis the campion in the stour,   *battle*
The capitane closit in the tour,
The lady in bour full of bewte;
   Timor mortis conturbat me.

He sparis no lord for his piscence,   *power*
Na clerk for his intelligence;
His awfull strak may no man fle;   *stroke*
   Timor mortis conturbat me.

Art, magicianis, and astrologgis,
Rethoris, logicianis, and theologgis,
Thame helpis no conclusionis sle;   *Them*
   Timor mortis conturbat me.

In medicyne the most practicianis,
Lechis, surrigianis, and phisicianis,
Thame self fra ded may not supple;
   Timor mortis conturbat me.

I se that makaris amang the laif   *rest*
Playis heir ther pageant, syne gois to graif;
Sparit is nocht ther faculte;
   Timor mortis conturbat me.

He hes done petuously devour,
The noble Chaucer, of makaris flour,
The Monk of Bery, and Gower, all thre;
  Timor mortis conturbat me.

The gude Syr Hew of Eglintoun,
And eik Heryot, and Wyntoun,
He hes tane out of this cuntre;
  Timor mortis conturbat me.

That scorpion fell hes done infek
Maister Johne Clerk, and James Afflek,
Fra balat making and tragidie;
  Timor mortis conturbat me.

Holland and Barbour he hes berevit;
Allace! that he nocht with us levit
Schir Mungo Lokert of the Le;
  Timor mortis conturbat me.

Clerk of Tranent eik he hes tane,
That maid the Anteris of Gawane;
Schir Gilbert Hay endit hes he;
  Timor mortis conturbat me.

He hes Blind Hary and Sandy Traill
Slaine with his schour of mortall haill,
Quhilk Patrik Johnestoun myght nocht fle;
  Timor mortis conturbat me.

He hes reft Merseir his endite,
That did in luf so lifly write,
So schort, so quyk, of sentence hie;
  Timor mortis conturbat me.

He hes tane Roull of Aberdene,
And gentill Roull of Corstorphin;
Two bettir fallowis did no man se;
  Timor mortis conturbat me.

In Dumfermelyne he hes done roune
With Maister Robert Henrisoun;
Schir Johne the Ros enbrast hes he;
  Timor mortis conturbat me.

And he hes now tane, last of aw,
Gud gentill Stobo and Quintyne Schaw,
Of quham all wichtis hes pete: *piety*
  Timor mortis conturbat me.

Gud Maister Walter Kennedy
In poynt of dede lyis veraly,
Gret reuth it wer that so suld be;
Timor mortis conturbat me.

Sen he hes all my brether tane,
He will nocht lat me lif alane,
On forse I man his nyxt pray be;
Timor mortis conturbat me.

Sen for the deid remeid is none,
Best is that we for dede dispone,
Eftir our deid that lif may we;
Timor mortis conturbat me.

42   *To a Ladye*

Sweit rois of vertew and of gentilnes,
Delytsum lyllie of everie lustynes,
    Richest in bontie and in bewtie cleir,
    And everie vertew that is [held most] deir,
Except onlie that ye ar mercyles.

In to your garthe this day I did persew,
Thair saw I flowris that fresche wer of hew;
    Baith quhyte and reid moist lusty wer to seyne,
    And halsum herbis upone stalkis grene;   *wholesome*
Yit leif nor flour fynd could I nane of rew.

I dout that Merche, with his caild blastis keyne,
Hes slane this gentill herbe that I of mene,
    Quhois petewous deithe dois to my hart sic pane
    That I wald mak to plant his rute agane,
So confortand his levis unto me bene.

43 From *The Tretis of the Tua Mariit Wemen and the Wedo*

Bot of ane bowrd in to bed I sall yow breif yit: *tell*
Quhen he ane hail year was hanyt, and him behuffit rage,   *spent*
And I wes laith to be loppin with sic a lob avoir,
                                    leaping; clumsy carthorse
Alse lang as he wes on loft, I lukit on him never,
Na leit never enter in my thoght that he my thing persit,   *pierced*

Bot ay in mynd ane other man ymagynit that I haid;
Or ellis had I never mery bene at that myrthles raid.
Quhen I that grome geldit had of gudis and of natur,   *man*
Me thought him gracelese one to goif, sa me God help: *gaze*
Quhen he had warit all one me his welth and his substance,   *spend*
Me thoght his wit wes all went away with the laif;   *rest*
And so I did him despise, I spittit quhen I saw
That super spendit evill spreit, spulyeit of all vertu.
For, weill ye wait, wiffis, that he that wantis riches
And valyeandnes in Venus play, is ful vile haldin: *held, reputed*
Full fruster is his fresch array and fairnes of persoune,   *vain*
All is bot frutlese his effeir and falyeis at the up with.

   I buskit up my barnis like baronis sonnis,   *dressed*
And maid bot fulis of the fry of his first wif.
I banyst fra my boundis his brethir ilkane;
His frendis as my fais I held at feid evir;   *foes; enmity*
Be this, ye belief may, I luffit nought him self,
For never I likit a leid that langit till his blude: *person; belonged to*
And yit thir wisemen, thai wait that all wiffis evill
Ar kend with ther conditionis and knawin with the samin.   *same*

   Deid is now that dyvour and dollin in erd: *bankrupt; buried*
With him deit all my dule and my drery thoghtis;   *sorrow*
Now done is my dolly nyght, my day is upsprungin,   *dismal*
Adew dolour, adew! my daynte now begynis:
Now am I a wedow, I wise and weill am at ese;
I weip as I were woful, but wel is me for ever;
I busk as I wer bailfull, bot blith is my hert;   *sorrowful*
My mouth it makis murnyng, and my mynd lauchis;
My clokis thai ar caerfull in colour of sabill,
Bot courtly and ryght curyus my corse is ther undir:
I drup with a ded luke in my dule habit,
As with manis daill [I] had done for dayis of my lif.   *part*

   Quhen that I go to the kirk, cled in cair weid,
As foxe in a lambis fleise fenye I my cheir;   *feign; expression*
Than lay I furght my bright buke one breid one my kne,
With mony lusty letter ellummynit with gold;
And drawis my clok forthwart our my face quhit,
That I may spy, unaspyit, a space me beside:
Full oft I blenk by my buke, and blynis of devotioun,   *glance; cease*
To se quhat berne is best brand or bredest in schulderis,   *brawned*
Or forgeit is maist forcely to furnyse a bancat   *banquet*
In Venus chalmer, valyeandly, withoutin vane ruse:
And, as the new mone all pale, oppressit with change,
Kythis quhilis her cleir face through cluddis of sable,   *shows*
So keik I through my clokis, and castis kynd lukis   *veils*
To knychtis, and to cleirkis, and cortly personis.

   Quhen frendis of my husbandis behaldis me one fer,
I haif a watter spunge for wa, within my wyde clokis,

Than wring I it full wylely and wetis my chekis,
With that watteris myn ene and welteris doune teris.   *pours*
Than say thai all, that sittis about, 'Se ye nought, allace!
Yone lustlese led so lelely scho luffit hir husband:
Yone is a pete to enprent in a princis hert,   *pity*
That sic a perle of plesance suld yone pane dre!'
I sane me as I war ane sanct, and semys ane angell;
At langage of lichory I leit as I war crabit:
I sich, without sair hert or seiknes in body;
According to my sable weid I mon haif sad maneris,
Or thai will se all the suth; for certis, we wemen
We set us all fra the syght to syle men of treuth:
We dule for na evill deid, sa it be derne haldin.   *grieve; kept secret*
    Wise wemen has wayis and wonderfull gydingis
With gret engyne to bejaip their jolyus husbandis;
And quyetly, with sic craft, convoyis our materis
That, under Crist, no creatur kennis of our doingis.
Bot folk a cury may miscuke, that knawledge wantis,
And has na colouris for to cover thair awne kindly fautis;
As dois thir damysellis, for derne dotit lufe,   *foolish*
That dogonis haldis in dainte and delis with thaim so lang,
                                              worthless fellows
Quhill all the cuntre knaw ther kyndnes and faith:
Faith has a fair name, bot falsheid faris bettir:
Fy one hir that can nought feyne her fame for to saif!
Yit am I wise in sic werk and wes all my tyme;
Thogh I want wit in warldlynes, I wylis haif in luf,
As ony happy woman has that is of hie blude:
Hutit be the halok las a hunder yeir of eild!   *Hooted; foolish*
    I have ane secrete servand, rycht sobir of his toung,
That me supportis of sic nedis, quhen I a syne mak:
Thogh he be sympill to the sicht, he has a tong sickir;
Full mony semelyar sege wer service dois mak: *man*
Though I haif cair, under cloke, the cleir day quhill nyght,
Yit haif I solace, under serk, quhill the sone ryse.   *shirt*
    Yit am I haldin a haly wif our all the haill schyre,
I am sa peteouse to the pur, quhen ther is personis mony.
In passing of pilgrymage I pride me full mekle,
Mair for the prese of peple na ony perdoun wynyng.
    Bot yit me think the best bourd, quhen baronis and knychtis,
And othir bachilleris, blith blumyng in youth,
And all my luffaris lele, my lugeing persewis,   *lodging*
And fyllis me wyne wantonly with weilfair and joy:
Sum rownis; and sum ralyeis; and sum redis ballatis;   *whispers; jests*
Sum raiffis furght rudly with riatus speche;   *raves*
Sum plenis, and sum prayis; sum prasis mi bewte,   *complains*
Sum kissis me; sum clappis me; sum kyndnes me proferis;
Sum kerffis to me curtasli; sum me the cop giffis;   *carves*

Sum stalwardly steppis ben, with a stout curage,
And a stif standand thing staiffis in my neiff;   *stuffs; fist*
And mony blenkis ben our, that but full fer sittis,
That mai, for the thik thrang, nought thrif as thai wald.   *thrive*
Bot, with my fair calling, I comfort thaim all:
For he that sittis me nixt, I nip on his finger;
I serf him on the tothir syde on the samin fasson;
And he that behind me sittis, I hard on him lene;
And him befor, with my fut fast on his I stramp;
And to the bernis far but sueit blenkis I cast:
To every man in speciall speke I sum wordis
So wisly and so womanly, quhill warmys ther hertis.

44   From *Ane Ballat of Our Lady*

Empryce of prys, imperatrice,
  Brycht polist precious stane;
Victrice of vyce, hie genetrice
  Of Jhesu, lord soverayne:
Our wys pavys fra enemys,
  Agane the feyndis trayne;
Oratrice, mediatrice, salvatrice,
  To God gret suffragane!
    Ave Maria, gracia plena!
  Haile, sterne meridiane!   *star*
Spyce, flour delice of paradys,
  That baire the gloryus grayne.

Imperiall wall, place palestrall,
  Of peirles pulcritud;
Tryumphale hall, hie trone regall
  Of Godis celsitud;
Hospitall riall, the lord of all
  Thy closet did include;
Bricht ball cristall, ros virginall,
  Fulfillit of angell fude.
    Ave Maria, gracia plena!
  Thy birth has with his blude
Fra fall mortall, originall,
  Us raunsound on the rude.

Late Mediaeval Ballads

45   *The Wee Wee Man*

As I was walking all alane
  Between a water and a wa';
And there I spied a wee wee man
  And he was the least that ere I saw.

His legs were scarce a shathmont's length
  And thick and thimber was his thigh,
Between his brows there was a span
  And between his shoulders there was three.

He took up a meikle stane
  And he flang 't as far as I could see;
Tho I had been as Wallace wight
  I couldna liften it to my knee.

'O wee wee man but thou be strong,
  O tell me whare thy dwelling be';
'My dwelling's down at yon bonny bower
  O will you go with me and see?'

On we lap and awa we rade
  Till we came to yon bonny green;
We lighted down for to bait our horse
  And out there came a lady fine;

Four and twenty at her back
  And they were a' clad out in green;
Tho the King of Scotland had been there
  The warst o' them might hae been his Queen.

On we lap and awa we rade
  Till we cam to yon bonny ha'
Whare the roof was o' the beaten gold
  And the floor was o' the cristal a'.

When we came to the stair foot
  Ladies were dancing jimp and sma',
But in the twinkling of an eye
  My wee wee man was clean awa'.

46   *The Twa Brothers*

There were twa brethren in the north,
  They went to school thegithar;
The one unto the other said,
  Will you try a warsle afore?

They wrestled up, they wrestled down,
  Till Sir John fell to the ground,
And there was a knife in Sir Willie's pouch,
  Gied him a deadlie wound.

'Oh brither dear, take me on your back,
  Carry me to yon burn clear,
And wash the blood from off my wound,
  And it will bleed nae mair.'

He took him up upon his back,
  Carried him to yon burn clear,
And washd the blood from off his wound,
  And aye it bled the mair.

'Oh brother dear, take me on your back,
  Carry me to yon kirk-yard,
And dig a grave baith wide and deep,
  And lay my body there.'

He's taen him up upon his back,
  Carried him to yon kirk-yard,
And dug a grave both deep and wide,
  And laid his body there.

'But what will I say to my father dear,
  Should he chance to say, Willie, whar's John?'
'Oh say that he's to England gone,
  To buy him a cask of wine.'

'And what shall I say to my mother dear,
  Should she chance to say, Willie, whar's John?'
'Oh say that he's to England gone,
  To buy her a new silk gown.'

'And what will I say to my sister dear,
  Should she chance to say, Willie, whar's John?'
'Oh say that he's to England gone,
  To buy her a wedding ring.'

'What will I say to her you loe dear,
  Should she cry, Why tarries my John?'
'Oh tell her I lie in fair Kirk-land,
  And home will never come.'

47   *Sir Patrick Spens*

The king sits in Dumferling toune,
　　Drinking the blude-reid wine:
'O whar will I get guid sailor,
　　To sail this schip of mine?'

Up and spak an eldern knicht,
　　Sat at the kings richt kne:
'Sir Patrick Spence is the best sailor
　　That sails upon the se.'

The king has written a braid letter,
　　And signd it wi his hand,
And sent it to Sir Patrick Spence,
　　Was walking on the sand.

The first line that Sir Patrick red,
　　A loud lauch lauched he;
The next line that Sir Patrick red,
　　The teir blinded his ee.

'O wha is this has don this deid,
　　This ill deid don to me,
To send me out this time o' the yeir,
　　To sail upon the se!

Mak hast, mak hast, my mirry men all,
　　Our guid schip sails the morne:'
'O say na sae, my master deir,
　　For I feir a deadlie storme.

Late late yestreen I saw the new moone,
　　Wi the auld moone in hir arme,
And I feir, I feir, my deir master,
　　That we will cum to harme.'

O our Scots nobles wer richt laith
　　To weet their cork-heild schoone;
Bot lang owre a' the play wer playd,
　　Thair hats they swam aboone.

O lang, lang may their ladies sit,
　　Wi thair fans into their hand,
Or eir they se Sir Patrick Spence
　　Cum sailing to the land.

O lang, lang may the ladies stand,
　　Wi thair gold kems in their hair,
Waiting for thair ain deir lords,
　　For they'll se thame na mair.

Haf owre, haf owre to Aberdour,
    It's fiftie fadom deip,
And thair lies guid Sir Patrick Spence,
    Wi the Scots lords at his feit.

48   *Jellon Grame*

O Jellon Grame sat in Silver Wood,
    He whistled and he sang,
And he has calld his little foot-page,
    His errand for to gang.

'Win up, my bonny boy,' he says,
    'As quick as eer you may;
For ye maun gang for Lillie Flower,
    Before the break of day.'

The boy he's buckled his belt about,
    And thro the green-wood ran,
And he came to the ladie's bower-door,
    Before the day did dawn.

'O sleep ye, or wake ye, Lillie Flower?
    The red run's i the rain':
'I sleep not aft, I wake right aft;
    Wha's that that kens my name?'

'Ye are bidden come to Silver Wood,
    But I fear you'll never win hame;
Ye are bidden come to Silver Wood,
    And speak wi Jellon Grame.'

'O I will gang to Silver Wood,
    Though I shoud never win hame;
For the thing I most desire on earth
    Is to speak wi Jellon Grame.'

She had no ridden a mile, a mile,
    A mile but barely three,
Ere she came to a new made grave,
    Beneath a green oak tree.

O then up started Jellon Grame,
    Out of a bush hard bye:
'Light down, light down now, Lillie Flower,
    For it's here that ye maun ly.'

She lighted aff her milk-white steed,
  And knelt upon her knee:
'O mercy, mercy, Jellon Grame!
  For I'm nae prepar'd to die.

Your bairn, that stirs between my sides,
  Maun shortly see the light;
But to see it weltring in my blude
  Woud be a piteous sight.'

'O shoud I spare your life,' he says,
  'Until that bairn be born,
I ken fu well your stern father
  Woud hang me on the morn.'

'O spare my life now, Jellon Grame!
  My father ye neer need dread;
I'll keep my bairn i the good green wood,
  Or wi it I'll beg my bread.'

He took nae pity on that ladie,
  Tho she for life did pray;
But pierced her thro the fair body,
  As at his feet she lay.

He felt nae pity for that ladie,
  Tho she was lying dead;
But he felt some for the bonny boy,
  Lay weltring in her blude.

Up has he taen that bonny boy,
  Gien him to nurices nine,
Three to wake, and three to sleep,
  And three to go between.

And he's brought up that bonny boy,
  Calld him his sister's son;
He thought nae man would eer find out
  The deed that he had done.

But it sae fell out upon a time,
  As a hunting they did gay,
That they rested them in Silver Wood,
  Upon a summer-day.

Then out it spake that bonny boy,
  While the tear stood in his eye,
'O tell me this now, Jellon Grame,
  And I pray you dinna lie.

The reason that my mother dear
  Does never take me hame?
To keep me still in banishment
  Is baith a sin and shame.'

'You wonder that your mother dear
  Does never send for thee;
Lo, there's the place I slew thy mother,
  Beneath that green oak tree.'

Wi that the boy has bent his bow,
  It was baith stout and lang,
And through and thro him Jellon Grame
  He's gard an arrow gang.

Says, 'Lye you thare now, Jellon Grame,
  My mellison you wi;
The place my mother lies buried in
  Is far too good for thee.'

49   *The Wife of Usher's Well*

There lived a wife at Usher's Well,
  And a wealthy wife was she;
She had three stout and stalwart sons,
  And sent them oer the sea.

They hadna been a week from her,
  A week but barely ane,
Whan word came to the carline wife
  That her three sons were gane.

They hadna been a week from her,
  A week but barely three,
Whan word came to the carlin wife
  That her sons she'd never see.

'I wish the wind may never cease,
  Nor fashes in the flood,
Till my three sons come hame to me,
  In earthly flesh and blood.'

It fell about the Martinmass,
  When nights are lang and mirk,
The carlin wife's three sons came hame,
  And their hats were o the birk.

It neither grew in syke nor ditch,
　　Nor yet in ony sheugh;
But at the gates o Paradise,
　　That birk grew fair eneugh.

[· · ·]

'Blow up the fire, my maidens,
　　Bring water from the well;
For a' my house shall feast this night,
　　Since my three sons are well.'

And she has made to them a bed,
　　She's made it large and wide,
And she's taen her mantle her about,
　　Sat down at the bed-side.

[· · ·]

Up then crew the red, red cock,
　　And up and crew the gray;
The eldest to the youngest said,
　　''T is time we were away.'

The cock he hadna crawd but once,
　　And clappd his wings at a',
When the youngest to the eldest said,
　　'Brother, we must awa.

The cock doth craw, the day doth daw,
　　The channerin worm doth chide;
Gin we be mist out o our place,
　　A sair pain we maun bide.

Fare ye weel, my mother dear!
　　Fareweel to barn and byre!
And fare ye weel, the bonny lass
　　That kindles my mother's fire!'

50　　　　　*The Cherry-Tree Carol*

Joseph was an old man,
　　and an old man was he,
And he married Mary,
　　the Queen of Galilee.

When Joseph was married,
　　and Mary home had brought,

Mary proved with child,
  and Joseph knew it not.

Joseph and Mary walked
  through a garden gay,
Where the cherries they grew
  upon every tree.

O then bespoke Mary,
  with words both meek and mild:
'O gather me cherries, Joseph,
  they run so in my mind.'

And then replied Joseph,
  with words so unkind:
'Let him gather thee cherries
  that got thee with child.'

O then bespoke our Saviour,
  all in his mother's womb:
'Bow down, good cherry-tree,
  to my mother's hand.'

The uppermost sprig
  bowed down to Mary's knee:
'Thus you may see, Joseph,
  these cherries are for me.'

'O eat your cherries, Mary,
  O eat your cherries now;
O eat your cherries, Mary,
  that grow upon the bough.'

As Joseph was a walking,
  he heard an angel sing:
'This night shall be born
  our heavenly king.

He neither shall be born
  in housen nor in hall,
Nor in the place of Paradise,
  but in an ox's stall.

He neither shall be clothed
  in purple nor in pall,
But all in fair linen,
  as were babies all.

He neither shall be rocked
  in silver nor in gold,
But in a wooden cradle,
  that rocks on the mould.

He neither shall be christened
   in white wine nor red,
But with fair spring water,
   with which we were christened.'

Then Mary took her young son,
   and set him on her knee:
'I pray thee now, dear child,
   tell how this world shall be.'

'O I shall be as dead, mother,
   as the stones in the wall;
O the stones in the street, mother,
   shall mourn for me all.

And upon a Wednesday
   my vow I will make,
And upon Good Friday
   my death I will take.

Upon Easter-day, mother,
   my rising shall be;
O the sun and the moon
   shall uprise with me.

The people shall rejoice,
   and the birds they shall sing,
To see the uprising
   of the heavenly king.'

51   *Lord Randal*

'O where ha you been, Lord Randal, my son?
And where ha you been, my handsome young man?'
'I ha been at the greenwood; mother, mak my bed soon,
For I'm wearied wi hunting, and fain wad lie down.'

'An wha met ye there, Lord Randal, my son?
An wha met you there, my handsome young man?'
'O I met wi my true-love; mother, mak my bed soon,
For I'm wearied wi huntin, and fain wad lie down.'

'And what did she give you, Lord Randal, my son?
And what did she give you, my handsome young man?'
'Eels fried in a pan; mother, mak my bed soon,
For I'm wearied wi huntin, and fain wad lie down.'

'And wha gat your leavins, Lord Randal, my son?
And wha gat your leavins, my handsome young man?'
'My hawks and my hounds; mother, mak my bed soon,
For I'm wearied wi hunting, and fain wad lie down.'

'And what becam of them, Lord Randal, my son?
And what becam of them, my handsome young man?'
'They stretched their legs out an died; mother, mak my bed soon,
For I'm wearied wi huntin, and fain wad lie down.'

'O I fear you are poisoned, Lord Randal, my son!
I fear you are poisoned, my handsome young man!'
'O yes, I am poisoned; mother, mak my bed soon,
For I'm sick at the heart, and I fain wad lie down.'

'What d'ye leave to your mother, Lord Randal, my son?
What d'ye leave to your mother, my handsome young man?'
'Four and twenty milk kye; mother, mak my bed soon,
For I'm sick at the heart, and I fain wad lie down.'

'What d'ye leave to your sister, Lord Randal, my son?
What d'ye leave to your sister, my handsome young man?'
'My gold and my silver; mother, mak my bed soon,
For I'm sick at the heart, and I fain wad lie down.'

'What d'ye leave to your brother, Lord Randal, my son?
What d'ye leave to your brother, my handsome young man?'
'My houses and my lands; mother, mak my bed soon,
For I'm sick at the heart, and I fain wad lie down.'

'What d'ye leave to your true-love, Lord Randal, my son?
What d'ye leave to your true-love, my handsome young man?'
'I leave her hell and fire; mother, mak my bed soon,
For I'm sick at the heart, and I fain wad lie down.'

52   *Edward*

'Why dois your brand sae drap wi bluid,
Edward, Edward,
Why dois your brand sae drap wi bluid,
And why sae sad gang yee O?'
'O I hae killed my hauke sai guid,
Mither, mither,
O I hae killed my hauke sae guid,
And I had nae mair bot hee O.'

'Your haukis bluid was nevir sae reid,
        Edward, Edward,
Your haukis bluid was nevir sae reid,
    My deir son I tell thee O.'
'O I hae killed my reid-roan steid,
        Mither, mither,
O I hae killed my reid-roan steid,
    That erst was sae fair and frie O.'

'Your steid was auld, and ye hae gat mair,
        Edward, Edward,
Your steid was auld, and ye hae gat mair,
    Sum other dule ye drie O.'
'Oh I hae killed my fadir deir,
        Mither, mither,
O I hae killed my fadir deir,
    Alas, and wae is mee O!'

'And whatten penance wul ye drie for that,
        Edward, Edward?
And whatten penance will ye drie for that?
    My deir son, now tell me O.'
'Ile set my feit in yonder boat,
        Mither, mither,
Ile set my feit in yonder boat,
    And Ile fare ovir the sea O.'

'And what wul ye doe wi your towirs and your ha,
        Edward, Edward?
And what wul ye doe wi your towirs and your ha,
    That were sae fair to see O?'
'Ile let thame stand tul they doun fa,
        Mither, mither,
Ile let thame stand tul they doun fa,
    For here nevir mair maun I bee O.'

'And what wul ye leive to your bairns and your wife,
        Edward, Edward?
And what wul ye leive to your bairns and your wife,
    Whan ye gang ovir the sea O?'
'The warldis room, late them beg thrae life,
        Mither, mither,
The warldis room, late them beg thrae life,
    For thame nevir mair wul I see O.'

'And what wul ye leive to your ain mither deir,
        Edward, Edward?
And what wul ye leive to your ain mither deir?
    My deir son, now tell me O.'

'The curse of hell frae me sall ye beir,
Mither, mither,
The curse of hell frae me sall ye beir,
Sic counseils ye gave to me O.'

John Skelton

53   From *The Tunning of Elinor Rumming*

Then Margery Milkduck
Her kirtle she did uptuck
An inch above her knee,
Her legs that ye might see;
But they were sturdy and stubbed,
Mighty pestles and clubbed,
As fair and as white
As the foot of a kite,
She was somewhat foul,
Crooken-necked like an owl;
And yet she brought her fees,
A cantle of Essex cheese,
Was well a foot thick
Full of maggots quick:
It was huge and great,
And mighty strong meat
For the devil to cat:
It was tart and pungete!

Another set of sluts:
Some brought walnuts,
Some apples, some pears,
Some brought their clipping shears,
Some brought this and that,
Some brought I wot ne'er what;
Some brought their husband's hat,
Some puddings and links,
Some tripes that stinks.
But of all this throng
One came them among,
She seemed half a leech
And began to preach
Of the Tuesday in the week
When the mare doth kick;
Of the virtue of an unset leek,
Of her husband's breek;

With the feathers of a quail
She could to Bordeaux sail;
And with good ale barmè
She could make a charmè
To help withal a stitch:
She seemed to be a witch.

Another brought two goslings
That were noughty frostlings;
She brought them in a wallet,
She was a comely callet:
The goslings were untied;
Elinour began to chide,
'They be wretchocks thou hast brought,
They are sheer shaking nought!'

54   *To Mistress Margaret Hussey*

Merry Margaret,
  As midsummer flower,
Gentle as falcon
Or hawk of the tower:
With solace and gladness,
Much mirth and no madness,
All good and no badness;
  So joyously,
  So maidenly,
  So womanly
  Her demeaning
  In every thing,
  Far, far passing
  That I can indite,
  Or suffice to write
Of Merry Margaret
  As midsummer flower,
Gentle as falcon
Or hawk of the tower.
  As patient and still
And as full of good will
As fair Isaphill,
Coriander,
Sweet pomander,
Good Cassander,
Steadfast of thought,
Well made, well wrought,

Far may be sought
Ere that ye can find
So courteous, so kind
As Merry Margaret,
   This midsummer flower,
Gentle as falcon
Or hawk of the tower.

55   *To Mistress Margery Wentworth*

With marjoram gentle,
   The flower of goodlihead,
Embroidered the mantle
   Is of your maidenhead.
Plainly I cannot glose;
   Ye be, as I devine,
The pretty primrose,
   The goodly columbine.
With marjoram gentle,
   The flower of goodlihead,
Embroidered the mantle
   Is of your maidenhead.
Benign, courteous, and meek,
   With wordès well devis'd;
In you, who list to seek,
   Be virtues well compris'd.
With marjoram gentle,
   The flower of goodlihead,
Embroidered the mantle
   Is of your maidenhead.

Stephen Hawes

56   *The Epitaph of Graunde Amoure*

O mortal folk! you may behold and see
   How I lie here, sometime a mighty knight;
The end of joy and all prosperity
   Is death at last, thorough his course and might;
   After the day there cometh the dark night;
   For though the day be never so long,
   At last the bells ringeth to evensong.

And my self called La Graunde Amoure,
  Seeking adventure in the worldly glory,
For to attain the riches and honour,
  Did think full little that I should here lie,
  Till death did mate me full right privily.
    Lo what I am! and whereto you must!
    Like as I am so shall you be all dust.

Then in your mind inwardly despise
  The brittle world, so full of doubleness,
With the vile flesh, and right soon arise
  Out of your sleep of mortal heaviness;
  Subdue the devil with grace and meekness,
    That after your life frail and transitory
    You may then live in joy perdurably.

Anonymous

57

When as I do record
  The pleasures I have had
At this side slippery board,
  My mind is merry and glad.
With many a lusty lass
  My pleasure I have ta'en:
I would give mine old white Jade
  That Jenny were here again!

She brews and bakes to sell
  For such as do pass by;
Good fellows love her well;
  In faith and so do I!
For ever when I was dry,
  Of drink I would have ta'en,
I would tread both shoes awry,
  That Jenny were here again.

Full often she and I
  Within the buttery play'd,
At traytrip of a day,
  And sent away the maid.
For she is of the dealing trade,
  She will give you three for one:
She is no sullen Jade;
  If Jenny were here again!

A man might for a penny
  Have had a pot of ale,
Or tasted of a coney
  Of either leg or tail.
For she would never fail
  If she were in the vein:
Alas, all flesh were frail
  If Jenny were here again!

Full oft I have been her man,
  Her market for to make;
And after I have ridden
  A journey for her sake,
Her panel I could take,
  And gallop all amain;
I'd make both bedsides crack:
  That Jenny were here again!

You hostesses that mean
  For to live by your trade,
If you scorn to kiss,
  Then keep a pretty maid.
For drink is not worth a louse
  If lasses there be none!
I would drink a whole carrouse
  That Jenny were here again.

58

Of all the seas that's coming,
Of all the woods that's rising,
Of all the fishes in the sea,
Give me a woman's swiving.   *making love*

For she hath pretty fancies
To pass away the night;
And she hath pretty pleasures
To conjure down a sprite.

My father gave me land,
My mother gave me money,
And I have spent it every whit
In hunting of a coney.

I hunted up a hill,
A coney did espy;
My ferret seeing that,
Into her hole did hie.

I put it in again;
It found her out at last;
The coney then betwixt her legs
Did hold my ferret fast,

Till that it was so weak,
Alack, it could not stand!
My ferret then out of her hole
Did come into my hand.

All you that be good fellows,
Give hearing unto me;
And if you would a coney hunt,
A black one let it be.

For black ones are the best,
Their skins will yield most money.
I would to God that he were hang'd
That does not love a coney.

59   *Tom Long*

Come in, Tom longtail, come short hose and round,
Come flat guts and slender, and all to be found,
Come flat cap and feather, and all to be found,
    Strike home thy pipe, Tom Long.

Come lowcy, come lac'd shirt, come damn me, come ruff!
Come holy geneva, a thing without cuff,
Come doughty Dom Diego, with linens enough,
    Strike home thy pipe, Tom Long.

Bring a face out of England, a back out of France,
A belly from Flanders, come all in a dance!
Pin buttocks of Spain, advance! advance!
    Strike home thy pipe, Tom Long.

Come bring in a wench shall fit every nation,
For shape and for making, a tailor's creation,
And new made again to fit every nation,
    Strike home thy pipe, Tom Long.

Come trick it, and tire it, in antic array!
Come trim it, and truss it, and make up the day,
For Tom and Nell, Nick and Gill, make up the hay,
    Strike home thy pipe, Tom Long.

A health to all captains that never was in wars,
That's known by their scarlets and not by their scars!
A health to all Ladies that never us'd merkin,   *pubic wig*
Yet their stuff ruffles like buff leather jerkin!
    Strike home thy pipe, Tom Long.

A health to all courtiers that never bend knees!
And a health to all scholars that scorns their degrees!
And a health to all lawyers that never took fees!
And a health to all Welshmen that loves toasted cheese!
    Strike home thy pipe, Tom Long!

60

Western wind, when will thou blow,
    The small rain down can rain?
Christ, if my love were in my arms
    And I in my bed again!

Sir Thomas Wyatt

61

My lute awake! perform the last
Labour that thou and I shall waste,
And end that I have now begun:
And when this song is sung and past,
My lute be still, for I have done.

As to be heard where ear is none,
As lead to grave in marble stone,
My song may pierce her heart as soon.
Should we then sigh, or sing, or moan?
No, no, my lute, for I have done.

The rocks do not so cruelly
Repulse the waves continually
As she my suit and affection,
So that I am past remedy;
Whereby my lute and I have done.

Proud of the spoil that thou hast got
Of simple hearts thorough Love's shot,
By whom, unkind, thou hast them won:
Think not he hath his bow forgot,
Although my lute and I have done.

Vengeance shall fall on thy disdain
That makest but game on earnest pain;
Think not alone under the sun
Unquit to cause thy lovers plain;
Although my lute and I have done.

May chance thee lie withered and old
In winter nights that are so cold,
Plaining in vain unto the moon;
Thy wishes then dare not be told:
Care then who list, for I have done.

And then may chance thee to repent
The time that thou hast lost and spent
To cause thy lovers sigh and swoon:
Then shalt thou know beauty but lent,
And wish and want as I have done.

Now cease, my lute: this is the last
Labour that thou and I shall waste,
And ended is that we begun.
Now is this song both sung and past:
My lute be still, for I have done.

62   Whoso list to hunt, I know where is an hind,
But as for me, helas, I may no more.
The vain travail hath wearied me so sore,
I am of them that farthest comes behind.
Yet may I by no means my wearied mind
Draw from the Deer, but as she fleeth afore
Fainting I follow. I leave off therefore,
Since in a net I seek to hold the wind.
Who list her hunt (I put him out of doubt)
As well as I may spend his time in vain.
And graven with diamonds in letters plain
There is written her fair neck round about:
'Noli me tangere, for Caesar's I am,
And wild for to hold, though I seem tame.'

63   Blame not my lute, for he must sound
      Of this or that as liketh me;
      For lack of wit the lute is bound
      To give such tunes as pleaseth me;
      Though my songs be somewhat strange,
      And speak such words as touch thy change,
          Blame not my lute.

      My lute, alas, doth not offend,
      Though that perforce he must agree
      To sound such tunes as I intend,
      To sing to them that heareth me;
      Then though my songs be somewhat plain,
      And toucheth some that use to feign,
          Blame not my lute.

      My lute and strings may not deny,
      But as I strike they must obey;
      Break not them then so wrongfully,
      But wreak thyself some other way;
      And though the songs which I indite
      Do quit thy change with rightful spite,
          Blame not my lute.

      Spite asketh spite and changing change,
      And falsed faith must needs be known;
      The faults so great, the case so strange,
      Of right it must abroad be blown:
      Then since that by thine own desert
      My songs do tell how true thou art,
          Blame not my lute.

      Blame but thyself that hast misdone,
      And well deserved to have blame;
      Change thou thy way so evil begun,
      And then my lute shall sound that same:
      But if till then my fingers play
      By thy desert their wonted way,
          Blame not my lute.

      Farewell, unknown, for though thou break
      My strings in spite with great disdain,
      Yet have I found out for thy sake,
      Strings for to string my lute again.
      And if perchance this sely rhyme
      Do make thee blush at any time,
          Blame not my lute.

King Henry VIII

64   *Green Groweth the Holly*

Green groweth the holly, so doth the ivy.
Though winter blasts blow never so high,
Green groweth the holly.

As the holly groweth green
And never changeth hue,
So am I, ever have been,
Unto my lady true.
    Green groweth the holly, etc.

As the holly groweth green
With ivy all alone,
When flowers can not be seen,
And green wood leaves be gone.
    Green groweth the holly, etc.

Now unto my lady
Promise to her I make
From all other only
To her I me betake.
    Green groweth the holly, etc.

Adieu mine own lady,
Adieu my special,
Who hath my heart truly,
Be sure, and ever shall.
    Green groweth the holly, etc.

65   *To His Lady*

Whereto should I express
    My inward heaviness?
No mirth can make me fain,
    Till that we meet again.

Do way, dear heart! Not so!
    Let no thought you dismay.
Though ye now part me fro,
    We shall meet when we may.

When I remember me
    Of your most gentle mind,

It may in no wise agree
  That I should be unkind.

The daisy delectable,
  The violet wan and blo,
Ye are not variable.
  I love you and no mo.

I make you fast and sure.
  It is to me great pain
Thus long to endure
  Till that we meet again.

66   *Pastime*

Pastime with good company
I love and shall, until I die.
Grudge who list, but none deny!
So God be pleas'd, thus live will I.
  For my pastance,
  Hunt, sing and dance,
  My heart is set.
    All goodly sport
    For my comfort
  Who shall me let?

Youth must have some dalliance,
Of good or ill some pastance.
Company me thinks the best,
All thoughts and fancies to digest;
  For idleness
  Is chief mistress
  Of vices all.
    Then who can say
    But mirth and play
  Is best of all?

Company with honesty
Is virtue, vices to flee;
Company is good and ill,
But every man has his free will.
  The best ensue,
  The worst eschew!
  My mind shall be,
    Virtue to use,
    Vice to refuse;
  Thus shall I use me.

Henry Howard, Earl of Surrey

67

When raging love with extreme pain
Most cruelly distrains my heart,
When that my tears, as floods of rain,
Bear witness of my woeful smart,
When sighs have wasted so my breath
That I lie at the point of death:

I call to mind the navy great
That the Grekes brought to Troye town,
And how the boisterous winds did beat
Their ships, and rent their sails adown,
Till Agamemnon's daughter's blood
Appeas'd the gods that them withstood:

And how that in those ten years' war
Full many a bloody deed was done,
And many a lord that came full far
There caught his bane, alas, too soon,
And many a good knight overrun,
Before the Grekes had Helen won.

Then think I thus: 'Sith such repair,
So long time war of valiant men,
Was all to win a lady fair,
Shall I not learn to suffer then?
And think my life well spent, to be
Serving a worthier wight than she?'

Therefore I never will repent,
But pains, contented, still endure;
For like as when, rough winter spent,
The pleasant spring straight draweth in ure;
So, after raging storms of care,
Joyful at length may be my fare.

68

O happy dames, that may embrace
The fruit of your delight,
Help to bewail the woeful case
And eke the heavy plight
Of me, that wonted to rejoice
The fortunes of my pleasant choice.
Good ladies, help to fill my mourning voice.

In ship freight with rememberance
Of thoughts and pleasures past

He sails, that hath in governance
My life while it will last;
With scalding sighs, for lack of gale,
Furthering his hope, that is his sail,
Toward me, the sweet port of his avail.

Alas, how oft in dreams I see
Those eyes that were my food,
Which sometime so delighted me
That yet they do me good:
Wherewith I wake with his return
Whose absent flame did make me burn:
But when I find the lack, Lord how I mourn!

When other lovers, in arms across,
Rejoice their chief delight,
Drowned in tears, to mourn my loss,
I stand the bitter night
In my window, where I may see
Before the winds how the clouds flee:
Lo, what a mariner love hath made of me!

And in green waves, when the salt flood
Doth rise by rage of wind,
A thousand fancies in that mood
Assail my restless mind.
Alas, now drencheth my sweet foe
That with the spoil of my heart did go,
And left me! But, alas, why did he so?

And when the seas wax calm again,
To chase fro me annoy,
My doubtful hope doth cause me plain:
So dread cuts off my joy.
Thus is my wealth mingled with woe,
And of each thought a doubt doth grow:
Now he comes! will he come? alas, no, no!

69   Alas, so all things now do hold their peace:
Heaven and earth disturbed in no thing:
The beasts, the air, the birds their song do cease;
The nightes car the stars about doth bring.
Calm is the sea, the waves work less and less:
So am not I, whom love, alas, doth wring,
Bringing before my face the great increase
Of my desires, whereat I weep and sing
In joy and woe, as in a doubtful case.

For my sweet thoughts sometime do pleasure bring,
But, by and by, the cause of my disease
Gives me a pang that inwardly doth sting,
When that I think what grief it is again
To live and lack the thing should rid my pain.

George Gascoigne

70
    'And if I did, what then?
      Are you aggriev'd therefore?
    The sea hath fish for every man,
      And what would you have more?'

    Thus did my mistress once
      Amaze my mind with doubt;
    And popp'd a question for the nonce,
      To beat my brains about.

    Whereto I thus replied:
      'Each fisherman can wish,
    That all the seas at every tide
      Were his alone to fish.

    And so did I, in vain,
      But since it may not be,
    Let such fish there as find the gain,
      And leave the loss for me.

    And with such luck and loss
      I will content myself,
    Till tides of turning time may toss
      Such fishers on the shelf.

    And when they stick on sands,
      That every man may see,
    Then will I laugh and clap my hands,
      As they do now at me.'

71
The Lullaby of a Lover

    Sing lullaby, as women do,
      Wherewith they bring their babes to rest;
    And lullaby can I sing too,
      As womanly as can the best.

With lullaby they still the child;
And if I be not much beguil'd,
Full many a wanton babe have I,
Which must be still'd with lullaby.

First lullaby my youthful years,
    It is now time to go to bed:
For crooked age and hoary hairs
    Have won the haven within my head.
With lullaby, then, youth be still;
With lullaby content thy will;
Since courage quails and comes behind,
Go sleep, and so beguile thy mind!

Next lullaby my gazing eyes,
    Which wonted were to glance apace;
For every glass may now suffice
    To show the furrows in thy face.
With lullaby then wink awhile;
With lullaby your looks beguile;
Let no fair face, nor beauty bright,
Entice you eft with vain delight.

And lullaby my wanton will;
    Let reason's rule now reign thy thought;
Since all too late I find by skill
    How dear I have thy fancies bought;
With lullaby now take thine ease,
With lullaby thy doubts appease;
For trust to this, if thou be still,
My body shall obey thy will.

Eek lullaby, my loving boy,
    My little Robin take thy rest,
Since age is cold, and nothing coy,
    Keep close thy coin, for so is best
With lullaby be thou content,
With lullaby thy lusts relent,
Let others pay which hath more pence,
Thou art too poor for such expense.

Thus lullaby my youth, mine eyes,
    My will, my ware, and all that was:
I can no more delays devise;
    But welcome pain, let pleasure pass,
With lullaby now take your leave;
With lullaby your dreams deceive;
And when you rise with waking eye,
Remember Gascoigne's lullaby.

Giles Fletcher

72   From *Licia*

In time the strong and stately turrets fall,
In time the rose and silver lilies die,
In time the monarchs captives are, and thrall,
In time the sea and rivers are made dry;
  The hardest flint in time doth melt asunder;
Still-living fame in time doth fade away;
The mountains proud we see in time come under;
And earth, for age, we see in time decay.
  The sun in time forgets for to retire
From out the East, where he was wont to rise;
The basest thoughts we see in time aspire,
And greedy minds in time do wealth despise.
    Thus all, sweet fair, in time must have an end,
    Except thy beauty, virtues, and thy friend.

Sir Walter Raleigh

73   *The Lie*

Go, Soul, the body's guest,
Upon a thankless arrant:
Fear not to touch the best;
The truth shall be thy warrant:
Go, since I needs must die,
And give the world the lie.

Say to the court, it glows
And shines like rotten wood;
Say to the church, it shows
What's good, and doth no good:
If church and court reply,
Then give them both the lie.

Tell potentates, they live
Acting by others' action;
Not lov'd unless they give,
Not strong but by a faction:
If potentates reply,
Give potentates the lie.

Tell men of high condition,
That manage the estate,

Their purpose is ambition,
Their practice only hate:
And if they once reply,
Then give them all the lie.

Tell them that brave it most,
They beg for more by spending,
Who, in their greatest cost,
Seek nothing but commending:
And if they make reply,
Then give them all the lie.

Tell zeal it wants devotion;
Tell love it is but lust:
Tell time it is but motion;
Tell flesh it is but dust:
And wish them not reply,
For thou must give the lie.

Tell age it daily wasteth;
Tell honour how it alters;
Tell beauty how she blasteth;
Tell favour how it falters:
And as they shall reply,
Give every one the lie.

Tell wit how much it wrangles
In tickle points of niceness;
Tell wisdom she entangles
Herself in over-wiseness:
And when they do reply,
Straight give them both the lie.

Tell physic of her boldness;
Tell skill it is pretension;
Tell charity of coldness;
Tell law it is contention:
And as they do reply,
So give them still the lie.

Tell fortune of her blindness;
Tell nature of decay;
Tell friendship of unkindness;
Tell justice of delay:
And if they will reply,
Then give them all the lie.

Tell arts they have no soundness,
But vary by esteeming;
Tell schools they want profoundness,
And stand too much on seeming:

If arts and schools reply,
Give arts and schools the lie.

Tell faith it's fled the city;
Tell how the country erreth;
Tell manhood shakes off pity
And virtue least preferreth:
And if they do reply,
Spare not to give the lie.

So when thou hast, as I
Commanded thee, done blabbing
– Although to give the lie
Deserves no less than stabbing –
Stab at thee he that will,
No stab the soul can kill.

74   What is our life? A play of passion.
And what our mirth but music of division?
Our mother's wombs the tiring-houses be
Where we are drest for this short comedy.
Heaven the judicious sharp spectator is
Who sits and marks what here we do amiss.
The graves that hide us from the searching sun
Are like drawn curtains when the play is done.
Thus playing post we to our latest rest,
And then we die, in earnest, not in jest.

Edmund Spenser

From *Amoretti*

75   I

Happy ye leaves! whenas those lily hands,
Which hold my life in their dead-doing might,
Shall handle you, and hold in love's soft bands,
Like captives trembling at the victor's sight.
And happy lines! on which, with starry light,
Those lamping eyes will deign sometimes to look,
And read the sorrows of my dying sprite,
Written with tears in heart's close-bleeding book.

And happy rhymes! bath'd in the sacred brook
Of Helicon, whence she derived is;
When ye behold that angel's blessed look,
My soul's long-lacked food, my heaven's bliss;
   Leaves, lines, and rhymes, seek her to please alone,
   Whom if ye please, I care for other none!

76
LXIV

Coming to kiss her lips, (such grace I found,)
Meseem'd, I smelt a garden of sweet flowers,
That dainty odours from them threw around,
For damsels fit to deck their lovers' bowers.
Her lips did smell like unto gillyflowers;
Her ruddy cheeks like unto roses red;
Her snowy brows like budded bellamoures;
Her lovely eyes like pinks but newly spread;
Her goodly bosom like a strawberry bed;
Her neck like to a bunch of columbines;
Her breast like lilies, ere their leaves be shed;
Her nipples like young blossom'd jessamines:
   Such fragrant flowers do give most odorous smell;
   But her sweet odour did them all excel.

77
LXXV

One day I wrote her name upon the strand;
But came the waves, and washed it away:
Again, I wrote it with a second hand;
But came the tide, and made my pains his prey.
Vain man, said she, that dost in vain assay
A mortal thing so to immortalize;
For I myself shall like to this decay,
And eke my name be wiped out likewise.
Not so, quoth I; let baser things devise
To die in dust, but you shall live by fame:
My verse your virtues rare shall eternize,
And in the heavens write your glorious name.
   Where, whenas death shall all the world subdue,
   Our love shall live, and later life renew.

78   *Iambicum Trimetrum*

Unhappy verse, the witness of my unhappy state,
    make thyself fluttering wings of thy fast flying
    thought, and fly forth unto my love, whereso'er she be:

Whether lying restless in heavy bed, or else
    sitting so cheerless at the cheerful board, or else
    playing alone careless on her heavenly virginals.

If in bed, tell her that my eyes can take no rest;
    if at board, tell her that my mouth can eat no meat;
    if at her virginals, tell her I can hear no mirth.

Asked why, say waking love suffereth no sleep;
    say that raging love doth appal the weak stomach;
    say that lamenting love marreth the musical.

Tell her that her pleasures were wont to lull me asleep;
    tell her that her beauty was wont to feed mine eyes;
    tell her that her sweet tongue was wont to make me mirth.

Now do I nightly waste, wanting my kindly rest;
    now do I daily starve, wanting my lively food;
    now do I always die, wanting my timely mirth.

And if I waste, who will bewail my heavy chance?
    and if I starve, who will record my cursed end?
    and if I die, who will say: *This was Immerito*?

79   *Prothalamion*

Calm was the day, and through the trembling air
Sweet-breathing Zephyrus did softly play
A gentle spirit, that lightly did delay
Hot Titan's beams, which then did glister fair;
When I (whom sullen care,
Through discontent of my long fruitless stay
In prince's court, and expectation vain
Of idle hopes, which still do fly away,
Like empty shadows, did afflict my brain),
Walk'd forth to ease my pain
Along the shore of silver-streaming Thames;
Whose rutty bank, the which his river hems,
Was painted all with variable flowers,
And all the meads adorn'd with dainty gems
Fit to deck maidens' bowers,

And crown their paramours
Against the bridal day, which is not long:
   Sweet Thames! run softly, till I end my song.

There, in a meadow, by the river's side,
A flock of nymphs I chanced to espy,
All lovely daughters of the flood thereby,
With goodly greenish locks, all loose untied,
As each had been a bride;
And each one had a little wicker basket,
Made of fine twigs, entrailed curiously,
In which they gather'd flowers to fill their flasket,
And with fine fingers cropt full feateously
The tender stalks on high.
Of every sort, which in that meadow grew,
They gather'd some; the violet, pallid blue,
The little daisy, that at evening closes,
The virgin lily, and the primrose true,
With store of vermeil roses,
To deck their bridegrooms' posies
Against the bridal day, which was not long:
   Sweet Thames! run softly, till I end my song.

With that I saw two swans of goodly hue
Come softly swimming down along the lee;
Two fairer birds I yet did never see;
The snow, which doth the top of Pindus strew,
Did never whiter shew,
Nor Jove himself, when he a swan would be,
For love of Leda, whiter did appear;
Yet Leda was (they say) as white as he,
Yet not so white as these, nor nothing near;
So purely white they were,
That even the gentle stream, the which them bare,
Seem'd foul to them, and bad his billows spare
To wet their silken feathers, lest they might
Soil their fair plumes with water not so fair,
And mar their beauties bright,
That shone as heaven's light,
Against their bridal day, which was not long:
   Sweet Thames! run softly, till I cnd my song.

Eftsoons the nymphs, which now had flowers their fill,
Ran all in haste to see that silver brood,
As they came floating on the crystal flood;
Whom when they saw, they stood amazed still,
Their wond'ring eyes to fill;
Them seemed they never saw a sight so fair,
Of fowls so lovely, that they sure did deem

Them heavenly born, or to be that same pair
Which through the sky draw Venus' silver team;
For sure they did not seem
To be begot of any earthly seed,
But rather angels, or of angels' breed;
Yet were they bred of summer's-heat, they say,
In sweetest season, when each flower and weed
The earth did fresh array;
So fresh they seem'd as day,
Even as their bridal day, which was not long:
   Sweet Thames! run softly, till I end my song.

Then forth they all out of their baskets drew
Great store of flowers, the honour of the field,
That to the sense did fragrant odours yield,
All which upon those goodly birds they threw
And all the waves did strew,
That like old Peneus' waters they did seem,
When down along by pleasant Tempe's shore,
Scatt'red with flowers, through Thessaly they stream,
That they appear through lilies' plenteous store,
Like a bride's chamber floor.
Two of those nymphs, meanwhile, two garlands bound
Of freshest flowers which in that mead they found,
The which presenting all in trim array,
Their snowy foreheads therewithal they crowned,
Whilst one did sing this lay,
Prepar'd against that day,
Against their bridal day, which was not long:
   Sweet Thames! run softly, till I end my song.

'Ye gentle birds! the world's fair ornament,
And heaven's glory, whom this happy hour
Doth lead unto your lovers' blissful bower,
Joy may you have, and gentle heart's content
Of your love's complement;
And let fair Venus, that is Queen of Love,
With her heart-quelling son upon you smile,
Whose smile, they say, hath virtue to remove
All love's dislike, and friendship's faulty guile
For ever to assoil.
Let endless peace your steadfast hearts accord,
And blessed plenty wait upon your board:
And let your bed with pleasures chaste abound,
That fruitful issue may to you afford,
Which may your foes confound,
And make your joys redound
Upon your bridal day, which is not long:
   Sweet Thames! run softly, till I end my song.'

So ended she; and all the rest around
To her redoubled that her undersong,
Which said their bridal day should not be long:
And gentle Echo from the neighbour ground
Their accents did resound.
So forth those joyous birds did pass along,
Adown the lee, that to them murmured low,
As he would speak, but that he lackt a tongue,
Yet did by signs his glad affection show,
Making his stream run slow.
And all the fowl which in his flood did dwell
Gan flock about these twain, that did excel
The rest, so far as Cynthia doth shend
The lesser stars. So they, enranged well,
Did on those two attend,
And their best service lend
Against their wedding day, which was not long:
   Sweet Thames! run softly, till I end my song.

At length they all to merry London came,
To merry London, my most kindly nurse,
That to me gave this life's first native source,
Though from another place I take my name,
An house of ancient fame:
There when they came, whereas those bricky towers
The which on Thames' broad aged back do ride,
Where now the studious lawyers have their bowers,
There whilom wont the Templar Knights to bide,
Till they decay'd through pride;
Next whereunto there stands a stately place,
Where oft I gained gifts and goodly grace
Of that great lord, which therein wont to dwell,
Whose want too well now feels my friendless case:
But ah! here fits not well
Old woes, but joys, to tell
Against the bridal day, which is not long:
   Sweet Thames! run softly, till I end my song.

Yet therein now doth lodge a noble peer,
Great England's glory, and the world's wide wonder,
Whose dreadful name late through all Spain did thunder,
And Hercules' two pillars standing near
Did make to quake and fear:
Fair branch of honour, flower of chivalry!
That fillest England with thy triumph's fame,
Joy have thou of thy noble victory,
And endless happiness of thine own name
That promiseth the same;

That through thy prowess, and victorious arms,
Thy country may be freed from foreign harms;
And great Eliza's glorious name may ring
Through all the world, fill'd with thy wide alarms,
Which some brave Muse may sing
To ages following,
Upon the bridal day, which is not long:
   Sweet Thames! run softly, till I end my song.

From those high towers this noble lord issuing,
Like radiant Hesper, when his golden hair
In th' ocean billows he hath bathed fair,
Descended to the river's open viewing,
With a great train ensuing,
Above the rest were goodly to be seen
Two gentle knights of lovely face and feature,
Beseeming well the bower of any queen,
With gifts of wit, and ornaments of nature,
Fit for so goodly stature,
That like the twins of Jove they seem'd in sight,
Which deck the baldric of the heavens bright;
They two, forth pacing to the river's side,
Receiv'd those two fair brides, their love's delight;
Which, at th' appointed tide,
Each one did make his bride
Against their bridal day, which is not long:
   Sweet Thames! run softly, till I end my song.

From *The Faerie Queene*

80

[1]

The Patrone of true Holinesse
Foule Errour doth defeate:
Hypocrisie, him to entrappe,
Doth to his home entreate.

A gentle Knight was pricking on the plaine,
Ycladd in mightie armes and silver shielde,
Wherein old dints of deepe woundes did remaine,
The cruell markes of many' a bloody fielde;
Yet armes till that time did he never wield.
His angry steede did chide his foming bitt,
As much disdayning to the curbe to yield:
Full jolly knight he seemed, and faire did sitt,
As one for knightly giusts and fierce encounters fitt.

And on his brest a bloodie Crosse he bore,
The deare remembrance of his dying Lord,
For whose sweete sake that glorious badge he wore,
And dead, as living, ever him ador'd:
Upon his shield the like was also scor'd,
For soveraine hope which in his helpe he had.
Right faithfull true he was in deede and word,
But of his cheere did seeme too solemne sad;
Yet nothing did he dread, but ever was ydrad.

Upon a great adventure he was bond,
That greatest Gloriana to him gave,
(That greatest Glorious Queene of Faery lond)
To winne him worshippe, and her grace to have,
Which of all earthly thinges he most did crave:
And ever as he rode his hart did earne
To prove his puissance in battell brave
Upon his foe, and his new force to learne,
Upon his foe, a Dragon horrible and stearne.

A lovely Ladie rode him faire beside,
Upon a lowly Asse more white then snow,
Yet she much whiter; but the same did hide
Under a vele, that wimpled was full low;
And over all a blacke stole shee did throw
As one that inly mournd, so was she sad,
And heavie sate upon her palfrey slow;
Seemed in heart some hidden care she had,
And by her, in a line, a milkewhite lambe she lad.

So pure and innocent, as that same lambe,
She was in life and every vertuous lore;
And by descent from Royall lynage came
Of ancient Kinges and Queenes, that had of yore
Their scepters stretcht from East to Westerne shore,
And all the world in their subjection held;
Till that infernall feend with foule uprore
Forwasted all their land, and them expeld;
Whom to avenge she had this Knight from far compeld.

Behind her farre away a Dwarfe did lag,
That lasie seemd, in being ever last,
Or wearied with bearing of her bag
Of needments at his backe. Thus as they past,
The day with cloudes was suddeine overcast,
And angry Jove an hideous storme of raine
Did poure into his Lemans lap so fast,
That everie wight to shrowd it did constrain;
And this faire couple eke to shroud themselves were fain.

Enforst to seeke some covert nigh at hand,
A shadie grove not farr away they spide,
That promist ayde the tempest to withstand;
Whose loftie trees, yclad with sommers pride,
Did spred so broad, that heavens light did hide,
Not perceable with power of any starr:
And all within were pathes and alleies wide,
With footing worne, and leading inward farr.
Faire harbour that them seems, so in they entered ar.

And foorth they passe, with pleasure forward led,
Joying to heare the birdes sweete harmony,
Which, therein shrouded from the tempest dred,
Seemd in their song to scorne the cruell sky.
Much can they praise the trees so straight and hy,
The sayling Pine; the Cedar proud and tall;
The vine-propp Elme; the Poplar never dry;
The builder Oake, sole king of forrests all;
The Aspine good for staves; the Cypresse funerall;

The Laurell, meed of mightie Conquerours
And Poets sage; the Firre that weepeth still:
The Willow, worne of forlorne Paramours;
The Eugh, obedient to the benders will;
The Birch for shaftes; the Sallow for the mill;
The Mirrhe sweete-bleeding in the bitter wound;
The warlike Beech; the Ash for nothing ill;
The fruitfull Olive; and the Platane round;
The carver Holme; the Maple seeldom inward sound.

Led with delight, they thus beguile the way,
Untill the blustring storme is overblowne;
When, weening to returne whence they did stray,
They cannot finde that path, which first was showne,
But wander too and fro in waies unknowne,
Furthest from end then, when they neerest weene,
That makes them doubt their wits be not their owne:
So many pathes, so many turnings seene,
That which of them to take in diverse doubt they been.

At last resolving forward still to fare,
Till that some end they finde, or in or out,
That path they take that beaten seemd most bare,
And like to lead the labyrinth about;
Which when by tract they hunted had throughout,
At length it brought them to a hollowe cave
Amid the thickest woods. The Champion stout
Eftsoones dismounted from his courser brave,
And to the Dwarfe a while his needlesse spere he gave.

'Be well aware,' quoth then that Ladie milde,
'Least suddaine mischiefe ye too rash provoke:
The danger hid, the place unknowne and wilde,
Breedes dreadfull doubts. Oft fire is without smoke,
And perill without show: therefore your stroke,
Sir Knight, with-hold, till further tryall made.'
'Ah Ladie,' (sayd he) 'shame were to revoke
The forward footing for an hidden shade:
Vertue gives her selfe light through darknesse for to wade.'

'Yea but' (quoth she) 'the perill of this place
I better wot then you: though nowe too late
To wish you backe returne with foule disgrace,
Yet wisedome warnes, whilest foot is in the gate,
To stay the steppe, ere forced to retrate.
This is the wandring wood, this *Errours* den,
A monster vile, whom God and man does hate:
Therefore I read beware.' 'Fly, fly!' (quoth then
The fearefull Dwarfe) 'this is no place for living men.'

But, full of fire and greedy hardiment,
The youthfull Knight could not for aught be staide;
But forth unto the darksom hole he went,
And looked in: his glistring armor made
A litle glooming light, much like a shade;
By which he saw the ugly monster plaine,
Halfe like a serpent horribly displaide,
But th' other halfe did womans shape retaine,
Most lothsom, filthie, foule, and full of vile disdaine.

And, as she lay upon the durtie ground,
Her huge long taile her den all overspred,
Yet was in knots and many boughtes upwound,
Pointed with mortall sting. Of her there bred
A thousand yong ones, which she dayly fed,
Sucking upon her poisnous dugs; each one
Of sundrie shapes, yet all ill-favored:
Soone as that uncouth light upon them shone,
Into her mouth they crept, and suddain all were gone.

Their dam upstart out of her den effraide,
And rushed forth, hurling her hideous taile
About her cursed head; whose folds displaid
Were stretcht now forth at length without entraile.
She lookt about, and seeing one in mayle,
Armed to point, sought backe to turne againe;
For light she hated as the deadly bale,
Ay wont in desert darknes to remaine,
Where plain none might her see, nor she see any plaine.

Which when the valiant Elfe perceiv'd, he lept
As Lyon fierce upon the flying pray,
And with his trenchand blade her boldly kept
From turning backe, and forced her to stay:
Therewith enrag'd she loudly gan to bray,
And turning fierce her speckled taile advaunst,
Threatning her angrie sting, him to dismay;
Who, nought aghast, his mightie hand enhaunst:
The stroke down from her head unto her shoulder glaunst.

Much daunted with that dint her sence was dazd;
Yet kindling rage her selfe she gathered round,
And all attonce her beastly bodie raizd
With doubled forces high above the ground:
Tho, wrapping up her wrethed sterne arownd,
Lept fierce upon his shield, and her huge traine
All suddenly about his body wound,
That hand or foot to stirr he strove in vaine.
God helpe the man so wrapt in Errours endlesse traine!

His Lady, sad to see his sore constraint,
Cride out, 'Now, now, Sir knight, shew what ye bee;
Add faith unto your force, and be not faint;
Strangle her, els she sure will strangle thee.'
That when he heard, in great perplexitie,
His gall did grate for griefe and high disdaine;
And, knitting all his force, got one hand free,
Wherewith he grypt her gorge with so great paine,
That soone to loose her wicked bands did her constraine.

Therewith she spewd out of her filthie maw
A floud of poyson horrible and blacke,
Full of great lumps of flesh and gobbets raw,
Which stunck so vildly, that it forst him slacke
His grasping hold, and from her turne him backe.
Her vomit full of bookes and papers was,
With loathly frogs and toades, which eyes did lacke,
And creeping sought way in the weedy gras:
Her filthie parbreake all the place defiled has.

81   [2]

There the most daintie Paradise on ground
It selfe doth offer to his sober eye,
In which all pleasures plenteously abownd,
And none does others happinesse envye;
The painted flowres, the trees upshooting hye,
The dales for shade, the hilles for breathing space,
The trembling groves, the christall running by,
And, that which all faire workes doth most aggrace,
The art which all that wrought appeared in no place.

One would have thought, (so cunningly the rude
And scorned partes were mingled with the fine)
That nature had for wantonesse ensude
Art, and that Art at nature did repine;
So striving each th' other to undermine,
Each did the others worke more beautify;
So diff'ring both in willes agreed in fine:
So all agreed, through sweet diversity,
This Gardin to adorne with all variety.

And in the midst of all a fountaine stood,
Of richest substance that on earth might bee,
So pure and shiny that the silver flood
Through every channell running one might see;
Most goodly it with curious ymageree
Was overwrought, and shapes of naked boyes,
Of which some seemd with lively jollitee
To fly about, playing their wanton toyes,
Whylest others did them selves embay in liquid joyes.

And over all of purest gold was spred
A trayle of yvie in his native hew;
For the rich metall was so coloured,
That wight who did not well avis'd it vew
Would surely deeme it to bee yvie trew:
Low his lascivious armes adown did creepe,
That themselves dipping in the silver dew
Their fleecy flowres they fearefully did steepe,
Which drops of Christall seemd for wantones to weep.

Infinit streames continually did well
Out of this fountaine, sweet and faire to see,
The which into an ample laver fell,
And shortly grew into so great quantitie,
That like a litle lake it seemd to bee;
Whose depth exceeded not three cubits hight,
That through the waves one might the bottom see,
All pav'd beneath with Jaspar shining bright,
That seemd the fountaine in that sea did sayle upright.

And all the margent round about was sett
With shady Laurell trees, thence to defend
The sunny beames which on the billowes bett,
And those which therein bathed mote offend.
As Guyon hapned by the same to wend,
Two naked Damzelles he therein espyde,
Which therein bathing seemed to contend
And wrestle wantonly, ne car'd to hyde
Their dainty partes from vew of any which them eyd.

Sometimes the one would lift the other quight
Above the waters, and then downe againe
Her plong, as over-maystered by might,
Where both awhile would covered remaine,
And each the other from to rise restraine;
The whiles their snowy limbes, as through a vele,
So through the christall waves appeared plaine:
Then suddeinly both would themselves unhele,
And th' amarous sweet spoiles to greedy eyes revele.

As that faire Starre, the messenger of morne,
His deawy face out of the sea doth reare;
Or as the Cyprian goddesse, newly borne
Of th' Ocean's fruitfull froth, did first appeare:
Such seemed they, and so their yellow heare
Christalline humor dropped downe apace.
Whom such when Guyon saw, he drew him neare,
And somewhat gan relent his earnest pace;
His stubborne brest gan secret pleasaunce to embrace.

The wanton Maidens, him espying, stood
Gazing awhile at his unwonted guise;
Then th' one her selfe low ducked in the flood,
Abasht that her a straunger did avise;
But thother rather higher did arise,
And her two lilly paps aloft displayd,
And all that might his melting hart entyse
To her delights she unto him bewrayd;
The rest hidd underneath him more desirous made.

With that the other likewise up arose,
And her faire lockes, which formerly were bownd
Up in one knott, she low adowne did lose,
Which flowing long and thick her cloth'd arownd,
And th' yvorie in golden mantle gownd:
So that faire spectacle from him was reft,
Yet that which reft it no lesse faire was fownd.
So hidd in lockes and waves from lookers theft,
Nought but her lovely face she for his looking left.

Withall she laughed, and she blusht withall,
That blushing to her laughter gave more grace,
And laughter to her blushing, as did fall.
Now when they spyde the knight to slacke his pace
Them to behold, and in his sparkling face
The secrete signes of kindled lust appeare,
Their wanton meriments they did encreace,
And to him beckned to approch more neare,
And shewd him many sights that corage cold could reare.

On which when gazing him the Palmer saw,
He much rebukt those wandring eyes of his,
And counseld well him forward thence did draw.
Now are they come nigh to the Bowre of blis,
Of her fond favorites so nam'd amis,
When thus the Palmer: 'Now, Sir, well avise;
For here the end of all our traveill is:
Here wonnes Acrasia, whom we must surprise,
Els she will slip away, and all our drift despise.'

Eftsoones they heard a most melodious sound,
Of all that mote delight a daintie eare,
Such as attonce might not on living ground,
Save in this Paradise, be heard elsewhere:
Right hard it was for wight which did it heare,
To read what manner musicke that mote bee;
For all that pleasing is to living eare
Was there consorted in one harmonee;
Birdes, voices, instruments, windes, waters, all agree:

The joyous birdes, shrouded in chearefull shade
Their notes unto the voice attempred sweet;
Th' Angelicall soft trembling voyces made
To th' instruments divine respondence meet;
The silver sounding instruments did meet
With the base murmure of the waters fall;
The waters fall with difference discreet,
Now soft, now loud, unto the wind did call;
The gentle warbling wind low answered to all.

There, whence that Musik seemed heard to bee,
Was the faire Witch her selfe now solacing
With a new Lover, whom, through sorceree
And witchcraft, she from farre did thither bring:
There she had him now laid aslombering
In secret shade after long wanton joyes;
Whilst round about them pleasauntly did sing
Many faire Ladies and lascivious boyes,
That ever mixt their song with light licentious toyes.

And all that while right over him she hong
With her false eyes fast fixed in his sight,
As seeking medicine whence she was stong,
Or greedily depasturing delight;
And oft inclining downe, with kisses light
For feare of waking him, his lips bedewd,
And through his humid eyes did sucke his spright,
Quite molten into lust and pleasure lewd;
Wherewith she sighed soft, as if his case she rewd.

The whiles some one did chaunt this lovely lay:
Ah! see, whoso fayre thing doest faine to see,
In springing flowre the image of thy day.
Ah! see the Virgin Rose, how sweetly shee
Doth first peepe foorth with bashfull modestee,
That fairer seemes the lesse ye see her may.
Lo! see soone after how more bold and free
Her bared bosome she doth broad display;
Lo! see soone after how she fades and falls away.

So passeth, in the passing of a day,
Of mortall life the leafe, the bud, the flowre;
Ne more doth florish after first decay,
That earst was sought to deck both bed and bowre
Of many a lady', and many a Paramowre.
Gather therefore the Rose whilest yet is prime,
For soone comes age that will her pride deflowre;
Gather the Rose of love whilest yet is time,
Whilest loving thou mayst loved be with equall crime.

He ceast; and then gan all the quire of birdes
Their diverse notes t'attune unto his lay,
As in approvaunce of his pleasing wordes,
The constant payre heard all that he did say,
Yet swarved not, but kept their forward way
Through many covert groves and thickets close,
In which they creeping did at last display
That wanton Lady with her lover lose,
Whose sleepie head she in her lap did soft dispose.

Upon a bed of Roses she was layd,
As faint through heat, or dight to pleasant sin;
And was arayd, or rather disarayd,
All in a vele of silke and silver thin,
That hid no whit her alablaster skin,
But rather shewd more white, if more might bee:
More subtile web Arachne cannot spin;
Nor the fine nets, which oft we woven see
Of scorched deaw, do not in th' ayre more lightly flee.

Her snowy brest was bare to ready spoyle
Of hungry eies, which n'ote therewith be fild;
And yet, through languour of her late sweet toyle,
Few drops, more cleare then Nectar, forth distild,
That like pure Orient perles adowne it trild;
And her faire eyes, sweet smyling in delight,
Moystened their fierie beames, with which she thrild
Fraile harts, yet quenched not; like starry light,
Which, sparckling on the silent waves, does seeme more
    bright.

The young man, sleeping by her, seemd to be
Some goodly swayne of honorable place,
That certes it great pitty was to see
Him his nobility so fowle deface:
A sweet regard and amiable grace,
Mixed with manly sternesse, did appeare,
Yet sleeping, in his well proportiond face;
And on his tender lips the downy heare
Did now but freshly spring, and silken blossoms beare.

His warlike Armes, the ydle instruments
Of sleeping praise, were hong upon a tree;
And his brave shield, full of old moniments,
Was fowly ras't, that none the signes might see:
Ne for them ne for honour cared hee,
Ne ought that did to his advauncement tend;
But in lewd loves, and wastfull luxuree,
His dayes, his goods, his bodie, he did spend:
O horrible enchantment, that him so did blend!

Sir Philip Sidney

82   From *Astrophel and Stella*

Loving in truth, and fain in verse my love to show,
That She, dear She, might take some pleasure of my pain,
Pleasure might cause her read, reading might make her know,
Knowledge might pity win, and pity grace obtain,
I sought fit words to paint the blackest face of woe;
Studying inventions fine, her wits to entertain,
Oft turning others' leaves, to see if thence would flow
Some fresh and fruitful showers upon my sun-burn'd brain.
But words came halting out, wanting Invention's stay;
Invention, Nature's child, fled stepdame Study's blows;
And others' feet still seem'd but strangers in my way.
Thus, great with child to speak, and helpless in my throes,
Biting my truand pen, beating myself for spite,
'Fool,' said my Muse to me, 'look in thy heart and write.'

83   *The Nightingale*

The nightingale, as soon as April bringeth
Unto her rested sense a perfect waking,
While late bare earth, proud of new clothing, springeth,
Sings out her woes, a thorn her song-book making;
  And, mournfully bewailing,
  Her throat in tunes expresseth
  What grief her breast oppresseth
For Tereus' force on her chaste will prevailing.
O Philomela fair, O take some gladness,
That here is juster cause of plaintful sadness:
  Thine earth now springs, mine fadeth;
Thy thorn without, my thorn my heart invadeth.

Alas, she hath no other cause of anguish
But Tereus' love, on her by strong hand wroken,
Wherein she suffering, all her spirits languish,
Full womanlike complains her will was broken.
  But I, who, daily craving,
  Cannot have to content me,
  Have more cause to lament me,
Since wanting is more woe than too much having.
O Philomela fair, O take some gladness,
That here is juster cause of plaintful sadness:
  Thine earth now springs, mine fadeth;
Thy thorn without, my thorn my heart invadeth.

Fulke Greville, Lord Brooke

84
When all this All doth pass from age to age,
And revolution in a circle turn,
Then heavenly justice doth appear like rage,
The caves do roar, the very seas do burn,
    Glory grows dark, the sun becomes a night,
    And makes this great world feel a greater might.

When love doth change his seat from heart to heart,
And worth about the wheel of fortune goes,
Grace is diseas'd, desert seems overthwart,
Vows are forlorn, and truth doth credit lose;
    Chance then gives law, desire must be wise,
    And look more ways than one, or lose her eyes.

My age of joy is past, of woe begun,
Absence my presence is, strangeness my grace;
With them that walk against me, is my sun:
The wheel is turn'd, I hold the lowest place;
    What can be good to me, since my love is,
    To do me harm, content to do amiss?

John Lyly

85
My shag-hair Cyclops, come, let's ply
Our Lemnian hammers lustily;
      By my wife's sparrows,
      I swear these arrows
      Shall singing fly
    Through many a wanton's eye.
These headed are with golden blisses,
These silver ones feathered with kisses,
      But this of lead
      Strikes a clown dead,
      When in a dance
      He falls in a trance,
To see his black-brow lass not buss him,
And then whines out for death t' untruss him.
So, so, our work, being done let's play,
Holiday (boys), cry Holiday!

Mark Alexander Boyd

86   *Sonet*

Fra bank to bank, fra wood to wood I rin,
    Ourhaillit with my feeble fantasie,
    Lyke til a leif that fallis from a tree,
    Or til a reid ourblawen by the win'.

Twa gods guides me: the ane of them is blin',
    Yea and a bairn, brocht up in fantasie:
    The next a wyf ingenrit of the sea,
    And lichter nor a dauphin with her fin.

Unhappie is the man for evermair
    That tils the sand and sawis in the air:
    But twice unhappier is he, I lairn,

That feidis in his hairt a mad desire,
    And follows on a woman through the fire,
    Led be a blind and teachit be a bairn.

Chidiock Tichbourne

87   My prime of youth is but a frost of cares;
    My feast of joy is but a dish of pain;
My crop of corn is but a field of tares;
    And all my good is but vain hope of gain;
My life is fled, and yet I saw no sun;
And now I live, and now my life is done.

The spring is past, and yet it hath not sprung;
    The fruit is dead, and yet the leaves be green;
My youth is gone, and yet I am but young;
    I saw the world and yet I was not seen;
My thread is cut, and yet it is not spun;
And now I live, and now my life is done.

I sought my death and found it in my womb,
    I look'd for life and saw it was a shade,
I trod the earth and knew it was my tomb,
    And now I die, and now I was but made;
My glass is full, and now my glass is run,
And now I live, and now my life is done.

William Shakespeare

Sonnets

88   XIX

Devouring Time, blunt thou the lion's paws,
And make the earth devour her own sweet brood;
Pluck the keen teeth from the fierce tiger's jaws,
And burn the long-liv'd phœnix in her blood;
Make glad and sorry seasons as thou fleet'st,
And do what'er thou wilt, swift-footed Time,
To the wide world and all her fading sweets;
But I forbid thee one most heinous crime:
O, carve not with thy hours my love's fair brow,
Nor draw no lines there with thine antique pen;
Him in thy course untainted do allow
For beauty's pattern to succeeding men.
        Yet do thy worst, old Time: despite thy wrong,
        My love shall in my verse ever live young.

89   XXIX

When, in disgrace with fortune and men's eyes,
I all alone beweep my outcast state,
And trouble deaf heaven with my bootless cries,
And look upon myself, and curse my fate,
Wishing me like to one more rich in hope,
Featured like him, like him with friends possess'd,
Desiring this man's art and that man's scope,
With what I most enjoy contented least;
Yet in these thoughts myself almost despising,
Haply I think on thee, and then my state,
Like to the lark at break of day arising
From sullen earth, sings hymns at heaven's gate;
        For thy sweet love remember'd such wealth brings
        That then I scorn to change my state with kings.

90   XXX

When to the sessions of sweet silent thought
I summon up remembrance of things past,
I sigh the lack of many a thing I sought,
And with old woes new wail my dear time's waste:
Then can I drown an eye, unus'd to flow,
For precious friends hid in death's dateless night,
And weep afresh love's long since cancell'd woe,
And moan the expense of many a vanish'd sight:
Then can I grieve at grievances foregone,
And heavily from woe to woe tell o'er
The sad account of fore-bemoaned moan,
Which I new pay as if not paid before.
        But if the while I think on thee, dear friend,
        All losses are restor'd and sorrows end.

91   XXXIII

Full many a glorious morning have I seen
Flatter the mountain-tops with sovereign eye,
Kissing with golden face the meadows green,
Gilding pale streams with heavenly alchemy;
Anon permit the basest clouds to ride
With ugly rack on his celestial face,
And from the forlorn world his visage hide,
Stealing unseen to west with this disgrace:
Even so my son one early morn did shine
With all-triumphant splendour on my brow;
But, out, alack! he was but one hour mine,
The region cloud hath mask'd him from me now.
        Yet him for this my love no whit disdaineth;
        Suns of the world may stain when heaven's sun staineth.

92   LIII

What is your substance, whereof are you made,
That millions of strange shadows on you tend?
Since every one hath, every one, one shade,
And you, but one, can every shadow lend.
Describe Adonis, and the counterfeit
Is poorly imitated after you;
On Helen's cheek all art of beauty set,
And you in Grecian tires are painted new:

Speak of the spring and foison of the year,
The one doth shadow of your beauty show,
The other as your bounty doth appear;
And you in every blessed shape we know.
    In all external grace you have some part,
    But you like none, none you, for constant heart.

93   LX

Like as the waves make towards the pebbled shore,
So do our minutes hasten to their end;
Each changing place with that which goes before,
In sequent toil all forwards do contend.
Nativity, once in the main of light,
Crawls to maturity, wherewith being crown'd,
Crooked eclipses 'gainst his glory fight,
And Time that gave doth now his gift confound.
Time doth transfix the flourish set on youth
And delves the parallels in beauty's brow,
Feeds on the rarities of nature's truth,
And nothing stands but for his scythe to mow:
    And yet to times in hope my verse shall stand,
    Praising thy worth, despite his cruel hand.

94   LXII

Sin of self-love possesseth all mine eye
And all my soul and all my every part;
And for this sin there is no remedy,
It is so grounded inward in my heart.
Methinks no face so gracious is as mine,
No shape so true, no truth of such account;
And for myself mine own worth do define,
As I all other in all worths surmount.
But when my glass shows me myself indeed,
Beated and chopp'd with tann'd antiquity,
Mine own self-love quite contrary I read;
Self so self-loving were iniquity.
    'Tis thee, myself, that for myself I praise,
    Painting my age with beauty of thy days.

95   LXVI

Tired with all these, for restful death I cry,
As, to behold desert a beggar born,
And needy nothing trimm'd in jollity,
And purest faith unhappily forsworn,
And gilded honour shamefully misplac'd,
And maiden virtue rudely strumpeted,
And right perfection wrongfully disgrac'd,
And strength by limping sway disabled,
And art made tongue-tied by authority,
And folly, doctor-like, controlling skill,
And simple truth miscall'd simplicity,
And captive good attending captain ill:
        Tir'd with all these, from these would I be gone,
        Save that, to die, I leave my love alone.

96   LXXI

No longer mourn for me when I am dead
Than you shall hear the surly sullen bell
Give warning to the world that I am fled
From this vile world, with vilest worms to dwell:
Nay, if you read this line, remember not
The hand that writ it; for I love you so,
That I in your sweet thoughts would be forgot,
If thinking on me then should make you woe.
O, if, I say, you look upon this verse
When I perhaps compounded am with clay,
Do not so much as my poor name rehearse,
But let your love even with my life decay;
        Lest the wise world should look into your moan,
        And mock you with me after I am gone.

97   LXXIII

That time of year thou mayst in me behold
When yellow leaves, or none, or few, do hang
Upon those boughs which shake against the cold,
Bare ruin'd choirs, where late the sweet birds sang.
In me thou see'st the twilight of such day
As after sunset fadeth in the west;
Which by and by black night doth take away,
Death's second self, that seals up all in rest.

In me thou see'st the glowing of such fire,
That on the ashes of his youth doth lie,
As the death-bed whereon it must expire,
Consum'd with that which it was nourish'd by.
    This thou perceiv'st, which makes thy love more strong,
    To love that well which thou must leave ere long.

98   LXXVI

Why is my verse so barren of new pride,
So far from variation or quick change?
Why with the time do I not glance aside
To new-found methods and to compounds strange?
Why write I still all one, ever the same,
And keep invention in a noted weed,
That every word doth almost tell my name,
Showing their birth and where they did proceed?
O, know, sweet love, I always write of you,
And you and love are still my argument;
So all my best is dressing old words new,
Spending again what is already spent:
    For as the sun is daily new and old,
    So is my love still telling what is told.

99   LXXXVII

Farewell! thou art too dear for my possessing,
And like enough thou know'st thy estimate:
The charter of thy worth gives thee releasing;
My bonds in thee are all determinate.
For how do I hold thee but by thy granting?
And for that riches where is my deserving?
The cause of this fair gift in me is wanting,
And so my patent back again is swerving.
Thyself thou gavest, thy own worth then not knowing,
Or me, to whom thou gavest it, else mistaking;
So thy great gift, upon misprision growing,
Comes home again, on better judgement making.
    Thus have I had thee, as a dream doth flatter,
    In sleep a king, but waking no such matter.

100   XC

Then hate me when thou wilt; if ever, now;
Now, while the world is bent my deeds to cross,
Join with the spite of fortune, make me bow,
And do not drop in for an after-loss:
Ah, do not, when my heart hath 'scaped this sorrow,
Come in the rearward of a conquer'd woe;
Give not a windy night a rainy morrow,
To linger out a purpos'd overthrow.
If thou wilt leave me, do not leave me last,
When other petty griefs have done their spite,
But in the onset come: so shall I taste
At first the very worst of fortune's might;
    And other strains of woe, which now seem woe,
    Compar'd with loss of thee will not seem so.

101   XCVIII

From you have I been absent in the spring,
When proud-pied April, dress'd in all his trim,
Hath put a spirit of youth in every thing,
That heavy Saturn laugh'd and leap'd with him.
Yet nor the lay of birds, nor the sweet smell
Of different flowers in odour and in hue,
Could make me any summer's story tell,
Or from their proud lap pluck them where they grew:
Nor did I wonder at the lily's white,
Nor praise the deep vermilion in the rose;
They were but sweet, but figures of delight,
Drawn after you, you pattern of all those.
    Yet seem'd it winter still, and, you away,
    As with your shadow I with these did play.

102   CVII

Not mine own fears, nor the prophetic soul
Of the wide world dreaming on things to come,
Can yet the lease of my true love control,
Suppos'd as forfeit to a confin'd doom.
The mortal moon hath her eclipse endur'd,
And the sad augurs mock their own presage;
Incertainties now crown themselves assur'd,
And peace proclaims olives of endless age.

Now with the drops of this most balmy time
My love looks fresh, and Death to me subscribes,
Since, spite of him, I'll live in this poor rhyme,
While he insults o'er dull and speechless tribes:
    And thou in this shalt find thy monument,
    When tyrants' crests and tombs of brass are spent.

103   CX

Alas, 'tis true I have gone here and there,
And made myself a motley to the view,
Gor'd mine own thoughts, sold cheap what is most dear,
Made old offences of affections new;
Most true it is that I have look'd on truth
Askance and strangely: but, by all above,
These blenches gave my heart another youth,
And worse essays prov'd thee my best of love.
Now all is done, have what shall have no end:
Mine appetite I never more will grind
On newer proof, to try an older friend,
A god in love, to whom I am confin'd.
    Then give me welcome, next my heaven the best,
    Even to thy pure and most most loving breast.

104   CXXIX

The expense of spirit in a waste of shame
Is lust in action; and till action, lust
Is perjur'd, murderous, bloody, full of blame,
Savage, extreme, rude, cruel, not to trust;
Enjoy'd no sooner but despised straight;
Past reason hunted; and no sooner had,
Past reason hated, as a swallow'd bait,
On purpose laid to make the taker mad:
Mad in pursuit, and in possession so;
Had, having, and in quest to have, extreme;
A bliss in proof, and prov'd, a very woe;
Before, a joy propos'd; behind, a dream.
    All this the world well knows; yet none knows well
    To shun the heaven that leads men to this hell.

105

CXXX

My mistress' eyes are nothing like the sun;
Coral is far more red than her lips' red:
If snow be white, why then her breasts are dun;
If hairs be wires, black wires grow on her head.
I have seen roses damask'd, red and white,
But no such roses see I in her cheeks;
And in some perfumes is there more delight
Than in the breath that from my mistress reeks.
I love to hear her speak, yet well I know
That music hath a far more pleasing sound:
I grant I never saw a goddess go,
My mistress, when she walks, treads on the ground:
    And yet, by heaven, I think my love as rare
    As any she belied with false compare.

106

CXXXVIII

When my love swears that she is made of truth,
I do believe her, though I know she lies,
That she might think me some untutor'd youth,
Unlearned in the world's false subtleties.
Thus vainly thinking that she thinks me young,
Although she knows my days are past the best,
Simply I credit her false-speaking tongue:
On both sides thus is simple truth suppress'd.
But wherefore says she not she is unjust?
And wherefore say not I that I am old?
O, love's best habit is in seeming trust,
And age in love loves not to have years told:
    Therefore I lie with her and she with me,
    And in our faults by lies we flatter'd be.

107

CXLIV

Two loves I have of comfort and despair,
Which like two spirits do suggest me still:
The better angel is a man right fair,
The worser spirit a woman colour'd ill.
To win me soon to hell, my female evil
Tempteth my better angel from my side,
And would corrupt my saint to be a devil,
Wooing his purity with her foul pride.

And whether that my angel be turn'd fiend
Suspect I may, yet not directly tell;
But being both from me, both to each friend,
I guess one angel in another's hell:
    Yet this shall I ne'er know, but live in doubt,
    Till my bad angel fire my good one out.

108   CXLVII

My love is as a fever, longing still
For that which longer nurseth the disease;
Feeding on that which doth preserve the ill,
The uncertain sickly appetite to please.
My reason, the physician to my love,
Angry that his prescriptions are not kept,
Hath left me, and I desperate now approve,
Desire his death, which physic did except.
Past cure I am, now reason is past care,
And frantic-mad with evermore unrest;
My thoughts and my discourse as madmen's are,
At random from the truth vainly express'd;
    For I have sworn thee fair, and thought thee bright,
    Who art as black as hell, as dark as night.

109   CLI

Love is too young to know what conscience is;
Yet who knows not conscience is born of love?
Then, gentle cheater, urge not my amiss,
Lest guilty of my faults thy sweet self prove:
For, thou betraying me, I do betray
My nobler part to my gross body's treason;
My soul doth tell my body that he may
Triumph in love; flesh stays no farther reason,
But rising at thy name doth point out thee
As his triumphant prize. Proud of this pride,
He is contented thy poor drudge to be,
To stand in thy affairs, fall by thy side.
    No want of conscience hold it that I call
    Her 'love' for whose dear love I rise and fall.

110   From *Venus and Adonis*

At this Adonis smiles as in disdain,
That in each cheek appears a pretty dimple:
Love made those hollows, if himself were slain,
He might be buried in a tomb so simple;
    Foreknowing well, if there he came to lie,
    Why, there Love liv'd, and there he could not die.

These lovely caves, these round enchanting pits,
Open'd their mouths to swallow Venus' liking.
Being mad before, how doth she now for wits?
Struck dead at first, what needs a second striking?
    Poor queen of love, in thine own law forlorn,
    To love a cheek that smiles at thee in scorn!

Now which way shall she turn? what shall she say?
Her words are done, her woes the more increasing;
The time is spent, her object will away,
And from her twining arms doth urge releasing.
    'Pity,' she cries, 'some favour, some remorse!'
    Away he springs, and hasteth to his horse.

But, lo, from forth a copse that neighbours by,
A breeding jennet, lusty, young, and proud,
Adonis' trampling courser doth espy,
And forth she rushes, snorts, and neighs aloud:
    The strong neck'd steed, being tied unto a tree,
    Breaketh his rein, and to her straight goes he.

Imperiously he leaps, he neighs, he bounds,
And now his woven girths he breaks asunder;
The bearing earth with his hard hoof he wounds,
Whose hollow womb resounds like heaven's thunder;
    The iron bit he crusheth 'tween his teeth,
    Controlling what he was controlled with.

His ears up-prick'd; his braided hanging mane
Upon his compass'd crest now stand on end;
His nostrils drink the air, and forth again,
As from a furnace, vapours doth he send;
    His eye, which scornfully glisters like fire,
    Shows his hot courage and his high desire.

Sometime he trots, as if he told the steps,
With gentle majesty and modest pride;
Anon he rears upright, curvets and leaps,
As who should say, 'Lo, thus my strength is tried;
    And this I do to captivate the eye
    Of the fair breeder that is standing by.'

What recketh he his rider's angry stir,
His flattering 'Holla' or his 'Stand, I say'?
What cares he now for curb or pricking spur?
For rich caparisons or trapping gay?
   He sees his love, and nothing else he sees,
   For nothing else with his proud sight agrees.

Look, when a painter would surpass the life
In limning out a well-proportion'd steed,
His art with nature's workmanship at strife,
As if the dead the living should exceed;
   So did this horse excel a common one
   In shape, in courage, colour, pace, and bone.

Round-hoof'd, short-jointed, fetlocks shag and long,
Broad breast, full eye, small head, and nostril wide,
High crest, short ears, straight legs, and passing strong,
Thin mane, thick tail, broad buttock, tender hide:
   Look, what a horse should have he did not lack,
   Save a proud rider on so proud a back.

Sometime he scuds far off, and there he stares;
Anon he starts at stirring of a feather;
To bid the wind a base he now prepares,
And whe'r he run or fly they know not whether;
   For through his mane and tail the high wind sings,
   Fanning the hairs, who wave like feath'red wings.

He looks upon his love, and neighs unto her;
She answers him, as if she knew his mind:
Being proud, as females are, to see him woo her,
She puts on outward strangeness, seems unkind;
   Spurns at his love, and scorns the heat he feels,
   Beating his kind embracements with her heels.

Then, like a melancholy malcontent,
He vails his tail, that, like a falling plume,
Cool shadow to his melting buttock lent:
He stamps, and bites the poor flies in his fume.
   His love, perceiving how he is enraged,
   Grew kinder, and his fury was assuaged.

His testy master goeth about to take him;
When, lo, the unback'd breeder, full of fear,
Jealous of catching, swiftly doth forsake him,
With her the horse, and left Adonis there:
   As they were mad, unto the wood they hie them,
   Out-stripping crows that strive to over-fly them.

All swoll'n with chafing, down Adonis sits,
Banning his boist'rous and unruly beast:
And now the happy season once more fits,
That love-sick Love by pleading may be blest;
  For lovers say, the heart hath treble wrong
  When it is barr'd the aidance of the tongue.

An oven that is stopp'd, or river stay'd,
Burneth more hotly, swelleth with more rage:
So of concealed sorrow may be said;
Free vent of words love's fire doth assuage;
  But when the heart's attorney once is mute,
  The client breaks, as desperate in his suit.

He sees her coming, and begins to glow,
Even as a dying coal revives with wind,
And with his bonnet hides his angry brow;
Looks on the dull earth with disturbed mind;
  Taking no notice that she is so nigh,
  For all askance he holds her in his eye.

O, what a sight it was, wistly to view
How she came stealing to the wayward boy!
To note the fighting conflict of her hue,
How white and red each other did destroy!
  But now her cheek was pale, and by and by
  It flash'd forth fire, as lightning from the sky.

Now she was just before him as he sat,
And like a lowly lover down she kneels;
With one fair hand she heaveth up his hat,
Her other tender hand his fair cheek feels:
  His tenderer cheek receives her soft hand's print,
  As apt as new-fall'n snow takes any dint.

O, what a war of looks was then between them!
Her eyes petitioners to his eyes suing;
His eyes saw her eyes as they had not seen them;
Her eyes woo'd still, his eyes disdain'd the wooing:
  And all this dumb-play had his acts made plain
  With tears, which, chorus-like, her eyes did rain.

Full gently now she takes him by the hand,
A lily prison'd in a gaol of snow,
Or ivory in an alabaster band;
So white a friend engirts so white a foe:
  This beauteous combat, wilful and unwilling,
  Show'd like two silver doves that sit a-billing.

From *Henry V*

111   [1]

Chorus   Thus with imagin'd wing our swift scene flies
         In motion of no less celerity
         Than that of thought. Suppose that you have seen
         The well-appointed king at Hampton pier
         Embark his royalty; and his brave fleet
         With silken streamers the young Phœbus fanning:
         Play with your fancies; and in them behold
         Upon the hempen tackle ship-boys climbing;
         Hear the shrill whistle which doth order give
         To sounds confus'd; behold the threaden sails,
         Borne with th' invisible and creeping wind,
         Draw the huge bottoms through the furrow'd sea,
         Breasting the lofty surge: O, do but think
         You stand upon the rivage, and behold
         A city on th' inconstant billows dancing;
         For so appears this fleet majestical,
         Holding due course to Harfleur. Follow, follow!
         Grapple your minds to sternage of this navy;
         And leave your England, as dead midnight still,
         Guarded with grandsires, babies, and old women,
         Either past, or not arriv'd to, pith and puissance;
         For who is he, whose chin is but enrich'd
         With one appearing hair, that will not follow
         These cull'd and choice-drawn cavaliers to France?
         Work, work your thoughts, and therein see a siege;
         Behold the ordnance on their carriages,
         With fatal mouths gaping on girded Harfleur.
         Suppose th' ambassador from the French comes back;
         Tells Harry that the king doth offer him
         Katharine his daughter; and with her, to dowry,
         Some petty and unprofitable dukedoms.
         The offer likes not: and the nimble gunner
         With linstock now the devilish cannon touches,
         And down goes all before them. Still be kind,
         And eke out our performance with your mind.

112   [2]

Chorus   Now entertain conjecture of a time
         When creeping murmur and the poring dark
         Fills the wide vessel of the universe.
         From camp to camp, through the foul womb of night,
         The hum of either army stilly sounds,

That the fix'd sentinels almost receive
The secret whispers of each other's watch:
Fire answers fire; and through their paly flames
Each battle sees the other's umber'd face:
Steed threatens steed, in high and boastful neighs
Piercing the night's dull ear; and from the tents,
The armourers, accomplishing the knights,
With busy hammers closing rivets up,
Give dreadful note of preparation:
The country cocks do crow, the clocks do toll,
And the third hour of drowsy morning name.
Proud of their numbers, and secure in soul,
The confident and over-lusty French
Do the low-rated English play at dice;
And chide the cripple tardy-gaited night,
Who, like a foul and ugly witch, doth limp
So tediously away. The poor condemned English,
Like sacrifices, by their watchful fires
Sit patiently, and inly ruminate
The morning's danger; and their gesture sad
Investing lank-lean cheeks, and war-worn coats,
Presenteth them unto the gazing moon
So many horrid ghosts. O, now, who will behold
The royal captain of this ruin'd band
Walking from watch to watch, from tent to tent,
Let him cry, 'Praise and glory on his head!'
For forth he goes and visits all his host;
Bids them good morrow with a modest smile,
And calls them brothers, friends, and countrymen.
Upon his royal face there is no note
How dread an army hath enrounded him;
Nor doth he dedicate one jot of colour
Unto the weary and all-watched night;
But freshly looks, and over-bears attaint
With cheerful semblance and sweet majesty;
That every wretch, pining and pale before,
Beholding him, plucks comfort from his looks:
A largess universal, like the sun,
His liberal eye doth give to every one,
Thawing cold fear. Then, mean and gentle all,
Behold, as may unworthiness define,
A little touch of Harry in the night:

From *Hamlet*

113   [1]

Enter Ghost

Hamlet   Angels and ministers of grace defend us! –
          Be thou a spirit of health or goblin damn'd,
          Bring with thee airs from heaven or blasts from hell,
          Be thy intents wicked or charitable,
          Thou comest in such a questionable shape,
          That I will speak to thee: I'll call thee Hamlet,
          King, father, royal Dane: O, answer me!
          Let me not burst in ignorance; but tell
          Why thy canoniz'd bones, hearsed in death,
          Have burst their cerements; why the sepulchre,
          Wherein we saw thee quietly inurn'd,
          Hath op'd his ponderous and marble jaws
          To cast thee up again! What may this mean,
          That thou, dead corse, again, in complete steel,
          Revisits thus the glimpses of the moon,
          Making night hideous; and we fools of nature
          So horridly to shake our disposition
          With thoughts beyond the reaches of our souls?
          Say, why is this? wherefor? what should we do?
                                    [Ghost *beckons* Hamlet]

Horatio   It beckons you to go away with it,
          As if it some impartment did desire
          To you alone.

Marcellus   Look, with what courteous action
          It waves you to a more removed ground:
          But do not go with it.

Horatio   No, by no means.

Hamlet   It will not speak; then I will follow it.

Horatio   Do not, my lord.

Hamlet   Why, what should be the fear?
          I do not set my life at a pin's fee;
          And for my soul, what can it do to that,
          Being a thing immortal as itself?
          It waves me forth again; – I'll follow it.

Horatio   What if it tempt you toward the flood, my lord,
          Or to the dreadful summit of the cliff
          That beetles o'er his base into the sea,
          And there assume some other horrible form,
          Which might deprive your sovereignty of reason,
          And draw you into madness? think of it:

The very place puts toys of desperation,
Without more motive, into every brain,
That looks so many fathoms to the sea,
And hears it roar beneath.

Hamlet   It waves me still. —
Go on; I'll follow thee.

114   [2]

Laertes   What ceremony else?
First Priest   Her obsequies have been as far enlarg'd
As we have warrantise: her death was doubtful;
And, but that great command o'ersways the order,
She should in ground unsanctified have lodg'd
Till the last trumpet; for charitable prayers,
Shards, flints, and pebbles should be thrown on her:
Yet here she is allow'd her virgin crants,
Her maiden strewments, and the bringing home
Of bell and burial.

Laertes   Must there no more be done?
First Priest   No more be done:
We should profane the service of the dead
To sing a requiem, and such rest to her
As to peace-parted souls.

Laertes   Lay her i' th' earth; —
And from her fair and unpolluted flesh
May violets spring! — I tell thee, churlish priest,
A minist'ring angel shall my sister be,
When thou liest howling.

From *Othello*

115   [1]

Othello   Her father lov'd me; oft invited me;
Still question'd me the story of my life,
From year to year, — the battles, sieges, fortunes,
That I have pass'd.
I ran it through, even from my boyish days
To the very moment that he bade me tell it:
Wherein I spake of most disastrous chances,
Of moving accidents by flood and field;
Of hair-breadth scapes i' th' imminent deadly breach;

Of being taken by the insolent foe,
And sold to slavery; of my redemption thence,
And portance in my travel's history:
Wherein of antres vast and deserts idle,
Rough quarries, rocks, and hills whose heads touch heaven,
It was my hint to speak, – such was the process;
And of the Cannibals that each other eat,
The Anthropophagi, and men whose heads
Do grow beneath their shoulders. This to hear
Would Desdemona seriously incline:
But still the house-affairs would draw her thence;
Which ever as she could with haste dispatch,
She'ld come again, and with a greedy ear
Devour up my discourse: – which I observing,
Took once a pliant hour; and found good means
To draw from her a prayer of earnest heart
That I would all my pilgrimage dilate,
Whereof by parcels she had something heard,
But not intentively: I did consent;
And often did beguile her of her tears,
When I did speak of some distressful stroke
That my youth suffer'd. My story being done,
She gave me for my pains a world of sighs:
She swore, – in faith, 'twas strange, 'twas passing strange;
'Twas pitiful, 'twas wondrous pitiful:
She wish'd she had not heard it: yet she wish'd
That heaven had made her such a man: she thank'd me;
And bade me, if I had a friend that lov'd her,
I should but teach him how to tell my story,
And that would woo her. Upon this hint I spake:
She lov'd me for the dangers I had pass'd;
And I lov'd her that she did pity them.
This only is the witchcraft I have used:–

116   [2]

Othello   It is the cause, it is the cause, my soul, –
Let me not name it to you, you chaste stars!
It is the cause. – Yet I'll not shed her blood:
Nor scar that whiter skin of hers than snow,
And smooth as monumental alabaster.
Yet she must die, else she'll betray more men. –
Put out the light, and then put out the light:
If I quench thee, thou flaming minister,
I can again thy former light restore,
Should I repent me: – but once put out thy light,

Thou cunning'st pattern of excelling nature,
I know not where is that Promethean heat
That can thy light relume. When I have pluck'd the rose,
I cannot give it vital growth again,
It needs must wither: — I'll smell it on the tree. —

[*Kissing her*]

O balmy breath, that dost almost persuade
Justice to break her sword! — One more, one more: —
Be thus when thou art dead, and I will kill thee,
And love thee after: — one more, and this the last:
So sweet was ne'er so fatal. I must weep,
But they are cruel tears: this sorrow's heavenly;
It strikes where it doth love. — She wakes.

Desdemona   Who's there? Othello?
Othello   Ay, Desdemona.
Desdemona   Will you come to bed, my lord?
Othello   Have you pray'd to-night, Desdemona?
Desdemona   Ay, my lord.
Othello   If you bethink yourself of any crime
Unreconcil'd as yet to heaven and grace,
Solicit for it straight.
Desdemona   Alack, my lord, what may you mean by that?
Othello   Well, do it, and be brief; I will walk by:
I would not kill thy unprepared spirit;
No, — heaven forfend! — I would not kill thy soul.

From *Macbeth*

117   [1]

Macbeth   I have done the deed. — Didst thou not hear a noise?
Lady Macbeth   I heard the owl scream and the crickets cry.
Did not you speak?
Macbeth   When?
Lady Macbeth   Now.
Macbeth   As I descended?
Lady Macbeth   Ay.
Macbeth   Hark! —
Who lies i' th' second chamber?
Lady Macbeth   Donalbain.
Macbeth   This is a sorry sight.   [*Looking on his hands*]
Lady Macbeth   A foolish thought, to say a sorry sight.
Macbeth   There's one did laugh in 's sleep, and one cried 'Murder!'
That they did wake each other: I stood and heard them:
But they did say their prayers, and address'd them
Again to sleep.

Lady Macbeth	There are two lodg'd together.
Macbeth	One cried 'God bless us!' and 'Amen!' the other;
	As they had seen me, with these hangman's hands.
	Listening their fear, I could not say 'Amen!'
	When they did say 'God bless us!'
Lady Macbeth	Consider it not so deeply.
Macbeth	But wherefore could not I pronounce 'Amen'?
	I had most need of blessing, and 'Amen'
	Stuck in my throat.
Lady Macbeth	These deeds must not be thought
	After these ways; so, it will make us mad.
Macbeth	Methought I heard a voice cry, 'Sleep no more!
	Macbeth does murder sleep,' – the innocent sleep,
	Sleep that knits up the ravell'd sleave of care,
	The death of each day's life, sore labour's bath,
	Balm of hurt minds, great nature's second course.
	Chief nourisher in life's feast, –
Lady Macbeth	What do you mean?
Macbeth	Still it cried 'Sleep no more!' to all the house:
	'Glamis hath murder'd sleep, and therefore Cawdor
	Shall sleep no more, – Macbeth shall sleep no more!'
Lady Macbeth	Who was it that thus cried? Why, worthy thane,
	You do unbend your noble strength, to think
	So brainsickly of things. – Go get some water,
	And wash this filthy witness from your hand. –
	Why did you bring these daggers from the place?
	They must lie there: go carry them, and smear
	The sleepy grooms with blood.
Macbeth	I'll go no more:
	I am afraid to think what I have done;
	Look on 't again I dare not.
Lady Macbeth	Infirm of purpose!
	Give me the daggers: the sleeping and the dead
	Are but as pictures: 'tis the eye of childhood
	That fears a painted devil. If he do bleed,
	I'll gild the faces of the grooms withal;
	For it must seem their guilt. [*Exit. Knock within*]
Macbeth	Whence is that knocking?
	How is 't with me, when every noise appals me?
	What hands are here? ha! they pluck out mine eyes!
	Will all great Neptune's ocean wash this blood
	Clean from my hand? No; this my hand will rather
	The multitudinous seas incarnadine,
	Making the green one red.

118   [2]

Macbeth   Hang out our banners on the outward walls;
           The cry is still, 'They come': our castle's strength
           Will laugh a siege to scorn: here let them lie
           Till famine and the ague eat them up:
           Were they not forc'd with those that should be ours,
           We might have met them dareful, beard to beard,
           And beat them backward home.
                                        [A cry within of women]
                                        What is that noise?
Seyton   It is the cry of women, my good lord.   [Exit]
Macbeth   I have almost forgot the taste of fears:
           The time has been, my senses would have cool'd
           To hear a night-shriek; and my fell of hair
           Would at a dismal treatise rouse and stir
           As life were in 't: I have supp'd full with horrors;
           Direness, familiar to my slaughterous thoughts,
           Cannot once start me.
                         [Enter Seyton]
                                    Wherefore was that cry?
Seyton   The queen, my lord, is dead.
Macbeth   She should have died hereafter;
           There would have been a time for such a word. –
           To-morrow, and to-morrow, and to-morrow,
           Creeps in this petty pace from day to day,
           To the last syllable of recorded time;
           And all our yesterdays have lighted fools
           The way to dusty death. Out, out, brief candle!
           Life's but a walking shadow; a poor player,
           That struts and frets his hour upon the stage,
           And then is heard no more: it is a tale
           Told by an idiot, full of sound and fury,
           Signifying nothing.

119   From King Lear

Doctor   Please you, draw near. – Louder the music there!
Cordelia   O my dear father! Restoration hang
           Thy medicine on my lips; and let this kiss
           Repair those violent harms that my two sisters
           Have in thy reverence made!
Kent   Kind and dear princess!
Cordelia   Had you not been their father, these white flakes
           Had challeng'd pity of them. Was this a face
           To be oppos'd against the warring winds?

To stand against the deep dread-bolted thunder?
In the most terrible and nimble stroke
Of quick, cross lightning? to watch – poor perdu! –
With this thin helm? Mine enemy's dog,
Though he had bit me, should have stood that night
Against my fire; and wast thou fain, poor father,
To hovel thee with swine, and rogues forlorn,
In short and musty straw? Alack, alack!
'Tis wonder that thy life and wits at once
Had not concluded all. – He wakes; speak to him.

Doctor   Madam, do you: 'tis fittest.

Cordelia   How does my royal lord? how fares your majesty?

King Lear   You do me wrong to take me out o' the grave: –
Thou art a soul in bliss; but I am bound
Upon a wheel of fire, that mine own tears
Do scald like molten lead.

Cordelia   Sir, do you know me?

King Lear   You are a spirit, I know: when did you die?

Cordelia   Still, still, far wide!

Doctor   He's scarce awake: let him alone awhile.

King Lear   Where have I been? Where am I? – Fair daylight? –
I am mightily abus'd. – I should e'en die with pity,
To see another thus. – I know not what to say. –
I will not swear these are my hands: – let's see;
I feel this pin prick. Would I were assured
Of my condition.

Cordelia   O, look upon me, sir,
And hold your hands in benediction o'er me: –
No, sir, you must not kneel.

King Lear   Pray, do not mock me:
I am a very foolish fond old man,
Fourscore and upward, not an hour more nor less;
And, to deal plainly,
I fear I am not in my perfect mind.
Methinks I should know you, and know this man;
Yet I am doubtful: for I am mainly ignorant
What place this is; and all the skill I have
Remembers not these garments; nor I know not
Where I did lodge last night. Do not laugh at me;
For, as I am a man, I think this lady
To be my child Cordelia.

Cordelia   And so I am, I am.

King Lear   Be your tears wet? yes, faith. I pray, weep not:
If you have poison for me, I will drink it.
I know you do not love me; for your sisters
Have, as I do remember, done me wrong:
You have some cause, they have not.

Cordelia   No cause, no cause.

King Lear	Am I in France?
Kent	In your own Kingdom, sir.
King Lear	Do not abuse me.
Doctor	Be comforted, good madam: the great rage,
	You see, is kill'd in him: and yet it is danger
	To make him even o'er the time he has lost.
	Desire him to go in; trouble him no more
	Till further settling.
Cordelia	Will 't please your highness walk?
King Lear	You must bear with me:
	Pray you now, forget and forgive; I am old and foolish.

From *Antony and Cleopatra*

120   [1]

Antony	Eros, thou yet behold'st me?
Eros	Ay, noble lord.
Antony	Sometime we see a cloud that's dragonish;
	A vapour sometime like a bear or lion,
	A tower'd citadel, a pendant rock,
	A forked mountain, or blue promontory
	With trees upon 't, that nod unto the world,
	And mock our eyes with air: thou hast seen these signs;
	They are black vesper's pageants.
Eros	Ay, my lord.
Antony	That which is now a horse, even with a thought
	The rack dislimns, and makes it indistinct
	As water is in water.
Eros	It does, my lord.
Antony	My good knave Eros, now thy captain is
	Even such a body: here I am Antony;
	Yet cannot hold this visible shape, my knave.
	I made these wars for Egypt; and the queen, –
	Whose heart I thought I had, for she had mine;
	Which, whilst it was mine, had annex'd unto 't
	A million moe, now lost, – she, Eros, has
	Pack'd cards with Cæsar, and false-play'd my glory
	Unto an enemy's triumph. –
	Nay, weep not, gentle Eros; there is left us
	Ourselves to end ourselves.

121   [2]

Antony   The miserable change now at my end
          Lament nor sorrow at; but please your thoughts
          In feeding them with those my former fortunes,
          Wherein I liv'd the greatest prince o' the world,
          The noblest; and do now not basely die,
          Not cowardly put off my helmet to
          My countryman, – a Roman by a Roman
          Valiantly vanquish'd. Now my spirit is going,
          I can no more.
Cleopatra   Noblest of men, woo 't die?
          Hast thou no care of me? shall I abide
          In this dull world, which in thy absence is
          No better than a sty? – O, see, my women,
                                              [Antony dies]

          The crown o' the earth doth melt. – My lord!
          O, wither'd is the garland of the war,
          The soldier's pole is fall'n: young boys and girls
          Are level now with men; the odds is gone,
          And there is nothing left remarkable
          Beneath the visiting moon.   [Faints]

122   From *Timon of Athens*

Timon   Warr'st thou 'gainst Athens?
Alcibiades   Ay, Timon, and have cause.
Timon   The gods confound them all in thy conquest;
           And thee after, when thou hast conquered!
Alcibiades Why me, Timon?
Timon   That, by killing of villains, thou wast born to conquer
           My country.
           Put up thy gold: go on, – here's gold, – go on;
           Be as a planetary plague, when Jove
           Will o'er some high-vic'd city hang his poison
           In the sick air: let not thy sword skip one:
           Pity not honour'd age for his white beard, –
           He is an usurer: strike me the counterfeit matron, –
           It is her only habit that is honest,
           Herself's a bawd: let not the virgin's cheek
           Make soft thy trenchant sword; for those milk-paps
           That through the window-bars bore at men's eyes,
           Are not within the leaf of pity writ,
           But set down horrible traitors: spare not the babe,
           Whose dimpled smiles from fools exhaust their mercy;
           Think it a bastard, whom the oracle
           Hath doubtfully pronounc'd thy throat shall cut,

And mince it sans remorse: swear against objects;
Put armour on thine ears and on thine eyes,
Whose proof, nor yells of mothers, maids, nor babes,
Nor sight of priests in holy vestments bleeding,
Shall pierce a jot. There's gold to pay thy soldiers:
Make large confusion; and, thy fury spent,
Confounded be thyself! Speak not, be gone.

Alcibiades Hast thou gold yet? I'll take the gold thou givest me,
Not all thy counsel.

Timon Dost thou, or dost thou not, heaven's curse upon thee!

Phrynia }
Timandra } Give us some gold, good Timon: hast thou more?

Timon Enough to make a whore forswear her trade,
And to make whores, a bawd. Hold up, you sluts,
Your aprons mountant: you are not oathable, –
Although, I know, you'll swear, terribly swear,
Into strong shudders and to heavenly agues,
Th' immortal gods that hear you; – spare your oaths,
I'll trust to your conditions: be whores still;
And he whose pious breath seeks to convert you,
Be strong in whore, allure him, burn him up;
Let your close fire predominate his smoke,
And be no turncoats: yet may your pains, six months,
Be quite contrary: and thatch your poor thin roofs
With burdens of the dead; – some that were hang'd,
No matter: – wear them, betray with them: whore still;
Paint till a horse may mire upon your face:
A pox of wrinkles!

123   From *Pericles*

Pericles A terrible childbed hast thou had, my dear;
No light, no fire: th' unfriendly elements
Forgot thee utterly; nor have I time
To give thee hallow'd to thy grave, but straight
Must cast thee, scarcely coffin'd, in the ooze;
Where, for a monument upon thy bones,
And aye-remaining lamps, the belching whale
And humming water must o'erwhelm thy corpse,
Lying with simple shells. – O Lychorida,
Bid Nestor bring my spices, ink and paper,
My casket and my jewels; and bid Nicander
Bring me the satin coffer: lay the babe
Upon the pillow: hie thee, whiles I say
A priestly farewell to her: suddenly, woman.

From *Cymbeline*

124   [1]

Arviragus   With fairest flowers,
Whilst summer lasts, and I live here, Fidele,
I'll sweeten thy sad grave: thou shalt not lack
The flower that's like thy face, pale primrose; nor
The azur'd harebell, like thy veins; no, nor
The leaf of eglantine, whom not to slander,
Out-sweeten'd not thy breath: the ruddock would,
With charitable bill, – O bill, sore-shaming
Those rich-left heirs that let their fathers lie
Without a monument! – bring thee all this;
Yea, and furr'd moss besides, when flowers are none,
To winter-ground thy corse.
Guiderius   Prithee, have done;
And do not play in wench-like words with that
Which is so serious. Let us bury him,
And not protract with admiration what
Is now due debt. – To the grave!
Arviragus   Say, where shall's lay him?
Guiderius By good Euriphile, our mother.
Arviragus   Be 't so:
And let us, Polydore, though now our voices
Have got the mannish crack, sing him to the ground,
As once our mother; use like note and words,
Save that Euriphile must be Fidele.
Guiderius Cadwal,
I cannot sing: I'll weep, and word it with thee;
For notes of sorrow out of tune are worse
Than priests and fanes that lie.
Arviragus   We'll speak it, then.

125   [2]

Guiderius Fear no more the heat o' the sun,
            Nor the furious winter's rages;
         Thou thy worldly task hast done,
            Home art gone, and ta'en thy wages:
         Golden lads and girls all must,
            As chimney-sweepers, come to dust.
Arviragus Fear no more the frown o' the great,
            Thou art past the tyrant's stroke;
         Care no more to clothe and eat;
            To thee the reed is as the oak:

	The sceptre, learning, physic, must
	All follow this, and come to dust.
Guiderius	Fear no more the lightning-flash,
Arviragus	Nor th' all-dreaded thunder-stone;
Guiderius	Fear not slander, censure rash;
Arviragus	Thou hast finish'd joy and moan:
Both	All lovers young, all lovers must,
	Consign to thee, and come to dust.
Guiderius	No exorciser harm thee!
Arviragus	Nor no witchcraft charm thee!
Guiderius	Ghost unlaid forbear thee!
Arviragus	Nothing ill come near thee!
Both	Quiet consummation have;
	And renowned be thy grave!

126   From *The Tempest*

Prospero   Ye elves of hills, brooks, standing lakes, and groves;
And ye that on the sands with printless foot
Do chase the ebbing Neptune, and do fly him
When he comes back; you demi-puppets that
By moonshine do the green sour ringlets make,
Whereof the ewe not bites; and you whose pastime
Is to make midnight mushrumps, that rejoice
To hear the solemn curfew; by whose aid –
Weak masters though ye be – I have bedimm'd
The noontide sun, call'd forth the mutinous winds,
And 'twixt the green sea and the azur'd vault
Set roaring war: to the dread-rattling thunder
Have I given fire, and rifted Jove's stout oak
With his own bolt: the strong-bas'd promontory
Have I made shake; and by the spurs pluck'd up
The pine and cedar: graves at my command
Have wak'd their sleepers, op'd, and let 'em forth
By my so potent art. But this rough magic
I here abjure; and, when I have required
Some heavenly music, – which even now I do, –
To work mine end upon their senses that
This airy charm is for, I'll break my staff,
Bury it certain fadoms in the earth,
And deeper than did ever plummet sound
I'll drown my book.   [*Solemn music*]

Songs from the Plays

127   [1]

When that I was and a little tiny boy,
　With hey, ho! the wind and the rain,
A foolish thing was but a toy,
　For the rain it raineth every day.

But when I came to man's estate,
　With hey, ho! the wind and the rain,
'Gainst knaves and thieves men shut their gates,
　For the rain it raineth every day.

But when I came, alas! to wive,
　With hey, ho! the wind and the rain,
By swaggering could I never thrive,
　For the rain it raineth every day.

For when I came unto my beds,
　With hey, ho! the wind and the rain,
With toss-pots still had drunken heads,
　For the rain it raineth every day.

A great while ago the world begun,
　With hey, ho! the wind and the rain,
But that's all one, our play is done,
　And we'll strive to please you every day.

Sung by Feste in 'Twelfth Night'

128   [2]

How should I your true love know
　From another one?
'By his cockle hat and staff
　And his sandal shoon.'

He is dead and gone, lady,
　He is dead and gone;
At his head a grass-green turf,
　At his heels a stone.

White his shroud as the mountain snow,
　Larded with sweet flowers,
Which bewept to the grave did go
　With true-love showers.

Sung by Ophelia in 'Hamlet'

129

[3]

Take, O take, those lips away,
   That so sweetly were forsworn;
And those eyes, the break of day,
   Lights that do mislead the morn:
But my kisses bring again
           Bring again:
Seals of love but sealed in vain,
           – Sealed in vain!

Sung by 'a Boy', servant to Mariana, in
           'Measure for Measure'

130

[4]

Full fathom five thy father lies,
Of his bones are coral made:
Those are pearls that were his eyes.
Nothing of him that doth fade
But doth suffer a sea-change
Into something rich and strange:
Sea-nymphs hourly ring his knell.
         'Ding-dong.'
Hark! now I hear them – 'ding-dong bell'.

Sung by Ariel in 'The Tempest'

Christopher Marlowe

Translations from Ovid's *Amores*

131

To His Mistress (i.3)

I ask but right: let her that caught me late
Either love, or cause that I may never hate.
I ask too much, would she but let me love her;
Love knows with such like prayers I daily move her.
Accept him that will serve thee all his youth,
Accept him that will love with spotless truth.
If lofty titles cannot make me thine
That am descended but of knightly line
(Soon may you plough the little land I have;
I gladly grant my parents given to save),

Apollo, Bacchus and the Muses may,
And Cupid, who hath mark'd me for thy prey,
My spotless life, which but to gods gives place,
Naked simplicity, and modest grace.
I love but one, and her I love change never,
If men have faith, I'll live with thee for ever.
The years that fatal destiny shall give
I'll live with thee, and die, or thou shalt grieve.
Be thou the happy subject of my books,
That I may write things worthy thy fair looks.
By verses horned Io got her name,
And she to whom in shape of swan Jove came,
And she that on a feign'd bull swam to land,
Griping his false horns with her virgin hand.
So likewise we will through the world be rung,
And with my name shall thine be always sung.

132   *The Visitation* (i.5)

In summer's heat, and mid-time of the day,
To rest my limbs upon a bed I lay;
One window shut, the other open stood,
Which gave such light as twinkles in a wood
Like twilight glimpse at setting of the sun,
Or night being past, and yet not day begun.
Such light to shamefast maidens must be shown,
Where they may sport and seem to be unknown.
Then came Corinna in a long loose gown,
Her white neck hid with tresses hanging down,
Resembling fair Semiramis going to bed,
Or Lais of a thousand wooers sped.
I snatch'd her gown; being thin, the harm was small,
Yet striv'd she to be covered therewithal,
And striving thus as one that would be cast,
Betray'd herself, and yielded at the last.
Stark naked as she stood before mine eye,
Not one wen in her body could I spy.
What arms and shoulders did I touch and see,
How apt her breasts were to be press'd by me!
How smooth a belly under her waist saw I,
How large a leg, and what a lusty thigh!
To leave the rest, all lik'd me passing well;
I cling'd her naked body, down she fell.
Judge you the rest: being tir'd she bade me kiss;
Jove send me more such afternoons as this.

133   *To Cypassis, Corinna's Maid* (ii.8)

Cypassis, that a thousand ways trimm'st hair,
Worthy to kemb none but a goddess fair,
Our pleasant scapes show thee no clown to be,
Apt to thy mistress, but more apt to me.
Who that our bodies were compress'd bewray'd?
Whence knows Corinna that with thee I play'd?
Yet blush'd I not, nor us'd I any saying
That might be urg'd to witness our false playing.
What if a man with bondwomen offend,
To prove him foolish did I e'er contend?
Achilles burn'd with face of captive Briseis,
Great Agamemnon lov'd his servant Chryseis.
Greater than these myself I not esteem;
What graced kings, in me no shame I deem.
But when on thee her angry eyes did rush,
In both thy cheeks she did perceive thee blush.
But being present, might that work the best,
By Venus' deity how did I protest!
Thou, goddess, dost command a warm south blast
My false oaths in Carpathian seas to cast.
For which good turn by sweet reward repay,
Let me lie with thee, brown Cypass, today.
Ungrate, why feign'st new fears, and dost refuse?
Well mayst thou one thing for thy mistress use.
If thou deniest, fool, I'll our deeds express,
And as a traitor mine own fault confess,
Telling thy mistress where I was with thee,
How oft, and by what means we did agree.

134   *To Graecinus, on Loving Two Women at Once* (ii.10)

Graecinus (well I wot) thou told'st me once
I could not be in love with two at once.
By thee deceiv'd, by thee surpris'd am I,
For now I love two women equally.
Both are well favoured, both rich in array,
Which is the loveliest it is hard to say.
This seems the fairest, so doth that to me,
And this doth please me most, and so doth she.
Even as a boat toss'd by contrary wind,
So with this love and that, wavers my mind.
Venus, why doublest thou my endless smart?
Was not one wench enough to grieve my heart?
Why add'st thou stars to heaven, leaves to green woods,
And to the vast deep sea fresh water floods?

Yet this is better far than lie alone;
Let such as be mine enemies have none.
Yea, let my foes sleep in an empty bed,
And in the midst their bodies largely spread.
But may soft love rouse up my drowsy eyes,
And from my mistress' bosom let me rise.
Let one wench cloy me with sweet love's delight
If one can do 't, if not, two every night.
Though I am slender, I have store of pith,
Nor want I strength, but weight, to press her with.
Pleasure adds fuel to my lustful fire,
I pay them home with that they most desire.
Oft have I spent the night in wantonness,
And in the morn been lively ne'er the less.
He's happy who love's mutual skirmish slays,
And to the gods for that death Ovid prays.
Let soldier chase his enemies amain,
And with his blood eternal honour gain;
Let merchants seek wealth and with perjur'd lips,
Being wrack'd, carouse the sea tir'd by their ships;
But when I die, would I might droop with doing,
And in the midst thereof, set my soul going,
That at my funerals some may weeping cry,
'Even as he led his life, so did he die.'

135   From *Tamburlaine the Great, Part I*

Tamburlaine   Ah, fair Zenocrate, divine Zenocrate!
Fair is too foul an epithet for thee,
That in thy passion for thy country's love,
And fear to see thy kingly father's harm,
With hair dishevell'd wip'st thy watery cheeks,
And like to Flora in her morning's pride,
Shaking her silver tresses in the air,
Rain'st on the earth resolved pearl in showers,
And sprinklest sapphires on thy shining face,
Where Beauty, mother to the Muses, sits,
And comments volumes with her ivory pen,
Taking instructions from thy flowing eyes;
Eyes, when that Ebena steps to heaven,
In silence of thy solemn evening's walk,
Making the mantle of the richest night,
The moon, the planets, and the meteors, light;
There angels in their crystal armours fight
A doubtful battle with my tempted thoughts
For Egypt's freedom and the Soldan's life,

His life that so consumes Zenocrate,
Whose sorrows lay more siege unto my soul
Than all my army to Damascus walls;
And neither Persians' sovereign nor the Turk
Troubled my senses with conceit of foil
So much by much as doth Zenocrate.
What is beauty, saith my sufferings, then?
If all the pens that ever poets held
Had fed the feeling of their masters' thoughts,
And every sweetness that inspir'd their hearts,
Their minds, and muses on admired themes;
If all the heavenly quintessence they still
From their immortal flowers of poesy,
Wherein as in a mirror we perceive
The highest reaches of a human wit;
If these had made one poem's period,
And all combin'd in beauty's worthiness,
Yet should there hover in their restless heads
One thought, one grace, one wonder, at the least,
Which into words no virtue can digest.
But how unseemly is it for my sex,
My discipline of arms and chivalry,
My nature, and the terror of my name,
To harbour thoughts effeminate and faint!
Save only that in beauty's just applause,
With whose instinct the soul of man is touch'd,
And every warrior that is rapt with love
Of fame, of valour, and of victory,
Must needs have beauty beat on his conceits:
I thus conceiving and subduing both,
That which hath stoop'd the topmost of the gods,
Even from the fiery-spangled veil of heaven,
To feel the lovely warmth of shepherd's flames,
And march in cottages of strowed weeds,
Shall give the world to note, for all my birth,
That virtue solely is the sum of glory,
And fashions men with true nobility.
Who's within there?

136   From *The Tragical History of Doctor Faustus*

[*Re-enter* Helen]

Faustus   Was this face that launch'd a thousand ships,
And burnt the topless towers of Ilium?
Sweet Helen, make me immortal with a kiss:
Her lips suck forth my soul, see where it flies.

Come, Helen, come, give me my soul again.
Here will I dwell, for heaven is in these lips,
And all is dross that is not Helena.
I will be Paris, and for love of thee
Instead of Troy shall Wittenberg be sack'd,
And I will combat with weak Menelaus,
And wear thy colours on my plumed crest.
Yea, I will wound Achilles in the heel,
And then return to Helen for a kiss.
O, thou art fairer than the evening's air,
Clad in the beauty of a thousand stars.
Brighter art thou than flaming Jupiter,
When he appear'd to hapless Semele:
More lovely than the monarch of the sky,
In wanton Arethusa's azur'd arms,
And none but thou shalt be my paramour.

137   From *Hero and Leander, Sestiad II*

By this, Leander, being near the land,
Cast down his weary feet, and felt the sand.
Breathless albeit he were, he rested not
Till to the solitary tower he got,
And knock'd and call'd, at which celestial noise
The longing heart of Hero much more joys
Than nymphs and shepherds when the timbrel rings,
Or crooked dolphin when the sailor sings.
She stay'd not for her robes, but straight arose,
And drunk with gladness to the door she goes,
Where seeing a naked man she screech'd for fear —
Such sights as this to tender maids are rare —
And ran into the dark herself to hide;
Rich jewels in the dark are soonest spied.
Unto her was he led, or rather drawn,
By those white limbs, which sparkled through the lawn.
The nearer that he came, the more she fled,
And seeking refuge, slipp'd into her bed.
Whereon Leander sitting thus began,
Through numbing cold all feeble, faint and wan:
'If not for love, yet, love, for pity sake,
Me in thy bed and maiden bosom take;
At least vouchsafe these arms some little room,
Who, hoping to embrace thee, cheerly swum.
This head was beat with many a churlish billow,
And therefore let it rest upon thy pillow.'

Herewith affrighted Hero shrunk away,
And in her lukewarm place Leander lay,
Whose lively heat, like fire from heaven fet,
Would animate gross clay, and higher set
The drooping thoughts of base-declining souls
Than dreary Mars carousing nectar bowls.
His hands he cast upon her like a snare;
She, overcome with shame and sallow fear,
Like chaste Diana when Actaeon spied her,
Being suddenly betray'd, div'd down to hide her.
And as her silver body downward went,
With both her hands she made the bed a tent,
And in her own mind thought herself secure,
O'ercast with dim and darksome coverture.
And now she lets him whisper in her ear,
Flatter, entreat, promise, protest and swear;
Yet ever as he greedily assay'd
To touch those dainties, she the harpy play'd,
And every limb did as a soldier stout
Defend the fort, and keep the foeman out.
For though the rising iv'ry mount he scal'd,
Which is with azure circling lines empal'd,
Much like a globe (a globe may I term this,
By which love sails to regions full of bliss),
Yet there with Sisyphus he toil'd in vain,
Till gentle parley did the truce obtain.
Wherein Leander on her quivering breast
Breathless spoke something, and sigh'd out the rest;
Which so prevail'd as he with small ado
Enclos'd her in his arms and kiss'd her too.
And every kiss to her was as a charm,
And to Leander as a fresh alarm,
So that the truce was broke, and she alas
(Poor silly maiden) at his mercy was.
Love is not full of pity (as men say)
But deaf and cruel where he means to prey.
Even as a bird, which in our hands we wring,
Forth plungeth, and oft flutters with her wing,
She trembling strove; this strife of hers (like that
Which made the world) another world begat
Of unknown joy. Treason was in her thought,
And cunningly to yield herself she sought.
Seeming not won, yet won she was at length;
In such wars women use but half their strength.
Leander now, like Theban Hercules,
Ent'red the orchard of th' Hesperides,
Whose fruit none rightly can describe but he
That pulls or shakes it from the golden tree.

And now she wish'd this night were never done,
And sigh'd to think upon th' approaching sun,
For much it griev'd her that the bright daylight
Should know the pleasure of this blessed night,
And them like Mars and Erycine display'd,
Both in each other's arms chain'd as they laid.
Again she knew not how to frame her look,
Or speak to him who in a moment took
That which so long so charily she kept,
And fain by stealth away she would have crept,
And to some corner secretly have gone,
Leaving Leander in the bed alone.
But as her naked feet were whipping out,
He on the sudden cling'd her so about
That mermaid-like unto the floor she slid;
One half appear'd, the other half was hid.
Thus near the bed she blushing stood upright,
And from her countenance behold ye might
A kind of twilight break, which through the hair,
As from an orient cloud, glimps'd here and there.
And round about the chamber this false morn
Brought forth the day before the day was born.
So Hero's ruddy cheek Hero betray'd,
And her all naked to his sight display'd,
Whence his admiring eyes more pleasure took
Than Dis on heaps of gold fixing his look.
By this Apollo's golden harp began
To sound forth music to the Ocean,
Which watchful Hesperus no sooner heard,
But he the day-bright-bearing car prepar'd,
And ran before, as harbinger of light,
And with his flaring beams mock'd ugly Night,
Till she, o'ercome with anguish, shame and rage,
Dang'd down to hell her loathsome carriage.

George Chapman

138   From *Hero and Leander, Sestiad IV*

Now from Leander's place she rose, and found
Her hair and rent robe scatter'd on the ground;
Which taking up, she every piece did lay
Upon an altar, where in youth of day
She us'd t' exhibit private sacrifice:
Those would she offer to the deities

Of her fair goddess and her powerful son,
As relics of her late-felt passion;
And in that holy sort she vow'd to end them,
In hope her violent fancies, that did rend them,
Would as quite fade in her love's holy fire,
As they should in the flames she meant t' inspire.
Then she put on all her religious weeds,
That deck'd her in her secret sacred deeds;
A crown of icicles, that sun nor fire
Could ever melt, and figur'd chaste desire;
A golden star shin'd in her naked breast,
In honour of the queen-light of the east.
In her right hand she held a silver wand,
On whose bright top Peristera did stand,
Who was a nymph, but now transform'd a dove,
And in her life was dear in Venus' love;
And for her sake she ever since that time
Choos'd doves to draw her coach through heaven's blue
    clime.
Her plenteous hair in curled billows swims
On her bright shoulder: her harmonious limbs
Sustain'd no more but a most subtile veil,
That hung on them, as it durst not assail
Their different concord; for the weakest air
Could raise it swelling from her beauties fair;
Nor did it cover, but adumbrate only
Her most heart-piercing parts, that a blest eye
Might see, as it did shadow, fearfully,
All that all-love-deserving paradise:
It was as blue as the most freezing skies;
Near the sea's hue, for thence her goddess came:
On it a scarf she wore of wondrous frame;
In midst whereof she wrought a virgin's face,
From whose each cheek a fiery blush did chase
Two crimson flames, that did two ways extend,
Spreading the ample scarf to either end;
Which figur'd the division of her mind,
Whiles yet she rested bashfully inclin'd,
And stood not resolute to wed Leander;
This serv'd her white neck for a purple sphere,
And cast itself at full breadth down her back:
There, since the first breath that begun the wrack
Of her free quiet from Leander's lips,
She wrought a sea, in one flame, full of ships;
But that one ship where all her wealth did pass,
Like simple merchants' goods, Leander was;
For in that sea she naked figur'd him;
Her diving needle taught him how to swim,

And to each thread did such resemblance give,
For joy to be so like him it did live:
Things senseless live by art, and rational die
By rude contempt of art and industry.
Scarce could she work, but, in her strength of thought,
She fear'd she prick'd Leander as she wrought,
And oft would shriek so, that her guardian, frighted,
Would staring haste, as with some mischief cited:
They double life that dead things' grief sustain;
They kill that feel not their friends' living pain.
Sometimes she fear'd he sought her infamy;
And then, as she was working of his eye.
She thought to prick it out to quench her ill;
But, as she prick'd, it grew more perfect still:
Trifling attempts no serious acts advance;
The fire of love is blown by dalliance.
In working his fair neck she did so grace it,
She still was working her own arms t' embrace it.
That, and his shoulders, and his hands were seen
Above the stream; and with a pure sea-green
She did so quaintly shadow every limb,
All might be seen beneath the waves to swim.

Anonymous

139

Hey nonny no!
Men are fools that wish to die!
Is 't not fine to dance and sing
When the bells of death do ring?
Is 't not fine to swim in wine,
And turn upon the toe
And sing hey nonny no,
When the winds blow and the seas flow?
Hey nonny no!

140

Sing we and chant it
While love doth grant it,
                        Fa la la!

Not long youth lasteth
And old age hasteth.
                        Fa la la!

Now is best leisure
To take our pleasure.
                    Fa la la!

All things invite us
Now to delight us.
                    Fa la la!

Hence care be packing,
No mirth be lacking.
                    Fa la la!

Let spare no treasure
To live in pleasure.
                    Fa la la!

141

Now is the month of maying,
When merry lads are playing
Each with his bonny lass
Upon the greeny grass.
                    Fa la la!

The spring clad all in gladness
Doth laugh at winter's sadness,
And to the bagpipe's sound
The nymphs tread out their ground.
                    Fa la la!

Fie then, why sit we musing,
Youth's sweet delight refusing?
Say, dainty nymphs, and speak,
Shall we play barley-break.
                    Fa la la!

142

I saw my Lady weep,
And Sorrow proud to be advanced so
In those fair eyes where all perfections keep.
Her face was full of woe,
But such a woe (believe me) as wins more hearts
Than Mirth can do with her enticing parts.

Sorrow was there made fair,
And Passion wise; Tears a delightful thing;
Silence beyond all speech, a wisdom rare;
She made her sighs to sing,
And all things with so sweet a sadness move
As made my heart at once both grieve and love.

O fairer than aught else
The world can show, leave off in time to grieve.
Enough, enough: your joyful look excels:
Tears kill the heart, believe.
O strive not to be excellent in woe,
Which only breeds your beauty's overthrow.

143 Fine knacks for ladies, cheap, choice, brave and new,
  Good pennyworths, – but money cannot move:
I keep a fair but for the Fair to view, –
  A beggar may be liberal of love.
Though all my wares be trash, the heart is true,
    The heart is true.

Great gifts are guiles and look for gifts again,
  My trifles come as treasures from my mind;
It is a precious jewel to be plain;
  Sometimes in shell the orient'st pearls we find:
Of others take a sheaf, of me a grain!
    Of me a grain!

Within this pack pins, points, laces, and gloves,
  And divers toys fitting a country fair,
But my heart, wherein duty serves and loves,
  Turtles and twins, court's brood, a heavenly pair –
Happy the heart that thinks of no removes!
    Of no removes!

144 A sparrow-hawk proud did hold in wicked jail
Music's sweet chorister, the nightingale,
To whom with sighs she said: 'O set me free!
And in my song I'll praise no bird but thee.'
The hawk replied, 'I will not lose my diet
To let a thousand such enjoy their quiet.'

145   When love on time and measure makes his ground,
     Time that must end, though love can never die,
    'Tis love betwixt a shadow and a sound,
     A love not in the heart but in the eye;
    A love that ebbs and flows, now up, now down,
    A morning's favour and an evening's frown.

    Sweet looks show love, yet they are but as beams:
     Fair words seem true, yet they are but as wind;
    Eyes shed their tears, yet are but outward streams;
     Sighs paint a shadow in the falsest mind.
    Looks, words, tears, sighs show love when love they leave;
    False hearts can weep, sigh, swear, and yet deceive.

Attributed to John Lilliatt

146   Weep you no more, sad fountains;
      What need you flow so fast?
     Look how the snowy mountains
      Heaven's sun doth gently waste.
       But my sun's heavenly eyes
       View not your weeping,
       That now lies sleeping
      Softly, now softly lies
       Sleeping.

     Sleep is a reconciling,
      A rest that peace begets.
     Doth not the sun rise smiling
      When fair at ev'n he sets?
       Rest you then, rest, sad eyes,
       Melt not in weeping,
       While she lies sleeping
      Softly, now softly lies
       Sleeping.

147   The lowest trees have tops, the ant her gall,
     The fly her spleen, the little spark his heat;
    And slender hairs cast shadows, though but small,
     And bees have stings, although they be not great;
    Seas have their source, and so have shallow springs;
    And love is love in beggars and in kings!

Where waters smoothest run, deep are the fords;
  The dial stirs, yet none perceives it move;
The firmest faith is in the fewest words;
  The turtles cannot sing, and yet they love;
True hearts have eyes and ears, no tongues to speak;
They hear, and see, and sigh, and then they break!

148

Fain would I change that note
To which fond love hath charm'd me
Long long to sing by rote,
Fancying that that harm'd me:
Yet when this thought doth come,
'Love is the perfect sum
Of all delight,'
I have no other choice
Either for pen or voice
To sing or write.

O Love, they wrong thee much
That say thy sweet is bitter,
When thy rich fruit is such
As nothing can be sweeter.
Fair house of joy and bliss,
Where truest pleasure is,
I do adore thee;
I know thee what thou art,
I serve thee with my heart,
And fall before thee.

149

There is a Lady sweet and kind,
Was never face so pleas'd my mind;
I did but see her passing by,
And yet I love her till I die.

Her gesture, motion and her smiles,
Her wit, her voice my heart beguiles,
Beguiles my heart, I know not why,
And yet I love her till I die.

Her free behaviour, winning looks,
Will make a Lawyer burn his books;
I touch'd her not, alas! not I,
And yet I love her till I die.

Had I her fast betwixt mine arms,
Judge you that think such sports were harms;
Were 't any harm? no, no, fie, fie,
For I will love her till I die.

Should I remain confined there
So long as Phœbus in his sphere,
I to request, she to deny,
Yet would I love her till I die.

Cupid is winged and doth range,
Her country so my love doth change:
But change she earth, or change she sky,
Yet will I love her till I die.

150

Once did my thoughts both ebb and flow,
  As passion did them move;
Once did I hope, straight fear again, –
  And then I was in love.

Once did I waking spend the night,
  And tell how many minutes move.
Once did I wishing waste the day, –
  And then I was in love.

Once, by my carving true love's knot,
  The weeping trees did prove
That wounds and tears were both our lot, –
  And then I was in love.

Once did I breathe another's breath
  And in my mistress move,
Once was I not mine own at all, –
  And then I was in love.

Once wore I bracelets made of hair,
  And collars did approve,
Once wore my clothes made out of wax, –
  And then I was in love.

Once did I sonnet to my saint,
  My soul in numbers move,
Once did I tell a thousand lies, –
  And then I was in love.

Once in my ear did dangling hang
  A little turtle-dove,
Once, in a word, I was a fool, –
  And then I was in love.

151   *The Marriage of the Frog and the Mouse*

It was the frog in the well,
  Humbledum, humbledum,
And the merry mouse in the mill,
        Tweedle, tweedle, twino.

The frog would a-wooing ride
Sword and buckler by his side.

When he upon his high horse set,
His boots they shone as black as jet.

When he came to the merry mill-pin, –
'Lady Mouse, been you within?'

Then came out the dusty mouse:
'I am Lady of this house:

Hast thou any mind of me?'
'I have e'en great mind of thee.'

'Who shall this marriage make?'
'Our Lord which is the rat.'

'What shall we have to our supper?'
'Three beans in a pound of butter.'

When supper they were at,
The frog, the mouse, and e'en the rat;

Then came in Gib our cat,
And catch'd the mouse e'en by the back.

Then did they separate,
And the frog leap'd on the floor so flat.

Then came in Dick our drake,
And drew the frog e'en to the lake.

The rat run up the wall,
  Humbledum, humbledum;
A goodly company, the Devil go with all!
  Tweedle tweedle twino.

152   *The Bellman's Song*

Maids to bed and cover coal;
Let the mouse out of her hole;
Crickets in the chimney sing
Whilst the little bell doth ring:
If fast asleep, who can tell
When the clapper hits the bell?

153   Sweet Suffolk owl, so trimly dight
With feathers like a lady bright,
Thou sing'st alone, sitting by night,
    Te whit, te whoo!
Thy note, that forth so freely rolls,
With shrill command the mouse controls,
And sings a dirge for dying souls,
    Te whit, te whoo!

154   I heard a noise and wished for a sight.
    I look'd aside and did a shadow see,
Whose substance was the sum of my delight;
    It came unseen, and so it went from me.
But yet conceit persuaded my intent
There was a substance where the shadow went.
I did not play Narcissus in conceit,
    I did not see my shadow in a spring;
I knew my eyes were dimm'd with no deceit,
    I saw the shadow of some worthy thing;
For as I saw the shadow passing by,
I had a glance of something in my eye.
Shadow, or she, or both, or choose you whether,
Blest be the thing that brought the shadow hither.

Thomas Campion

155   Thrice toss these oaken ashes in the air,
Thrice sit thou mute in this enchanted chair,
Then thrice-three times tie up this true love's knot,
And murmur soft 'She will or she will not.'

Go, burn these poisonous weeds in yon blue fire,
These screech-owl's feathers and this prickling briar,
This cypress gather'd at a dead man's grave,
That all my fears and cares an end may have.

Then come, you Fairies! dance with me a round!
Melt her hard heart with your melodious sound!
In vain are all the charms I can devise:
She hath an art to break them with her eyes.

156   Shall I come, sweet Love, to thee
                When the evening beams are set?
          Shall I not excluded be,
                Will you find no feigned let?
          Let me not, for pity, more
          Tell the long hours at your door.

          Who can tell what thief or foe,
                In the covert of the night,
          For his prey will work my woe,
                Or through wicked foul despite?
          So may I die unredrest
          Ere my long love be possest.

          But to let such dangers pass,
                Which a lover's thoughts disdain,
          'Tis enough in such a place
                To attend love's joys in vain:
          Do not mock me in thy bed,
          While these cold nights freeze me dead.

157   Follow your saint, follow with accents sweet!
Haste you, sad notes, fall at her flying feet!
There, wrapp'd in cloud of sorrow, pity move,
And tell the ravisher of my soul I perish for her love:
But, if she scorns my never-ceasing pain,
Then burst with sighing in her sight and ne'er return again.

All that I sang still to her praise did tend,
Still she was first, still she my songs did end;
Yet she my love and music both doth fly,
The music that her echo is and beauty's sympathy.
Then let my notes pursue her scornful flight!
It shall suffice that they were breath'd and died for her delight.

158

Now winter nights enlarge
The number of their hours,
And clouds their storms discharge
Upon the airy towers.
Let now the chimneys blaze,
And cups o'erflow with wine;
Let well-tun'd words amaze
With harmony divine.
Now yellow waxen lights
Shall wait on honey love,
While youthful revels, masques, and courtly sights
Sleep's leaden spells remove.

This time doth well dispense
With lovers' long discourse;
Much speech hath some defence,
Though beauty no remorse.
All do not all things well;
Some measures comely tread,
Some knotted riddles tell,
Some poems smoothly read.
The summer hath his joys
And winter his delights;
Though love and all his pleasures are but toys,
They shorten tedious nights.

159   *Vivamus, Mea Lesbia, atque Amemus*

My sweetest Lesbia, let us live and love,
And though the sager sort our deeds reprove
Let us not weigh them. Heaven's great lamps do dive
Into their west, and straight again revive;
But, soon as once set is our little light,
Then must we sleep one ever-during night.

If all would lead their lives in love like me,
Then bloody swords and armour should not be;
No drum nor trumpet peaceful sleeps should move,
Unless alarm came from the Camp of Love:
But fools do live and waste their little light,
And seek with pain their ever-during night.

When timely death my life and fortunes ends,
Let not my hearse be vext with mourning friends;
But let all lovers, rich in triumph, come
And with sweet pastimes grace my happy tomb:
And, Lesbia, close up thou my little light
And crown with love my ever-during night.

160   Hark, all you ladies that do sleep!
                    The fairy-queen Proserpina
                Bids you awake and pity them that weep:
                    You may do in the dark
                        What the day doth forbid;
                    Fear not the dogs that bark,
                        Night will have all hid.

                But if you let your lovers moan,
                    The fairy-queen Proserpina
                Will send abroad her fairies every one,
                    That shall pinch black and blue
                        Your white hands and fair arms
                    That did not kindly rue
                        Your paramours' harms.

                In myrtle arbours on the downs
                    The fairy-queen Proserpina,
                This night by moonshine leading merry rounds,
                    Holds a watch with sweet love,
                        Down the dale, up the hill;
                    No plaints or groans may move
                        Their holy vigil.

                All you that will hold watch with love,
                    The fairy-queen Proserpina
                Will make you fairer than Dione's dove;
                    Roses red, lilies white,
                        And the clear damask hue,
                    Shall on your cheeks alight:
                        Love will adorn you.

                All you that love or lov'd before,
                    The fairy-queen Proserpina
                Bids you increase that loving humour more:
                    They that yet have not fed
                        On delight amorous,
                  She vows that they shall lead
                        Apes in Avernus.

161   When thou must home to shades of underground,
                And there arriv'd, a new admired guest,
                The beauteous spirits do engirt thee round,
                White Iope, blithe Helen, and the rest,
                To hear the stories of thy finish'd love
                From that smooth tongue whose music hell can move;

Then wilt thou speak of banqueting delights,
Of masques and revels which sweet youth did make,
Of tourneys and great challenges of knights,
And all these triumphs for thy beauty's sake:
When thou hast told these honours done to thee,
Then tell, O tell, how thou didst murder me.

162   What if a day, or a month, or a year
            Crown thy delights with a thousand sweet contentings;
      Cannot a chance of a night or an hour
            Cross thy desires with as many sad tormentings?
            Fortune, honour, beauty, youth
                Are but blossoms dying;
            Wanton pleasure, doting love
                Are but shadows flying.
                    All our joys
                    Are but toys,
                Idle thoughts deceiving.
                    None have power
                    Of an hour
                In their lives bereaving.

      Earth's but a point to the world; and a man
            Is but a point to the world's compared centre.
      Shall then a point of a point be so vain
            As to triumph in a seely point's adventure?
            All is hazard that we have,
                There is nothing biding;
            Days of pleasure are like streams
                Through fair meadows gliding.
                    Weal and woe,
                    Time doth go,
                Time is never turning.
                    Secret fates
                    Guide our states
                Both in mirth and mourning.

Thomas Nashe

163

Adieu, farewell earth's bliss,
This world uncertain is;
Fond are life's lustful joys,
Death proves them all but toys,
None from his darts can fly.
I am sick, I must die.
    Lord, have mercy on us!

Rich men, trust not in wealth,
Gold cannot buy you health;
Physic himself must fade,
All things to end are made.
The plague full swift goes by.
I am sick, I must die.
    Lord, have mercy on us!

Beauty is but a flower
Which wrinkles will devour;
Brightness falls from the air,
Queens have died young and fair,
Dust hath clos'd Helen's eye.
I am sick, I must die.
    Lord, have mercy on us!

Strength stoops unto the grave,
Worms feed on Hector brave,
Swords may not fight with fate,
Earth still holds ope her gate;
'Come! come!' the bells do cry.
I am sick, I must die.
    Lord, have mercy on us!

Wit with his wantonness
Tasteth death's bitterness;
Hell's executioner
Hath no ears for to hear
What vain art can reply.
I am sick, I must die.
    Lord, have mercy on us!

Haste, therefore, each degree,
To welcome destiny:
Heaven is our heritage,
Earth but a player's stage;
Mount we unto the sky.
I am sick, I must die.
    Lord, have mercy on us!

Barnabe Barnes

164

A blast of wind, a momentary breath,
A watery bubble symboliz'd with air,
A sun-blown rose, but for a season fair,
A ghostly glance, a skeleton of death;
A morning dew, pearling the grass beneath,
Whose moisture sun's appearance doth impair;
A lightning glimpse, a muse of thought and care,
A planet's shot, a shade which followeth,
A voice which vanisheth so soon as heard,
The thriftless heir of time, a rolling wave,
A show, no more in action than regard,
A mass of dust, world's momentary slave,
  Is man, in state of our old Adam made,
  Soon born to die, soon flourishing to fade.

John Donne

165

The Broken Heart

He is stark mad, who ever says,
 That he hath been in love an hour,
Yet not that love so soon decays,
 But that it can ten in less space devour;
Who will believe me, if I swear
That I have had the plague a year?
 Who would not laugh at me, if I should say,
 I saw a flask of powder burn a day?

Ah, what a trifle is a heart,
 If once into love's hands it come!
All other griefs allow a part
 To other griefs, and ask themselves but some;
They come to us, but us Love draws,
He swallows us, and never chaws:
 By him, as by chain'd shot, whole ranks do die,
 He is the tyrant Pike, our hearts the Fry.

If 'twere not so, what did become
 Of my heart, when I first saw thee?
I brought a heart into the room,
 But from the room, I carried none with me:

If it had gone to thee, I know
Mine would have taught thine heart to show
　More pity unto me: but Love, alas,
　At one first blow did shiver it as glass.

Yet nothing can to nothing fall,
　Nor any place be empty quite,
Therefore I think my breast hath all
　Those pieces still, though they be not unite;
And now as broken glasses show
A hundred lesser faces, so
　My rags of heart can like, wish, and adore,
　But after one such love, can love no more.

166   *The Flea*

Mark but this flea, and mark in this,
How little that which thou deny'st me is;
It suck'd me first, and now sucks thee,
And in this flea, our two bloods mingled be;
Thou know'st that this cannot be said
A sin, nor shame, nor loss of maidenhead,
　Yet this enjoys before it woo,
　And pamper'd swells with one blood made of two,
　And this, alas, is more than we would do.

Oh stay, three lives in one flea spare,
Where we almost, yea more than married are.
This flea is you and I, and this
Our marriage bed, and marriage temple is;
Though parents grudge, and you, we're met,
And cloistered in these living walls of jet.
　Though use make you apt to kill me,
　Let not to that, self murder added be,
　And sacrilege, three sins in killing three.

Cruel and sudden, hast thou since
Purpled thy nail, in blood of innocence?
Wherein could this flea guilty be,
Except in that drop which it suck'd from thee?
Yet thou triumph'st, and say'st that thou
Find'st not thyself, nor me the weaker now;
　'Tis true, then learn how false, fears be;
　Just so much honour, when thou yield'st to me,
　Will waste, as this flea's death took life from thee.

167　　　　　　　　*The Funeral*

Whoever comes to shroud me, do not harm
　　　　Nor question much
That subtle wreath of hair, which crowns my arm;
The mystery, the sign you must not touch,
　　　　For 'tis my outward Soul,
Viceroy to that, which then to heaven being gone,
　　　　Will leave this to control,
And keep these limbs, her Provinces, from dissolution.

For if the sinewy thread my brain lets fall
　　　　Through every part,
Can tie those parts, and make me one of all;
These hairs which upward grew, and strength and art
　　　　Have from a better brain,
Can better do 't; except she meant that I
　　　　By this should know my pain,
As prisoners then are manacled, when they're condemn'd
　　　　　　　to die.

Whate'er she meant by it, bury it with me,
　　　　For since I am
Love's martyr, it might breed idolatry,
If into others' hands these Reliques came;
　　　　As 'twas humility
To afford to it all that a Soul can do,
　　　　So, 'tis some bravery,
That since you would save none of me, I bury some of you.

168　　　　　　　　*The Good-Morrow*

I wonder by my troth, what thou and I
Did, till we lov'd? were we not wean'd till then?
But suck'd on country pleasures, childishly?
Or snorted we in the seven sleepers' den?
'Twas so; but this, all pleasures fancies be.
If ever any beauty I did see,
Which I desir'd, and got, 'twas but a dream of thee.

And now good-morrow to our waking souls,
Which watch not one another out of fear;
For love all love of other sights controls,
And makes one little room an everywhere.
Let sea-discoverers to new worlds have gone,
Let maps to other, worlds on worlds have shown,
Let us possess one world, each hath one, and is one.

My face in thine eye, thine in mine appears,
And true plain hearts do in the faces rest;
Where can we find two better hemispheres
Without sharp North, without declining West?
What ever dies, was not mixt equally;
If our two loves be one, or thou and I
Love so alike that none do slacken, none can die.

169   *A Nocturnal upon St Lucy's Day,*
            Being the Shortest Day

'Tis the year's midnight, and it is the day's,
Lucy's, who scarce seven hours herself unmasks;
    The Sun is spent, and now his flasks
    Send forth light squibs, no constant rays;
        The world's whole sap is sunk:
The general balm th' hydroptic earth hath drunk,
Whither, as to the bed's-feet, life is shrunk,
Dead and interr'd; yet all these seem to laugh,
Compar'd with me, who am their Epitaph.

Study me then, you who shall lovers be
At the next world, that is, at the next Spring:
    For I am every dead thing,
    In whom love wrought new alchemy.
        For his art did express
A quintessence even from nothingness,
From dull privations, and lean emptiness:
He ruin'd me, and I am re-begot
Of absence, darkness, death; things which are not.

All others, from all things, draw all that's good,
Life, soul, form, spirit, whence they being have;
    I, by love's limbec, am the grave
    Of all, that's nothing. Oft a flood
        Have we two wept, and so
Drown'd the whole world, us two; oft did we grow
To be two Chaoses, when we did show
Care to aught else; and often absences
Withdrew our souls, and made us carcases.

But I am by her death (which word wrongs her)
Of the first nothing, the Elixir grown;
    Were I a man, that I were one,
    I needs must know; I should prefer,
        If I were any beast,

Some ends, some means; yea plants, yea stones detest,
And love; all, all some properties invest;
If I an ordinary nothing were,
As shadow, a light, and body must be here.

But I am None; nor will my Sun renew.
You lovers, for whose sake, the lesser Sun
 At this time to the Goat is run
 To fetch new lust, and give it you,
  Enjoy your summer all;
Since she enjoys her long night's festival,
Let me prepare towards her, and let me call
This hour her Vigil, and her Eve, since this
Both the year's, and the day's deep midnight is.

170   *Song*

Go, and catch a falling star,
 Get with child a mandrake root,
Tell me, where all past years are,
 Or who cleft the Devil's foot,
Teach me to hear Mermaids singing,
Or to keep off envy's stinging,
   And find
   What wind
Serves to advance an honest mind.

If thou be'st born to strange sights,
 Things invisible to see,
Ride ten thousand days and nights,
 Till age snow white hairs on thee,
Thou, when thou return'st, wilt tell me
All strange wonders that befell thee,
   And swear
   No where
Lives a woman true, and fair.

If thou find'st one, let me know,
 Such a Pilgrimage were sweet;
Yet do not, I would not go,
 Though at next door we might meet,
Though she were true, when you met her,
And last, till you write your letter,
   Yet she
   Will be
False, ere I come, to two, or three.

171   *Twickenham Garden*

Blasted with sighs, and surrounded with tears,
    Hither I come to seek the spring,
    And at mine eyes, and at mine ears,
Receive such balms, as else cure everything;
    But O, self-traitor, I do bring
The spider love, which transubstantiates all,
    And can convert Manna to gall,
And that this place may thoroughly be thought
    True Paradise, I have the serpent brought.

'Twere wholesomer for me, that winter did
    Benight the glory of this place,
    And that a grave frost did forbid
These trees to laugh, and mock me to my face;
    But that I may not this disgrace
Endure, nor yet leave loving, Love, let me
    Some senseless piece of this place be;
Make me a mandrake, so I may groan here,
    Or a stone fountain weeping out my year.

Hither with crystal vials, lovers come,
    And take my tears, which are love's wine.
And try your mistress' tears at home,
For all are false, that taste not just like mine;
    Alas, hearts do not in eyes shine,
Nor can you more judge woman's thoughts by tears,
    Than by her shadow, what she wears.
O perverse sex, where none is true but she,
    Who's therefore true, because her truth kills me.

172   *The Will*

Before I sigh my last gasp, let me breathe,
Great love, some Legacies; Here I bequeath
Mine eyes to *Argus*, if mine eyes can see,
If they be blind, then Love, I give them thee;
My tongue to Fame; to Ambassadors mine ears;
    To women or the sea, my tears.
Thou, Love, hast taught me heretofore
By making me serve her who had twenty more,
That I should give to none, but such, as had too much before.

My constancy I to the planets give;
My truth to them, who at the Court do live;

Mine ingenuity and openness,
To Jesuits; to Buffoons my pensiveness;
My silence to any, who abroad hath been;
   My money to a Capuchin.
Thou Love taught'st me, by appointing me
To love there, where no love receiv'd can be,
Only to give to such as have an incapacity.

My faith I give to Roman Catholics;
All my good works unto the Schismatics
Of Amsterdam: my best civility
And Courtship, to an University;
My modesty I give to soldiers bare;
   My patience let gamesters share.
Thou Love taught'st me, by making me
Love her that holds my love disparity,
Only to give to those that count my gifts indignity.

I give my reputation to those
Which were my friends; mine industry to foes;
To Schoolmen I bequeath my doubtfulness;
My sickness to Physicians, or excess;
To Nature, all that I in Rhyme have writ;
   And to my company my wit.
Thou Love, by making me adore
Her, who begot this love in me before,
Taught'st me to make, as though I gave, when I did but restore.

To him for whom the passing bell next tolls,
I give my physic books; my written rolls
Of Moral counsels, I to Bedlam give;
My brazen medals, unto them which live
In want of bread; to them which pass among
   All foreigners, mine English tongue.
Thou, Love, by making me love one
Who thinks her friendship a fit portion
For younger lovers, dost my gifts thus disproportion.

Therefore I'll give no more; but I'll undo
The world by dying; because love dies too.
Then all your beauties will be no more worth
Than gold in Mines, where none doth draw it forth;
And all your graces no more use shall have
   Than a Sun-dial in a grave.
Thou Love taught'st me, by making me
Love her, who doth neglect both me and thee,
To invent, and practise this one way, to annihilate all three.

173   *Elegy III   Change*

Although thy hand and faith, and good works too,
Have seal'd thy love which nothing should undo,
Yea though thou fall back, that apostasy
Confirm thy love; yet much, much I fear thee.
Women are like the Arts, forc'd unto none,
Open to all searchers, unpriz'd, if unknown.
If I have caught a bird, and let him fly,
Another fowler using these means, as I,
May catch the same bird; and, as these things be,
Women are made for men, not him, nor me.
Foxes and goats, all beasts change when they please,
Shall women, more hot, wily, wild than these,
Be bound to one man, and did Nature then
Idly make them apter to endure than men?
They're our clogs, not their own; if a man be
Chain'd to a galley, yet the galley's free;
Who hath a plow-land, casts all his seed corn there,
And yet allows his ground more corn should bear;
Though Danuby into the sea must flow,
The sea receives the Rhine, Volga, and Po.
By nature, which gave it, this liberty
Thou lov'st, but Oh! canst thou love it and me?
Likeness glues love: and if that thou so do,
To make us like and love, must I change too?
More than thy hate, I hate it, rather let me
Allow her change, than change as oft as she,
And so not teach, but force my opinion
To love not any one, nor every one.
To live in one land, is captivity,
To run all countries, a wild roguery;
Waters stink soon, if in one place they bide,
And in the vast sea are more putrefied:
But when they kiss one bank, and leaving this
Never look back, but the next bank do kiss,
Then are they purest; Change is the nursery
Of music, joy, life and eternity.

174   *Elegy XII   His Parting from Her*

Since she must go, and I must mourn, come Night,
Environ me with darkness, whilst I write:
Shadow that hell unto me, which alone
I am to suffer when my Love is gone.
Alas the darkest Magic cannot do it,
Thou and great Hell to boot are shadows to it.
Should Cynthia quit thee, Venus, and each star,
It would not form one thought dark as mine are.
I could lend thee obscureness now, and say,
Out of my self, There should be no more Day,
Such is already my felt want of sight,
Did not the fires within me force a light.
O Love, that fire and darkness should be mix'd,
Or to thy Triumphs so strange torments fix'd!
Is 't because thou thyself art blind, that we
Thy Martyrs must no more each other see?
Or tak'st thou pride to break us on the wheel,
And view old Chaos in the Pains we feel?
Or have we left undone some mutual Rite,
Through holy fear, that merits thy despite?
No, no. The fault was mine, impute it to me,
Or rather to conspiring destiny,
Which (since I lov'd for form before) decreed,
That I should suffer when I lov'd indeed:
And therefore now, sooner than I can say,
I saw the golden fruit, 'tis rapt away.
Or as I had watch'd one drop in a vast stream,
And I left wealthy only in a dream.
Yet Love, thou 'rt blinder than thyself in this,
To vex my Dove-like friend for my amiss:
And, where my own sad truth may expiate
Thy wrath, to make her fortune run my fate:
So blinded Justice doth, when Favourites fall,
Strike them, their house, their friends, their followers all.
Was 't not enough that thou didst dart thy fires
Into our bloods, inflaming our desires,
And madest us sigh and glow, and pant, and burn,
And then thyself into our flame didst turn?
Was 't not enough, that thou didst hazard us
To paths in love so dark, so dangerous:
And those so ambush'd round with household spies,
And over all, thy husband's towering eyes
That flam'd with oily sweat of jealousy:
Yet went we not still on with constancy?
Have we not kept our guards, like spy on spy?
Had correspondence whilst the foe stood by?

Stol'n (more to sweeten them) our many blisses
Of meetings, conference, embracements, kisses?
Shadow'd with negligence our most respects?
Varied our language through all dialects,
Of becks, winks, looks, and often under-boards
Spoke dialogues with our feet far from our words?
Have we prov'd all these secrets of our Art,
Yea, thy pale inwards, and thy panting heart?
And, after all this passed Purgatory,
Must sad divorce make us the vulgar story?
First let our eyes be riveted quite through
Our turning brains, and both our lips grow to:
Let our arms clasp like Ivy, and our fear
Freeze us together, that we may stick here,
Till Fortune, that would rive us, with the deed,
Strain her eyes open, and it make them bleed.
For Love it cannot be, whom hitherto
I have accus'd, should such a mischief do.
O Fortune, thou 'rt not worth my least exclaim
And plague enough thou hast in thy own shame.
Do thy great worst, my friend and I have arms,
Though not against thy strokes, against thy harms
Rend us in sunder, thou canst not divide
Our bodies so, but that our souls are tied,
And we can love by letters still and gifts,
And thoughts and dreams; Love never wanteth shifts.
I will not look upon the quickening Sun,
But straight her beauty to my sense shall run;
The air shall note her soft, the fire most pure;
Water suggest her clear, and the earth sure.
Time shall not lose our passages; the Spring
Shall tell how fresh our love was in the beginning;
The Summer how it ripened in the ear;
And Autumn, what our golden harvests were.
The Winter I'll not think on to spite thee,
But count it a lost season, so shall she.
And dearest Friend, since we must part, drown night
With hope of Day, burthens well borne are light.
Though cold and darkness longer hang somewhere,
Yet Phœbus equally lights all the Sphere.
And what he cannot in like Portions pay,
The world enjoys in Mass, and so we may.
Be then ever yourself, and let no woe
Win on your health, your youth, your beauty: so
Declare yourself base fortune's Enemy,
No less by your contempt than constancy;
That I may grow enamour'd on your mind,
When my own thoughts I there reflected find.

For this to th' comfort of my Dear I vow,
My Deeds shall still be what my words are now;
The Poles shall move to teach me ere I start;
And when I change my Love, I'll change my heart;
Nay, if I wax but cold in my desire,
Think, heaven hath motion lost, and the world, fire:
Much more I could, but many words have made
That, oft, suspected which men would persuade;
Take therefore all in this: I love so true,
As I will never look for less in you.

175   *Elegy XVI   On His Mistress*

By our first strange and fatal interview,
By all desires which thereof did ensue,
By our long starving hopes, by that remorse
Which my words' masculine persuasive force
Begot in thee, and by the memory
Of hurts, which spies and rivals threatened me,
I calmly beg: but by thy father's wrath,
By all pains, which want and divorcement hath,
I conjure thee, and all the oaths which I
And thou have sworn to seal joint constancy,
Here I unswear, and overswear them thus,
Thou shalt not love by ways so dangerous.
Temper, O fair Love, love's impetuous rage,
Be my true Mistress still, not my feign'd Page;
I'll go, and, by thy kind leave, leave behind
Thee, only worthy to nurse in my mind
Thirst to come back; O if thou die before,
My soul from other lands to thee shall soar.
Thy (else Almighty) beauty cannot move
Rage from the Seas, nor thy love teach them love,
Nor tame wild Boreas' harshness; thou hast read
How roughly he in pieces shivered
Fair Orithea, whom he swore he lov'd.
Fall ill or good, 'tis madness to have prov'd
Dangers unurg'd; feed on this flattery,
That absent Lovers one in th' other be.
Dissemble nothing, not a boy, nor change
Thy body's habit, nor mind's; be not strange
To thyself only; all will spy in thy face
A blushing womanly discovering grace;
Richly cloth'd Apes, are call'd Apes, and as soon
Eclips'd as bright we call the Moon the Moon.

Men of France, changeable chameleons,
Spitals of diseases, shops of fashions,
Love's fuellers, and the rightest company
Of Players, which upon the world's stage be,
Will quickly know thee, and no less, alas!
Th' indifferent Italian, as we pass
His warm land, well content to think thee Page,
Will hunt thee with such lust, and hideous rage,
As Lot's fair guests were vex'd. But none of these
Nor spongy hydroptic Dutch shall thee displease,
If thou stay here. O stay here, for, for thee
England is only a worthy gallery,
To walk in expectation, till from thence
Our greatest King call thee to his presence.
When I am gone, dream me some happiness,
Nor let thy looks our long-hid love confess,
Nor praise, nor dispraise me, nor bless nor curse
Openly love's force, nor in bed fright thy Nurse
With midnight's startings, crying out, oh, oh
Nurse, O my love is slain, I saw him go
O'er the white Alps alone; I saw him, I,
Assail'd, fight, taken, stabb'd, bleed, fall, and die.
Augur me better chance, except dread Jove
Think it enough for me to have had thy love.

176   *Elegy XIX   Going to Bed*

Come, Madam, come, all rest my powers defy,
Until I labour, I in labour lie.
The foe oft-times having the foe in sight,
Is tired with standing though he never fight.
Off with that girdle, like heaven's Zone glistering,
But a far fairer world encompassing.
Unpin that spangled breastplate which you wear,
That th' eyes of busy fools may be stopt there.
Unlace yourself, for that harmonious chime
Tells me from you, that now it is bed time.
Off with that happy busk, which I envy,
That still can be, and still can stand so nigh.
Your gown going off, such beauteous state reveals,
As when from flowry meads th' hill's shadow steals.
Off with that wiry Coronet and show
The hairy Diadem which on you doth grow:
Now off with those shoes, and then safely tread
In this love's hallow'd temple, this soft bed.

In such white robes, heaven's Angels used to be
Receiv'd by men; thou Angel bring'st with thee
A heaven like Mahomet's Paradise; and though
Ill spirits walk in white, we easily know,
By this these Angels from an evil sprite,
Those set our hairs, but these our flesh upright.
   Licence my roving hands, and let them go,
Before, behind, between, above, below.
O my America! my new-found-land,
My kingdom, safeliest when with one man mann'd,
My Mine of precious stones, My Empery,
How blest am I in this discovering thee!
To enter in these bonds, is to be free;
Then where my hand is set, my seal shall be.
   Full nakedness! All joys are due to thee,
As souls unbodied, bodies uncloth'd must be,
To taste whole joys. Gems which you women use
Are like Atlanta's balls, cast in men's views,
That when a fool's eye lighteth on a Gem,
His earthly soul may covet theirs, not them.
Like pictures, or like books' gay coverings made
For lay-men, are all women thus array'd;
Themselves are mystic books, which only we
(Whom their imputed grace will dignify)
Must see reveal'd. Then since that I may know,
As liberally, as to a Midwife, show
Thyself: cast all, yea, this white linen hence,
There is no penance due to innocence.
   To teach thee, I am naked first; why then
What needst thou have more covering than a man.

177   *A Burnt Ship*

Out of a fired ship, which, by no way
But drowning, could be rescued from the flame,
Some men leap'd forth, and ever as they came
Near the foes' ships, did by their shot decay;
So all were lost, which in the ship were found,
   They in the sea being burnt, they in the burnt ship drown'd.

178   *Antiquary*

If in his study he hath so much care
To hang all old strange things, let his wife beware.

179   *Satire III*

Kind pity chokes my spleen; brave scorn forbids
Those tears to issue which swell my eye-lids;
I must not laugh, nor weep sins, and be wise,
Can railing then cure these worn maladies?
Is not our Mistress fair Religion,
As worthy of all our Soul's devotion,
As virtue was to the first blinded age?
Are not heaven's joys as valiant to assuage
Lusts, as earth's honour was to them? Alas,
As we do them in means, shall they surpass
Us in the end, and shall thy father's spirit
Meet blind Philosophers in heaven, whose merit
Of strict life may be imputed faith, and hear
Thee, whom he taught so easy ways and near
To follow, damn'd? O if thou dar'st, fear this;
This fear great courage, and high valour is.
Dar'st thou aid mutinous Dutch, and dar'st thou lay
Thee in ships' wooden sepulchres, a prey
To leaders' rage, to storms, to shot, to dearth?
Dar'st thou dive seas, and dungeons of the earth?
Hast thou courageous fire to thaw the ice
Of frozen North discoveries? and thrice
Colder than Salamanders, like divine
Children in th' oven, fires of Spain, and the line,
Whose countries limbecks to our bodies be,
Canst thou for gain bear? and must every he
Which cries not, Goddess, to thy Mistress, draw,
Or eat thy poisonous words? courage of straw!
O desperate coward, wilt thou seem bold, and
To thy foes and his (who made thee to stand
Sentinel in his world's garrison) thus yield,
And for the forbidden wars, leave th' appointed field?
Know thy foes: the foul Devil (whom thou
Strivest to please,) for hate, not love, would allow
Thee fain, his whole Realm to be quit; and as
The world's all parts wither away and pass,
So the world's self, thy other lov'd foe, is
In her decrepit wane, and thou loving this,

Dost love a withered and worn strumpet; last,
Flesh (itself's death) and joys which flesh can taste,
Thou lovest; and thy fair goodly soul, which doth
Give this flesh power to taste joy, thou dost loathe.
Seek true religion. O where? Mirreus
Thinking her unhous'd here, and fled from us,
Seeks her at Rome; there, because he doth know
That she was there a thousand years ago;
He loves her rags so, as we here obey
The statecloth where the Prince sate yesterday.
Crantz to such brave Loves will not be enthrall'd,
But loves her only, who at Geneva is call'd
Religion, plain, simple, sullen, young,
Contemptuous, yet unhandsome; as among
Lecherous humours, there is one that judges
No wenches wholesome, but coarse country drudges.
Graius stays still at home here, and because
Some Preachers, vile ambitious bawds, and laws
Still new like fashions, bid him think that she
Which dwells with us, is only perfect, he
Embraceth her, whom his Godfathers will
Tender to him, being tender, as Wards still
Take such wives as their Guardians offer, or
Pay values. Careless Phrygius doth abhor
All, because all cannot be good, as one
Knowing some women whores, dares marry none.
Gracchus loves all as one, and thinks that so
As women do in divers countries go
In divers habits, yet are still one kind,
So doth, so is Religion; and this blind-
ness too much light breeds; but unmoved thou
Of force must one, and forc'd but one allow;
And the right; ask thy father which is she,
Let him ask his; though truth and falsehood be
Near twins, yet truth a little elder is;
Be busy to seek her, believe me this,
He's not of none, nor worst, that seeks the best.
To adore, or scorn an image, or protest,
May all be bad; doubt wisely; in strange way
To stand inquiring right, is not to stray;
To sleep, or run wrong is. On a huge hill,
Cragged, and steep, Truth stands, and he that will
Reach her, about must, and about must go;
And what the hill's suddenness resists, win so;
Yet strive so, that before age, death's twilight,
Thy Soul rest, for none can work in that night.
To will, implies delay, therefore now do:
Hard deeds, the body's pains; hard knowledge too

The mind's endeavours reach, and mysteries
Are like the Sun, dazzling, yet plain to all eyes.
Keep the truth which thou hast found; men do not stand
In so ill case here, that God hath with His hand
Sign'd Kings blank-charters to kill whom they hate,
Nor are they Vicars, but hangmen to Fate.
Fool and wretch, wilt thou let thy Soul be tied
To man's laws, by which she shall not be tried
At the last day? Oh, will it then boot thee
To say a Philip, or a Gregory,
A Harry, or a Martin taught thee this?
Is not this excuse for mere contraries,
Equally strong? cannot both sides say so?
That thou mayest rightly obey power, her bounds know;
Those past, her nature, and name is chang'd; to be
Then humble to her is idolatry.
As streams are, Power is; those blest flowers that dwell
At the rough stream's calm head, thrive and do well,
But having left their roots, and themselves given
To the stream's tyrannous rage, alas are driven
Through mills, and rocks, and woods, and at last, almost
Consum'd in going, in the sea are lost:
So perish Souls, which more choose men's unjust
Power from God claimed, than God Himself to trust.

Holy Sonnets

180   I

Thou hast made me, and shall Thy work decay?
Repair me now, for now mine end doth haste,
I run to death, and death meets me as fast,
And all my pleasures are like yesterday;
I dare not move my dim eyes any way,
Despair behind, and death before doth cast
Such terror, and my feeble flesh doth waste
By sin in it, which it towards hell doth weigh;
Only Thou art above, and when towards Thee
By Thy leave I can look, I rise again;
But our old subtle foe so tempteth me,
That not one hour myself I can sustain;
Thy Grace may wing me to prevent his art,
And thou like Adamant draw mine iron heart.

181

IV

Oh my black Soul! now thou art summoned
By sickness, death's herald, and champion;
Thou art like a pilgrim, which abroad hath done
Treason, and durst not turn to whence he is fled,
Or like a thief, which till death's doom be read,
Wisheth himself delivered from prison;
But damn'd and hal'd to execution,
Wisheth that still he might be imprisoned.
Yet grace, if thou repent, thou canst not lack;
But who shall give thee that grace to begin?
Oh make thyself with holy mourning black,
And red with blushing, as thou art with sin;
Or wash thee in Christ's blood, which hath this might
That being red, it dyes red souls to white.

182

VI

This is my play's last scene, here heavens appoint
My pilgrimage's last mile; and my race
Idly, yet quickly run, hath this last pace,
My span's last inch, my minute's latest point,
And gluttonous death, will instantly unjoint
My body, and soul, and I shall sleep a space,
But my ever-waking part shall see that face,
Whose fear already shakes my every joint:
Then, as my soul, to heaven her first seat, takes flight,
And earth-born body, in the earth shall dwell,
So, fall my sins, that all may have their right,
To where they're bred, and would press me, to hell.
Impute me righteous, thus purg'd of evil,
For thus I leave the world, the flesh, the devil.

183

VII

At the round earth's imagin'd corners, blow
Your trumpets, Angels, and arise, arise
From death, you numberless infinities
Of souls, and to your scatter'd bodies go,
All whom the flood did, and fire shall o'erthrow,
All whom war, dearth, age, agues, tyrannies,
Despair, law, chance, hath slain, and you whose eyes,
Shall behold God, and never taste death's woe.

But let them sleep, Lord, and me mourn a space,
For, if above all these, my sins abound,
'Tis late to ask abundance of Thy grace,
When we are there; here on this lowly ground,
Teach me how to repent; for that's as good
As if Thou hadst seal'd my pardon, with Thy blood.

184   IX

If poisonous minerals, and if that tree,
Whose fruit threw death on else immortal us,
If lecherous goats, if serpents envious
Cannot be damn'd; alas! why should I be?
Why should intent or reason, born in me,
Make sins, else equal, in me more heinous?
And mercy being easy, and glorious
To God; in His stern wrath, why threatens He?
But who am I, that dare dispute with Thee
O God? Oh! of thine only worthy blood,
And my tears, make a heavenly Lethean flood,
And drown in it my sin's black memory;
That Thou remember them, some claim as debt,
I think it mercy, if Thou wilt forget.

185   XIII

What if this present were the world's last night?
Mark in my heart, O Soul, where thou dost dwell,
The picture of Christ crucified, and tell
Whether that countenance can thee affright,
Tears in His eyes quench the amazing light,
Blood fills His frowns, which from His pierc'd head fell.
And can that tongue adjudge thee unto hell,
Which pray'd forgiveness for His foes' fierce spite?
No, no; but as in my idolatry
I said to all my profane mistresses,
Beauty, of pity, foulness only is
A sign of rigour: so I say to thee,
To wicked spirits are horrid shapes assign'd,
This beauteous form assures a piteous mind.

186   XIV

    Batter my heart, three-person'd God; for, you
    As yet but knock, breathe, shine, and seek to mend;
    That I may rise, and stand, o'erthrow me, and bend
    Your force, to break, blow, burn and make me new.
    I, like an usurp'd town, to another due,
    Labour to admit you, but Oh, to no end,
    Reason your viceroy in me, me should defend,
    But is captiv'd, and proves weak or untrue.
    Yet dearly I love you, and would be loved fain,
    But am betroth'd unto your enemy:
    Divorce me, untie, or break that knot again,
    Take me to you, imprison me, for I
    Except you enthral me, never shall be free,
    Nor ever chaste, except you ravish me.

187   *To Mr Tilman after He Had Taken Orders*

    Thou, whose diviner soul hath caus'd thee now
    To put thy hand unto the holy Plough,
    Making Lay-scornings of the Ministry,
    Not an impediment, but victory;
    What bringst thou home with thee? how is thy mind
    Affected since the vintage? Dost thou find
    New thoughts and stirrings in thee? and as Steel
    Touch'd with a Loadstone, dost new motions feel?
    Or, as a Ship after much pain and care,
    For Iron and Cloth brings home rich Indian ware,
    Hast thou thus traffick'd, but with far more gain
    Of noble goods, and with less time and pain?
    Thou art the same materials, as before,
    Only the stamp is changed; but no more.
    And as new crowned Kings alter the face,
    But not the money's substance; so hath grace
    Chang'd only God's old Image by Creation,
    To Christ's new stamp, at this thy Coronation;
    Or, as we paint Angels with wings, because
    They bear God's message, and proclaim His laws,
    Since thou must do the like and so must move,
    Art thou new feather'd with celestial love?
    Dear, tell me where thy purchase lies, and show
    What thy advantage is above, below.
    But if thy gainings do surmount expression,
    Why doth the foolish world scorn that profession,

Whose joys pass speech? Why do they think unfit
That Gentry should join families with it?
As if their day were only to be spent
In dressing, Mistressing and compliment;
Alas poor joys, but poorer men, whose trust
Seems richly placed in sublimed dust:
(For, such are clothes and beauty, which though gay,
Are, at the best, but of sublimed clay.)
Let then the world thy calling disrespect,
But go thou on, and pity their neglect.
What function is so noble, as to be
Ambassador to God and destiny?
To open life, to give kingdoms to more
Than Kings give dignities; to keep heaven's door?
Mary's prerogative was to bear Christ, so
'Tis preachers' to convey Him, for they do
As Angels out of clouds, from Pulpits speak;
And bless the poor beneath, the lame, the weak.
If then th' Astronomers, whereas they spy
A new-found Star, their Optics magnify,
How brave are those, who with their Engine, can
Bring man to heaven, and heaven again to man?
These are thy titles and pre-eminences,
In whom must meet God's graces, men's offences,
And so the heavens which beget all things here,
And the earth our mother, which these things doth bear,
Both these in thee, are in thy Calling knit,
And make thee now a blest Hermaphrodite.

188   *A Hymn to Christ*
    at the Author's Last Going into Germany

In what torn ship soever I embark,
That ship shall be my emblem of Thy Ark;
What sea soever swallow me, that flood
Shall be to me an emblem of Thy blood;
Though Thou with clouds of anger do disguise
Thy face; yet through that mask I know those eyes,
   Which, though they turn away sometimes,
      They never will despise.

I sacrifice this Island unto Thee,
And all whom I lov'd there, and who lov'd me;
When I have put our seas 'twixt them and me,
Put thou Thy sea betwixt my sins and Thee.

As the tree's sap doth seek the root below
In winter, in my winter now I go,
    Where none but Thee, th' Eternal root
    Of true Love I may know.

Nor Thou nor Thy religion dost control,
The amorousness of an harmonious Soul,
But thou would'st have that love Thyself: as Thou
Art jealous, Lord, so I am jealous now,
Thou lov'st not, till from loving more, Thou free
My soul: who ever gives, takes liberty:
    O, if Thou car'st not whom I love
    Alas, Thou lov'st not me.

Seal then this bill of my Divorce to All,
On whom those fainter beams of love did fall;
Marry those loves, which in youth scattered be
On Fame, Wit, Hopes (false mistresses) to Thee.
Churches are best for Prayer, that have least light:
To see God only, I go out of sight:
    And to 'scape stormy days, I choose
    An Everlasting night.

189   *Hymn to God My God, in My Sickness*

Since I am coming to that Holy room,
    Where, with thy Quire of Saints for evermore,
I shall be made thy Music; as I come
    I tune the Instrument here at the door,
    And what I must do then, think here before.

Whilst my Physicians by their love are grown
    Cosmographers, and I their Map, who lie
Flat on this bed, that by them may be shown
    That this is my South-west discovery
    Per fretum febris, by these straits to die,

I joy, that in these straits, I see my West;
    For, though their currents yield return to none,
What shall my West hurt me? As West and East
    In all flat Maps (and I am one) are one,
    So death doth touch the Resurrection.

Is the Pacific Sea my home? Or are
    The Eastern riches? Is Jerusalem?
Anyan, and Magellan, and Gibraltar,
    All straits, and none but straits, are ways to them,
    Whether where Japhet dwelt, or Cham, or Shem.

We think that Paradise and Calvary,
   Christ's Cross, and Adam's tree, stood in one place;
Look Lord, and find both Adams met in me;
   As the first Adam's sweat surrounds my face,
   May the last Adam's blood my soul embrace.

So, in His purple wrapp'd receive me Lord,
   By these His thorns give me His other Crown;
And as to others' souls I preach'd Thy word,
   Be this my Text, my Sermon to mine own,
   Therefore that He may raise the Lord throws down.

190   *A Hymn to God the Father*

Wilt Thou forgive that sin where I begun,
   Which is my sin, though it were done before?
Wilt Thou forgive that sin, through which I run,
   And do run still: though still I do deplore?
     When Thou hast done, Thou hast not done,
      For, I have more.

Wilt Thou forgive that sin by which I have won
   Others to sin? and, made my sin their door?
Wilt Thou forgive that sin which I did shun
   A year, or two: but wallowed in, a score?
     When Thou hast done, Thou hast not done,
      For I have more.

I have a sin of fear, that when I have spun
   My last thread, I shall perish on the shore;
Swear by Thyself, that at my death Thy son
   Shall shine as He shines now, and heretofore;
     And, having done that, Thou hast done,
      I fear no more.

Anonymous

191   *Tom o' Bedlam*

From the hag and hungry goblin
That into rags would rend ye,
The spirit that stands by the naked man
In the Book of Moons defend ye,

That of your five sound senses
You never be forsaken,
Nor wander from yourselves with Tom
Abroad to beg your bacon,
>   *While I do sing, Any food, any feeding,*
>   *Feeding, drink, or clothing;*
>   *Come dame or maid, be not afraid,*
>   *Poor Tom will injure nothing.*

Of thirty bare years have I
Twice twenty been enraged,
And of forty been three times fifteen
In durance soundly caged
On the lordly lofts of Bedlam
With stubble soft and dainty,
Brave bracelets strong, sweet whips ding dong
With wholesome hunger plenty,
>   *And now I sing, etc.*

With a thought I took for Maudlin
And a cruse of cockle pottage,
With a thing thus tall, sky bless you all,
I befell into this dotage.
I slept not since the Conquest,
Till then I never waked,
Till the roguish boy of love where I lay
Me found and strip't me naked.
>   *And now I sing, etc.*

When I short have shorn my sow's face
And swigg'd my horny barrel,
In an oaken inn I pound my skin
As a suit of gilt apparel;
The moon's my constant mistress
And the lovely owl my marrow;
The flaming drake and the night crow make
Me music to my sorrow.
>   *While I do sing, etc.*

The palsy plagues my pulses
When I prig your pigs or pullen,
Your culvers take, or matchless make
Your Chanticleer or Sullen.
When I want provant with Humphrey
I sup, and when benighted,
I repose in Paul's with waking souls
Yet never am affrighted.
>   *But I do sing, etc.*

I know more than Apollo,
For oft when he lies sleeping
I see the stars at bloody wars
In the wounded welkin weeping;
The moon embrace her shepherd,
And the Queen of Love her warrior,
While the first doth horn the star of morn,
And the next the heavenly Farrier.
     While I do sing, etc.

The gypsies, Snap and Pedro,
Are none of Tom's comradoes,
The punk I scorn and the cutpurse sworn,
And the roaring boy's bravadoes.
The meek, the white, the gentle
Me handle, touch, and spare not;
But those that cross Tom Rynosseross
  Do what the panther dare not.
     Although I sing, etc.

With an host of furious fancies
Whereof I am commander,
With a burning spear and a horse of air,
To the wilderness I wander.
By a knight of ghosts and shadows
I summon'd am to a tourney
Ten leagues beyond the wide world's end:
Methinks it is no journey.
     Yet will I sing, etc.

Ben Jonson

192   From *The Alchemist*

Mammon   I will have all my beds blown up, not stuft:
Down is too hard: and then, mine oval room
Fill'd with such pictures as Tiberius took
From Elephantis, and dull Aretine
But coldly imitated. Then, my glasses
Cut in more subtle angles, to disperse
And multiply the figures, as I walk
Naked between my succubae. My mists
I'll have of perfume, vapour'd 'bout the room,
To lose ourselves in; and my baths, like pits
To fall into; from whence we will come forth,
And roll us dry in gossamer and roses. –

Is it arrived at ruby? – Where I spy
A wealthy citizen, or a rich lawyer,
Have a sublim'd pure wife, unto that fellow
I'll send a thousand pound to be my cuckold.

Face   And I shall carry it?
Mammon   No. I'll have no bawds,
But fathers and mothers: they will do it best,
Best of all others. And my flatterers
Shall be the pure and gravest of divines,
That I can get for money. My mere fools,
Eloquent burgesses, and then my poets
The same that writ so subtly of the fart,
Whom I will entertain still for that subject.
The few that would give out themselves to be
Court and town-stallions, and, each-where, bely
Ladies who are known most innocent for them;
Those will I beg, to make me eunuchs of:
And they shall fan me with ten estrich tails
A-piece, made in a plume to gather wind.
We will be brave, Puffe, now we have the med'cine.
My meat shall all come in, in Indian shells,
Dishes of agat set in gold, and studded
With emeralds, sapphires, hyacinths, and rubies.
The tongues of carps, dormice, and camels' heels,
Boil'd in the spirit of sol, and dissolv'd pearl,
Apicius' diet, 'gainst the epilepsy:
And I will eat these broths with spoons of amber,
Headed with diamond and carbuncle.
My foot-boy shall eat pheasants, calver'd salmons,
Knots, godwits, lampreys: I myself will have
The beards of barbels served, instead of sallads;
Oil'd mushrooms; and the swelling unctuous paps
Of a fat pregnant sow, newly cut off,
Drest with an exquisite, and poignant sauce;
For which, I'll say unto my cook, *There's gold,*
Go forth, and be a knight.

193   *On My First Daughter*

Here lies, to each her parents' ruth,
Mary, the daughter of their youth;
Yet, all heaven's gifts being heaven's due,
It makes the father less to rue.
At six months' end she parted hence,
With safety of her innocence;

Whose soul heaven's Queen (whose name she bears)
In comfort of her mother's tears,
Hath plac'd amongst her virgin-train;
Where, while that sever'd doth remain,
This grave partakes the fleshly birth;
Which cover lightly, gentle earth.

194   *On My First Son*

Farewell, thou child of my right hand, and joy;
  My sin was too much hope of thee, lov'd boy.
Seven years thou wert lent to me, and I thee pay,
  Exacted by thy fate, on the just day.
Oh, could I lose all father now! For why
  Will man lament the state he should envy?
To have so soon 'scap'd world's and flesh's rage,
  And, if no other misery, yet age!
Rest in soft peace, and asked, say, Here doth lie
  Ben Jonson his best piece of poetry –
For whose sake, henceforth, all his vows be such,
  As what he loves may never like too much.

195   From *The Gipsies Metamorphosed*

The faery beam upon you,
The stars to glisten on you,
  A moon of light
  In the noon of night
Till the firedrake hath o'er gone you.

The wheel of fortune guide you,
The boy with the bow beside you
  Run aye in the way
  Till the bird of day
And the luckier lot betide you.

196   From *A Celebration of Charis in Ten Lyric Pieces*

II Her Triumph

See the Chariot at hand here of Love,
    Wherein my Lady rideth!
Each that draws is a swan or a dove,
    And well the car Love guideth.
As she goes, all hearts do duty
        Unto her beauty;
And enamour'd do wish, so they might
        But enjoy such a sight,
That they still were to run by her side,
Thorough swords, thorough seas, whither she would ride.

Do but look on her eyes, they do light
    All that Love's world compriseth!
Do but look on her hair, it is bright
    As Love's star when it riseth!
Do but mark, her forehead's smoother
        Than words that soothe her;
And from her arch'd brows such a grace
        Sheds itself through the face,
As alone there triumphs to the life
All the gain, all the good, of the elements' strife.

Have you seen but a bright lily grow
    Before rude hands have touch'd it?
Have you mark'd but the fall of the snow
    Before the soil hath smutch'd it?
Have you felt the wool of the beaver,
        Or swan's down ever?
Or have smelt of the bud of the brier,
        Or the nard in the fire?
Or have tasted the bag of the bee?
O so white, O so soft, O so sweet is she!

Joseph Hall

197   From *Toothless Satires*

Book I   Satire VII

Great is the folly of a feeble brain,
O'er-rul'd with love, and tyrannous disdain.
For love, however in the basest breast,
It breeds high thoughts that feed the fancy best:
Yet is he blind, and leads poor fools awry,
While they hang gazing on their mistress' eye.
The love-sick poet, whose importune prayer
Repulsed is with resolute despair,
Hopeth to conquer his disdainful dame,
With public plaints of his conceived flame.
Then pours he forth in patched sonettings,
His love, his lust, and loathsome flatterings:
As though the staring world hang'd on his sleeve,
When once he smiles, to laugh: and when he sighs, to grieve.
Careth the world, thou love, thou live or die?
Careth the world how fair thy fair-one be?
Fond wittol that wouldst load thy witless head
With timely horns, before thy bridal bed!
Then can he term his dirty ill-faced bride
Lady and Queen, and virgin deify'd:
Be she all sooty black, or berry brown,
She's white as morrow's milk, or flakes new blown:
And though she be some dunghill drudge at home,
Yet can he her resign some refuse room
Amidst the well-known stars; or if not there,
Sure will he saint her in his Kalendere!

John Webster

198   From *The White Devil*

Cornelia   Call for the robin redbreast, and the wren,
Since o'er shady groves they hover,
And with leaves and flowers do cover
The friendless bodies of unburied men.
Call unto his funeral dole
The ant, the fieldmouse, and the mole,
To rear him hillocks that shall keep him warm,
And (when gay tombs are robb'd) sustain no harm;
But keep the wolf far thence, that's foe to men,
For with his nails he'll dig them up again.

Robert Herrick

199   *The Argument of His Book*

I sing of brooks, of blossoms, birds and bowers,
Of April, May, of June and July-flowers;
I sing of May-poles, hock-carts, wassails, wakes,
Of bridegrooms, brides and of their bridal cakes;
I write of youth, of love, and have access
By these to sing of cleanly wantonness;
I sing of dews, of rains, and piece by piece
Of balm, of oil, of spice and ambergris;
I sing of times trans-shifting, and I write
How roses first came red and lilies white;
I write of groves, of twilights, and I sing
The Court of Mab, and of the Fairy King;
I write of hell; I sing (and ever shall)
Of heaven, and hope to have it after all.

200

A sweet disorder in the dress
Kindles in clothes a wantonness:
A lawn about the shoulders thrown
Into a fine distraction:
An erring lace which here and there
Enthralls the crimson stomacher:
A cuff neglectful, and thereby
Ribbons to flow confusedly:
A winning wave, deserving note,
In the tempestuous petticoat:
A careless shoe-string, in whose tie
I see a wild civility:
Do more bewitch me than when art
Is too precise in every part.

201

Whenas in silks my Julia goes,
Then, then, methinks, how sweetly flows
The liquefaction of her clothes.

Next, when I cast mine eyes and see
That brave vibration each way free;
O how that glittering taketh me!

202   *The Hock-cart or Harvest Home.*
To the Right Honourable Mildmay,
Earl of Westmoreland

Come, sons of summer, by whose toil
We are the lords of wine and oil:
By whose tough labours and rough hands
We rip up first, then reap our lands.
Crown'd with the ears of corn, now come,
And to the pipe sing harvest home.
Come forth, my lord, and see the cart
Dress'd up with all the country art:
See here a maukin, there a sheet,
As spotless pure as it is sweet:
The horses, mares, and frisking fillies,
Clad all in linen white as lilies.
The harvest swains and wenches bound
For joy, to see the hock-cart crown'd.
About the cart, hear how the rout
Of rural younglings raise the shout;
Pressing before, some coming after,
Those with a shout, and these with laughter.
Some bless the cart, some kiss the sheaves,
Some prank them up with oaken leaves:
Some cross the fill-horse, some with great
Devotion stroke the home-borne wheat:
While other rustics, less attent
To prayers than to merriment,
Run after with their breeches rent.
Well, on, brave boys, to your lord's hearth,
Glitt'ring with fire, where, for your mirth,
Ye shall see first the large and chief
Foundation of your feast, fat beef:
With upper stories, mutton, veal
And bacon (which makes full the meal),
With sev'ral dishes standing by,
As here a custard, there a pie,
And here all-tempting frumenty.
And for to make the merry cheer,
If smirking wine be wanting here,
There's that which drowns all care, stout beer;
Which freely drink to your lord's health,
Then to the plough, the commonwealth,
Next to your flails, your fans, your fats,
Then to the maids with wheaten hats:
To the rough sickle, and crook'd scythe,
Drink, frolic boys, till all be blithe.

Feed, and grow fat; and as ye eat
Be mindful that the lab'ring neat,
As you, may have their fill of meat.
And know, besides, ye must revoke
The patient ox unto the yoke,
And all go back unto the plough
And harrow, though they're hang'd up now.
And, you must know, your lord's word's true,
Feed him ye must, whose food fills you;
And that this pleasure is like rain,
Not sent ye for to drown your pain,
But for to make it spring again.

Henry King

203   *The Surrender*

My once dear love – hapless that I no more
Must call thee so – the rich affection's store
That fed our hopes, lies now exhaust and spent,
Like sums of treasure unto bankrupts lent.
   We that did nothing study but the way
To love each other, with which thoughts the day
Rose with delight to us, and with them set,
Must learn the hateful art, how to forget.
   We that did nothing wish that Heav'n could give
Beyond ourselves, nor did desire to live
Beyond that wish, all these now cancel must,
As if not writ in faith, but words and dust.
   Yet witness those clear vows which lovers make,
Witness the chaste desires, that never brake
Into unruly heats; witness that breast
Which in thy bosom anchor'd his whole rest,
'Tis no default in us. I dare acquite
Thy maiden faith, thy purpose fair and white
As thy pure self. Cross planets did envy
Us to each other, and Heav'n did untie
Faster than vows could bind. O that the stars
When lovers meet, should stand oppos'd in wars!
   Since then some higher Destinies command,
Let us not strive, nor labour to withstand
What is past help. The longest date of grief
Can never yield a hope of our relief:
And though we waste ourselves in moist laments,
Tears may drown us, but not our discontents.

Fold back our arms, take home our fruitless loves,
That must new fortunes try, like turtle doves
Dislodged from their haunts. We must in tears
Unwind a love knit up in many years.
In this last kiss I here surrender thee
Back to thyself. Lo, thou again art free.
Thou in another, sad as that, resend
The truest heart that lover e'er did lend.
 Now turn from each. So fare our sever'd hearts
As the divorc'd soul from her body parts.

Francis Quarles

204   *Emblem IV*

I Am My Beloved's, and His Desire Is towards Me

Like to the arctic needle, that doth guide
 The wandering shade by his magnetic power,
And leaves his silken gnomon to decide
 The question of the controverted hour,
First frantics up and down from side to side,
  And restless beats his crystall'd ivory case
  With vain impatience; jets from place to place,
And seeks the bosom of his frozen bride;
  At length he slacks his motion, and doth rest
His trembling point at his bright pole's beloved breast.

Even so my soul, being hurried here and there,
 By every object that presents delight,
Fain would be settled, but she knows not where;
 She likes at morning what she loathes at night:
She bows to honour, then she lends an ear
  To that sweet swan-like voice of dying pleasure,
  Then tumbles in the scatter'd heaps of treasure;
Now flatter'd with false hope, now foil'd with fear:
  Thus finding all the world's delight to be
But empty toys, good God, she points alone to thee.

But hath the virtued steel a power to move?
 Or can the untouch'd needle point aright?
Or can my wandering thoughts forbear to rove,
 Unguided by the virtue of thy sprite?
Oh hath my laden soul the art to improve
  Her wasted talent, and, unrais'd, aspire
  In this sad moulting time of her desire?
Not first belov'd, have I the power to love?

I cannot stir but as thou please to move me,
Nor can my heart return thee love until thou love me.

The still commandress of the silent night
  Borrows her beams from her bright brother's eye;
His fair aspéct fills her sharp horns with light,
  If he withdraw, her flames are quench'd and die:
Even so the beams of thy enlightening sprite,
    Infus'd and shot into my dark desire,
    Inflame my thoughts, and fill my soul with fire,
That I am ravish'd with a new delight;
    But if thou shroud thy face, my glory fades,
And I remain a nothing, all compos'd of shades.

Eternal God! O thou that only art,
  The sacred fountain of eternal light,
And blessed loadstone of my better part,
  O thou, my heart's desire, my soul's delight!
Reflect upon my soul, and touch my heart,
    And then my heart shall prize no good above thee;
    And then my soul shall know thee; knowing, love thee;
And then my trembling thoughts shall never start
    From thy commands, or swerve the least degree,
Or once presume to move, but as they move in thee.

George Herbert

205   *Prayer (I)*

Prayer the Churches banquet, Angels age,
Gods breath in man returning to his birth,
The soul in paraphrase, heart in pilgrimage,
The Christian plummet sounding heav'n and earth;
Engine against th' Almightie, sinners towre,
Reversed thunder, Christ-side-piercing spear,
The six-daies world-transposing in an houre,
A kinde of tune, which all things heare and fear;
Softnesse, and peace, and joy, and love, and blisse,
Exalted Manna, gladnesse of the best,
Heaven in ordinarie, man well drest,
The milkie way, the bird of Paradise,
    Church-bels beyond the starres heard, the souls bloud,
    The land of spices; something understood.

206   *The Church-floore*

Mark you the floore? that square & speckled stone,
          Which looks so firm and strong,
                    Is *Patience*:

And th' other black and grave, wherewith each one
          Is checker'd all along,
                    Humilitie:

The gentle rising, which on either hand
          Leads to the Quire above,
                    Is *Confidence*:

But the sweet cement, which in one sure band
          Ties the whole frame, is *Love*
                    And *Charitie*.

          Hither sometimes Sinne steals, and stains
          The marbles neat and curious veins:
But all is cleansed when the marble weeps.
          Sometimes Death, puffing at the doore,
          Blows all the dust about the floore:
But while he thinks to spoil the room, he sweeps.
          Blest be the *Architect*, whose art
          Could build so strong in a weak heart.

207   *The Collar*

          I struck the board, and cry'd, No more.
                    I will abroad.
          What? shall I ever sigh and pine?
My lines and life are free; free as the rode,
          Loose as the winde, as large as store.
                    Shall I be still in suit?
          Have I no harvest but a thorn
          To let me bloud, and not restore
What I have lost with cordiall fruit?
                    Sure there was wine
Before my sighs did drie it: there was corn
          Before my tears did drown it.
          Is the yeare onely lost to me?
                    Have I no bayes to crown it?
No flowers, no garlands gay? all blasted?
                    All wasted?
          Not so, my heart: but there is fruit,
                    And thou hast hands.

Recover all thy sigh-blown age
On double pleasures: leave thy cold dispute
Of what is fit, and not forsake thy cage,
Thy rope of sands,
Which pettie thoughts have made, and made to thee
Good cable, to enforce and draw,
And be thy law,
While thou didst wink and wouldst not see.
Away; take heed:
I will abroad.
Call in thy deaths head there: tie up thy fears.
He that forbears
To suit and serve his need,
Deserves his load.
But as I rav'd and grew more fierce and wilde
At every word,
Me thoughts I heard one calling, *Child*:
And I reply'd, *My Lord*.

208   *Love (III)*

Love bade me welcome: yet my soul drew back,
Guiltie of dust and sinne.
But quick-ey'd Love, observing me grow slack
From my first entrance in,
Drew nearer to me, sweetly questioning,
If I lack'd any thing.

A guest, I answer'd, worthy to be here:
Love said, You shall be he.
I the unkinde, ungratefull? Ah my deare,
I cannot look on thee.
Love took my hand, and smiling did reply,
Who made the eyes but I?

Truth Lord, but I have marr'd them: let my shame
Go where it doth deserve.
And know you not, sayes Love, who bore the blame?
My deare, then I will serve.
You must sit down, sayes Love, and taste my meat:
So I did sit and eat.

209   *The Pearl. Matth. 13*

I know the wayes of learning; both the head
And pipes that feed the presse, and make it runne;
What reason hath from nature borrowed,
Or of it self, a good huswife, spunne
In laws and policie; what the starres conspire,
What willing nature speaks, what forc'd by fire;
Both th' old discoveries, and the new-found seas,
The stock and surplus, cause and historie:
All these stand open, or I have the keyes:
             Yet I love thee.

I know the wayes of honour, what maintains
The quick returns of courtesie and wit:
In vies of favours whether partie gains,
When glorie swells the heart, and moldeth it
To all expressions both of hand and eye,
Which on the world a true-love-knot may tie,
And bear the bundle, wheresoe'er it goes:
How many drammes of spirit there must be
To sell my life unto my friends or foes:
             Yet I love thee.

I know the wayes of pleasure, the sweet strains,
The lullings and the relishes of it;
The propositions of hot bloud and brains;
What mirth and musick mean; what love and wit
Have done these twentie hundred yeares, and more:
I know the projects of unbridled store:
My stuffe is flesh, not brasse; my senses live,
And grumble oft, that they have more in me
Then he that curbs them being but one to five:
             Yet I love thee.

I know all these, and have them in my hand:
Therefore not sealed, but with open eyes
I flie to thee, and fully understand
Both the main sale, and the commodities;
And at what rate and price I have thy love;
With all the circumstances that may move:
Yet through the labyrinths, not my groveling wit,
But thy silk twist let down from heav'n to me,
Did both conduct and teach me, how by it
             To climbe to thee.

Edmund Waller

210   *Of the Last Verses in the Book*

When we for age could neither read nor write
The subject made us able to indite:
The soul with nobler resolutions deck'd,
The body stooping, does herself erect,
No mortal parts are requisite to raise
Her that unbodied can her Maker praise.
  The seas are quiet when the winds give o'er:
So, calm are we when passions are no more,
For then we know how vain it was to boast
Of fleeting things, so certain to be lost.
Clouds of affection from our younger eyes
Conceal that emptiness which age descries.
  The soul's dark cottage, batter'd and decay'd,
Lets in new light through chinks that time has made:
Stronger by weakness wiser men become
As they draw near to their eternal home.
Leaving the old, both worlds at once they view
That stand upon the threshold of the new.

211   *To a Fair Lady Playing with a Snake*

Strange, that such horror and such grace
Should dwell together in one place;
A fury's arm, an angel's face!

'Tis innocence and youth which makes
In Chloris' fancy such mistakes,
To start at love and play with snakes.

By this and by her coldness barr'd,
Her servants have a task too hard:
The tyrant has a double guard.

Thrice happy snake, that in her sleeve
May boldly creep: we dare not give
Our thoughts so unconfin'd a leave.

Contented in that nest of snow
He lies, as he his bliss did know,
And to the wood no more would go.

Take heed, fair Eve, you do not make
Another tempter of this snake;
A marble one so warm'd would speak.

John Milton

212   *The Fifth Ode of Horace Lib. I*

Quis multa gracilis te puer in Rosa. *Rendred*
almost word for word without Rhyme according
to the Latin Measure, as near as the Language will
permit.

What slender Youth bedew'd with liquid odours
Courts thee on Roses in some pleasant Cave,
    Pyrrha for whom bind'st thou
    In wreaths thy golden Hair,
Plain in thy neatness; O how oft shall he
On Faith and changed Gods complain: and Seas
    Rough with black winds and storms
    Unwonted shall admire:
Who now enjoyes thee credulous, all Gold,
Who always vacant, always amiable
    Hopes thee; of flattering gales
    Unmindfull. Hapless they
To whom thou untry'd seem'st fair. Me in my vow'd
Picture the sacred wall declares t' have hung
    My dank and dropping weeds
    To the stern God of Sea.

213   *On the University Carrier*

who sickn'd in the time of his vacancy,
being forbid to go to London, by reason of the Plague.

Here lies old *Hobson*, Death hath broke his girt,
And here alas, hath laid him in the dirt,
Or els the ways being foul, twenty to one,
He's here stuck in a slough, and overthrown.
'Twas such a shifter, that if truth were known,
Death was half glad when he had got him down;
For he had any time this ten yeers full,
Dodg'd with him, betwixt *Cambridge* and the Bull.
And surely, Death could never have prevail'd,
Had not his weekly cours of carriage fail'd;
But lately finding him so long at home,
And thinking now his journeys end was come,
And that he had tane up his latest Inne,
In the kind office of a Chamberlin
Shew'd him his room where he must lodge that night,
Pull'd off his Boots, and took away the light:
If any ask for him, it shall be sed,
Hobson has supt, and 's newly gon to bed.

Sonnets

214   XVI

When I consider how my light is spent,
   E're half my days, in this dark world and wide,
   And that one Talent which is death to hide,
   Lodg'd with me useless, though my Soul more bent
To serve therewith my Maker, and present
   My true account, least he returning chide,
   Doth God exact day-labour, light deny'd,
   I fondly ask; But patience to prevent
That murmur, soon replies, God doth not need
   Either man's work or his own gifts, who best
   Bear his milde yoak, they serve him best, his State
Is Kingly. Thousands at his bidding speed
   And post o're Land and Ocean without rest:
   They also serve who only stand and waite.

215   XIX

Methought I saw my late espoused Saint
   Brought to me like *Alcestis* from the grave,
   Whom *Joves* great Son to her glad Husband gave,
   Rescu'd from death by force though pale and faint.
Mine as whom washt from spot of child-bed taint,
   Purification in the old Law did save,
   And such, as yet once more I trust to have
   Full sight of her in Heaven without restraint,
Came vested all in white, pure as her mind:
   Her face was vail'd, yet to my fancied sight,
   Love, sweetness, goodness, in her person shin'd
So clear, as in no face with more delight.
   But O as to embrace me she enclin'd
   I wak'd, she fled, and day brought back my night.

216

Lycidas

In this Monody the Author bewails a learned Friend, unfortunately drown'd in his Passage from *Chester* on the *Irish* Seas, 1637. And by occasion foretels the ruine of our corrupted Clergy then in their height.

Yet once more, O ye Laurels, and once more
Ye Myrtles brown, with Ivy never-sear,
I com to pluck your Berries harsh and crude,
And with forc'd fingers rude,
Shatter your leaves before the mellowing year.
Bitter constraint, and sad occasion dear,
Compels me to disturb your season due:
For *Lycidas* is dead, dead ere his prime
Young *Lycidas,* and hath not left his peer:
Who would not sing for *Lycidas*? he knew
Himself to sing, and build the lofty rhyme.
He must not flote upon his watry bear
Unwept, and welter to the parching wind,
Without the meed of som melodious tear.
　　Begin then, Sisters of the sacred well,
That from beneath the seat of *Jove* doth spring,
Begin, and somwhat loudly sweep the string.
Hence with denial vain, and coy excuse,
So may som gentle Muse
With lucky words favour my destin'd Urn,
And as he passes turn,
And bid fair peace be to my sable shrowd.
For we were nurst upon the self-same hill,
Fed the same flock, by fountain, shade, and rill.
　　Together both, ere the high Lawns appear'd
Under the opening eye-lids of the morn,
We drove a field, and both together heard
What time the Gray-fly winds her sultry horn,
Batt'ning our flocks with the fresh dews of night,
Oft till the Star that rose, at Ev'ning, bright
Toward Heav'ns descent had slop'd his westering wheel.
Mean while the Rural ditties were not mute,
Temper'd to th' Oaten Flute,
Rough *Satyrs* danc'd, and *Fauns* with clov'n heel,
From the glad sound would not be absent long,
And old *Damœtas* lov'd to hear our song.
　　But O the heavy change, now thou art gon,
Now thou art gon, and never must return!
Thee Shepherd, thee the Woods, and desert Caves,
With wilde Thyme and the gadding Vine o'regrown,
And all their echoes mourn.

The Willows, and the Hazle Copses green,
Shall now no more be seen,
Fanning their joyous Leaves to thy soft layes.
As killing as the Canker to the Rose,
Or Taint-worm to the weanling Herds that graze,
Or Frost to Flowers, that their gay wardrop wear,
When first the White thorn blows;
Such, *Lycidas*, thy loss to Shepherds ear.
   Where were ye Nymphs when the remorseless deep
Clos'd o're the head of your lov'd *Lycidas*?
For neither were ye playing on the steep,
Where your old *Bards*, the famous *Druids* ly,
Nor on the shaggy top of *Mona* high,
Nor yet where *Deva* spreads her wisard stream:
Ay me, I fondly dream!
Had ye bin there — for what could that have don?
What could the Muse her self that *Orpheus* bore,
The Muse her self, for her inchanting son
Whom Universal nature did lament,
When by the rout that made the hideous roar,
His goary visage down the stream was sent,
Down the swift *Hebrus* to the *Lesbian* shore.
   Alas! What boots it with uncessant care
To tend the homely slighted Shepherds trade,
And strictly meditate the thankles Muse,
Were it not better don as others use,
To sport with *Amaryllis* in the shade,
Or with the tangles of *Neæra's* hair?
Fame is the spur that the clear spirit doth raise
(That last infirmity of Noble mind)
To scorn delights, and live laborious dayes;
But the fair Guerdon when we hope to find,
And think to burst out into sudden blaze,
Comes the blind *Fury* with th' abhorred shears,
And slits the thin spun life. But not the praise,
Phœbus repli'd, and touch'd my trembling ears:
Fame is no plant that grows on mortal soil,
Nor in the glistering foil
Set off to th' world, nor in broad rumour lies,
But lives and spreds aloft by those pure eyes,
And perfet witnes of all judging *Jove*;
As he pronounces lastly on each deed,
Of so much fame in Heav'n expect thy meed.
   O Fountain *Arethuse*, and thou honour'd floud,
Smooth-sliding *Mincius*, crown'd with vocall reeds,
That strain I heard was of a higher mood:
But now my Oate proceeds,
And listens to the Herald of the Sea
That came in *Neptune's* plea,

He ask'd the Waves, and ask'd the Fellon winds,
What hard mishap hath doom'd this gentle swain?
And question'd every gust of rugged wings
That blows from off each beaked Promontory,
They knew not of his story,
And sage *Hippotades* their answer brings,
That not a blast was from his dungeon stray'd,
The Ayr was calm, and on the level brine,
Sleek *Panope* with all her sisters play'd.
It was that fatall and perfidious Bark
Built in th' eclipse, and rigg'd with curses dark,
That sunk so low that sacred head of thine.
  Next *Camus*, reverend Sire, went footing slow,
His Mantle hairy, and his Bonnet sedge,
Inwrought with figures dim, and on the edge
Like to that sanguine flower inscrib'd with woe.
Ah! Who hath reft (quoth he) my dearest pledge?
Last came, and last did go,
The Pilot of the *Galilean* lake,
Two massy Keyes he bore of metals twain,
(The Golden opes, the Iron shuts amain)
He shook his Miter'd locks, and stern bespake,
How well could I have spar'd for thee young swain,
Anow of such as for their bellies sake,
Creep and intrude, and climb into the fold?
Of other care they little reck'ning make,
Then how to scramble at the shearers feast,
And shove away the worthy bidden guest.
Blind mouthes! that scarce themselves know how to hold
A Sheep-hook, or have learn'd ought els the least
That to the faithfull Herdmans art belongs!
What recks it them? What need they? They are sped;
And when they list, their lean and flashy songs
Grate on their scrannel Pipes of wretched straw,
The hungry Sheep look up, and are not fed,
But swoln with wind, and the rank mist they draw,
Rot inwardly, and foul contagion spread:
Besides what the grim Woolf with privy paw
Daily devours apace, and nothing sed,
But that two-handed engine at the door,
Stands ready to smite once, and smite no more.
  Return *Alpheus*, the dread voice is past,
That shrunk thy streams; Return *Sicilian* Muse,
And call the Vales, and bid them hither cast
Their Bels, and Flourets of a thousand hues.
Ye valleys low where the milde whispers use,
Of shades and wanton winds, and gushing brooks,
On whose fresh lap the swart Star sparely looks,
Throw hither all your quaint enameld eyes,

That on the green terf suck the honied showres,
And purple all the ground with vernal flowres.
Bring the rathe Primrose that forsaken dies.
The tufted Crow-toe, and pale Gessamine,
The white Pink, and the Pansie freakt with jeat,
The glowing Violet.
The Musk-rose, and the well attir'd Woodbine,
With Cowslips wan that hang the pensive hed,
And every flower that sad embroidery wears:
Bid *Amaranthus* all his beauty shed,
And Daffadillies fill their cups with tears,
To strew the Laureat Herse where *Lycid* lies.
For so to interpose a little ease,
Let our frail thoughts dally with false surmise.
Ay me! Whilst thee the shores, and sounding Seas
Wash far away, where ere thy bones are hurld,
Whether beyond the stormy *Hebrides*,
Where thou perhaps under the whelming tide
Visit'st the bottom of the monstrous world;
Or whether thou to our moist vows deny'd,
Sleep'st by the fable of *Bellerus* old,
Where the great vision of the guarded Mount
Looks toward *Namancos* and *Bayona's* hold;
Look homeward Angel now, and melt with ruth.
And, O ye *Dolphins*, waft the haples youth.
  Weep no more, woful Shepherds weep no more,
For *Lycidas* your sorrow is not dead,
Sunk though he be beneath the watry floar,
So sinks the day-star in the Ocean bed,
And yet anon repairs his drooping head,
And tricks his beams, and with new spangled Ore,
Flames in the forehead of the morning sky:
So *Lycidas* sunk low, but mounted high,
Through the dear might of him that walk'd the waves
Where other groves, and other streams along,
With *Nectar* pure his oozy Lock's he laves,
And hears the unexpressive nuptiall Song,
In the blest Kingdoms meek of joy and love.
There entertain him all the Saints above,
In solemn troops, and sweet Societies
That sing, and singing in their glory move,
And wipe the tears for ever from his eyes.
Now *Lycidas* the Shepherds weep no more;
Hence forth thou art the Genius of the shore,
In thy large recompense, and shalt be good
To all that wander in that perilous flood.

Thus sang the uncouth Swain to th' Okes and rills,
While the still morn went out with Sandals gray,
He touch'd the tender stops of various Quills,
With eager thought warbling his *Dorick* lay:
And now the Sun had stretch'd out all the hills,
And now was dropt into the Western bay;
At last he rose, and twitch'd his Mantle blew:
To morrow to fresh Woods, and Pastures new.

217   From *Comus*

The Spirit sings   *Sabrina fair*
                    Listen where thou art sitting
            Under the glassie, cool, translucent wave,
                    In twisted braids of Lillies knitting
            The loose train of thy amber-dropping hair,
                    Listen for dear honours sake,
                    Goddess of the silver lake,
                                Listen and save.

            Listen and appear to us
            In name of great *Oceanus,*
            By th' earth-shaking *Neptunes* mace,
            And *Tethys* grave majestic pace,
            By hoary *Nereus* wrinkl'd look,
            And the *Carpathian* wizards hook,
            By scaly *Tritons* winding shell,
            And old sooth-saying *Glaucus* spell,
            By *Leucothea's* lovely hands,
            And her son that rules the strands,
            By *Thetis* tinsel-slipperd feet
            And the Songs of *Sirens* sweet,
            By dead *Parthenope's* dear tomb,
            And fair *Ligea's* golden comb,
            Wherwith she sits on diamond rocks
            Sleeking her soft alluring locks,
            By all the *Nymphs* that nightly dance
            Upon thy streams with wily glance,
            Rise, rise, and heave thy rosie head
            From thy coral-paven bed,
            And bridle in thy headlong wave
            Till thou our summons answer have.
                                Listen and save.

Sabrina replies   *By the rushy-fringed bank,*
Where grows the Willow and the Osier dank,
My sliding Chariot stays,
Thick set with Agat, and the azurn sheen
Of Turkis blue, and Emrauld green
That in the channel strays,

Whilst from off the waters fleet
Thus I set my printless feet
Ore the Cowslips Velvet head,
That bends not as I tread,
Gentle swain at thy request,
I am here.

From *Paradise Lost*

218   [1]

Of Mans First Disobedience, and the Fruit
Of that Forbidden Tree, whose mortal tast
Brought Death into the World, and all our woe,
With loss of *Eden*, till one greater Man
Restore us, and regain the blissful Seat,
Sing Heav'nly Muse, that on the secret top
Of *Oreb*, or of *Sinai*, didst inspire
That Shepherd, who first taught the chosen Seed,
In the Beginning how the Heav'ns and Earth
Rose out of *Chaos*: Or if *Sion* Hill
Delight three more, and *Siloa's* Brook that flow'd
Fast by the Oracle of God; I thence
Invoke thy aid to my adventrous Song,
That with no middle flight intends to soar
Above th' *Aonian* Mount, while it pursues
Things unattempted yet in Prose or Rhime.
And chiefly Thou O Spirit, that dost prefer
Before all Temples th' upright heart and pure,
Instruct me, for Thou know'st; Thou from the first
Wast present, and with mighty wings outspread
Dove-like satst brooding on the vast Abyss
And mad'st it pregnant: What in me is dark
Illumine, what is low raise and support;
That to the highth of this great Argument
I may assert Eternal Providence,
And justifie the wayes of God to men.

Say first, for Heav'n hides nothing from thy view
Nor the deep Tract of Hell, say first what cause
Mov'd our Grand Parents in that happy State,
Favour'd of Heav'n so highly, to fall off
From their Creator, and transgress his Will
For one restraint, Lords of the World besides?
Who first seduc'd them to that fowl revolt?
Th' infernal Serpent; he it was, whose guile
Stird up with Envy and Revenge, deceiv'd
The Mother of Mankinde, what time his Pride
Had cast him out from Heav'n, with all his Host
Of Rebel Angels, by whose aid aspiring
To set himself in Glory above his Peers,
He trusted to have equal'd the most High,
If he oppos'd; and with ambitious aim
Against the Throne and Monarchy of God
Rais'd impious War in Heav'n and Battel proud
With vain attempt. Him the Almighty Power
Hurld headlong flaming from th' Ethereal Skie
With hideous ruine and combustion down
To bottomless perdition, there to dwell
In Adamantine Chains and penal Fire,
Who durst defie th' Omnipotent to Arms.
Nine times the Space that measures Day and Night
To mortal men, he with his horrid crew
Lay vanquisht, rowling in the fiery Gulfe
Confounded though immortal: But his doom
Reserv'd him to more wrath; for now the thought
Both of lost happiness and lasting pain
Torments him; round he throws his baleful eyes
That witness'd huge affliction and dismay
Mixt with obdurate pride and stedfast hate:
At once as far as Angels kenn he views
The dismal Situation waste and wilde,
A Dungeon horrible, on all sides round
As one great Furnace flam'd, yet from those flames
No light, but rather darkness visible
Serv'd only to discover sights of woe,
Regions of sorrow, doleful shades, where peace
And rest can never dwell, hope never comes
That comes to all; but torture without end
Still urges, and a fiery Deluge, fed
With ever-burning Sulphur unconsum'd:
Such place Eternal Justice had prepar'd
For those rebellious, here their Prison ordain'd
In utter darkness, and their portion set
As far remov'd from God and light of Heav'n
As from the Center thrice to th' utmost Pole.

O how unlike the place from whence they fell!
There the companions of his fall, o'rewhelm'd
With Floods and Whirlwinds of tempestuous fire,
He soon discerns, and weltring by his side
One next himself in power, and next in crime,
Long after known in *Palestine*, and nam'd
Bëëlzebub. To whom th' Arch-Enemy,
And thence in Heav'n call'd Satan, with bold words
Breaking the horrid silence thus began.
  If thou beest he; But O how fall'n! how chang'd
From him, who in the happy Realms of Light
Cloth'd with transcendent brightness didst outshine
Myriads though bright: If he whom mutual league,
United thoughts and counsels, equal hope,
And hazard in the Glorious Enterprize,
Joynd with me once, now misery hath joynd
In equal ruin: into what Pit thou seest
From what highth fal'n, so much the stronger provd
He with his Thunder: and till then who knew
The force of those dire Arms? yet not for those
Nor what the Potent Victor in his rage
Can else inflict do I repent or change,
Though chang'd in outward lustre; that fixt mind
And high disdain, from sence of injur'd merit,
That with the mightiest rais'd me to contend,
And to the fierce contention brought along
Innumerable force of Spirits arm'd
That durst dislike his reign, and me preferring,
His utmost power with adverse power oppos'd
In dubious Battel on the Plains of Heav'n,
And shook his throne. What though the field be lost?
All is not lost; the unconquerable Will,
And study of revenge, immortal hate,
And courage never to submit or yield:
And what is else not to be overcome?
That Glory never shall his wrath or might
Extort from me. To bow and sue for grace
With suppliant knee, and deifie his power
Who from the terrour of this Arm so late
Doubted his Empire, that were low indeed,
That were an ignominy and shame beneath
This downfall; since by Fate the strength of Gods
And this Empyreal substance cannot fail,
Since through experience of this great event
In Arms not worse, in foresight much advanc't,
We may with more successful hope resolve
To wage by force or guile eternal Warr
Irreconcileable, to our grand Foe,

Who now triumphs, and in th' excess of joy
Sole reigning holds the Tyranny of Heav'n.
  So spake th' Apostate Angel, though in pain,
Vaunting aloud, but rackt with deep despare:
And him thus answer'd soon his bold Compeer.
  O Prince, O Chief of many Throned Powers,
That led th' imbattelld Seraphim to Warr
Under thy conduct, and in dreadful deeds
Fearless, endanger'd Heav'ns perpetual King;
And put to proof his high Supremacy,
Whether upheld by strength, or Chance, or Fate,
Too well I see and rue the dire event,
That with sad overthrow and foul defeat
Hath lost us Heav'n, and all this mighty Host
In horrible destruction laid thus low,
As far as Gods and Heav'nly Essences
Can Perish: for the mind and spirit remains
Invincible, and vigour soon returns,
Though all our Glory extinct, and happy state
Here swallow'd up in endless misery.
But what if he our Conquerour, (whom I now
Of force believe Almighty, since no less
Then such could hav orepow'rd such force as ours)
Have left us this our spirit and strength intire
Strongly to suffer and support our pains,
That we may so suffice his vengeful ire,
Or do him mightier service as his thralls
By right of Warr, what e're his business be
Here in the heart of Hell to work in Fire,
Or do his Errands in the gloomy Deep;
What can it then avail though yet we feel
Strength undiminisht, or eternal being
To undergo eternal punishment?
Whereto with speedy words th' Arch-fiend reply'd.
  Fall'n Cherube, to be weak is miserable
Doing or Suffering: but of this be sure,
To do ought good never will be our task,
But ever to do ill our sole delight,
As being the contrary to his high will
Whom we resist. If then his Providence
Out of our evil seek to bring forth good,
Our labour must be to pervert that end,
And out of good still to find means of evil;
Which oft times may succeed, so as perhaps
Shall grieve him, if I fail not, and disturb
His inmost counsels from their destind aim.
But see the angry Victor hath recall'd
His Ministers of vengeance and pursuit

Back to the Gates of Heav'n: The Sulphurous Hail
Shot after us in storm, oreblown hath laid
The fiery Surge, that from the Precipice
Of Heav'n receiv'd us falling, and the Thunder,
Wing'd with red Lightning and impetuous rage,
Perhaps hath spent his shafts, and ceases now
To bellow through the vast and boundless Deep.
Let us not slip th' occasion, whether scorn,
Or satiate fury yield it from our Foe.
Seest thou yon dreary Plain, forlorn and wilde,
The seat of desolation, voyd of light,
Save what the glimmering of these livid flames
Casts pale and dreadful? Thither let us tend
From off the tossing of these fiery waves,
There rest, if any rest can harbour there,
And reassembling our afflicted Powers,
Consult how we may henceforth most offend
Our Enemy, our own loss how repair,
How overcome this dire Calamity,
What reinforcement we may gain from Hope,
If not what resolution from despare.
    Thus Satan talking to his neerest Mate
With Head up-lift above the wave, and Eyes
That sparkling blaz'd, his other Parts besides
Prone on the Flood, extended long and large
Lay floating many a rood, in bulk as huge
As whom the Fables name of monstrous size,
Titanian, or *Earth-born*, that warr'd on *Jove*,
Briarios or *Typhon*, whom the Den
By ancient *Tarsus* held, or that Sea-beast
Leviathan, which God of all his works
Created hugest that swim th' Ocean stream:
Him haply slumbring on the *Norway* foam
The Pilot of some small night-founder'd Skiff,
Deeming some Island, oft, as Sea-men tell,
With fixed Anchor in his skaly rind
Moors by his side under the Lee, while Night
Invests the Sea, and wished Morn delayes:
So stretcht out huge in length the Arch-fiend lay
Chain'd on the burning Lake, nor ever thence
Had ris'n or heav'd his head, but that the will
And high permission of all-ruling Heaven
Left him at large to his own dark designs,
That with reiterated crimes he might
Heap on himself damnation, while he sought
Evil to others, and enrag'd might see
How all his malice serv'd but to bring forth
Infinite goodness, grace and mercy shewn

On Man by him seduc't, but on himself
Treble confusion, wrath and vengeance pour'd.
Forthwith upright he rears from off the Pool
His mighty Stature; on each hand the flames
Drivn backward slope their pointing spires, & rowld
In billows, leave i' th' midst a horrid Vale.
Then with expanded wings he stears his flight
Aloft, incumbent on the dusky Air
That felt unusual weight, till on dry Land
He lights, if it were Land that ever burn'd
With solid, as the Lake with liquid fire;
And such appear'd in hue, as when the force
Of subterranean wind transports a Hill
Torn from *Pelorus*, or the shatter'd side
Of thundring *Ætna*, whose combustible
And fewel'd entrals thence conceiving Fire,
Sublim'd with Mineral fury, aid the Winds,
And leave a singed bottom all involv'd
With stench and smoak: Such resting found the sole
Of unblest feet. Him followed his next Mate,
Both glorying to have scap't the *Stygian* flood
As Gods, and by their own recover'd strength,
Not by the sufferance of supernal Power.
    Is this the Region, this the Soil, the Clime,
Said then the lost Arch Angel, this the seat
That we must change for Heav'n, this mournful gloom
For that celestial light? Be it so, since hee
Who now is Sovran can dispose and bid
What shall be right: fardest from him is best
Whom reason hath equald, force hath made supream
Above his equals. Farewel happy Fields
Where Joy for ever dwells: Hail horrours, hail
Infernal world, and thou profoundest Hell
Receive thy new Possessor: One who brings
A mind not to be chang'd by Place or Time.
The mind is its own place, and in it self
Can make a Heav'n of Hell, a Hell of Heav'n.
What matter where, if I be still the same,
And what I should be, all but less then hee
Whom Thunder hath made greater? Here at least
We shall be free; th' Almighty hath not built
Here for his envy, will not drive us hence:
Here we may reign secure, and in my choyce
To reign is worth ambition though in Hell:
Better to reign in Hell, then serve in Heav'n.
But wherefore let we then our faithful friends,
Th' associates and copartners of our loss
Lye thus astonisht on th' oblivious Pool,

And call them not to share with us their part
In this unhappy Mansion, or once more
With rallied Arms to try what may be yet
Regaind in Heav'n, or what more lost in Hell?

219   [2]

Next came one
Who mourn'd in earnest, when the Captive Ark
Maim'd his brute Image, head and hands lopt off
In his own Temple, on the grunsel edge,
Where he fell flat, and sham'd his Worshipers:
Dagon his Name, Sea Monster, upward Man
And downward Fish: yet had his Temple high
Rear'd in *Azotus*, dreaded through the Coast
Of *Palestine*, in *Gath* and *Ascalon*,
And *Accaron* and *Gaza*'s frontier bounds.
Him follow'd *Rimmon*, whose delightful Seat
Was fair *Damascus*, on the fertil Banks
Of *Abbana* and *Pharphar*, lucid streams.
He also against the house of God was bold;
A Leper once he lost and gain'd a King,
Ahaz his sottish Conquerour, whom he drew
Gods Altar to disparage and displace
For one of *Syrian* mode, whereon to burn
His odious offrings, and adore the Gods
Whom he had vanquisht. After these appear'd
A crew who under Names of old Renown,
Osiris, Isis, Orus and their Train
With monstrous shapes and sorceries abus'd
Fanatic *Egypt* and her Priests, to seek
Thir wandring Gods disguis'd in brutish forms
Rather then human. Nor did *Israel* scape
Th' infection when their borrow'd Gold compos'd
The Calf in *Oreb*: and the Rebel King
Doubl'd that sin in *Bethel* and in *Dan*,
Lik'ning his Maker to the Grazed Ox,
Jehovah, who in one Night when he pass'd
From *Egypt* marching, equal'd with one stroke
Both her first born and all her bleating Gods.

220   [3]

 Mean while the Adversary of God and Man,
Satan with thoughts inflam'd of highest design,
Puts on swift wings, and toward the Gates of Hell
Explores his solitary flight; som times
He scours the right hand coast, som times the left,
Now shaves with level wing the Deep, then soares
Up to the fiery concave touring high.
As when farr off at Sea a Fleet descri'd
Hangs in the Clouds, by *Æquinoctial* Winds
Close sailing from *Bengala*, or the Iles
Of *Ternate* and *Tidore*, whence Merchants bring
Thir spicie Drugs: they on the trading Flood
Through the wide *Ethiopian* to the Cape
Ply stemming nightly toward the Pole. So seem'd
Farr off the flying Fiend: at last appeer
Hell bounds high reaching to the horrid Roof,
And thrice threefold the Gates; three folds were Brass,
Three Iron, three of Adamantine Rock,
Impenitrable, impal'd with circling fire,
Yet unconsum'd. Before the Gates there sat
On either side a formidable shape;
The one seem'd Woman to the waste, and fair,
But ended foul in many a scaly fould
Voluminous and vast, a Serpent arm'd
With mortal sting: about her middle round
A cry of Hell Hounds never ceasing bark'd
With wide *Cerberean* mouths full loud, and rung
A hideous Peal: yet, when they list, would creep,
If aught disturb'd thir noyse, into her woomb,
And kennel there, yet there still bark'd and howl'd
Within unseen. Farr less abhorrd then these
Vex'd *Scylla* bathing in the Sea that parts
Calabria from the hoarce *Trinacrian* shore:
Nor uglier follow the Night-Hag, when call'd
In secret, riding through the Air she comes
Lur'd with the smell of infant blood, to dance
With *Lapland* Witches, while the labouring Moon
Eclipses at thir charms. The other shape,
If shape it might be call'd that shape had none
Distinguishable in member, joynt, or limb,
Or substance might be call'd that shadow seem'd,
For each seem'd either; black it stood as Night,
Fierce as ten Furies, terrible as Hell,
And shook a dreadful Dart; what seem'd his head
The likeness of a Kingly Crown had on.

Satan was now at hand, and from his seat
The Monster moving onward came as fast,
With horrid strides, Hell trembled as he strode.
Th' undaunted Fiend what this might be admir'd,
Admir'd, not fear'd; God and his Son except,
Created thing naught vallu'd he nor shun'd;
And with disdainful look thus first began.
      Whence and what art thou, execrable shape,
That dar'st, though grim and terrible, advance
Thy miscreated Front athwart my way
To yonder Gates? through them I mean to pass,
That be assur'd, without leave askt of thee:
Retire, or taste thy folly, and learn by proof,
Hell-born, not to contend with Spirits of Heav'n.
      To whom the Goblin full of wrauth reply'd,
Art thou that Traitor Angel, art thou hee,
Who first broke peace in Heav'n, and Faith, till then
Unbrok'n, and in proud rebellious Arms
Drew after him the third part of Heav'ns Sons
Conjur'd against the highest, for which both Thou
And they outcast from God, are here condemn'd
To waste Eternal daies in woe and pain?
And reck'n'st thou thy self with Spirits of Heav'n,
Hell-doomd, and breath'st defiance here and scorn,
Where I reign King, and to enrage thee more,
Thy King and Lord? Back to thy punishment,
False fugitive, and to thy speed add wings,
Least with a whip of Scorpions I pursue
Thy lingring, or with one stroke of this Dart
Strange horror seise thee, and pangs unfelt before.
      So spake the grieslie terrour, and in shape,
So speaking and so threatning, grew ten fold
More dreadful and deform: on th' other side
Incenc't with indignation *Satan* stood
Unterrifi'd, and like a Comet burn'd,
That fires the length of *Ophiucus* huge
In th' Artick Sky, and from his horrid hair
Shakes Pestilence and Warr. Each at the Head
Level'd his deadly aime; thir fatall hands
No second stroke intend, and such a frown
Each cast at th' other, as when two black Clouds
With Heav'ns Artillery fraught, come rattling on
Over the *Caspian*, then stand front to front
Hov'ring a space, till Winds the signal blow
To joyn thir dark Encounter in mid air:
So frownd the mighty Combatants, that Hell
Grew darker at thir frown, so matcht they stood;

For never but once more was either like
To meet so great a foe: and now great deeds
Had been achiev'd, whereof all Hell had rung,
Had not the Snakie Sorceress that sat
Fast by Hell Gate, and kept the fatal Key,
Ris'n, and with hideous outcry rush'd between.
   O Father, what intends thy hand, she cry'd
Against thy only Son? What fury O Son,
Possesses thee to bend that mortal Dart
Against thy Fathers head? and know'st for whom;
For him who sits above and laughs the while
At thee ordain'd his drudge, to execute
What e're his wrath, which he calls Justice, bids,
His wrath which one day will destroy ye both.

221   [4]

   Thus saying, from her side the fatal Key,
Sad instrument of all our woe, she took;
And towards the Gate rouling her bestial train,
Forthwith the huge Porcullis high up drew,
Which but her self not all the *Stygian* powers
Could once have mov'd; then in the key-hole turns
Th' intricate wards, and every Bolt and Bar
Of massie Iron or sollid Rock with ease
Unfast'ns: on a sudden op'n flie
With impetuous recoile and jarring sound
Th' infernal dores, and on thir hinges grate
Harsh Thunder, that the lowest bottom shook
Of *Erebus*. She op'nd, but to shut
Excel'd her power; the Gates wide op'n stood,
That with extended wings a Bannerd Host
Under spread Ensigns marching might pass through
With Horse and Chariots rankt in loose array;
So wide they stood, and like a Furnace mouth
Cast forth redounding smoak and ruddy flame.
Before thir eyes in sudden view appear
The secrets of the hoarie deep, a dark
Illimitable Ocean without bound,
Without dimension, where length, breadth, and highth
And time and place are lost; where eldest Night
And *Chaos*, Ancestors of Nature, hold
Eternal *Anarchie*, amidst the noise
Of endless warrs, and by confusion stand.

For hot, cold, moist, and dry, four Champions fierce
Strive here for Maistrie, and to Battel bring
Thir embryon Atoms; they around the flag
Of each his faction, in thir several Clanns,
Light-arm'd or heavy, sharp, smooth, swift or slow,
Swarm populous, unnumber'd as the Sands
Of *Barca* or *Cyrene*'s torrid soil,
Levied to side with warring Winds, and poise
Thir lighter wings. To whom these most adhere,
Hee rules a moment; *Chaos* Umpire sits,
And by decision more imbroiles the fray
By which he Reigns: next him high Arbiter
Chance governs all. Into this wilde Abyss,
The Womb of nature and perhaps her Grave,
Of neither Sea, nor Shore, nor Air, nor Fire,
But all these in thir pregnant causes mixt
Confus'dly, and which thus must ever fight,
Unless th' Almighty Maker them ordain
His dark materials to create more Worlds,
Into this wilde Abyss the warie fiend
Stood on the brink of Hell and look'd a while,
Pondering his Voyage; for no narrow frith
He had to cross. Nor was his eare less peal'd
With noises loud and ruinous (to compare
Great things with small) then when *Bellona* storms,
With all her battering Engines bent to rase
Som Capital City, or less then if this frame
Of Heav'n were falling, and these Elements
In mutinie had from her Axle torn
The stedfast Earth. At last his Sail-broad Vannes
He spreads for flight, and in the surging smoak
Uplifted spurns the ground, thence many a League
As in a cloudy Chair ascending rides
Audacious, but that seat soon failing, meets
A vast vacuitie: all unawares
Fluttring his pennons vain plumb down he drops
Ten thousand fadom deep, and to this hour
Down had been falling, had not by ill chance
The strong rebuff of som tumultuous cloud
Instinct with Fire and Nitre hurried him
As many miles aloft: that furie stay'd,
Quencht in a Boggie *Syrtis*, neither Sea,
Nor good dry Land: nigh founderd on he fares,
Treading the crude consistence, half on foot,
Half flying; behoves him now both Oare and Saile.
As when a Gryfon through the Wilderness
With winged course ore Hill or moarie Dale,

Pursues the *Arimaspian*, who by stelth
Had from his wakeful custody purloind
The guarded Gold: So eagerly the fiend
Ore bog or steep, through strait, rough, dense, or rare,
With head, hands, wings, or feet pursues his way,
And swims or sinks, or wades, or creeps, or flyes:
At length a universal hubbub wilde
Of stunning sounds and voices all confus'd
Born through the hollow dark assaults his eare
With loudest vehemence: thither he plyes,
Undaunted to meet there what ever power
Or Spirit of the nethermost Abyss
Might in that noise reside, of whom to ask
Which way the neerest coast of darkness lyes
Bordering on light; when strait behold the Throne
Of *Chaos*, and his dark Pavilion spread
Wide on the wasteful Deep; with him Enthron'd
Sat Sable-vested Night, eldest of things,
The consort of his Reign; and by them stood
Orcus and *Ades*, and the dreaded name
Of *Demogorgon*; Rumor next and Chance,
And Tumult and Confusion all imbroild,
And Discord with a thousand various mouths.
  T' whom *Satan* turning boldly, thus. Ye Powers
And Spirits of this nethermost Abyss,
Chaos and *ancient Night*, I come no Spie,
With purpose to explore or to disturb
The secrets of your Realm, but by constraint
Wandring this darksome desart, as my way
Lies through your spacious Empire up to light,
Alone, and without guide, half lost, I seek
What readiest path leads where your gloomie bounds
Confine with Heav'n; or if som other place
From your Dominion won, th' Ethereal King
Possesses lately, thither to arrive
I travel this profound, direct my course;
Directed, no mean recompence it brings
To your behoof, if I that Region lost,
All usurpation thence expell'd, reduce
To her original darkness and your sway
(Which is my present journey) and once more
Erect the Standerd there of *ancient Night*;
Yours be th' advantage all, mine the revenge.
  Thus *Satan*; and him thus the Anarch old
With faultring speech and visage incompos'd
Answer'd. I know thee, stranger, who thou art,
That mighty leading Angel, who of late
Made head against Heav'ns King, though overthrown.

I saw and heard, for such a numerous host
Fled not in silence through the frighted deep
With ruin upon ruin, rout on rout,
Confusion worse confounded; and Heav'n Gates
Pourd out by millions her victorious Bands
Pursuing. I upon my Frontieres here
Keep residence; if all I can will serve,
That little which is left so to defend
Encroacht on still through our intestine broiles
Weakning the Scepter of old Night: first Hell
Your dungeon stretching far and wide beneath;
Now lately Heaven and Earth, another World
Hung ore my Realm, link'd in a golden Chain
To that side Heav'n from whence your Legions fell:
If that way be your walk, you have not farr;
So much the neerer danger; goe and speed;
Havock and spoil and ruin are my gain.
    He ceas'd; and *Satan* staid not to reply,
But glad that now his Sea should find a shore,
With fresh alacritie and force renew'd
Springs upward like a Pyramid of fire
Into the wilde expanse, and through the shock
Of fighting Elements, on all sides round
Environ'd wins his way; harder beset
And more endanger'd, then when *Argo* pass'd
Through *Bosporus* betwixt the justling Rocks:
Or when *Ulysses* on the Larbord shunnd
Charybdis, and by th' other whirlpool steard.
So he with difficulty and labour hard
Mov'd on, with difficulty and labour hee;
But hee once past, soon after when man fell,
Strange alteration! Sin and Death amain
Following his track, such was the will of Heav'n,
Pav'd after him a broad and beat'n way
Over the dark Abyss, whose boiling Gulf
Tamely endur'd a Bridge of wondrous length
From Hell continu'd reaching th' utmost Orbe
Of this frail World; by which the Spirits perverse
With easie intercourse pass to and fro
To tempt or punish mortals, except whom
God and good Angels guard by special grace.
But now at last the sacred influence
Of light appears, and from the walls of Heav'n
Shoots farr into the bosom of dim Night
A glimmering dawn; here Nature first begins
Her fardest verge, and *Chaos* to retire
As from her utmost works a brok'n foe
With tumult less and with less hostile din,

That *Satan* with less toil, and now with ease
Wafts on the calmer wave by dubious light
And like a weather-beaten Vessel holds
Gladly the Port, though Shrouds and Tackle torn;
Or in the emptier waste, resembling Air,
Weighs his spread wings, at leasure to behold
Farr off th' Empyreal Heav'n, extended wide
In circuit, undetermind square or round,
With Opal Towrs and Battlements adorn'd
Of living Saphire, once his native Seat;
And fast by hanging in a golden Chain
This pendant world, in bigness as a Starr
Of smallest Magnitude close by the Moon.
Thither full fraught with mischievous revenge,
Accurst, and in a cursed hour he hies.

222   [5]

   Thus they in Heav'n, above the starry Sphear,
Thir happie hours in joy and hymning spent.
Mean while upon the firm opacous Globe
Of this round World, whose first convex divides
The luminous inferior Orbs, enclos'd
From *Chaos* and th' inroad of Darkness old,
Satan alighted walks: a Globe farr off
It seem'd, now seems a boundless Continent
Dark, waste, and wild, under the frown of Night
Starless expos'd, and ever-threatning storms
Of *Chaos* blustring round, inclement skie;
Save on that side which from the wall of Heav'n
Though distant farr som small reflection gaines
Of glimmering air less vext with tempest loud:
Here walk'd the Fiend at large in spacious field.
As when a Vultur on *Imaus* bred,
Whose snowie ridge the roving *Tartar* bounds,
Dislodging from a Region scarce of prey
To gorge the flesh of Lambs or yeanling Kids
On Hills where Flocks are fed, flies toward the Springs
Of *Ganges* or *Hydaspes*, *Indian* streams;
But in his way lights on the barren plaines
Of *Sericana*, where *Chineses* drive
With Sails and Wind thir canie Waggons light:
So on this windie Sea of Land, the Fiend
Walk'd up and down alone bent on his prey,
Alone, for other Creature in this place
Living or liveless to be found was none,

None yet, but store hereafter from the earth
Up hither like Aereal vapours flew
Of all things transitorie and vain, when Sin
With vanity had filld the works of men:
Both all things vain, and all who in vain things
Built thir fond hopes of Glorie or lasting fame,
Or happiness in this or th' other life;
All who have thir reward on Earth, the fruits
Of painful Superstition and blind Zeal,
Naught seeking but the praise of men, here find
Fit retribution, emptie as thir deeds;
All th' unaccomplisht works of Natures hand,
Abortive, monstrous, or unkindly mixt,
Dissolvd on earth, fleet hither, and in vain,
Till final dissolution, wander here,   .
Not in the neighbouring Moon, as some have dreamd;
Those argent Fields more likely habitants,
Translated Saints, or middle Spirits hold
Betwixt th' Angelical and Human kinde:
Hither of ill-joynd Sons and Daughters born
First from the ancient World those Giants came
With many a vain exploit, though then renowned:
The builders next of *Babel* on the Plain
Of *Sennaar*, and still with vain designe
New *Babels*, had they wherewithall, would build:
Others came single; hee who to be deemd
A God, leap'd fondly into *Ætna* flames
Empedocles, and hee who to enjoy
Plato's Elysium, leap'd into the Sea,
Cleombrotus, and many more too long,
Embryo's, and Idiots, Eremits and Friers
White, Black and Grey, with all thir trumperie.
Here Pilgrims roam, that stray'd so farr to seek
In *Golgotha* him dead, who lives in Heav'n;
And they who to be sure of Paradise
Dying put on the weeds of *Dominic*,
Or in *Franciscan* think to pass disguis'd;
They pass the Planets seven, and pass the fixt
And that Crystalline Sphear whose ballance weighs
The Trepidation talkt, and that first mov'd;
And now Saint *Peter* at Heav'ns Wicket seems
To wait them with his Keys, and now at foot
Of Heav'ns ascent they lift thir Feet, when loe
A violent cross wind from either Coast
Blows them transverse ten thousand Leagues awry
Into the devious Air; then might ye see
Cowles, Hoods and Habits with thir wearers tost
And flutterd into Raggs, then Reliques, Beads,
Indulgences, Dispenses, Pardons, Bulls,

The sport of Winds: all these upwhirld aloft
Fly o're the backside of the World farr off
Into a *Limbo* large and broad, since calld
The Paradise of Fools, to few unknown
Long after, now unpeopl'd, and untrod;
All this dark Globe the Fiend found as he pass'd,
And long he wanderd, till at last a gleame
Of dawning light turnd thither-ward in haste
His travell'd steps; farr distant hee descries
Ascending by degrees magnificent
Up to the wall of Heaven a Structure high,
At top whereof, but farr more rich appeerd
The work as of a Kingly Palace Gate
With Frontispice of Diamond and Gold
Imbellisht, thick with sparkling orient Gemmes
The Portal shon, inimitable on Earth
By Model, or by shading Pencil drawn.
The Stairs were such as whereon *Jacob* saw
Angels ascending and descending, bands
Of Guardians bright, when he from *Esau* fled
To *Padan-Aram* in the field of *Luz*,
Dreaming by night under the open Skie,
And waking cri'd, This is the Gate of Heav'n.

223   [6]

Thus talking hand in hand alone they pass'd
On to thir blissful Bower; it was a place
Chos'n by the sovran Planter, when he fram'd
All things to mans delightful use; the roofe
Of thickest covert was inwoven shade
Laurel and Mirtle, and what higher grew
Of firm and fragrant leaf; on either side
Acanthus, and each odorous bushie shrub
Fenc'd up the verdant wall; each beauteous flour,
Iris all hues, Roses, and Gessamin
Rear'd high thir flourisht heads between, and wrought
Mosaic; underfoot the Violet,
Crocus, and Hyacinth with rich inlay
Broiderd the ground, more colour'd then with stone
Of costliest Emblem: other Creature here
Beast, Bird, Insect, or Worm durst enter none;
Such was thir awe of man. In shadier Bower
More sacred and sequesterd, though but feignd,
Pan or *Silvanus* never slept, nor Nymph,

Nor *Faunus* haunted. Here in close recess
With Flowers, Garlands, and sweet-smelling Herbs
Espoused *Eve* deckt first her Nuptial Bed,
And heav'nly Quires the Hymenæan sung,
What day the genial Angel to our Sire
Brought her in naked beauty more adorn'd,
More lovely then *Pandora*, whom the Gods
Endowd with all thir gifts, and O too like
In sad event, when to the unwiser Son
Of *Japhet* brought by *Hermes*, she ensnar'd
Mankind with her faire looks, to be aveng'd
On him who had stole *Joves* authentic fire.
   Thus at thir shadie Lodge arriv'd, both stood,
Both turnd, and under op'n Skie ador'd
The God that made both Skie, Air, Earth & Heav'n
Which they beheld, the Moons resplendent Globe
And starrie Pole: Thou also mad'st the Night,
Maker Omnipotent, and thou the Day,
Which we in our appointed work imployd
Have finisht happie in our mutual help
And mutual love, the Crown of all our bliss
Ordain'd by thee, and this delicious place
For us too large, where thy abundance wants
Partakers, and uncropt falls to the ground.
But thou hast promis'd from us two a Race
To fill the Earth, who shall with us extoll
Thy goodness infinite, both when we wake,
And when we seek, as now, thy gift of sleep.
   This said unanimous, and other Rites
Observing none, but adoration pure
Which God likes best, into thir inmost bower
Handed they went; and eas'd the putting off
These troublesom disguises which wee wear,
Strait side by side were laid, nor turnd I weene
Adam from his fair Spouse, nor *Eve* the Rites
Mysterious of connubial Love refus'd:
Whatever Hypocrites austerely talk
Of puritie and place and innocence,
Defaming as impure what God declares
Pure, and commands to som, leaves free to all.
Our Maker bids increase, who bids abstain
But our Destroyer, foe to God and Man?
Haile wedded Love, mysterious Law, true sourse
Of human ofspring, sole proprietie,
In Paradise of all things common else.
By thee adulterous lust was driv'n from men
Among the bestial herds to raunge, by thee
Founded in Reason, Loyal, Just, and Pure,

Relations dear, and all the Charities
Of Father, Son, and Brother first were known.
Farr be it, that I should write thee sin or blame,
Or think thee unbefitting holiest place,
Perpetual Fountain of Domestic sweets,
Whose Bed is undefil'd and chast pronounc't,
Present, or past, as Saints and Patriarchs us'd.
Here Love his golden shafts imploies, here lights
His constant Lamp, and waves his purple wings,
Reigns here and revels; not in the bought smile
Of Harlots, loveless, joyless, unindeard,
Casual fruition, nor in Court Amours
Mixt Dance, or wanton Mask, or Midnight Bal,
Or Serenate, which the starv'd Lover sings
To his proud fair, best quitted with disdain.
These lulld by Nightingales imbraceing slept,
And on thir naked limbs the flourie roof
Showrd Roses, which the Morn repair'd. Sleep on,
Blest pair; and O yet happiest if ye seek
No happier state, and know to know no more.

224   [7]

 Descend from Heav'n *Urania*, by that name
If rightly thou art call'd, whose Voice divine
Following, above th' *Olympian* Hill I soare,
Above the flight of *Pegasean* wing.
The meaning, not the Name I call: for thou
Nor of the Muses nine, nor on the top
Of old *Olympus* dwell'st, but Heav'nlie borne,
Before the Hills appeerd, or Fountain flow'd,
Thou with Eternal wisdom didst converse,
Wisdom thy Sister, and with her didst play
In presence of th' Almightie Father, pleas'd
With thy Celestial Song. Up led by thee
Into the Heav'n of Heav'ns I have presum'd,
An Earthlie Guest, and drawn Empyreal Aire,
Thy tempring; with like safetie guided down
Return me to my Native Element:
Least from this flying Steed unrein'd, (as once
Bellerophon, though from a lower Clime)
Dismounted, on th' *Aleian* Field I fall
Erroneous, there to wander and forlorne.
Half yet remaines unsung, but narrower bound
Within the visible Diurnal Spheare;
Standing on Earth, not rapt above the Pole,

More safe I Sing with mortal voice, unchang'd
To hoarce or mute, though fall'n on evil dayes,
On evil dayes though fall'n, and evil tongues;
In darkness, and with dangers compast round,
And solitude; yet not alone, while thou
Visit'st my slumbers Nightly, or when Morn
Purples the East: still govern thou my Song,
Urania, and fit audience find, though few.
But drive farr off the barbarous dissonance
Of *Bacchus* and his Revellers, the Race
Of that wilde Rout that tore the *Thracian* Bard
In *Rhodope*, where Woods and Rocks had Eares
To rapture, till the savage clamor dround
Both Harp and Voice; nor could the Muse defend
Her Son. So fail not thou, who thee implores:
For thou art Heav'nlie, shee an empty dreame.

225   From *Paradise Regain'd*

    It was the hour of night, when thus the Son
Commun'd in silent walk, then laid him down
Under the hospitable covert nigh
Of Trees thick interwoven; there he slept,
And dream'd, as appetite is wont to dream,
Of meats and drinks, Natures refreshment sweet;
Him thought, he by the Brook of *Cherith* stood
And saw the Ravens with their horny beaks
Food to *Elijah* bringing Even and Morn,
Though ravenous, taught to abstain from what they brought:
He saw the Prophet also how he fled
Into the Desert, and how there he slept
Under a Juniper; then how awakt,
He found his Supper on the coals prepar'd,
And by the Angel was bid rise and eat,
And eat the second time after repose,
The strength whereof suffic'd him forty days,
Sometimes that with *Elijah* he partook,
Or as a guest with *Daniel* at his pulse.
Thus wore out night, and now the Herald Lark
Left his ground-nest, high towring to descry
The morns approach, and greet her with his Song:
As lightly from his grassy Couch up rose
Our Saviour, and found all was but a dream,
Fasting he went to sleep, and fasting wak'd.
Up to a hill anon his steps he rear'd,
From whose high top to ken the prospect round,
If Cottage were in view, Sheep-cote or Herd;

But Cottage, Herd or Sheep-cote none he saw,
Only in a bottom saw a pleasant Grove,
With chaunt of tuneful Birds resounding loud;
Thither he bent his way, determin'd there
To rest at noon, and entr'd soon the shade
High rooft and walks beneath, and alleys brown
That open'd in the midst a woody Scene,
Natures own work it seem'd (Nature taught Art)
And to a Superstitious eye the haunt
Of Wood-Gods and Wood-Nymphs; he view'd it round,
When suddenly a man before him stood,
Not rustic as before, but seemlier clad,
As one in City, or Court, or Palace bred,
And with fair speech these words to him address'd.
    With granted leave officious I return,
But much more wonder that the Son of God
In this wild solitude so long should bide
Of all things destitute, and well I know,
Not without hunger. Others of some note,
As story tells, have trod this Wilderness;
The Fugitive Bond-woman with her Son
Out cast *Nebaioth*, yet found he relief
By a providing Angel; all the race
Of *Israel* here had famish'd, had not God
Rain'd from Heaven Manna, and that Prophet bold
Native of *Thebez* wandring here was fed
Twice by a voice inviting him to eat.
Of thee these forty days none hath regard,
Forty and more deserted here indeed.
    To whom thus Jesus; what conclud'st thou hence?
They all had need, I as thou seest have none.
    How hast thou hunger then? Satan reply'd,
Tell me if Food were now before thee set,
Would'st thou not eat? Thereafter as I like
The giver, answer'd Jesus. Why should that
Cause thy refusal, said the subtle Fiend,
Hast thou not right to all Created things,
Owe not all Creatures by just right to thee
Duty and Service, nor to stay till bid,
But tender all their power? nor mention I
Meats by the Law unclean, or offer'd first
To Idols, those young *Daniel* could refuse;
Nor proffer'd by an Enemy, though who
Would scruple that, with want opprest? behold
Nature asham'd, or better to express,
Troubl'd that thou should'st hunger, hath purvey'd
From all the Elements her choicest store
To treat thee as beseems, and as her Lord
With honour, only deign to sit and eat.

He spake no dream, for as his words had end,
Our Saviour lifting up his eyes beheld
In ample space under the broadest shade
A Table richly spred, in regal mode,
With dishes pil'd, and meats of noblest sort
And savour, Beasts of chase, or Fowl of game,
In pastry built, or from the spit, or boyl'd,
Gris-amber-steam'd; all Fish from Sea or Shore,
Freshet, or purling Brook, of shell or fin,
And exquisitest name, for which was drain'd
Pontus and *Lucrine* Bay, and *Afric* Coast.
Alas how simple, to these Cates compar'd,
Was that crude Apple that diverted *Eve*!
And at a stately side-board by the wine
That fragrant smell diffus'd, in order stood
Tall stripling youths rich clad, of fairer hew
Then *Ganymed* or *Hylas*, distant more
Under the Trees now trip'd, now solemn stood
Nymphs of *Diana*'s train, and *Naiades*
With fruits and flowers from *Amalthea*'s horn,
And Ladies of th' *Hesperides*, that seem'd
Fairer then feign'd of old, or fabl'd since
Of Fairy Damsels met in Forest wide
By Knights of *Logres*, or of *Lyones*,
Lancelot or *Pelleas*, or *Pellenore*,
And all the while Harmonious Airs were heard
Of chiming strings, or charming pipes and winds.
Of gentlest gale *Arabian* odors fann'd
From their soft wings, and *Flora*'s earliest smells.
Such was the Splendour, and the Tempter now
His invitation earnestly renew'd.
　　What doubts the Son of God to sit and eat?
These are not Fruits forbidden, no interdict
Defends the touching of these viands pure,
Thir taste no knowledge works, at least of evil,
But life preserves, destroys life's enemy,
Hunger, with sweet restorative delight.
All these are Spirits of Air, and Woods, and Springs,
Thy gentle Ministers, who come to pay
Thee homage, and acknowledge thee thir Lord:
What doubt'st thou Son of God? sit down and eat.
　　To whom thus Jesus temperately reply'd:
Said'st thou not that to all things I had right?
And who withholds my pow'r that right to use?
Shall I receive by gift what of my own,
When and where likes me best, I can command?
I can at will, doubt not, assoon as thou,
Command a Table in this Wilderness,

And call swift flights of Angels ministrant
Array'd in Glory on my cup to attend:
Why shouldst thou then obtrude this diligence,
In vain, where no acceptance it can find,
And with my hunger what hast thou to do?

From *Samson Agonistes*

226   [1]

Chorus	But see here comes thy reverend Sire
	With careful step, Locks white as doune,
	Old *Manoah*: advise
	Forthwith how thou oughtst to receive him.
Samson	Ay me, another inward grief awak't,
	With mention of that name renews th' assault.
Manoah	Brethren and men of *Dan*, for such ye seem,
	Though in this uncouth place; if old respect,
	As I suppose, towards your once gloried friend,
	My Son now Captive, hither hath inform'd
	Your younger feet, while mine cast back with age
	Came lagging after; say if he be here.
Chorus	As signal now in low dejected state,
	As earst in highest, behold him where he lies.
Manoah	O miserable change! is this the man,
	That invincible *Samson*, far renown'd,
	The dread of *Israel*'s foes, who with a strength
	Equivalent to Angels walk'd thir streets,
	None offering fight; who single combatant
	Duell'd thir Armies rank't in proud array,
	Himself an Army, now unequal match
	To save himself against a coward arm'd
	At one spears length. O ever failing trust
	In mortal strength! and oh what not in man
	Deceivable and vain! Nay what thing good
	Pray'd for, but often proves our woe, our bane?
	I pray'd for Children, and thought barrenness
	In wedlock a reproach; I gain'd a Son,
	And such a Son as all Men hail'd me happy;
	Who would be now a Father in my stead?
	O wherefore did God grant me my request,
	And as a blessing with such pomp adorn'd?
	Why are his gifts desirable, to tempt
	Our earnest Prayers, then giv'n with solemn hand
	As Graces, draw a Scorpions tail behind?

For this did the Angel twice descend? for this
Ordain'd thy nurture holy, as of a Plant;
Select, and Sacred, Glorious for a while,
The miracle of men: then in an hour
Ensnar'd, assaulted, overcome, led bound,
Thy Foes derision, Captive, Poor, and Blind
Into a Dungeon thrust, to work with Slaves?

227   [2]

Manoah   Wilt thou then serve the *Philistines* with that gift
Which was expresly giv'n thee to annoy them?
Better at home lie bed-rid, not only idle,
Inglorious, unimploy'd, with age out-worn.
But God who caus'd a fountain at thy prayer
From the dry ground to spring, thy thirst to allay
After the brunt of battel, can as easie
Cause light again within thy eies to spring,
Wherewith to serve him better then thou hast;
And I perswade me so; why else this strength
Miraculous yet remaining in those locks?
His might continues in thee not for naught,
Nor shall his wondrous gifts be frustrate thus.

Samson   All otherwise to me my thoughts portend,
That these dark orbs no more shall treat with light,
Nor th' other light of life continue long,
But yield to double darkness nigh at hand:
So much I feel my genial spirits droop,
My hopes all flat, nature within me seems
In all her functions weary of herself;
My race of glory run, and race of shame,
And I shall shortly be with them that rest.

228   [3]

Dalilah   Let me obtain forgiveness of thee, *Samson*,
Afford me place to shew what recompence
Towards thee I intend for what I have misdone,
Misguided; only what remains past cure
Bear not too sensibly, nor still insist
To afflict thy self in vain: though sight be lost,
Life yet hath many solaces, enjoy'd
Where other senses want not their delights
At home in leisure and domestic ease,

Exempt from many a care and chance to which
Eye-sight exposes daily men abroad.
I to the Lords will intercede, not doubting
Thir favourable ear, that I may fetch thee
From forth this loathsom prison-house, to abide
With me, where my redoubl'd love and care
With nursing diligence, to me glad office,
May ever tend about thee to old age
With all things grateful chear'd, and so suppli'd,
That what by me thou hast lost thou least shalt miss.

Samson   No, no, of my condition take no care;
It fits not; thou and I long since are twain;
Nor think me so unwary or accurst
To bring my feet again into the snare
Where once I have been caught; I know thy trains
Though dearly to my cost, thy ginns, and toyls;
Thy fair enchanted cup, and warbling charms
No more on me have power, their force is null'd,
So much of Adders wisdom I have learn't
To fence my ear against thy sorceries.
If in my flower of youth and strength, when all men
Lov'd, honour'd, fear'd me, thou alone could hate me
Thy Husband, slight me, sell me, and forgo me;
How wouldst thou use me now, blind, and thereby
Deceiveable, in most things as a child
Helpless, thence easily contemn'd, and scorn'd,
And last neglected? How wouldst thou insult
When I must live uxorious to thy will
In perfet thraldom, how again betray me,
Bearing my words and doings to the Lords
To gloss upon, and censuring, frown or smile?
This Gaol I count the house of Liberty
To thine whose doors my feet shall never enter.

Dalilah   Let me approach at least, and touch thy hand.
Samson   Not for thy life, lest fierce remembrance wake
My sudden rage to tear thee joint by joint.
At distance I forgive thee, go with that;
Bewail thy falshood, and the pious works
It hath brought forth to make thee memorable
Among illustrious women, faithful wives:
Cherish thy hast'n'd widowhood with the gold
Of Matrimonial treason: so farewel.

Dalilah   I see thou art implacable, more deaf
To prayers, then winds and seas, yet winds to seas
Are reconcil'd at length, and Sea to Shore:
Thy anger, unappeasable, still rages,
Eternal tempest never to be calm'd.
Why do I humble thus my self, and suing
For peace, reap nothing but repulse and hate?

Bid go with evil omen and the brand
Of infamy upon my name denounc't?
To mix with thy concernments I desist
Henceforth, nor too much disapprove my own.
Fame if not double-fac't is double-mouth'd,
And with contrary blast proclaims most deeds,
On both his wings, one black, th' other white,
Bears greatest names in his wild aerie flight.
My name perhaps among the Circumcis'd
In *Dan*, in *Judah*, and the bordering Tribes,
To all posterity may stand defam'd,
With malediction mention'd, and the blot
Of falshood most unconjugal traduc't.
But in my countrey where I most desire,
In *Ecron*, *Gaza*, *Asdod*, and in *Gath*
I shall be nam'd among the famousest
Of Women, sung at solemn festivals,
Living and dead recorded, who to save
Her countrey from a fierce destroyer, chose
Above the faith of wedlock-bands, my tomb
With odours visited and annual flowers.
Not less renown'd then in Mount *Ephraim*,
Jael, who with inhospitable guile
Smote *Sisera* sleeping through the Temples nail'd.
Nor shall I count it hainous to enjoy
The public marks of honour and reward
Conferr'd upon me, for the piety
Which to my countrey I was judg'd to have shewn.
At this who ever envies or repines
I leave him to his lot, and like my own.

229   [4]

Messenger   The Feast and noon grew high, and Sacrifice
Had fill'd thir hearts with mirth, high chear, & wine,
When to thir sports they turn'd. Immediately
Was *Samson* as a public servant brought,
In thir state Livery clad; before him Pipes
And Timbrels, on each side went armed guards,
Both horse and foot before him and behind
Archers, and Slingers, Cataphracts and Spears.
At sight of him the people with a shout
Rifted the Air clamouring thir god with praise,
Who had made thir dreadful enemy thir thrall.
He patient but undaunted where they led him,
Came to the place, and what was set before him

Which without help of eye, might be assay'd,
To heave, pull, draw, or break, he still perform'd
All with incredible, stupendious force,
None daring to appear Antagonist.
At length for intermission sake they led him
Between the pillars; he his guide requested
(For so from such as nearer stood we heard)
As over-tir'd to let him lean a while
With both his arms on those two massie Pillars
That to the arched roof gave main support.
He unsuspitious led him; which when *Samson*
Felt in his arms, with head a while enclin'd,
And eyes fast fixt he stood, as one who pray'd,
Or some great matter in his mind revolv'd.
At last with head erect thus cryed aloud,
Hitherto, Lords, what your commands impos'd
I have perform'd, as reason was, obeying,
Not without wonder or delight beheld.
Now of my own accord such other tryal
I mean to shew you of my strength, yet greater;
As with amaze shall strike all who behold.
This utter'd, straining all his nerves he bow'd,
As with the force of winds and waters pent,
When Mountains tremble, those two massie Pillars
With horrible convulsion to and fro,
He tugg'd, he shook, till down they came and drew
The whole roof after them, with burst of thunder
Upon the heads of all who sate beneath,
Lords, Ladies, Captains, Councellors, or Priests,
Thir choice nobility and flower, not only
Of this but each *Philistian* City round
Met from all parts to solemnize this Feast.
Samson with these immixt, inevitably
Pulld down the same destruction on himself;
The vulgar only scap'd who stood without.

     Chorus   O dearly-bought revenge, yet glorious!
Living or dying thou hast fulfill'd
The work for which thou wast foretold
To *Israel*, and now ly'st victorious
Among thy slain self-kill'd
Not willingly, but tangl'd in the fold
Of dire necessity, whose law in death conjoin'd
Thee with thy slaughter'd foes in number more
Then all thy life had slain before.

Semichorus While thir hearts were jocund and sublime,
Drunk with Idolatry, drunk with Wine,
And fat regorg'd of Bulls and Goats,
Chaunting thir Idol, and preferring

Before our living Dread who dwells
In *Silo* his bright Sanctuary:
Among them he a spirit of phrenzie sent,
Who hurt thir minds,
And urg'd them on with mad desire
To call in hast for thir destroyer;
They only set on sport and play
Unweetingly importun'd
Thir own destruction to come speedy upon them.
So fond are mortal men
Fall'n into wrath divine,
As thir own ruin on themselves to invite,
Insensate left, or to sense reprobate,
And with blindness internal struck.

Semichorus   But he though blind of sight,
Despis'd and thought extinguish't quite,
With inward eyes illuminated
His fierie vertue rouz'd
From under ashes into sudden flame,
And as an ev'ning Dragon came,
Assailant on the perched roosts,
And nests in order rang'd
Of tame villatic Fowl; but as an Eagle
His cloudless thunder bolted on thir heads.
So vertue giv'n for lost,
Deprest, and overthrown, as seem'd,
Like that self-begott'n bird
In the *Arabian* woods embost,
That no second knows nor third,
And lay e're while a Holocaust,
From out her ashie womb now teem'd
Revives, reflourishes, then vigorous most
When most unactive deem'd,
And though her body die, her fame survives,
A secular bird ages of lives.

Manoah   Come, come, no time for lamentation now,
Nor much more cause, *Samson* hath quit himself
Like *Samson*, and heroicly hath finish'd
A life Heroic, on his Enemies
Fully reveng'd, hath left them years of mourning,
And lamentation to the Sons of *Caphtor*
Through all *Philistian* bounds. To *Israel*
Honour hath left, and freedom, let but them
Find courage to lay hold on this occasion,
To himself and Fathers house eternal fame;
And which is best and happiest yet, all this
With God not parted from him, as was feard,
But favouring and assisting to the end.

Nothing is here for tears, nothing to wail
Or knock the breast, no weakness, no contempt,
Dispraise, or blame, nothing but well and fair,
And what may quiet us in a death so noble.
Let us go find the body where it lies
Sok't in his enemies blood, and from the stream
With lavers pure and cleansing herbs wash off
The clotted gore. I with what speed the while
(*Gaza* is not in plight to say us nay)
Will send for all my kindred, all my friends
To fetch him hence and solemnly attend
With silent obsequie and funeral train
Home to his Fathers house: there will I build him
A Monument, and plant it round with shade
Of Laurel ever green, and branching Palm,
With all his Trophies hung, and Acts enroll'd
In copious Legend, or sweet Lyric Song.
Thither shall all the valiant youth resort,
And from his memory inflame thir breasts
To matchless valour, and adventures high:
The Virgins also shall on feastful days
Visit his Tomb with flowers, only bewailing
His lot unfortunate in nuptial choice,
From whence captivity and loss of eyes.

Chorus   All is best, though we oft doubt,
What th' unsearchable dispose
Of highest wisdom brings about,
And ever best found in the close.
Oft he seems to hide his face,
But unexpectedly returns
And to his faithful Champion hath in place
Bore witness gloriously; whence *Gaza* mourns
And all that band them to resist
His uncontroulable intent,
His servants he with new acquist
Of true experience from this great event
With peace and consolation hath dismist,
And calm of mind all passion spent.

The End

Sir John Suckling

230   *A Ballad upon a Wedding*

I tell thee, Dick, where I have been;
Where I the rarest things have seen,
      Oh, things without compare!
Such sights again cannot be found
In any place on English ground,
      Be it at wake or fair.

At Charing Cross, hard by the way
Where we, thou know'st, do sell our hay,
      There is a house with stairs;
And there did I see coming down
Such folk as are not in our town,
      Vorty at least, in pairs.

Amongst the rest, one pest'lent fine
(His beard no bigger though than thine)
      Walk'd on before the rest:
Our landlord looks like nothing to him;
The King (God bless him!), 'twould undo him,
      Should he go still so dress'd.

At course-a-park, without all doubt,
He should have first been taken out
      By all the maids i' th' town,
Though lusty Roger there had been,
Or little George upon the Green,
      Or Vincent of the Crown.

But wot you what? the youth was going
To make an end of all his wooing;
      The parson for him stay'd:
Yet by his leave, for all his haste,
He did not so much wish all past,
      Perchance, as did the maid.

The maid – and thereby hangs a tale;
For such a maid no Whitsun-ale
      Could ever yet produce:
No grape that's kindly ripe could be
So round, so plump, so soft as she,
      Nor half so full of juice.

Her finger was so small, the ring
Would not stay on which they did bring,
    It was too wide a peck;
And to say truth (for out it must)
It look'd like the great collar (just)
    About our young colt's neck.

Her feet beneath her petticoat
Like little mice stole in and out,
    As if they fear'd the light;
But oh! she dances such a way,
No sun upon an Easter day
    Is half so fine a sight.

He would have kiss'd her once or twice,
But she would not, she was so nice,
    She would not do 't in sight;
And then she look'd as who should say,
I will do what I list to-day,
    And you shall do 't at night.

Her cheeks so rare a white was on,
No daisy makes comparison,
    (Who sees them is undone);
For streaks of red were mingled there,
Such as are on a Kather'ne pear
    (The side that's next the sun).

Her lips were red, and one was thin
Compar'd to that was next her chin –
    Some bee had stung it newly;
But, Dick, her eyes so guard her face,
I durst no more upon them gaze
    Than on the sun in July.

Her mouth so small, when she does speak,
Thou'dst swear her teeth her words did break,
    That they might passage get;
But she so handled still the matter,
They came as good as ours, or better,
    And are not spent a whit.

If wishing should be any sin,
The parson himself had guilty bin,
    She look'd that day so purely;
And did the youth so oft the feat
At night, as some did in conceit,
    It would have spoil'd him surely.

Passion o' me! how I run on!
There's that that would be thought upon,
  I trow, besides the bride:
The business of the kitchen's great,
For it is fit that men should eat;
  Nor was it there deni'd.

Just in the nick the cook knock'd thrice,
And all the waiters in a trice
  His summons did obey;
Each serving-man, with dish in hand,
March'd boldly up, like our train'd band,
  Presented, and away.

When all the meat was on the table,
What man of knife or teeth was able
  To stay to be entreated?
And this the very reason was
Before the parson could say grace
  The company was seated.

Now hats fly off, and youths carouse;
Healths first go round, and then the house,
  The bride's came thick and thick;
And when 'twas nam'd another's health,
Perhaps he made it hers by stealth:
  (And who could help it, Dick?)

O' th' sudden up they rise and dance;
Then sit again, and sigh, and glance;
  Then dance again and kiss:
Thus several ways the time did pass,
Whilst ev'ry woman wish'd her place,
  And ev'ry man wish'd his.

By this time all were stol'n aside
To counsel and undress the bride;
  But that he must not know:
But yet 'twas thought he guess'd her mind,
And did not mean to stay behind
  Above an hour or so.

When in he came, Dick, there she lay
Like new-fall'n snow melting away,
  ('Twas time, I trow, to part);
Kisses were now the only stay,
Which soon she gave, as who would say,
  God b' w' y', with all my heart.

But just as Heav'ns would have, to cross it,
In came the bridesmaids with the posset:
    The bridegroom eat in spite;
For had he left the women to 't,
It would have cost two hours to do 't,
    Which were too much that night.

At length the candle's out, and now
All that they had not done they do:
    What that is, who can tell?
But I believe it was no more
Than thou and I have done before
    With Bridget and with Nell.

Samuel Butler

From *Hudibras*

231

[1]

[Sir Hudibras, His Mind and Character]

The Argument
Sir Hudibras his passing worth,
The manner how he sallied forth;
His arms and equipage are shown;
His horse's virtues, and his own.
Th' adventure of the bear and fiddle
Is sung, but breaks off in the middle.

When civil fury first grew high,
And men fell out, they knew not why;
When hard words, jealousies, and fears,
Set folks together by the ears,
And made them fight, like mad or drunk,
For Dame Religion, as for punk;
Whose honesty they all durst swear for,
Though not a man of them knew wherefore:
When Gospel-Trumpeter, surrounded
With long-eared rout, to battle sounded,
And pulpit, drum ecclesiastic,
Was beat with fist, instead of a stick;
Then did Sir Knight abandon dwelling,
And out he rode a colonelling.

A wight he was, whose very sight would
Entitle him Mirror of Knighthood;
That never bent his stubborn knee
To any thing but Chivalry;
Nor put up blow, but that which laid
Right worshipful on shoulder-blade:
Chief of domestic knights and errant,
Either for cartel or for warrant;
Great on the bench, great in the saddle,
That could as well bind o'er, as swaddle;
Mighty he was at both of these,
And styl'd of war, as well as peace.
So some rats, of amphibious nature,
Are either for the land or water.
But here our authors make a doubt
Whether he were more wise, or stout:
Some hold the one, and some the other;
But howsoe'er they make a pother,
The difference was so small, his brain
Outweigh'd his rage but half a grain;
Which made some take him for a tool
That knaves do work with, call'd a fool:
For 't has been held by many, that
As Montaigne, playing with his cat,
Complains she thought him but an ass,
Much more she would Sir Hudibras;
For that's the name our valiant knight
To all his challenges did write.
But they're mistaken very much,
'Tis plain enough he was not such;
We grant, although he had much wit,
H' was very shy of using it;
As being loth to wear it out,
And therefore bore it not about,
Unless on holy-days, or so,
As men their best apparel do.
Beside, 'tis known he could speak Greek
As naturally as pigs squeak;
That Latin was no more difficile,
Than to a blackbird 'tis to whistle:
Being rich in both, he never scanted
His bounty unto such as wanted;
But much of either would afford
To many, that had not one word.
For Hebrew roots, although they're found
To flourish most in barren ground,
He had such plenty, as suffic'd
To make some think him circumcis'd;
And truly so, perhaps, he was,
'Tis many a pious Christian's case.

He was in logic a great critic,
Profoundly skill'd in analytic;
He could distinguish, and divide
A hair 'twixt south, and south-west side;
On either which he would dispute.
Confute, change hands, and still confute;
He'd undertake to prove, by force
Of argument, a man's no horse;
He'd prove a buzzard is no fowl,
And that a lord may be an owl,
A calf an alderman, a goose a justice,
And rooks Committee-men and Trustees.
He'd run in debt by disputation,
And pay with ratiocination.
All this by syllogism, true
In mood and figure, he would do.
   For rhetoric, he could not ope
His mouth, but out there flew a trope;
And when he happen'd to break off
I' th' middle of his speech, or cough,
H' had hard words ready to show why,
And tell what rules he did it by;
Else, when with greatest art he spoke,
You'd think he talk'd like other folk.
For all a rhetorician's rules
Teach nothing but to name his tools.
But, when he pleas'd to show't, his speech
In loftiness of sound was rich;
A Babylonish dialect,
Which learned pedants much affect.
It was a parti-colour'd dress
Of patch'd and piebald languages;
'Twas English cut on Greek and Latin,
Like fustian heretofore on satin;
It had an old promiscuous tone
As if h' had talk'd three parts in one;
Which made some think, when he did gabble,
Th' had heard three labourers of Babel;
Or Cerberus himself pronounce
A leash of languages at once.
This he as volubly would vent
As if his stock would ne'er be spent:
And truly, to support that charge,
He had supplies as vast and large;
For he could coin, or counterfeit
New words, with little or no wit;
Words so debas'd and hard, no stone
Was hard enough to touch them on;
And when with hasty noise he spoke 'em;
The ignorant for current took 'em;

That had the orator, who once
Did fill his mouth with pebble stones
When he harangu'd, but known his phrase,
He would have us'd no other ways.
    In mathematics he was greater
Than Tycho Brahe, or Erra Pater:
For he, by geometric scale,
Could take the size of pots of ale;
Resolve, by sines and tangents straight,
If bread or butter wanted weight;
And wisely tell what hour o' th' day
The clock does strike, by Algebra.
    Beside, he was a shrewd philosopher,
And had read ev'ry text and gloss over;
Whate'er the crabbed'st author hath,
He understood b'implicit faith:
Whatever sceptic could inquire for,
For ev'ry why he had a wherefore;
Knew more than forty of them do,
As far as words and terms could go.
All which he understood by rote,
And, as occasion serv'd, would quote;
No matter whether right or wrong,
They might be either said or sung.
His notions fitted things so well,
That which was which he could not tell;
But oftentimes mistook the one
For th' other, as great clerks have done.
He could reduce all things to acts,
And knew their natures by abstracts;
Where entity and quiddity,
The ghost of defunct bodies fly;
Where truth in person does appear,
Like words congeal'd in northern air.
He knew what's what, and that's as high
As metaphysic wit can fly.
In school-divinity as able
As he that hight Irrefragable;
A second Thomas, or, at once
To name them all, another Duns;
Profound in all the Nominal
And Real ways, beyond them all:
And, with as delicate a hand,
Could twist as tough a rope of sand;
And weave fine cobwebs, fit for skull
That's empty when the moon is full;
Such as take lodgings in a head
That's to be let unfurnished.

He could raise scruples dark and nice,
And after solve 'em in a trice;
As if Divinity had catch'd
The itch, on purpose to be scratch'd;
Or, like a mountebank, did wound
And stab herself with doubts profound,
Only to show with how small pain
The sores of Faith are cur'd again;
Although by woful proof we find,
They always leave a scar behind.
He knew the seat of Paradise,
Could tell in what degree it lies;
And, as he was dispos'd, could prove it,
Below the moon, or else above it:
What Adam dreamt of, when his bride
Came from her closet in his side:
Whether the devil tempted her
By an High Dutch interpreter;
If either of them had a navel:
Who first made music malleable:
Whether the serpent, at the fall,
Had cloven feet, or none at all.
All this, without a gloss, or comment,
He could unriddle in a moment,
In proper terms, such as men smatter
When they throw out, and miss the matter.
    For his Religion, it was fit
To match his learning and his wit;
'Twas Presbyterian, true blue;
For he was of that stubborn crew
Of errant saints, whom all men grant
To be the true Church Militant;
Such as do build their faith upon
The holy text of pike and gun;
Decide all controversies by
Infallible artillery;
And prove their doctrine orthodox
By apostolic blows, and knocks;
Call fire, and sword, and desolation,
A godly, thorough Reformation,
Which always must be carried on,
And still be doing, never done;
As if Religion were intended
For nothing else but to be mended.
A sect, whose chief devotion lies
In odd perverse antipathies;
In falling out with that or this,
And finding somewhat still amiss;

More peevish, cross, and splenetic,
Than dog distract or monkey sick.
That with more care keep holy-day
The wrong, than others the right way;
Compound for sins they are inclin'd to,
By damning those they have no mind to:
Still so perverse and opposite,
As if they worshipp'd God for spite.
The self-same thing they will abhor
One way, and long another for.
Free-will they one way disavow,
Another, nothing else allow.
All piety consists therein
In them, in other men all sin.
Rather than fail, they will defy
That which they love most tenderly,
Quarrel with minc'd-pies, and disparage
Their best and dearest friend — plum-porridge;
Fat pig and goose itself oppose,
And blaspheme custard through the nose.
Th' apostles of this fierce religion,
Like Mahomet's, were ass and widgeon,
To whom our knight, by fast instinct
Of wit and temper, was so link'd,
As if hypocrisy and nonsense
Had got the advowson of his conscience.

232   [2]

[The Chaos of Theories that Preceded the Restoration]

Some were for setting up a king,
But all the rest for no such thing,
Unless king Jesus: others tamper'd
For Fleetwood, Desborough, and Lambert;
Some for the Rump; and some more crafty,
For agitators, and the safety;
Some for the gospel, and massacres
Of spiritual affidavit-makers,
That swore to any human regence
Oaths of suprem'cy and allegiance, —
Yea, though the ablest swearing saint,
That vouch'd the bulls o' th' covenant;
Others for pulling down th' high places
Of synods and provincial classes,
That used to make such hostile inroads
Upon the saints, like bloody Nimrods;

Some for fulfilling prophecies,
And th' extirpation of th' excise;
And some against th' Egyptian bondage
Of holy-days, and paying poundage;
Some for the cutting down of groves,
And rectifying bakers' loaves,
And some for finding out expedients
Against the slavery of obedience;
Some were for gospel-ministers,
And some for redcoat seculars,
As men most fit t' hold forth the word,
And wield the one and th' other sword;
Some were for carrying on the work
Against the pope, and some the Turk;
Some for engaging to suppress
The camisado of surplices,
That gifts and dispensations hinder'd,
And turned to th' outward man the inward:
More proper for the cloudy night
Of popery than gospel-light;
Others were for abolishing
That tool of matrimony, a ring,
With which th' unsanctifi'd bridegroom
Is married only to a thumb, –
As wise as ringing of a pig,
That used to break up ground, and dig, –
The bride to nothing but her will,
That nulls the after-marriage still;
Some were for th' utter extirpation
Of linsey-woolsey in the nation;
And some against all idolising
The cross in shop-books, or baptising;
Others, to make all things recant
The Christian or surname of saint,
And force all churches, streets, and towns,
The holy title to renounce;
Some 'gainst a third estate of souls,
And bringing down the price of coals;
Some for abolishing black-pudding,
And eating nothing with the blood in,
To abrogate them roots and branches;
While others were for eating haunches
Of warriors, and, now and then,
The flesh of kings and mighty men;
And some for breaking of their bones
With rods of iron, by secret ones;
For thrashing mountains, and with spells
For hallowing carriers' packs and bells;
Things that the legend never heard of
But made the wicked sore afeard of.

The quacks of government, who sate
At the unregarded helm of state,
And understood this wild confusion
Of fatal madness and delusion
Must, sooner than a prodigy,
Portend destruction to be nigh,
Consider'd timely how t' withdraw,
And save their windpipes from the law;
For one rencounter at the bar
Was worse than all th' had 'scaped in war;
And therefore met in consultation
To cant and quack upon the nation;
Not for the sickly patient's sake,
Nor what to give, but what to take;
To feel the purses of their fees,
More wise than fumbling arteries;
Prolong the snuff of life in pain,
And from the grave recover – gain.

Richard Crashaw

233   *Hymn to St Teresa*

Love, thou art absolute, sole lord
Of life and death. To prove the word
We need to go to none of all
Those thy old soldiers, stout and tall,
Ripe and full-grown, that could reach down
With strong arms their triumphant crown;
Such as could with lusty breath
Speak loud unto the face of death
Their great lord's glorious name; to none
Of those whose large breasts built a throne
For love their Lord, glorious and great:
We'll see him take a private seat,
And make a mansion in the mild
And milky soul of a soft child.

Since she had learnt to lisp a name
Of martyr, yet she thinks it shame
Life should so long play with that breath,
Which, spent, can buy so brave a death.

She never undertook to know
What death with love should have to do;
Nor hath she e'er yet understood
Why to show love she should shed blood;

Yet though she cannot tell you why,
She can love and she can die.

    Scarce had she blood enough to make
    A guilty sword blush for her sake,
    Yet has she a heart dares hope to prove
    How much less strong is death than love.

Be love but there, let poor six years
Be pos'd with the maturest fears
Man trembles at, we straight shall find
Love knows no nonage, nor the mind.
'Tis love, not years or limbs, that can
Make the martyr or the man.
    Love touch'd her heart, and lo it beats
    High, and burns with such brave heats,
    Such thirst to die as dare drink up
    A thousand cold deaths in one cup.
    Good reason for she breathes all fire:
    Her weak breast heaves with strong desire
    Of what she may with fruitless wishes
    Seek for amongst her mother's kisses.

Since 'tis not to be had at home
She'll travel to a martyrdom.
No home for her confesses she
But where she may a martyr be.
    She'll to the Moors, and trade with them
    For this unvalu'd diadem:
    She offers them her dearest breath,
    With Christ's name in 't, in change for death.
    She'll bargain with them and will give
    Them God, and teach them how to live
    In him; or if they this deny
    For him she'll teach them how to die.
    So shall she leave amongst them sown
    Her Lord's blood, or at least her own.

Farewell then all the world, adieu,
Teresa is no more for you.
Farewell all pleasures, sports and joys,
Never till now esteemed toys.
Farewell whatever dear may be –
Mother's arms or father's knee.
Farewell house and farewell home,
She's for the Moors and martyrdom.

    Sweet, not so fast, lo thy fair spouse,
    Whom thou seek'st with so swift vows,

Calls thee back and bids thee come
T'embrace a milder martyrdom.

Bless'd powers forbid thy tender life
Should bleed upon a barbarous knife,
Or some base hand have power to race
Thy breast's chaste chamber and uncase
A soul kept there so sweet. O no,
Wise heaven will never have it so.
Thou art Love's victim and must die
A death more mystical and high:
Into Love's hand thou shalt let fall
A still surviving funeral.

His is the dart must make the death,
Whose stroke shall taste thy hallow'd breath;
A dart thrice dipp'd in that rich flame
Which writes thy spouse's radiant name
Upon the roof of heaven, where ay
It shines, and with a sovereign ray
Beats bright upon the burning faces
Of souls, which in that name's sweet graces

Find everlasting smiles. So rare,
So spiritual, pure and fair
Must be the immortal instrument
Upon whose choice point shall be spent
A life so lov'd; and that there be
Fit executioners for thee,
The fairest and the first-born loves of fire,
Bless'd seraphims, shall leave their choir
And turn Love's soldiers upon thee
To exercise their archery.

O how oft shalt thou complain
Of a sweet and subtle pain?
Of intolerable joys?
Of a death in which who dies
Loves his death and dies again
And would forever be so slain?
And lives and dies and knows not why
To live, but that he still may die.

How kindly will thy gentle heart
Kiss the sweetly-killing dart;
And close in his embraces keep
Those delicious wounds that weep
Balsam, to heal themselves with. Thus
When these thy deaths so numerous
Shall all at last die into one,
And melt thy soul's sweet mansion –
Like a soft lump of incense, hasted
By too hot a fire and wasted

Into perfuming clouds – so fast
Shalt thou exhale to heaven at last
In a dissolving sigh, and then

   O what? Ask not the tongues of men:
Angels cannot tell. Suffice
Thyself shalt feel thine own full joys,
And hold them fast forever there
As soon as thou shalt first appear,
The moon of maiden stars; thy white
Mistress, attended by such bright
Souls as thy shining self, shall come
And in her first ranks make thee room;
Where 'mongst her snowy family
Immortal welcomes wait on thee.
O what delight when she shall stand
And teach thy lips heaven with her hand,
On which thou now mayst to thy wishes
Heap up thy consecrated kisses.
What joy shall seize thy soul when she,
Bending her blessed eyes on thee
Those second smiles of heaven shall dart,
Her mild rays, through thy melting heart.

   Angels, thy old friends, there shall greet thee,
Glad at their own home now to meet thee.
All thy good works which went before,
And waited for thee at the door,
Shall own thee there, and all in one
Weave a constellation
Of crowns, with which the king thy spouse
Shall build up thy triumphant brows.

All thy old woes shall now smile on thee,
And thy pains set bright upon thee;
All thy sorrows here shall shine,
And thy sufferings be divine.
Tears shall take comfort and turn gems,
And wrongs repent to diadems.
Even thy deaths shall live, and new-
Dress the soul which late they slew.
Thy wounds shall blush to such bright scars
As keep account of the Lamb's wars.
   Those rare works, where thou shalt leave writ
Love's noble history, with wit
Taught thee by none but him, while here
They feed our souls, shall clothe thine there.

   Each heavenly word, by whose hid flame
Our hard hearts shall strike fire, the same

Shall flourish on thy brows, and be
Both fire to us and flame to thee;
Whose light shall live bright, in thy face
By glory, in our hearts by grace.

Thou shalt look round about, and see
Thousands of crown'd souls throng to be
Themselves thy crown, sons of thy vows:
The virgin births with which thy spouse
Made fruitful thy fair soul: go now
And with them all about thee bow
To him. Put on (he'll say) put on
My rosy love, that thy rich zone,
Sparkling with the sacred flames
Of thousand souls whose happy names
Heaven keeps upon thy score (thy bright
Life, brought them first to kiss the light

That kindled them to stars), and so
Thou with the Lamb thy Lord shall go;
And wheresoe'er he sets his white
Steps, walk with him those ways of light:
Which who in death would live to see
Must learn in life to die like thee.

234   *An Epitaph upon Husband and Wife,*
        which Died and Were Buried Together

To these whom death again did wed,
This grave's their second marriage bed;
For though the hand of fate could force
'Twixt soul and body a divorce,
It could not sunder man and wife
Because they both liv'd but one life.
Peace, good reader, do not weep;
Peace, the lovers are asleep.
They, sweet turtles, folded lie
In the last knot that love could tie.
And though they lie as they were dead,
Their pillows stone, their sheets of lead,
(Pillow hard, and sheets not warm)
Love made the bed; they'll take no harm.
Let them sleep, let them sleep on
Till this stormy night be gone,
Till th' eternal morrow dawn:
Till the curtains will be drawn,
And they awake into a light
Whose day shall never die in night.

235   *Wishes to His (Supposed) Mistress*

Who e'er she be,
That not impossible she
That shall command my heart and me;

Where'er she lie,
Lock'd up from mortal eye
In shady leaves of destiny,

Till that ripe birth
Of studied fate stands forth
And teach her fair steps to our earth;

Till that divine
Idea take a shrine
Of crystal flesh through which to shine,

Meet you her my wishes,
Bespeak her to my blisses,
And be ye call'd my absent kisses.

I wish her beauty,
That owes not all his duty
To gaudy tire or glistering shoe-tie.

Something more than
Taffeta or tissue can,
Or rampant feather or rich fan.

More than the spoil
Of shop, or silkworm's toil,
Or a bought blush, or a set smile.

A face that's best
By its own beauty dress'd,
And can alone command the rest.

A face made up
Out of no other shop,
Than what nature's white hand sets ope.

A cheek where youth
And blood, with pen of truth,
Write what the reader sweetly ru'th.

A cheek where grows
More than a morning rose;
Which to no box his being owes.

Lips where all day
A lover's kiss may play,
Yet carry nothing thence away.

Looks that oppress
Their richest tires, but dress
And clothe their simplest nakedness.

Eyes that displaces
The neighbour diamond, and outfaces
That sunshine by their own sweet graces.

Tresses that wear
Jewels but to declare
How much themselves more precious are;

Whose native ray
Can tame the wanton day
Of gems that in their bright shades play.

Each ruby there,
Or pearl that dare appear,
Be its own blush, be its own tear.

A well-tam'd heart,
For whose more noble smart
Love may be long choosing a dart.

Eyes that bestow
Full quivers on love's bow,
Yet pay less arrows than they owe.

Smiles that can warm
The blood, yet teach a charm,
That chastity shall take no harm.

Blushes that bin
The burnish of no sin,
Nor flames of aught too hot within.

Joys that confess
Virtue their mistress,
And have no other head to dress.

Fears fond and flight,
As the coy bride's when night
First does the longing lover right.

Tears quickly fled,
And vain as those are shed
For a dying maidenhead.

Days that need borrow
No part of their good morrow
From a forspent night of sorrow.

Days that in spite
Of darkness, by the light
Of a clear mind are day all night.

Nights sweet as they
Made short by lovers' play,
Yet long by the absence of the day.

Life that dares send
A challenge to his end,
And when it comes say 'Welcome friend'.

Sidneyan showers
Of sweet discourse, whose powers
Can crown old winter's head with flowers.

Soft silken hours,
Open suns, shady bowers
'Bove all, nothing within that lours.

Whate'er delight
Can make day's forehead bright,
Or give down to the wings of night.

In her whole frame
Have nature all the name,
Art and ornament the shame.

Her flattery
Picture and poesy,
Her council her own virtue be.

I wish her store
Of worth may leave her poor
Of wishes: and I wish – no more.

Now if time knows
That her whose radiant brows
Weave them a garland of my vows;

Her whose just bays
My future hopes can raise
A trophy to her present praise;

Her that dares be
What these lines wish to see:
I seek no further, it is she.

'Tis she, and here
Lo I unclothe and clear
My wishes' cloudy character.

May she enjoy it,
Whose merit dare apply it,
But modesty dares still deny it.

Such worth as this is
Shall fix my flying wishes
And determine them to kisses.

Let her full glory,
My fancies, fly before ye,
Be ye my fictions, but her story.

Richard Lovelace

236   *La Bella Bona-Roba*

I cannot tell who loves the skeleton
Of a poor marmoset, naught but bone, bone:
Give me a nakedness with her clothes on.

Such whose white-satin upper coat of skin,
Cut upon velvet rich incarnadin,
Has yet a body (and of flesh) within.

Sure it is meant good husbandry in men,
Who so incorporate with aery lean,
T' repair their sides, and get their rib again.

Hard hap unto that huntsman that decrees
Fat joys for all his sweat, whenas he sees,
After his 'say, naught but his keeper's fees.

Then Love, I beg, when next thou takest thy bow,
Thy angry shafts, and dost heart-chasing go,
Pass rascal deer, strike me the largest doe.

237   *The Grasshopper*

To My Noble Friend Mr Charles Cotton.   Ode

O thou that swing'st upon the waving hair
    Of some well-filled oaten beard,
Drunk every night with a delicious tear
    Dropp'd thee from heav'n where now th' art rear'd;

The joys of earth and air are thine entire,
    That with thy feet and wings dost hop and fly;
And when thy poppy works, thou dost retire
    To thy carv'd acorn-bed to lie.

Up with the day, the sun thou welcomest then,
    Sport'st in the gilt plats of his beams,
And all these merry days mak'st merry men,
    Thyself, and melancholy streams.

But ah the sickle! golden ears are cropp'd,
    Ceres and Bacchus bid good night;
Sharp frosty fingers all your flow'rs have topp'd,
    And what scythes spar'd, winds shave off quite.

Poor verdant fool, and now green ice! thy joys,
    Large and as lasting as thy perch of grass,
Bid us lay in 'gainst winter rain, and poise
    Their floods with an o'erflowing glass.

Thou best of men and friends! we will create
    A genuine summer in each other's breast;
And spite of this cold time and frozen fate,
    Thaw us a warm seat to our rest.

Our sacred hearths shall burn eternally
    As vestal flames; the North-wind, he
Shall strike his frost-stretch'd wings, dissolve, and fly
    This Ætna in epitome.

Dropping December shall come weeping in,
    Bewail th' usurping of his reign;
But when in showers of old Greek we begin,
    Shall cry he hath his crown again.

Night as clear Hesper shall our tapers whip
    From the light casements where we play,
And the dark hag from her black mantle strip,
    And stick there everlasting day.

Thus richer than untempted kings are we,
    That asking nothing, nothing need:
Though lord of all what seas embrace, yet he
    That wants himself is poor indeed.

Abraham Cowley

238　　　　　From *Anacreontiques*

Or, some Copies of Verses translated
Paraphrastically out of Anacreon

XI The Swallow

Foolish Prater, what dost thou
So early at my Window do
With thy tuneless Serenade?
Well 't had been had Tereus made
Thee as Dumb as Philomel;
There his Knife had done but well.
In thy undiscover'd Nest
Thou dost all the Winter rest,
And dreamest o'er thy Summer Joys
Free from the stormy Seasons noise:
Free from th' Ill thou'st done to me;
Who disturbs, or seeks out Thee?
Had'st thou all the charming Notes
Of the Woods Poetick Throats,
All thy Art could never pay
What thou'st ta'en from me away.
Cruel Bird, thou'st ta'en away
A Dream out of my Arms to Day,
A Dream that ne'er must equall'd be
By all that waking Eyes may see.
Thou this Damage to repair,
Nothing half so sweet or fair,
Nothing half so good can'st bring,
Though Men say, Thou bring'st the Spring.

239　　　　*On the Death of Mr William Hervey*

Immodicis brevis est aetas, & rara Senectus. Mart.

It was a dismal and a fearful Night,
Scarce could the Morn drive on th' unwilling Light,
When Sleep, Death's Image, left my troubled Breast
　　　By something liker Death possesst.
My Eyes with Tears did uncommanded flow,
　　　And on my Soul hung the dull weight
　　　　　Of some intolerable Fate.
What Bell was that? Ah me! Too much I know.

My sweet Companion, and my gentle Peer,
Why hast thou left me thus unkindly here,
Thy End for ever, and my Life to moan?
    O thou hast left me all alone!
Thy Soul and Body, when Death's Agony
     Besieg'd around thy Noble Heart,
     Did not with more Reluctance part,
Than I, my dearest Friend, do part from Thee.

My dearest Friend, would I had dy'd for Thee!
Life and this World henceforth will tedious be.
Nor shall I know hereafter what to do,
    If once my Grief prove tedious too.
Silent and sad I walk about all Day,
     As sullen Ghosts stalk speechless by
     Where their hid Treasures lye;
Alas, my Treasure's gone, Why do I stay?

He was my Friend, the truest Friend on Earth:
A strong and mighty Influence join'd our Birth.
Nor did we envy the most sounding Name
    By Friendship giv'n of old to Fame.
None but his Brethren he, and Sisters knew,
     Whom the kind Youth preferr'd to me;
     And ev'n in that we did agree,
For much above myself I lov'd them too.

Say, for you saw us, ye immortal Lights,
How oft unweary'd have we spent the Nights?
'Till the Ledean Stars so fam'd for Love,
    Wonder'd at us from above.
We spent them not in Toys, in Lusts, or Wine;
     But Search of deep Philosophy,
     Wit, Eloquence, and Poetry;
Arts which I lov'd, for they, my Friend, were Thine.

Ye Fields of Cambridge, our dear Cambridge, say,
Have ye not seen us Walking ev'ry Day?
Was there a Tree about which did not know
    The Love betwixt us Two?
Henceforth, ye gentle Trees, for ever fade;
     Or your sad Branches thicker join,
     And into darksome Shades combine;
Dark as the Grave wherein my Friend is laid.

Henceforth no Learned Youths beneath you sing,
'Till all the Tuneful Birds t' your Boughs they bring;
No Tuneful Birds play with their wonted Chear,
     And call the Learned Youths to hear;

No whistling Winds through the glad Branches fly,
 But all with sad Solemnity,
  Mute and unmoved be,
Mute as the Grave wherein my Friend does lye.

To him my Muse made haste with ev'ry Strain
Whilst it was New, and Warm yet from the Brain.
He lov'd my worthless Rhimes, and like a Friend
 Would find out something to Commend.
Hence now, my Muse; thou canst not me delight;
 Be this my latest Verse
  With which I now Adorn his Herse,
And this my Grief without thy Help shall write.

Had I a Wreath of Bays about my Brow,
I should contemn that flourishing Honour now,
Condemn it to the Fire, and joy to hear
 It rage and crackle there.
Instead of Bays, crown with sad Cypress me;
 Cypress which Tombs does beautifie;
  Not Phoebus griev'd so much as I
For him, who first was made that Mournful Tree.

Large was his Soul; as large a Soul as e'er
Submitted to inform a Body here.
High as the Place 'twas shortly in Heav'n to have,
 But Low, and Humble as his Grave.
So High, that all the Virtues there did come,
 As to the chiefest Seat
  Conspicuous and Great;
So Low, that for Me too it made a room.

He scorn'd this busie World below, and all
That we, Mistaken Mortals, Pleasure call;
Was fill'd with innocent Gallantry and Truth,
 Triumphant o'er the Sins of Youth.
He like the Stars, to which he now is gone,
 That shine with Beams like Flame,
  Yet burn not with the same,
Had all the Light of Youth, of the Fire none.

Knowledge he only sought, and so soon caught,
As if for him Knowledge had rather sought.
Nor did more Learning ever crowded lye
 In such a short Mortality.
Whene'er the Skilful Youth discours'd or writ,
 Still did the Notions throng
  About his El'quent Tongue,
Nor could his Ink flow faster than his Wit.

So strong a Wit did Nature to him frame,
As all things but his Judgment overcame;
His Judgment like the Heav'nly Moon did show,
    Temp'ring that Mighty Sea below.
O had he liv'd in Learning's World, what Bound
    Would have been able to controul
    His over-pow'ring Soul?
We've lost in him Arts that not yet are found.

His Mirth was the pure Spirits of various Wit,
Yet never did his God or Friends forget.
And when deep Talk and Wisdom came in view,
    Retir'd and gave to them their due.
For the rich help of Books he always took,
    Though his own searching Mind before
    Was so with Notions written o'er
As if wise Nature had made that her Book.

So many Virtues join'd in him, as we
Can scarce pick here and there in History.
More than old Writers Practice e'er could reach,
    As much as they could ever Teach.
These did Religion, Queen of Virtues, sway,
    And all their Sacred Motions steer,
    Just like the First and Highest Sphere
Which wheels about, and turns all Heav'n one way.

With as much Zeal, Devotions, Piety,
He always Liv'd, as other Saints do Die.
Still with his Soul severe Account he kept,
    Weeping all Debts out e'er he slept.
Then down in Peace and Innocence he lay,
    Like the Sun's laborious Light,
    Which still in Water sets at Night,
Unsully'd with his Journey of the Day.

Wondrous young Man, why wert thou made so good,
To be snatch'd hence e'er better understood?
Snatch'd before half of Thee enough was seen!
    Thou Ripe, and yet thy Life but Green!
Nor could thy Friends take their last sad Farewel,
    But Danger and Infectious Death
    Maliciously seiz'd on that Breath
Where Life, Sp'rit, Pleasure always us'd to dwell.

But Happy Thou, ta'en from this frantick Age,
Where Ign'rance and Hypocrisie does rage!
A fitter Time for Heav'n no Soul e'er chose,
    The Place now only free from those.

There 'mong the Blest thou dost for ever shine,
 And whereso'er thou cast'st thy view
 Upon that White and Radiant Crew,
See'st not a Soul cloath'd with more Light than Thine.

And if the Glorious Saints cease not to know
Their wretched Friends who fight with Life below;
Thy Flame to Me does still the same abide,
 Only more Pure and Rarify'd.
There whilst Immortal Hymns thou dost rehearse,
 Thou dost with Holy Pity see
 Our dull and Earthly Poesie,
Where Grief and Mis'ry can be join'd with Verse.

Andrew Marvell

240   *The Definition of Love*

My Love is of a birth as rare
As 'tis for object strange and high:
It was begotten by despair
Upon Impossibility.

Magnanimous Despair alone
Could show me so divine a thing,
Where feeble Hope could ne'r have flown
But vainly flapt its Tinsel Wing.

And yet I quickly might arrive
Where my extended Soul is fixt,
But Fate does Iron wedges drive,
And alwaies crouds it self betwixt.

For Fate with jealous Eye does see
Two perfect Loves; nor lets them close;
Their union would her ruine be,
And her Tyrannick pow'r depose.

And therefore her Decrees of Steel
Us as the distant Poles have plac'd,
(Though Loves whole World on us doth wheel)
Not by themselves to be embrac'd.

Unless the giddy Heaven fall,
And Earth some new Convulsion tear;
And, us to joyn, the World should all
Be cramp'd into a *Planisphere*.

As Lines so Loves *oblique* may well
Themselves in every Angle greet:
But ours so truly *Paralel*,
Though infinite can never meet.

Therefore the Love which us doth bind.
But Fate so enviously debarrs,
Is the Conjunction of the Mind,
And Opposition of the Stars.

241   *To His Coy Mistress*

    Had we but World enough, and Time,
This coyness Lady were no crime.
We would sit down, and think which way
To walk, and pass our long Loves Day.
Thou by the *Indian Ganges* side
Should'st Rubies find: I by the Tide
Of *Humber* would complain. I would
Love you ten years before the Flood:
And you should, if you please, refuse
Till the Conversion of the *Jews*.
My vegetable Love should grow
Vaster than Empires, and more slow.
An hundred years should go to praise
Thine Eyes, and on thy Forehead Gaze.
Two hundred to adore each Breast:
But thirty thousand to the rest.
An Age at least to every part,
And the last Age should show your Heart.
For Lady you deserve this State;
Nor would I love at lower rate.
    But at my back I alwaies hear
Times winged Charriot hurrying near:
And yonder all before us lye
Deserts of vast Eternity.
Thy Beauty shall no more be found;
Nor, in thy marble Vault, shall sound
My ecchoing Song: then Worms shall try
That long preserv'd Virginity:
And your quaint Honour turn to dust;
And into ashes all my Lust.
The Grave's a fine and private place,
But none I think do there embrace.

Now therefore, while the youthful hew
Sits on thy skin like morning dew,
And while thy willing Soul transpires
At every pore with instant Fires,
Now let us sport us while we may;
And now, like am'rous birds of prey,
Rather at once our Time devour,
Than languish in his slow-chapt pow'r.
Let us roll all our Strength, and all
Our sweetness, up into one Ball:
And tear our Pleasures with rough strife,
Thorough the Iron gates of Life.
Thus, though we cannot make our Sun
Stand still, yet we will make him run.

242   *The Match*

Nature had long a Treasure made
    Of all her choisest store;
Fearing, when She should be decay'd,
    To beg in vain for more.

Her *Orientest* Colours there,
    And Essences most pure,
With sweetest Perfumes hoarded were,
    All as she thought secure.

She seldom them unlock'd, or us'd,
    But with the nicest care;
For, with one grain of them diffus'd,
    She could the World repair.

But likeness soon together drew
    What she did sep'rate lay;
Of which one perfect Beauty grew,
    And that was *Celia*.

Love wisely had of long fore-seen
    That he must once grow old;
And therefore stor'd a Magazine,
    To save him from the cold.

He kept the several Cells repleat
    With Nitre thrice refin'd;
The Naphta's and the Sulphur's heat,
    And all that burns the Mind.

He fortifi'd the double Gate,
  And rarely thither came;
For, with one Spark of these, he streight
  All Nature could inflame.

Till, by vicinity so long,
  A nearer Way they sought;
And, grown magnetically strong,
  Into each other wrought.

Thus all his fewel did unite
  To make one fire high:
None ever burn'd so hot, so bright:
  And *Celia* that am I.

So we alone the happy rest,
  Whilst all the World is poor,
And have within our Selves possest
  All Love's and Nature's store.

243   *An Horatian Ode*
      upon Cromwell's Return from Ireland

The forward Youth that would appear
Must now forsake his Muses dear,
  Nor in the Shadows sing
  His Numbers languishing.
'Tis time to leave the Books in dust,
And oyl th' unused Armours rust:
  Removing from the Wall
  The Corslet of the Hall.
So restless Cromwel could not cease
In the inglorious Arts of Peace,
  But through adventrous War
  Urged his active Star:
And, like the three-fork'd Lightning, first
Breaking the Clouds where it was nurst,
  Did thorough his own Side
  His fiery way divide.
For 'tis all one to Courage high
The Emulous or Enemy;
  And with such to inclose
  Is more then to oppose.
Then burning through the Air he went,
And Pallaces and Temples rent:
  And Caesars head at last
  Did through his Laurels blast.

'Tis Madness to resist or blame
The force of angry Heavens flame;
  And, if we would speak true,
  Much to the Man is due:
Who, from his private Gardens, where
He liv'd reserved and austere,
  As if his highest plot
  To plant the Bergamot,
Could by industrious Valour climbe
To ruine the great Work of Time,
  And cast the Kingdoms old
  Into another Mold.
Though Justice against Fate complain,
And plead the antient Rights in vain:
  But those do hold or break
  As Men are strong or weak.
Nature that hateth emptiness,
Allows of penetration less:
  And therefore must make room
  Where greater Spirits come.
What Field of all the Civil Wars
Where his were not the deepest Scars?
  And Hampton shows what part
  He had of wiser Art:
Where, twining subtile fears with hope,
He wove a Net of such a scope,
  That Charles himself might chase
  To Caresbrooks narrow case:
That thence the *Royal Actor* born
The Tragick Scaffold might adorn,
  While round the armed Bands
  Did clap their bloody hands.
He nothing common did, or mean,
Upon the memorable Scene:
  But with his keener Eye
  The Axes edge did try:
Nor call'd the Gods with vulgar spight
To vindicate his helpless Right,
  But bow'd his comely Head
  Down, as upon a Bed.
This was that memorable Hour
Which first assur'd the forced Pow'r.
  So when they did design
  The Capitols first Line,
A bleeding Head where they begun,
Did fright the Architects to run;
  And yet in that the State
  Foresaw its happy Fate.

And now the Irish are asham'd
To see themselves in one Year tam'd:
   So much one Man can do,
   That does both act and know.
They can affirm his Praises best,
And have, though overcome, confest
   How good he is, how just,
   And fit for highest Trust:
Nor yet grown stiffer with Command,
But still in the Republick's hand:
   How fit he is to sway
   That can so well obey.
He to the Commons Feet presents
A Kingdome, for his first years rents:
   And, what he may, forbears
   His Fame to make it theirs:
And has his Sword and Spoyls ungirt,
To lay them at the Publick's skirt.
   So when the Falcon high
   Falls heavy from the Sky,
She, having kill'd, no more does search,
But on the next green Bow to pearch;
   Where, when he first does lure,
   The Falckner has her sure.
What may not then our Isle presume
While Victory his Crest does plume;
   What may not others fear,
   If thus he crown each Year!
A Caesar he ere long to Gaul,
To Italy an Hannibal,
   And to all States not free
   Shall Clymacterick be.
The Pict no shelter now shall find
Within his party-colour'd Mind;
   But from this Valour sad
   Shrink underneath the Plad:
Happy if in the tufted brake
The English Hunter him mistake,
   Nor lay his Hounds in near
   The Caledonian Deer.
But thou the Wars and Fortunes Son
March indefatigably on,
   And for the last effect
   Still keep thy Sword erect:
Besides the force it has to fright
The Spirits of the shady Night;
   The same Arts that did gain
   A Pow'r must it maintain.

244   *The Mower against Gardens*

Luxurious Man, to bring his Vice in use,
   Did after him the World seduce:
And from the fields the Flow'rs and Plants allure,
   Where Nature was most plain and pure.
He first enclos'd within the Gardens square
   A dead and standing pool of Air:
And a more luscious Earth for them did knead,
   Which stupifi'd them while it fed.
The Pink grew then as double as his Mind;
   The nutriment did change the kind.
With strange perfumes he did the Roses taint.
   And Flow'rs themselves were taught to paint.
The Tulip, white, did for complexion seek;
   And learn'd to interline its cheek:
Its Onion root they then so high did hold,
   That one was for a Meadow sold.
Another World was search'd, through Oceans new,
   To find the Marvel of Peru.
And yet these Rarities might be allow'd,
   To Man, that sov'raign thing and proud;
Had he not dealt between the Bark and Tree,
   Forbidden mixtures there to see.
No Plant now knew the Stock from which it came;
   He grafts upon the Wild the Tame:
That the uncertain and adult'rate fruit
   Might put the Palate in dispute.
His green Seraglio has its Eunuchs too;
   Lest any Tyrant him out-doe.
And in the Cherry he does Nature vex,
   To procreate without a Sex.
'Tis all enforc'd; the Fountain and the Grot;
   While the sweet Fields do lye forgot:
Where willing Nature does to all dispence
   A wild and fragrant Innocence:
And Fauns and Faryes do the Meadows till,
   More by their presence than their skill.
Their Statues polish'd by some ancient hand,
   May to adorn the Gardens stand:
But howso'ere the Figures do excel,
   The Gods themselves with us do dwell.

Henry Vaughan

245   *The Night. John, III, 2*

Through that pure Virgin-shrine,
That sacred veil drawn o'er thy glorious noon
That men might look and live as Glow-worms shine,
    And face the Moon:
  Wise Nicodemus saw such light
  As made him know his God by night.

    Most blest believer he!
Who in that land of darkness and blind eyes
Thy long expected healing wings could see,
    When thou didst rise,
  And what can never more be done,
  Did at mid-night speak with the Sun!

    O who will tell me, where
He found thee at that dead and silent hour!
What hallow'd solitary ground did bear
    So rare a flower,
  Within whose sacred leafs did lie
  The fulness of the Deity.

    No mercy-seat of gold,
No dead and dusty Cherub, nor carv'd stone,
But his own living works did my Lord hold
    And lodge alone;
  Where trees and herbs did watch and peep
  And wonder, while the Jews did sleep.

    Dear night! this world's defeat;
The stop to busy fools; care's check and curb;
The day of spirits; my soul's calm retreat
    Which none distrub!
Christ's progress, and his prayer time;
The hours to which high Heaven doth chime.

    God's silent, searching flight:
When my Lord's head is fill'd with dew, and all
His locks are wet with the clear drops of night;
    His still, soft call;
His knocking time; The soul's dumb watch,
  When spirits their fair kindred catch.

Were all my loud, evil days
Calm and unhaunted as is thy dark Tent,
Whose peace but by some Angel's wing or voice
    Is seldom rent;
  Then I in Heaven all the long year
  Would keep, and never wander here.

    But living where the Sun
Doth all things wake, and where all mix and tire
Themselves and others, I consent and run
    To every mire,
  And by this world's ill-guiding light,
  Err more than I can do by night.

    There is in God (some say)
A deep, but dazzling darkness; As men here
Say it is late and dusky, because they
    See not all clear.
  O for that night! where I in him
  Might live invisible and dim.

246   *Peace*

My soul, there is a country
  Far beyond the stars,
 Where stands a winged sentry
  All skilful in the wars.
There above noise and danger
  Sweet peace sits crown'd with smiles,
And one born in a manger
  Commands the beauteous files.
He is thy gracious friend
  And (O my soul, awake!)
Did in pure love descend
  To die here for thy sake.
If thou canst get but thither,
  There grows the flower of peace,
The rose that cannot wither,
  Thy fortress and thy ease.
Leave then thy foolish ranges,
  For none can thee secure,
But one who never changes,
  Thy God, thy life, thy cure.

247   *The World*

I saw eternity the other night
  Like a great ring of pure and endless light,
    All calm as it was bright;
And round beneath it Time in hours, days, years,
    Driven by the spheres
Like a vast shadow mov'd, in which the world
  And all her train were hurl'd:
The doting lover in his quaintest strain
    Did there complain;
Near him his lute, his fancy and his flights,
    Wits so our delights,
With gloves and knots, the silly snares of pleasure –
    Yet his dear treasure
All scatter'd lay, while he his eyes did pour
    Upon a flower.

The darksome statesmen, hung with weights and woe,
Like a thick midnight fog moved there so slow
  He did not stay nor go:
Condemning thoughts, like sad eclipses, scowl
    Upon his soul,
And clouds of crying witnesses without
    Pursu'd him with one shout.
Yet digg'd the mole and lest his ways be found
    Work'd underground,
Where he did clutch his prey, but one did see
    That policy;
Churches and altars fed him; perjuries
    Were gnats and flies;
It rain'd about him blood and tears but he
    Drank them as free.

The fearful miser on a heap of rust
Sat pining all his life there, did scarce trust
  His own hands with the dust,
Yet would not place one piece above, but lives
    In fear of thieves.
Thousands there were as frantic as himself
    And hugg'd each one his pelf.
The downright epicure plac'd heaven in sense
    And scorn'd pretence,
While others, slipp'd into a wide excess,
    Said little less.
The weaker sort slight, trivial wares enslave
    Who think them brave,
And poor, despised truth sat counting by
    Their victory.

Yet some, who all this while did weep and sing,
And sing and weep, soar'd up into the king,
    But most would use no wing.
'O fools,' said I, 'thus to prefer dark night
    Before true light;
To live in grots and caves and hate the day
    Because it shows the way;
The way which from this dead and dark abode
    Leads up to God;
A way where you might tread the sun and be
    More bright than he.'
But as I did their madness so discuss,
    One whisper'd thus:
'The ring the bridegroom did for none provide
    But for his bride.'

John Bunyan

Songs from *The Pilgrim's Progress*

248   [1]

    He that is down needs fear no fall,
He that is low, no pride;
He that is humble, ever shall
Have God to be his Guide,

    I am content with what I have,
Little be it, or much:
And Lord, contentment still I crave,
Because thou savest such.

    Fulness to such a burden is
That go on Pilgrimage;
Here little, and hereafter Bliss,
Is best from age to age.

249   [2]

    Who would true Valour see,
Let him come hither;
One here will constant be,
Come Wind, come Weather.

There's no Discouragement,
Shall make him once relent,
His first avow'd intent,
To be a Pilgrim.

Who so beset him round
With dismal Stories,
Do but themselves confound,
His Strength the more is;
No Lion can him fright,
He'll with a Giant fight,
But he will have a right,
To be a Pilgrim.

Hobgoblin nor foul Fiend
Can daunt his spirit;
He knows he at the end
Shall Life inherit.
Then Fancies fly away,
He'll fear not what men say,
He'll labour night and day
To be a Pilgrim.

250

[3]

What danger is the Pilgrim in,
How many are his Foes,
How many ways there are to sin,
No living mortal knows.

Some of the Ditch shy are, yet can
Lie tumbling in the Mire;
Some, though they shun the Frying-pan,
Do leap into the Fire.

Charles Cotton

251   *An Epitaph on M.H.*

In this cold monument lies one,
That I knew who has lain upon,
The happier He: her sight would charm,
And touch have kept King David warm.
Lovely, as is the dawning East,
Was this marble's frozen guest;

As soft, and snowy, as that down
Adorns the blow-ball's frizzled crown;
As straight and slender as the crest,
Or antlet of the one-beam'd beast;
Pleasant as th' odorous month of May:
As glorious, and as light as day.

Whom I admir'd, as soon as knew,
And now her memory pursue
With such a superstitious lust,
That I could fumble with her dust.

She all perfections had, and more,
Tempting, as if design'd a whore,
For so she was; and since there are
Such, I could wish them all as fair.

Pretty she was, and young, and wise,
And in her calling so precise,
That industry had made her prove
The sucking school-mistress of love:
And Death, ambitious to become
Her pupil, left his ghastly home,
And, seeing how we us'd her here,
The raw-boned rascal ravisht her.

Who, pretty soul, resign'd her breath,
To seek new lechery in Death.

John Dryden

252   From *Annus Mirabilis*

Swell'd with our late Successes on the Foe,
Which *France* and *Holland* wanted power to cross,
We urge an unseen Fate to lay us low,
And feed their envious Eyes with *English* loss.

Each Element his dread Command obeys,
Who makes or ruines with a Smile or Frown;
Who as by one he did our Nation raise,
So now, he with another pulls us down.

Yet *London*, Empress of the Northern Clime,
By an high Fate thou greatly didst expire:
Great as the Worlds, which, at the death of time,
Must fall, and rise a nobler frame by fire.

As when some dire Usurper Heav'n provides
To scourge his Country with a lawless sway:
His birth perhaps some petty Village hides,
And sets his Cradle out of Fortune's way.

Till fully ripe his swelling Fate breaks out,
And hurries him to mighty Mischiefs on:
His Prince, surpriz'd at first, no ill could doubt,
And wants the pow'r to meet it when 'tis known.

Such was the Rise of his prodigious fire,
Which in mean Buildings first obscurely bred,
From thence did soon to open Streets aspire,
And straight to Palaces and Temples spread.

The diligence of Trades and noiseful Gain,
And luxury, more late, asleep were laid:
All was the nights, and in her silent reign
No sound the rest of Nature did invade.

In this deep quiet, from what source unknown,
Those seeds of Fire their fatal Birth disclose;
And first, few scatt'ring Sparks about were blown,
Big with the flames that to our Ruin rose.

Then, in some close-pent Room it crept along,
And, smouldring as it went, in silence fed;
Till th' infant Monster, with devouring strong,
Walk'd boldly upright with exalted head.

Now like some rich or mighty Murderer,
Too great for Prison, which he breaks with Gold,
Who fresher for new Mischiefs does appear
And dares the World to tax him with the old:

So scapes th' insulting Fire his narrow Jail
And makes small out-lets into open air:
There the fierce Winds his tender Force assail,
And beat him down-ward to his first repair.

The Winds, like crafty Courtezans, withheld
His Flames from burning, but to blow them more:
And every fresh attempt he is repell'd
With faint Denials, weaker than before.

And now, no longer letted of his Prey,
He leaps up at it with inrag'd desire:
O'relooks the Neighbours with a wide survey,
And nods at every House his threatening Fire.

The Ghosts of Traitors from the *Bridge* descend,
With bold Fanatick Spectres to rejoyce:
About the fire into a Dance they bend,
And sing their Sabbath Notes with feeble voice.

Our Guardian Angel saw them where he sate
Above the Palace of our slumbring King;
He sigh'd, abandoning his charge to Fate,
And, drooping, oft lookt back upon the wing.

At length the crackling noise and dreadful blaze
Call'd up some waking Lover to the sight;
And long it was ere he the rest could raise,
Whose heavy Eye-lids yet were full of Night.

The next to Danger, hot persu'd by Fate,
Half-cloth'd, half-naked, hastily retire:
And frighted Mothers strike their Breasts, too late,
For helpless Infants left amidst the Fire.

Their Cries soon waken all the Dwellers near;
Now murmuring Noises rise in every Street;
The more remote run stumbling with their fear,
And, in the dark, Men justle as they meet.

So weary Bees in little Cells repose;
But if Night-robbers lift the well-stor'd Hive,
An humming through their waxen City grows,
And out upon each others wings they drive.

Now Streets grow throng'd and busie as by day:
Some run for Buckets to the hallow'd Quire:
Some cut the Pipes, and some the Engines play;
And some more bold mount Ladders to the fire.

In vain: For from the East a *Belgian* wind
His hostile Breath through the dry Rafters sent;
The Flames impell'd soon left their Foes behind
And forward, with a wanton fury went.

A Key of Fire ran all along the Shore,
And lighten'd all the River with a blaze:
The waken'd Tides began again to roar,
And wond'ring Fish in shining waters gaze.

Old Father Thames rais'd up his reverend head,
But fear'd the fate of *Simoeis* would return:
Deep in his *Ooze* he sought his sedgy Bed,
And shrunk his Waters back into his Urn.

The Fire, mean time walks in a broader gross;
To either hand his Wings he opens wide:
He wades the Streets, and streight he reaches cross,
And plays his longing Flames on th' other side.

At first they warm, then scorch, and then they take;
Now with long Necks from side to side they feed:
At length, grown strong, their Mother-fire forsake,
And a new Colony of Flames succeed.

To every nobler Portion of the Town
The curling Billows roll their restless Tide:
In parties now they straggle up and down,
As Armies, unoppos'd, for Prey divide.

One mighty Squadron with a Side-wind sped,
Through narrow Lanes his cumber'd Fire does haste:
By pow'rful charms of Gold and Silver led,
The *Lombard* Banquers and the *Change* to waste.

Another backward to the *Tow'r* would go,
And slowly eats his way against the Wind:
But the main body of the marching Foe
Against th' Imperial Palace is design'd.

Now Day appears, and with the day the King,
Whose early Care had robb'd him of his rest:
Far off the Cracks of Falling houses ring,
And Shrieks of Subjects pierce his tender Breast.

Near as he draws, thick harbingers of Smoke
With gloomy Pillars cover all the place:
Whose little intervals of Night are broke
By Sparks, that drive against his Sacred Face.

More than his Guards his Sorrows made him known,
And pious Tears, which down his Cheeks did show'r:
The Wretched in his Grief forgot their own;
(So much the Pity of a King has pow'r.)

He wept the Flames of what he lov'd so well
And what so well had merited his love:
For never Prince in Grace did more excel,
Or Royal City more in Duty strove.

Nor with an idle Care did he behold:
(Subjects may grieve, but Monarchs must redress;)
He chears the Fearful and commends the Bold,
And makes Despairers hope for good Success.

Himself directs what first is to be done,
And orders all the Succours which they bring:
The Helpful and the Good about him run,
And form an Army worthy such a King.

He sees the dire Contagion spread so fast
That where it seizes, all Relief is vain:
And therefore must unwillingly lay waste
That Country, which would, else, the Foe maintain.

The Powder blows up all before the Fire:
Th' amazed flames stand gather'd on a heap;
And from the precipices-brink retire,
Afraid to venture on so large a leap.

Thus fighting Fires a while themselves consume,
But streight like *Turks*, forc'd on to win or die,
They first lay tender Bridges of their fume,
And o're the Breach in unctuous vapours flie.

Part stays for Passage, 'till a gust of wind
Ships o're their Forces in a shining Sheet:
Part, creeping under ground, their Journey blind,
And, climbing from below, their Fellows meet.

Thus to some desert Plain, or old Wood-side,
Dire Night-hags come from far to dance their round:
And o're broad rivers, on their Fiends, they ride,
Or sweep in Clouds above the blasted ground.

No help avails: for, *Hydra*-like, the Fire
Lifts up his Hundred heads to aim his way:
And scarce the wealthy can one half retire,
Before he rushes in to share the Prey.

The Rich grow suppliant, and the Poor grow proud:
Those offer mighty gain, and these ask more;
So void of pity is th' ignoble Crowd,
When others Ruin may increase their Store.

As those who live by Shores with joy behold
Some wealthy Vessel split or stranded nigh;
And from the Rocks leap down for shipwrack'd Gold,
And seek the Tempest which the others flie:

So these but wait the Owners last despair,
And what's permitted to the flames invade:
Ev'n from their Jaws they hungry morsels tear,
And, on their backs, the Spoils of *Vulcan* lade.

The days were all in this lost labour spent;
And when the weary King gave place to Night,
His Beams he to his Royal Brother lent,
And so shone still in his reflective Light.

Night came, but without darkness or repose,
A dismal Picture of the gen'ral Doom;
Where Souls distracted when the Trumpet blows,
And half unready with their Bodies come.

Those who have Homes, when Home they do repair,
To a last Lodging call their wand'ring Friends:
Their short uneasie Sleeps are broke with Care,
To look how near their own Destruction tends.

Those who have none, sit round where once it was,
And with full Eyes each wonted Room require:
Haunting the yet warm Ashes of the place,
As murder'd Men walk where they did expire.

Some stir up Coals, and watch the Vestal fire,
Others in vain from sight of Ruin run;
And, while through burning Lab'rinths they retire,
With loathing Eyes repeat what they would shun.

The most in Feilds like herded Beasts lie down,
To Dews obnoxious on the grassie Floor;
And while their Babes in Sleep their Sorrows drown,
Sad Parents watch the remnants of their Store.

While by the Motion of the Flames they guess
What Streets are burning now, and what are near,
An infant waking to the Paps would press,
And meets, instead of Milk, a falling Tear.

No thought can ease them but their Sovereign's Care,
Whose Praise th' afflicted as their Comfort sing;
Ev'n those, whom Want might drive to just despair,
Think Life a Blessing under such a King.

Mean time he sadly suffers in their Grief,
Out-weeps an Hermite, and out-prays a Saint:
All the long night he studies their relief,
How they may be suppli'd, and he may want.

O God, said he, thou Patron of my Days,
Guide of my Youth in Exile and Distress!
Who me unfriended brought'st by wondrous ways,
The Kingdom of my Fathers to possess:

Be thou my Judge, with what unwearied Care
I since have labour'd for my People's good;
To bind the Bruises of a Civil War,
And stop the Issues of their wasting Blood.

Thou, who has taught me to forgive the Ill,
And recompense, as Friends, the Good misled:
If Mercy be a Precept of thy Will,
Return that Mercy on thy Servants head.

Or, if my heedless Youth has stept astray,
Too soon forgetful of thy gracious hand;
On me alone thy just Displeasure lay,
But take thy Judgments from this mourning Land.

We all have sinn'd, and thou hast laid us low,
As humble Earth from whence at first we came:
Like flying Shades before the Clouds we shew,
And shrink like Parchment in consuming Flame.

O let it be enough what thou hast done;
When spotted Deaths ran arm'd thro' every Street,
With poison'd Darts which not the Good could shun,
The Speedy could out-flie, or Valiant meet.

The living few, and frequent Funerals then,
Proclaim'd thy Wrath on this forsaken place:
And now those few, who are return'd agen,
Thy searching Judgments to their dwellings trace.

O pass not, Lord, an absolute Decree,
Or bind thy Sentence unconditional:
But in thy Sentence our Remorse foresee,
And, in that foresight, this thy Doom recall.

Thy Threatings, Lord, as thine thou maist revoke:
But, if immutable and fix'd they stand,
Continue still thy self to give the stroke,
And let not Foreign-foes oppress Thy Land.

Th' Eternal heard, and from the Heav'nly Quire
Chose out the Cherub with the flaming Sword:
And bad him swiftly drive th' approaching Fire
From where our Naval Magazines were stor'd.

The blessed Minister his Wings displai'd,
And like a shooting Star he cleft the night;
He charg'd the Flames, and those that disobey'd
He lash'd to duty with his Sword of light.

The fugitive Flames, chastis'd, went forth to prey
On pious Structures, by our Fathers rear'd;
By which to Heav'n they did affect the way,
Ere Faith in Church-men without Works was heard.

The wanting Orphans saw with watry Eyes
Their Founders Charity in Dust laid low,
And sent to God their ever-answer'd cries,
(For he protects the Poor, who made them so.)

Nor could thy Fabrick, *Paul's*, defend thee long,
Though thou wert Sacred to thy Makers praise:
Though made Immortal by a Poet's Song,
And Poets Songs the *Theban* walls could raise.

The daring Flames peep't in, and saw from far
The awful Beauties of the Sacred Quire:
But, since it was prophan'd by Civil War,
Heav'n thought it fit to have it purg'd by fire.

Now down the narrow Streets it swiftly came,
And, widely opening, did on both sides prey:
This benefit we sadly owe the Flame,
If only Ruin must enlarge our way.

And now four days the Sun had seen our Woes;
Four nights the Moon beheld th' incessant fire;
It seem'd as if the Stars more sickly rose,
And farther from the feav'rish North retire.

In th' Empyrean Heav'n (the Bless'd abode),
The Thrones and the Dominions prostrate lie.
Not daring to behold their angry God:
And an hush'd silence damps the tuneful Sky.

At length th' Almighty cast a pitying Eye,
And Mercy softly touch'd his melting Breast:
He saw the Towns one half in Rubbish lie,
And eager flames drive on to storm the rest.

An hollow chrystal Pyramid he takes,
In firmamental Waters dipt above;
Of it a broad Extinguisher he makes
And hoods the Flames that to their quarry strove.

The vanquish'd Fires withdraw from every place,
Or, full with feeding, sink into a sleep:
Each household Genius shows again his face,
And, from the hearths, the little Lares creep.

Our King this more than natural change beholds;
With sober Joy his heart and eyes abound:
To the All-good his lifted hands he folds,
And thanks him low on his redeemed ground.

As when sharp Frosts had long constrain'd the earth,
A kindly Thaw unlocks it with mild Rain,
And first the tender Blade peeps up to birth,
And streight the Green fields laugh with promis'd grain:

By such degrees the spreading Gladness grew
In every heart, which Fear had froze before:
The standing Streets with so much joy they view,
That with less grief the Perish'd they deplore.

The Father of the People open'd wide
His stores, and all the Poor with Plenty fed;
Thus God's Anointed God's own place suppli'd,
And fill'd the Empty with his daily Bread.

253   From *To My Honour'd Kinsman,*
            John Driden, of Chesterton,
        in the County of Huntingdon, Esquire

No porter guards the Passage of your Door;
T' admit the Wealthy, and exclude the Poor;
For God, who gave the Riches, gave the Heart
To sanctifie the Whole, by giving Part:
Heav'n, who foresaw the Will, the Means has wrought,
And to the Second Son, a Blessing brought:
The First-begotten had his Father's Share,
But you, like *Jacob,* are *Rebecca's* Heir.
   So may your Stores, and fruitful Fields increase;
And ever be you bless'd, who live to bless.
As *Ceres* sow'd where e'er her Chariot flew;
As Heav'n in Desarts rain'd the Bread of Dew,
So free to Many, to Relations most,
You feed with Manna your own *Israel*-Host.
   With Crowds attended of your ancient Race,
You see the Champian-Sports, or Sylvan-Chace:
With well-breath'd Beagles, you surround the Wood,
Ev'n then, industrious of the Common Good:
And often have you brought the wily Fox
To suffer for the Firstlings of the Flocks;
Chas'd ev'n amid the Folds; and made to bleed,
Like Felons, where they did the murd'rous Deed.

This fiery Game, your active Youth maintain'd:
Not yet, by years extinguish'd, though restrain'd:
You season still with Sports your serious Hours;
For Age but tastes of Pleasures, Youth devours.
The Hare, in Pastures or in Plains is found,
Emblem of Humane Life, who runs the Round;
And, after all his wand'ring Ways are done, ⎫
His Circle fills, and ends where he begun, ⎬
Just as the Setting meets the Rising Sun. ⎭

    Thus Princes ease their Cares: But happier he,
Who seeks not Pleasure thro' Necessity,
Than such as once on slipp'ry Thrones were plac'd;
And chasing, sigh to think themselves are chas'd.

    So liv'd our Sires, e'er Doctors learn'd to kill,
And multiply'd with theirs, the Weekly Bill:
The first Physicans by Debauch were made:
Excess began, and Sloth sustains the Trade.
Pity the gen'rous Kind their Cares bestow
To search forbidden Truths; (a Sin to know:)
To which, if Humane Science cou'd attain,
The Doom of Death, pronounc'd by God, were vain.
In vain the Leech wou'd interpose Delay;
Fate fastens first, and vindicates the Prey.
What Help from Arts Endeavours can we have!
Guibbons but guesses, nor is sure to save:
But *Maurus* sweeps whole Parishes, and Peoples ev'ry Grave,
And no more Mercy to Mankind will use,
Than when he robb'd and murder'd *Maro's* Muse.
Wou'dst thou be soon dispatch'd, and perish whole?
Trust *Maurus* with thy Life, and M—lb—rn with thy Soul.
By Chace our long-liv'd Fathers earned their Food,
Toil strung the Nerves, and purif'd the Blood:
But we, their Sons, a pamper'd Race of Men,
Are dwindl'd down to threescore Years and ten.
Better to hunt in Fields, for Health unbought,
Than fee the Doctor for a nauseous Draught.
The Wise, for Cure, on Exercise depend;
God never made his Work, for Man to mend.

    The Tree of Knowledge, once in *Eden* plac'd,
Was easie found, but was forbid the Taste:
O, had our Grandsire walk'd without his Wife,
He first had sought the better Plant of Life!
Now, both are lost: Yet, wandring in the dark,
Physicians for the Tree have found the Bark.
They, lab'ring for Relief of Humane Kind, ⎫
With sharpen'd sight some Remedies may find; ⎬
Th' Apothecary-Train is wholly blind. ⎭
From Files, a Random-*Recipe* they take,
And Many Deaths of One Prescription make.

Garth, gen'rous as his Muse, prescribes and gives;
The Shop-man sells; and by Destruction lives:
Ungrateful Tribe! who, like the Viper's Brood,
From Med'cine issuing, suck their Mother's Blood!
Let These obey; and let the Learn'd prescribe;
That Men may die, without a double Bribe:
Let Them, but under their Superiours, kill;
When Doctors first have sign'd the bloody Bill:
He scapes the best, who Nature to repair,
Draws Phisick from the Fields, in Draughts of Vital Air.
  You hoard not Health, for your own private use,
But on the Publick spend the rich Produce.
When, often urg'd, unwilling to be Great,
Your Country calls you from your lov'd Retreat,
And sends to Senates, charg'd with Common Care,
Which none more shuns; and none can better bear.
Where cou'd they find another form'd so fit,
To poise, with solid Sense, a spritely Wit!
Were these both wanting, (as they both abound)
Where cou'd so firm Integrity be found?
  Well-born and Wealthy; wanting no Support,
You steer betwixt the Country and the Court:
Nor gratifie whate'er the Great desire,
Nor grudging give, what Publick Needs require.
Part must be left, a Fund when Foes invade;
And Part employ'd to roll the Watry Trade;
Ev'n *Canaans* happy Land, when worn with Toil,
Requir'd a Sabbath-Year, to mend the meagre Soil.

254   *To My Dear Friend Mr Congreve*
      on His Comedy Called The Double-Dealer

Well then, the promis'd Hour is come at last;
The present Age of Wit obscures the past:
Strong were our Syres, and as they fought they Writ,
Conqu'ring with Force of Arms and Dint of Wit:
Theirs was the Giant Race before the Flood;
And thus, when *Charles* Return'd, our Empire stood.
Like *Janus*, he the stubborn Soil manur'd,
With Rules of Husbandry the Rankness cur'd:
Tam'd us to Manners, when the Stage was rude,
And boistrous *English* Wit with Art indu'd.
Our Age was cultivated thus at length,
But what we gain'd in Skill we lost in Strength.

Our Builders were with Want of Genius curst;
The second Temple was not like the first;
Till you, the best *Vitruvius*, come at length,
Our Beauties equal, but excel our Strength.
Firm *Dorique* Pillars found Your solid Base,
The fair *Corinthian* crowns the higher Space; ⎫
Thus all below is Strength, and all above is Grace. ⎬
In easie Dialogue is *Fletcher's* Praise:
He mov'd the Mind, but had no Pow'r to raise.
Great *Johnson* did by Strength of Judgment please,
Yet, doubling *Fletcher's* Force, he wants his Ease.
In diff'ring Talents both adorn'd their Age,
One for the Study, t'other for the Stage.
But both to *Congreve* justly shall submit,
One match'd in Judgment, both o'er-match'd in Wit.
In Him all Beauties of this Age we see, ⎫
Etherege his Courtship, *Southern's* Purity, ⎬
The Satyre, Wit, and Strength of Manly *Wycherly*. ⎭
All this in blooming Youth you have Atchiev'd;
Nor are your foil'd Contemporaries griev'd;
So much the Sweetness of your Manners move,
We cannot Envy you, because we Love.
Fabius might joy in *Scipio*, when he saw
A Beardless Consul made against the Law,
And join his Suffrage to the Votes of *Rome*,
Though he with *Hannibal* was overcome.
Thus old *Romano* bow'd to *Raphael's* Fame,
And Scholar to the Youth he taught, became.
   O that your Brows my Lawrel had sustain'd,
Well had I been depos'd, if you had reign'd!
The Father had descended for the Son,
For only You are lineal to the Throne.
Thus, when the State one *Edward* did depose,
A greater *Edward* in his Room arose:
But now, not I, but Poetry is curst;
For *Tom* the Second reigns like *Tom* the First.
But let 'em not mistake my Patron's Part,
Nor call his Charity their own Desert.
Yet this I Prophesie: Thou shalt be seen,
(Tho' with some short Parenthesis between:)
High on the Throne of Wit; and, seated there,
Not mine (that's little) but thy Lawrel wear.
Thy first Attempt an early Promise made;
That early Promise this has more than paid.
So bold, yet so judiciously you dare,
That your least Praise, is to be Regular.
Time, Place, and Action may with Pains be wrought,
But Genius must be born, and never can be taught.

This is Your Portion, this Your Native Store:
Heav'n, that but once was Prodigal before,
To *Shakespear* gave as much; she cou'd not give him more. }
   Maintain your Post: that's all the Fame you need;
For 'tis impossible you shou'd proceed.
Already I am worn with Cares and Age,
And just abandoning th' ungrateful Stage:
Unprofitably kept at Heav'n's Expence,
I live a Rent-charge on his Providence:
But You, whom ev'ry Muse and Grace adorn,
Whom I foresee to better Fortune born,
Be kind to my Remains; and oh defend,
Against your Judgment, your departed Friend!
Let not th' insulting Foe my Fame pursue;
But shade those Lawrels which descend to You:
And take for Tribute what these Lines express;
You merit more; nor cou'd my Love do less.

John Dryden

255   *Song*

Sylvia the fair, in the bloom of Fifteen
Felt an innocent warmth, as she lay on the green;
She had heard of a pleasure, and something she guest
By the towzing and tumbling and touching her Breast:
She saw the men eager, but was at a loss,
What they meant by their sighing and kissing so close;
    By their praying and whining,
    And clasping and twining,
    And panting and wishing,
    And sighing and kissing,
    And sighing and kissing so close.

Ah she cry'd, ah for a languishing Maid
In a Country of Christians to die without aid!
Not a Whig, or a Tory, or Trimmer at least,
Or a Protestant Parson or Catholick Priest,
To instruct a young Virgin that is at a loss
What they meant by their sighing and kissing so close:
    By their praying and whining,
    And clasping and twining,
    And panting and wishing,
    And sighing and kissing,
    And sighing and kissing so close.

Cupid in Shape of a Swayn did appear,
He saw the sad wound, and in pity drew near,
Then show'd her his Arrow, and bid her not fear,
For the pain was no more than a Maiden may bear;
When the balm was infus'd, she was not at a loss
What they meant by their sighing and kissing so close,
 By their praying and whining,
 And clasping and twining,
 And panting and wishing,
 And sighing and kissing,
 And sighing and kissing so close.

From *Absalom and Achitophel*

256
      [1]

Some of their Chiefs were Princes of the Land;
In the first Rank of these did *Zimri* stand:
A man so various, that he seem'd to be
Not one, but all Mankind's Epitome.
Stiff in Opinions, always in the wrong;
Was Everything by starts, and Nothing long:
But, in the course of one revolving Moon,
Was Chymist, Fidler, States-man, and Buffoon;
Then all for Women, Painting, Rhiming, Drinking,
Besides ten thousand Freaks that died in thinking.
Blest Madman, who coud every hour employ,
With something New to wish, or to enjoy!
Railing and praising were his usual Theams;
And both (to shew his Judgment) in Extreams:
So over Violent, or over Civil,
That every Man, with him, was God or Devil.
In squandring Wealth was his peculiar Art:
Nothing went unrewarded, but Desert.
Begger'd by fools, whom still he found too late:
He had his Jest, and they had his Estate.
He laugh'd himself from Court; then sought Relief
By forming Parties, but could ne'r be Chief:
For, spight of him, the weight of Business fell
On *Absalom* and wise *Achitophel*:
Thus wicked but in Will, of Means bereft,
He left not Faction, but of that was left.
 Titles and Names 'twere tedious to Reherse
Of Lords, below the Dignity of Verse.

Wits, Warriors, Commonwealths-men were the best:
Kind Husbands and meer Nobles all the rest.
And, therefore in the name of Dulness, be
The well-hung *Balaam* and cold *Caleb* free;
And Canting *Nadab* let Oblivion damn,
Who made new Porridge for the Paschal Lamb.
Let Friendships holy Band some Names assure,
Some their own Worth, and some let Scorn secure.
Nor shall the Rascal Rabble here have Place,
Whom Kings no Titles gave, and God no Grace:
Not Bull-fac'd *Jonas*, who coud Statutes draw
To mean Rebellion, and make Treason Law.
But he, though bad, is follow'd by a worse,
The Wretch, who Heav'ns Anointed dar'd to Curse.
Shimei, whose Youth did early Promise bring
Of Zeal to God, and Hatred to his King;
Did wisely from Expensive Sins refrain,
And never broke the Sabbath, but for Gain:
Nor ever was he known an Oath to vent,
Or Curse, unless against the Government.
Thus, heaping Wealth, by the most ready way
Among the *Jews*, which was to Cheat and Pray;
The City, to reward his pious Hate
Against his Master, chose him Magistrate:
His Hand a Vare of Justice did uphold;
His Neck was loaded with a Chain of Gold.
During his Office, Treason was no Crime.
The Sons of *Belial* had a Glorious Time:
For *Shimei*, though not prodigal of pelf,
Yet lov'd his wicked Neighbour as himself:
When two or three were gather'd to declaim
Against the Monarch of *Jerusalem*,
Shimei was always in the midst of them.
And, if they Curst the King when he was by,
Woud rather Curse, than break good Company.
If any durst his Factious Friends accuse,
He pact a jury of dissenting *Jews*:
Whose fellow-feeling, in the godly Cause
Would free the suff'ring Saint from Humane Laws.
For Laws are onely made to Punish those
Who serve the King, and to protect his Foes.
If any leisure time he had from Pow'r,
(Because 'tis Sin to misimploy an hour;)
His bus'ness was by Writing to persuade
That kings were Useless, and a Clog to Trade:
And that his noble Stile he might refine,
No *Rechabite* more shund the fumes of Wine.

Chaste were his Cellars; and his Shrieval Board
The Grossness of a City Feast abhor'd:
His Cooks, with long disuse, their Trade forgot;
Cool was his Kitchin, though his Brains were hot.
Such frugal Vertue Malice may accuse;
But sure 'twas necessary to the *Jews*:
For Towns once burnt, such Magistrates require
As dare not tempt Gods Providence by Fire.
With Spiritual Food he fed his Servants well,
But free from Flesh that made the *Jews* rebel:
And *Moses's* Laws he held in more account,
For forty days of Fasting in the Mount.
To speak the rest, who better are forgot,
Would tire a well-breath'd Witness of the Plot:
Yet, *Corah*, thou shalt from Oblivion pass;
Erect thy self thou Monumental Brass:
High as the Serpent of thy Metal made,
While Nations stand secure bencath thy shade.
What though his Birth were base, yet Comets rise
From Earthy Vapours, e'r they shine in Skies.
Prodigious Actions may as well be done
By Weaver's issue as by Prince's son.
This Arch-Attestor for the Publick Good
By that one Deed enobles all his Bloud.
Who ever ask'd the Witnesses high race
Whose Oath with Martyrdom did *Stephen* grace?
Ours was a *Levite*, and as times went then,
His tribe were God-almighties Gentlemen.
Sunk were his Eyes, his Voice was harsh and loud,
Sure signs he neither Cholerick was, nor Proud:
His long Chin prov'd his Wit; his Saint-like Grace
A Church Vermilion, and a *Moses's* Face.
His Memory, miraculously great,
Coud Plots, exceeding mans belief, repeat;
Which, therefore cannot be accounted Lies,
For humane Wit could never such devise.
Some future Truths arc mingled in his Book;
But where the Witness fail'd, the Prophet spoke:
Some things like Visionary flights appear;
The Spirit caught him up, the Lord knows where:
And gave him his *Rabinical* degree,
Unknown to Foreign University.

257

[2]

With all these loads of Injuries opprest,
And long revolving in his careful brest
Th' event of things; at last his patience tir'd,
Thus from his Royal Throne, by Heav'n inspir'd,
The God-like *David* spoke; with awful fear
His Train their Maker in their Master hear.

Thus long have I by Native Mercy sway'd,
My Wrongs dissembl'd, my Revenge delay'd;
So willing to forgive th' Offending Age;
So much the Father did the King asswage.
But now so far my Clemency they slight,
Th' Offenders question my Forgiving Right.
That one was made for many, they contend;
But 'tis to Rule, for that's a Monarch's End.
They call my tenderness of Blood, my Fear,
Though Manly tempers can the longest bear.
Yet since they will divert my Native course,
'Tis time to show I am not Good by Force.
Those heap'd Affronts that haughty Subjects bring,
Are burdens for a Camel, not a King:
Kings are the publick Pillars of the State,
Born to sustain and prop the Nations weight:
If my young *Sampson* will pretend a Call
To shake the Column, let him share the Fall:
But oh that yet he woud repent and live!
How easie 'tis for Parents to forgive!
With how few Tears a Pardon might be won
From Nature, pleading for a Darling Son!
Poor pitied youth, by my Paternal care,
Rais'd up to all the Height his Frame coud bear:
Had God ordain'd his Fate for Empire born,
He woud have giv'n his Soul another turn:
Gull'd with a Patriot's name, whose Modern sense
Is one that woud by Law supplant his Prince:
The Peoples Brave, the Politicians Tool;
Never was Patriot yet, but was a Fool.
Whence comes it that Religion and the Laws
Should more be *Absalom's* then *David's* Cause?
His old Instructor, e'r he lost his Place,
Was never thought indu'd with so much Grace.
Good heav'ns, how Faction can a Patriot Paint!
My Rebel ever proves my Peoples Saint:
Woud *They* impose an Heir upon the Throne
Let Sanhedrins be taught to give their Own.

A king's at least a part of Government;
And mine as requisite as their Consent:
Without my leave a future King to choose,
Infers a Right the present to Depose:
True, they petition me t' approve their Choice:
But *Esau's* Hands suit ill with *Jacob's* Voice.
My Pious Subjects for my Safety pray,
Which to Secure, they take my Pow'r away.
From Plots and Treasons Heav'n preserve my Years,
But save me most from my Petitioners.
Unsatiate as the barren Womb or Grave;
God cannot Grant so much as they can Crave.
What then is left but with a Jealous Eye
To guard the Small remains of Royalty?
The Law shall still direct my peaceful Sway,
And the same Law teach Rebels to obey:
Votes shall no more Established Pow'r controul,
Such Votes as make a Part exceed the Whole:
No groundless Clamours shall my Friends remove
Nor Crouds have pow'r to Punish e'r they Prove;
For Gods and God-like kings their Care express,
Still to defend their Servants in distress.
Oh that my Pow'r to Saving were confin'd:
Why am I forc'd, like Heav'n, against my mind, }
To make Examples of another Kind?
Must I at length the Sword of Justice draw?
Oh curst Effects of necessary Law!
How ill my Fear they by my Mercy scan,
Beware the Fury of a Patient Man.
Law they require, let Law then shew her Face;
They could not be content to look on Grace,
Her hinder parts, but with a daring Eye
To tempt the terror of her Front, and Die.
By their own Arts 'tis Righteously decreed,
Those dire Artificers of Death shall bleed.
Against themselves their Witnesses will Swear,
Till, Viper-like, their Mother Plot they tear,
And suck for Nutriment that bloudy gore
Which was their Principle of Life before.
Their *Belial* with their *Belzebub* will fight;
Thus on my Foes, my Foes shall do me Right.
Nor doubt th' event; for Factious crouds engage
In their first Onset, all their Brutal Rage;
Then let 'em take an unresisted Course;
Retire and Traverse, and Delude their Force:
But when they stand all Breathless, urge the fight,
And rise upon 'em with redoubled might:

For Lawful Pow'r is still Superiour found,
When long driv'n back, at length it stands the ground.

He said. Th' Almighty, nodding, gave consent;
And peals of Thunder shook the Firmament.
Henceforth a Series of new time began,
The mighty Years in long Procession ran:
Once more the God-like *David* was Restor'd,
And willing Nations knew their Lawful Lord.

258   *To the Memory of Mr Oldham*

Farewell, too little and too lately known,
Whom I began to think and call my own:
For sure our Souls were near alli'd, and thine
Cast in the same poetick mold with mine.
One common Note on either Lyre did strike,
And Knaves and Fools we both abhorr'd alike.
To the same Goal did both our Studies drive:
The last set out the soonest did arrive.
Thus *Nisus* fell upon the slippery place,
Whilst his young Friend perform'd and won the Race.
O early ripe! to thy abundant Store
What could advancing Age have added more?
It might (what Nature never gives the Young)
Have taught the Numbers of thy Native Tongue.
But Satire needs not those, and Wit will shine
Through the harsh Cadence of a rugged Line.
A noble Error, and but seldom made,
When Poets are by too much force betray'd.
Thy gen'rous Fruits, though gather'd ere their prime,
Still shew'd a Quickness; and maturing Time
But mellows what we write to the dull Sweets of Rhyme.
Once more, hail, and farewell! farewell, thou young,
But ah! too short, *Marcellus* of our Tongue!
Thy Brows with Ivy and with Laurels bound;
But Fate and gloomy Night encompass thee around.

Thomas Traherne

259   *Walking*

To *walk* abroad is, not with eyes,
But thoughts, the fields to see and prize;
  Else may the silent feet,
    Like logs of wood,
Move up and down, and see no good,
  Nor joy nor glory meet.

Ev'n carts and wheels their place do change,
But cannot see; though very strange
  The glory that is by:
    Dead puppets may
Move in the bright and glorious day,
  Yet not behold the sky.

And are not men than they more blind,
Who having eyes yet never find
  The bliss in which they move:
    Like statues dead
They up and down are carried,
  Yet neither see nor love.

To *walk* is by a thought to go;
To move in spirit to and fro;
  To mind the good we see;
    To taste the sweet;
Observing all the things we meet
  How choice and rich they be.

To note the beauty of the day,
And golden fields of corn survey;
  Admire the pretty flow'rs
    With their sweet smell;
To praise their Maker, and to tell
  The marks of His great pow'rs.

To fly abroad like active bees,
Among the hedges and the trees,
  To cull the dew that lies
    On every blade,
From ev'ry blossom; till we lade
  Our *minds*, as they their *thighs*.

Observe those rich and glorious things,
The rivers, meadows, woods and springs,
 The fructifying sun;
  To note from far
The rising of each twinkling star
 For us his race to run.

A little child these well perceives,
Who, tumbling among grass and leaves,
 May rich as kings be thought,
  But there's a sight
Which perfect manhood may delight,
 To which we shall be brought.

While in those pleasant paths we talk
'Tis *that* tow'rds which at last we walk;
 But we may by degrees
  Wisely proceed
Pleasures of love and praise to heed,
 From viewing herbs and trees.

Aphra Behn

260   *And Forgive Us Our Trespasses*

How prone we are to Sin, how sweet were made
The pleasures, our resistless hearts invade!
Of all my Crimes, the breach of all thy Laws,
Love, soft bewitching Love! has been the cause;
Of all the Paths that Vanity has trod,
That sure will soonest be forgiven of God;
If things on Earth may be to Heaven resembled,
It must be love, pure, constant, undissembled:
But if to Sin by chance the Charmer press,
Forgive, O Lord, forgive our Trespasses.

John Wilmot, Earl of Rochester

261 *The Mistress*

An age in her embraces pass'd
  Would seem a winter's day,
Where life and light with envious haste
  Are torn and snatch'd away.

But oh, how slowly minutes roll
  When absent from her eyes,
That feed my love, which is my soul:
  It languishes and dies.

For then no more a soul, but shade,
  It mournfully does move
And haunts my breast, by absence made
  The living tomb of love.

You wiser men, despise me not
  Whose lovesick fancy raves
On shades of souls, and heaven knows what:
  Short ages live in graves.

Whene'er those wounding eyes, so full
  Of sweetness, you did see,
Had you not been profoundly dull,
  You had gone mad like me.

Nor censure us, you who perceive
  My best belov'd and me
Sigh and lament, complain and grieve:
  You think we disagree.

Alas! 'tis sacred jealousy,
  Love rais'd to an extreme:
The only proof 'twixt her and me
  We love, and do not dream.

Fantastic fancies fondly move
  And in frail joys believe,
Taking false pleasure or true love;
  But pain can ne'er deceive.

Kind jealous doubts, tormenting fears,
  And anxious cares, when past,
Prove our hearts' treasure fix'd and dear,
  And make us blest at last.

262   *A Translation from Seneca's 'Troades',*
                      Act II, Chorus

After death nothing is, and nothing, death:
The utmost limit of a gasp of breath.
Let the ambitious zealot lay aside
His hopes of heaven, whose faith is but his pride;
   Let slavish souls lay by their fear,
   Nor be concern'd which way nor where
   After this life they shall be hurl'd.
Dead, we become the lumber of the world,
And to that mass of matter shall be swept
Where things destroy'd with things unborn are kept.
   Devouring time swallows us whole;
Impartial death confounds body and soul.
   For Hell and the foul fiend that rules
   God's everlasting fiery jails
   (Devis'd by rogues, dreaded by fools),
With his grim, grisly dog that keeps the door,
   Are senseless stories, idle tales,
      Dreams, whimseys, and no more.

263   *A Song of a Young Lady to Her Ancient Lover*

Ancient person, for whom I
All the flattering youth defy,
Long be it ere thou grow old,
Aching, shaking, crazy, cold;
   But still continue as thou art,
   Ancient person of my heart.

On thy wither'd lips and dry,
Which like barren furrows lie,
Brooding kisses I will pour
Shall thy youthful heat restore
(Such kind showers in autumn fall,
And a second spring recall);
   Nor from thee will ever part,
   Ancient person of my heart.

Thy nobler part, which but to name
In our sex would be counted shame,
By age's frozen grasp possess'd,
From his ice shall be releas'd,
And sooth'd by my reviving hand,
In former warmth and vigor stand.

All a lover's wish can reach
For thy joy my love shall teach,
And for thy pleasure shall improve
All that art can add to love.
   Yet still I love thee without art,
   Ancient person of my heart.

Anne, Countess of Winchilsea

264   *A Nocturnal Reverie*

In such a *Night*, when every louder Wind
Is to its distant Cavern safe confin'd;
And only gentle *Zephyr* fans his Wings,
And lonely *Philomel*, still waking, sings;
Or from some Tree, fam'd for the *Owl's* delight,
She, hollowing clear, directs the Wand'rer right:
In such a *Night*, when passing Clouds give place,
Or thinly vail the Heav'ns mysterious Face;
When in some River, overhung with Green,
The waving Moon and trembling Leaves are seen;
When freshen'd Grass now bears it self upright,
And makes cool Banks to pleasing Rest invite,
Whence springs the *Woodbind*, and the *Bramble*-Rose,
And where the sleepy *Cowslip* shelter'd grows;
Whilst now a paler Hue the *Foxglove* takes,
Yet checquers still with Red the dusky brakes,
When scatter'd *Glow-worms*, but in Twilight fine,
Shew trivial Beauties watch their Hour to shine;
Whilst *Salisb'ry* stands the Test of every Light,
In perfect Charms, and perfect Virtue bright:
When Odours, which declin'd repelling Day,
Thro' temp'rate Air uninterrupted stray;
When darken'd Groves their softest Shadows wear,
And falling Waters we distinctly hear;
When thro' the Gloom more venerable shows
Some ancient Fabrick, awful in Repose,
While Sunburnt Hills their swarthy Looks conceal,
And swelling Haycocks thicken up the Vale:
When the loos'd *Horse* now, as his Pasture leads,
Comes slowly grazing thro' th' adjoining Meads,
Whose stealing Pace, and lengthen'd Shade we fear,
Till torn up Forage in his Teeth we hear:
When nibbling *Sheep* at large pursue their Food,
And unmolested Kine rechew the Cud;

When *Curlews* cry beneath the Village-walls,
And to her straggling Brood the *Partridge* calls;
Their shortliv'd Jubilee the Creatures keep,
Which but endures, whilst Tyrant-*Man* do's sleep;
When a sedate Content the Spirit feels,
And no fierce Light disturb, whilst it reveals;
But silent Musings urge the Mind to seek
Something, too high for Syllables to speak;
Till the free Soul to a compos'dness charm'd
Finding the Elements of Rage disarm'd,
O'er all below a solemn Quiet grown,
Joys in th' inferiour World, and thinks it like her Own:
In such a *Night* let Me abroad remain,
Till Morning breaks, and All's confus'd again;
Our Cares, our Toils, our Clamours are renew'd,
Or Pleasures, seldom reach'd, again pursu'd.

Jonathan Swift

265   *A Description of the Morning*

Now hardly here and there a Hackney-Coach
Appearing, show'd the Ruddy Morns Approach.
Now *Betty* from her Masters Bed had flown,
And softly stole to discompose her own.
And slipshod Prentice from his Masters Door,
Had par'd the Dirt, and Sprinkled round the Floor.
Now *Moll* had whirl'd her Mop with dext'rous Airs,
Prepar'd to Scrub the Entry and the Stairs.
The Youth with Broomy Stumps began to trace
The Kennel-Edge, where Wheels had worn the Place.
The Small-coal-Man was heard with Cadence deep,
'Till drown'd in Shriller Notes of *Chimney-sweep*.
Duns at his Lordships Gate began to meet,
And Brickdust *Moll* had Scream'd through half a Street.
The Turnkey now his Flock returning sees,
Duly let out a Nights to Steal for Fees.
The watchful Bailiffs take their silent Stands,
And School-Boys lag with Satchels in their Hands.

266   From *Verses on the Death of Dr Swift*

    The Time is not remote, when I
Must by the Course of Nature dye:
When I foresee my special Friends,
Will try to find their private Ends:
Tho' it is hardly understood,
Which way my Death can do them good;
Yet, thus methinks, I hear 'em speak;
See, how the Dean begins to break:
Poor Gentleman, he droops apace,
You plainly find it in his Face:
That old Vertigo in his Head,
Will never leave him, till he's dead:
Besides, his Memory decays,
He recollects not what he says;
He cannot call his Friends to Mind;
Forgets the Place where last he din'd:
Plyes you with Stories o'er and o'er,
He told them fifty Times before.
How does he fancy we can sit,
To hear his out-of-fashion'd Wit?
But he takes up with younger Fokes,
Who for his Wine will bear his Jokes:
Faith, he must make his Stories shorter,
Or change his Comrades once a Quarter:
In half the Time, he talks them round;
There must another Sett be found.

    For Poetry, he's past his Prime,
He takes an Hour to find a Rhime:
His Fire is out, his Wit decay'd,
His Fancy sunk, his Muse a Jade.
I'd have him throw away his Pen;
But there's no talking to some Men.

    And, then their Tenderness appears,
By adding largely to my Years:
'He's older than he would be reckon'd,
And well remembers *Charles* the Second.

    'He hardly drinks a Pint of Wine;
And that, I doubt, is no good Sign.
His Stomach too begins to fail:
Last Year we thought him strong and hale;
But now, he's quite another Thing;
I wish he may hold out till Spring.'

Then hug themselves, and reason thus;
'It is not yet so bad with us.'

In such a Case they talk in Tropes,
And, by their Fears express their Hopes:
Some great Misfortune to portend,
No Enemy can match a Friend;
With all the Kindness they profess,
The Merit of a lucky Guess,
(When daily Howd'y's come of Course,
And Servants answer; *Worse and Worse*)
Wou'd please 'em better than to tell,
That, GOD be prais'd, the Dean is well.
Then he who prophecy'd the best,
Approves his Foresight to the rest:
'You know, I always fear'd the worst,
And often told you so at first:'
He'd rather chuse that I should dye,
Than his Prediction prove a Lye.
Not one foretels I shall recover;
But, all agree, to give me over.

Yet shou'd some Neighbour feel a Pain,
Just in the Parts, where I complain;
How many a Message would he send?
What hearty Prayers that I should mend?
Enquire what Regimen I kept;
What gave me Ease, and how I slept?
And more lament, when I was dead,
Than all the Sniv'llers round my Bed.

My good Companions, never fear,
For though you may mistake a Year;
Though your Prognosticks run too fast,
They must be verify'd at last.

'Behold the fatal Day arrive!
How is the Dean? He's just alive.
Now the departing Prayer is read:
He hardly breathes. The Dean is dead.
Before the Passing-Bell begun,
The News thro' half the Town has run.
O, may we all for Death prepare!
What has he left? And who's his Heir?
I know no more than what the News is,
'Tis all bequeath'd to publick Uses.
To publick Use! A perfect Whim!
What had the Publick done for him!
Meer Envy, Avarice, and Pride!
He gave it all: − But first he dy'd.

And had the Dean, in all the Nation,
No worthy Friend, no poor Relation?
So ready to do Strangers good,
Forgetting his own Flesh and Blood?'

    Now Grub-Street Wits are all employ'd;
With Elegies, the Town is cloy'd:
Some Paragraph in ev'ry Paper,
To *curse* the *Dean*, or *bless* the *Drapier*.

    The Doctors tender of their Fame,
Wisely on me lay all the Blame:
'We must confess his Case was nice;
But he would never take Advice:
Had he been rul'd, for ought appears,
He might have liv'd these Twenty Years:
For when we open'd him we found,
That all his vital Parts were sound.'

    From *Dublin* soon to *London* spread,
'Tis told at Court, the Dean is dead.

    Kind Lady *Suffolk* in the Spleen,
Runs laughing up to tell the Queen.
The Queen, so Gracious, Mild, and Good,
Cries, 'Is he gone? 'Tis time he shou'd.
He's dead you say; why let him rot;
I'm glad the Medals were forgot.
I promis'd them, I own; but when?
I only was the Princess then;
But now as Consort of the King,
You know 'tis quite a different Thing.'

    Now, *Chartres* at Sir *Robert*'s Levee,
Tells, with a Sneer, the Tidings heavy:
'Why, is he dead without his Shoes?'
(Cries *Bob*) 'I'm Sorry for the News;
Oh, were the Wretch but living still,
And in his Place my good Friend *Will*;
Or, had a Mitre on his Head
Provided *Bolingbroke* were dead.'

    Now *Curl* his Shop from Rubbish drains;
Three genuine Tomes of *Swift*'s Remains.
And then to make them pass the glibber,
Revis'd by *Tibbalds*, *Moore*, and *Cibber*.
He'll treat me as he does my Betters.
Publish my Will, my Life, my Letters.
Revive the Libels born to dye;
Which Pope must bear, as well as I.

Here shift the Scene, to represent
How those I love, my Death lament.
Poor POPE will grieve a Month; and GAY
A Week; and ARBUTHNOTT a Day.

St JOHN himself will scarce forbear,
To bite his Pen, and drop a Tear.
The rest will give a Shrug and cry
I'm sorry; but we all must dye.
Indifference clad in Wisdom's Guise,
All Fortitude of Mind supplies:
For how can stony Bowels melt,
In those who never Pity felt;
When *We* are lash'd, *They* kiss the Rod;
Resigning to the Will of God.

The Fools, my Juniors by a Year,
Are tortur'd with Suspence and Fear.
Who wisely thought my Age a Screen,
When Death approach'd, to stand between:
The Screen remov'd, their Hearts are trembling,
They mourn for me without dissembling.

My female Friends, whose tender Hearts
Have better learn'd to act their Parts,
Receive the News in *doleful Dumps*,
'The Dean is dead, (*and what is Trumps?*)
Then Lord have Mercy on his Soul.
(Ladies I'll venture for the *Vole*.)
Six Deans they say must bear the Pall.
(I wish I knew what *King* to call.)
Madam, your Husband will attend
The Funeral of so good a Friend.
No Madam, 'tis a shocking Sight,
And he's engag'd To-morrow Night!
My Lady *Club* wou'd take it ill,
If he shou'd fail her at *Quadrill*.
He lov'd the Dean. (*I lead a Heart.*)
But dearest Friends, they say, must part.
His Time was come, he ran his Race;
We hope he's in a better Place.'

Why do we grieve that Friends should dye?
No Loss more easy to supply.
One Year is past; a different Scene;
No further mention of the Dean;
Who now, alas, no more is mist,
Than if he never did exist.
Where's now this Fav'rite of *Apollo?*
Departed; *and his Works must follow:*

Must undergo the common Fate;
His Kind of Wit is out of Date.
Some Country Squire to *Lintot* goes,
Enquires for SWIFT in Verse and Prose:
Says *Lintot*, 'I have heard the Name:
He dy'd a Year ago.' The same.
He searcheth all his Shop in vain;
'Sir you may find them in *Duck-lane*:
I sent them with a Load of Books,
Last *Monday* to the Pastry-cooks.
To fancy they cou'd live a Year!
I find you're but a Stranger here.
The Dean was famous in his Time;
And had a Kind of Knack at Rhyme:
His way of Writing now is past;
The Town hath got a better Taste:
I keep no antiquated Stuff;
But, spick and span I have enough.
Pray, do but give me leave to shew 'em;
Here's *Colley Cibber*'s Birth-day Poem.
This Ode you never yet have seen,
By *Stephen Duck*, upon the Queen.
Then, here's a Letter finely penn'd
Against the *Craftsman* and his Friend;
It clearly shews that all Reflection
On Ministers, is disaffection.
Next, here's Sir *Robert*'s Vindication,
And Mr *Henly's* last Oration:
The Hawkers have not got 'em yet,
Your Honour please to buy a Set?

John Gay

267   *Mr Pope's Welcome from Greece*
            Upon his having finished his translation of Homer's 'Iliad'

Long hast thou, friend! been absent from thy soil,
   Like patient Ithacus at siege of Troy;
I have been witness of thy six years' toil,
   Thy daily labours, and thy night's annoy,
Lost to thy native land, with great turmoil,
   On the wide sea, oft threat'ning to destroy:
Methinks with thee I've trod Sigæan ground,
And heard the shores of Hellespont resound.

Did I not see thee when thou first sett'st sail
   To seek adventures fair in Homer's land?
Did I not see thy sinking spirits fail,
   And wish thy bark had never left the strand?
Ev'n in mid ocean often didst thou quail,
   And oft lift up thy holy eye and hand,
Praying the Virgin dear, and saintly choir,
Back to the port to bring thy bark entire.

Cheer up, my friend, thy dangers now are o'er;
   Methinks – nay, sure the rising coasts appear;
Hark how the guns salute from either shore,
   As thy trim vessel cuts the Thames so fair:
Shouts answ'ring shouts, from Kent and Essex roar,
   And bells break loud thro' every gust of air:
Bonfires do blaze, and bones and cleavers ring,
As at the coming of some mighty king.

Now pass we Gravesend with a friendly wind,
   And Tilbury's white fort, and long Blackwall;
Greenwich, where dwells the friend of human kind,
   More visited than or her park or hall,
Withers the good, and (with him ever join'd)
   Facetious Disney, greet thee first of all:
I see his chimney smoke, and hear him say,
Duke! that's the room for Pope, and that for Gay.

Come in, my friends, here shall ye dine and lie,
   And here shall breakfast, and here dine again;
And sup, and breakfast on, (if ye comply)
   For I have still some dozens of champagne:
His voice still lessens as the ship sails by;
   He waves his hand to bring us back in vain;
For now I see, I see proud London's spires;
Greenwich is lost, and Deptford dock retires.

Oh, what a concourse swarms on yonder key!
   The sky re-echoes with new shouts of joy:
By all this show, I ween, 'tis Lord May'r's day,
   I hear the voice of trumpet and hautboy. –
No, now I see them near – oh, these are they
   Who come in crowds to welcome thee from Troy.
Hail to the bard whom long as lost we mourn'd,
From siege, from battle, and from storm return'd!

Of goodly Dames, and courteous Knights, I view
   The silken petticoat and broider'd vest,
Yea peers and mighty Dukes with ribands blue
   (True blue fair emblem of unstained breast.)

Others I see as noble and more true,
  By no court badge distinguish'd from the rest.
First see I Methwen of sincerest mind
As Arthur grave, yet soft as woman kind.

What lady's that to whom he gently bends?
  Who knows not her? ah! those are Wortley's eyes.
How art thou honour'd number'd with her friends?
  For she distinguishes the good and wise.
The sweet tongu'd Murray near her side attends.
  Now to my heart the glance of Howard flies.
Now Harvey fair of face I mark full well,
With thee youth's youngest daughter, sweet Lepell.

I see two lovely sisters hand in hand,
  The fair hair'd Martha and Teresa brown,
Madge Bellenden the tallest of the land
  And smiling Mary soft and fair as down.
Yonder I see the cheerful Duchess stand
  For friendship, zeal and blithsome humour known.
Whence that loud shout in such a hearty strain?
Why, all the Hamiltons are in her train.

See next the decent Scudamore advance,
  With Winchelsea still meditating song.
With her Miss Howe came there by chance,
  Nor knows with whom or why she comes along.
Far off from these see Santlow fam'd for dance,
  And frolic Bicknell and her sister young,
With other names by me not to be nam'd,
Much lov'd in private, not in public fam'd.

But now behold the female band retire,
  And the shrill music of their voice is still'd:
Methinks I see famed Buckingham admire
  That in Troy's ruin thou had'st not been kill'd,
Sheffield who knows to strike the living lyre
  With hand judicious like thy Homer skill'd.
Bathurst impetuous hastens to the coast
Whom you and I strive who shall love the most.

See generous Burlington, with goodly Bruce,
  (But Bruce comes wafted in a soft sedan)
Dan Prior next, belov'd by every muse,
  And friendly Congreve, unreproachful man!
(Oxford by Cunningham hath sent excuse)
  See hearty Watkins comes with cup and can;
And Lewis, who has never friend forsaken;
And Laughton whisp'ring asks – Is Troy town taken?

Earl Warwick comes, of free and honest mind;
   Bold, gen'rous Craggs, whose heart was ne'er disguis'd:
Ah why, sweet St John, cannot I thee find?
   St John for ev'ry social virtue priz'd. –
Alas! to foreign climates he's confin'd,
   Or else to see thee here I well surmiz'd:
Thou too, my Swift, dost breathe Bœotian air;
When wilt thou bring back wit and humour here?

Harcourt I see for eloquence renown'd,
   The mouth of justice, oracle of law!
Another Simon is beside him found,
   Another Simon, like as straw to straw.
How Lansdowne smiles, with lasting laurel crown'd!
   What mitred prelate there commands our awe?
See Rochester approving nods his head,
And ranks one modern with the mighty dead.

Carlton and Chandos thy arrival grace;
   Hanmer, whose eloquence th' unbiass'd sways;
Harley, whose goodness opens in his face,
   And shews his heart the seat where virtue stays.
Ned Blount advances next, with busy pace,
   In haste, but saunt'ring, hearty in his ways:
I see the friendly Carylls come by dozens,
Their wives, their uncles, daughters, sons, and cousins.

Arbuthnot there I see, in physic's art,
   As Galen learn'd, or famed Hippocrate;
Whose company drives sorrow from the heart,
   As all disease his medicines dissipate:
Kneller amid the triumph bears his part,
   Who could (were mankind lost) a new create:
What can th' extent of his vast soul confine?
A painter, critic, engineer, divine!

Thee Jervas hails, robust and debonair,
   Now have we conquer'd Homer, friends, he cries:
Dartneuf, grave joker, joyous Ford is there,
   And wond'ring Maine, so fat with laughing eyes:
(Gay, Maine, and Cheney, boon companions dear,
   Gay fat, Maine fatter, Cheney huge of size)
Yea Dennis, Gildon, (hearing thou hast riches)
And honest, hatless Cromwell, with red breeches.

O Wanley, whence com'st thou with shorten'd hair,
   And visage from thy shelves with dust besprent?
'Forsooth (quoth he) from placing Homer there,
   For ancients to compyle is myne entente:

Of ancients only hath Lord Harley care;
  But hither me hath my meeke lady sent: –
In manuscript of Greeke rede we thilke same,
But book yprint best plesyth myn gude dame.'

Yonder I see, among th' expecting crowd,
  Evans with laugh jocose, and tragic Young;
High-buskin'd Booth, grave Mawbert, wand'ring Frowd,
  And Titcomb's belly waddles slow along.
See Digby faints at Southern talking loud,
  Yea Steele and Tickell mingle in the throng;
Tickell whose skiff (in partnership they say)
Set forth for Greece, but founder'd in the way.

Lo the two Doncastles in Berkshire known!
  Lo Bickford, Fortescue, of Devon land!
Lo Tooker, Eccleshall, Sykes, Rawlinson:
  See hearty Morley takes thee by the hand.
Ayrs, Grahame, Buckridge joy thy voyage done,
  But who can count the leaves, the stars, the sand.
Lo Stonor, Fenton, Caldwell, Ward, and Broome,
Lo thousands more, but I want rhyme and room.

How lov'd! how honour'd thou! yet be not vain;
  And sure thou art not, for I hear thee say,
All this, my friends, I owe to Homer's strain,
  On whose strong pinions I exalt my lay.
What from contending cities did he gain;
  And what rewards his grateful country pay?
None, none were paid – why then all this for me?
These honours, Homer, had been just to thee.

Alexander Pope

268   From *Epistle to Augustus*

  Of little use the Man you may suppose,
Who says in verse what others say in prose;
Yet let me show, a Poet's of some weight,
And (tho' no Soldier) useful to the State.
What will a Child learn sooner than a Song?
What better teach a Foreigner the tongue?
What's long or short, each accent where to place,
And speak in public with some sort of grace?
I scarce can think him such a worthless thing,
Unless he praise some Monster of a King;

Or Virtue, or Religion turn to sport,
To please a lewd or unbelieving Court.
Unhappy Dryden! – In all Charles's days,
Roscommon only boasts unspotted bays;
And in our own (excuse some Courtly stains)
No whiter page than Addison remains.
He, from the taste obscene reclaims our youth,
And sets the Passions on the side of Truth,
Forms the soft bosom with the gentlest art,
And pours each human Virtue in the heart.
Let Ireland tell, how Wit upheld her cause,
Her Trade supported, and supplied her Laws;
And leave on SWIFT this grateful verse engrav'd:
'The Rights a Court attack'd, a Poet sav'd.'
Behold the hand that wrought a Nation's cure,
Stretch'd to relieve the Idiot and the Poor,
Proud Vice to brand, or injur'd Worth adorn,
And stretch the Ray to Ages yet unborn.
Not but there are, who merit other palms;
Hopkins and Sternhold glad the heart with Psalms:
The Boys and Girls whom charity maintains,
Implore your help in these pathetic strains:
How could Devotion touch the country pews,
Unless the Gods bestow'd a proper Muse?
Verse cheers their leisure, Verse assists their work,
Verse prays for Peace, or sings down Pope and Turk.
The silenc'd Preacher yields to potent strain,
And feels that grace his pray'r besought in vain;
The blessing thrills thro' all the lab'ring throng,
And Heav'n is won by Violence of Song.
  Our rural Ancestors, with little blest,
Patient of labour when the end was rest,
Indulg'd the day that hous'd their annual grain,
With feasts, and off'rings, and a thankful strain:
The joy their wives, their sons, and servants share,
Ease of their toil, and part'ners of their care:
The laugh, the jest, attendants on the bowl,
Smooth'd ev'ry brow, and open'd ev'ry soul:
With growing years the pleasing Licence grew,
And Taunts alternate innocently flew.
But Times corrupt, and Nature, ill-inclin'd,
Produc'd the point that left a sting behind;
Till friend with friend, and families at strife,
Triumphant Malice rag'd thro' private life.
Who felt the wrong, or fear'd it, took th' alarm,
Appeal'd to Law, and Justice lent her arm.
At length, by wholesome dread of statutes bound,
The Poets learn'd to please, and not to wound:

Most warp'd to Flatt'ry's side; but some, more nice,
Preserv'd the freedom, and forbore the vice.
Hence Satire rose, that just the medium hit,
And heals with Morals what it hurts with Wit.
  We conquer'd France, but felt our Captive's charms;
Her Arts victorious triumph'd o'er our Arms;
Britain to soft refinements less a foe,
Wit grew polite, and Numbers learn'd to flow.
Waller was smooth; but Dryden taught to join ⎫
The varying verse, the full-resounding line,   ⎬
The long majestic March, and Energy divine. ⎭
Tho' still some traces of our rustic vein
And splay-foot verse, remain'd, and will remain.
Late, very late, correctness grew our care,
When the tir'd Nation breath'd from civil war.
Exact Racine, and Corneille's noble fire,
Show'd us that France had something to admire.
Not but the Tragic spirit was our own,
And full in Shakespear, fair in Otway shone:
But Otway fail'd to polish or refine,
And fluent Shakespeare scarce effac'd a line.
Ev'n copious Dryden wanted, or forgot,
The last and greatest Art, the Art to blot.
Some doubt, if equal pains, or equal fire
The humbler Muse of Comedy require.
But in known Images of life, I guess
The labour greater, as th' indulgence less.
Observe how seldom ev'n the best succeed:
Tell me if Congreve's Fools are Fools indeed?
What pert, low Dialogue has Farquhar writ!
How Van wants grace, who never wanted wit!
The stage how loosely does Astraea tread,
Who fairly puts all Characters to bed!
And idle Cibber, how he breaks the laws,
To make poor Pinky eat with vast applause!
But fill their purse, our Poet's work is done,
Alike to them, by Pathos or by Pun.
  Oh you! whom Vanity's light bark conveys
On Fame's mad voyage by the wind of praise,
With what a shifting gale your course you ply,
For ever sunk too low, or borne too high!
Who pants for glory finds but short repose,
A breath revives him, or a breath o'erthrows.
Farewell the stage! if just as thrives the play,
The silly bard grows fat, or falls away.

269   From *Epistle to Dr Arbuthnot*

    Why do I write? what sin to me unknown
Dipt me in ink, my parents', or my own?
As yet a child, nor yet a fool to fame,
I lisp'd in numbers, for the numbers came.
I left no calling for this idle trade,
No duty broke, no father disobey'd.
The Muse but serv'd to ease some friend, not Wife,
To help me thro' this long disease, my Life,
To second, ARBUTHNOT! thy Art and Care,
And teach the Being you preserv'd, to bear.
    But why then publish? Granville the polite,
And knowing Walsh, would tell me I could write;
Well-natur'd Garth inflam'd with early praise;
And Congreve lov'd, and Swift endur'd my lays;
The courtly Talbot, Somers, Sheffield read;
Ev'n mitred Rochester would nod the head,
And St John's self (great Dryden's friend before)
With open arms receiv'd one Poet more.
Happy my studies, when by these approv'd!
Happier their author, when by these belov'd!
From these the world will judge of men and books,
Not from the Burnets, Oldmixons, and Cookes.
    Soft were my numbers; who could take offence,
While pure Description held the place of Sense?
Like gentle Fanny's was my flow'ry theme,
A painted mistress, or a purling stream.
Yet then did Gildon draw his venal quill; –
I wish'd the man a dinner, and sat still.
Yet then did Dennis rave in furious fret;
I never answer'd, – I was not in debt.
If want provok'd, or madness made them print,
I wag'd no war with Bedlam or the Mint.
    Did some more sober Critic come abroad;
If wrong, I smil'd; if right, I kiss'd the rod.
Pains, reading, study, are their just pretence,
And all they want is spirit, taste, and sense.
Commas and points they set exactly right,
And 'twere a sin to rob them of their mite.
Yet ne'er one sprig of laurel grac'd these ribalds,
From slashing Bentley down to pidling Tibalds:
Each wight, who reads not, and but scans and spells,
Each Word-catcher, that lives on syllables,
Ev'n such small Critics some regard may claim,
Preserv'd in Milton's or in Shakespeare's name.
Pretty! in amber to observe the forms
Of hairs, or straws, or dirt, or grubs, or worms!

The things, we know, are neither rich nor rare,
But wonder how the devil they got there.
   Were others angry: I excus'd them too;
Well might they rage, I gave them but their due.
A man's true merit 'tis not hard to find;
But each man's secret standard in his mind,
That Casting-weight pride adds to emptiness,
This, who can gratify? for who can guess?
The Bard whom pilfer'd Pastorals renown,
Who turns a Persian tale for half a Crown,
Just writes to make his barrenness appear,
And strains, from hard-bound brains, eight lines a year;
He, who still wanting, tho' he lives on theft,
Steals much, spends little, yet has nothing left:
And He, who now to sense, now nonsense leaning,
Means not, but blunders round about a meaning:
And He, whose fustian's so sublimely bad,
It is not Poetry, but prose run mad:
All these, my modest Satire bade translate,
And own'd that nine such Poets made a Tate.
How did they fume, and stamp, and roar, and chafe!
And swear, not ADDISON himself was safe.
   Peace to all such! but were there One whose fires
True Genius kindles, and fair Fame inspires;
Blest with each talent and each art to please,
And born to write, converse, and live with ease:
Should such a man, too fond to rule alone,
Bear, like the Turk, no brother near the throne,
View him with scornful, yet with jealous eyes,
And hate for arts that caus'd himself to rise;
Damn with faint praise, assent with civil leer,
And without sneering, teach the rest to sneer:
Willing to wound, and yet afraid to strike,
Just hint a fault, and hesitate dislike;
Alike reserv'd to blame, or to commend,
A tim'rous foe, and a suspicious friend;
Dreading ev'n fools, by Flatterers besieg'd,
And so obliging, that he ne'er oblig'd;
Like Cato, give his little Senate laws,
And sit attentive to his own applause;
While Wits and Templars ev'ry sentence raise,
And wonder with a foolish face of praise: —
Who but must laugh, if such a man there be?
Who would not weep, if ATTICUS were he?

270   From *The Rape of the Lock*

Not with more glories, in th' etherial plain,
The Sun first rises o'er the purpled main,
Than, issuing forth, the rival of his beams
Launch'd on the bosom of the silver Thames.
Fair Nymphs, and well-drest Youths around her shone,
But ev'ry eye was fix'd on her alone.
On her white breast a sparkling Cross she wore,
Which Jews might kiss, and Infidels adore.
Her lively looks a sprightly mind disclose,
Quick as her eyes, and as unfix'd as those:
Favours to none, to all she smiles extends;
Oft she rejects, but never once offends.
Bright as the sun, her eyes the gazers strike,
And, like the sun, they shine on all alike.
Yet graceful ease, and sweetness void of pride,
Might hide her faults, if Belles had faults to hide:
If to her share some female errors fall,
Look on her face, and you'll forget 'em all.
    This Nymph, to the destruction of mankind,
Nourish'd two Locks, which graceful hung behind
In equal curls, and well conspir'd to deck
With shining ringlets the smooth iv'ry neck.
Love in these labyrinths his slaves detains,
And mighty hearts are held in slender chains.
With hairy springes we the birds betray,
Slight lines of hair surprise the finny prey,
Fair tresses man's imperial race ensnare,
And beauty draws us with a single hair.
    Th' advent'rous Baron the bright locks admir'd;
He saw, he wish'd, and to the prize aspir'd.
Resolv'd to win, he meditates the way,
By force to ravish, or by fraud betray;
For when success a Lover's toil attends,
Few ask, if fraud or force attain'd his ends.
    For this, ere Phoebus rose, he had implor'd
Propitious heav'n, and ev'ry pow'r ador'd,
But chiefly Love – to Love an Altar built,
Of twelve vast French Romances, neatly gilt.
There lay three garters, half a pair of gloves;
And all the trophies of his former loves;
With tender Billet-doux he lights the pyre,
And breathes three am'rous sighs to raise the fire.
Then prostrate falls, and begs with ardent eyes
Soon to obtain, and long possess the prize:
The pow'rs gave ear, and granted half his pray'r,
The rest, the winds dispers'd in empty air.

But now secure the painted vessel glides,
The sun-beams trembling on the floating tides:
While melting music steals upon the sky,
And soften'd sounds along the waters die;
Smooth flow the waves, the Zephyrs gently play,
Belinda smil'd, and all the world was gay.
All but the Sylph – with careful thoughts opprest,
Th' impending woe sat heavy on his breast.
He summons strait his Denizens of air;
The lucid squadrons round the sails repair:
Soft o'er the shrouds aërial whispers breathe,
That seem'd but Zephyrs to the train beneath.
Some to the sun their insect-wings unfold,
Waft on the breeze, or sink in clouds of gold;
Transparent forms, too fine for mortal sight,
Their fluid bodies half dissolv'd in light,
Loose to the wind their airy garments flew,
Thin glitt'ring textures of the filmy dew,
Dipt in the richest tincture of the skies,
Where light disports in ever-mingling dyes,
While ev'ry beam new transient colours flings,
Colours that change whene'er they wave their wings.
Amid the circle, on the gilded mast,
Superior by the head, was Ariel plac'd;
His purple pinions op'ning to the sun,
He rais'd his azure wand, and thus begun.
    Ye Sylphs and Sylphids, to your chief give ear!
Fays, Fairies, Genii, Elves, and Daemons, hear!
Ye know the spheres and various tasks assign'd
By laws eternal to th' aërial kind.
Some in the fields of purest Aether play,
And bask and whiten in the blaze of day.
Some guide the course of wand'ring orbs on high,
Or roll the planets thro' the boundless sky.
Some less refin'd, beneath the moon's pale light
Pursue the stars that shoot athwart the night,
Or suck the mists in grosser air below,
Or dip their pinions in the painted bow,
Or brew fierce tempests on the wintry main,
Or o'er the glebe distil the kindly rain.
Others on earth o'er human race preside,
Watch all their ways, and all their actions guide:
Of these the chief the care of Nations own,
And guard with Arms divine the British Throne.
    Our humbler province is to tend the Fair,
Not a less pleasing, tho' less glorious care;
To save the powder from too rude a gale,
Nor let th' imprison'd essences exhale;

To draw fresh colours from the vernal flow'rs;
To steal from rainbows e'er they drop in show'rs
A brighter wash; to curl their waving hairs,
Assist their blushes, and inspire their airs;
Nay oft, in dreams, invention we bestow,
To change a Flounce, or add a Furbelow.
   This day, black Omens threat the brightest Fair,
That e'er deserv'd a watchful spirit's care;
Some dire disaster, or by force, or slight;
But what, or where, the fates have wrapt in night.
Whether the nymph shall break Diana's law,
Or some frail China jar receive a flaw;
Or stain her honour or her new brocade;
Forget her pray'rs, or miss a masquerade;
Or lose her heart, or necklace, at a ball;
Or whether Heav'n has doom'd that Shock must fall.
Haste, then, ye spirits! to your charge repair:
The flutt'ring fan be Zephyretta's care;
The drops to thee, Brillante, we consign;
And, Momentilla, let the watch be thine;
Do thou, Crispissa, tend her fav'rite Lock;
Ariel himself shall be the guard of Shock.
   To fifty chosen Sylphs, of special note,
We trust th' important charge, the Petticoat:
Oft have we known that seven-fold fence to fail,
Tho' stiff with hoops, and arm'd with ribs of whale;
Form a strong line about the silver bound,
And guard the wide circumference around.
   Whatever spirit, careless of his charge,
His post neglects, or leaves the fair at large,
Shall feel sharp vengeance soon o'ertake his sins,
Be stopp'd in vials, or transfix'd with pins;
Or plung'd in lakes of bitter washes lie,
Or wedg'd whole ages in a bodkin's eye:
Gums and Pomatums shall his flight restrain,
While clogg'd he beats his silken wings in vain;
Or Alum styptics with contracting pow'r
Shrink his thin essence like a rivell'd flow'r:
Or, as Ixion fix'd, the wretch shall feel
The giddy motion of the whirling Mill,
In fumes of burning Chocolate shall glow,
And tremble at the sea that froths below!
   He spoke; the spirits from the sails descend;
Some, orb in orb, around the nymph extend;
Some thrid the mazy ringlets of her hair;
Some hang upon the pendants of her ear:
With beating hearts the dire event they wait,
Anxious, and trembling for the birth of Fate.

271   *Lines Written in Windsor Forest*

All hail, once pleasing, once inspiring shade!
Scene of my youthful loves and happier hours!
Where the kind Muses met me as I stray'd,
    And gently press'd my hand, and said 'Be ours! –
Take all thou e'er shalt have, a constant Muse:
    At Court thou may'st be liked, but nothing gain:
Stock thou may'st buy and sell, but always lose,
    And love the brightest eyes, but love in vain.'

272   From *The Dunciad*

To Dr Jonathan Swift

    In vain, in vain – the all-composing Hour
Resistless falls: the Muse obeys the Pow'r.
She comes! she comes! the sable Throne behold
Of Night primaeval and of Chaos old!
Before her, Fancy's gilded clouds decay,
And all its varying Rain-bows die away.
Wit shoots in vain its momentary fires,
The meteor drops, and in a flash expires.
As one by one, at dread Medea's strain,
The sick'ning stars fade off th' ethereal plain;
As Argus' eyes by Hermes' wand opprest,
Clos'd one by one to everlasting rest;
Thus at her felt approach, and secret might,
Art after Art goes out, and all is Night.
See skulking Truth to her old cavern fled,
Mountains of Casuistry heap'd o'er her head!
Philosophy, that lean'd on Heav'n before,
Shrinks to her second cause, and is no more.
Physic of Metaphysic begs defence,
And Metaphysic calls for aid on Sense!
See Mystery to Mathematics fly!
In vain! they gaze, turn giddy, rave, and die.
Religion blushing veils her sacred fires,
And unawares Morality expires.
For public Flame, nor private, dares to shine;
Nor human Spark is left, nor Glimpse divine!
Lo! thy dread Empire, CHAOS! is restor'd;
Light dies before thy uncreating word;
Thy hand, great Anarch! lets the curtain fall,
And universal Darkness buries All.

273   *Epistle to Miss Teresa Blount,*
        on Her Leaving the Town after the Coronation

As some fond Virgin, whom her mother's care
Drags from the Town to wholesome Country air,
Just when she learns to roll a melting eye,
And fear a spark, yet think no danger nigh;
From the dear man unwilling she must sever,
Yet takes one kiss before she parts for ever:
Thus from the world fair Zephalinda flew,
Saw others happy, and with sighs withdrew;
Not that their Pleasures caus'd her discontent,
She sigh'd not that they stay'd, but that she went.
    She went, to plain-work, and to purling brooks,
Old fashion'd halls, dull Aunts, and croaking rooks:
She went from Op'ra, Park, Assembly, Play,
To morning-walks, and pray'rs three hours a day;
To part her time 'twixt reading and bohea;
To muse, and spill her solitary tea;
Or o'er cold coffee trifle with the spoon,
Count the slow clock, and dine exact at noon;
Divert her eyes with pictures in the fire,
Hum half a tune, tell stories to the squire;
Up to her godly garret after sev'n,
There starve and pray, for that's the way to heav'n.
    Some Squire, perhaps you take delight to rack;
Whose game is Whisk, whose treat a toast in sack;
Who visits with a Gun, presents you birds,
Then gives a smacking buss, and cries, – 'No words!'
Or with his hound comes hollowing from the stable,
Makes love with nods, and knees beneath a table;
Whose laughs are hearty, tho' his jests are coarse,
And loves you best of all things – but his horse.
    In some fair ev'ning, on your elbow laid,
You dream of Triumphs in the rural shade;
In pensive thought recall the fancy'd scene,
See Coronations rise on ev'ry green;
Before you pass th' imaginary sights
Of Lords, and Earls, and Dukes, and garter'd Knights,
While the spread fan o'ershades your closing eyes;
Then give one flirt, and all the vision flies.
Thus vanish sceptres, coronets, and balls,
And leave you in lone woods, or empty walls!
    So when your Slave, at some dear idle time,
(Not plagu'd with head-achs, or the want of rhyme)
Stands in the streets, abstracted from the crew,
And while he seems to study, thinks of you;

Just when his fancy points your sprightly eyes,
Or sees the blush of soft Parthenia rise,
Gay pats my shoulder, and you vanish quite,
Streets, Chairs, and Coxcombs, rush upon my sight;
Vex'd to be still in town, I knit my brow,
Look sour, and hum a Tune, as you may now.

Philip Stanhope, Earl of Chesterfield

274   *Verses Written in a Lady's*
           *Sherlock upon Death**

Mistaken fair, lay Sherlock by,
    His doctrine is deceiving;
For whilst he teaches us to die,
    He cheats us of our living.

To die's a lesson we shall know
    Too soon without a master;
Then let us only study now
    How we may live the faster.

To live's to love, to bless, be bless'd
    With mutual inclination;
Share then my ardour in your breast,
And kindly meet my passion.

But if thus bless'd I may not live,
    And pity you deny,
To me at least your Sherlock give;
    'Tis I must learn to die.

* William Sherlock's *Discourse Concerning Death*, 1689

James Thomson

The Seasons

275

[1]

From *Summer*

'Tis raging noon; and, vertical, the sun
Darts on the head direct his forceful rays.
O'er heaven and earth, far as the ranging eye
Can sweep, a dazzling deluge reigns; and all
From pole to pole is undistinguish'd blaze.
In vain the sight dejected to the ground
Stoops for relief; thence hot ascending steams
And keen reflection pain. Deep to the root
Of vegetation parch'd, the cleaving fields
And slippery lawn an arid hue disclose,
Blast fancy's blooms, and wither even the soul.
Echo no more returns the cheerful sound
Of sharpening scythe: the mower, sinking, heaps
O'er him the humid hay, with flowers perfum'd;
And scarce a chirping grasshopper is heard
Through the dumb mead. Distressful nature pants.
The very streams look languid from afar,
Or, through the unshelter'd glade, impatient seem
To hurl into the covert of the grove.
   All-conquering heat, oh, intermit thy wrath!
And on my throbbing temples potent thus
Beam not so fierce! Incessant still you flow,
And still another fervent flood succeeds,
Poured on the head profuse. In vain I sigh,
And restless turn, and look around for night:
Night is far off; and hotter hours approach.
Thrice happy he, who on the sunless side
Of a romantic mountain, forest-crown'd,
Beneath the whole collected shade reclines;
Or in the gelid caverns, woodbine-wrought
And fresh bedew'd with ever-spouting streams,
Sits coolly calm; while all the world without,
Unsatisfied and sick, tosses in noon.
Emblem instructive of the virtuous man,
Who keeps his temper'd mind serene and pure,
And every passion aptly harmoniz'd
Amid a jarring world with vice inflam'd.
   Welcome, ye shades! ye bowery thickets, hail!
Ye lofty pines! ye venerable oaks!
Ye ashes wild, resounding o'er the steep!

Delicious is your shelter to the soul
As to the hunted hart the sallying spring
Or stream full-flowing, that his swelling sides
Laves as he floats along the herbag'd brink.
Cool through the nerves your pleasing comfort glides;
The heart beats glad; the fresh-expanded eye
And ear resume their watch; the sinews knit;
And life shoots swift through all the lighten'd limbs.
    Around the adjoining brook, that purls along
The vocal grove, now fretting o'er a rock,
Now scarcely moving through a reedy pool,
Now starting to a sudden stream, and now
Gently diffus'd into a limpid plain,
A various group the herds and flocks compose,
Rural confusion! On the grassy bank
Some ruminating lie, while others stand
Half in the flood and, often bending, sip
The circling surface. In the middle droops
The strong laborious ox, of honest front,
Which incompos'd he shakes; and from his sides
The troublous insects lashes with his tail,
Returning still. Amid his subjects safe
Slumbers the monarch-swain, his careless arm
Thrown round his head on downy moss sustain'd;
Here laid his scrip with wholesome viands fill'd,
There, listening every noise, his watchful dog.
    Light fly his slumbers, if perchance a flight
Of angry gad-flies fasten on the herd,
That startling scatters from the shallow brook
In search of lavish stream. Tossing the foam,
They scorn the keeper's voice, and scour the plain
Through all the bright severity of noon;
While from their labouring breasts a hollow moan
Proceeding runs low-bellowing round the hills.
    Oft in this season too, the horse, provok'd,
While his big sinews full of spirits swell,
Trembling with vigour, in the heat of blood
Springs the high fence, and, o'er the field effus'd,
Darts on the gloomy flood with steadfast eye
And heart estrang'd to fear: his nervous chest,
Luxuriant and erect, the seat of strength,
Bears down the opposing stream; quenchless his thirst,
He takes the river at redoubl'd draughts,
And with wide nostrils, snorting, skims the wave.
    Still let me pierce into the midnight depth
Of yonder grove, of wildest largest growth,
That, forming high in air a woodland quire,
Nods o'er the mount beneath. At every step,
Solemn and slow the shadows blacker fall,
And all is awful listening gloom around.

These are the haunts of meditation, these
The scenes where ancient bards the inspiring breath
Ecstatic felt, and, from this world retir'd,
Convers'd with angels and immortal forms,
On gracious errands bent – to save the fall
Of virtue struggling on the brink of vice;
In waking whispers and repeated dreams
To hint pure thought, and warn the favour'd soul,
For future trials fated, to prepare;
To prompt the poet, who devoted gives
His muse to better themes; to soothe the pangs
Of dying worth, and from the patriot's breast
(Backward to mingle in detested war,
But foremost when engag'd) to turn the death;
And numberless such offices of love,
Daily and nightly, zealous to perform.

276   [2]

From *Winter*

The keener tempests come: and, fuming dun
From all the livid east or piercing north,
Thick clouds ascend, in whose capacious womb
A vapoury deluge lies, to snow congeal'd.
Heavy they roll their fleecy world along,
And the sky saddens with the gather'd storm.
Through the hush'd air the whitening shower descends,
At first thin-wavering; till at last the flakes
Fall broad and wide and fast, dimming the day
With a continual flow. The cherish'd fields
Put on their winter-robe of purest white.
'Tis brightness all; save where the new snow melts
Along the mazy current. Low the woods
Bow their hoar head; and, ere the languid sun
Faint from the west emits his evening ray,
Earth's universal face, deep-hid and chill,
Is one wild dazzling waste, that buries wide
The works of man. Drooping, the labourer-ox
Stands covered o'er with snow, and then demands
The fruit of all his toil. The fowls of heaven,
Tam'd by the cruel season, crowd around
The winnowing store, and claim the little boon
Which Providence assigns them. One alone,
The redbreast, sacred to the household gods,
Wisely regardful of the embroiling sky,

In joyless fields and thorny thickets leaves
His shivering mates, and pays to trusted man
His annual visit. Half afraid, he first
Against the window beats; then brisk alights
On the warm hearth; then, hopping o'er the floor,
Eyes all the smiling family askance,
And pecks, and starts, and wonders where he is –
Till, more familiar grown, the table-crumbs
Attract his slender feet. The foodless wilds
Pour forth their brown inhabitants. The hare,
Though timorous of heart, and hard beset
·By death in various forms, dark snares, and dogs,
And more unpitying men, the garden seeks,
Urg'd on by fearless want. The bleating kind
Eye the bleak heaven, and next the glistening earth,
With looks of dumb despair; then, sad-dispers'd,
Dig for the wither'd herb through heaps of snow.
    Now, shepherds, to your helpless charge be kind:
Baffle the raging year, and fill their pens
With food at will; lodge them below the storm,
And watch them strict: for, from the bellowing east,
In this dire season, oft the whirlwind's wing
Sweeps up the burden of whole wintry plains
In one wide waft, and o'er the hapless flocks,
Hid in the hollow of two neighbouring hills,
The billowy tempest whelms; till, upward urg'd,
The valley to a shining mountain swells,
Tipt with a wreath high-curling in the sky.
    As thus the snows arise, and, foul and fierce,
All Winter drives along the darken'd air,
In his own loose-revolving fields the swain
Disastered stands; sees other hills ascend,
Of unknown joyless brow; and other scenes,
Of horrid prospect, shag the trackless plain;
Nor finds the river nor the forest, hid
Beneath the formless wild; but wanders on
From hill to dale, still more and more astray –
Impatient flouncing through the drifted heaps,
Stung with the thoughts of home: the thoughts of home
Rush on his nerves and call their vigour forth
In many a vain attempt. How sinks his soul!
What black despair, what horror fills his heart,
When, for the dusky spot which fancy feign'd
His tufted cottage rising through the snow,
He meets the roughness of the middle waste,
Far from the track and blest abode of man;
While round him night resistless closes fast,
And every tempest, howling o'er his head,
Renders the savage wilderness more wild.

Then throng the busy shapes into his mind
Of covered pits, unfathomably deep,
A dire descent! beyond the power of frost;
Of faithless bogs; of precipices huge,
Smooth'd up with snow; and (what is land unknown,
What water) of the still unfrozen spring,
In the loose marsh or solitary lake,
Where the fresh fountain from the bottom boils.
These check his fearful steps; and down he sinks
Beneath the shelter of the shapeless drift,
Thinking o'er all the bitterness of death,
Mix'd with the tender anguish nature shoots
Through the wrung bosom of the dying man –
His wife, his children, and his friends unseen.
In vain for him the officious wife prepares
The fire fair-blazing and the vestment warm;
In vain his little children, peeping out
Into the mingling storm, demand their sire
With tears of artless innocence. Alas!
Nor wife nor children more shall he behold,
Nor friends, nor sacred home. On every nerve
The deadly Winter seizes, shuts up sense,
And, o'er his inmost vitals creeping cold,
Lays him along the snows a stiffen'd corse,
Stretch'd out, and bleaching in the northern blast.

Samuel Johnson

277   *Prologue Spoken by Mr Garrick*
at the Opening of the Theatre
in Drury-Lane, 1747

When Learning's Triumph o'er her barb'rous Foes
First rear'd the Stage, immortal Shakespear rose;
Each Change of many-colour'd Life he drew,
Exhausted Worlds, and then imagin'd new:
Existence saw him spurn her bounded Reign,
And panting Time toil'd after him in vain:
His pow'rful Strokes presiding Truth impress'd,
And unresisted Passion storm'd the Breast.
   Then Johnson came, instructed from the School,
To please in Method, and invent by Rule;
His studious Patience, and laborious Art,
By regular Approach essay'd the Heart;

Cold Approbation gave the ling'ring Bays,
For those who durst not censure, scarce cou'd praise.
A Mortal born he met the general Doom,
But left, like *Egypt's* Kings, a lasting Tomb.
   The Wits of *Charles* found easier Ways to Fame,
Nor wish'd for Johnson's Art, or Shakespear's Flame;
Themselves they studied, as they felt, they writ,
Intrigue was Plot, Obscenity was Wit.
Vice always found a sympathetick Friend;
They pleas'd their Age, and did not aim to mend.
Yet Bards like these aspir'd to lasting Praise,
And proudly hop'd to pimp in future Days.
Their Cause was gen'ral, their Supports were strong,
Their Slaves were willing, and their Reign was long;
Till Shame regain'd the Post that Sense betray'd,
And Virtue call'd Oblivion to her Aid.
   Then crush'd by Rules, and weaken'd as refin'd,
For Years the Pow'r of Tragedy declin'd;
From Bard, to Bard, the frigid Caution crept,
Till Declamation roar'd, while Passion slept.
Yet still did Virtue deign the Stage to tread,
Philosophy remain'd, though Nature fled.
But forc'd at length her antient Reign to quit,
She saw great *Faustus* lay the Ghost of Wit:
Exulting Folly hail'd the joyful Day,
And Pantomime, and Song, confirm'd her Sway.
   But who the coming Changes can presage,
And mark the future Periods of the Stage? –
Perhaps if Skill could distant Times explore,
New *Behns*, new *Durfeys*, yet remain in Store.
Perhaps, where *Lear* has rav'd, and *Hamlet* dy'd,
On flying Cars new Sorcerers may ride.
Perhaps, for who can guess th' Effects of Chance?
Here *Hunt* may box, or *Mahomet* may dance.
   Hard is his lot, that here by Fortune plac'd,
Must watch the wild Vicissitudes of Taste;
With ev'ry Meteor of Caprice must play,
And chase the new-blown Bubbles of the Day.
Ah! let not Censure term our Fate our Choice,
The Stage but echoes back the publick Voice.
The Drama's Laws the Drama's Patrons give,
For we that live to please, must please to live.
   Then prompt no more the Follies you decry,
As Tyrants doom their Tools of Guilt to die;
'Tis yours this Night to bid the Reign commence
Of rescu'd Nature, and reviving Sense;
To chase the Charms of Sound, the Pomp of Show,
For useful Mirth, and salutary Woe;
Bid scenic Virtue form the rising Age,
And Truth diffuse her Radiance from the Stage.

278   *The Vanity of Human Wishes*
           The Tenth Satire of Juvenal, Imitated

Let Observation with extensive View,
Survey Mankind, from *China* to *Peru*;
Remark each anxious Toil, each eager Strife,
And watch the busy Scenes of crouded Life;
Then say how Hope and Fear, Desire and Hate,
O'erspread with Snares the clouded Maze of Fate,
Where wav'ring Man, betray'd by vent'rous Pride,
To tread the dreary Paths without a Guide;
As treach'rous Phantoms in the Mist delude,
Shuns fancied Ills, or chases airy Good.
How rarely Reason guides the stubborn Choice,
Rules the bold Hand, or prompts the suppliant Voice,
How Nations sink, by darling Schemes oppress'd,
When Vengeance listens to the Fool's Request.
Fate wings with ev'ry Wish th' afflictive Dart,
Each Gift of Nature, and each Grace of Art,
With fatal Heat impetuous Courage glows,
With fatal Sweetness Elocution flows,
Impeachment stops the Speaker's pow'rful Breath,
And restless Fire precipitates on Death.
   But scarce observ'd the Knowing and the Bold,
Fall in the gen'ral Massacre of Gold;
Wide-wasting Pest! that rages unconfin'd,
And crouds with Crimes the Records of Mankind,
For Gold his Sword the Hireling Ruffian draws,
For Gold the hireling Judge distorts the Laws;
Wealth heap'd on Wealth, nor Truth nor Safety buys,
The Dangers gather as the Treasures rise.
   Let Hist'ry tell where rival Kings command,
And dubious Title shakes the madded Land,
When Statutes glean the Refuse of the Sword,
How much more safe the Vassal than the Lord,
Low sculks the Hind beneath the Rage of Pow'r,
And leaves the wealthy Traytor in the *Tow'r*,
Untouch'd his Cottage, and his Slumbers sound,
Tho' Confiscation's Vulturs hover round.
   The needy Traveller, serene and gay,
Walks the wild Heath, and sings his Toil away.
Does Envy seize thee? crush th' upbraiding Joy,
Increase his Riches and his Peace destroy,
Now Fears in dire Vicissitude invade,
The rustling Brake alarms, and quiv'ring Shade,
Nor Light nor Darkness bring his Pain Relief,
One shews the Plunder, and one hides the Thief.
   Yet still one gen'ral Cry the Skies assails,
And Gain and Grandeur load the tainted Gales;

Few know the toiling Statesman's Fear or Care,
Th' insidious Rival and the gaping Heir.
    Once more, *Democritus*, arise on Earth,
With chearful Wisdom and instructive Mirth,
See motly Life in modern Trappings dress'd,
And feed with varied Fools th' eternal Jest:
Thou who couldst laugh where Want enchain'd Caprice,
Toil crush'd Conceit, and Man was of a Piece;
Where Wealth unlov'd without a Mourner dy'd;
And scarce a Sycophant was fed by Pride;
Where ne'er was known the Form of mock Debate,
Or seen a new-made Mayor's unwieldly State;
Where Change of Fav'rites made no Change of Laws,
And Senates heard before they judg'd a Cause;
How wouldst thou shake at *Britain*'s modish Tribe,
Dart the quick Taunt, and edge the piercing Gibe?
Attentive Truth and Nature to descry,
And pierce each Scene with Philosophic Eye.
To thee were solemn Toys or empty Shew,
The Robes of Pleasure and the Veils of Woe:
All aid the Farce, and all thy Mirth maintain,
Whose Joys are causeless, or whose Griefs are vain.
    Such was the Scorn that fill'd the Sage's Mind,
Renew'd at ev'ry Glance on Humankind;
How just that Scorn ere yet thy Voice declare,
Search every State, and canvass ev'ry Pray'r.
    Unnumber'd Suppliants croud Preferment's Gate,
Athirst for Wealth, and burning to be great;
Delusive Fortune hears th' incessant Call,
They mount, they shine, evaporate, and fall.
On ev'ry Stage the Foes of Peace attend,
Hate dogs their Flight, and Insult mocks their End.
Love ends with Hope, the sinking Statesman's Door
Pours in the Morning Worshiper no more;
For growing Names the weekly Scribbler lies,
To growing Wealth the Dedicator flies,
From every Room descends the painted Face,
That hung the bright *Palladium* of the Place,
And smoak'd in Kitchens, or in Auctions sold,
To better Features yields the Frame of Gold;
For now no more we trace in ev'ry Line
Heroic Worth, Benevolence Divine:
The Form distorted justifies the Fall,
And Detestation rids th' indignant Wall.
    But will not *Britain* hear the last Appeal,
Sign her Foes Doom, or guard her Fav'rites Zeal;
Through Freedom's Sons no more Remonstrance rings,
Degrading Nobles and controuling Kings;

Our supple Tribes repress their Patriot Throats,
And ask no Questions but the Price of Votes;
With Weekly Libels and Septennial Ale,
Their Wish is full to riot and to rail.
    In full-blown Dignity, see *Wolsey* stand,
Law in his Voice, and Fortune in his Hand:
To him the Church, the Realm, their Pow'rs consign,
Thro' him the Rays of regal Bounty shine,
Turn'd by his Nod the Stream of Honour flows,
His Smile alone Security bestows:
Still to new Heights his restless Wishes tow'r,
Claim leads to Claim, and Pow'r advances Pow'r;
Till Conquest unresisted ceas'd to please,
And Rights submitted, left him none to seize.
At length his Sov'reign frowns – the Train of State
Mark the keen Glance, and watch the Sign to hate;
Where-e'er he turns he meets a Stranger's Eye,
His Suppliants scorn him, and his Followers fly;
Now drops at once the Pride of aweful State,
The golden Canopy, the glitt'ring Plate,
The regal Palace, the luxurious Board,
The liv'ried Army, and the menial Lord.
With Age, with Cares, with Maladies oppress'd,
He seeks the Refuge of Monastic Rest.
Grief aids Disease, remember'd Folly stings,
And his last Sighs reproach the Faith of Kings.
    Speak thou, whose Thoughts at humble Peace repine,
Shall *Wolsey's* Wealth, with *Wolsey's* End be thine?
Or liv'st thou now, with safer Pride content,
The wisest Justice on the Banks of *Trent*?
For why did *Wolsey* near the Steeps of Fate,
On weak Foundations raise th' enormous Weight?
Why but to sink beneath Misfortune's Blow,
With louder Ruin to the Gulphs below?
    What gave great *Villiers* to th' Assassin's Knife,
And fix'd Disease on *Harley's* closing Life?
What murder'd *Wentworth*, and what exil'd *Hyde*,
By Kings protected, and to Kings ally'd?
What but their Wish indulg'd in Courts to shine,
And Pow'r too great to keep or to resign?
    When first the College Rolls receive his Name,
The young Enthusiast quits his Ease for Fame;
Through all his Veins the Fever of Renown
Burns from the strong Contagion of the Gown;
O'er *Bodley's* Dome his future Labours spread,
And *Bacon's* Mansion trembles o'er his Head.
Are these thy Views? proceed, illustrious Youth,
And Virtue guard thee to the Throne of Truth!

Yet should thy Soul indulge the gen'rous Heat,
Till captive Science yields her last Retreat;
Should Reason guide thee with her brightest Ray,
And pour on misty Doubt resistless Day;
Should no false Kindness lure to loose Delight,
Nor Praise relax, nor Difficulty fright;
Should tempting Novelty thy Cell refrain,
And Sloth effuse her opiate Fumes in vain;
Should Beauty blunt on Fops her fatal Dart,
Nor claim the Triumph of a letter'd Heart;
Should no Disease thy torpid Veins invade,
Nor Melancholy's Phantoms haunt thy Shade;
Yet hope not Life from Grief or Danger free,
Nor think the Doom of Man revers'd for thee:
Deign on the passing World to turn thine Eyes,
And pause awhile from Letters, to be wise;
There mark what Ills the Scholar's Life assail,
Toil, Envy, Want, the Patron, and the Jail.
See Nations slowly wise, and meanly just,
To buried Merit raise the tardy Bust.
If Dreams yet flatter, once again attend,
Hear *Lydiat*'s life, and *Galileo*'s end.
    Nor deem, when Learning her last Prize bestows
The glitt'ring Eminence exempt from Foes;
See when the Vulgar 'scape, despis'd or aw'd,
Rebellion's vengeful Talons seize on *Laud*.
From meaner Minds, tho' smaller Fines content
The plunder'd Palace or sequester'd Rent;
Mark'd out by dangerous Parts he meets the Shock,
And fatal Learning leads him to the Block:
Around his Tomb let Art and Genius weep,
But hear his Death, ye Blockheads, hear and sleep.
    The festal Blazes, the triumphal Show,
The ravish'd Standard, and the captive Foe,
The Senate's Thanks, the Gazette's pompous Tale,
With Force resistless o'er the Brave prevail.
Such Bribes the rapid *Greek* o'er *Asia* whirl'd,
For such the steady *Romans* shook the World;
For such in distant Lands the *Britons* shine,
And stain with Blood the *Danube* or the *Rhine*;
This Pow'r has Praise, that Virtue scarce can warm,
Till Fame supplies the universal Charm.
Yet Reason frowns on War's unequal Game,
Where wasted Nations raise a single Name,
And mortgag'd States their Grandsires Wreaths regret,
From Age to Age in everlasting Debt;
Wreaths which at last the dear-bought Right convey
To rust on Medals, or on Stones decay.

On what Foundation stands the Warrior's Pride,
How just his Hopes let *Swedish Charles* decide;
A Frame of Adamant, a Soul of Fire,
No Dangers fright him, and no Labours tire;
O'er Love, o'er Fear extends his wide Domain,
Unconquer'd Lord of Pleasure and of Pain;
No Joys to him pacific Scepters yield,
War sounds the Trump, he rushes to the Field;
Behold surrounding Kings their Pow'rs combine,
And One capitulate, and One resign;
Peace courts his Hand, but spreads her Charms in vain;
'Think Nothing gain'd,' he cries, 'till nought remain,
On *Moscow*'s Walls till *Gothic* Standards fly,
And All be mine beneath the Polar Sky.'
The March begins in Military State,
And Nations on his Eye suspended wait;
Stern Famine guards the solitary Coast,
And Winter barricades the Realms of Frost;
He comes, nor Want nor Cold his Course delay; –
Hide, blushing Glory, hide *Pultowa*'s Day:
The vanquish'd Hero leaves his broken Bands,
And shews his Miseries in distant Lands;
Condemn'd a needy Supplicant to wait,
While Ladies interpose, and Slaves debate.
But did not Chance at length her Error mend?
Did no subverted Empire mark his End?
Did rival Monarchs give the fatal Wound?
Or hostile Millions press him to the Ground?
His Fall was destin'd to a barren Strand,
A petty Fortress, and a dubious Hand;
He left the Name, at which the World grew pale,
To point a Moral, or adorn a Tale.
    All Times their Scenes of pompous Woes afford,
From *Persia*'s Tyrant to *Bavaria*'s Lord.
In gay Hostility, and barb'rous Pride,
With half Mankind embattled at his Side,
Great *Xerxes* comes to seize the certain Prey,
And starves exhausted Regions in his Way;
Attendant Flatt'ry counts his Myriads o'er,
Till counted Myriads sooth his Pride no more;
Fresh Praise is try'd till Madness fires his Mind,
The Waves he lashes, and enchains the Wind;
New Pow'rs are claim'd, new Pow'rs are still bestow'd,
Till rude Resistance lops the spreading God;
The daring *Greeks* deride the Martial Shew,
And heap their Vallies with the gaudy Foe;
Th' insulted Sea with humbler Thoughts he gains,
A single Skiff to speed his Flight remains;

Th' incumber'd Oar scarce leaves the dreaded Coast
Through purple Billows and a floating Host.
   The bold *Bavarian*, in a luckless Hour,
Tries the dread Summits of *Cesarean* Pow'r,
With unexpected Legions bursts away,
And sees defenceless Realms receive his Sway;
Short Sway! fair *Austria* spreads her mournful Charms,
The Queen, the Beauty, sets the World in Arms;
From Hill to Hill the Beacons rousing Blaze
Spreads wide the Hope of Plunder and of Praise;
The fierce *Croatian*, and the wild *Hussar*,
With all the Sons of Ravage croud the War;
The baffled Prince in Honour's flatt'ring Bloom
Of hasty Greatness finds the fatal Doom,
His Foes Derision, and his Subjects Blame,
And steals to Death from Anguish and from Shame.
   Enlarge my Life with Multitude of Days,
In Health, in Sickness, thus the Suppliant prays;
Hides from himself his State, and shuns to know,
That Life protracted is protracted Woe.
Time hovers o'er, impatient to destroy,
And shuts up all the Passages of Joy:
In vain their Gifts the bounteous Seasons pour,
The Fruit Autumnal, and the Vernal Flow'r,
With listless Eyes the Dotard views the Store,
He views, and wonders that they please no more;
Now pall the tastless Meats, and joyless Wines,
And Luxury with Sighs her Slave resigns.
Approach, ye Minstrels, try the soothing Strain,
Diffuse the tuneful Lenitives of Pain:
No Sounds alas would touch th' impervious Ear,
Though dancing Mountains witness'd *Orpheus* near;
Nor Lute nor Lyre his feeble Pow'rs attend,
Nor sweeter Musick of a virtuous Friend,
But everlasting Dictates croud his Tongue,
Perversely grave, or positively wrong.
The still returning Tale, and ling'ring Jest,
Perplex the fawning Niece and pamper'd Guest,
While growing Hopes scarce awe the gath'ring Sneer,
And scarce a Legacy can bribe to hear;
The watchful Guests still hint the last Offence,
The Daughter's Petulance, the Son's Expence,
Improve his heady Rage with treach'rous Skill,
And mould his Passions till they make his Will.
   Unnumber'd Maladies his Joints invade,
Lay Siege to Life and press the dire Blockade;
But unextinguish'd Av'rice still remains,
And dreaded Losses aggravate his Pains;

He turns, with anxious Heart and cripled Hands,
His Bonds of Debt, and Mortgages of Lands;
Or views his Coffers with suspicious Eyes,
Unlocks his Gold, and counts it till he dies.
   But grant, the Virtues of a temp'rate Prime
Bless with an Age exempt from Scorn or Crime;
An Age that melts with unperceiv'd Decay,
And glides in modest Innocence away;
Whose peaceful Day Benevolence endears,
Whose Night congratulating Conscience cheers;
The gen'ral Fav'rite as the gen'ral Friend:
Such Age there is, and who shall wish its End?
   Yet ev'n on this her Load Misfortune flings,
To press the weary Minutes flagging Wings:
New Sorrow rises as the Day returns,
A Sister sickens, or a Daughter mourns.
Now Kindred Merit fills the sable Bier,
Now lacerated Friendship claims a Tear.
Year chases Year, Decay pursues Decay,
Still drops some Joy from with'ring Life away;
New Forms arise, and diff'rent Views engage,
Superfluous lags the Vet'ran on the Stage,
Till pitying Nature signs the last Release,
And bids afflicted Worth retire to Peace.
   But few there are whom Hours like these await,
Who set unclouded in the Gulphs of Fate.
From *Lydia*'s Monarch should the Search descend,
By *Solon* caution'd to regard his End,
In Life's last Scene what Prodigies surprise,
Fears of the Brave, and Follies of the Wise?
From *Marlb'rough*'s Eyes the Streams of Dotage flow,
And *Swift* expires a Driv'ler and a Show.
   The teeming Mother, anxious for her Race,
Begs for each Birth the Fortune of a Face:
Yet *Vane* could tell what Ills from Beauty spring;
And *Sedley* curs'd the Form that pleas'd a King.
Ye Nymphs of rosy Lips and radiant Eyes,
Whom Pleasure keeps too busy to be wise,
Whom Joys with soft Varieties invite,
By Day the Frolick, and the Dance by Night,
Who frown with Vanity, who smile with Art,
And ask the latest Fashion of the Heart,
What Care, what Rules your heedless Charms shall save,
Each Nymph your Rival, and each Youth your Slave?
Against your Fame with Fondness Hate combines,
The Rival batters, and the Lover mines.
With distant Voice neglected Virtue calls,
Less heard and less, the faint Remonstrance falls;

Tir'd with Contempt, she quits the slipp'ry Reign,
And Pride and Prudence take her Seat in vain.
In croud at once, where none the Pass defend,
The harmless Freedom, and the private Friend.
The Guardians yield, by Force superior ply'd;
To Int'rest, Prudence; and to Flatt'ry, Pride.
Here Beauty falls betray'd, despis'd, distress'd,
And hissing Infamy proclaims the rest.
　Where then shall Hope and Fear their Objects find?
Must dull Suspence corrupt the stagnant Mind?
Must helpless Man, in Ignorance sedate,
Roll darkling down the Torrent of his Fate?
Must no Dislike alarm, no Wishes rise,
Nor Cries invoke the Mercies of the Skies?
Enquirer, cease, Petitions yet remain,
Which Heav'n may hear, nor deem Religion vain.
Still raise for Good the supplicating Voice,
But leave to Heav'n the Measure and the Choice.
Safe in his Pow'r, whose Eyes discern afar
The secret Ambush of a specious Pray'r.
Implore his Aid, in his Decisions rest,
Secure whate'er he gives, he gives the best.
Yet when the Sense of sacred Presence fires,
And Strong Devotion to the Skies aspires,
Pour forth thy Fervours for a healthful Mind,
Obedient Passions, and a Will resign'd;
For Love, which scarce collective Man can fill;
For Patience sov'reign o'er transmuted Ill;
For Faith, that panting for a happier Seat,
Counts Death kind Nature's Signal of Retreat:
These Goods for Man the Laws of Heav'n ordain,
These Goods he grants, who grants the Pow'r to gain;
With these celestial Wisdom calms the Mind,
And makes the Happiness she does not find.

279　　　　　*Epitaph on William Hogarth*

The Hand of Art here torpid lies
　That wav'd th' essential Form of Grace,
Here death has clos'd the curious eyes
　That saw the manners in the face.
If Genius warm thee, Reader, stay,
　If Merit touch thee, shed a tear,
Be Vice and Dulness far away
　Great Hogarth's honour'd Dust is here.

280   *Burlesque Translation of Lines from*
           Lope de Vega's 'Arcadia'

> If the Man who Turneps cries
> Cry not when his Father dies;
> 'Tis a Sign that he had rather
> Have a Turnep than a Father.

281   *Prologue to Hugh Kelly's 'A Word to the Wise'*

> This night presents a play, which publick rage,
> Or right, or wrong, once hooted from the stage;
> From zeal or malice now no more we dread,
> For English vengeance *wars not with the dead.*
> A generous foe regards, with pitying eye,
> The man whom fate has laid, where all must lye.
> To wit, reviving from its author's dust,
> Be kind, ye judges, or at least be just:
> Let no resentful petulance invade
> Th' oblivious grave's inviolable shade.
> Let one great payment every claim appease,
> And him who cannot hurt, allow to please;
> To please by scenes unconscious of offence,
> By harmless merriment, or useful sense.
> Where aught of bright, or fair, the piece displays,
> Approve it only – 'tis too late to praise.
> If want of skill, or want of care appear,
> Forbear to hiss – the Poet cannot hear.
> By all, like him, must praise and blame be found;
> At best, a fleeting gleam, or empty sound.
> Yet then shall calm reflection bless the night,
> When liberal pity dignify'd delight;
> When pleasure fired her torch at Virtue's flame,
> And mirth was bounty with a humbler name.

282   *A Short Song of Congratulation*

> Long-expected one and twenty
> Ling'ring year at last is flown,
> Pomp and Pleasure, Pride and Plenty
> Great Sir John, are all your own.

Loosen'd from the Minor's tether,
Free to mortgage or to sell,
Wild as wind, and light as feather
Bid the slaves of thrift farewel.

Call the Bettys, Kates, and Jennys
Ev'ry name that laughs at Care,
Lavish of your Grandsire's guineas,
Show the Spirit of an heir.

All that prey on vice and folly
Joy to see their quarry fly,
Here the Gamester light and jolly,
There the Lender grave and sly.

Wealth, Sir John, was made to wander,
Let it wander as it will;
See the Jocky, see the Pander,
Bid them come, and take their fill.

When the bonny Blade carouses,
Pockets full, and Spirits high,
What are acres? what are houses?
Only dirt, or wet or dry.

If the Guardian or the Mother
Tell the woes of wilful waste,
Scorn their counsel and their pother,
You can hang or drown at last.

283   *On the Death of Dr Robert Levet*

Condemn'd to hope's delusive mine,
    As on we toil from day to day,
By sudden blasts, or slow decline,
    Our social comforts drop away.

Well tried through many a varying year,
    See LEVET to the grave descend;
Officious, innocent, sincere,
    Of ev'ry friendless name the friend.

Yet still he fills affection's eye,
    Obscurely wise, and coarsely kind;
Nor, letter'd arrogance, deny
    Thy praise to merit unrefin'd.

When fainting nature call'd for aid,
  And hov'ring death prepar'd the blow,
His vig'rous remedy display'd
  The power of art without the show.

In misery's darkest caverns known,
  His useful care was ever nigh,
Where hopeless anguish pour'd his groan,
  And lonely want retir'd to die.

No summons mock'd by chill delay,
  No petty gain disdain'd by pride,
The modest wants of ev'ry day
  The toil of ev'ry day supplied.

His virtues walk'd their narrow round,
  Nor made a pause, nor left a void;
And sure th' Eternal Master found
  The single talent well employ'd.

The busy day, the peaceful night,
  Unfelt, uncounted, glided by;
His frame was firm, his powers were bright,
  Tho' now his eightieth year was nigh.

Then with no throbbing fiery pain,
  No cold gradations of decay,
Death broke at once the vital chain,
  And free'd his soul the nearest way.

Walter Harte

284   *The Enchanted Region: or, Mistaken Pleasures*

The mistress of witchcrafts.
    NAHUM iii. 4
Draw near hither, ye sons of the Sorceress.
    ISAIAH lvii. 3
According to their pasture, so were they filled;
  they were filled, and their heart was exalted:
  Therefore have they forgotten ME.
    HOSEA xiii. 6

Empty, illusory *Life*,
Pregnant with fraud, in mischiefs rife;
Form'd t' ensnare us, and deceive us:
NAHUM's Enchantress! which beguiles
With all her harlotry of wiles! –
First SHE loves, and then SHE leaves us!

Erring happiness beguiles
The wretch that strays o'er CIRCE's isles;
All things smile, and all annoy him;
The rose has thorns, the doves can bite;
Riot is a fatigue till night,
Sleep an opium to destroy him.

Louring in the groves of death
Eugh-trees breathe funereal breath,
Brambles and thorns perplex the shade:
Asphaltic waters creep and rest;
Birds, in gaudy plumage drest,
Scream un-meaning thro' the glade.

Earth *fallacious herbage* yields,
And deep in grass its influence shields;
Acrid juices, scent annoying; –
Corrósive *crow-feet* choak the plains,
And *hemlock* strip'd with lurid stains,
And luscious *mandrakes*, life-destroying.

Gaudy *bella-donna* blowing,
Or with glossy berries glowing,
Lures th' *Un-wise* to tempt their doom:
Love's apple masks the fruit of death;
Sick *hen-bane* murders with her breath,
Actæa with an harlot's bloom.

One PLANT alone is wrapt in shade;
Few eyes its privacy invade;
Plant of joy, of life, and health!
More than the fabled LOTOS fam'd,
Which (tasted once) mankind reclaim'd
From parents, country, pow'r, and wealth.

On yonder *Alp* I see it rise,
Aspiring to congenial skies,
But cover'd half with ivy-walls; –
There, where EUSEBIO rais'd a shrine,
Snatch'd from the gulph by Pow'r Divine,
Where REIGA's tumbling torrent falls.

Compar'd with *thee*, how dimly shows
Poor ANACREON's life-less rose?
What is HOMER's *plant* to thee? —
In vain the MANTUAN poet try'd
To paint AMELLUS' *starry* pride,
Emblem of wit's futility!

Men saw, alas, and knew not thee,
Mystic evangelic tree!
Thou hadst no charms for paynim-eyes;
Till, guided by the lamp of Heav'n,
To chaste URANIA pow'r was giv'n
To see, t' admire, and moralize.

All-beauteous FLOW'R, whose centre glows
With studs of gold; thence streaming flows
Ray-like effulgence. Next is seen
A rich expanse of varying hue,
Enfring'd with an empurpled-blue,
And streak'd with young POMONA's green.

High o'er the pointal, deck'd with gold,
(Emblem mysterious to behold,)
A radiant CROSS its form expands; —
Its opening arms appear t' embrace
The whole collective human race,
Refuge of all men in all lands!

Grant me, kind Heav'n, in prosp'rous hour
To pluck this consecrated flow'r,
And wear it thankful on my breast;
Then shall my steps securely stray,
No pleasures shall pervert my way,
No joys seduce, no cares molest.

Like TOBIT (when the hand, approv'd
By Heav'n, th' obstructing films remov'd)
I now see objects as I ought:
Ambition's hideous; pleasure vain;
Av'rice is but a blockhead's gain,
Possessing all, bestowing nought.

Passions and *frauds* surround us all,
Their empire is reciprocal:
Shun their blandishments and wiles;
Riches but serve to steel the heart;
Want has its meanness and its art;
Health betrays, and strength beguiles.

In highest stations *snares* misguide;
Midst solitude they nurture pride,
Breeding vanity in knowledge;
A poison in delicious meat,
Midst wines a fraud, midst mirth a cheat,
In courts, in cabinet, and college.

The toils are fixt, the sportsmen keen:
Abroad unsafe, betray'd within,
Whither, *O Mortal*! art thou flying?
Thy *resolutions* oft are snares,
Thy *doubts, petitions, gifts,* and *pray'rs*; –
Alas, there may be *snares* in *dying*!

Deceiving none, by none ensnar'd,
O PARACLETE, be thou my guard,
Patron of ev'ry just endeavour!
The *Cross* of CHRIST is man's reward:
No heights obstruct, no depths retard;
Christian joys are joys for ever!

Thomas Gray

285　　*Elegy Written in a Country Churchyard*
[Original Version]

The *Curfeu* tolls the Knell of parting Day,
The lowing Herd winds slowly o'er the Lea,
The Plow-man homeward plods his weary Way,
And leaves the World to Darkness, and to me.

Now fades the glimmering Landscape on the Sight,
And all the Air a solemn Stillness holds;
Save where the Beetle wheels his droning Flight,
And drowsy Tinklings lull the distant Folds.

Save that from yonder Ivy-mantled Tow'r
The mopeing Owl does to the Moon complain
Of such, as wand'ring near her sacred Bow'r,
Molest her ancient solitary Reign.

Beneath those rugged Elms, that Yew-Tree's Shade,
Where heaves the Turf in many a mould'ring Heap,
Each in his narrow Cell for ever laid,
The rude Forefathers of the Hamlet sleep.

The breezy Call of Incense-breathing Morn,
The Swallow twitt'ring from the Straw-built Shed,
The Cock's shrill Clarion, or the ecchoing Horn,
No more shall wake them from their lowly Bed.

For them no more the blazing Hearth shall burn,
Or busy Housewife ply her Evening Care:
No Children run to lisp their Sire's Return,
Or climb his Knees the envied Kiss to share.

Oft did the Harvest to their Sickle yield,
Their Furrow oft the stubborn Glebe has broke;
How jocund did they drive their Team afield!
How bow'd the Woods beneath their sturdy Stroke!

Let not Ambition mock their useful Toil,
Their homely Joys and Destiny obscure;
Nor Grandeur hear with a disdainful Smile,
The short and simple Annals of the Poor.

The Boast of Heraldry, the Pomp of Pow'r,
And all that Beauty, all that Wealth e'er gave,
Awaits alike th' inevitable Hour.
The Paths of Glory lead but to the Grave.

Forgive, ye Proud, th' involuntary Fault,
If Memory to these no Trophies raise,
Where thro' the long-drawn Isle and fretted Vault
The pealing Anthem swells the Note of Praise.

Can storied Urn or animated Bust
Back to its Mansion call the fleeting Breath?
Can Honour's Voice provoke the silent Dust,
Or Flatt'ry sooth the dull cold Ear of Death!

Perhaps in this neglected Spot is laid
Some Heart once pregnant with celestial Fire,
Hands that the Reins of Empire might have sway'd,
Or wak'd to Extacy the living Lyre.

But Knowledge to their Eyes her ample Page
Rich with the Spoils of Time did ne'er unroll;
Chill Penury repress'd their noble Rage,
And froze the genial Current of the Soul.

Full many a Gem of purest Ray serene,
The dark unfathom'd Caves of Ocean bear:
Full many a Flower is born to blush unseen,
And waste its Sweetness on the desart Air.

Some Village-*Hampden* that with dauntless Breast
The little Tyrant of his Fields withstood;
Some mute inglorious *Milton* here may rest,
Some *Cromwell* guiltless of his Country's Blood.

Th' Applause of list'ning Senates to command,
The Threats of Pain and Ruin to despise,
To scatter Plenty o'er a smiling Land,
And read their Hist'ry in a Nation's Eyes

Their Lot forbad: nor circumscrib'd alone
Their growing Virtues, but their Crimes confin'd;
Forbad to wade through Slaughter to a Throne,
And shut the Gates of Mercy on Mankind,

The struggling Pangs of conscious Truth to hide,
To quench the Blushes of ingenuous Shame,
Or heap the Shrine of Luxury and Pride
With Incense, kindled at the Muse's Flame.

The thoughtless World to Majesty may bow,
Exalt the brave, and idolize Success;
But more to Innocence, their Safety owe
Than Power and Genius e'er conspired to bless.

And thou, who mindful of the unhonour'd Dead
Dost in these Notes their artless Tale relate,
By Night and lonely Contemplation led
To linger in the gloomy Walks of Fate,

Hark how the sacred Calm that broods around
Bids ev'ry fierce tumultuous Passion cease
In still small Accents whisp'ring from the Ground
A grateful Earnest of eternal Peace

No more with Reason and thyself at Strife
Give anxious Cares and endless Wishes room
But thro the cool sequester'd Vale of Life
Pursue the silent Tenour of thy Doom.

286   *Ode on the Death of a Favourite Cat,*
       Drowned in a Tub of Gold Fishes

'Twas on a lofty vase's side,
Where China's gayest art had dy'd
    The azure flowers, that blow;
Demurest of the tabby kind,
The pensive Selima reclin'd,
    Gazed on the lake below.

Her conscious tail her joy declar'd;
The fair round face, the snowy beard,
    The velvet of her paws,
Her coat, that with the tortoise vies,
Her ears of jet, and emerald eyes,
    She saw; and purr'd applause.

Still had she gaz'd; but 'midst the tide
Two angel forms were seen to glide,
    The Genii of the stream:
Their scaly armour's Tyrian hue
Thro' richest purple to the view
    Betray'd a golden gleam.

The hapless Nymph with wonder saw:
A whisker first and then a claw,
    With many an ardent wish,
She stretch'd in vain to reach the prize.
What female heart can gold despise?
    What Cat's averse to fish?

Presumptuous Maid! with looks intent
Again she stretch'd, again she bent,
    Nor knew the gulf between.
(Malignant Fate sat by, and smil'd)
The slipp'ry verge her feet beguil'd,
    She tumbled headlong in.

Eight times emerging from the flood
She mew'd to ev'ry watry God,
    Some speedy aid to send.
No Dolphin came, no Nereid stirr'd:
Nor cruel *Tom*, nor *Susan* heard.
    A Fav'rite has no friend!

From hence, ye Beauties, undeceiv'd,
Know, one false step is ne'er retriev'd,
    And be with caution bold.
Not all that tempts your wand'ring eyes
And heedless hearts, is lawful prize;
    Nor all, that glisters, gold.

William Collins

287   *Ode to Evening*

If ought of Oaten Stop, or Pastoral Song,
May hope, chaste *Eve*, to sooth thy modest Ear,
    Like thy own solemn Springs,
    Thy Springs, and dying Gales,
O *Nymph* reserv'd, while now the bright-hair'd Sun
Sits in yon western Tent, whose cloudy Skirts,
    With Brede ethereal wove,
    O'erhang his wavy Bed:
Now Air is hush'd, save where the weak-ey'd Bat,
With short shrill Shriek flits by on leathern Wing,
    Or where the Beetle winds
    His small but sullen Horn,
As oft he rises 'midst the twilight Path,
Against the Pilgrim born in heedless Hum:
    Now teach me, *Maid* compos'd,
    To breathe some soften'd Strain,
Whose Numbers stealing thro' thy darkning Vale,
May not unseemly with its Stillness suit,
    As musing slow, I hail
    Thy genial lov'd Return!
For when thy folding Star arising shews
His paly Circlet, at his warning Lamp
    The fragrant *Hours*, and *Elves*
    Who slept in Flowers the Day,
And many a *Nymph* who wreaths her Brows with Sedge,
And sheds the fresh'ning Dew, and lovelier still,
    The *Pensive Pleasures* sweet
    Prepare thy shadowy Car.
Then lead, calm *Vot'ress* where some sheety Lake
Cheers the lone Heath, or some time-hallowed Pile,
    Or upland Fallows grey
    Reflect its last cool Gleam.
But when chill blustring Winds, or driving Rain,
Forbid my willing Feet, be mine the Hut,
    That from the Mountain's Side,
    Views Wilds, and swelling Floods,
And Hamlets brown, and dim-discover'd Spires,
And hears their simple Bell, and marks o'er all
    Thy Dewy Fingers draw
    The gradual dusky Veil.
While *Spring* shall pour his Show'rs, as oft he wont,
And bathe thy breathing Tresses, meekest *Eve*!
    While *Summer* loves to sport,
    Beneath thy ling'ring Light:

While sallow *Autumn* fills thy Lap with Leaves,
Or *Winter* yelling thro' the troublous Air,
   Affrights thy shrinking Train,
   And rudely rends thy Robes.
So long, sure-found beneath the sylvan Shed,
Shall *Fancy, Friendship, Science,* rose-lipp'd *Health,*
   Thy gentlest Influence own,
   And love thy fav'rite Name!

Christopher Smart

288   From *A Song to David*

DAVID the Son of JESSE said, and the MAN who was
RAISED UP ON HIGH, the ANOINTED OF THE GOD
OF JACOB and the SWEET PSALMIST OF ISRAEL, said,
THE SPIRIT OF THE LORD spake by ME, and HIS
WORD was in my TONGUE.   *2 SAM. xxiii. 1,2*

O Thou, that sit'st upon a throne,
With harp of high majestic tone,
   To praise the King of kings;
And voice of heav'n-ascending swell,
Which, while its deeper notes excell,
   Clear, as a clarion, rings:

To bless each valley, grove and coast,
And charm the cherubs to the post
   Of gratitude in throngs;
To *keep* the days on Zion's mount,
And send the year to his account,
   With dances and with songs:

O Servant of God's holiest charge,
The minister of praise at large,
   Which thou may'st now receive;
From thy blest mansion hail and hear,
From topmost eminence appear
   To this the wreath I weave.

Great, valiant, pious, good, and clean,
Sublime, contemplative, serene,
   Strong, constant, pleasant, wise!
Bright effluence of exceeding grace;
Best man! – the swiftness and the race,
   The peril, and the prize!

Great – from the lustre of his crown,
From Samuel's horn and God's renown,
   Which is the people's voice;
For all the host, from rear to van,
Applauded and embrac'd the man –
   The man of God's own choice.

Valiant – the word, and up he rose –
The fight – he triumph'd o'er the foes,
   Whom God's just laws abhor;
And arm'd in gallant faith he took
Against the boaster, from the brook,
   The weapons of the war.

Pious – magnificent and grand;
'Twas he the famous temple plan'd:
   (The seraph in his soul)
Foremost to give the Lord his dues,
Foremost to bless the welcome news,
   And foremost to condole.

Good – from Jehudah's genuine vein,
From God's best nature good in grain,
   His aspect and his heart;
To pity, to forgive, to save,
Witness En-gedi's conscious cave,
   And Shimei's blunted dart.

Clean – if perpetual prayer be pure,
And love, which could itself innure,
   To fasting and to fear –
Clean in his gestures, hands, and feet,
To smite the lyre, the dance compleat,
   To play the sword and spear.

Sublime – invention ever young,
Of vast conception, tow'ring tongue,
   To God th' eternal theme;
Notes from yon exaltations caught,
Unrival'd royalty of thought,
   O'er meaner strains supreme.

Contemplative – on God to fix
His musings, and above the six
   The sabbath-day he blest;
'Twas then his thoughts self-conquest prun'd,
And heavenly melancholy tun'd,
   To bless and bear the rest.

Serene – to sow the seeds of peace,
Rememb'ring, when he watch'd the fleece,
　　How sweetly Kidron purl'd –
To further knowledge, silence vice,
And plant perpetual paradise
　　When God had calm'd the world.

Strong – in the Lord, who could defy
Satan, and all his powers that lie
　　In sempiternal night;
And hell, and horror, and despair
Were as the lion and the bear
　　To his undaunted might.

Constant – in love to God THE TRUTH,
Age, manhood, infancy, and youth –
　　To Jonathan his friend
Constant, beyond the verge of death;
And Ziba, and Mephibosheth,
　　His endless fame attend.

Pleasant – and various as the year;
Man, soul, and angel, without peer,
　　Priest, champion, sage and boy;
In armour, or in ephod clad,
His pomp, his piety was glad;
　　Majestic was his joy.

Wise – in recovery from his fall,
Whence rose his eminence o'er all,
　　Of all the most revil'd;
The light of Israel in his ways,
Wise are his precepts, prayer and praise,
　　And counsel to his child.

His muse, bright angel of his verse,
Gives balm for all the thorns that pierce,
　　For all the pangs that rage;
Blest light, still gaining on the gloom,
The more than Michal of his bloom,
　　Th' Abishag of his age.

He sung of God – the mighty source
Of all things – the stupendous force
　　On which all strength depends;
From whose right arm, beneath whose eyes,
All period, pow'r and enterprize
　　Commences, reigns, and ends.

Angels – their ministry and meed,
Which to and fro with blessings speed,
  Or with their citterns wait;
Where Michael with his millions bows,
Where dwells the seraph and his spouse,
  The cherub and her mate.

Of man – the semblance and effect
Of God and Love – the Saint elect
  For infinite applause –
To rule the land, and briny broad,
To be laborious in his laud,
  And heroes in his cause.

The world – the clustring spheres he made,
The glorious light, the soothing shade,
  Dale, champaign, grove, and hill;
The multitudinous abyss,
Where secrecy remains in bliss,
  And wisdom hides her skill.

Trees, plants, and flow'rs – of virtuous root;
Gem yielding blossom, yielding fruit,
  Choice gums and precious balm;
Bless ye the nosegay in the vale,
And with the sweetners of the gale
  Enrich the thankful psalm.

Of fowl – e'en ev'ry beak and wing
Which chear the winter, hail the spring,
  That live in peace or prey;
They that make music, or that mock,
The quail, the brave domestic cock,
  The raven, swan, and jay.

Of fishes – ev'ry size and shape,
Which nature frames of light escape,
  Devouring man to shun:
The shells are in the wealthy deep,
The shoals upon the surface leap,
  And love the glancing sun.

Of beasts – the beaver plods his task;
While the sleek tygers roll and bask,
  Nor yet the shades arouse:
Her cave the mining coney scoops;
Where o'er the mead the mountain stoops,
  The kids exult and brouse.

Of gems – their virtue and their price,
Which hid in earth from man's device,
    Their darts of lustre sheathe;
The jasper of the master's stamp,
The topaz blazing like a lamp
    Among the mines beneath.

Blest was the tenderness he felt
When to his graceful harp he knelt,
    And did for audience call;
When Satan with his hand he quell'd,
And in serene suspence he held
    The frantic throes of Saul.

289   *The Nativity of Our Lord*

Where is this stupendous stranger,
    Swains of Solyma, advise,
Lead me to my Master's manger,
    Show me where my Saviour lies?

O Most Mighty! O MOST HOLY!
    Far beyond the seraph's thought,
Art thou then so mean and lowly
    As unheeded prophets taught?

O the magnitude of meekness!
    Worth from worth immortal sprung;
O the strength of infant weakness,
    If eternal is so young!

If so young and thus eternal,
    Michael tune the shepherd's reed,
Where the scenes are ever vernal,
    And the loves be love indeed!

See the God blasphem'd and doubted
    In the schools of Greece and Rome;
See the pow'rs of darkness routed,
    Taken at their utmost gloom.

Nature's decorations glisten
    Far above their usual trim;
Birds on box and laurel listen,
    As so near the cherubs hymn.

Boreas now no longer winters
  On the desolated coast;
Oaks no more are riv'n in splinters
  By the whirlwind and his host.

Spinks and ouzels sing sublimely,
  'We too have a Saviour born;'
Whither blossoms burst untimely
  On the blest Mosaic thorn.

God all-bounteous, all-creative,
  Whom no ills from good dissuade,
Is incarnate, and a native
  Of the very world he made.

Oliver Goldsmith

From *The Deserted Village*

290
[1]

  Sweet AUBURN! parent of the blissful hour,
Thy glades forlorn confess the tyrant's power.
Here as I take my solitary rounds,
Amidst thy tangling walks, and ruined grounds,
And, many a year elaps'd, return to view
Where once the cottage stood, the hawthorn grew,
Remembrance wakes with all her busy train,
Swells at my breast, and turns the past to pain.

  In all my wanderings round this world of care,
In all my griefs – and GOD has given my share –
I still had hopes my latest hours to crown,
Amidst these humble bowers to lay me down;
To husband out life's taper at the close,
And keep the flame from wasting by repose.
I still had hopes, for pride attends us still,
Amidst the swains to shew my book-learn'd skill,
Around my fire an evening group to draw,
And tell of all I felt, and all I saw;
And, as an hare whom hounds and horns pursue,
Pants to the place from whence at first she flew,
I still had hopes, my long vexations past,
Here to return – and die at home at last.

O blest retirement, friend to life's decline,
Retreats from care that never must be mine,
How happy he who crowns in shades like these,
A youth of labour with an age of ease;
Who quits a world where strong temptations try,
And, since 'tis hard to combat, learns to fly.
For him no wretches, born to work and weep,
Explore the mine, or tempt the dangerous deep;
No surly porter stands in guilty state
To spurn imploring famine from the gate,
But on he moves to meet his latter end,
Angels around befriending virtue's friend;
Bends to the grave with unperceiv'd decay,
While resignation gently slopes the way;
And all his prospects brightening to the last,
His Heaven commences ere the world be past!

Sweet was the sound when oft at evening's close,
Up yonder hill the village murmur rose;
There as I past with careless steps and slow,
The mingling notes came soften'd from below;
The swain responsive as the milk-maid sung,
The sober herd that low'd to meet their young;
The noisy geese that gabbl'd o'er the pool,
The playful children just let loose from school;
The watch-dog's voice that bayed the whispering wind,
And the loud laugh that spoke the vacant mind,
These all in sweet confusion sought the shade,
And fill'd each pause the nightingale had made.
But now the sounds of population fail,
No chearful murmurs fluctuate in the gale,
No busy steps the grass-grown foot-way tread,
For all the bloomy flush of life is fled.
All but yon widow'd, solitary thing
That feebly bends beside the plashy spring;
She, wretched matron, forc'd, in age, for bread,
To strip the brook with mantling cresses spread,
To pick her wintry faggot from the thorn,
To seek her nightly shed, and weep till morn;
She only left of all the harmless train,
The sad historian of the pensive plain.

Near yonder copse, where once the garden smil'd,
And still where many a garden flower grows wild;
There, where a few torn shrubs the place disclose,
The village preacher's modest mansion rose.
A man he was, to all the country dear,
And passing rich with forty pounds a year;

Remote from towns he ran his godly race,
Nor ere had chang'd, nor wish'd to change his place;
Unpractis'd he to fawn, or seek for power,
By doctrines fashion'd to the varying hour;
Far other aims his heart had learned to prize,
More skill'd to raise the wretched than to rise.
His house was known to all the vagrant train,
He chid their wanderings, but reliev'd their pain;
The long remember'd beggar was his guest,
Whose beard descending swept his aged breast;
The ruin'd spendthrift, now no longer proud,
Claim'd kindred there, and had his claims allowed;
The broken soldier, kindly bade to stay,
Satc by his fire, and talked the night away;
Wept o'er his wounds, or tales of sorrow done,
Shoulder'd his crutch, and shew'd how fields were won.
Pleas'd with his guests, the good man learn'd to glow,
And quite forgot their vices in their woe;
Careless their merits, or their faults to scan,
His pity gave ere charity began.

   Thus to relieve the wretched was his pride,
And even his failings lean'd to Virtue's side;
But in his duty prompt at every call,
He watch'd and wept, he pray'd and felt, for all.
And, as a bird each fond endearment tries,
To tempt its new fledg'd offspring to the skies;
He tried each art, reprov'd each dull delay,
Allur'd to brighter worlds, and led the way.

   Beside the bed where parting life was lay'd,
And sorrow, guilt, and pain, by turns dismay'd,
The reverend champion stood. At his control,
Despair and anguish fled the struggling soul;
Comfort came down the trembling wretch to raise,
And his last faultering accents whisper'd praise.

   At church, with meek and unaffected grace,
His looks adorn'd the venerable place;
Truth from his lips prevail'd with double sway,
And fools, who came to scoff, remain'd to pray.
The service past, around the pious man,
With steady zeal each honest rustic ran;
Even children follow'd with endearing wile,
And pluck'd his gown, to share the good man's smile.
His ready smile a parent's warmth exprest,
Their welfare pleased him, and their cares distrest;
To them his heart, his love, his griefs were given,
But all his serious thoughts had rest in Heaven.

As some tall cliff that lifts its awful form,
Swells from the vale, and midway leaves the storm,
Tho' round its breast the rolling clouds are spread,
Eternal sunshine settles on its head.

   Beside yon straggling fence that skirts the way,
With blossom'd furze unprofitably gay,
There, in his noisy mansion, skill'd to rule,
The village master taught his little school;
A man severe he was, and stern to view,
I knew him well, and every truant knew;
Well had the boding tremblers learn'd to trace
The day's disasters in his morning face;
Full well they laugh'd with counterfeited glee,
At all his jokes, for many a joke had he;
Full well the busy whisper circling round,
Convey'd the dismal tidings when he frown'd;
Yet he was kind, or if severe in aught,
The love he bore to learning was in fault;
The village all declar'd how much he knew;
'Twas certain he could write, and cypher too;
Lands he could measure, terms and tides presage,
And even the story ran that he could gauge.
In arguing too, the parson own'd his skill,
For e'en tho' vanquished, he could argue still;
While words of learned length, and thundering sound,
Amazed the gazing rustics rang'd around,
And still they gazed, and still the wonder grew,
That one small head could carry all he knew.

   But past is all his fame. The very spot
Where many a time he triumph'd, is forgot.
Near yonder thorn, that lifts its head on high,
Where once the sign-post caught the passing eye,
Low lies that house where nut-brown draughts inspir'd,
Where grey-beard mirth and smiling toil retir'd,
Where village statesmen talk'd with looks profound,
And news much older than their ale went round.
Imagination fondly stoops to trace
The parlour splendours of that festive place;
The white-wash'd wall, the nicely sanded floor,
The varnish'd clock that click'd behind the door;
The chest contriv'd a double debt to pay,
A bed by night, a chest of drawers by day;
The pictures plac'd for ornament and use,
The twelve good rules, the royal game of goose;
The hearth, except when winter chill'd the day,
With aspen boughs, and flowers, and fennel gay,
While broken tea-cups, wisely kept for shew,
Rang'd o'er the chimney, glisten'd in a row.

Vain transitory splendours! Could not all
Reprieve the tottering mansion from its fall!
Obscure it sinks, nor shall it more impart
An hour's importance to the poor man's heart;
Thither no more the peasant shall repair
To sweet oblivion of his daily care;
No more the farmer's news, the barber's tale,
No more the wood-man's ballad shall prevail;
No more the smith his dusky brow shall clear,
Relax his ponderous strength, and lean to hear;
The host himself no longer shall be found
Careful to see the mantling bliss go round;
Nor the coy maid, half willing to be prest,
Shall kiss the cup to pass it to the rest.

Yes! let the rich deride, the proud disdain;
These simple blessings of the lowly train,
To me more dear, congenial to my heart,
One native charm, than all the gloss of art;
Spontaneous joys, where Nature has its play,
The soul adopts, and owns their first born sway,
Lightly they frolic o'er the vacant mind,
Unenvied, unmolested, unconfin'd.
But the long pomp, the midnight masquerade,
With all the freaks of wanton wealth array'd,
In these, ere triflers half their wish obtain,
The toiling pleasure sickens into pain;
And, even while fashion's brightest arts decoy,
The heart distrusting asks, if this be joy.

291   [2]

Even now the devastation is begun,
And half the business of destruction done;
Even now, methinks, as pondering here I stand,
I see the rural virtues leave the land.
Down where yon anchoring vessel spreads the sail
That idly waiting flaps with every gale,
Downward they move, a melancholy band,
Pass from the shore, and darken all the strand.
Contented Toil, and hospitable Care,
And kind connubial Tenderness, are there;
And Piety with wishes plac'd above,
And steady Loyalty, and faithful Love.
And thou, sweet Poetry, thou loveliest maid,
Still first to fly where sensual joys invade;

Unfit in these degenerate times of shame,
To catch the heart, or strike for honest fame;
Dear charming nymph, neglected and decried,
My shame in crowds, my solitary pride.
Thou source of all my bliss, and all my woe,
That found'st me poor at first, and keep'st me so;
Thou guide by which the nobler arts excell,
Thou nurse of every virtue, fare thee well.
Farewell, and O where'er thy voice be tried,
On Torno's cliffs, or Pambamarca's side,
Whether where equinoctial fervours glow,
Or winter wraps the polar world in snow,
Still let thy voice prevailing over time,
Redress the rigours of the inclement clime;
Aid slighted truth, with thy persuasive strain
Teach erring man to spurn the rage of gain;
Teach him that states of native strength possest,
Tho' very poor, may still be very blest;
That trade's proud empire hastes to swift decay,
As ocean sweeps the labour'd mole away;
While self dependent power can time defy,
As rocks resist the billows and the sky.

William Cowper

292   *On the Loss of the 'Royal George'*
            Written When the News Arrived

Toll for the brave —
The brave! that are no more:
All sunk beneath the wave,
Fast by their native shore.
Eight hundred of the brave,
Whose courage well was tried,
Had made the vessel heel
And laid her on her side;
A land-breeze shook the shrouds,
And she was overset;
Down went the Royal George,
With all her crew complete.

Toll for the brave —
Brave Kempenfelt is gone,
His last sea-fight is fought,
His work of glory done.

It was not in the battle,
No tempest gave the shock,
　She sprang no fatal leak,
She ran upon no rock;
　His sword was in the sheath,
His fingers held the pen,
　When Kempenfelt went down
With twice four hundred men.

　Weigh the vessel up,
Once dreaded by our foes,
　And mingle with your cup
The tears that England owes;
　Her timbers yet are sound,
And she may float again,
　Full charg'd with England's thunder,
And plough the distant main;
　But Kempenfelt is gone,
His victories are o'er;
　And he and his eight hundred
Must plough the wave no more.

293　　*Lines Written During a Period of Insanity*

Hatred and vengeance, my eternal portion,
Scarce can endure delay of execution,
Wait, with impatient readiness, to seize my
　　　　　　Soul in a moment.

Damn'd below Judas: more abhorr'd than he was,
Who for a few pence sold his holy Master.
Twice betrayed Jesus me, the last delinquent,
　　　　　　Deems the profanest.

Man disavows, and Deity disowns me:
Hell might afford my miseries a shelter;
Therefore hell keeps her ever hungry mouths all
　　　　　　Bolted against me.

Hard lot! encompass'd with a thousand dangers;
Weary, faint, trembling with a thousand terrors;
I'm called, if vanquish'd, to receive a sentence
　　　　　　Worse than Abiram's.

Him the vindictive rod of angry justice
Sent quick and howling to the centre headlong;
I, fed with judgment, in a fleshly tomb, am
　　　　　　Buried above ground.

294   *Light Shining out of Darkness*

God moves in a mysterious way,
   His wonders to perform;
He plants his footsteps in the sea,
   And rides upon the storm.

Deep in unfathomable mines
   Of never failing skill,
He treasures up his bright designs,
   And works his sovereign will.

Ye fearful saints, fresh courage take,
   The clouds ye so much dread
Are big with mercy, and shall break
   In blessings on your head.

Judge not the LORD by feeble sense,
   But trust him for his grace;
Behind a frowning providence,
   He hides a smiling face.

His purposes will ripen fast,
   Unfolding ev'ry hour;
The bud may have a bitter taste,
   But sweet will be the flow'r.

Blind unbelief is sure to err,
   And scan his work in vain;
GOD is his own interpreter,
   And he will make it plain.

Thomas Chatterton

295   *An Excelente Balade of Charitie*
          As wroten bie the goode Prieste Thomas Rowley, 1464

In Virgyne the sweltrie sun gan sheene,
And hotte upon the mees did caste his raie;
The apple rodded from its palie greene,
And the mole peare did bende the leafy spraie;
The peede chelandri sunge the livelong daie;
   'Twas nowe the pride, the manhode of the yeare,
And eke the grounde was dighte in its mose defte aumere.

The sun was glemeing in the midde of daie,
Deadde still the aire, and eke the welken blue,
When from the sea arist in drear arraie
A hepe of cloudes of sable sullen hue,
The which full fast unto the woodlande drewe,
Hiltring attenes the sunnis fetive face,
And the blacke tempeste swolne and gatherd up apace.

Beneathe an holme, faste by a pathwaie side,
Which did unto Seyncte Godwine's covent lede,
A hapless pilgrim moneynge did abide,
Pore in his viewe, ungentle in his weede,
Longe bretful of the miseries of neede,
Where from the hail-stone coulde the almer flie?
He had no housen theere, ne anie covent nie.

Look in his glommed face, his sprighte there scanne;
Howe woe-be-gone, how withered, forwynd, deade!
Haste to thie church-glebe-house, ashrewed mannc!
Haste to thie kiste, thie onlie dortoure bedde.
Cale, as the claie whiche will gre on thie hedde,
Is Charitie and Love aminge highe elves;
Knightis and Barons live for pleasure and themselves.

The gatherd storme is rype; the bigge drops falle;
The forswat meadowes smethe, and drenche the raine;
The comyng ghastness do the cattle pall,
And the full flockes are drivynge ore the plaine;
Dashde from the cloudes the waters flott againe;
The welkin opes; the yellow levynne flies;
And the hot fierie smothe in the wide lowings dies.

Liste! now the thunder's rattling clymmynge sound
Cheves slowlie on, and then embollen clangs,
Shakes the hie spyre, and losst, dispended, drown'd,
Still on the gallard eare of terroure hanges;
The windes are up; the lofty elmen swanges;
Again the levynne and the thunder poures,
And the full cloudes are braste attenes in stonen showers.

Spurreynge his palfrie oere the watrie plaine,
The Abbote of Seyncte Godwynes convente came;
His chapournette was drented with the reine,
And his pencte gyrdle met with mickle shame;
He ayneward tolde his bederoll at the same;
The storme encreasen, and he drew aside,
With the mist almes craver neere to the holme to bide.

His cope was all of Lyncolne clothe so fyne,
With a gold button fasten'd neere his chynne;
His autremete was edged with golden twynne,
And his shoone pyke a loverds mighte have binne;
Full well it shewn he thoughten coste no sinne:
The trammels of the palfrye pleasde his sighte,
For the horse-millanare his head with roses dighte.

An almes, sir prieste! the droppynge pilgrim saide,
O! let me waite within your covente dore,
Till the sunne sheneth hie above our heade,
And the loude tempeste of the aire is oer;
Helpless and ould am I alas! and poor;
No house, ne friend, ne moneie in my pouche;
All yatte I call my owne is this my silver crouche.

Varlet, replyd the Abbatte, cease your dinne;
This is no season almes and prayers to give;
Mie porter never lets a faitour in;
None touch mie rynge who not in honour live.
And now the sonne with the black cloudes did stryve,
And shettynge on the grounde his glairie raie,
The Abbatte spurrde his steede, and eftsoons roadde awaie.

Once moe the skie was blacke, the thounder rolde:
Faste reyneynge oer the plaine a prieste was seen;
Ne dighte full proude, ne buttoned up in golde;
His cope and jape were graie, and eke were clene;
A Limitoure he was of order seene;
And from the pathwaie side then turned hee,
Where the pore almer laie binethe the holmen tree.

An almes, sir priest! the droppynge pilgrim sayde,
For sweet Seyncte Marie and your order sake.
The Limitoure then loosen'd his pouche threade,
And did thereoute a groate of silver take;
The mister pilgrim dyd for halline shake.
Here take this silver, it maie eathe thie care;
We are Goddes stewards all, nete of oure owne we bare.

But ah! unhailie pilgrim, lerne of me,
Scathe anie give a rentrolle to their Lorde.
Here take my semescope, thou art bare I see;
Tis thyne; the Seynctes will give me mie rewarde.
He left the pilgrim, and his waie aborde.
Virgynne and hallie Seyncte, who sitte yn gloure,
Or give the mittee will, or give the gode man power.

George Crabbe

296   From *Phoebe Dawson*

Lo! now with red rent cloak and bonnet black,
And torn green gown loose hanging at her back,
One who an infant in her arms sustains,
And seems in patience striving with her pains;
Pinch'd are her looks, as one who pines for bread,
Whose cares are growing and whose hopes are fled;
Pale her parch'd lips, her heavy eyes sunk low,
And tears unnotic'd from their channels flow;
Serene her manner, till some sudden pain
Frets the meek soul, and then she's calm again;
Her broken pitcher to the pool she takes,
And every step with cautious terror makes;
For not alone that infant in her arms,
But nearer cause her anxious soul alarms;
With water burden'd then she picks her way,
Slowly and cautious, in the clinging clay;
Till, in mid-green, she trusts a place unsound,
And deeply plunges in the adhesive ground;
Thence, but with pain, her slender foot she takes,
While hope the mind as strength the frame forsakes;
For when so full the cup of sorrow grows,
Add but a drop, it instantly o'erflows.
And now her path but not her peace she gains,
Safe from her task, but shivering with her pains;
Her home she reaches, open leaves the door,
And placing first her infant on the floor,
She bares her bosom to the wind, and sits,
And sobbing struggles with the rising fits;
In vain, they come, she feels the inflating grief,
That shuts the swelling bosom from relief;
That speaks in feeble cries a soul distress'd,
Or the sad laugh that cannot be repress'd;
The neighbour-matron leaves her wheel, and flies
With all the aid her poverty supplies;
Unfee'd, the calls of nature she obeys,
Not led by profit, not allur'd by praise;
And waiting long, till these contentions cease,
She speaks of comfort, and departs in peace.
   Friend of distress! the mourner feels thy aid,
She cannot pay thee, but thou wilt be paid.
   But who this child of weakness, want, and care?
'Tis Phœbe Dawson, pride of Lammas fair;
Who took her lover for his sparkling eyes,
Expressions warm, and love-inspiring lies:

Compassion first assail'd her gentle heart
For all his suffering, all his bosom's smart:
'And then his prayers! they would a savage move,
And win the coldest of the sex to love:'
But ah! too soon his looks success declar'd,
Too late her loss the marriage-rite repair'd;
The faithless flatterer then his vows forgot,
A captious tyrant or a noisy sot:
If present, railing till he saw her pain'd;
If absent, spending what their labours gain'd;
Till that fair form in want and sickness pin'd,
And hope and comfort fled that gentle mind.
    Then fly temptation, youth; resist! refrain!
    Nor let me preach for ever and in vain!

William Blake

From *Songs of Experience*

297   [1]

Introduction

Hear the voice of the Bard!
Who Present, Past & Future sees,
Whose ears have heard
The Holy Word
That walk'd among the ancient trees,

Calling the lapsed Soul,
And weeping in the evening dew,
That might controll
The starry pole
And fallen fallen light renew!

'O Earth, O Earth return!
Arise from out the dewy grass;
Night is worn
And the morn
Rises from the slumberous mass.

Turn away no more:
Why wilt thou turn away?
The starry floor
The wat'ry shore
Is giv'n thee till the break of day.'

298   [2]

Ah Sun-flower! weary of time,
Who countest the steps of the Sun,
Seeking after that sweet golden clime
Where the traveller's journey is done:

Where the Youth pin'd away with desire,
And the pale Virgin shrouded in snow,
Arise from their graves and aspire
Where my Sun-flower wishes to go.

299   *Auguries of Innocence*

To see a World in a Grain of Sand
And a Heaven in a Wild Flower,
Hold Infinity in the palm of your hand
And Eternity in an hour.
A Robin Red breast in a Cage
Puts all Heaven in a Rage.
A Dove house fill'd with Doves & Pigeons
Shudders Hell thro' all its regions.
A Dog starv'd at his Master's Gate
Predicts the ruin of the State.
A Horse misus'd upon the Road
Calls to Heaven for Human blood.
Each outcry of the hunted Hare
A fibre from the Brain does tear.
A Skylark wounded in the wing,
A Cherubim does cease to sing.
The Game Cock clip'd & arm'd for fight
Does the Rising Sun affright.
Every Wolf's & Lion's howl
Raises from Hell a Human Soul.
The wild Deer wand'ring here & there
Keeps the Human Soul from Care.
The Lamb misus'd breeds Public strife
And yet forgives the Butcher's Knife.
The Bat that flits at close of Eve
Has left the Brain that won't Believe.
The Owl that calls upon the Night
Speaks the Unbeliever's fright.
He who shall hurt the little Wren
Shall never be belov'd by Men.
He who the Ox to wrath has mov'd
Shall never be by Woman lov'd.

The wanton Boy that kills the Fly
Shall feel the Spider's enmity.
He who torments the Chafer's sprite
Weaves a Bower in endless Night.
The Catterpiller on the Leaf
Repeats to thee thy Mother's grief.
Kill not the Moth nor Butterfly
For the Last Judgment draweth nigh.
He who shall train the Horse to war
Shall never pass the Polar Bar.
The Beggar's Dog & Widow's Cat,
Feed them, & thou wilt grow fat.
The Gnat that sings his Summer's song
Poison gets from Slander's tongue.
The poison of the Snake & Newt
Is the sweat of Envy's Foot.
The Poison of the Honey Bee
Is the Artist's Jealousy.
The Prince's Robes & Beggar's Rags
Are Toadstools on the Miser's Bags.
A truth that's told with bad intent
Beats all the Lies you can invent.
It is right it should be so;
Man was made for Joy & Woe,
And when this we rightly know,
Thro' the World we safely go.
Joy & Woe are woven fine,
A Clothing for the Soul divine;
Under every grief & pine
Runs a joy with silken twine.
The Babe is more than Swadling Bands,
Throughout all these Human Lands;
Tools were made, & Born were hands,
Every Farmer Understands.
Every Tear from Every Eye
Becomes a Babe in Eternity;
This is caught by Females bright
And return'd to its own delight.
The Bleat, the Bark, Bellow & Roar
Are Waves that Beat on Heaven's Shore.
The Babe that weeps the Rod beneath
Writes Revenge in realms of Death.
The Beggar's Rags fluttering in Air
Does to Rags the Heavens tear.
The Soldier arm'd with Sword & Gun
Palsied strikes the Summer's Sun.
The poor Man's Farthing is worth more
Than all the Gold on Afric's Shore.

One Mite wrung from the Lab'rer's hands
Shall buy & sell the Miser's Lands
Or if protected from on high
Does that whole Nation sell & buy.
He who mocks the Infant's Faith
Shall be mock'd in Age & Death.
He who shall teach the Child to Doubt
The rotting Grave shall ne'er get out.
He who respects the Infant's faith
Triumphs over Hell & Death.
The Child's Toys & the Old Man's Reasons
Are the Fruits of the Two seasons.
The Questioner who sits so sly
Shall never know how to Reply.
He who replies to words of Doubt
Doth put the Light of Knowledge out.
The Strongest Poison ever known
Came from Cæsar's Laurel Crown.
Nought can deform the Human Race
Like to the Armour's iron brace.
When Gold & Gems adorn the Plow
To peaceful Arts shall Envy Bow.
A Riddle or the Cricket's Cry
Is to Doubt a fit Reply.
The Emmet's Inch & Eagle's Mile
Make Lame Philosophy to smile.
He who Doubts from what he sees
Will ne'er Believe, do what you Please.
If the Sun & Moon should doubt,
They'd immediately Go out.
To be in a Passion you Good may do,
But no Good if a Passion is in you.
The Whore & Gambler, by the State
Licenc'd, build that Nation's Fate.
The Harlot's cry from Street to Street
Shall weave Old England's winding Sheet.
The Winner's Shout, the Loser's Curse,
Dance before dead England's Hearse.
Every Night & every Morn
Some to Misery are Born.
Every Morn & every Night
Some are Born to sweet delight.
Some are Born to sweet delight,
Some are Born to Endless Night.
We are led to Believe a Lie
When we see not Thro' the Eye
Which was Born in a Night, to perish in a Night,
When the Soul Slept in Beams of Light.

God Appears, & God is Light
To those poor Souls who dwell in Night,
But does a Human Form Display
To those who Dwell in Realms of Day.

300   From *Milton*

This Wine-press is call'd War on Earth: it is the Printing Press
Of Los, and here he lays his words in order above the mortal brain,
As cogs are form'd in a wheel to turn the cogs of the adverse wheel.

Timbrels and violins sport round the Wine-presses; the little Seed,
The sportive Root, the Earth-worm, the gold Beetle, the wise Emmet,
Dance round the Wine-presses of Luvah: the Centipede is there,
The ground Spider with many eyes, the Mole clothed in velvet,
The ambitious Spider in his sullen web, the lucky golden Spinner,
The Earwig arm'd, the tender Maggot, emblem of immortality,
The Flea, Louse, Bug, the Tape-Worm, all the Armies of Disease
Visible or invisible to the slothful vegetating Man:
The slow Slug, the Grasshopper that sings & laughs & drinks:
Winter comes, he folds his slender bones without a murmur:
The cruel Scorpion is there, the Gnat, Wasp, Hornet & the Honey Bee,
The Toad & venomous Newt, the Serpent cloth'd in gems & gold:
They throw off their gorgeous raiment: they rejoice with loud jubilee
Around the Wine-presses of Luvah, naked & drunk with wine.

There is the Nettle that stings with soft down, and there
The indignant Thistle whose bitterness is bred in his milk,
Who feeds on contempt of his neighbour: there all the idle Weeds
That creep around the obscure places shew their various limbs
Naked in all their beauty dancing round the Wine-presses.

Poems from Blake's MS Book (1793)

301   [1]

Abstinence sows sand all over
The ruddy limbs & flaming hair;
But Desire Gratified
Plants fruits of life & beauty there.

302

[2]

He who binds to himself a joy
Does the winged life destroy;
But he who kisses the joy as it flies
Lives in eternity's sun rise.

Robert Burns

303   *Holy Willie's Prayer*

'And send the godly in a pet to pray.' – *Pope*

O Thou, that in the heavens does dwell,
Wha, as it pleases best Thysel',
Sends ane to heaven an' ten to hell,
          A' for thy glory,
And no for onie guid or ill
          They've done afore Thee!

I bless and praise Thy matchless might,
When thousands Thou hast left in night,
That I am here afore Thy sight,
          For gifts an' grace
A burning and a shining light
          To a' this place.

What was I, or my generation,
That I should get sic exaltation,
I wha deserv'd most just damnation
          For broken laws,
Sax thousand years ere my creation,
          Thro' Adam's cause.

When from my mither's womb I fell,
Thou might hae plung'd me deep in hell,
To gnash my gooms, and weep and wail,
          In burnin lakes,
Where damned devils roar and yell,
          Chain'd to their stakes.

Yet I am here a chosen sample,
To show thy grace is great and ample;
I'm here a pillar o' Thy temple,
          Strong as a rock,
A guide, a buckler, and example,
          To a' Thy flock.

O Lord, Thou kens what zeal I bear,
When drinkers drink, an' swearers swear,
An' singing here, an' dancin' there,
    Wi' great and sma';
For I am keepit by Thy fear
    Free frae them a'.

But yet, O Lord! confess I must,
At times I'm fash'd wi' fleshly lust:
An' sometimes, too, in wardly trust,
    Vile self gets in;
But Thou remembers we are dust,
    Defil'd wi' sin.

O Lord! yestreen, Thou kens, wi' Meg –
Thy pardon I sincerely beg;
O! may't ne'er be a livin plague
    To my dishonour,
An' I'll ne'er lift a lawless leg
    Again upon her.

Besides, I farther maun allow,
Wi' Leezie's lass, three times I trow –
But Lord, that Friday I was fou,   *mad*
    When I cam near her;
Or else, Thou kens, Thy servant true
    Wad never steer her.   *stir, rouse*

Maybe Thou lets this fleshly thorn
Buffet Thy servant e'en and morn,
Lest he owre proud and high shou'd turn,
    That he's sae gifted:
If sae, Thy han' maun e'en be borne,
    Until Thou lift it.

Lord, bless Thy chosen in this place,
For here Thou hast a chosen race:
But God confound their stubborn face,
    An' blast their name,
Wha bring Thy elders to disgrace
    An' public shame.

Lord, mind Gaw'n Hamilton's deserts;
He drinks, an' swears, an' plays at cartes,
Yet has sae mony takin arts,
    Wi' great and sma',
Frae God's ain priest the people's hearts
    He steals awa.

An' when we chasten'd him therefor,
Thou kens how he bred sic a splore,   *frolic*
An' set the warld in a roar
      O' laughing at us; –
Curse Thou his basket and his store,
      Kail an' potatoes.

Lord, hear my earnest cry and pray'r,
Against that Presbyt'ry o' Ayr;
Thy strong right hand, Lord, make it bare
      Upo' their heads;
Lord, visit them, an' dinna spare,
      For their misdeeds.

O Lord, my God! that glib-tongu'd Aiken,
My vera heart and flesh are quakin,
To think how we stood sweatin, shakin,
      An' p—'d wi' dread,
While he, wi' hingin lip an' snakin,
      Held up his head.

Lord, in Thy day o' vengeance try him,
Lord, visit them wha did employ him,
And pass not in Thy mercy by them,
      Nor hear their pray'r,
But for thy people's sake destroy them,
      An' dinna spare.

But, Lord, remember me an' mine
Wi' mercies temporal and divine,
That I for grace an' gear may shine,
      Excell'd by nane,
And a' the glory shall be thine,
      Amen, Amen!

304   *Epistle to a Young Friend*

               May——, 1786

I lang hae thought, my youthfu' friend,
    A something to have sent you,
Tho' it should serve nae ither end
    Than just a kind memento:
But how the subject-theme may gang,
    Let time and chance determine;
Perhaps it may turn out a sang:
    Perhaps turn out a sermon.

Ye'll try the world soon, my lad;
 And, Andrew dear, believe me,
Ye'll find mankind an unco squad,   *strange*
 And muckle they may grieve ye:
For care and trouble set your thought,
 Ev'n when your end's attained;
And a' your views may come to nought,
 Where ev'ry nerve is strained.

I'll no say, men are villains a';
 The real, harden'd wicked,
Wha hae nae check but human law,
 Are to a few restricked;
But, och! mankind are unco weak,
 An' little to be trusted;
If *self* the wavering balance shake,
 It's rarely right adjusted!

Yet they wha fa' in fortune's strife,
 Their fate we shouldna censure;
For still, th' important end of life
 They equally may answer;
A man may hae an honest heart,
 Tho' poortith hourly stare him;   *poverty*
A man may tak a neibor's part,
 Yet hae nae cash to spare him.

Aye free, aff-han', your story tell,
 When wi' a bosom crony;
But still keep something to yoursel',
 Ye scarcely tell to ony:
Conceal yoursel' as weel's ye can
 Frae critical dissection;
But keek thro' ev'ry other man,   *peer*
 Wi' sharpen'd, sly inspection.

The sacred lowe o' weel-plac'd love,   *flame*
 Luxuriantly indulge it;
But never tempt th' illicit rove,
 Tho' naething should divulge it:
I waive the quantum o' the sin,
 The hazard of concealing;
But, och! it hardens a' within,
 And petrifies the feeling!

To catch dame Fortune's golden smile,
 Assiduous wait upon her;
And gather gear by ev'ry wile   *money, possessions*
 That's justified by honour;

Not for to hide it in a hedge,
   Nor for a train attendant;
But for the glorious privilege
   Of being independent.

The fear o' hell's a hangman's whip,
   To haud the wretch in order;
But where ye feel your honour grip,
   Let that aye be your border;
Its slightest touches, instant pause —
   Debar a' side-pretences;
And resolutely keep its laws,
   Uncaring consequences.

The great Creator to revere,
   Must sure become the creature;
But still the preaching cant forbear,
   And ev'n the rigid feature:
Yet ne'er with wits profanc to range,
   Be complaisance extended;
An atheist-laugh's a poor exchange
   For Deity offended!

When ranting round in pleasure's ring,
   Religion may be blinded;
Or if she gie a random sting,
   It may be little minded;
But when on life we're tempest-driv'n —
   A conscience but a canker,
A correspondence fix'd wi' Heav'n,
   Is sure a noble anchor!

Adieu, dear, amiable youth!
   Your heart can ne'er be wanting!
May prudence, fortitude, and truth,
   Erect your brow undaunting!
In ploughman phrase, 'God send you speed,'
   Still daily to grow wiser;
And may ye better reck the rede,
   Than ever did th' adviser!

305   *Epitaph for James Smith*

Lament him, Mauchline husbands a',
    He aften did assist ye;
For had ye staid hale weeks awa,
    Your wives they ne'er had miss'd ye.

Ye Mauchline bairns, as on ye pass
    To school in bands thegither,
O tread ye lightly on his grass, –
    Perhaps he was your father!

306   *Highland Harry Back Again*

My Harry was a gallant gay,
    Fu' stately strade he on the plain;
But now he's banish'd far away,
    I'll never see him back again.

      O for him back again!
      O for him back again!
      I wad gie a' Knockhaspie's land
      For Highland Harry back again.

When a' the lave gae to their bed,   *others*
    I wander dowie up the glen;
I set me down and greet my fill,   *wept*
    And aye I wish him back again.
      O for him, etc.

O were some villains hangit high,
    And ilka body had their ain!
Then I might see the joyfu' sight,
    My Highland Harry back again.
      O for him, etc.

Attributed to Burns

307   *No Cold Approach*

No cold approach, no altered mien,
    Just what would make suspicion start;
No pause the dire extremes between,
    He made me blest – and broke my heart.

Attributed to Burns

308   ## *O Wert Thou in the Cauld Blast*

O wert thou in the cauld blast,
  On yonder lea, on yonder lea,
My plaidie to the angry airt,
  I'd shelter thee, I'd shelter thee;
Or did Misfortune's bitter storms
  Around thee blaw, around thee blaw,
Thy bield should be my bosom,
  To share it a', to share it a'.

Or were I in the wildest waste,
  Sae black and bare, sae black and bare,
The desert were a Paradise,
  If thou wert there, if thou wert there;
Or were I Monarch o' the globe,
  Wi' thee to reign, wi' thee to reign,
The brightest jewel in my Crown
  Wad be my Queen, wad be my Queen.

William Wordsworth

309   ## *The Two April Mornings*

We walked along, while bright and red
Uprose the morning sun;
And Matthew stopped, he looked, and said,
'The will of God be done!'

A village schoolmaster was he,
With hair of glittering grey;
As blithe a man as you could see
On a spring holiday.

And on that morning, through the grass,
And by the steaming rills,
We travelled merrily, to pass
A day among the hills.

'Our work,' said I, 'was well begun,
Then, from thy breast what thought,
Beneath so beautiful a sun,
So sad a sigh has brought?'

A second time did Matthew stop;
And fixing still his eye
Upon the eastern mountain-top,
To me he made reply:

'Yon cloud with that long purple cleft
Brings fresh into my mind
A day like this which I have left
Full thirty years behind.

And just above yon slope of corn
Such colours, and no other,
Were in the sky, that April morn,
Of this the very brother.

With rod and line I sued the sport
Which that sweet season gave,
And, to the churchyard come, stopped short
Beside my daughter's grave.

Nine summers had she scarcely seen,
The pride of all the vale;
And then she sang; – she would have been
A very nightingale.

Six feet in earth my Emma lay;
And yet I loved her more,
For so it seemed, than till that day
I e'er had loved before.

And, turning from her grave, I met,
Beside the churchyard yew,
A blooming Girl, whose hair was wet
With points of morning dew.

A basket on her head she bare;
Her brow was smooth and white:
To see a child so very fair,
It was a pure delight!

No fountain from its rocky cave
E'er tripped with foot so free;
She seemed as happy as a wave
That dances on the sea.

There came from me a sigh of pain
Which I could ill confine;
I looked at her, and looked again:
And did not wish her mine!'

Matthew is in his grave, yet now,
Methinks, I see him stand,
As at that moment, with a bough
Of wilding in his hand.

310   Strange fits of passion have I known:
                        And I will dare to tell,
                    But in the Lover's ear alone,
                        What once to me befell.

When she I loved looked every day
    Fresh as a rose in June,
I to her cottage bent my way,
    Beneath an evening-moon.

Upon the moon I fixed my eye,
    All over the wide lea;
With quickening pace my horse drew nigh
    Those paths so dear to me.

And now we reached the orchard-plot;
    And, as we climbed the hill,
The sinking moon to Lucy's cot
    Came near, and nearer still.

In one of those sweet dreams I slept,
    Kind Nature's gentlest boon!
And all the while my eyes I kept
    On the descending moon.

My horse moved on; hoof after hoof
    He raised, and never stopped:
When down behind the cottage roof,
    At once, the bright moon dropped.

What fond and wayward thoughts will slide
    Into a Lover's head!
'O mercy!' to myself I cried,
    'If Lucy should be dead!'

311   *The Farmer of Tilsbury Vale*

'Tis not for the unfeeling, the falsely refined,
The squeamish in taste, and the narrow of mind,
And the small critic wielding his delicate pen,
That I sing of old Adam, the pride of old men.

He dwells in the centre of London's wide Town;
His staff is a sceptre – his grey hairs a crown;
And his bright eyes look brighter, set off by the streak
Of the unfaded rose that still blooms on his cheek.

'Mid the dews, in the sunshine of morn, – 'mid the joy
Of the fields, he collected that bloom, when a boy,
That countenance there fashioned, which, spite of a stain
That his life hath received, to the last will remain.

A Farmer he was; and his house far and near
Was the boast of the country for excellent cheer:
How oft have I heard in sweet Tilsbury Vale
Of the silver-rimmed horn whence he dealt his mild ale!

Yet Adam was far as the farthest from ruin,
His fields seemed to know what their Master was doing:
And turnips, and corn-land, and meadow, and lea,
All caught the infection – as generous as he.

Yet Adam prized little the feast and the bowl, –
The fields better suited the ease of his soul:
He strayed through the fields like an indolent wight,
The quiet of nature was Adam's delight.

For Adam was simple in thought; and the poor,
Familiar with him, made an inn of his door:
He gave them the best that he had; or, to say
What less may mislead you, they took it away.

Thus thirty smooth years did he thrive on his farm:
The Genius of plenty preserved him from harm:
At length, what to most is a season of sorrow,
His means are run out, – he must beg, or must borrow.

To the neighbours he went, – all were free with their money;
For his hive had so long been replenished with honey,
That they dreamt not of dearth; – He continued his rounds,
Knocked here – and knocked there, pounds still adding to pounds.

He paid what he could with his ill-gotten pelf,
And something, it might be, reserved for himself:
Then (what is too true) without hinting a word,
Turned his back on the country – and off like a bird.

You lift up your eyes! – but I guess that you frame
A judgment too harsh of the sin and the shame;
In him it was scarcely a business of art,
For this he did all in the *ease* of his heart.

To London – a sad emigration I ween –
With his grey hairs he went from the brook and the green;
And there, with small wealth but his legs and his hands,
As lonely he stood as a crow on the sands.

All trades, as need was, did old Adam assume, –
Served as stable-boy, errand-boy, porter, and groom;

But nature is gracious, necessity kind,
And, in spite of the shame that may lurk in his mind,

He seems ten birthdays younger, is green and is stout;
Twice as fast as before does his blood run about;
You would say that each hair of his beard was alive,
And his fingers are as busy as bees in a hive.

For he's not like an Old Man that leisurely goes
About work that he knows, in a track that he knows;
But often his mind is compelled to demur,
And you guess that the more then his body must stir.

In the throng of the town like a stranger is he,
Like one whose own country's far over the sea;
And Nature, while through the great city he hies,
Full ten times a day takes his heart by surprise.

This gives him the fancy of one that is young,
More of soul in his face than of words on his tongue;
Like a maiden of twenty he trembles and sighs,
And tears of fifteen will come into his eyes.

What's a tempest to him, or the dry parching heats?
Yet he watches the clouds that pass over the streets;
With a look of such earnestness often will stand,
You might think he'd twelve reapers at work in the Strand.

Where proud Covent-garden, in desolate hours
Of snow and hoar-frost, spreads her fruits and her flowers,
Old Adam will smile at the pains that have made
Poor winter look fine in such strange masquerade.

'Mid coaches and chariots, a waggon of straw,
Like a magnet, the heart of old Adam can draw;
With a thousand soft pictures his memory will teem,
And his hearing is touched with the sounds of a dream.

Up the Haymarket hill he oft whistles his way,
Thrusts his hands in a waggon, and smells at the hay;
He thinks of the fields he so often hath mown,
And is happy as if the rich freight were his own.

But chiefly to Smithfield he loves to repair, –
If you pass by at morning, you'll meet with him there.
The breath of the cows you may see him inhale,
And his heart all the while is in Tilsbury Vale.

Now farewell, old Adam! when low thou art laid,
May one blade of grass spring up over thy head;
And I hope that thy grave, wheresoever it be,
Will hear the wind sigh through the leaves of a tree.

312   *Resolution and Independence*

There was a roaring in the wind all night;
The rain came heavily and fell in floods;
But now the sun is rising calm and bright;
The birds are singing in the distant woods;
Over his own sweet voice the Stock-dove broods;
The Jay makes answer as the Magpie chatters;
And all the air is filled with pleasant noise of waters.

All things that love the sun are out of doors;
The sky rejoices in the morning's birth;
The grass is bright with rain-drops; – on the moors
The hare is running races in her mirth;
And with her feet she from the plashy earth
Raises a mist; that, glittering in the sun,
Runs with her all the way, wherever she doth run.

I was a Traveller then upon the moor,
I saw the hare that raced about with joy;
I heard the woods and distant waters roar;
Or heard them not, as happy as a boy:
The pleasant season did my heart employ:
My old remembrances went from me wholly;
And all the ways of men, so vain and melancholy.

But, as it sometimes chanceth, from the might
Of joy in minds that can no further go,
As high as we have mounted in delight
In our dejection do we sink as low;
To me that morning did it happen so;
And fears and fancies thick upon me came;
Dim sadness – and blind thoughts, I knew not, nor could name.

I heard the sky-lark warbling in the sky;
And I bethought me of the playful hare:
Even such a happy Child of earth am I;
Even as these blissful creatures do I fare;
Far from the world I walk, and from all care;
But there may come another day to me –
Solitude, pain of heart, distress, and poverty.

My whole life I have lived in pleasant thought,
As if life's business were a summer mood;
As if all needful things would come unsought
To genial faith, still rich in genial good;
But how can He expect that others should
Build for him, sow for him, and at his call
Love him, who for himself will take no heed at all?

I thought of Chatterton, the marvellous Boy,
The sleepless Soul that perished in his pride;
Of Him who walked in glory and in joy
Following his plough, along the mountain-side:
By our own spirits are we deified:
We Poets in our youth begin in gladness;
But thereof come in the end despondency and madness.

Now, whether it were by peculiar grace,
A leading from above, a something given,
Yet it befell, that, in this lonely place,
When I with these untoward thoughts had striven,
Beside a pool bare to the eye of heaven
I saw a Man before me unawares:
The oldest man he seemed that ever wore grey hairs.

As a huge stone is sometimes seen to lie
Couched on the bald top of an eminence;
Wonder to all who do the same espy,
By what means it could thither come, and whence;
So that it seems a thing endued with sense:
Like a sea-beast crawled forth, that on a shelf
Of rock or sand reposeth, there to sun itself;

Such seemed this Man, not all alive nor dead,
Nor all asleep – in his extreme old age:
His body was bent double, feet and head
Coming together in life's pilgrimage;
As if some dire constraint of pain, or rage
Of sickness felt by him in times long past,
A more than human weight upon his frame had cast.

Himself he propped, limbs, body, and pale face,
Upon a long grey staff of shaven wood:
And, still as I drew near with gentle pace,
Upon the margin of that moorish flood
Motionless as a cloud the old Man stood,
That heareth not the loud winds when they call
And moveth all together, if it move at all.

At length, himself unsettling, he the pond
Stirred with his staff, and fixedly did look
Upon the muddy water, which he conned,
As if he had been reading in a book:
And now a stranger's privilege I took;
And, drawing to his side, to him did say,
'This morning gives us promise of a glorious day.'

A gentle answer did the old Man make,
In courteous speech which forth he slowly drew:
And him with further words I thus bespake,
'What occupation do you there pursue?
This is a lonesome place for one like you.'
Ere he replied, a flash of mild surprise
Broke from the sable orbs of his yet-vivid eyes.

His words came feebly, from a feeble chest,
But each in solemn order followed each,
With something of a lofty utterance drest –
Choice word and measured phrase, above the reach
Of ordinary men; a stately speech;
Such as grave Livers do in Scotland use,
Religious men, who give to God and man their dues.

He told, that to these waters he had come
To gather leeches, being old and poor:
Employment hazardous and wearisome!
And he had many hardships to endure:
From pond to pond he roamed, from moor to moor;
Housing, with God's good help, by choice or chance,
And in this way he gained an honest maintenance.

The old Man still stood talking by my side;
But now his voice to me was like a stream
Scarce heard; nor word from word could I divide;
And the whole body of the Man did seem
Like one whom I had met with in a dream;
Or like a man from some far region sent,
To give me human strength, by apt admonishment.

My former thoughts returned: the fear that kills;
And hope that is unwilling to be fed;
Cold, pain, and labour, and all fleshly ills;
And mighty Poets in their misery dead.
– Perplexed, and longing to be comforted,
My question eagerly did I renew,
'How is it that you live, and what is it you do?'

He with a smile did then his words repeat;
And said, that, gathering leeches, far and wide
He travelled; stirring thus about his feet
The waters of the pools where they abide.
'Once I could meet with them on every side;
But they have dwindled long by slow decay;
Yet still I persevere, and find them where I may.'

While he was talking thus, the lonely place,
The old Man's shape, and speech – all troubled me:
In my mind's eye I seemed to see him pace
About the weary moors continually,
Wandering about alone and silently.
While I these thoughts within myself pursued,
He, having made a pause, the same discourse renewed.

And soon with this he other matter blended,
Cheerfully uttered, with demeanour kind,
But stately in the main; and when he ended,
I could have laughed myself to scorn to find
In the decrepit Man so firm a mind.
'God,' said I, 'be my help and stay secure;
I'll think of the Leech-gatherer on the lonely moor!'

From *The Prelude (1805)*

313   [1]

Summer Vacation

                              In a throng,
A festal company of Maids and Youths,
Old Men, and Matrons staid, promiscuous rout,
A medley of all tempers, I had passed
The night in dancing, gaiety and mirth;
With din of instruments, and shuffling feet,
And glancing forms, and tapers glittering,
And unaimed prattle flying up and down,
Spirits upon the stretch, and here and there
Slight shocks of young love-liking interspersed,
That mounted up like joy into the head,
And tingled through the veins. Ere we retired,
The cock had crowed, the sky was bright with day.
Two miles I had to walk along the fields
Before I reached my home. Magnificent
The morning was, in memorable pomp,
More glorious than I ever had beheld.
The Sea was laughing at a distance; all
The solid Mountains were as bright as clouds,
Grain-tinctured, drenched in empyrean light;
And, in the meadows and the lower grounds,
Was all the sweetness of a common dawn,
Dews, vapours, and the melody of birds,
And Labourers going forth into the fields.

– Ah! need I say, dear Friend, that to the brim
My heart was full; I made no vows, but vows
Were then made for me; bond unknown to me
Was given, that I should be, else sinning greatly,
A dedicated Spirit. On I walked
In blessedness, which even yet remains.

314   [2]

Conclusion

In one of these excursions, travelling then
Through Wales on foot, and with a youthful Friend,
I left Bethhelert's huts at couching-time,
And westward took my way to see the sun
Rise from the top of Snowdon. Having reached
The Cottage at the Mountain's foot, we there
Rouzed up the Shepherd, who by ancient right
Of office is the Stranger's usual guide;
And after short refreshment sallied forth.

    It was a Summer's night, a close warm night,
Wan, dull and glaring, with a dripping mist
Low-hung and thick that covered all the sky,
Half threatening storm and rain; but on we went
Unchecked, being full of heart and having faith
In our tried Pilot. Little could we see
Hemmed round on every side with fog and damp,
And, after ordinary travellers' chat
With our Conductor, silently we sank
Each into commerce with his private thoughts:
Thus did we breast the ascent, and by myself
Was nothing either seen or heard the while
Which took me from my musings, save that once
The Shepherd's Cur did to his own great joy
Unearth a hedgehog in the mountain crags
Round which he made a barking turbulent.
This small adventure, for even such it seemed
In that wild place and at the dead of night,
Being over and forgotten, on we wound
In silence as before. With forehead bent
Earthward, as if in opposition set
Against an enemy, I panted up
With eager pace, and no less eager thoughts.
Thus might we wear perhaps an hour away,
Ascending at loose distance each from each,

And I, as chanced, the foremost of the Band;
When at my feet the ground appeared to brighten,
And with a step or two seemed brighter still;
Nor had I time to ask the cause of this,
For instantly a Light upon the turf
Fell like a flash: I looked about, and lo!
The Moon stood naked in the Heavens, at height
Immense above my head, and on the shore
I found myself of a huge sea of mist,
Which, meek and silent, rested at my feet:
A hundred hills their dusky backs upheaved
All over this still Ocean, and beyond,
Far, far beyond, the vapours shot themselves,
In headlands, tongues, and promontory shapes,
Into the Sea, the real Sea, that seemed
To dwindle, and give up its majesty,
Unsurped upon as far as sight could reach.
Meanwhile, the Moon looked down upon this shew
In single glory, and we stood, the mist
Touching our very feet; and from the shore
At distance not the third part of a mile
Was a blue chasm; a fracture in the vapour,
A deep and gloomy breathing-place through which
Mounted the roar of waters, torrents, streams
Innumerable, roaring with one voice.
The universal spectacle throughout
Was shaped for admiration and delight,
Grand in itself alone, but in that breach
Through which the homeless voice of waters rose,
That dark deep thoroughfare had Nature lodged
The Soul, the Imagination of the whole.

   A meditation rose in me that night
Upon the lonely Mountain when the scene
Had passed away, and it appeared to me
The perfect image of a mighty Mind,
Of one that feeds upon infinity,
That is exalted by an underpresence,
The sense of God, or whatsoe'er is dim
Or vast in its own being, above all
One function of such mind had Nature there
Exhibited by putting forth, and that
With circumstance most awful and sublime,
That domination which she oftentimes
Exerts upon the outward face of things,
So moulds them, and endues, abstracts, combines,
Or by abrupt and unhabitual influence
Doth make one object so impress itself
Upon all others, and pervade them so

That even the grossest minds must see and hear
And cannot chuse but feel. The Power which these
Acknowledge when thus moved, which Nature thus
Thrusts forth upon the senses, is the express
Resemblance, in the fulness of its strength
Made visible, a genuine Counterpart
And Brother of the glorious faculty
Which higher minds bear with them as their own.
That is the very spirit in which they deal
With all the objects of the universe;
They from their native selves can send abroad
Like transformations, for themselves create
A like existence, and, whene'er it is
Created for them, catch it by an instinct;
Them the enduring and the transient both
Serve to exalt; they build up greatest things
From least suggestions, ever on the watch,
Willing to work and to be wrought upon,
They need not extraordinary calls
To rouze them, in a world of life they live,
By sensible impressions not enthralled,
But quickened, rouzed, and made thereby more apt
To hold communion with the invisible world.
Such minds are truly from the Deity,
For they are Powers; and hence the highest bliss
That can be known is theirs, the consciousness
Of whom they are habitually infused
Through every image, and through every thought,
And all impressions; hence religion, faith,
And endless occupation for the soul
Whether discursive or intuitive;
Hence sovereignty within and peace at will
Emotion which best foresight need not fear
Most worthy then of trust when most intense.
Hence chearfulness in every act of life
Hence truth in moral judgements and delight
That fails not in the external universe.

315   Nuns fret not at their convent's narrow room;
           And hermits are contented with their cells;
           And students with their pensive citadels;
           Maids at the wheel, the weaver at his loom,
           Sit blithe and happy; bees that soar for bloom,
           High as the highest Peak of Furness-fells.
           Will murmur by the hour in foxglove bells:
           In truth the prison, unto which we doom

Ourselves, no prison is: and hence for me,
In sundry moods, 'twas pastime to be bound
Within the Sonnet's scanty plot of ground;
Pleased if some Souls (for such there needs must be)
Who have felt the weight of too much liberty,
Should find brief solace there, as I have found.

316   *Mutability*

From low to high doth dissolution climb,
And sink from high to low, along a scale
Of awful notes, whose concord shall not fail;
A musical but melancholy chime,
Which they can hear who meddle not with crime,
Nor avarice, nor over-anxious care.
Truth fails not; but her outward forms that bear
The longest date do melt like frosty rime,
That in the morning whitened hill and plain
And is no more; drop like the tower sublime
Of yesterday, which royally did wear
His crown of weeds, but could not even sustain
Some casual shout that broke the silent air,
Or the unimaginable touch of Time.

317   Scorn not the Sonnet; Critic, you have frowned,
Mindless of its just honours; with this key
Shakespeare unlocked his heart; the melody
Of this small lute gave ease to Petrarch's wound;
A thousand times this pipe did Tasso sound;
With it Camöens soothed an exile's grief;
The Sonnet glittered a gay myrtle leaf
Amid the cypress with which Dante crowned
His visionary brow: a glow-worm lamp,
It cheered mild Spenser, called from Faeryland
To struggle through dark ways; and, when a damp
Fell round the path of Milton, in his hand
The Thing became a trumpet; whence he blew
Soul-animating strains – alas, too few!

318   ## On the Departure of Sir Walter Scott
from Abbotsford, for Naples

A trouble, not of clouds, or weeping rain,
Nor of the setting sun's pathetic light
Engendered, hangs o'er Eildon's triple height:
Spirits of Power, assembled there, complain
For kindred Power departing from their sight;
While Tweed, best pleased in chanting a blithe strain,
Saddens his voice again, and yet again.
Lift up your hearts, ye Mourners! for the might
Of the whole world's good wishes with him goes;
Blessings and prayers, in nobler retinue
Than sceptred king or laurelled conqueror knows,
Follow this wondrous Potentate. Be true,
Ye winds of ocean, and the midland sea,
Wafting your Charge to soft Parthenope!

319   ## Extempore Effusion upon the Death
of James Hogg

When first, descending from the moorlands,
I saw the Stream of Yarrow glide
Along a bare and open valley,
The Ettrick Shepherd was my guide.

When last along its banks I wandered,
Through groves that had begun to shed
Their golden leaves upon the pathways,
My steps the Border-minstrel led.

The mighty Minstrel breathes no longer,
'Mid mouldering ruins low he lies;
And death upon the braes of Yarrow,
Has closed the Shepherd-poet's eyes:

Nor has the rolling year twice measured,
From sign to sign, its steadfast course,
Since every mortal power of Coleridge
Was frozen at its marvellous source;

The rapt One, of the godlike forehead,
The heaven-eyed creature sleeps in earth:
And Lamb, the frolic and the gentle,
Has vanished from his lonely hearth.

Like clouds that rake the mountain-summits,
Or waves that own no curbing hand,
How fast has brother followed brother
From sunshine to the sunless land!

Yet I, whose lids from infant slumber
Were earlier raised, remain to hear
A timid voice, that asks in whispers,
'Who next will drop and disappear?'

Our haughty life is crowned with darkness,
Like London with its own black wreath,
On which with thee, O Crabbe! forth-looking,
I gazed from Hampstead's breezy heath.

As if but yesterday departed,
Thou too art gone before; but why,
O'er ripe fruit, seasonably gathered,
Should frail survivors heave a sigh?

Mourn rather for that holy Spirit,
Sweet as the spring, as ocean deep;
For Her who, ere her summer faded,
Has sunk into a breathless sleep.

No more of old romantic sorrows,
For slaughtered Youth or love-lorn Maid!
With sharper grief is Yarrow smitten,
And Ettrick mourns with her their Poet dead.

Samuel Taylor Coleridge

320   *The Rime of the Ancyent Marinere*
                    In Seven Parts

Argument

How a Ship having passed the Line was driven by Storms to
the cold Country towards the South Pole; and how from
thence she made her course to the Tropical Latitude of the
Great Pacific Ocean; and of the strange things that befell;
and in what manner the Ancyent Marinere came back to his
own Country.

I

It is an ancyent Marinere,
    And he stoppeth one of three:
'By thy long grey beard and thy glittering eye
    Now wherefore stoppest me?

The Bridegroom's doors are open'd wide,
   And I am next of kin;
The Guests are met, the Feast is set, –
   May'st hear the merry din.'

But still he holds the wedding-guest –
   There was a Ship, quoth he –
'Nay, if thou'st got a laughsome tale,
   Marinere! come with me.'

He holds him with his skinny hand,
   Quoth he, there was a Ship –
'Now get thee hence, thou grey-beard Loon!
   Or my Staff shall make thee skip.'

He holds him with his glittering eye –
   The wedding-guest stood still
And listens like a three year's child;
   The Marinere hath his will.

The wedding-guest sate on a stone.
   He cannot chuse but hear:
And thus spake on that ancyent man,
   The bright-eyed Marinere.

The Ship was cheer'd, the Harbour clear'd –
   Merrily did we drop
Below the Kirk, below the Hill,
   Below the Light-house top.

The Sun came up upon the left,
   Out of the Sea came he:
And he shone bright, and on the right
   Went down into the Sea.

Higher and higher every day,
   Till over the mast at noon –
The wedding-guest here beat his breast,
   For he heard the loud bassoon.

The Bride hath pac'd into the Hall,
   Red as a rose is she;
Nodding their heads before her goes
   The merry Minstralsy.

The wedding-guest he beat his breast,
   Yet he cannot chuse but hear:
And thus spake on that ancyent Man,
   The bright-eyed Marinere.

Listen, Stranger! Storm and Wind,
   A Wind and Tempest strong!
For days and weeks it play'd us freaks —
   Like Chaff we drove along.

Listen, Stranger! Mist and Snow,
   And it grew wond'rous cauld:
And Ice mast-high came floating by
   As green as Emerauld.

And thro' the drifts the snowy clifts
   Did send a dismal sheen;
Ne shapes of men ne beasts we ken —
   The Ice was all between.

The Ice was here, the Ice was there,
   The Ice was all around:
It crack'd and growl'd, and roar'd and howl'd —
   Like noises of a swound.

At length did cross an Albatross,
   Thorough the Fog it came;
And an it were a Christian Soul,
   We hail'd it in God's name.

The Marineres gave it biscuit-worms,
   And round and round it flew:
The Ice did split with a Thunder-fit,
   The Helmsman steer'd us thro'.

And a good south wind sprung up behind,
   The Albatross did follow;
And every day for food or play
   Came to the Marinere's hollo!

In mist or cloud on mast or shroud,
   It perch'd for vespers nine,
Whiles all the night thro' fog-smoke white,
   Glimmer'd the white moon-shine.

'God save thee, ancyent Marinere!
   From the fiends that plague thee thus —
Why look'st thou so?' — with my cross-bow
   I shot the Albatross.

II

The Sun came up upon the right,
   Out of the Sea came he;
And broad as a weft upon the left
   Went down into the Sea.

And the good south wind still blew behind,
  But no sweet Bird did follow
Ne any day for food or play
  Came to the Marinere's hollo!

And I had done an hellish thing
  And it would work 'em woe:
For all averr'd, I had kill'd the Bird
  That made the Breeze to blow.

Ne dim ne red, like God's own head,
  The glorious Sun uprist:
Then all averr'd, I had kill'd the Bird
  That brought the fog and mist.
'Twas right, said they, such birds to slay
  That bring the fog and mist.

The breezes blew, the white foam flew,
  The furrow follow'd free:
We were the first that ever burst
  Into that silent Sea.

Down dropt the breeze, the Sails dropt down,
  'Twas sad as sad could be
And we did speak only to break
  The silence of the Sea.

All in a hot and copper sky
  The bloody sun at noon,
Right up above the mast did stand,
  No bigger than the moon.

Day after day, day after day,
  We stuck, ne breath ne motion,
As idle as a painted Ship
  Upon a painted Ocean.

Water, water, everywhere,
  And all the boards did shrink;
Water, water, everywhere,
  Ne any drop to drink.

The very deeps did rot: O Christ!
  That ever this should be!
Yea, slimy things did crawl with legs
  Upon the slimy Sea.

About, about, in reel and rout,
  The Death-fires danc'd at night;
The water, like a witch's oils,
  Burnt green and blue and white.

And some in dreams assured were
  Of the Spirit that plagued us so:
Nine fathom deep he had follow'd us
  From the Land of Mist and Snow.

And every tongue thro' utter drouth
  Was wither'd at the root;
We could not speak no more than if
  We had been choked with soot.

Ah wel-a-day! what evil looks
  Had I from old and young;
Instead of the Cross the Albatross
  About my neck was hung.

III

I saw a something in the Sky
  No bigger than my fist;
At first it seem'd a little speck
  And then it seem'd a mist:
It mov'd and mov'd, and took at last
  A certain shape, I wist.

A speck, a mist, a shape, I wist!
  And still it ner'd and ner'd;
And, an it dodg'd a water-sprite,
  It plung'd and tack'd and veer'd.

With throat unslack'd, with black lips bak'd
  Ne could we laugh, ne wail:
Then while thro' drouth all dumb they stood
I bit my arm and suck'd the blood
  And cry'd, A sail! a sail!

With throat unslack'd, with black lips bak'd
  Agape they hear'd me call:
Gramercy! they for joy did grin
And all at once their breath drew in
  As they were drinking all.

She doth not tack from side to side –
  Hither to work us weal
Withouten wind, withouten tide
  She steddies with upright keel.

The western wave was all a flame,
  The day was well nigh done!
Almost upon the western wave
  Rested the broad bright Sun;

When that strange shape drove suddenly
  Betwixt us and the Sun.

And strait the Sun was fleck'd with bars
  (Heaven's mother send us grace)
As if thro' a dungeon grate he peer'd
  With broad and burning face.

Alas! (thought I, and my heart beat loud)
  How fast she neres and neres!
Are those *her* Sails that glance in the Sun
  Like restless gossameres?

Are those *her* naked ribs, which fleck'd
  The sun that did behind them peer?
And are these two all, all the crew,
  That woman and her fleshless Pheere?

His bones were black with many a crack,
  All black and bare, I ween;
Jet-black and bare, save where with rust
Of mouldy damps and charnel crust
  They're patch'd with purple and green.

Her lips are red, *her* looks are free,
  Her locks are yellow as gold:
Her skin is as white as leprosy,
And she is far liker Death than he;
  Her flesh makes the still air cold.

The naked Hulk alongside came
  And the Twain were playing dice;
'The Game is done! I've won, I've won!'
  Quoth she, and whistled thrice.

A gust of wind sterte up behind
  And whistled thro' his bones;
Thro' the holes of his eyes and the hole of his mouth
  Half-whistles and half-groans.

With never a whisper in the Sea
  Off darts the Spectre-ship;
While clombe above the Eastern bar
The horned Moon, with one bright Star
  Almost atween the tips.

One after one by the horned Moon
  (Listen, O Stranger! to me)
Each turn'd his face with a ghastly pang
  And curs'd me with his ee.

Four times fifty living men,
   With never a sigh or groan,
With heavy thump, a lifeless lump
   They dropp'd down one by one.

Their souls did from their bodies fly, —
   They fled to bliss or woe;
And every soul it pass'd me by,
   Like the whiz of my Cross-bow.

IV

'I fear thee, ancyent Marinere!
   I fear thy skinny hand;
And thou art long, and lank, and brown,
   As is the ribb'd Sea-sand.

I fear thee and thy glittering eye
   And thy skinny hand so brown –'
Fear not, fear not, thou wedding-guest!
   This body dropt not down.

Alone, alone, all all alone
   Alone on the wide wide Sea;
And Christ would take no pity on
   My soul in agony.

The many men so beautiful,
   And they all dead did lie!
And a million million slimy things
   Liv'd on – and so did I.

I look'd upon the rotting Sea,
   And drew my eyes away;
I look'd upon the eldritch deck,
   And there the dead men lay.

I look'd to Heav'n, and try'd to pray;
   But or ever a prayer had gusht,
A wicked whisper came and made
   My heart as dry as dust.

I clos'd my lids and kept them close,
   Till the balls like pulses beat;
For the sky and the sea, and the sea and the sky
Lay like a load on my weary eye,
   And the dead were at my feet.

The cold sweat melted from their limbs,
 Ne rot, ne reek did they;
The look with which they look'd on me,
 Had never pass'd away.

An orphan's curse would drag to Hell
 A spirit from on high:
But O! more horrible than that
 Is the curse in a dead man's eye!
Seven days, seven nights I saw that curse,
 And yet I could not die.

The moving Moon went up the sky,
 And no where did abide:
Softly she was going up
 And a star or two beside —

Her beams bemock'd the sultry main
 Like morning frosts yspread;
But where the ship's huge shadow lay,
The charmed water burnt alway
 A still and awful red.

Beyond the shadow of the ship
 I watch'd the water-snakes:
They mov'd in tracks of shining white;
And when they rear'd, the elfish light
 Fell off in hoary flakes.

Within the shadow of the ship
 I watch'd their rich attire:
Blue, glossy green, and velvet black
They coil'd and swam; and every track
 Was a flash of golden fire.

O happy living things! no tongue
 Their beauty might declare:
A spring of love gusht from my heart,
 And I bless'd them unaware!
Sure my kind saint took pity on me,
 And I bless'd them unaware.

The self-same moment I could pray;
 And from my neck so free
The Albatross fell off, and sank
 Like lead into the sea.

V

O sleep, it is a gentle thing,
  Belov'd from pole to pole!
To Mary-queen the praise be yeven
She sent the gentle sleep from heaven
  That slid into my soul.

The silly buckets on the deck
  That had so long remain'd,
I dreamt that they were fill'd with dew
  And when I awoke it rain'd.

My lips were wet, my throat was cold,
  My garments all were dank;
Sure I had drunken in my dreams
  And still my body drank.

I mov'd and could not feel my limbs,
  I was so light, almost
I thought that I had died in sleep,
  And was a blessed Ghost.

The roaring wind! it roar'd far off,
  It did not come anear;
But with its sound it shook the sails
  That were so thin and sere.

The upper air bursts into life,
  And a hundred fire-flags sheen
To and fro they are hurried about;
And to and fro, and in and out
  The stars dance on between.

The coming wind doth roar more loud;
  The sails do sigh, like sedge:
The rain pours down from one black cloud
  And the Moon is at its edge.

Hark! hark! the thick black cloud is cleft,
  And the Moon is at its side:
Like waters shot from some high crag,
The lightning falls with never a jag
  A river steep and wide.

The strong wind reach'd the ship: it roar'd
  And dropp'd down, like a stone!
Beneath the lightning and the moon
  The dead men gave a groan.

It ceas'd: yet still the sails made on
    A pleasant noise till noon,
A noise like of a hidden brook
    In the leafy month of June,
That to the sleeping woods all night
    Singeth a quiet tune.

Listen, O listen, thou Wedding-guest!
    'Marinere! thou hast thy will:
For that, which comes out of thine eye, doth make
    My body and soul to be still.'

Never sadder tale was told
    To a man of woman born:
Sadder and wiser thou wedding-guest!
    Thou'lt rise to-morrow morn.

Never sadder tale was heard
    By a man of woman born:
The Marineres all return'd to work
    As silent as beforne.

The Marineres all 'gan pull the ropes,
    But look at me they n'old:
Thought I, I am as thin as air –
    They cannot me behold.

Till noon we silently sail'd on
    Yet never a breeze did breathe:
Slowly and smoothly went the ship
    Mov'd onward from beneath.

Under the keel nine fathom deep
    From the land of mist and snow
The spirit slid: and it was He
    That made the Ship to go.
The sails at noon left off their tune
    And the Ship stood still also.

They groan'd, they stirr'd, they all uprose,
    Ne spake, ne mov'd their eyes:
It had been strange, even in a dream
    To have seen those dead men rise.

The helmsman steer'd, the ship mov'd on;
    Yet never a breeze up-blew;
The Marineres all 'gan work the ropes,
    Where they were wont to do:
They rais'd their limbs like lifeless tools –
    We were a ghastly crew.

The body of my brother's son
  Stood by me knee to knee:
The body and I pull'd at one rope,
  But he said nought to me –
And I quak'd to think of my own voice
  How frightful it would be!

The day-light dawn'd – they dropp'd their arms,
  And cluster'd round the mast:
Sweet sounds rose slowly thro' their mouths
  And from their bodies pass'd.

Around, around, flew each sweet sound,
  Then darted to the sun:
Slowly the sounds came back again
  Now mix'd, now one by one.

Sometimes a dropping from the sky
  I heard the Lavrock sing;
Sometimes all little birds that are
How they seem'd to fill the sea and air
  With their sweet jargoning.

And now 'twas like all instruments,
  Now like a lonely flute;
And now it is an angel's song
  That makes the heavens be mute.

The sun right up above the mast
  Had fix'd her to the ocean:
But in a minute she 'gan stir
  With a short uneasy motion –
Backwards and forwards half her length
  With a short uneasy motion.

Then, like a pawing horse let go,
  She made a sudden bound:
It flung the blood into my head,
  And I fell into a swound.

How long in that same fit I lay,
  I have not to declare;
But ere my living life return'd,
I heard and in my soul discern'd
  Two voices in the air,

'Is it he?' quoth one, 'Is this the man?
  By him who died on cross,
With his cruel bow he lay'd full low
  The harmless Albatross.

The spirit who 'bideth by himself
  In the land of mist and snow,
He lov'd the bird that lov'd the man
  Who shot him with his bow.'

The other was a softer voice,
  As soft as honey-dew:
Quoth he 'The man hath penance done,
  And penance more will do.'

VI

First Voice

'But tell me, tell me! speak again,
  Thy soft response renewing —
What makes that ship drive on so fast?
  What is the Ocean doing?'

Second Voice

'Still as a Slave before his Lord,
  The Ocean hath no blast:
His great bright eye most silently
  Up to the moon is cast —

If he may know which way to go,
  For she guides him smooth or grim.
See, brother, see! how graciously
  She looketh down on him.'

First Voice

'But why drives on that ship so fast
  Withouten wave or wind?'

Second Voice

'The air is cut away before,
  And closes from behind.'

'Fly, brother, fly! more high, more high,
  Or we shall be belated:
For slow and slow that ship will go,
  When the Marinere's trance is abated.'

I woke, and we were sailing on
  As in a gentle weather:
'Twas night, calm night, the moon was high;
  The dead men stood together.

All stood together on the deck,
  For a charnel-dungeon fitter:
All fix'd on me their stony eyes
  That in the moon did glitter.

The pang, the curse, with which they died,
  Had never pass'd away:
I could not draw my een from theirs
  Ne turn them up to pray.

And in its time the spell was snapt,
  And I could move my een:
I look'd far-forth, but little saw
  Of what might else be seen.

Like one, that on a lonely road
  Doth walk in fear and dread,
And having once turn'd round, walks on
  And turns no more his head:
Because he knows, a frightful fiend
  Doth close behind him tread.

But soon there breath'd a wind on me,
  Ne sound ne motion made:
Its path was not upon the sea
  In ripple or in shade.

It rais'd my hair, it fann'd my cheek,
  Like a meadow-gale of spring –
It mingled strangely with my fears,
  Yet it felt like a welcoming.

Swiftly, swiftly flew the ship,
  Yet she sail'd softly too:
Sweetly, sweetly blew the breeze –
  On me alone it blew.

O dream of joy! is this indeed
  The light-house top I see?
Is this the Hill? Is this the Kirk?
  Is this mine own countrée?

We drifted o'er the Harbour-bar,
  And I with sobs did pray –
'O let me be awake, my God!
  Or let me sleep alway!'

The harbour-bay was clear as glass,
  So smoothly it was strewn!
And on the bay the moon light lay,
  And the shadow of the moon.

The moonlight bay was white all o'er,
  Till rising from the same,
Full·many shapes, that shadows were,
  Like as of torches came.

A little distance from the prow
    Those dark-red shadows were;
But soon I saw that my own flesh
    Was red as in a glare.

I turn'd my head in fear and dread,
    And by the holy rood,
The bodies had advanc'd, and now
    Before the mast they stood.

They lifted up their stiff right arms,
    They held them strait and tight;
And each right-arm burnt like a torch,
    A torch that's borne upright.
Their stony eye-balls glitter'd on
    In the red and smoky light.

I pray'd and turn'd my head away
    Forth looking as before.
There was no breeze upon the bay,
    No wave against the shore.

The rock shone bright, the kirk no less
    That stands above the rock:
The moonlight steep'd in silentness
    The steady weathercock.

And the bay was white with silent light,
    Till rising from the same
Full many shapes, that shadows were,
    In crimson colours came.

A little distance from the prow
    Those crimson shadows were:
I turn'd my eyes upon the deck –
    O Christ! what saw I there?

Each corse lay flat, lifeless and flat;
    And by the Holy rood
A man all light, a seraph-man,
    On every corse there stood.

This seraph-band, each wav'd his hand:
    It was a heavenly sight:
They stood as signals to the land,
    Each one a lovely light:

This seraph-band, each wav'd his hand,
    No voice did they impart –
No voice; but O! the silence sank,
    Like music on my heart.

Eftsones I heard the dash of oars,
   I heard the pilot's cheer:
My head was turn'd perforce away
   And I saw a boat appear.

Then vanish'd all the lovely lights;
   The bodies rose anew:
With silent pace, each to his place,
   Came back the ghastly crew.
The wind, that shade nor motion made,
   On me alone it blew.

The pilot, and the pilot's boy
   I heard them coming fast:
Dear Lord in Heaven! it was a joy,
   The dead men could not blast.

I saw a third – I heard his voice:
   It is the Hermit good!
He singeth loud his godly hymns
   That he makes in the wood.
He'll shrieve my soul, he'll wash away
   The Albatross's blood.

VII

This Hermit good lives in that wood
   Which slopes down to the Sea.
How loudly his sweet voice he rears!
He loves to talk with Marineres
   That come from a far Countrée.

He kneels at morn and noon and eve –
   He hath a cushion plump:
It is the moss, that wholly hides
   The rotted old Oak-stump.

The Skiff-boat ne'rd: I heard them talk,
   'Why, this is strange, I trow!
Where are those lights so many and fair
   That signal made but now?'

'Strange, by my faith!' the Hermit said –
   'And they answer'd not our cheer.
The planks look warp'd, and see those sails
   How thin they are and sere!
I never saw aught like to them
   Unless perchance it were

The skeletons of leaves that lag
  My forest-brook along:
When the Ivy-tod is heavy with snow,
And the Owlet whoops to the wolf below
  That eats the she-wolf's young.'

'Dear Lord! it has a fiendish look —'
  (The Pilot made reply)
'I am afear'd —' 'Push on, push on!'
  Said the Hermit cheerily.

The Boat came closer to the Ship,
  But I ne spake ne stirr'd!
The Boat came close beneath the Ship.
  And strait a sound was heard!

Under the water it rumbled on,
  Still louder and more dread:
It reach'd the Ship, it split the bay;
  The Ship went down like lead.

Stunn'd by that loud and dreadful sound,
  Which sky and ocean smote:
Like one that had been seven days drown'd
  My body lay afloat:
But, swift as dreams, myself I found
  Within the Pilot's boat.

Upon the whirl, where sank the Ship,
  The boat spun round and round:
And all was still, save that the hill
  Was telling of the sound.

I mov'd my lips: the Pilot shriek'd
  And fell down in a fit.
The Holy Hermit rais'd his eyes
  And pray'd where he did sit.

I took the oars: the Pilot's boy,
  Who now doth crazy go,
Laugh'd loud and long, and all the while
  His eyes went to and fro,
'Ha! ha!' quoth he — 'full plain I see,
  The devil knows how to row.'

And now all in mine own Countrée
  I stood on the firm land!
The Hermit stepp'd forth from the boat,
  And scarcely he could stand.

'O shrieve me, shrieve me, holy Man!'
  The Hermit cross'd his brow —
'Say quick,' quoth he, 'I bid thee say
  What manner man art thou?'

Forthwith this frame of mine was wrench'd
  With a woeful agony,
Which forc'd me to begin my tale
  And then it left me free.

Since then at an uncertain hour,
  Now oftimes and now fewer,
That anguish comes and makes me tell
  My ghastly aventure.

I pass, like night, from land to land;
  I have strange power of speech;
The moment that his face I see
I know the man that must hear me;
  To him my tale I teach.

What loud uproar bursts from that door!
  The Wedding-guests are there;
But in the Garden-bower the Bride
  And Bride-maids singing are:
And hark the little Vesper-bell
  Which biddeth me to prayer.

O Wedding-guest! this soul hath been
  Alone on a wide wide sea:
So lonely 'twas, that God himself
  Scarce seemed there to be.

O sweeter than the Marriage-feast,
  'Tis sweeter far to me
To walk together to the Kirk
  With a goodly company.

To walk together to the Kirk
  And all together pray,
While each to his great Father bends,
Old men, and babes, and loving friends,
  And Youths, and Maidens gay.

Farewell, farewell! but this I tell
  To thee, thou wedding-guest!
He prayeth well who loveth well,
  Both man and bird and beast.

He prayeth best who loveth best,
  All things both great and small:
For the dear God, who loveth us,
  He made and loveth all.

The Marinere, whose eye is bright,
  Whose beard with age is hoar,
Is gone; and now the wedding-guest
  Turn'd from the bridegroom's door.

He went, like one that hath been stunn'd
  And is of sense forlorn:
A sadder and a wiser man
  He rose the morrow morn.

321   *Frost at Midnight*

The Frost performs its secret ministry,
Unhelped by any wind. The owlet's cry
Came loud – and hark again! loud as before.
The inmates of my cottage, all at rest,
Have left me to that solitude, which suits
Abstruser musings: save that at my side
My cradled infant slumbers peacefully.
'Tis calm indeed! so calm, that it disturbs
And vexes meditation with its strange
And extreme silentness. Sea, hill, and wood,
This populous village! Sea, and hill, and wood,
With all the numberless goings-on of life,
Inaudible as dreams! the thin blue flame
Lies on my low-burnt fire, and quivers not;
Only that film,* which fluttered on the grate,
Still flutters there, the sole unquiet thing.
Methinks, its motion in this hush of nature
Gives it dim sympathies with me who live,
Making it a companionable form,
Whose puny flaps and freaks the idling Spirit
By its own moods interprets, every where
Echo or mirror seeking of itself,
And makes a toy of Thought.

                            But O! how oft,
How oft, at school, with most believing mind,
Presageful, have I gazed upon the bars,
To watch that fluttering *stranger*! and as oft

* In all parts of the kingdom these films are called *strangers* and supposed
to portend the arrival of some absent friend. [S. T. C.]

With unclosed lids, already had I dreamt
Of my sweet birth-place, and the old church-tower,
Whose bells, the poor man's only music, rang
From morn to evening, all the hot Fair-day,
So sweetly, that they stirred and haunted me
With a wild pleasure, falling on mine ear
Most like articulate sounds of things to come!
So gazed I, till the soothing things, I dreamt,
Lulled me to sleep, and sleep prolonged my dreams!
And so I brooded all the following morn,
Awed by the stern preceptor's face, mine eye
Fixed with mock study on my swimming book:
Save if the door half opened, and I snatched
A hasty glance, and still my heart leaped up,
For still I hoped to see the *stranger's* face,
Townsman, or aunt, or sister more beloved,
My play-mate when we both were clothed alike!

Dear Babe, that sleepest cradled by my side,
Whose gentle breathings, heard in this deep calm,
Fill up the interspersèd vacancies
And momentary pauses of the thought!
My babe so beautiful! it thrills my heart
With tender gladness, thus to look at thee,
And think that thou shalt learn far other lore,
And in far other scenes! For I was reared
In the great city, pent 'mid cloisters dim,
And saw nought lovely but the sky and stars.
But *thou*, my babe! shalt wander like a breeze
By lakes and sandy shores, beneath the crags
Of ancient mountain, and beneath the clouds,
Which image in their bulk both lakes and shores
And mountain crags: so shalt thou see and hear
The lovely shapes and sounds intelligible
Of that eternal language, which thy God.
Utters, who from eternity doth teach
Himself in all, and all things in himself.
Great universal Teacher! he shall mould
Thy spirit, and by giving make it ask.

Therefore all seasons shall be sweet to thee,
Whether the summer clothe the general earth
With greenness, or the redbreast sit and sing
Betwixt the tufts of snow on the bare branch
Of mossy apple-tree, while the nigh thatch
Smokes in the sun-thaw; whether the eave-drops fall
Heard only in the trances of the blast,
Or if the secret ministry of frost
Shall hang them up in silent icicles,
Quietly shining to the quiet Moon.

Joseph Blanco White

322   *To Night*

Mysterious Night! when our first parent knew
Thee from report divine, and heard thy name,
Did he not tremble for this lovely frame,
This glorious canopy of light and blue?
Yet 'neath a curtain of translucent dew,
Bathed in the rays of the great setting flame,
Hesperus with the host of heaven came,
And lo! Creation widened in man's view.
Who could have thought such darkness lay concealed
Within thy beams, O Sun! or who could find,
Whilst fly and leaf and insect stood revealed,
That to such countless orbs thou mad'st us blind!
　Why do we then shun Death with anxious strife?
　If Light can thus deceive, wherefore not Life?

Walter Savage Landor

323   *Dirce*

Stand close around, ye Stygian set,
　With Dirce in one boat conveyed!
Or Charon, seeing, may forget
　That he is old and she a shade.

324   *On His Seventy-fifth Birthday*

I strove with none, for none was worth my strife:
　Nature I loved, and next to Nature, Art:
I warmed both hands before the fire of Life;
　It sinks; and I am ready to depart.

325   *Memory*

> The Mother of the Muses, we are taught,
> Is Memory: she has left me; they remain,
> And shake my shoulder, urging me to sing
> About the summer days, my loves of old.
> *Alas! alas!* is all I can reply.
> Memory has left with me that name alone,
> Harmonious name, which other bards may sing,
> But her bright image in my darkest hour
> Comes back, in vain comes back, called or uncalled.
> Forgotten are the names of visitors
> Ready to press my hand but yesterday;
> Forgotten are the names of earlier friends
> Whose genial converse and glad countenance
> Are fresh as ever to mine ear and eye;
> To these, when I have written and besought
> Rembrance of me, the word *Dear* alone
> Hangs on the upper verge, and waits in vain.
> A blessing wert thou, O oblivion,
> If thy stream carried only weeds away,
> But vernal and autumnal flowers alike
> It hurries down to wither on the strand.

Ebenezer Elliott

326   *How Different!*

> Poor weaver, with the hopeless brow,
>   And bare wo-whitened head;
> Thou art a pauper all allow,
>   All see thou begg'st thy bread;
> And yet thou dost not plunder slaves,
>   Then tell them they are free;
> Nor hast thou joined with tax-fed knaves,
>   To Corn-Bill mine and me.
>
> What borough dost thou represent?
>   Who bidd'st thou toil and pay?
> Why sitt'st not thou in pauperment,
>   If baser beggars may?
> Where are thy hounds, thy palaced w——e,
>   To feed on mine and me?
> Thy reverend pimp, thy coach and four,
>   Thy thieves in livery?

No house hast thou, no food, no fire:
   None bow to thee alas!
A beggar? yet nor Lord, nor Squire!
   Say, how comes this to pass?
While you proud pauper, dead to shame,
   Is fed by mine and me?
And yet behind the rascal's name
   The scoundrel writes M.P.!

327   *Caged Rats*

Ye coop us up, and tax our bread,
   And wonder why we pine;
But ye are fat, and round, and red,
   And filled with tax-bought wine.
Thus twelve rats starve while three rats thrive,
   (Like you on mine and me,)
When fifteen rats are caged alive,
   With food for nine and three.

Haste! Havoc's torch begins to glow –
   The ending is begun;
Make haste! Destruction thinks ye slow;
   Make haste to be undone!
Why are ye called 'my Lord' and 'Squire',
   While fed by mine and me,
And wringing food, and clothes, and fire,
   From bread-taxed misery?

Make haste, slow rogues! *prohibit* trade,
   Prohibit honest gain;
Turn all the good that God hath made
   To fear, and hate, and pain;
Till beggars all, assassins all,
   All cannibals we be,
And death shall have no funeral
   From shipless sea to sea.

328   *Song*

When working blackguards come to blows,
And give or take a bloody nose,
Shall juries try such dogs as those,
    Now Nap lies at Saint Helena?

No – let the Great Unpaid decide,
Without appeal, on tame bull's hide,
Ash-planted well, or fistified,
    Since Nap died at Saint Helena.

When Sabbath stills the dizzy mill,
Shall Cutler Tom, or Grinder Bill,
On footpaths wander where they will,
    Now Nap lies at Saint Helena?

No – let them curse, but *feel* our power;
Dogs! let them spend their idle hour
Where burns the highway's dusty shower;
    For Nap died at Saint Helena.

Huzza! the rascal Whiglings work
For better men than Hare and Burke,
And envy Algerine and Turk,
    Since Nap died at Saint Helena.

Then close each path that sweetly climbs
Suburban hills, where village chimes
Remind the rogues of other times,
    Ere Nap died at Saint Helena.

We tax their bread, restrict their trade;
To toil for us, their hands were made;
Their doom is sealed, their prayer is prayed;
    Nap perished at Saint Helena.

Dogs! would they toil and fatten too?
They grumble still, as dogs will do;
We conquered *them* at Waterloo:
    And Nap lies at Saint Helena.

But shall the villains meet and prate,
In crowds about affairs of State?
Ride, yeomen, ride! act, magistrate!
    Nap perished at Saint Helena.

Leigh Hunt

329 *The Nile*

It flows through old hushed Egypt and its sands,
   Like some grave mighty thought threading a dream,
   And times and things, as in that vision, seem
Keeping along it their eternal stands, –
Caves, pillars, pyramids, the shepherd bands
   That roamed through the young world, the glory extreme
   Of high Sesostris, and that southern beam,
The laughing queen that caught the world's great hands.
Then comes a mightier silence, stern and strong,
As of a world left empty of its throng,
   And the void weighs on us; and then we wake,
And hear the fruitful stream lapsing along
      Twixt villages, and think how we shall take
      Our own calm journey on for human sake.

George Gordon, Lord Byron

330   *Maid of Athens, Ere We Part*
        Ζώη μοῦ, σάς ἀγαπῶ.*

Maid of Athens, ere we part,
Give, oh, give me back my heart!
Or, since that has left my breast,
Keep it now, and take the rest!
Hear my vow before I go,
Ζώη μοῦ, σάς ἀγαπῶ.

By those tresses unconfined,
Woo'd by each Aegean wind;
By those lids whose jetty fringe
Kiss thy soft cheeks' blooming tinge;
By those wild eyes like the roe,
Ζώη μοῦ, σάς ἀγαπῶ.

By that lip I long to taste;
By that zone-encircled waist;
By all the token-flowers that tell
What words can never speak so well;
By love's alternate joy and woe,
Ζώη μοῦ, σάς ἀγαπῶ.

*My life, I love you

Maid of Athens! I am gone:
Think of me, sweet! when alone.
Though I fly to Istambol,
Athens holds my heart and soul:
Can I cease to love thee? No!
Ζώη μοῦ, σάς ἀγαπῶ.

Athens, 1810

331   From *Childe Harold's Pilgrimage*

There was a sound of revelry by night,
And Belgium's capital had gathered then
Her Beauty and her Chivalry, and bright
The lamps shone o'er fair women and brave men;
A thousand hearts beat happily; and when
Music arose with its voluptuous swell,
Soft eyes looked love to eyes which spake again,
And all went merry as a marriage-bell;
But hush! hark! a deep sound strikes like a rising knell!

Did ye not hear it? – No; 'twas but the wind
Or the car rattling o'er the stony street;
On with the dance! let joy be unconfined;
No sleep till morn, when Youth and Pleasure meet
To chase the glowing Hours with flying feet –
But, hark! – that heavy sound breaks in once more
As if the clouds its echo would repeat;
And nearer, clearer, deadlier than before!
Arm! Arm! it is – it is – the cannon's opening roar!

Within a windowed niche of that high hall
Sate Brunswick's fated chieftain; he did hear
That sound the first amidst the festival,
And caught its tone with Death's prophetic ear;
And when they smiled because he deemed it near,
His heart more truly knew that peal too well
Which stretched his father on a bloody bier,
And roused the vengeance blood alone could quell:
He rushed into the field, and, foremost fighting, fell.

Ah! then and there was hurrying to and fro,
And gathering tears, and tremblings of distress,
And cheeks all pale, which but an hour ago
Blushed at the praise of their own loveliness;

And there were sudden partings, such as press
The life from out young hearts, and choking sighs
Which ne'er might be repeated; who could guess
If ever more should meet those mutual eyes,
Since upon night so sweet such awful morn could rise!

And there was mounting in hot haste: the steed,
The mustering squadron, and the clattering car,
Went pouring forward with impetuous speed,
And swiftly forming in the ranks of war;
And the deep thunder peal on peal afar;
And near, the beat of the alarming drum
Roused up the soldier ere the morning star;
While thronged the citizens with terror dumb,
Or whispering, with white lips – 'The foe! they come!
    they come!'

And wild and high the 'Cameron's gathering' rose!
The war-note of Lochiel, which Albyn's hills
Have heard, and heard, too, have her Saxon foes:–
How in the noon of night that pibroch thrills,
Savage and shrill! But with the breath which fills
Their mountain-pipe, so fill the mountaineers
With the fierce native daring which instils
The stirring memory of a thousand years,
And Evan's, Donald's fame rings in each clansman's ears!

And Ardennes waves above them her green leaves,
Dewy with nature's tear-drops, as they pass,
Grieving, if aught inanimate e'er grieves,
Over the unreturning brave, – alas!
Ere evening to be trodden like the grass
Which now beneath them, but above shall grow
In its next verdure, when this fiery mass
Of living valour, rolling on the foe
And burning with high hope shall moulder cold and low.

Last noon beheld them full of lusty life,
Last eve in Beauty's circle proudly gay,
The midnight brought the signal-sound of strife,
The morn the marshalling in arms, – the day
Battle's magnificently stern array!
The thunder-clouds close o'er it, which when rent
The earth is covered thick with other clay,
Which her own clay shall cover, heaped and pent,
Rider and horse, – friend, foe, – in one red burial blent!

And thou wert sad – yet I was not with thee:
And thou wert sick, and yet I was not near;
Methought that joy and health alone could be
Where I was not – and pain and sorrow here!
And is it thus? – it is as I foretold,
And shall be more so; for the mind recoils
Upon itself, and the wrecked heart lies cold,
While heaviness collects the shattered spoils.
It is not in the storm nor in the strife
We feel benumbed, and wish to be no more,
But in the after-silence on the shore,
When all is lost, except a little life.

I am too well avenged! – but 'twas my right;
Where'er my sins might be, *thou* wert not sent
To be the Nemesis who should requite –
Nor did Heaven choose so near an instrument.
Mercy is for the merciful! – if thou
Hast been of such, 'twill be accorded now.
Thy nights are banished from the realms of sleep! –
Yes! they may flatter thee, but thou shalt feel
A hollow agony which will not heal,
For thou art pillowed on a curse too deep;
Thou hast sown in my sorrow, and must reap
The bitter harvest in a woe as real!
I have had many foes, but none like thee;
For 'gainst the rest myself I could defend,
And be avenged, or turn them into friend;
But thou in safe implacability
Hadst nought to dread – in thy own weakness shielded,
And in my love, which hath but too much yielded,
And spared, for thy sake, some I should not spare –
And thus upon the world – trust in thy truth –
And the wild fame of my ungoverned youth –
On things that were not, and on things that are –
Even upon such a basis hast thou built
A monument, whose cement hath been guilt!
The moral Clytemnestra of thy lord,
And hewed down, with an unsuspected sword,
Fame, peace, and hope – and all the better life
Which, but for this cold treason of thy heart,
Might still have risen from out the grave of strife,
And found a nobler duty than to part.
But of thy virtues didst thou make a vice,
Trafficking with them in a purpose cold,
For present anger, and for future gold –
And buying other's grief at any price.

And thus once entered into crooked ways,
The early truth, which was thy proper praise,
Did not still walk beside thee – but at times,
And with a breast unknowing its own crimes.
Deceit, averments incompatible,
Equivocations, and the thoughts which dwell
In Janus-spirits – the significant eye
Which learns to lie with silence – the pretext
Of Prudence, with advantages annexed –
The acquiescence in all things which tend,
No matter how, to the desired end –
All found a place in thy philosophy.
The means were worthy, and the end is won –
I would not do by thee as thou hast done!

333   From *Don Juan*

They were alone once more; for them to be
  Thus was another Eden; they were never
Weary, unless when separate: the tree
  Cut from its forest root of years – the river
Damm'd from its fountain – the child from the knee
  And breast maternal weaned at once for ever, –
Would wither less than these two torn apart;
Alas! there is no instinct like the heart –

The heart – which may be broken: happy they!
  Thrice fortunate! who of that fragile mould,
The precious porcelain of human clay,
  Break with the first fall: they can ne'er behold
The long year linked with heavy day on day,
  And all which must be borne, and never told;
While life's strange principle will often lie
Deepest in those who long the most to die.

'Whom the gods love die young,' was said of yore,
  And many deaths do they escape by this:
The death of friends, and that which slays even more –
  The death of friendship, love, youth, all that is,
Except mere breath; and since the silent shore
  Awaits at last even those who longest miss
The old archer's shafts, perhaps the early grave
Which men weep over may be meant to save.

Haidée and Juan thought not of the dead.
  The heavens, and earth, and air, seemed made for them:
They found no fault with Time, save that he fled;
  They saw not in themselves aught to condemn:

Each was the other's mirror, and but read
   Joy sparkling in their dark eyes like a gem,
And knew such brightness was but the reflection
Of their exchanging glances of affection.

The gentle pressure, and the thrilling touch,
   The least glance better understood than words,
Which still said all, and ne'er could say too much;
   A language, too, but like to that of birds,
Known but to them, at least appearing such
   As but to lovers a true sense affords;
Sweet playful phrases, which would seem absurd
To those who have ceased to hear such, or ne'er heard:

All these were theirs, for they were children still,
   And children still they should have ever been;
They were not made in the real world to fill
   A busy character in the dull scene,
But like two beings born from out a rill,
   A nymph and her beloved, all unseen
To pass their lives in fountains and on flowers,
And never know the weight of human hours.

Moons changing had rolled on, and changeless found
   Those their bright rise had lighted to such joys
As rarely they beheld throughout their round;
   And these were not of the vain kind which cloys,
For theirs were buoyant spirits, never bound
   By the mere senses; and that which destroys
Most love, possession, unto them appeared
A thing which each endearment more endeared.

Oh beautiful! and rare as beautiful!
   But theirs was love in which the mind delights
To lose itself, when the old world grows dull,
   And we are sick of its hack sounds and sights,
Intrigues, adventures of the common school,
   Its petty passions, marriages, and flights,
Where Hymen's torch but brands one strumpet more
Whose husband only knows her not a wh—re.

Hard words; harsh truth; a truth which many know.
   Enough. – The faithful and the fairy pair,
Who never found a single hour too slow,
   What was it made them thus exempt from care?
Young innate feelings all have felt below,
   Which perish in the rest, but in them were
Inherent; what we mortals call romantic,
And always envy, though we deem it frantic.

This is in others a factitious state,
   An opium dream of too much youth and reading,
But was in them their nature or their fate:
   No novels e'er had set their young hearts bleeding,
For Haidée's knowledge was by no means great,
   And Juan was a boy of saintly breeding;
So that there was no reason for their loves
More than for those of nightingales or doves.

They gazed upon the sunset; 'tis an hour
   Dear unto all, but dearest to *their* eyes,
For it had made them what they were: the power
   Of love had first o'erwhelmed them from such skies,
When happiness had been their only dower,
   And twilight saw them linked in passion's ties;
Charmed with each other, all things charmed that brought
The past still welcome as the present thought.

I know not why, but in that hour to-night,
   Even as they gazed, a sudden tremor came,
And swept, as 'twere, across their heart's delight,
   Like the wind o'er a harp-string, or a flame,
When one is shook in sound, and one in sight:
   And thus some boding flashed through either frame,
And called from Juan's breast a faint low sigh,
While one new tear arose in Haidée's eye.

That large black prophet eye seemed to dilate
   And follow far the disappearing sun,
As if their last day of a happy date
   With his broad, bright, and dropping orb were gone.
Juan gazed on her as to ask his fate –
   He felt a grief, but knowing cause for none,
His glance inquired of hers for some excuse
For feelings causeless, or at least abstruse.

She turned to him, and smiled, but in that sort
   Which makes not others smile; then turned aside:
Whatever feeling shook her, it seemed short,
   And mastered by her wisdom or her pride;
When Juan spoke, too – it might be in sport –
   Of this their mutual feeling, she replied –
'If it should be so, – but – it cannot be –
Or I at least shall not survive to see.'

Juan would question further, but she pressed
   His lips to hers, and silenced him with this,
And then dismissed the omen from her breast,
   Defying augury with that fond kiss;

And no doubt of all methods 'tis the best:
  Some people prefer wine — 'tis not amiss;
I have tried both; so those who would a part take
May choose between the headache and the heartache.

One of the two, according to your choice,
  Women or wine, you'll have to undergo;
Both maladies are taxes on our joys:
  But which to choose, I really hardly know;
And if I had to give a casting voice,
  For both sides I could many reasons show,
And then decide, without great wrong to either.
It were much better to have both than neither.

Juan and Haidée gazed upon each other
  With swimming looks of speechless tenderness,
Which mixed all feelings, friend, child, lover, brother,
  All that the best can mingle and express
When two pure hearts are poured in one another,
  And love too much, and yet cannot love less;
But almost sanctify the sweet access
By the immortal wish and power to bless.

Mixed in each other's arms, and heart in heart,
  Why did they not then die? — they had lived too long
Should an hour come to bid them breathe apart;
  Years could but bring them cruel things or wrong;
The world was not for them, nor the world's art
  For beings passionate as Sappho's song;
Love was born *with* them, *in* them, so intense,
It was their very spirit — not a sense.

They should have lived together deep in woods,
  Unseen as sings the nightingale; they were
Unfit to mix in these thick solitudes
  Called social, haunts of Hate, and Vice, and Care:
How lonely every freeborn creature broods!
  The sweetest song-birds nestle in a pair;
The eagle soars alone; the gull and crow
Flock o'er their carrion, just like men below.

334   [*Love and Death*]

I watched thee when the foe was at our side,
  Ready to strike at him — or thee and me,
Were safety hopeless — rather than divide
  Aught with one loved save love and liberty.

I watched thee on the breakers, when the rock
  Received our prow and all was storm and fear,
And bade thee cling to me through every shock;
  This arm would be thy bark, or breast thy bier.

I watched thee when the fever glazed thine eyes,
  Yielding my couch, and stretched me on the ground,
When overworn with watching, ne'er to rise
  From thence if thou an early grave hadst found.

The earthquake came, and rocked the quivering wall,
  And men and nature reeled as if with wine.
Whom did I seek around the tottering hall?
  For thee. Whose safety first provide for? Thine.

And when convulsive throes denied my breath
  The faintest utterance to my fading thought,
To thee — to thee — e'en in the gasp of death
  My spirit turned, oh! oftener than it ought.

Thus much and more; and yet thou lov'st me not,
  And never wilt! Love dwells not in our will.
Nor can I blame thee, though it be my lot
  To strongly, wrongly, vainly love thee still.

Percy Bysshe Shelley

335   *Ode to the West Wind*

I

O wild West Wind, thou breath of Autumn's being,
Thou, from whose unseen presence the leaves dead
Are driven, like ghosts from an enchanter fleeing,

Yellow, and black, and pale, and hectic red,
Pestilence-stricken multitudes: O thou,
Who chariotest to their dark wintry bed

The wingèd seeds, where they lie cold and low,
Each like a corpse within its grave, until
Thine azure sister of the Spring shall blow

Her clarion o'er the dreaming earth, and fill
(Driving sweet buds like flocks to feed in air)
With living hues and odours plain and hill:

Wild Spirit, which art moving everywhere;
Destroyer and Preserver; hear, O hear!

II

Thou on whose stream, 'mid the steep sky's commotion,
Loose clouds like Earth's decaying leaves are shed,
Shook from the tangled boughs of Heaven and Ocean,

Angels of rain and lightning: there are spread
On the blue surface of thine airy surge,
Like the bright hair uplifted from the head

Of some fierce Mænad, even from the dim verge
Of the horizon to the zenith's height,
The locks of the approaching storm. Thou dirge

Of the dying year, to which this closing night
Will be the dome of a vast sepulchre
Vaulted with all thy congregated might

Of vapours, from whose solid atmosphere
Black rain, and fire, and hail will burst: O hear!

III

Thou who didst waken from his summer dreams
The blue Mediterranean, where he lay,
Lulled by the coil of his crystalline streams,

Beside a pumice isle in Baiæ's bay,
And saw in sleep old palaces and towers
Quivering within the wave's intenser day,

All overgrown with azure moss and flowers
So sweet, the sense faints picturing them! Thou
For whose path the Atlantic's level powers

Cleave themselves into chasms, while far below
The sea-blooms and the oozy woods which wear
The sapless foliage of the ocean, know

Thy voice, and suddenly grow grey with fear,
And tremble and despoil themselves: O hear!

IV

If I were a dead leaf thou mightest bear;
If I were a swift cloud to fly with thee;
A wave to pant beneath thy power, and share

The impulse of thy strength, only less free
Than thou, O Uncontrollable! If even
I were as in my boyhood, and could be

The comrade of thy wanderings over Heaven,
As then, when to outstrip thy skiey speed
Scarce seemed a vision; I would ne'er have striven

As thus with thee in prayer in my sore need.
Oh! lift me as a wave, a leaf, a cloud!
I fall upon the thorns of life! I bleed!

A heavy weight of hours has chained and bowed
One too like thee: tameless, and swift, and proud.

V

Make me thy lyre, even as the forest is:
What if my leaves are falling like its own!
The tumult of thy mighty harmonies

Will take from both a deep, autumnal tone,
Sweet though in sadness. Be thou, Spirit fierce,
My spirit! Be thou me, impetuous one!

Drive my dead thoughts over the universe
Like withered leaves to quicken a new birth!
And, by the incantation of this verse,

Scatter, as from an unextinguished hearth
Ashes and sparks, my words among mankind!
Be through my lips to unawakened Earth

The trumpet of a prophecy! O Wind,
If Winter comes, can Spring be far behind?

336   From *Letter to Maria Gisborne*

                              You are now
In London, that great sea, whose ebb and flow
At once is deaf and loud, and on the shore
Vomits its wrecks, and still howls on for more.
Yet in its depth what treasures! – You will see
That which was Godwin, – greater none than he
Though fallen – and fallen on evil times – to stand
Among the spirits of our age and land,
Before the dread tribunal of *to come*
The foremost – while Rebuke cowers, pale and dumb.
You will see Coleridge – he who sits obscure
In the exceeding lustre and the pure
Intense irradiation of a mind,
Which, with its own internal lightning blind,

Flags wearily through darkness and despair –
A cloud-encircled meteor of the air,
A hooded eagle among blinking owls. –
You will see Hunt – one of those happy souls
Who are the salt of the earth, and without whom
This world would smell like what it is – a tomb;
Who is, what others seem; his room no doubt
Is still adorned with many a cast from Shout,
With graceful flowers, tastefully placed about;
And coronals of bay from ribbons hung,
And brighter wreaths in neat disorder flung,
The gifts of the most learn'd among some dozens
Of female friends, sisters-in-law and cousins.
And there is he with his eternal puns,
Which beat the dullest brain for smiles, like duns
Thundering for money at a poet's door;
Alas, it is no use to say 'I'm poor!'
Or oft in graver mood, when he will look
Things wiser than were ever read in book,
Except in Shakespeare's wisest tenderness. –
You will see Hogg – and I cannot express
His virtues, though I know that they are great,
Because he locks, then barricades, the gate
Within which they inhabit; – of his wit
And wisdom, you'll cry out when you are bit.
He is a pearl within an oyster shell,
One of the richest of the deep. And there
Is English Peacock with his mountain Fair,
Turned into a Flamingo, – that shy bird
That gleams i' the Indian air. Have you not heard
When a man marries, dies, or turns Hindoo,
His best friends hear no more of him? – but you
Will see him and will like him too, I hope,
With the milk-white Snowdonian Antelope
Matched with this Cameleopard. – His fine wit
Makes such a wound, the knife is lost in it;
A strain too learned for a shallow age,
Too wise for selfish bigots; let his page
Which charms the chosen spirits of the time
Fold itself up for the serener clime
Of years to come, and find its recompense
In that just expectation. – Wit and sense,
Virtue and human knowledge, all that might
Make this dull world a business of delight,
Are all combined in Horace Smith. – And these,
With some exceptions which I need not tease
Your patience by descanting on, are all
You and I know in London –

I recall

My thoughts, and bid you look upon the night.
As water does a sponge, so the moonlight
Fills the void, hollow, universal air –
What see you? – unpavilioned heaven is fair,
Whether the moon, into her chamber gone,
Leaves midnight to the golden stars, or wan
Climbs with diminished beams the azure steep;
Or whether clouds sail o'er the inverse deep,
Piloted by the many-wandering blast,
And the rare stars rush through them dim and fast: –
All this is beautiful in every land. –
But what see you beside? – a shabby stand
Of hackney coaches – a brick house or wall
Fencing some lordly court, white with the scrawl
Of our unhappy politics; or worse –
A wretched woman reeling by, whose curse
Mixed with the watchman's, partner of her trade,
You must accept in place of serenade –
Or yellow-haired Pollonia murmuring
To Henry some unutterable thing. –
I see a chaos of green leaves and fruit
Built round dark caverns, even to the root
Of the living stems which feed them – in whose bowers
There sleep in their dark dew the folded flowers;
Beyond, the surface of the unsickled corn
Trembles not in the slumbering air, and borne
In circles quaint, and ever-changing dance,
Like wingèd stars the fire-flies flash and glance
Pale in the open moonshine, but each one
Under the dark trees seems a little sun,
A meteor tamed, a fixed star gone astray
From the silver regions of the Milky Way;–
Afar the Contadino's song is heard,
Rude, but made sweet by distance – and a bird
Which cannot be the nightingale, and yet
I know none else that sings so sweet as it
At this late hour; – and then all is still –
Now, Italy or London – which you will!

Next winter you must pass with me; I'll have
My house by that time turned into a grave
Of dead despondence and low-thoughted care,
And all the dreams which our tormentors are.
Oh, that Hunt, Hogg, Peacock and Smith were there,
With every thing belonging to them fair!
We will have books, Spanish, Italian, Greek;
And ask one week to make another week

As like his father as I'm unlike mine,
Which is not his fault, as you may divine.
Though we eat little flesh and drink no wine,
Yet let's be merry: we'll have tea and toast,
Custards for supper, and an endless host
Of syllabubs and jellies and mince-pies,
And other such lady-like luxuries —
Feasting on which, we will philosophize!
And we'll have fires out of the Grand Duke's wood
To thaw the six weeks' winter in our blood.
And then we'll talk; — what shall we talk about?
Oh! there are themes enough for many a bout
Of thought-entangled descant; — as to nerves,
With cones and parallelograms and curves
I've sworn to strangle them if once they dare
To bother me — when you are with me there,
And they shall never more sip laudanum
From Helicon or Himeros; — well, come,
And in despite of God and of the devil,
We'll make our friendly philosophic revel
Outlast the leafless time; — till buds and flowers
Warn the obscure inevitable hours
Sweet meeting by sad parting to renew —
'Tomorrow to fresh woods and pastures new.'

337   *Adonais*

I weep for Adonais — he is dead!
O, weep for Adonais! though our tears
Thaw not the frost which binds so dear a head!
And thou, sad Hour, selected from all years
To mourn our loss, rouse thy obscure compeers,
And teach them thine own sorrow, say: with me
Died Adonais; till the Future dares
Forget the Past, his fate and fame shall be
An echo and a light unto eternity!

Where wert thou, mighty Mother, when he lay,
When thy Son lay, pierced by the shaft which flies
In darkness? where was lorn Urania
When Adonais died? With veilèd eyes,
Mid listening Echoes, in her Paradise
She sate, while one, with soft enamoured breath,
Rekindled all the fading melodies
With which, like flowers that mock the corse beneath,
He had adorned and hid the coming bulk of death.

O, weep for Adonais – he is dead!
Wake, melancholy Mother, wake and weep!
Yet wherefore? Quench within their burning bed
Thy fiery tears, and let thy loud heart keep
Like his, a mute and uncomplaining sleep;
For he is gone, where all things wise and fair
Descend; – oh, dream not that the amorous Deep
Will yet restore him to the vital air;
Death feeds on his mute voice, and laughs at our despair.

Most musical of mourners, weep again!
Lament anew, Urania! – He died,
Who was the Sire of an immortal strain,
Blind, old, and lonely, when his country's pride
The priest, the slave, and the liberticide
Trampled and mocked with many a loathèd rite
Of lust and blood; he went, unterrified,
Into the gulf of death; but his clear Sprite
Yet reigns o'er earth; the third among the sons of light.

Most musical of mourners, weep anew!
Not all to that bright station dared to climb;
And happier they their happiness who knew,
Whose tapers yet burn through that night of time
In which suns perished; others more sublime,
Struck by the envious wrath of man or God,
Have sunk, extinct in their refulgent prime;
And some yet live, treading the thorny road
Which leads, through toil and hate, to Fame's serene abode.

But now, thy youngest, dearest one, has perished –
The nursling of thy widowhood, who grew,
Like a pale flower by some sad maiden cherished,
And fed with true love tears, instead of dew;
Most musical of mourners, weep anew!
Thy extreme hope, the loveliest and the last,
The bloom, whose petals nipped before they blew
Died on the promise of the fruit, is waste;
The broken lily lies – the storm is overpast.

To that high Capital, where kingly Death
Keeps his pale court in beauty and decay,
He came; and bought, with price of purest breath,
A grave among the eternal. – Come away!
Haste, while the vault of blue Italian day
Is yet his fitting charnel-roof! while still
He lies, as if in dewy sleep he lay;
Awake him not! surely he takes his fill
Of deep and liquid rest, forgetful of all ill.

He will awake no more, oh, never more! –
Within the twilight chamber spreads apace
The shadow of white Death, and at the door
Invisible Corruption waits to trace
His extreme way to her dim dwelling-place;
The eternal Hunger sits, but pity and awe
Soothe her pale rage, nor dares she to deface
So fair a prey, till darkness, and the law
Of change, shall o'er his sleep the mortal curtain draw.

O, weep for Adonais! – The quick Dreams,
The passion-wingèd Ministers of thought,
Who were his flocks, whom near the living streams
Of his young spirit he fed, and whom he taught
The love which was its music, wander not, –
Wander no more, from kindling brain to brain,
But droop there, whence they sprung; and mourn their lot
Round the cold heart, where, after their sweet pain,
They ne'er will gather strength, or find a home again.

And one with trembling hands clasps his cold head,
And fans him with her moonlight wings, and cries,
'Our love, our hope, our sorrow, is not dead;
See, on the silken fringe of his faint eyes,
Like dew upon a sleeping flower, there lies
A tear some Dream has loosened from his brain.'
Lost Angel of a ruined Paradise!
She knew not 'twas her own; as with no stain
She faded, like a cloud which had outwept its rain.

One from a lucid urn of starry dew
Washed his light limbs as if embalming them;
Another clipped her profuse locks, and threw
The wreath upon him, like an anadem,
Which frozen tears instead of pearls begem;
Another in her wilful grief would break
Her bow and wingèd reeds, as if to stem
A greater loss with one which was more weak;
And dull the barbèd fire against his frozen cheek.

Another Splendour on his mouth alit,
That mouth, whence it was wont to draw the breath
Which gave it strength to pierce the guarded wit,
And pass into the panting heart beneath
With lightning and with music: the damp death
Quenched its caress upon his icy lips;
And, as a dying meteor stains a wreath
Of moonlight vapour, which the cold night clips,
It flushed through his pale limbs, and passed to its eclipse.

And others came . . . Desires and Adorations,
Wingèd Persuasions and veiled Destinies,
Splendours, and Glooms, and glimmering Incarnations
Of hopes and fears, and twilight Phantasies;
And Sorrow, with her family of Sighs,
And Pleasure, blind with tears, led by the gleam
Of her own dying smile instead of eyes,
Came in slow pomp; – the moving pomp might seem
Like pageantry of mist on an autumnal stream.

All he had loved, and moulded into thought,
From shape, and hue, and odour, and sweet sound,
Lamented Adonais. Morning sought
Her eastern watch-tower, and her hair unbound,
Wet with the tears which should adorn the ground,
Dimmed the aërial eyes that kindle day;
Afar the melancholy thunder moaned,
Pale Ocean in unquiet slumber lay,
And the wild winds flew round, sobbing in their dismay.

Lost Echo sits amid the voiceless mountains,
And feeds her grief with his remembered lay,
And will no more reply to winds or fountains,
Or amorous birds perched on the young green spray,
Or herdsman's horn, or bell at closing day,
Since she can mimic not his lips, more dear
Than those for whose disdain she pined away
Into a shadow of all sounds: – a drear
Murmur, between their songs, is all the woodmen hear.

Grief made the young Spring wild, and she threw down
Her kindling buds, as if she Autumn were,
Or they dead leaves; since her delight is flown,
For whom should she have waked the sullen year?
To Phoebus was not Hyacinth so dear
Nor to himself Narcissus, as to both
Thou, Adonais: wan they stand and sere
Amid the faint companions of their youth,
With dew all turned to tears; odour, to sighing ruth.

Thy spirit's sister, the lorn nightingale
Mourns not her mate with such melodious pain;
Not so the eagle, who like thee could scale
Heaven, and could nourish in the sun's domain
Her mighty youth with morning, doth complain,
Soaring and screaming round her empty nest,
As Albion wails for thee: the curse of Cain
Light on his head who pierced thy innocent breast,
And scared the angel soul that was its earthly guest!

Ah, woe is me! Winter is come und gone,
But grief returns with the revolving year;
The airs and streams renew their joyous tone;
The ants, the bees, the swallows reappear;
Fresh leaves and flowers deck the dead Season's bier;
The amorous birds now pair in every brake,
And build their mossy homes in field and brere;
And the green lizard, and the golden snake,
Like unimprisoned flames, out of their trance awake.

Through wood and stream and field and hill and Ocean
A quickening life from the Earth's heart has burst
As it has ever done, with change and motion,
From the great morning of the world when first
God dawned on Chaos; in its stream immersed,
The lamps of Heaven flash with a softer light;
All baser things pant with life's sacred thirst;
Diffuse themselves; and spend in love's delight
The beauty and the joy of their renewèd might.

The leprous corpse touched by this spirit tender
Exhales itself in flowers of gentle breath;
Like incarnations of the stars, when splendour
Is changed to fragrance, they illumine death
And mock the merry worm that wakes beneath;
Nought we know, dies. Shall that alone which knows
Be as a sword consumed before the sheath
By sightless lightning? – the intense atom glows
A moment, then is quenched in a most cold repose.

Alas! that all we loved of him should be,
But for our grief, as if it had not been,
And grief itself be mortal! Woe is me!
Whence are we, and why are we? of what scene
The actors or spectators? Great and mean
Meet massed in death, who lends what life must borrow.
As long as skies are blue, and fields are green,
Evening must usher night, night urge the morrow,
Month follow month with woe, and year wake year to sorrow.

He will awake no more, oh, never more!
'Wake thou,' cried Misery, 'childless Mother, rise
Out of thy sleep, and slake, in thy heart's core,
A wound more fierce than his with tears and sighs.'
And all the Dreams that watched Urania's eyes,
And all the Echoes whom their sister's song
Had held in holy silence, cried: 'Arise!'
Swift as a Thought by the snake Memory stung,
From her ambrosial rest the fading Splendour sprung.

She rose like an autumnal Night, that springs
Out of the East, and follows wild and drear
The golden Day, which, on eternal wings,
Even as a ghost abandoning a bier,
Has left the Earth a corpse. Sorrow and fear
So struck, so roused, so rapt Urania;
So saddened round her like an atmosphere
Of stormy mist; so swept her on her way
Even to the mournful place where Adonais lay.

Out of her secret Paradise she sped,
Through camps and cities rough with stone, and steel,
And human hearts, which to her aery tread
Yielding not, wounded the invisible
Palms of her tender feet where'er they fell:
And barbèd tongues, and thoughts more sharp than they,
Rent the soft Form they never could repel,
Whose sacred blood, like the young tears of May,
Paved with eternal flowers that undeserving way.

In the death-chamber for a moment Death,
Shamed by the presence of that living Might,
Blushed to annihilation, and the breath
Revisited those lips, and life's pale light
Flashed through those limbs, so late her dear delight.
'Leave me not wild and drear and comfortless,
As silent lightning leaves the starless night!
Leave me not!' cried Urania: her distress
Roused Death: Death rose and smiled, and met her vain caress.

'Stay yet awhile! speak to me once again;
Kiss me, so long but as a kiss may live;
And in my heartless breast and burning brain
That word, that kiss, shall all thoughts else survive,
With food of saddest memory kept alive,
Now thou art dead, as if it were a part
Of thee, my Adonais! I would give
All that I am to be as thou now art!
But I am chained to Time, and cannot thence depart!

Oh gentle child, beautiful as thou wert,
Why didst thou leave the trodden paths of men
Too soon, and with weak hands though mighty heart
Dare the unpastured dragon in his den?
Defenceless as thou wert, oh where was then
Wisdom the mirrored shield, or scorn the spear?
Or hadst thou waited the full cycle, when
Thy spirit should have filled its crescent sphere,
The monsters of life's waste had fled from thee like deer.

The herded wolves, bold only to pursue;
The obscene ravens, clamorous o'er the dead;
The vultures to the conqueror's banner true
Who feed where Desolation first has fed,
And whose wings rain contagion; – how they fled,
When like Apollo, from his golden bow,
The Pythian of the age one arrow sped
And smiled! – The spoilers tempt no second blow,
They fawn on the proud feet that spurn them lying low.

The sun comes forth, and many reptiles spawn;
He sets, and each ephemeral insect then
Is gathered into death without a dawn,
And the immortal stars awake again;
So is it in the world of living men:
A godlike mind soars forth, in its delight
Making earth bare and veiling heaven, and when
It sinks, the swarms that dimmed or shared its light
Leave to its kindred lamps the spirit's awful night.'

Thus ceased she: and the mountain shepherds came,
Their garlands sere, their magic mantles rent;
The Pilgrim of Eternity, whose fame
Over his living head like Heaven is bent,
An early but enduring monument,
Came, veiling all the lightnings of his song
In sorrow; from her wilds Ierne sent
The sweetest lyrist of her saddest wrong,
And love taught grief to fall like music from his tongue.

Midst others of less note, came one frail Form,
A phantom among men; companionless
As the last cloud of an expiring storm
Whose thunder is its knell; he, as I guess,
Had gazed on Nature's naked loveliness,
Actaeon-like, and now he fled astray
With feeble steps o'er the world's wilderness,
And his own thoughts, along that rugged way,
Pursued, like raging hounds, their father and their prey.

A pardlike Spirit beautiful and swift –
A Love in desolation masked; – a Power
Girt round with weakness; – it can scarce uplift
The weight of the superincumbent hour;
It is a dying lamp, a falling shower,
A breaking billow; – even whilst we speak
Is it not broken? On the withering flower
The killing sun smiles brightly: on a cheek
The life can burn in blood, even while the heart may break.

His head was bound with pansies overblown,
And faded violets, white, and pied, and blue;
And a light spear topped with a cypress cone,
Round whose rude shaft dark ivy tresses grew
Yet dripping with the forest's noonday dew,
Vibrated, as the ever-beating heart
Shook the weak hand that grasped it; of that crew
He came the last, neglected and apart;
A herd-abandoned deer struck by the hunter's dart.

All stood aloof, and at his partial moan
Smiled through their tears; well knew that gentle band
Who in another's fate now wept his own —
As in the accents of an unknown land
He sung new sorrow; sad Urania scanned
The Stranger's mien, and murmured: 'Who art thou?'
He answered not, but with a sudden hand
Made bare his branded and ensanguined brow,
Which was like Cain's or Christ's — Oh! that it should be so!

What softer voice is hushed over the dead?
Athwart what brow is that dark mantle thrown?
What form leans sadly o'er the white death-bed,
In mockery of monumental stone,
The heavy heart heaving without a moan?
If it be He, who gentlest of the wise,
Taught, soothed, loved, honoured the departed one,
Let me not vex, with inharmonious sighs,
The silence of that heart's accepted sacrifice.

Our Adonais has drunk poison — oh!
What deaf and viperous murderer could crown
Life's early cup with such a draught of woe?
The nameless worm would now itself disown:
It felt, yet could escape, the magic tone
Whose prelude held all envy, hate, and wrong,
But what was howling in one breast alone,
Silent alone amid an Heaven of song.
Assume thy wingèd throne, thou Vesper of our throng!'

Live thou, whose infamy is not thy fame!
Live! fear no heavier chastisement from me,
Thou noteless blot on a remembered name!
But be thyself, and know thyself to be!
And ever at thy season be thou free
To spill the venom when thy fangs o'erflow:
Remorse and Self-contempt shall cling to thee;
Hot Shame shall burn upon thy secret brow,
And like a beaten hound tremble thou shalt — as now.

Nor let us weep that our delight is fled
Far from these carrion kites that scream below;
He wakes or sleeps with the enduring dead;
Thou canst not soar where he is sitting now. –
Dust to the dust! but the pure spirit shall flow
Back to the burning fountain whence it came,
A portion of the Eternal, which must glow
Through time and change, unquenchably the same,
Whilst thy cold embers choke the sordid hearth of shame.

Peace, peace! he is not dead, he doth not sleep –
He hath awakened from the dream of life –
'Tis we, who lost in stormy visions, keep
With phantoms an unprofitable strife,
And in mad trance, strike with our spirit's knife
Invulnerable nothings. – We decay
Like corpses in a charnel; fear and grief
Convulse us and consume us day by day,
And cold hopes swarm like worms within our living clay.

He has outsoared the shadow of our night;
Envy and calumny and hate and pain,
And that unrest which men miscall delight,
Can touch him not and torture not again;
From the contagion of the world's slow stain
He is secure, and now can never mourn
A heart grown cold, a head grown grey in vain;
Nor, when the spirit's self has ceased to burn,
With sparkless ashes load an unlamented urn.

He lives, he wakes –'tis Death is dead, not he;
Mourn not for Adonais. – Thou young Dawn
Turn all thy dew to splendour, for from thee
The spirit thou lamentest is not gone;
Ye caverns and ye forests, cease to moan!
Cease ye faint flowers and fountains, and thou Air
Which like a mourning veil thy scarf hadst thrown
O'er the abandoned Earth, now leave it bare
Even to the joyous stars which smile on its despair!

He is made one with Nature: there is heard
His voice in all her music, from the moan
Of thunder, to the song of night's sweet bird;
He is a presence to be felt and known
In darkness and in light, from herb and stone,
Spreading itself where'er that Power may move
Which has withdrawn his being to its own;
Which wields the world with never wearied love,
Sustains it from beneath, and kindles it above.

He is a portion of the loveliness
Which once he made more lovely: he doth bear
His part, while the one Spirit's plastic stress
Sweeps through the dull dense world, compelling there
All new successions to the forms they wear;
Torturing th' unwilling dross that checks its flight
To its own likeness, as each mass may bear;
And bursting in its beauty and its might
From trees and beasts and men into the Heavens' light.

The splendours of the firmament of time
May be eclipsed, but are extinguished not;
Like stars to their appointed height they climb,
And death is a low mist which cannot blot
The brightness it may veil. When lofty thought
Lifts a young heart above its mortal lair,
And love and life contend in it, for what
Shall be its earthly doom, the dead live there
And move like winds of light on dark and stormy air.

The inheritors of unfulfilled renown
Rose from their thrones, built beyond mortal thought,
Far in the Unapparent. Chatterton
Rose pale, his solemn agony had not
Yet faded from him; Sidney as he fought
And as he fell and as he lived and loved
Sublimely mild, a Spirit without spot,
Arose; and Lucan, by his death approved:
Oblivion as they rose shrank like a thing reproved.

And many more, whose names on Earth are dark,
But whose transmitted effluence cannot die
So long as fire outlives the parent spark,
Rose, robed in dazzling immortality.
'Thou art become as one of us,' they cry,
'It was for thee yon kingless sphere has long
Swung blind in unascended majesty,
Silent alone amid an Heaven of song.
Assume thy wingèd throne, thou Vesper of our throng!'

Who mourns for Adonais? oh, come forth
Fond wretch! and know thyself and him aright.
Clasp with thy panting soul the pendulous Earth;
As from a centre, dart thy spirit's light
Beyond all worlds, until its spacious might
Satiate the void circumference: then shrink
Even to a point within our day and night;
And keep thy heart light lest it make thee sink
When hope has kindled hope, and lured thee to the brink;

Or go to Rome, which is the sepulchre,
O, not of him, but of our joy: 'tis nought
That ages, empires, and religions there
Lie buried in the ravage they have wrought;
For such as he can lend, — they borrow not
Glory from those who made the world their prey;
And he is gathered to the kings of thought
Who waged contention with their time's decay,
And of the past are all that cannot pass away.

Go thou to Rome, — at once the Paradise,
The grave, the city, and the wilderness;
And where its wrecks like shattered mountains rise,
And flowering weeds, and fragrant copses dress
The bones of Desolation's nakedness
Pass, till the Spirit of the spot shall lead
Thy footsteps to a slope of green access
Where, like an infant's smile, over the dead,
A light of laughing flowers along the grass is spread.

And grey walls moulder round, on which dull Time
Feeds, like slow fire upon a hoary brand:
And one keen pyramid with wedge sublime,
Pavilioning the dust of him who planned
This refuge for his memory, doth stand
Like flame transformed to marble; and beneath,
A field is spread, on which a newer band
Have pitched in Heaven's smile their camp of death,
Welcoming him we lose with scarce extinguished breath.

Here pause: these graves are all too young as yet
To have outgrown the sorrow which consigned
Its charge to each; and if the seal is set,
Here, on one fountain of a mourning mind,
Break it not thou! too surely shalt thou find
Thine own well full, if thou returnest home,
Of tears and gall. From the world's bitter wind
Seeks shelter in the shadow of the tomb.
What Adonais is, why fear we to become?

The One remains, the many change and pass;
Heaven's light forever shines, Earth's shadows fly;
Life, like a dome of many-coloured glass,
Stains the white radiance of Eternity,
Until Death tramples it to fragments. — Die,
If thou wouldst be with that which thou dost seek!
Follow where all is fled! — Rome's azure sky,
Flowers, ruins, statues, music, words, are weak
The glory they transfuse with fitting truth to speak.

Why linger, why turn back, why shrink, my Heart?
Thy hopes are gone before: from all things here
They have departed; thou shouldst now depart!
A light is passed from the revolving year,
And man, and woman; and what still is dear
Attracts to crush, repels to make thee wither.
The soft sky smiles, – the low wind whispers near:
'Tis Adonais calls! oh, hasten thither,
No more let Life divide what Death can join together.

That Light whose smiles kindles the Universe,
That Beauty in which all things work and move,
That Benediction which the eclipsing Curse
Of birth can quench not, that sustaining Love
Which through the web of being blindly wove
By man and beast and earth and air and sea,
Burns bright or dim, as each are mirrors of
The fire for which all thirst, now beams on me,
Consuming the last clouds of cold mortality.

The breath whose might I have invoked in song
Descends on me; my spirit's bark is driven
Far from the shore, far from the trembling throng
Whose sails were never to the tempest given;
The massy earth and spherèd skies are riven!
I am borne darkly, fearfully, afar;
Whilst burning through the inmost veil of Heaven,
The soul of Adonais, like a star,
Beacons from the abode where the Eternal are.

338   *The Aziola*

'Do you not hear the aziola cry?
Methinks she must be nigh –'
    Said Mary as we sate
In dusk, ere stars were lit or candles brought –
    And I who thought
This Aziola was some tedious woman
Asked, 'Who is Aziola?' – how elate
I felt to know that it was nothing human,
No mockery of myself to fear or hate!
    And Mary saw my soul,
And laughed and said – 'Disquiet yourself not,
    'Tis nothing but a little downy owl.'

Sad aziola, many an eventide
 Thy music I had heard
By wood and stream, meadow and mountainside,
 And fields and marshes wide,
Such as nor voice, nor lute, nor wind, nor bird
 The soul ever stirred –
Unlike and far sweeter than them all.
Sad aziola, from that moment I
Loved thee and thy sad cry.

339   *Chorus* from *'Hellas'*

The world's great age begins anew,
 The golden years return,
The earth doth like a snake renew
 Her winter weeds outworn;
Heaven smiles, and faiths and empires gleam
Like wrecks of a dissolving dream.

A brighter Hellas rears its mountains
 From waves serener far,
A new Peneus rolls his fountains
 Against the morning-star;
Where fairer Tempes bloom, there sleep
Young Cyclads on a sunnier deep.

A loftier Argo cleaves the main
 Fraught with a later prize;
Another Orpheus sings again,
 And loves, and weeps, and dies;
A new Ulysses leaves once more
Calypso for his native shore.

O, write no more the tale of Troy,
 If earth Death's scroll must be!
Nor mix with Laian rage the joy
 Which dawns upon the free;
Although a subtler Sphinx renew
Riddles of death Thebes never knew.

Another Athens shall arise,
 And to remoter time
Bequeath, like sunset to the skies,
 The splendour of its prime;
And leave, if nought so bright may live,
All earth can take or Heaven can give.

Saturn and Love their long repose
    Shall burst, more bright and good
Than all who fell, than One who rose,
    Than many unsubdued;
Not gold, not blood, their altar dowers,
But votive tears and symbol flowers.

O cease! must hate and death return?
    Cease! must men kill and die?
Cease! drain not to its dregs the urn
    Of bitter prophecy.
The world is weary of the past,
O might it die or rest at last!

John Clare

340   *The Eternity of Nature*

Leaves from eternity are simple things
To the world's gaze – whereto a spirit clings
Sublime and lasting. Trampled under foot,
The daisy lives, and strikes its little root
Into the lap of time: centuries may come,
And pass away into the silent tomb,
And still the child, hid in the womb of time,
Shall smile and pluck them when this simple rhyme
Shall be forgotten, like a churchyard stone,
Or lingering lie unnoticed and alone.
When eighteen hundred years, our common date,
Grow many thousands in their marching state,
Ay, still the child, with pleasure in his eye,
Shall cry – the daisy! a familiar cry –
And run to pluck it, in the self-same state
As when Time found it in his infant date;
And, like a child himself, when all was new,
Might smile with wonder, and take notice too.
Its little golden bosom, frilled with snow,
Might win e'en Eve to stoop adown, and show
Her partner, Adam, in the silky grass
This little gem that smiled where pleasure was,
And loving Eve, from Eden followed ill,
And bloomed with sorrow, and lives smiling still,
As once in Eden under heaven's breath,
So now on earth, and on the lap of death
It smiles for ever. – Cowslips of gold bloom,
That in the pasture and the meadow come,

Shall come when kings and empires fade and die;
And in the closen, as Time's partners, lie
As fresh two thousand years to come as now,
With those five crimson spots upon their brow.
The little brooks that hum a simple lay
In green unnoticed spots, from praise away,
Shall sing when poets in time's darkness hid
Shall lie like memory in a pyramid,
Forgetting yet not all forgot, though lost
Like a thread's end in ravelled windings crost.
The little humble-bee shall hum as long
As nightingales, for Time protects the song;
And Nature is their soul, to whom all clings
Of fair or beautiful in lasting things.
The little robin in the quiet glen,
Hidden from fame and all the strife of men,
Sings unto Time a pastoral, and gives
A music that lives on and ever lives.
Spring and autumnal years shall bloom, and fade,
Longer than songs that poets ever made.
Think ye not these, Time's playthings, pass proud skill?
Time loves them like a child, and ever will;
And so I seek them in each bushy spot,
And sing with them when all else notice not,
And feel the music of their mirth agree
With that sooth quiet that bestirs in me.
And if I touch aright that quiet tone,
That soothing truth that shadows forth their own,
Then many a year to come, in after-days,
Shall still find hearts to love my quiet lays.
Thus cheering mirth with thoughts sung not for fame,
But for the joy that with their utterance came,
That inward breath of rapture urged not loud –
Birds, singing lone, fly silent past a crowd –
In these same pastoral spots, which childish time
Makes dear to me, I wander out and rhyme;
What hour the dewy morning's infancy
Hangs on each blade of grass and every tree,
And sprents the red thighs of the humble-bee,
Who 'gins betimes unwearied minstrelsy;
Who breakfasts, dines, and most divinely sups,
With every flower save golden buttercups –
On whose proud bosoms he will never go,
But passes by with scarcely 'How do ye do?'
Since in their showy, shining, gaudy cells
Haply the summer's honey never dwells.
All nature's ways are mysteries! Endless youth
Lives in them all, unchangeable as truth.
With the odd number five, her curious laws
Play many freaks, nor once mistake the cause;

For in the cowslip-peeps this very day
Five spots appear, which Time wears not away,
Nor once mistakes in counting – look within
Each peep, and five, nor more nor less, are seen.
So trailing bindweed, with its pinky cup,
Five leaves of paler hue go streaking up;
And many a bird, too, keeps the rule alive,
Laying five eggs, nor more nor less than five.
But flowers, how many own that mystic power,
With five leaves ever making up the flower!
The five-leaved grass, mantling its golden cup
Of flowers – five leaves make all for which I stoop.
The bryony, in the hedge, that now adorns
The tree to which it clings, and now the thorns,
Owns five-starred pointed leaves of dingy white;
Count which I will, all make the number right.
The spreading goose-grass, trailing all abroad
In leaves of silver green about the road –
Five leaves make every blossom all along.
I stoop for many, none are counted wrong.
'Tis Nature's wonder, and her Maker's will,
Who bade earth be, and order owns him still,
As that superior Power, who keeps the key
Of wisdom and of might through all eternity.

341   *I Am*

I am – yet what I am none cares or knows,
  My friends forsake me like a memory lost;
I am the self-consumer of my woes,
  They rise and vanish in oblivions host,
Like shadows in love – frenzied stifled throes
And yet I am, and live like vapours tost

Into the nothingness of scorn and noise,
  Into the living sea of waking dreams,
Where there is neither sense of life or joys,
  But the vast shipwreck of my life's esteems;
And e'en the dearest – that I love the best –
Are strange – nay, rather stranger than the rest.

I long for scenes where man has never trod,
  A place where woman never smiled or wept;
There to abide with my Creator, God,
  And sleep as I in childhood sweetly slept:
Untroubling and untroubled where I lie,
The grass below – above the vaulted sky.

John Keats

342 *On Sitting Down to Read 'King Lear' Once Again*

O golden-tongued Romance with serene lute!
　Fair plumed Syren! Queen of far away!
　Leave melodizing on this wintry day,
Shut up thine olden pages, and be mute.
Adieu! for once again the fierce dispute,
　Betwixt damnation and impassioned clay
　Must I burn through; once more humbly assay
The bitter-sweet of this Shakespearian fruit.
Chief Poet! and ye clouds of Albion,
　Begetters of our deep eternal theme,
When through the old oak forest I am gone,
　Let me not wander in a barren dream,
But when I am consumèd in the fire
Give me new Phœnix wings to fly at my desire.

343

When I have fears that I may cease to be
　Before my pen has glean'd my teeming brain,
Before high-pilèd books, in charact'ry,
　Hold like rich garners the full-ripened grain;
When I behold, upon the night's starr'd face,
　Huge cloudy symbols of a high romance,
And think that I may never live to trace
　Their shadows, with the magic hand of chance;
And when I feel, fair creature of an hour!
　That I shall never look upon thee more,
Never have relish in the faery power
　Of unreflecting love! – then on the shore
Of the wide world I stand alone, and think,
Till Love and Fame to nothingness do sink.

344 *What the Thrush Said*

O thou whose face hath felt the Winter's wind,
Whose eye has seen the snow-clouds hung in mist,
And the black elm tops 'mong the freezing stars!
To thee the spring will be a harvest time.
O thou whose only book has been the light
Of supreme darkness, which thou feddest on
Night after night, when Phœbus was away!
To thee the spring shall be a triple morn.

O fret not after knowledge. I have none,
And yet my song comes native with the warmth.
O fret not after knowledge! I have none.
And yet the evening listens. He who saddens
At thought of idleness cannot be idle,
And he's awake who thinks himself asleep.

345   *To Homer*

Standing aloof in giant ignorance,
   Of thee I hear and of the Cyclades,
As one who sits ashore and longs perchance
   To visit dolphin-coral in deep seas.
So thou wast blind! – but then the veil was rent;
   For Jove uncurtain'd Heaven to let thee live,
And Neptune made for thee a spumy tent,
   And Pan made sing for thee his forest-hive;
Ay, on the shores of darkness there is light,
   And precipices show untrodden green;
There is a budding morrow in midnight;
   There is a triple sight in blindness keen;
Such seeing hadst thou, as it once befell,
To Dian, Queen of Earth, and Heaven, and Hell.

346   *[Verses from a Letter]*

There was a naughty Boy
A naughty boy was he
He would not stop at home
He could not quiet be –
He took
In his Knapsack
A Book
Full of vowels
And a shirt
With some towels –
A slight cap
For night cap –
A hair brush
Comb ditto
New Stockings
For old ones
Would split O!

This Knapsack
Tight at 's back
He rivetted close
And followéd his Nose
To the North
To the North
And follow'd his nose
To the North.

There was a naughty boy
And a naughty boy was he
For nothing would he do
But scribble poetry –
He took
An inkstand
In his hand
And a Pen
Big as ten
In the other
And away
In a Pother
He ran
To the mountains
And fountains
And ghostes
And Postes
And witches
And ditches
And wrote
In his coat
When the weather
Was ~~warm~~ cool
Fear of gout –
And without
When the w[e]ather
Was ~~cool~~ warm –
Och the charm
When we choose
To follow ones nose
To the north
To the north
To follow one's nose to the north!

There was a naughty boy
And a naughty boy we [for was] he
He kept little fishes
In washing tubs three
In spite
Of the might

Of the Maid
Nor affraid
Of his Granny-good –
He often would
Hurly burly
Get up early
And go
By hook or crook
To the brook
And bring home
Miller's thumb
Tittle bat
Not over fat
Minnows small
As the stall
Of a glove
Not above
The size
Of a nice
Little Baby's
Little finger –
O he made
'Twas his trade
Of Fish a pretty Kettle
A Kettle – A Kettle
Of Fish a pretty Kettle
A Kettle!

There was a naughty Boy
And a naughty Boy was he
He ran away to Scotland
The people for to see –
There he found
That the ground
Was as hard
That a yard
Was as long,
That a song
Was as merry,
That a cherry
Was as red –
That lead
Was as weighty
That fourscore
Was as eighty
That a door
Was as wooden
As in england –

So he stood in
His shoes
And he wonderd
He wonderd
He stood in his
Shoes and he wonder'd.

347   *Ode to a Nightingale*

My heart aches, and a drowsy numbness pains
    My sense, as though of hemlock I had drunk,
Or emptied some dull opiate to the drains
    One minute past, and Lethe-wards had sunk:
'Tis not through envy of thy happy lot,
    But being too happy in thy happiness, —
        That thou, light-wingèd Dryad of the trees,
            In some melodious plot
    Of beechen green, and shadows numberless,
        Singest of summer in full-throated ease.

O for a draught of vintage, that hath been
    Cooled a long age in the deep-delvèd earth,
Tasting of Flora and the country green,
    Dance, and Provençal song, and sunburnt mirth!
O for a beaker full of the warm South,
    Full of the true, the blushful Hippocrene,
        With beaded bubbles winking at the brim,
            And purple-stainèd mouth;
    That I might drink and leave the world unseen,
        And with thee fade away into the forest dim:

Fade far away, dissolve, and quite forget
    What thou among the leaves hast never known,
The weariness, the fever, and the fret
    Here, where men sit and hear each other groan;
Where palsy shakes a few, sad, last grey hairs,
    Where youth grows pale, and spectre-thin, and dies;
        Where but to think is to be full of sorrow
            And leaden-eyed despairs;
    Where Beauty cannot keep her lustrous eyes,
        Or new Love pine at them beyond to-morrow.

Away! away! for I will fly to thee,
    Not charioted by Bacchus and his pards,
But on the viewless wings of Poesy,
    Though the dull brain perplexes and retards:

Already with thee! tender is the night,
  And haply the Queen-Moon is on her throne,
    Clustered around by all her starry Fays;
      But here there is no light,
  Save what from heaven is with the breezes blown
    Through verdurous glooms and winding mossy ways.

I cannot see what flowers are at my feet,
  Nor what soft incense hangs upon the boughs,
But, in embalmèd darkness, guess each sweet
  Wherewith the seasonable month endows
The grass, the thicket, and the fruit-tree wild;
  White hawthorn, and the pastoral eglantine;
    Fast-fading violets covered up in leaves;
      And mid-May's eldest child,
  The coming musk-rose, full of dewy wine,
    The murmurous haunt of flies on summer eves.

Darkling I listen; and for many a time
  I have been half in love with easeful Death,
Called him soft names in many a musèd rhyme,
  To take into the air my quiet breath;
Now more than ever seems it rich to die,
  To cease upon the midnight with no pain,
    While thou art pouring forth thy soul abroad
      In such an ecstasy!
  Still wouldst thou sing, and I have ears in vain –
    To thy high requiem become a sod.

Thou wast not born for death, immortal Bird!
  No hungry generations tread thee down;
The voice I hear this passing night was heard
  In ancient days by emperor and clown:
Perhaps the self-same song that found a path
  Through the sad heart of Ruth, when sick for home,
    She stood in tears amid the alien corn;
      The same that oft-times hath
  Charmed magic casements, opening on the foam
    Of perilous seas, in faery lands forlorn.

Forlorn! the very word is like a bell
  To toll me back from thee to my sole self.
Adieu! the fancy cannot cheat so well
  As she is famed to do, deceiving elf,
Adieu! adieu! thy plaintive anthem fades
  Past the near meadows, over the still stream,
    Up the hill-side; and now 'tis buried deep
      In the next valley-glades:
  Was it a vision, or a waking dream?
    Fled is that music: – do I wake or sleep?

348   *Ode on a Grecian Urn*

Thou still unravished bride of quietness!
  Thou foster-child of Silence and slow Time,
Sylvan historian, who canst thus express
  A flowry tale more sweetly than our rhyme:
What leaf-fringed legend haunts about thy shape
    Of deities or mortals, or of both,
      In Tempe or the dales of Arcady?
    What men or gods are these? What maidens loth?
What mad pursuit? What struggle to escape?
    What pipes and timbrels? What wild ecstasy?

Heard melodies are sweet, but those unheard
  Are sweeter: therefore, ye soft pipes, play on;
Not to the sensual ear, but, more endeared,
  Pipe to the spirit ditties of no tone:
Fair youth, beneath the trees, thou canst not leave
    Thy song, nor ever can those trees be bare;
    Bold Lover, never, never canst thou kiss,
Though winning near the goal – yet, do not grieve;
    She cannot fade, though thou hast not thy bliss,
For ever wilt thou love, and she be fair!

Ah, happy, happy boughs! that cannot shed
  Your leaves, nor ever bid the Spring adieu;
And, happy melodist, unwearièd,
  For ever piping songs for ever new;
More happy love! more happy, happy love!
    For ever warm and still to be enjoyed,
    For ever panting and for ever young;
All breathing human passion far above,
    That leaves a heart high sorrowful and cloyed,
    A burning forehead, and a parching tongue.

Who are these coming to the sacrifice?
  To what green altar, O mysterious priest,
Lead'st thou that heifer lowing at the skies,
  And all her silken flanks with garlands drest?
What little town by river or sea-shore,
    Or mountain-built with peaceful citadel,
    Is emptied of its folk, this pious morn?
And, little town, thy streets for evermore
    Will silent be; and not a soul to tell
    Why thou art desolate, can e'er return.

O Attic shape! Fair attitude! with brede
  Of marble men and maidens overwrought,
With forest branches and the trodden weed;
    Thou, silent form, dost tease us out of thought

As doth eternity: Cold Pastoral!
　When old age shall this generation waste,
　　Thou shalt remain, in midst of other woe
　Than ours, a friend to man, to whom thou say'st,
'Beauty is truth, truth beauty, — that is all
　　Ye know on earth, and all ye need to know.'

349   *To Autumn*

Season of mists and mellow fruitfulness!
　Close bosom-friend of the maturing sun;
Conspiring with him how to load and bless
　With fruit the vines that round the thatch-eaves run;
To bend with apples the mossed cottage-trees,
　And fill all fruit with ripeness to the core;
　　To swell the gourd, and plump the hazel shells
　With a sweet kernel; to set budding more,
And still more, later flowers for the bees,
Until they think warm days will never cease,
　　For Summer has o'er-brimmed their clammy cells.

Who hath not seen thee oft amid thy store?
　Sometimes whoever seeks abroad may find
Thee sitting careless on a granary floor,
　Thy hair soft-lifted by the winnowing wind;
Or on a half-reaped furrow sound asleep,
　Drowsed with the fume of poppies, while thy hook
　　Spares the next swath and all its twinèd flowers;
And sometimes like a gleaner thou dost keep
　Steady thy laden head across a brook;
　Or by a cider-press, with patient look,
　　Thou watchest the last oozings, hours by hours.

Where are the songs of Spring? Ay, where are they?
　Think not of them, thou hast thy music too,
　While barrèd clouds bloom the soft-dying day,
And touch the stubble-plains with rosy hue;
　Then in a wailful choir the small gnats mourn
　Among the river sallows, borne aloft
　　Or sinking as the light wind lives or dies;
And full-grown lambs loud bleat from hilly bourn;
　Hedge-crickets sing; and now with treble soft
　The redbreast whistles from a garden-croft,
　　And gathering swallows twitter in the skies.

350   *To Fanny*

I cry your mercy – pity – love! – ay, love!
  Merciful love that tantalises not
One-thoughted, never-wandering, guileless love,
  Unmasked and being seen – without a blot!
O! let me have thee whole, – all – all – be mine!
  That shape, that fairness, that sweet minor zest
Of love, your kiss, – those hands, those eyes divine,
  That warm, white, lucent, million-pleasured breast, –
Yourself – your soul – in pity give me all,
  Withhold no atom's atom or I die,
Or living on, perhaps, your wretched thrall,
  Forget, in the mist of idle misery,
Life's purposes, – the palate of my mind
Losing its gust, and my ambition blind!

Thomas Hood

351   *The Bridge of Sighs*

'Drown'd! drown'd!' *Hamlet*

One more Unfortunate,
Weary of breath,
Rashly importunate,
Gone to her death!

Take her up tenderly,
Lift her with care;
Fashioned so slenderly,
Young, and so fair!

Look at her garments
Clinging like cerements;
Whilst the wave constantly
Drips from her clothing;
Take her up instantly,
Loving, not loathing. –

Touch her not scornfully;
Think of her mournfully,
Gently and humanly;
Not of the stains of her,
All that remains of her
Now is pure womanly.

Make no deep scrutiny
Into her mutiny
Rash and undutiful:
Past all dishonour
Death has left on her
Only the beautiful.

Still, for all slips of hers,
One of Eve's family –
Wipe those poor lips of hers
Oozing so clammily.

Loop up her tresses
Escaped from the comb,
Her fair auburn tresses;
Whilst wonderment guesses
Where was her home?

Who was her father?
Who was her mother?
Had she a sister?
Had she a brother?
Or was there a dearer one
Still, and a nearer one
Yet, than all other?

Alas! for the rarity
Of Christian charity
Under the sun!
Oh! it was pitiful!
Near a whole city full,
Home she had none!

Sisterly, brotherly,
Fatherly, motherly,
Feelings had changed:
Love, by harsh evidence,
Thrown from its eminence;
Even God's providence
Seeming estranged.

Where the lamps quiver
So far in the river,
With many a light
From window and casement,
From garret to basement,
She stood, with amazement,
Houseless by night.

The bleak wind of March
Made her tremble and shiver;
But not the dark arch,
Or the black flowing river:
Mad from life's history,
Glad to death's mystery,
Swift to be hurled –
Anywhere, anywhere,
Out of the world!

In she plunged boldly,
No matter how coldly
The rough river ran, –
Over the brink of it,
Picture it – think of it,
Dissolute man!
Lave in it, drink of it,
Then, if you can!

Take her up tenderly,
Lift her with care;
Fashioned so slenderly,
Young, and so fair!

Ere her limbs frigidly
Stiffen too rigidly,
Decently, – kindly, –
Smoothe and compose them:
And her eyes, close them,
Staring so blindly!

Dreadfully staring
Through muddy impurity,
As when with the daring
Last look of despairing,
Fixed on futurity.

Perishing gloomily,
Spurred by contumely,
Cold inhumanity,
Burning insanity,
Into her rest. –
Cross her hands humbly,
As if praying dumbly,
Over her breast!

Owning her weakness,
Her evil behaviour,
And leaving, with meekness,
Her sins to her Saviour!

352   *Silence*

There is a silence where hath been no sound,
   There is a silence where no sound may be,
    In the cold grave – under the deep deep sea,
Or in wide desert where no life is found,
Which hath been mute, and still must sleep profound;
   No voice is hushed – no life treads silently,
    But clouds and cloudy shadows wander free,
That never spoke, over the idle ground:
But in green ruins, in the desolate walls
   Of antique palaces, where Man hath been,
Though the dun fox, or wild hyena, calls,
   And owls, that flit continually between,
Shriek to the echo, and the low winds moan,
There the true Silence is, self-conscious and alone.

353   *The Haunted House*

                                    A Romance

'A jolly place, said he, in times of old,
But something ails it now; the spot is curst.'
        – *Hartleap Well, by Wordsworth*

                                        I

Some dreams we have are nothing else but dreams,
Unnatural, and full of contradictions;
Yet others of our most romantic schemes
Are something more than fictions.

It might be only on enchanted ground;
It might be merely by a thought's expansion;
But in the spirit, or the flesh, I found
An old deserted Mansion.

A residence for woman, child, and man,
A dwelling-place, – and yet no habitation;
A House, – but under some prodigious ban
Of excommunication.

Unhinged the iron gates half open hung,
Jarred by the gusty gales of many winters,
That from its crumbled pedestal had flung
One marble globe in splinters.

No dog was at the threshold, great or small;
No pigeon on the roof — no household creature —
No cat demurely dozing on the wall —
Not one domestic feature.

No human figure stirred, to go or come,
No face looked forth from shut or open casement;
No chimney smoked — there was no sign of Home
From parapet to basement.

With shattered panes the grassy court was starred;
The time-worn coping-stone had tumbled after!
And through the ragged roof the sky shone, barred
With naked beam and rafter.

O'er all there hung a shadow and a fear;
A sense of mystery the spirit daunted,
And said, as plain as whisper in the ear,
The place is Haunted!

The flower grew wild and rankly as the weed,
Roses with thistles struggled for espial,
And vagrant plants of parasitic breed
Had overgrown the Dial.

But gay or gloomy, steadfast or infirm,
No heart was there to heed the hour's duration;
All times and tides were lost in one long term
Of stagnant desolation.

The wren had built within the Porch, she found
Its quiet loneliness so sure and thorough;
And on the lawn, — within its turfy mound, —
The rabbit made its burrow.

The rabbit wild and gray, that flitted through
The shrubby clumps, and frisked, and sat, and vanished,
But leisurely and bold, as if he knew
His enemy was banished.

The wary crow, — the pheasant from the woods —
Lulled by the still and everlasting sameness,
Close to the Mansion, like domestic broods,
Fed with a 'shocking tameness'.

The coot was swimming in the reedy pond,
Beside the water-hen, so soon affrighted;
And in the weedy moat the heron, fond
Of solitude, alighted.

The moping heron, motionless and stiff,
That on a stone, as silently and stilly,
Stood, an apparent sentinel, as if
To guard the water-lily.

No sound was heard except, from far away,
The ringing of the Whitwall's shrilly laughter,
Or, now and then, the chatter of the jay,
That Echo murmured after.

But Echo never mocked the human tongue;
Some weighty crime, that Heaven could not pardon,
A secret curse on that old Building hung,
And its deserted Garden.

The beds were all untouched by hand or tool;
No footstep marked the damp and mossy gravel,
Each walk as green as is the mantled pool,
For want of human travel.

The vine unpruned, and the neglected peach,
Drooped from the wall with which they used to grapple;
And on the cankered tree, in easy reach,
Rotted the golden apple.

But awfully the truant shunned the ground,
The vagrant kept aloof, and daring Poacher,
In spite of gaps that through the fences round
Invited the encroacher.

For over all there hung a cloud of fear,
A sense of mystery the spirit daunted,
And said, as plain as whisper in the ear,
The place is Haunted!

The pear and quince lay squandered on the grass;
The mould was purple with unheeded showers
Of bloomy plums – a Wilderness it was
Of fruits, and weeds, and flowers!

The marigold amidst the nettles blew,
The gourd embraced the rose bush in its ramble.
The thistle and the stock together grew,
The holly-hock and bramble.

The bear-bine with the lilac interlaced,
The sturdy bur-dock choked its slender neighbour,
The spicy pink. All tokens were effaced
Of human care and labour.

The very yew Formality had trained
To such a rigid pyramidal stature,
For want of trimming had almost regained
The raggedness of nature.

The Fountain was a-dry – neglect and time
Had marred the work of artisan and mason,
And efts and croaking frogs, begot of slime,
Sprawled in the ruined bason.

The Statue, fallen from its marble base
Amidst the refuse leaves, and herbage rotten,
Lay like the Idol of some bygone race,
Its name and rites forgotten.

On ev'ry side the aspect was the same,
All ruined, desolate, forlorn, and savage:
No hand or foot within the precinct came
To rectify or ravage.

For over all there hung a cloud of fear,
A sense of mystery the spirit daunted,
And said as plain as whisper in the ear,
The place is Haunted!

II

O, very gloomy is the House of Woe,
Where tears are falling while the bell is knelling,
With all the dark solemnities which show
That Death is in the dwelling!

O very, very dreary is the room
Where Love, domestic Love, no longer nestles,
But smitten by the common stroke of doom,
The Corpse lies on the trestles!

But House of Woe, and hearse, and sable pall,
The narrow home of the departed mortal,
Ne'er looked so gloomy as that Ghostly Hall,
With its deserted portal!

The centipede along the threshold crept,
The cobweb hung across in mazy tangle,
And in its winding-sheet the maggot slept,
At every nook and angle.

The keyhole lodged the earwig and her brood,
The emmets of the steps had old possession,
And marched in search of their diurnal food
In undisturbed procession.

As undisturbed as the prehensile cell
Of moth or maggot, or the spider's tissue,
For never foot upon that threshold fell,
To enter or to issue.

O'er all there hung the shadow of a fear,
A sense of mystery the spirit daunted,
And said, as plain as whisper in the ear,
The place is Haunted!

Howbeit, the door I pushed – or so I dreamed –
Which slowly, slowly gaped, – the hinges creaking
With such a rusty eloquence, it seemed
That Time himself was speaking.

But Time was dumb within that Mansion old,
Or left his tale to the heraldic banners,
That hung from the corroded walls, and told
Of former men and manners:–

Those tattered flags, that with the opened door,
Seemed the old wave of battle to remember,
While fallen fragments danced upon the floor,
Like dead leaves in December.

The startled bats flew out – bird after bird –
The screech-owl overhead began to flutter,
And seemed to mock the cry that she had heard
Some dying victim utter!

A shriek that echoed from the joisted roof,
And up the stair, and further still and further,
Till in some ringing chamber far aloof
It ceased its tale of murther!

Meanwhile the rusty armour rattled round,
The banner shuddered, and the ragged streamer;
All things the horrid tenor of the sound
Acknowledged with a tremor.

The antlers, where the helmet hung and belt,
Stirred as the tempest stirs the forest branches,
Or as the stag had trembled when he felt
The blood-hound at his haunches.

The window jingled in its crumbled frame,
And through its many gaps of destitution
Dolorous moans and hollow sighings came,
Like those of dissolution.

The wood-louse dropped and rolled into a ball,
Touched by some impulse occult or mechanic;
And nameless beetles ran along the wall
In universal panic.

The subtle spider, that from overhead
Hung like a spy on human guilt and error,
Suddenly turned, and up its slender thread
Ran with a nimble terror.

The very stains and fractures on the wall
Assuming features solemn and terrific,
Hinted some tragedy of that old Hall,
Locked up in Hieroglyphic.

Some tale that might, perchance, have solved the doubt,
Wherefore amongst those flags so dull and livid,
The banner of the Bloody Hand shone out
So ominously vivid.

Some key to that inscrutable appeal,
Which made the very frame of Nature quiver;
And every thrilling nerve and fibre feel
So ague-like a shiver.

For over all there hung a cloud of fear,
A sense of mystery the spirit daunted,
And said, as plain as whisper in the ear,
The place is Haunted!

If but a rat had lingered in the house,
To lure the thought into a social channel!
But not a rat remained, or tiny mouse,
To squeak behind the panel.

Huge drops rolled down the walls, as if they wept;
And where the cricket used to chirp so shrilly,
The toad was squatting, and the lizard crept
On that damp hearth and chilly.

For years no cheerful blaze had sparkled there,
Or glanced on coat of buff or knightly metal;
The slug was crawling on the vacant chair, —
The snail upon the settle.

The floor was redolent of mould and must,
The fungus in the rotten seams had quickened;
While on the oaken table coats of dust
Perennially had thickened.

No mark of leathern jack or metal can,
No cup – no horn – no hospitable token –
All social ties between that board and Man
Had long ago been broken.

There was so foul a rumour in the air,
The shadow of a Presence so atrocious;
No human creature could have feasted there,
Even the most ferocious.

For over all there hung a cloud of fear,
A sense of mystery the spirit daunted,
And said, as plain as whisper in the ear,
The place is Haunted!

III

'Tis hard for human actions to account,
Whether from reason or from impulse only –
But some internal prompting bade me mount
The gloomy stairs and lonely.

Those gloomy stairs, so dark, and damp, and cold,
With odours as from bones and relics carnal,
Deprived of rite, and consecrated mould,
The chapel vault, or charnel.

Those dreary stairs, where with the sounding stress
Of ev'ry step so many echoes blended,
The mind, with dark misgivings, feared to guess
How many feet ascended.

The tempest with its spoils had drifted in,
Till each unwholesome stone was darkly spotted,
As thickly as the leopard's dappled skin,
With leaves that rankly rotted.

The air was thick – and in the upper gloom
The bat – or something in its shape – was winging,
And on the wall, as chilly as a tomb,
The Death's Head moth was clinging.

That mystic moth, which, with a sense profound
Of all unholy presence, augurs truly;
And with a grim significance flits round
The taper burning bluely.

Such omens in the place there seemed to be,
At ev'ry crooked turn, or on the landing,
The straining eyeball was prepared to see
Some Apparition standing.

For over all there hung a cloud of fear,
A sense of mystery the spirit daunted,
And said, as plain as whisper in the ear,
The place is Haunted!

Yet no portentous Shape the sight amazed;
Each object plain, and tangible, and valid;
But from their tarnished frames dark Figures gazed,
And Faces spectre-pallid.

Not merely with the mimic life that lies
Within the compass of Art's simulation;
Their souls were looking through their painted eyes
With awful speculation.

On every lip a speechless horror dwelt;
On ev'ry brow the burthen of affliction;
The old Ancestral Spirits knew and felt
The House's malediction.

Such earnest woe their features overcast,
They might have stirred, or sighed, or wept, or spoken;
But, save the hollow moaning of the blast,
The stillness was unbroken.

No other sound or stir of life was there,
Except my steps in solitary clamber,
From flight to flight, from humid stair to stair,
From chamber into chamber.

Deserted rooms of luxury and state,
That old magnificence had richly furnished
With pictures, cabinets of ancient date,
And carvings gilt and burnished.

Rich hangings, storied by the needle's art,
With scripture history, or classic fable;
But all had faded, save one ragged part,
Where Cain was slaying Abel.

The silent waste of mildew and the moth
Had marred the tissue with a partial ravage;
But undecaying frowned upon the cloth
Each feature stern and savage.

The sky was pale; the cloud a thing of doubt;
Some hues were fresh, and some decayed and duller;
But still the BLOODY HAND shone strangely out
With vehemence of colour!

The BLOODY HAND that with a lurid stain
Shone on the dusty floor, a dismal token,
Projected from the casement's painted pain,
Where all beside was broken.

The BLOODY HAND significant of crime,
That glaring on the old heraldic banner,
Had kept its crimson unimpaired by time,
In such a wondrous manner!

O'er all there hung the shadow of a fear,
A sense of mystery the spirit daunted,
And said, as plain as whisper in the ear,
The place is Haunted!

The Death Watch ticked behind the panel'd oak,
Inexplicable tremors shook the arras,
And echoes strange and mystical awoke,
The fancy to embarrass.

Prophetic hints that filled the soul with dread,
But through one gloomy entrance pointing mostly,
The while some secret inspiration said
That Chamber is the Ghostly!

Across the door no gossamer festoon
Swung pendulous – no web – no dusty fringes,
No silky chrysalis or white cocoon
About its nooks and hinges.

The spider shunned the interdicted room,
The moth, the beetle, and the fly were banished,
And where the sunbeam fell athwart the gloom,
The very midge had vanished.

One lonely ray that glanced upon a Bed,
As if with awful aim direct and certain,
To show the BLOODY HAND in burning red
Embroidered on the curtain.

And yet no gory stain was on the quilt –
The pillow in its place had slowly rotted;
The floor alone retained the trace of guilt,
Those boards obscurely spotted.

Obscurely spotted to the door, and thence
With mazy doubles to the grated casement –
Oh what a tale they told of fear intense,
Of horror and amazement!

What human creature in the dead of night
Had coursed like hunted hare that cruel distance?
Had sought the door, the window in his flight,
Striving for dear existence?

What shrieking Spirit in that bloody room
Its mortal frame had violently quitted? –
Across the sunbeam, with a sudden gloom,
A ghostly Shadow flitted.

Across the sunbeam, and along the wall,
But painted on the air so very dimly,
It hardly veiled the tapestry at all,
Or portrait frowning grimly.

O'er all there hung the shadow of a fear,
A sense of mystery the spirit daunted,
And said, as plain as whisper in the ear,
The place is Haunted!

Thomas Babington Macaulay

354   *Epitaph on a Jacobite*

To my true king I offered free from stain
Courage and faith; vain faith, and courage vain.
For him, I threw lands, honours, wealth, away.
And one dear hope, that was more prized than they.
For him I languished in a foreign clime,
Grey-haired with sorrow in my manhood's prime;
Heard on Lavernia Scargill's whispering trees,
And pined by Arno for my lovelier Tees;
Beheld each night my home in fevered sleep,
Each morning started from the dream to weep;
Till God who saw me tried too sorely, gave
The resting place I asked, an early grave.
Oh thou, whom chance leads to this nameless stone,
From that proud country which was once mine own,
By those white cliffs I never more must see,
By that dear language which I spake like thee,
Forget all feuds, and shed one English tear
O'er English dust. A broken heart lies here.

Anonymous

355

Jimmy's Enlisted
or
The Recruited Collier

Oh, what's the matter wi' you, my lass,
   An' where's your dashin Jimmy?
The sowdger boys have picked him up
   And sent him far, far frae me.

Last pay-day he set off to town,
   And them red-coated fellows
Enticed him in and made him drunk,
   And he'd better gone to the gallows.

The very sight o' his cockade,
   It set us all a-cryin;
And me, I fairly fainted twice,
   I thought that I was dyin.

My father would have paid the smart,
   And run for the golden guinea,
But the sergeant swore he'd kissed the book,
   And now they've got young Jimmy.

When Jimmy talks about the wars
   It's worse than death to hear him.
I must go out and hide my tears,
   Because I cannot bear him.

For aye he jibes and cracks his jokes,
   And bids me not forsake him.
A brigadier or grenadier,
   He says they're sure to make him.

As I walked over the stubble field,
   Below it runs the seam,
I thought o' Jimmy hewin there,
   But it was all a dream.

He hewed the very coals we burn,
   An when the fire I'se leetin,
To think the lumps was in his hands,
   It sets my heart to beatin.

So break my heart, and then it's ower,
   So break my heart, my dearie,
And I'll lie in the cold, cold grave,
   For of single life I'm weary.

Thomas Lovell Beddoes

356   *Song* from *'Death's Jest Book'*

Old Adam, the carrion crow,
  The old crow of Cairo;
He sat in the shower, and let it flow
Under his tail and over his crest;
    And through every feather
    Leaked the wet weather;
And the bough swung under his nest;
For his beak it was heavy with marrow.
  Is that the wind dying? O no;
  It's only two devils, that blow
  Through a murderer's bones, to and fro,
    In the ghosts' moonshine.

Ho! Eve, my grey carrion wife,
  When we have supped on king's marrow,
Where shall we drink and make merry our life?
Our nest it is queen Cleopatra's skull,
    'Tis cloven and cracked,
    And battered and hacked,
But with tears of blue eyes it is full:
Let us drink then, my raven of Cairo.
  Is that the wind dying? O no;
  It's only two devils, that blow
  Through a murderer's bones, to and fro,
    In the ghosts' moonshine.

Charles Tennyson Turner

357   *The White Horse of Westbury*

As from the Dorset shore I travelled home,
I saw the charger of the Wiltshire wold;
A far-seen figure, stately to behold,
Whose groom the shepherd is, the hoe his comb;
His wizard-spell even sober daylight owned;
That night I dreamed him into living will;
He neighed – and, straight, the chalk poured down the hill;
He shook himself, and all beneath was stoned;

Hengist and Horsa shouted o'er my sleep,
Like fierce Achilles; while that storm-blanched horse
Sprang to the van of all the Saxon force,
And pushed the Britons to the Western deep;
Then, dream-wise, as it were a thing of course,
He floated upwards, and regained the steep.

Edward Fitzgerald

From *The Rubáiyát of Omar Khayyám*

358   [1]

They say the Lion and the Lizard keep
The Courts where Jamshýd gloried and drank deep;
    And Bahrám, that great Hunter — the Wild Ass
Stamps o'er his Head, and he lies fast asleep.

I sometimes think that never blows so red
The Rose as where some buried Cæsar bled;
    That every Hyacinth the Garden wears
Dropt in its Lap from some once lovely Head.

And this delightful Herb whose tender Green
Fledges the River's Lip on which we lean —
    Ah, lean upon it lightly! for who knows
From what once lovely Lip it springs unseen!

Ah, my Beloved, fill the Cup that clears
TO-DAY of past Regrets and future Fears —
    To-morrow? — Why, To-morrow I may be
Myself with Yesterday's Sev'n Thousand Years.

Lo! some we loved, the loveliest and best
That Time and Fate of all their Vintage prest,
    Have drunk their Cup a Round or two before,
And one by one crept silently to Rest.

And we, that now make merry in the Room
They left, and Summer dresses in new Bloom,
    Ourselves must we beneath the Couch of Earth
Descend, ourselves to make a Couch — for whom?

Ah, make the most of what we yet may spend,
Before we too into the Dust descend;
    Dust into Dust, and under Dust, to lie,
Sans Wine, sans Song, sans Singer, and — sans End!

Alike for those who for TO-DAY prepare,
And those that after a TO-MORROW stare,
    A Muezzin from the Tower of Darkness cries
'Fools! your Reward is neither Here nor There!'

Why, all the Saints and Sages who discussed
Of the two Worlds so learnedly, are thrust
    Like foolish Prophets forth; their Words to Scorn
Are scattered, and their Mouths are stopt with Dust.

Oh, come with old Khayyám, and leave the Wise
To talk; one thing is certain, that Life flies;
    One thing is certain, and the Rest is Lies;
The Flower that once has blown for ever dies.

Myself when young did eagerly frequent
Doctor and Saint, and heard great Argument
    About it and about: but evermore
Came out by the same Door as in I went.

With them the Seed of Wisdom did I sow,
And with my own hand laboured it to grow:
    And this was all the Harvest that I reaped –
'I came like Water, and like Wind I go.'

359   [2]

Ah, with the Grape my fading Life provide,
And wash my Body whence the Life has died,
    And in a Winding-sheet of Vine-leaf wrapt,
So bury me by some sweet Garden-side.

That ev'n my buried Ashes such a Snare
Of Perfume shall fling up into the Air,
    As not a True Believer passing by
But shall be overtaken unaware.

Indeed the Idols I have loved so long
Have done my Credit in Men's Eye much wrong:
    Have drowned my Honour in a shallow Cup,
And sold my Reputation for a Song.

Indeed, indeed, Repentance oft before
I swore – but was I sober when I swore?
    And then and then came Spring, and Rose-in-hand
My thread-bare Penitence apieces tore.

And much as Wine has played the Infidel,
And Robbed me of my Robe of Honour – well,
  I often wonder what the Vintners buy
One half so precious as the Goods they sell.

Alas, that Spring should vanish with the Rose!
That Youth's sweet-scented Manuscript should close!
  The Nightingale that in the Branches sang,
Ah, whence, and whither flown again, who knows?

Ah Love! could thou and I with Fate conspire
To grasp this sorry Scheme of Things entire,
  Would not we shatter it to bits – and then
Re-mould it nearer to the Heart's Desire!

Ah, Moon of my Delight, who know'st no wane,
The Moon of Heav'n is rising once again:
  How oft hereafter rising shall she look
Through this same Garden after me – in vain!

And when Thyself with shining Foot shall pass
Among the Guests Star-scattered on the Grass,
  And in thy joyous Errand reach the Spot
Where I made one – turn down an empty Glass!

TAMÁM SHUD

Alfred, Lord Tennyson

360   *Ulysses*

It little profits that an idle king,
By this still hearth, among these barren crags,
Matched with an agèd wife, I mete and dole
Unequal laws unto a savage race,
That hoard, and sleep, and feed, and know not me.

I cannot rest from travel: I will drink
Life to the lees: all times I have enjoyed
Greatly, have suffered greatly, both with those
That loved me, and alone; on shore, and when
Through scudding drifts the rainy Hyades
Vext the dim sea: I am become a name;
For always roaming with a hungry heart
Much have I seen and known; cities of men
And manners, climates, councils, governments,
Myself not least, but honoured of them all;

And drunk delight of battle with my peers,
Far on the ringing plains of windy Troy.

I am a part of all that I have met;
Yet all experience is an arch wherethrough
Gleams that untravelled world, whose margin fades
For ever and for ever when I move.
How dull it is to pause, to make an end,
To rest unburnished, not to shine in use!
As though to breathe were life. Life piled on life
Were all too little, and of one to me
Little remains: but every hour is saved
From that eternal silence, something more,
A bringer of new things; and vile it were
For some three suns to store and hoard myself,
And this grey spirit yearning in desire
To follow knowledge like a sinking star,
Beyond the utmost bound of human thought.

    This is my son, mine own Telemachus,
To whom I leave the sceptre and the isle –
Well-loved of me, discerning to fulfil
This labour, by slow prudence to make mild
A rugged people, and through soft degrees
Subdue them to the useful and the good.
Most blameless is he, centred in the sphere
Of common duties, decent not to fail
In offices of tenderness, and pay
Meet adoration to my household gods,
When I am gone. He works his work, I mine.

    There lies the port; the vessel puffs her sail:
There gloom the dark broad seas. My mariners,
Souls that have toiled, and wrought, and thought with me –
That ever with a frolic welcome took
The thunder and the sunshine, and opposed
Free hearts, free foreheads – you and I are old;
Old age hath yet his honour and his toil;
Death closes all: but something ere the end,
Some work of noble note, may yet be done,
Not unbecoming men that strove with Gods.
The lights begin to twinkle from the rocks:
The long day wanes: the slow moon climbs: the deep
Moans round with many voices. Come, my friends,
'Tis not too late to seek a newer world.
Push off, and sitting well in order smite
The sounding furrows; for my purpose holds
To sail beyond the sunset, and the baths
Of all the western stars, until I die.
It may be that the gulfs will wash us down:

It may be we shall touch the Happy Isles,
And see the great Achilles, whom we knew.
Though much is taken, much abides; and though
We are not now that strength which in old days
Moved earth and heaven; that which we are, we are;
One equal temper of heroic hearts,
Made weak by time and fate, but strong in will
To strive, to seek, to find, and not to yield.

361   From *The Passing of Arthur*

And answer made King Arthur, breathing hard:
'My end draws nigh; 'tis time that I were gone.
Make broad thy shoulders to receive my weight,
And bear me to the margin; yet I fear
My wound hath taken cold, and I shall die.'

So saying, from the pavement he half rose,
Slowly, with pain, reclining on his arm,
And looking wistfully with wide blue eyes
As in a picture. Him Sir Bedivere
Remorsefully regarded through his tears,
And would have spoken, but he found not words;
Then took with care, and kneeling on one knee,
O'er both his shoulders drew the languid hands,
And rising bore him through the place of tombs.

But, as he walked, King Arthur panted hard,
Like one that feels a nightmare on his bed
When all the house is mute. So sighed the King,
Muttering and murmuring at his ear, 'Quick, quick!
I fear it is too late, and I shall die.'
But the other swiftly strode from ridge to ridge,
Clothed with his breath, and looking, as he walked,
Larger than human on the frozen hills.
He heard the deep behind him, and a cry
Before. His own thought drove him like a goad.
Dry clashed his harness in the icy caves
And barren chasms, and all to left and right
The bare black cliff clanged round him, as he based
His feet on juts of slippery crag that rang
Sharp-smitten with the dint of armèd heels —
And on a sudden, lo! the level lake,
And the long glories of the winter moon.

Then saw they how there hove a dusky barge,
Dark as a funeral scarf from stem to stern,
Beneath them; and descending they were ware
That all the decks were dense with stately forms,
Black-stoled, black-hooded, like a dream — by these
Three Queens with crowns of gold: and from them rose
A cry that shivered to the tingling stars,
And, as it were one voice, an agony
Of lamentation, like a wind that shrills
All night in a waste land, where no one comes,
Or hath come, since the making of the world.

Then murmured Arthur, 'Place me in the barge.'
So to the barge they came. There those three Queens
Put forth their hands, and took the King, and wept.
But she, that rose the tallest of them all
And fairest, laid his head upon her lap,
And loosed the shattered casque, and chafed his hands,
And called him by his name, complaining loud,
And dropping bitter tears against a brow
Striped with dark blood: for all his face was white
And colourless, and like the withered moon
Smote by the fresh beam of the springing east;
And all his greaves and cuisses dashed with drops
Of onset; and the light and lustrous curls —
That made his forehead like a rising sun
High from the daïs-throne — were parched with dust;
Or, clotted into points and hanging loose,
Mixed with the knightly growth that fringed his lips.
So like a shattered column lay the King;
Not like that Arthur who, with lance in rest,
From spur to plume a star of tournament,
Shot through the lists at Camelot, and charged
Before the eyes of ladies and of kings.

362   *The Northern Cobbler*

Waäit till our Sally cooms in, fur thou mun a' sights to tell.
Eh, but I be maäin glad to seeä tha sa 'arty an' well.
'Cast awaäy on a disolut land wi' a vartical soon!'
Strange fur to goä fur to think what saäilors a' seëan an' a' doon;
'Summat to drink — sa' 'ot?' I 'a nowt but Adam's wine:
What's the 'eät o' this little 'ill-side to the 'eät o' the line?

'What's i' tha bottle a-stanning theer?' I'll tell tha. Gin.
But if thou wants thy grog, tha mun goä fur it down to the Inn.

Naay – fur I be maäin-glad, but thaw tha was iver sa dry,
Thou gits naw gin fro' the bottle theer, an' I'll tell tha why.

Meä an' thy sister was married, when wur it? back-end o' June,
Ten year sin', and wa 'greed as well as a fiddle i' tune:
I could fettle and clump owd booöts and shoes wi' the best on 'em all,
As fer as fro' Thursby thurn hup to Harmsby and Hutterby Hall.
We was busy as beeäs i' the bloom an' as 'appy as 'art could think,
An' then the babby wur burn, and then I taäkes to the drink.

An' I weant gaäinsaäy it, my lad, thaw I be hafe shaämed on it now,
We could sing a good song at the Plow, we could sing a good song at the Plow;
Thaw once of a frosty night I slither'd an' hurted my huck,
An' I coom'd neck-an-crop soomtimes slaäpe down i' the squad an' the muck:
An' once I fowt wi' the Taäilor – not hafe ov a man, my lad –
Fur he scrawm'd an' scratted my faäce like a cat, an' it maäde 'er sa mad
That Sally she turn'd a tongue-banger, an' raäted ma, 'Sottin' thy braäins
Guzzlin' an' soäkin' an' smoäkin' an' hawmin' about i' the laänes,
Soä sow-droonk that tha doesn not touch thy 'at to the Squire;'
An' I looök'd cock-eyed at my noäse an' I seeäd 'im a-gittin' o' fire;
But sin' I wur hallus i' liquor an' hallus as droonk as a king,
Foälks' coostom flitted awaäy like a kite wi' a brokken string.

An' Sally she wesh'd foälks' cloäths to keep the wolf fro' the door,
Eh but the moor she riled me, she druv me to drink the moor,
Fur I fun', when 'er back wur turn'd, wheer Sally's own stockin' wur 'id,
An' I grabb'd the munny she maäde, and I weär'd it o' liquor, I did.

An' one night I cooms 'oäm like a bull gotten loose at a faäir,
An' she wur a-waäitin' fo'mma, an' cryin' and teärin' 'er 'aäir,
An' I tummled athurt the craädle an' sweär'd as I'd breäk ivry stick
O' furnitur 'ere i' the 'ouse, an' I gied our Sally a kick,
An' I mash'd the taäbles an' chairs, an' she an' the babby beäl'd,
Fur I knaw'd naw moor what I did nor a mortal beäst o' the feäld.

An' when I waäked i' the murnin' I seeäd that our Sally went laämed
Cos' o' the kick as I gied 'er, an' I wur dreädful ashaämed;
An' Sally wur sloomy an' draggle taäil'd in an owd turn gown,
An' the babby's faäce wurn't wesh'd an' the 'ole 'ouse hupside down.

An' then I minded our Sally sa pratty an' neät an' sweeät,
Straät as a pole an' cleän as a flower fro' 'eäd to feeät:
An' then I minded the fust kiss I gied 'er by Thursby thurn;
Theer wur a lark a-singin' 'is best of a Sunday at murn,
Couldn't see 'im, we 'eärd 'im a-mountin' oop 'igher an' 'igher,
An' then 'e turn'd to the sun, an' 'e shined like a sparkle o' fire.
'Doesn't tha see 'im,' she axes, 'fur I can see 'im?' an' I
Seeäd nobbut the smile o' the sun as danced in 'er pratty blue eye;
An' I says 'I mun gie tha a kiss,' an' Sally says 'Noä, thou moänt,'
But I gied 'er a kiss, an' then anoother, an' Sally says 'doänt!'

An' when we coom'd into Meeätin', at fust she wur all in a tew,
But, arter, we sing'd the 'ymn togither like birds on a beugh;
An' Muggins 'e preäch'd o' Hell-fire an' the loov o' God fur men,
An' then upo' commin' awaäy Sally gied me a kiss ov 'ersen.

Heer wur a fall fro' a kiss to a kick like Saätan as fell
Down out o' heaven i' Hell-fire – thaw theer's naw drinkin' i' Hell;
Meä fur to kick our Sally as kep the wolf fro' the door,
All along o' the drink, fur I loov'd 'er as well as afoor.

Sa like a greät num-cumpus I blubber'd awaäy o' the bed –
'Weänt niver do it naw moor;' an' Sally looökt up an' she said,
'I'll upowd it tha weänt; thou'rt like the rest o' the men,
Thou'll goä sniffin' about the tap till tha does it agëan.
Theer's thy hennemy, man, an' I knaws, as knaws tha sa well,
That, if tha seeäs 'im an' smells 'im tha'll foller 'im slick into Hell.'

'Naäy,' says I, 'fur I weänt goä sniffin' about the tap.'
'Weän't tha?' she says, an' mysen I thowt i' mysen 'mayhap.'
'Noä:' an' I started awaäy like a shot, an' down to the Hinn,
An' I browt what tha seeäs stannin' theer, yon big black bottle o' gin.

'That caps owt,' says Sally, an' saw she begins to cry,
But I puts it inter 'er 'ands an' I says to 'er, 'Sally,' says I,
'Stan' 'im theer i' the naäme o' the Lord an' the power ov 'is Graäce,
Stan' 'im theer, fur I'll looök my hennemy straït i' the faäce,
Stan' 'im theer i' the winder, an' let ma looök at 'im then,
'E seeäms naw moor nor watter, an' 'e's the Divil's oän sen.'

An' I wur down i' tha mouth, couldn't do naw work an' all,
Nasty an' snaggy an' shaäky, an' poonch'd my 'and wi' the hawl,
But she wur a power o' coomfut, an' sattled 'ersen o' my knee,
An' coäxd an' coodled me oop till ageän I feel'd mysen free.

An' Sally she tell'd it about, an' foälk stood a-gawmin' in,
As thaw it wur summat bewitch'd istead of a quart o' gin;
An' some on 'em said it wur watter – an' I wur chousin' the wife,
Fur I couldn't 'owd 'ands off gin, wur it nobbut to saäve my life;
An' blacksmith 'e strips me the thick ov 'is airm, an' 'e shaws it to me,
'Feëal thou this! thou can't graw this upo' watter!' says he.
An' Doctor 'e calls o' Sunday an' just as candles was lit,
'Thou moänt do it,' he says, 'tha mun breäk 'im off bit by bit.'

'Thou'rt but a Methody-man,' says Parson, and laäys down 'is 'at,
An' 'e points to the bottle o' gin, 'but I respecks tha fur that;'
An' Squire, his oän very sen, walks down fro' the 'All to see,
An' 'e spanks 'is 'and into mine, 'fur I respecks tha,' says 'e;
An' coostom ageän draw'd in like a wind fro' far an' wide,
And browt me the booöts to be cobbled fro' hafe the coontryside.

An' theer 'e stans an' theer 'e shall stan to my dying daäy;
I 'a gotten to loov 'im ageän in anoother kind of a waäy,
Proud on 'im, like, my lad, an' I keeäps 'im cleän an' bright,
Loovs 'im, an' roobs 'im, an' doosts 'im, an' puts 'im back i' the light.

Wouldn't a pint a' sarved as well as a quart? Naw doubt:
But I liked a bigger feller to fight wi' an' fowt it out.
Fine an' meller 'e mun be by this, if I cared to taäste,
But I moänt, my lad, and I weänt, fur I'd feäl mysen cleän disgraäced.

An' once I said to the Missis, 'My lass, when I cooms to die,
Smash the bottle to smithers, the Divil's in 'im,' said I.
But arter I chaänged my mind, an' if Sally be left aloän,
I'll hev 'im a-buried wi'mma an' taäke 'im afoor the Throän.

Coom thou 'eer — yon laädy a-steppin' along the streeät,
Doesn't tha knaw 'er — sa pratty, an' feät, an' neät, an' sweeät?
Look at the cloäths on 'er back, thebbe ammost spick-span-new,
An' Tommy's faäce be as fresh as a codlin wesh'd i' the dew.

'Ere be our Sally an' Tommy, an' we be a-goin to dine,
Baäcon an' taätes, an' a beslings puddin' an' Adam's wine;
But if tha wants ony grog tha mun goä fur it down to the Hinn,
Fur I weänt shed a drop on 'is blood, noä, not fur Sally's oän kin.

363   *Hendecasyllabics*

O you chorus of indolent reviewers,
Irresponsible, indolent reviewers,
Look, I come to the test, a tiny poem
All composed in a metre of Catullus,
All in quantity, careful of my motion,
Like the skater on ice that hardly bears him,
Lest I fall unawares before the people,
Waking laughter in indolent reviewers.
Should I flounder awhile without a tumble
Through this metrification of Catullus,
They should speak to me not without a welcome,
All that chorus of indolent reviewers.
Hard, hard, hard is it, only not to tumble,
So fantastical is the dainty metre.
Wherefore slight me not wholly, nor believe me
Too presumptuous, indolent reviewers.
O blatant Magazines, regard me rather —
Since I blush to belaud myself a moment —
As some rare little rose, a piece of inmost
Horticultural art, or half coquette-like
Maiden, not to be greeted unbenignly.

From *In Memoriam*

364   VII

Dark house, by which once more I stand
    Here in the long unlovely street,
    Doors, where my heart was used to beat
So quickly, waiting for a hand,

A hand that can be clasped no more —
    Behold me, for I cannot sleep,
    And like a guilty thing I creep
At earliest morning to the door.

He is not here; but far away
    The noise of life begins again,
    And ghastly through the drizzling rain
On the bald street breaks the blank day.

365   XI

Calm is the morn without a sound,
    Calm as to suit a calmer grief,
    And only through the faded leaf
The chestnut pattering to the ground:

Calm and deep peace on this high wold,
    And on these dews that drench the furze,
    And all the silvery gossamers
That twinkle into green and gold:

Calm and still light on yon great plain
    That sweeps with all its autumn bowers,
    And crowded farms and lessening towers,
To mingle with the bounding main:

Calm and deep peace in this wide air,
    These leaves that redden to the fall;
    And in my heart, if calm at all,
If any calm, a calm despair:

Calm on the seas, and silver sleep,
    And waves that sway themselves in rest,
    And dead calm in that noble breast
Which heaves but with the heaving deep.

366   XVI

What words are these have fallen from me?
  Can calm despair and wild unrest
  Be tenants of a single breast,
Or sorrow such a changeling be?

Or doth she only seem to take
  The touch of change in calm or storm;
  But knows no more of transient form
In her deep self, than some dead lake

That holds the shadow of a lark
  Hung in the shadow of a heaven?
  Or has the shock, so harshly given,
Confused me like the unhappy bark

That strikes by night a craggy shelf,
  And staggers blindly ere she sink?
  And stunned me from my power to think
And all my knowledge of myself;

And made me that delirious man
  Whose fancy fuses old and new,
  And flashes into false and true,
And mingles all without a plan?

367   From *The Princess*

Now sleeps the crimson petal, now the white;
Nor waves the cypress in the palace walk;
Nor winks the gold fin in the porphyry font:
The fire-fly wakens: waken thou with me.

Now droops the milkwhite peacock like a ghost,
And like a ghost she glimmers on to me.

Now lies the Earth all Danaë to the stars,
And all thy heart lies open unto me.

Now slides the silent meteor on, and leaves
A shining furrow, as thy thoughts in me.

Now folds the lily all her sweetness up,
And slips into the bosom of the lake:
So fold thyself, my dearest, thou, and slip
Into my bosom and be lost in me.

368   *Locksley Hall*

Comrades, leave me here a little, while as yet 'tis early morn:
Leave me here, and when you want me, sound upon the bugle-horn.

'Tis the place, and all around it, as of old, the curlews call,
Dreary gleams about the moorland flying over Locksley Hall;

Locksley Hall, that in the distance overlooks the sandy tracts,
And the hollow ocean-ridges roaring into cataracts.

Many a night from yonder ivied casement, ere I went to rest,
Did I look on great Orion sloping slowly to the West.

Many a night I saw the Pleiads, rising through the mellow shade,
Glitter like a swarm of fire-flies tangled in a silver braid.

Here about the beach I wandered, nourishing a youth sublime
With the fairy tales of science, and the long result of Time;

When the centuries behind me like a fruitful land reposed;
When I clung to all the present for the promise that it closed:

When I dipt into the future far as human eye could see;
Saw the Vision of the world, and all the wonder that would be. –

In the Spring a fuller crimson comes upon the robin's breast;
In the Spring the wanton lapwing gets himself another crest;

In the Spring a livelier iris changes on the burnished dove;
In the Spring a young man's fancy lightly turns to thoughts of love.

Then her cheek was pale and thinner than should be for one so young,
And her eyes on all my motions with a mute observance hung.

And I said, 'My cousin Amy, speak, and speak the truth to me,
Trust me, cousin, all the current of my being sets to thee.'

On her pallid cheek and forehead came a colour and a light,
As I have seen the rosy red flushing in the northern night.

And she turned – her bosom shaken with a sudden storm of sighs –
All the spirit deeply dawning in the dark of hazel eyes –

Saying, 'I have hid my feelings, fearing they should do me wrong;'
Saying, 'Dost thou love me, cousin?' weeping, 'I have loved thee long.'

Love took up the glass of Time, and turned it in his glowing hands;
Every moment, lightly shaken, ran itself in golden sands.

Love took up the harp of Life, and smote on all the chords with might;
Smote the chord of Self, that, trembling, passed in music out of sight.

Many a morning on the moorland did we hear the copses ring,
And her whisper thronged my pulses with the fullness of the Spring.

Many an evening by the waters did we watch the stately ships,
And our spirits rushed together at the touching of the lips.

O my cousin, shallow-hearted! O my Amy, mine no more!
O the dreary, dreary moorland! O the barren, barren shore!

Falser than all fancy fathoms, falser than all songs have sung,
Puppet to a father's threat, and servile to a shrewish tongue!

Is it well to wish thee happy? — having known me — to decline
On a range of lower feelings and a narrower heart than mine!

Yet it shall be: thou shalt lower to his level day by day,
What is fine within thee growing coarse to sympathise with clay.

As the husband is, the wife is: thou art mated with a clown,
And the grossness of his nature will have weight to drag thee down.

He will hold thee, when his passion shall have spent its novel force,
Something better than his dog, a little dearer than his horse.

What is this: his eyes are heavy: think not they are glazed with wine.
Go to him: it is thy duty: kiss him: take his hand in thine.

It may be my lord is weary, that his brain is overwrought:
Soothe him with thy finer fancies, touch him with thy lighter thought.

He will answer to the purpose, easy things to understand —
Better thou wert dead before me, though I slew thee with my hand!

Better thou and I were lying, hidden from the heart's disgrace,
Rolled in one another's arms, and silent in a last embrace.

Cursèd be the social wants that sin against the strength of youth!
Cursèd be the social lies that warp us from the living truth!

Cursèd be the sickly forms that err from honest Nature's rule!
Cursèd be the gold that gilds the straitened forehead of the fool!

Well — 'tis well that I should bluster! — Hadst thou less unworthy
     proved —
Would to God — for I had loved thee more than ever wife was loved.

Am I mad, that I should cherish that which bears but bitter fruit?
I will pluck it from my bosom, though my heart be at the root.

Never, though my mortal summers to such length of years should come
As the many-wintered crow that leads the clanging rookery home.

Where is comfort? in division of the records of the mind?
Can I part her from herself, and love her, as I knew her, kind?

I remember one that perished: sweetly did she speak and move:
Such a one do I remember, whom to look at was to love.

Can I think of her as dead, and love her for the love she bore?
No – she never loved me truly: love is love for evermore.

Comfort? comfort scorned of devils! this is truth the poet sings,
That a sorrow's crown of sorrow is remembering happier things.

Drug thy memories, lest thou learn it, lest thy heart be put to proof,
In the dead unhappy night, and when the rain is on the roof.

Like a dog, he hunts in dreams, and thou art staring at the wall,
Where the dying night-lamp flickers, and the shadows rise and fall.

Then a hand shall pass before thee, pointing to his drunken sleep,
To thy widowed marriage-pillows, to the tears that thou wilt weep.

Thou shalt hear the 'Never, never,' whispered by the phantom years,
And a song from out the distance in the ringing of thine ears;

And an eye shall vex thee, looking ancient kindness on thy pain.
Turn thee, turn thee on thy pillow: get thee to thy rest again.

Nay, but Nature brings thee solace; for a tender voice will cry.
'Tis a purer life than thine; a lip to drain thy trouble dry.

Baby lips will laugh me down: my latest rival brings thee rest.
Baby fingers, waxen touches, press me from the mother's breast.

O, the child too clothes the father with a dearness not his due.
Half is thine and half is his: it will be worthy of the two.

O, I see thee old and formal, fitted to thy petty part,
With a little hoard of maxims preaching down a daughter's heart.

'They were dangerous guides the feelings – she herself was not exempt –
Truly, she herself had suffered' – Perish in thy self-contempt!

Overlive it – lower yet – be happy! wherefore should I care?
I myself must mix with action, lest I wither by despair.

What is that which I should turn to, lighting upon days like these?
Every door is barred with gold, and opens but to golden keys.

Every gate is thronged with suitors, all the markets overflow.
I have but an angry fancy: what is that which I should do?

I had been content to perish, falling on the foeman's ground,
When the ranks are rolled in vapour, and the winds are laid with
    sound.

But the jingling of the guinea helps the hurt that Honour feels,
And the nations do but murmur, snarling at each other's heels.

Can I but relive in sadness? I will turn that earlier page.
Hide me from my deep emotion, O thou wondrous Mother-Age!

Make me feel the wild pulsation that I felt before the strife,
When I heard my days before me, and the tumult of my life;

Yearning for the large excitement that the coming years would yield,
Eager-hearted as a boy when first he leaves his father's field,

And at night along the dusky highway near and nearer drawn,
Sees in heaven the light of London flaring like a dreary dawn;

And his spirit leaps within him to be gone before him then,
Underneath the light he looks at, in among the throngs of men:

Men, my brothers, men the workers, ever reaping something new:
That which they have done but earnest of the things that they shall do:

For I dipt into the future, far as human eye could see,
Saw the Vision of the world, and all the wonder that would be;

Saw the heavens fill with commerce, argosies of magic sails,
Pilots of the purple twilight, dropping down with costly bales;

Heard the heavens fill with shouting, and there rained a ghastly dew
From the nations' airy navies grappling in the central blue;

Far along the world-wide whisper of the south-wind rushing warm,
With the standards of the peoples plunging through the thunder-storm;

Till the war-drum throbbed no longer, and the battle-flags were furled
In the Parliament of man, the Federation of the world.

There the common sense of most shall hold a fretful realm in awe,
And the kindly earth shall slumber, lapt in universal law.

So I triumphed ere my passion sweeping through me left me dry,
Left me with the palsied heart, and left me with the jaundiced eye;

Eye, to which all order festers, all things here are out of joint:
Science moves, but slowly slowly, creeping on from point to point:

Slowly comes a hungry people, as a lion creeping nigher,
Glares at one that nods and winks behind a slowly-dying fire.

Yet I doubt not through the ages one increasing purpose runs,
And the thoughts of men are widened with the process of the suns.

What is that to him that reaps not harvest of his youthful joys,
Though the deep heart of existence beat for ever like a boy's?

Knowledge comes, but wisdom lingers, and I linger on the shore,
And the individual withers, and the world is more and more.

Knowledge comes, but wisdom lingers, and he bears a laden breast,
Full of sad experience, moving toward the stillness of his rest.

Hark, my merry comrades call me, sounding on the bugle-horn,
They to whom my foolish passion were a target for their scorn:

Shall it not be scorn to me to harp on such a mouldered string?
I am shamed through all my nature to have loved so slight a thing.

Weakness to be wroth with weakness! woman's pleasure, woman's
    pain –
Nature made them blinder motions bounded in a shallower brain:

Woman is the lesser man, and all thy passions, matched with mine,
Are as moonlight unto sunlight, and as water unto wine –

Here at least, where nature sickens, nothing. Ah, for some retreat
Deep in yonder shining Orient, where my life began to beat;

Where in wild Mahratta-battle fell my father evil-starred; –
I was left a trampled orphan, and a selfish uncle's ward.

Or to burst all links of habit – there to wander far away,
On from island unto island at the gateways of the day.

Larger constellations burning, mellow moons and happy skies,
Breadths of tropic shade and palms in cluster, knots of Paradise.

Never comes the trader, never floats an European flag,
Slides the bird o'er lustrous woodland, swings the trailer from the crag;

Droops the heavy-blossomed bower, hangs the heavy-fruited tree –
Summer isles of Eden lying in dark-purple spheres of sea.

There methinks would be enjoyment more than in this march of mind,
In the steamship, in the railway, in the thoughts that shake mankind.

There the passions cramped no longer shall have scope and breathing
    space;
I will take some savage woman, she shall rear my dusky race.

Iron jointed, supple-sinewed, they shall dive, and they shall run,
Catch the wild goat by the hair, and hurl their lances in the sun;

Whistle back the parrot's call, and leap the rainbows of the brooks,
Not with blinded eyesight poring over miserable books –

Fool, again the dream, the fancy! but I *know* my words are wild,
But I count the gray barbarian lower than the Christian child.

I, to herd with narrow foreheads, vacant of our glorious gains,
Like a beast with lower pleasures, like a beast with lower pains!

Mated with a squalid savage – what to me were sun or clime?
I the heir of all the ages, in the foremost files of time –

I that rather held it better men should perish one by one,
Than that earth should stand at gaze like Joshua's moon in Ajalon!

Not in vain the distance beacons. Forward, forward let us range,
Let the great world spin for ever down the ringing grooves of change.

Through the shadow of the globe we sweep into the younger day:
Better fifty years of Europe than a cycle of Cathay.

Mother-Age (for mine I knew not) help me as when life begun:
Rift the hills, and roll the waters, flash the lightnings, weigh the Sun.

O, I see the crescent promise of my spirit hath not set.
Ancient founts of inspiration well through all my fancy yet.

Howsoever these things be, a long farewell to Locksley Hall!
Now for me the woods may wither, now for me the roof-tree fall.

Comes a vapour from the margin, blackening over heath and holt,
Cramming all the blast before it, in its breast a thunderbolt.

Let it fall on Locksley Hall, with rain or hail, or fire or snow;
For the mighty wind arises, roaring seaward, and I go.

Robert Browning

369   *Two in the Campagna*

I wonder do you feel to-day
    As I have felt, since, hand in hand,
We sat down on the grass, to stray
    In spirit better through the land,
This morn of Rome and May?

For me, I touched a thought, I know,
    Has tantalised me many times,
(Like turns of thread the spiders throw
    Mocking across our path) for rhymes
To catch at and let go.

Help me to hold it: first it left
    The yellowing fennel, run to seed
There, branching from the brickwork's cleft,
    Some old tomb's ruin: yonder weed
Took up the floating weft,

Where one small orange cup amassed
   Five beetles, – blind and green they grope
Among the honey-meal, – and last
   Everywhere on the grassy slope
I traced it. Hold it fast!

The champaign with its endless fleece
   Of feathery grasses everywhere!
Silence and passion, joy and peace,
   An everlasting wash of air –
Rome's ghost since her decease.

Such life there, through such lengths of hours,
   Such miracles performed in play,
Such primal naked forms of flowers,
   Such letting Nature have her way
While Heaven looks from its towers.

How say you? Let us, O my dove,
   Let us be unashamed of soul,
As earth lies bare to heaven above.
   How is it under our control
To love or not to love?

I would that you were all to me,
   You that are just so much, no more –
Nor yours, nor mine, – nor slave nor free!
   Where does the fault lie? what the core
Of the wound, since wound must be?

I would I could adopt your will,
   See with your eyes, and set my heart
Beating by yours, and drink my fill
   At your soul's springs, – your part, my part
In life, for good and ill.

No. I yearn upward – touch you close,
   Then stand away. I kiss your cheek,
Catch your soul's warmth, – I pluck the rose
   And love it more than tongue can speak –
Then the good minute goes.

Already how am I so far
   Out of that minute? Must I go
Still like the thistle-ball, no bar,
   Onward, whenever light winds blow,
Fixed by no friendly star?

Just when I seemed about to learn!
   Where is the thread now? Off again!
The old trick! Only I discern –
   Infinite passion and the pain
Of finite hearts that yearn.

370

Caliban upon Setebos;
or, Natural Theology in the Island

'Thou thoughtest that I was altogether such a one as thyself.'

['Will sprawl, now that the heat of day is best,
Flat on his belly in the pit's much mire,
With elbows wide, fists clenched to prop his chin.
And, while he kicks both feet in the cool slush,
And feels about his spine small eft-things course,
Run in and out each arm, and make him laugh:
And while above his head a pompion-plant,
Coating the cave-top as a brow its eye,
Creeps down to touch and tickle hair and beard,
And now a flower drops with a bee inside,
And now a fruit to snap at, catch and crunch, –
He looks out o'er yon sea which sunbeams cross
And recross till they weave a spider-web
(Meshes of fire, some great fish breaks at times)
And talks to his own self, howe'er he please,
Touching that other, whom his dam called God.
Because to talk about Him, vexes – ha,
Could He but know! and time to vex is now,
When talk is safer than in winter-time.
Moreover Prosper and Miranda sleep
In confidence he drudges at their task,
And it is good to cheat the pair, and gibe,
Letting the rank tongue blossom into speech.]

Setebos, Setebos, and Setebos!
'Thinketh, He dwelleth i' the cold o' the moon.
'Thinketh He made it, with the sun to match,
But not the stars; the stars came otherwise;
Only made clouds, winds, meteors, such as that:
Also this isle, what lives and grows thereon,
And snaky sea which rounds and ends the same.

'Thinketh, it came of being ill at ease:
He hated that He cannot change His cold,
Nor cure its ache. 'Hath spied an icy fish
That longed to 'scape the rock-stream where she lived,
And thaw herself within the lukewarm brine
O' the lazy sea her stream thrusts far amid,
A crystal spike 'twixt two warm walls of wave;
Only, she ever sickened, found repulse
At the other kind of water, not her life,
(Green-dense and dim-delicious, bred o' the sun)
Flounced back from bliss she was not born to breathe,
And in her old bounds buried her despair,
Hating and loving warmth alike: so He.

'Thinketh, He made thereat the sun, this isle,
Trees and the fowls here, beast and creeping thing.
Yon otter, sleek-wet, black, lithe as a leech;
Yon auk, one fire-eye in a ball of foam,
That floats and feeds; a certain badger brown
He hath watched hunt with that slant white-wedge eye
By moonlight; and the pie with the long tongue
That pricks deep into oakwarts for a worm,
And says a plain word when she finds her prize,
But will not eat the ants; the ants themselves
That build a wall of seeds and settled stalks
About their hole — He made all these and more,
Made all we see, and us, in spite: how else?
He could not, Himself, make a second self
To be His mate: as well have made Himself:
He would not make what he mislikes or slights,
An eyesore to Him, or not worth His pains:
But did, in envy, listlessness or sport,
Make what Himself would fain, in a manner, be —
Weaker in most points, stronger in a few,
Worthy, and yet mere playthings all the while,
Things He admires and mocks too, — that is it.
Because, so brave, so better though they be,
It nothing skills if He begin to plague.
Look now, I melt a gourd-fruit into mash,
Add honeycomb and pods, I have perceived,
Which bite like finches when they bill and kiss, —
Then, when froth rises bladdery, drink up all,
Quick, quick, till maggots scamper through my brain;
Last, throw me on my back i' the seeded thyme,
And wanton, wishing I were born a bird.
Put case, unable to be what I wish,
I yet could make a live bird out of clay:
Would not I take clay, pinch my Caliban
Able to fly? — for, there, see, he hath wings,
And great comb like the hoopoe's to admire,
And there, a sting to do his foes offence,
There, and I will that he begin to live,
Fly to yon rock-top, nip me off the horns
Of grigs high up that make the merry din,
Saucy through their veined wings, and mind me not.
In which feat, if his leg snapped, brittle clay,
And he lay stupid-like, — why, I should laugh;
And if he, spying me, should fall to weep,
Beseech me to be good, repair his wrong,
Bid his poor leg smart less or grow again, —
Well, as the chance were, this might take or else
Not take my fancy: I might hear his cry,

And give the mankin three sound legs for one,
Or pluck the other off, leave him like an egg,
And lessoned he was mine and merely clay.
Were this no pleasure, lying in the thyme,
Drinking the mash, with brain become alive,
Making and marring clay at will? So He.

'Thinketh, such shows nor right nor wrong in Him,
Nor kind, nor cruel: He is strong and Lord.
'Am strong myself compared to yonder crabs
That march now from the mountain to the sea;
'Let twenty pass, and stone the twenty-first,
Loving not, hating not, just choosing so.
'Say, the first straggler that boasts purple spots
Shall join the file, one pincer twisted off;
'Say, this bruised fellow shall receive a worm,
And two worms he whose nippers end in red;
As it likes me each time, I do: so He.

Well then, 'supposeth He is good i' the main,
Placable if His mind and ways were guessed,
But rougher than His handiwork, be sure!
Oh, He hath made things worthier than Himself,
And envieth that, so helped, such things do more
Than He who made them! What consoles but this?
That they, unless through Him, do nought at all,
And must submit: what other use in things?
'Hath cut a pipe of pithless elder joint
That, blown through, gives exact the scream o' the jay
When from her wing you twitch the feathers blue:
Sound this, and little birds that hate the jay
Flock within stone's throw, glad their foe is hurt:
Put case such pipe could prattle and boast forsooth
'I catch the birds, I am the crafty thing,
I make the cry my maker cannot make
With his great round mouth; he must blow through mine!'
Would not I smash it with my foot? So He.

But wherefore rough, why cold and ill at ease?
Aha, that is a question! Ask, for that,
What knows, – the something over Setebos
That made Him, or He, may be, found and fought,
Worsted, drove off and did to nothing, perchance.
There may be something quiet o'er His head,
Out of His reach, that feels nor joy nor grief,
Since both derive from weakness in some way.
I joy because the quails come; would not joy
Could I bring quails here when I have a mind:
This Quiet, all it hath a mind to, doth.

'Esteemeth stars the outposts of its couch,
But never spends much thought nor care that way.
It may look up, work up, — the worse for those
It works on! 'Careth but for Setebos
The many-handed as a cuttle-fish,
Who, making Himself feared through what He does,
Looks up, first, and perceives he cannot soar
To what is quiet and hath happy life;
Next looks down here, and out of very spite
Makes this a bauble-world to ape yon real,
These good things to match those as hips do grapes.
'Tis solace making baubles, ay, and sport.
Himself peeped late, eyed Prosper at his books
Careless and lofty, lord now of the isle:
Vexed, 'stitched a book of broad leaves, arrow-shaped,
Wrote thereon, he knows what, prodigious words;
Has peeled a wand and called it by a name;
Weareth at whiles for an enchanter's robe
The eyed skin of a supple oncelot;
And hath an ounce sleeker than youngling mole,
A four-legged serpent he makes cower and couch,
Now snarl, now hold its breath and mind his eye,
And saith she is Miranda and my wife:
'Keeps for his Ariel a tall pouch-bill crane
He bids go wade for fish and straight disgorge;
Also a sea-beast, lumpish, which he snared,
Blinded the eyes of, and brought somewhat tame,
And split its toe-webs, and now pens the drudge
In a hole o' the rock and calls him Caliban;
A bitter heart that bides its time and bites.
'Plays thus at being Prosper in a way,
Taketh his mirth with make-believes: so He.

His dam held that the Quiet made all things
Which Setebos vexed only: 'holds not so.
Who made them weak, meant weakness He might vex.
Had He meant other, while His hand was in,
Why not make horny eyes no thorn could prick,
Or plate my scalp with bone against the snow,
Or overscale my flesh 'neath joint and joint,
Like an orc's armour? Ay, — so spoil His sport!
He is the One now: only He doth all.

'Saith, He may like, perchance, what profits Him.
Ay, himself loves what does him good; but why?
'Gets good no otherwise. This blinded beast
Loves whoso places flesh-meat on his nose,
But, had he eyes, would want no help, but hate
Or love, just as it liked him: He hath eyes.

Also it pleaseth Setebos to work,
Use all His hands, and exercise much craft,
By no means for the love of what is worked.
'Tasteth, himself, no finer good i' the world
When all goes right, in this safe summer-time,
And he wants little, hungers, aches not much,
Than trying what to do with wit and strength.
'Falls to make something: 'piled yon pile of turfs,
And squared and stuck there squares of soft white chalk,
And, with a fish-tooth, scratched a moon on each,
And set up endwise certain spikes of tree,
And crowned the whole with a sloth's skull a-top,
Found dead i' the woods, too hard for one to kill.
No use at all i' the work, for work's sole sake;
'Shall some day knock it down again: so He.

'Saith He is terrible: watch His feats in proof!
One hurricane will spoil six good months' hope.
He hath a spite against me, that I know,
Just as He favours Prosper, who knows why?
So it is, all the same, as well I find.
'Wove wattles half the winter, fenced them firm
With stone and stake to stop she-tortoises
Crawling to lay their eggs here: well, one wave,
Feeling the foot of Him upon its neck,
Gaped as a snake does, lolled out its large tongue,
And licked the whole labour flat: so much for spite.
'Saw a ball flame down late (yonder it lies)
Where, half an hour before, I slept i' the shade:
Often they scatter sparkles: there is force!
'Dug up a newt He may have envied once
And turned to stone, shut up inside a stone.
Please Him and hinder this? – What Prosper does?
Aha, if He would tell me how! Not He!
There is the sport: discover how or die!
All need not die, for of the things o' the isle
Some flee afar, some dive, some run up trees;
Those at His mercy, – why, they please Him most
When . . . when . . . well, never try the same way twice!
Repeat what act has pleased, He may grow wroth.
You must not know His ways, and play Him off,
Sure of the issue. 'Doth the like himself:
'Spareth a squirrel that it nothing fears
But steals the nut from underneath my thumb,
And when I threat, bites stoutly in defence:
'Spareth an urchin that contrariwise,
Curls up into a ball, pretending death
For fright at my approach: the two ways please.
But what would move my choler more than this,

That either creature counted on its life
To-morrow and next day and all days to come,
Saying, forsooth, in the inmost of its heart,
'Because he did so yesterday with me,
And otherwise with such another brute,
So must he do henceforth and always.' – Ay?
Would teach the reasoning couple what 'must' means!
'Doth as he likes, or wherefore Lord? So He.

'Conceiveth all things will continue thus,
And we shall have to live in fear of Him
So long as He lives, keeps His strength: no change,
If He have done His best, make no new world
To please Him more, so leave off watching this, –
If He surprise not even the Quiet's self
Some strange day, – or, suppose, grow into it
As grubs grow butterflies: else, here are we,
And there is He, and nowhere help at all.

'Believeth with the life, the pain shall stop.
His dam held different, that after death
He both plagued enemies and feasted friends:
Idly! He doth His worst in this our life,
Giving just respite lest we die through pain,
Saving last pain for worst, – with which, an end.
Meanwhile, the best way to escape His ire
Is, not to seem too happy. 'Sees, himself,
Yonder two flies, with purple films and pink,
Bask on the pompion-bell above; kills both.
'Sees two black painful beetles roll their ball
On head and tail as if to save their lives:
Moves them the stick away they strive to clear.

Even so, 'would have Him misconceive, suppose
This Caliban strives hard and ails no less,
And always, above all else, envies Him;
Wherefore he mainly dances on dark nights,
Moans in the sun, gets under holes to laugh,
And never speaks his mind save housed as now:
Outside, 'groans, curses. If He caught me here,
O'erheard this speech, and asked 'What chucklest at?'
'Would, to appease Him, cut a finger off,
Or of my three kid yearlings burn the best,
Or let the toothsome apples rot on tree,
Or push my tame beast for the orc to taste:
While myself lit a fire, and made a song
And sung it, '*What I hate, be consecrate
To celebrate Thee and Thy state, no mate
For Thee; what see for envy in poor me?*'

Hoping the while, since evils sometimes mend,
Warts rub away and sores are cured with slime,
That some strange day, will either the Quiet catch
And conquer Setebos, or likelier He
Decrepit may doze, doze, as good as die.

[What, what? A curtain o'er the world at once!
Crickets stop hissing; not a bird – or, yes,
There scuds His raven that has told Him all!
It was fool's play, this prattling! Ha! The wind
Shoulders the pillared dust, death's house o' the move,
And fast invading fires begin! White blaze –
A tree's head snaps – and there, there, there, there, there,
His thunder follows! Fool to gibe at Him!
Lo! 'Lieth flat and loveth Setebos!
'Maketh his teeth meet through his upper lip,
Will let those quails fly, will not eat this month
One little mess of whelks, so he may 'scape!]

371   *Instans Tyrannus*

Of the million or two, more or less,
I rule and possess,
One man, for some cause undefined,
Was least to my mind.

I struck him, he grovelled of course –
For, what was his force?
I pinned him to earth with my weight
And persistence of hate –
And he lay, would not moan, would not curse,
As his lot might be worse.

'Were the object less mean, would he stand
At the swing of my hand!
For obscurity helps him and blots
The hole where he squats.'
So I set my five wits on the stretch
To inveigle the wretch.
All in vain! gold and jewels I threw,
Still he couched there perdue.
I tempted his blood and his flesh,
Hid in roses my mesh,
Choicest cates and the flagon's best spilth –
Still he kept to his filth!

Had he kith now or kin, were access
To his heart, if I press –
Just a son or a mother to seize –
No such booty as these!
Were it simply a friend to pursue
'Mid my million or two,
Who could pay me in person or pelf
What he owes me himself.
No! I could not but smile through my chafe –
For the fellow lay safe
As his mates do, the midge and the nit,
– Through minuteness, to wit.
Then a humour more great took its place
At the thought of his face,
The droop, the low cares of the mouth,
The trouble uncouth

'Twixt the brows, all that air one is fain
To put out of its pain –
And, no, I admonished myself,
'Is one mocked by an elf,
Is one baffled by toad or by rat?
The gravamen's in that!
How the lion, who crouches to suit
His back to my foot,
Would admire that I stand in debate!
But the Small is the Great
If it vexes you, – that is the thing!
Toad or rat vex the King?
Though I waste half my realm to unearth
Toad or rat, 'tis well worth!'

So I soberly laid my last plan
To extinguish the man.
Round his creep-hole, – with never a break
Ran my fires for his sake;
Over-head, did my thunders combine
With my under-ground mine:
Till I looked from my labour content
To enjoy the event.

When sudden . . . how think ye, the end?
Did I say 'without friend?'
Say rather, from marge to blue marge
The whole sky grew his targe
With the sun's self for visible boss,
While an Arm ran across
Which the earth heaved beneath like a breast
Where the wretch was safe prest!

Do you see? just my vengeance complete,
The man sprang to his feet,
Stood erect, caught at God's skirts and prayed!
– So, *I* was afraid!

Edward Lear

372   *The Jumblies*

They went to sea in a Sieve, they did,
  In a Sieve they went to sea:
In spite of all their friends could say,
On a winter's morn, on a stormy day,
  In a Sieve they went to sea!
And when the Sieve turned round and round,
And every one cried, 'You'll all be drowned!'
They called aloud, 'Our Sieve ain't big,
But we don't care a button! we don't care a fig!
  In a Sieve we'll go to sea!'
    Far and few, far and few,
      Are the lands where the Jumblies live;
      Their heads are green, and their hands are blue,
      And they went to sea in a Sieve.

They sailed away in a Sieve, they did,
  In a Sieve they sailed so fast,
With only a beautiful pea-green veil
Tied with a riband by way of a sail,
  To a small tobacco-pipe mast;
And every one said, who saw them go,
'O won't they be soon upset, you know!
For the sky is dark, and the voyage is long,
And happen what may, it's extremely wrong
  In a Sieve to sail so fast!'
    Far and few, far and few,
      Are the lands where the Jumblies live;
      Their heads are green, and their hands are blue,
      And they went to sea in a Sieve.

The water it soon came in, it did,
  The water it soon came in;
So to keep them dry, they wrapped their feet
In a pinky paper all folded neat,
  And they fastened it down with a pin.
And they passed the night in a crockery-jar,
And each of them said, 'How wise we are!

Though the sky be dark, and the voyage be long,
Yet we never can think we were rash or wrong,
   While round in our Sieve we spin!'
      Far and few, far and few,
         Are the lands where the Jumblies live;
         Their heads are green, and their hands are blue,
         And they went to sea in a Sieve.

And all night long they sailed away;
   And when the sun went down,
They whistled and warbled a moony song
To the echoing sound of a coppery gong,
   In the shade of the mountains brown.
'O Timballo! How happy we are,
When we live in a Sieve and a crockery-jar,
And all night long in the moonlight pale,
We sail away with a pea-green sail,
   In the shade of the mountains brown!'
      Far and few, far and few,
         Are the lands where the Jumblies live;
         Their heads are green, and their hands are blue,
         And they went to sea in a Sieve.

They sailed to the Western Sea, they did,
   To a land all covered with trees,
And they bought an Owl, and a useful Cart,
And a pound of Rice, and a Cranberry Tart,
   And a hive of silvery Bees.
And they bought a Pig, and some green Jack-daws,
And a lovely Monkey with lollipop paws,
And forty bottles of Ring-Bo-Ree,
   And no end of Stilton Cheese.
      Far and few, far and few,
         Are the lands where the Jumblies live;
         Their heads are green, and their hands are blue,
         And they went to sea in a Sieve.

And in twenty years they all came back,
   In twenty years or more,
And every one said, 'How tall they've grown!
For they've been to the Lakes, and the Torrible Zone,
   And the hills of the Chankly Bore;
And they drank their health, and gave them a feast
Of dumplings made of beautiful yeast;
And every one said, 'If we only live,
We too will go to sea in a Sieve, –
   To the hills of the Chankly Bore!'
      Far and few, far and few,
         Are the lands where the Jumblies live;
         Their heads are green, and their hands are blue,
         And they went to sea in a Sieve.

373   *The Quangle Wangle's Hat*

On the top of the Crumpetty Tree
    The Quangle Wangle sat,
But his face you could not see,
    On account of his Beaver Hat.
For his Hat was a hundred and two feet wide,
With ribbons and bibbons on every side
And bells, and buttons, and loops, and lace,
So that nobody ever could see the face
        Of the Quangle Wangle Quee.

The Quangle Wangle said
    To himself on the Crumpetty Tree, –
'Jam; and jelly; and bread;
    Are the best food for me!
But the longer I live on this Crumpetty Tree,
The plainer than ever it seems to me
That very few people come this way,
And that life on the whole is far from gay!'
        Said the Quangle Wangle Quee.

But there came to the Crumpetty Tree,
    Mr and Mrs Canary;
And they said, – 'Did you ever see
    Any spot so charmingly airy?
May we build a nest on your lovely Hat?
Mr Quangle Wangle, grant us that!
O please let us come and build a nest
Of whatever material suits you best,
        Mr Quangle Wangle Quee!'

And besides, to the Crumpetty Tree
    Came the Stork, the Duck, and the Owl;
The Snail, and the Bumble-Bee,
    The Frog, and the Fimble Fowl;
(The Fimble Fowl, with a Corkscrew leg);
And all of them said, – We humbly beg,
'We may build our homes on your lovely Hat, –
Mr Quangle Wangle, grant us that!
        Mr Quangle Wangle Quee!'

And the Golden Grouse came there,
    And the Pobble who has no toes, –
And the small Olympian bear, –
    And the Dong with a luminous nose.
And the Blue Baboon, who played the flute, –
And the Orient Calf from the Land of Tute, –
And the Attery Squash, and the Bisky Bat, –
All came and built on the lovely Hat
        Of the Quangle Wangle Quee.

And the Quangle Wangle said
   To himself on the Crumpetty Tree, –
   'When all these creatures move
     What a wonderful noise there'll be!'
And at night by the light of the Mulberry moon
They danced to the Flute of the Blue Baboon,
On the broad green leaves of the Crumpetty Tree,
And all were as happy as happy could be,
   With the Quangle Wangle Quee.

Limericks

374   There was an Old Person of Burton,
      Whose answers were rather uncertain;
         When they said, 'How d'ye do?'
         He replied, 'Who are you?'
      That distressing Old Person of Burton.

375   There was a Young Lady of Sweden,
      Who went by the slow train to Weedon;
         When they cried, 'Weedon Station!'
         She made no observation
      But thought she should go back to Sweden.

376   There was a Young Lady of Norway,
      Who casually sat in a doorway;
         When the door squeezed her flat,
         She exclaimed, 'What of that?'
      This courageous Young Lady of Norway.

377   There was an Old Person of Prague,
      Who was suddenly seized with the plague;
         But they gave him some butter,
         Which caused him to mutter,
      And cured that Old Person of Prague.

378
There was an Old Man of Peru,
Who never knew what he should do;
    So he tore off his hair,
    And behaved like a bear,
That intrinsic Old Man of Peru.

379
There was a Young Lady whose eyes
Were unique as to colour and size;
    When she opened them wide,
    People all turned aside,
And started away in surprise.

380
There was an Old Man of the West,
Who wore a pale plum-coloured vest;
    When they said, 'Does it fit?'
    He replied, 'Not a bit!'
That uneasy Old Man of the West.

381
There was an Old Man of Peru,
Who watched his wife making a stew;
    But once by mistake,
    In a stove she did bake
That unfortunate Man of Peru.

382
There was an Old Person of Rhodes,
Who strongly objected to toads;
    He paid several cousins
    To catch them by dozens,
That futile Old Person of Rhodes.

383
There was an Old Man of Cape Horn,
Who wished he had never been born;
    So he sat on a chair,
    Till he died of despair,
That dolorous Man of Cape Horn.

384   There was an Old Man of the East,
Who gave all his children a feast;
    But they all ate so much,
    And their conduct was such
That it killed that Old Man of the East.

385   There was a Young Lady whose bonnet
Came untied when the birds sat upon it;
    But she said, 'I don't care!
    All the birds in the air
Are welcome to sit on my bonnet!'

386   There was an Old Man in a boat,
Who said, 'I'm afloat! I'm afloat!'
    When they said, 'No, you ain't!'
    He was ready to faint,
That unhappy Old Man in a boat.

387   There was an Old Person of Basing,
Whose presence of mind was amazing;
    He purchased a steed,
    Which he rode at full speed,
And escaped from the people of Basing.

388   There was an Old Man of Whitehaven,
Who danced a quadrille with a raven;
    But they said, 'It's absurd
    To encourage this bird!'
So they smashed that Old Man of Whitehaven.

389   There was an Old Person of Dutton,
Whose head was as small as a button,
    So, to make it look big,
    He purchased a wig,
And rapidly rushed about Dutton.

390
There was an Old Man of Thermopylæ,
Who never did anything properly;
But they said, 'If you choose
To boil Eggs in your Shoes,
You shall never remain in Thermopylæ.'

391
There was an Old Man in a Barge,
Whose Nose was exceedingly large;
But in fishing by night,
It supported a light,
Which helped that Old Man in a Barge.

392
There was an Old Man who screamed out
Whenever they knocked him about;
So they took off his boots,
And fed him with fruits,
And continued to knock him about.

393
There was an Old Person of Cassel,
Whose Nose finished off in a Tassel;
But they call'd out, 'Oh well! –
Don't it look like a bell!'
Which perplexed that Old Person of Cassel.

394
There was an Old Man on the Border,
Who lived in the utmost disorder;
He danced with the Cat,
And made Tea in his Hat,
Which vexed all the folks on the Border.

395
There was an Old Man of West Dumpet,
Who possessed a large Nose like a Trumpet;
When he blew it aloud,
It astonished the crowd,
And was heard through the whole of West Dumpet.

396   There was an Old Man of Dunblane,
   Who greatly resembled a Crane;
    But they said, – 'Is it wrong,
    Since your legs are so long,
   To request you won't stay in Dunblane?'

397   There was an Old Person of Blythe,
   Who cut up his Meat with a Scythe;
    When they said, 'Well! I never!' –
    He cried, 'Scythes for ever!'
   That lively Old Person of Blythe.

398   There was an Old Person of Bow,
   Whom nobody happened to know;
    So they gave him some Soap,
    And said coldly, 'We hope
   You will go back directly to Bow!'

399   There was a Young Lady whose Nose
   Continually prospers and grows;
    When it grew out of sight,
    She exclaimed in a fright,
   'Oh! Farewell to the end of my Nose!'

400   There was an Old Man of Ibreem,
   Who suddenly threaten'd to scream;
    But they said, 'If you do,
    We will thump you quite blue,
   You disgusting Old Man of Ibreem!'

401   'How pleasant to know Mr Lear!'
    Who has written such volumes of stuff!
   Some think him ill-tempered and queer,
    But a few think him pleasant enough.

   His mind is concrete and fastidious,
    His nose is remarkably big;
   His visage is more or less hideous,
    His beard it resembles a wig.

He has ears, and two eyes, and ten fingers,
    Leastways if you reckon two thumbs;
Long ago he was one of the singers,
    But now he is one of the dumbs.

He sits in a beautiful parlour,
    With hundreds of books on the wall:
He drinks a great deal of Marsala,
    But never gets tipsy at all.

He has many friends, laymen and clerical,
    Old Foss is the name of his cat:
His body is perfectly spherical,
    He weareth a runcible hat.

When he walks in a waterproof white,
    The children run after him so!
Calling out, 'He's come out in his night-
    gown, that crazy old Englishman, oh!'

He weeps by the side of the ocean,
    He weeps on the top of the hill,
He purchases pancakes and lotion,
    And chocolate shrimps from the mill.

He reads but he cannot speak Spanish,
    He cannot abide ginger-beer:
Ere the days of his pilgrimage vanish,
    How pleasant to know Mr Lear!

Emily Brontë

402   *Remembrance*

Cold in the earth – and the deep snow piled above thee,
Far, far removed, cold in the dreary grave!
Have I forgot, my only Love, to love thee,
Severed at last by Time's all-severing wave?

Now, when alone, do my thoughts no longer hover
Over the mountains, on that northern shore,
Resting their wings where heath and fern-leaves cover
Thy noble heart for ever, ever more?

Cold in the earth – and fifteen wild Decembers
From those brown hills have melted into spring –
Faithful indeed is the spirit that remembers
After such years of change and suffering!

Sweet Love of youth, forgive if I forget thee
While the world's tide is bearing me along:
Other desires and other hopes beset me,
Hopes which obscure, but cannot do thee wrong!

No later light has lightened up my heaven;
No second morn has ever shone for me:
All my life's bliss from thy dear life was given –
All my life's bliss is in the grave with thee.

But, when the days of golden dreams had perished,
And even Despair was powerless to destroy,
Then did I learn how existence could be cherished,
Strengthened, and fed without the aid of joy;

Then did I check the tears of useless passion,
Weaned my young soul from yearning after thine;
Sternly denied its burning wish to hasten
Down to that tomb already more than mine!

And, even yet, I dare not let it languish,
Dare not indulge in Memory's rapturous pain;
Once drinking deep of that divinest anguish,
How could I seek the empty world again?

Arthur Hugh Clough

403   *The Latest Decalogue*

Thou shalt have one God only; who
Would be at the expense of two?
No graven images may be
Worshipped, except the currency:
Swear not at all; for, for thy curse
Thine enemy is none the worse:
At church on Sunday to attend
Will serve to keep the world thy friend:
Honour thy parents; that is, all
From whom advancement may befall;
Thou shalt not kill; but need'st not strive
Officiously to keep alive:

Do not adultery commit;
Advantage rarely comes of it:
Thou shalt not steal; an empty feat,
When it's so lucrative to cheat:
Bear not false witness; let the lie
Have time on its own wings to fly:
Thou shalt not covet, but tradition
Approves all forms of competition.

404   Put forth thy leaf, thou lofty plane,
    East wind and frost are safely gone;
With zephyr mild and balmy rain
    The summer comes serenely on;
Earth, air, and sun and skies combine
    To promise all that's kind and fair: —
But thou, O human heart of mine,
    Be still, contain thyself, and bear.

December days were brief and chill,
    The winds of March were wild and drear,
And, nearing and receding still,
    Spring never would, we thought, be here.
The leaves that burst, the suns that shine,
    Had, not the less, their certain date: —
And thou, O human heart of mine,
    Be still, refrain thyself, and wait.

405   From *Amours de Voyage*

Is it illusion? or does there a spirit from perfecter ages,
Here, even yet, amid loss, change, and corruption abide?
Does there a spirit we know not, though seek, though we find,
    comprehend not,
  Here to entice and confuse, tempt and evade us, abide?
Lives in the exquisite grace of the column disjointed and single,
  Haunts the rude masses of brick garlanded gaily with vine,
E'en in the turret fantastic surviving that springs from the ruin,
  E'en in the people itself? is it illusion or not?
Is it illusion or not that attracteth the pilgrim transalpine,
  Brings him a dullard and dunce hither to pry and to stare?
Is it illusion or not that allures the barbarian stranger,
  Brings him with gold to the shrine, brings him in arms to
    the gate?

I Claude to Eustace

What do the people say, and what does the government do? – you
Ask, and I know not at all. Yet fortune will favour your hopes; and
I, who avoided it all, am fated, it seems, to describe it.
I, who nor meddle nor make in politics, – I who sincerely
Put not my trust in leagues nor any suffrage by ballot,
Never predicted Parisian millenniums, never beheld a
New Jerusalem coming down dressed like a bride out of heaven
Right on the Place de la Concorde, – I, nevertheless, let me say it,
Could in my soul of souls, this day, with the Gaul at the gates shed
One true tear for thee, thou poor little Roman Republic;
What, with the German restored, with Sicily safe to the Bourbon,
Not leave one poor corner for native Italian exertion?
France, it is foully done! and you, poor foolish England, –
You, who a twelvemonth ago said nations must choose for themselves, you
Could not, of course, interfere, – you, now, when a nation has chosen –
Pardon this folly! The *Times* will, of course, have announced the occasion,
Told you the news of to-day; and although it was slightly in error
When it proclaimed as a fact the Apollo was sold to a Yankee,
You may believe when it tells you the French are at Civita Vecchia.

II Claude to Eustace

Dulce it is, and *decorum*, no doubt, for the country to fall, – to
Offer one's blood an oblation to Freedom, and die for the Cause; yet
Still, individual culture is also something, and no man
Finds quite distinct the assurance that he of all others is called on,
Or would be justified even, in taking away from the world that
Precious creature, himself. Nature sent him here to abide here;
Else why send him at all? Nature wants him still, it is likely;
On the whole, we are meant to look after ourselves; it is certain
Each has to eat for himself, digest for himself, and in general
Care for his own dear life, and see to his own preservation;
Nature's intentions, in most things uncertain, in this are decisive;
Which, on the whole, I conjecture the Romans will follow, and I shall.
     So we cling to our rocks like limpets; Ocean may bluster,
Over and under and round us; we open our shells to imbibe our
Nourishment, close them again, and are safe, fulfilling the purpose
Nature intended, – a wise one, of course, and a noble, we doubt not.
Sweet it may be and decorous, perhaps, for the country to die; but,
On the whole, we conclude the Romans won't do it, and I sha'n't.

III Claude to Eustace

Will they fight? They say so. And will the French? I can hardly,
Hardly think so; and yet – He is come, they say, to Palo,
He is passed from Monterone, at Santa Severa
He hath laid up his guns. But the Virgin, the Daughter of Roma,

She hath despised thee and laughed thee to scorn, – The Daughter of Tiber,
She hath shaken her head and built barricades against thee!
Will they fight? I believe it. Alas! 'tis ephemeral folly,
Vain and ephemeral folly, of course, compared with pictures,
Statues, and antique gems! – Indeed: and yet indeed too,
Yet, methought, in broad day did I dream, – tell it not in St James's,
Whisper it not in thy courts, O Christ Church! – yet did I, waking,
Dream of a cadence that sings, *Si tombent nos jeunes héros, la*
Terre en produit de nouveaux contre vous tous prêts à se battre;
Dreamt of great indignations and angers transcendental,
Dreamt of a sword at my side and a battle-horse underneath me.

IV Claude to Eustace

Now supposing the French or the Neapolitan soldier
Should by some evil chance come exploring the Maison Serny
(Where the family English are all to assemble for safety),
Am I prepared to lay down my life for the British female?
Really, who knows? One has bowed and talked, till, little by little,
All the natural heat has escaped of the chivalrous spirit.
Oh, one conformed, of course; but one doesn't die for good manners,
Stab or shoot, or be shot, by way of graceful attention.
No, if it should be at all, it should be on the barricades there;
Should I incarnadine ever this inky pacifical finger,
Sooner far should it be for this vapour of Italy's freedom,
Sooner far by the side of the d—d and dirty plebeians.
Ah, for a child in the street I could strike; for the full-blown lady –
Somehow, Eustace, alas! I have not felt the vocation.
Yet these people of course will expect, as of course, my protection,
Vernon in radiant arms stand forth for the lovely Georgina,
And to appear, I suppose, were but common civility. Yes, and
Truly I do not desire they should either be killed or offended.
Oh, and of course, you will say, 'When the time comes, you will be ready.'
Ah, but before it comes, am I to presume it will be so?
What I cannot feel now, am I to suppose that I shall feel?
Am I not free to attend for the ripe and indubious instinct?
Am I forbidden to wait for the clear and lawful perception?
Is it the calling of man to surrender his knowledge and insight,
For the mere venture of what may, perhaps, be the virtuous action?
Must we, walking our earth, discern a little, and hoping
Some plain visible task shall yet for our hands be assigned us, –
Must we abandon the future for fear of omitting the present,
Quit our own fireside hopes at the alien call of a neighbour,
To the mere possible shadow of Deity offer the victim?
And is all this, my friend, but a weak and ignoble refining,
Wholly unworthy the head or the heart of Your Own Correspondent?

Charles Kingsley

406   *Young and Old*

When all the world is young, lad,
    And all the trees are green;
And every goose a swan, lad,
    And every lass a queen;
Then hey for boot and horse, lad,
    And round the world away;
Young blood must have its course, lad,
    And every dog his day.

When all the world is old, lad,
    And all the trees are brown;
And all the sport is stale, lad,
    And all the wheels run down;
Creep home, and take your place there,
    The spent and maimed among:
God grant you find one face there,
    You loved when all was young.

Matthew Arnold

407   *The Forsaken Merman*

Come, dear children, let us away;
Down and away below!
Now my brothers call from the bay,
Now the great winds shoreward blow,
Now the salt tides seaward flow;
Now the wild white horses play,
Champ and chafe and toss in the spray.
Children dear, let us away!
This way, this way!

Call her once before you go –
Call once yet!
In a voice that she will know:
'Margaret! Margaret!'
Children's voices should be dear
(Call once more) to a mother's ear;
Children's voices, wild with pain –
Surely she will come again!

Call her once and come away;
This way, this way!
Mother dear, we cannot stay!
The wild white horses foam and fret.'
Margaret! Margaret!

Come, dear children, come away down;
Call no more!
One last look at the white wall'd town,
And the little grey church on the windy shore;
Then come down!
She will not come though you call all day;
Come away, come away!

Children dear, was it yesterday
We heard the sweet bells over the bay?
In the caverns where we lay,
Through the surf and through the swell,
The far-off sound of a silver bell?
Sand-strewn caverns, cool and deep,
Where the winds are all asleep;
Where the spent lights quiver and gleam,
Where the salt weed sways in the stream,
Where the sea-beasts, ranged all round,
Feed in the ooze of their pasture-ground;
Where the sea-snakes coil and twine,
Dry their mail and bask in the brine;
Where great whales come sailing by,
Sail and sail, with unshut eye,
Round the world for ever and aye?
When did music come this way?
Children dear, was it yesterday?

Children dear, was it yesterday
(Call yet once) that she went away?
Once she sate with you and me,
On the red gold throne in the heart of the sea,
And the youngest sate on her knee.
She comb'd its bright hair, and she tended it well,
When down swung the sound of a far-off bell.
She sigh'd, she look'd up through the clear green sea;
She said: 'I must go, for my kinsfolk pray
In the little grey church on the shore to-day.
'Twill be Easter-time in the world – ah me!
And I lose my poor soul, Merman! here with thee.
I said: 'Go up, dear heart, through the waves;
Say thy prayer, and come back to the kind sea-caves.
She smiled, she went up through the surf in the bay.
Children dear, was it yesterday?

Children dear, were we long alone?
'The sea grows stormy, the little ones moan;
Long prayers,' I said, 'in the world they say;
Come!' I said; and we rose through the surf in the bay
We went up the beach, by the sandy down
Where the sea-stocks bloom, to the white-wall'd town
Through the narrow paved streets, where all was still,
To the little grey church on the windy hill.
From the church came a murmur of folk at their prayers
But we stood without in the cold blowing airs.
We climb'd on the graves, on the stones worn with rains
And we gazed up the aisle through the small leaded panes.
She sate by the pillar; we saw her clear:
'Margaret, hist! come quick, we are here!
Dear heart,' I said, 'we are long alone;
The sea grows stormy, the little ones moan.'
But, ah, she gave me never a look,
For her eyes were seal'd to the holy book!
Loud prays the priest; shut stands the door.
Come away, children, call no more!
Come away, come down, call no more!

Down, down, down!
Down to the depths of the sea!
She sits at her wheel in the humming town,
Singing most joyfully.
Hark what she sings: 'O joy, O joy,
For the humming street, and the child with its toy!
For the priest, and the bell, and the holy well;
For the wheel where I spun
And the blessed light of the sun!'
And so she sings her fill,
Singing most joyfully,
Till the spindle drops from her hand,
And the whizzing wheel stands still.
She steals to the window, and looks at the sand,
And over the sand at the sea;
And her eyes are set in a stare;
And anon there breaks a sigh,
And anon there drops a tear,
From a sorrow-clouded eye,
And a heart sorrow-laden,
A long, long sigh;
For the cold strange eyes of a little Mermaiden
And the gleam of her golden hair

Come away, away children;
Come children, come down!
The hoarse wind blows coldly;
Lights shine in the town

She will start from her slumber
When gusts shake the door;
She will hear the winds howling,
Will hear the waves roar.
We shall see, while above us
The waves roar and whirl,
A ceiling of amber,
A pavement of pearl.
Singing: 'Here came a mortal,
But faithless was she!
And alone dwell for ever
The kings of the sea.'

But, children, at midnight,
When soft the winds blow,
When clear falls the moonlight,
When spring-tides are low;
When sweet airs come seaward
From heaths starr'd with broom,
And high rocks throw mildly
On the blanch'd sands a gloom;
Up the still, glistening beaches,
Up the creeks we will hie,
Over banks of bright seaweed
The ebb-tide leaves dry.
We will gaze, from the sand-hills,
At the white, sleeping town;
At the church on the hill-side –
And then come back down.
Singing: 'There dwells a loved one,
But cruel is she!
She left lonely for ever
The kings of the sea.'

408   *To Marguerite – Continued*

Yes! in the sea of life enisled,
With echoing straits between us thrown,
Dotting the shoreless watery wild,
We mortal millions live *alone*.
The islands feel the enclasping flow,
And then their endless bounds they know.

But when the moon their hollows lights,
And they are swept by balms of spring,
And in their glens, on starry nights,
The nightingales divinely sing;

And lovely notes, from shore to shore,
Across the sounds and channels pour –

Oh! then a longing like despair
Is to their farthest caverns sent;
For surely once, they feel, we were
Parts of a single continent!
Now round us spreads the watery plain –
Oh might our marges meet again!

Who order'd, that their longing's fire
Should be, as soon as kindled, cool'd?
Who renders vain their deep desire? –
A God, a God their severance ruled!
And bade betwixt their shores to be
The unplumb'd, salt, estranging sea.

409   *The Scholar-Gipsy*

Go, for they call you, shepherd, from the hill;
  Go, shepherd, and untie the wattled cotes!
    No longer leave thy wistful flock unfed,
  Nor let thy bawling fellows rack their throats,
    Nor the cropp'd herbage shoot another head.
      But when the fields are still,
  And the tired men and dogs all gone to rest,
    And only the white sheep are sometimes seen
    Cross and recross the strips of moon-blanch'd green,
Come, shepherd, and again begin the quest!

Here, where the reaper was at work of late –
  In this high field's dark corner, where he leaves
    His coat, his basket, and his earthen cruse,
  And in the sun all morning binds the sheaves,
    Then here, at noon, comes back his stores to use –
      Here will I sit and wait,
  While to my ear from uplands far away
    The bleating of the folded flocks is borne,
    With distant cries of reapers in the corn –
All the live murmur of a summer's day.

Screen'd is this nook o'er the high, half-reap'd field,
  And here till sun-down, shepherd! will I be.
    Through the thick corn the scarlet poppies peep,
  And round green roots and yellowing stalks I see
    Pale pink convolvulus in tendrils creep;
      And air-swept lindens yield

Their scent, and rustle down their perfumed showers
   Of bloom on the bent grass where I am laid,
     And bower me from the August sun with shade;
And the eye travels down to Oxford's towers.

And near me on the grass lies Glanvil's book –
   Come, let me read the oft-read tale again!
     The story of the Oxford scholar poor,
Of pregnant parts and quick inventive brain,
     Who, tired of knocking at preferment's door,
       One summer-morn forsook
His friends, and went to learn the gipsy-lore,
     And roam'd the world with that wild brotherhood,
     And came, as most men deem'd, to little good,
But came to Oxford and his friends no more.

But once, years after, in the country-lanes,
   Two scholars, whom at college erst he knew,
     Met him, and of his way of life enquired;
Whereat he answer'd, that the gipsy-crew,
     His mates, had arts to rule as they desired
       The workings of men's brains,
And they can bind them to what thoughts they will.
   'And I,' he said, 'the secret of their art,
     When fully learn'd, will to the world impart;
But it needs heaven-sent moments for this skill.'

This said, he left them, and return'd no more. –
   But rumours hung about the country-side,
     That the lost Scholar long was seen to stray,
Seen by rare glimpses, pensive and tongue-tied,
     In hat of antique shape, and cloak of grey,
       The same the gipsies wore.
Shepherds had met him on the Hurst in spring;
     At some lone alehouse in the Berkshire moors,
     On the warm ingle-bench, the smock-frock'd boors
Had found him seated at their entering,

But, 'mid their drink and clatter, he would fly.
   And I myself seem half to know thy looks,
     And put the shepherds, wanderer! on thy trace;
And boys who in lone wheatfields scare the rooks
     I ask if thou hast pass'd their quiet place;
       Or in my boat I lie
Moor'd to the cool bank in the summer-heats,
     'Mid wide grass meadows which the sunshine fills,
     And watch the warm, green-muffled Cumner hills,
And wonder if thou haunt'st their shy retreats.

For most, I know, thou lov'st retired ground!
  Thee at the ferry Oxford riders blithe,
    Returning home on summer-nights, have met
  Crossing the stripling Thames at Bab-lock-hithe,
    Trailing in the cool stream thy fingers wet,
      As the punt's rope chops round;
  And leaning backward in a pensive dream,
    And fostering in thy lap a heap of flowers
    Pluck'd in shy fields and distant Wychwood bowers,
  And thine eyes resting on the moonlit stream.

And then they land, and thou art seen no more! –
  Maidens, who from the distant hamlets come
    To dance around the Fyfield elm in May,
  Oft through the darkening fields have seen thee roam,
    Or cross a stile into the public way.
      Oft thou hast given them store
  Of flowers – the frail-leaf'd, white anemony,
    Dark bluebells drench'd with dews of summer eves,
    And purple orchises with spotted leaves –
  But none hath words she can report of thee.

And, above Godstow Bridge, when hay-time's here
  In June, and many a scythe in sunshine flames,
    Men who through those wide fields of breezy grass
  Where black-wing'd swallows haunt the glittering Thames,
    To bathe in the abandon'd lasher pass,
      Have often pass'd thee near
  Sitting upon the river bank o'ergrown;
    Mark'd thine outlandish garb, thy figure spare,
    Thy dark vague eyes, and soft abstracted air –
  But, when they came from bathing, thou wast gone!

At some lone homestead in the Cumner hills,
  Where at her open door the housewife darns,
    Thou hast been seen, or hanging on a gate
  To watch the threshers in the mossy barns.
    Children, who early range these slopes and late
      For cresses from the rills,
  Have known thee eyeing, all an April-day,
    The springing pastures and the feeding kine;
    And mark'd thee, when the stars come out and shine,
  Through the long dewy grass move slow away.

In autumn, on the skirts of Bagley Wood –
  Where most the gipsies by the turf-edged way
    Pitch their smoked tents, and every bush you see
  With scarlet patches tagg'd and shreds of grey,
    Above the forest-ground called Thessaly –
      The blackbird, picking food,

Sees thee, nor stops his meal, nor fears at all;
  So often has he known thee past him stray,
  Rapt, twirling in thy hand a wither'd spray,
And waiting for the spark from heaven to fall.

And once, in winter, on the causeway chill
  Where home through flooded fields foot-travellers go,
    Have I not pass'd thee on the wooden bridge,
  Wrapt in thy cloak and battling with the snow,
    Thy face tow'rd Hinksey and its wintry ridge?
      And thou hast climb'd the hill,
And gain'd the white brow of the Cumner range;
  Turn'd once to watch, while thick the snowflakes fall,
  The line of festal light in Christ-Church hall –
Then sought thy straw in some sequester'd grange.

But what – I dream! Two hundred years are flown
  Since first thy story ran through Oxford halls,
    And the grave Glanvil did the tale inscribe
That thou wert wander'd from the studious walls
    To learn strange arts, and join a gipsy-tribe;
      And thou from earth art gone
Long since, and in some quiet churchyard laid –
  Some country-nook, where o'er thy unknown grave
  Tall grasses and white flowering nettles wave,
Under a dark, red-fruited yew-tree's shade.

– No, no, thou hast not felt the lapse of hours!
  For what wears out the life of mortal men?
    'Tis that from change to change their being rolls;
  'Tis that repeated shocks, again, again,
    Exhaust the energy of strongest souls
      And numb the elastic powers.
Till having used our nerves with bliss and teen,
  And tired upon a thousand schemes our wit,
  To the just-pausing Genius we remit
Our worn-out life, and are – what we have been.

Thou hast not lived, why should'st thou perish, so?
  Thou hadst *one* aim, *one* business, *one* desire;
    Else wert thou long since number'd with the dead!
Else hadst thou spent, like other men, thy fire!
    The generations of thy peers are fled,
      And we ourselves shall go;
But thou possessest an immortal lot,
  And we imagine thee exempt from age
  And living as thou liv'st on Glanvil's page,
Because thou hadst – what we, alas! have not.

For early didst thou leave the world, with powers
   Fresh, undiverted to the world without,
      Firm to their mark, not spent on other things;
   Free from the sick fatigue, the languid doubt,
      Which much to have tried, in much been baffled, brings.
         O life unlike to ours!
   Who fluctuate idly without term or scope,
      Of whom each strives, nor knows for what he strives,
      And each half lives a hundred different lives;
   Who wait like thee, but not, like thee, in hope.

Thou waitest for the spark from heaven! and we,
   Light half-believers of our casual creeds,
      Who never deeply felt, nor clearly will'd,
   Whose insight never has borne fruit in deeds,
      Whose vague resolves never have been fulfill'd;
         For whom each year we see
   Breeds new beginnings, disappointments new;
      Who hesitate and falter life away,
      And lose to-morrow the ground won to-day —
   Ah! do not we, wanderer! await it too?

Yes, we await it! — but it still delays,
   And then we suffer! and amongst us one,
      Who most has suffer'd, takes dejectedly
   His seat upon the intellectual throne;
      And all his store of sad experience he
         Lays bare of wretched days;
   Tells us his misery's birth and growth and signs,
      And how the dying spark of hope was fed,
      And how the breast was soothed, and how the head,
   And all his hourly varied anodynes.

This for our wisest! and we others pine,
   And wish the long unhappy dream would end,
      And waive all claim to bliss, and try to bear;
   With close-lipp'd patience for our only friend,
      Sad patience, too near neighbour to despair —
         But none has hope like thine!
   Thou through the fields and through the woods dost stray,
      Roaming the country-side, a truant boy,
      Nursing thy project in unclouded joy,
   And every doubt long blown by time away.

O born in days when wits were fresh and clear,
   And life ran gaily as the sparkling Thames;
      Before this strange disease of modern life,
   With its sick hurry, its divided aims,
      Its heads o'ertax'd, its palsied hearts, was rife —
         Fly hence, our contact fear!

Still fly, plunge deeper in the bowering wood!
  Averse, as Dido did with gesture stern
  From her false friend's approach in Hades turn,
Wave us away, and keep thy solitude!

Still nursing the unconquerable hope,
  Still clutching the inviolable shade,
    With a free, onward impulse brushing through,
  By night, the silver'd branches of the glade –
    Far on the forest-skirts, where none pursue,
      On some mild pastoral slope
  Emerge, and resting on the moonlit pales
    Freshen thy flowers as in former years
    With dew, or listen with enchanted ears,
From the dark dingles, to the nightingales!

But fly our paths, our feverish contact fly!
  For strong the infection of our mental strife,
    Which, though it gives no bliss, yet spoils for rest;
  And we should win thee from thy own fair life,
    Like us distracted, and like us unblest.
      Soon, soon thy cheer would die,
  Thy hopes grow timorous, and unfix'd thy powers,
    And thy clear aims be cross and shifting made;
    And then thy glad perennial youth would fade,
Fade, and grow old at last, and die like ours.

Then fly our greetings, fly our speech and smiles!
  – As some grave Tyrian trader, from the sea,
    Descried at sunrise an emerging prow
  Lifting the cool-hair'd creepers stealthily,
    The fringes of a southward-facing brow
      Among the Aegaean isles;
  And saw the merry Grecian coaster come,
    Freighted with amber grapes, and Chian wine,
    Green, bursting figs, and tunnies steep'd in brine –
And knew the intruders on his ancient home,

The young light-hearted masters of the waves –
  And snatch'd his rudder, and shook out more sail;
    And day and night held on indignantly
  O'er the blue Midland waters with the gale,
    Betwixt the Syrtes and soft Sicily,
      To where the Atlantic raves
  Outside the western straits; and unbent sails
    There, where down cloudy cliffs, through sheets of foam,
    Shy traffickers, the dark Iberians come;
And on the beach undid his corded bales.

Coventry Patmore

410   *The Toys*

My little Son, who looked from thoughtful eyes
And moved and spoke in quiet grown-up wise,
Having my law the seventh time disobeyed,
I struck him, and dismissed
With hard words and unkissed,
His Mother, who was patient, being dead.
Then, fearing lest his grief should hinder sleep,
I visited his bed,
But found him slumbering deep,
With darkened eyelids, and their lashes yet
From his late sobbing wet.
And I, with moan,
Kissing away his tears, left others of my own;
For, on a table drawn beside his head,
He had put, within his reach,
A box of counters and a red-veined stone,
A piece of glass abraded by the beach,
And six or seven shells,
A bottle with bluebells
And two French copper coins, ranged there with careful art,
To comfort his sad heart.

So when that night I prayed
To God, I wept, and said:
Ah, when at last we lie with trancèd breath,
Not vexing Thee in death,
And Thou rememberest of what toys
We made our joys,
How weakly understood,
Thy great commanded good,
Then, fatherly not less
Than I whom Thou hast moulded from the clay,
Thou'lt leave Thy wrath, and say,
'I will be sorry for their childishness.'

From *The Angel in the House*

411

[1]

The Spirit's Epochs

Not in the crises of events,
    Of compassed hopes, or fears fulfilled,
Or acts of gravest consequence,
    Are life's delight and depth revealed.
The day of days was not the day;
    That went before, or was postponed;
The night Death took our lamp away
    Was not the night on which we groaned.
I drew my bride, beneath the moon,
    Across my threshold; happy hour!
But, ah, the walk that afternoon
    We saw the water-flags in flower!

412

[2]

The Tribute

Boon Nature to the woman bows;
    She walks in earth's whole glory clad,
And, chiefest far herself of shows,
    All others help her, and are glad:
No splendour 'neath the sky's proud dome
    But serves for her familiar wear;
The far-fetched diamond finds its home
    Flashing and smouldering in her hair;
For her the seas their pearls reveal;
    Art and strange lands her pomp supply
With purple, chrome, and cochineal,
    Ochre, and lapis lazuli;
The worm its golden woof presents;
    Whatever runs, flies, dives, or delves,
All doff for her their ornaments,
    Which suit her better than themselves;
And all, by this their power to give,
    Proving her right to take, proclaim
Her beauty's clear prerogative
    To profit so by Eden's blame.

George Meredith

413   From *Modern Love*

L

Thus piteously Love closed what he begat:
The union of this ever-diverse pair!
These two were rapid falcons in a snare,
Condemned to do the flitting of the bat.
Lovers beneath the singing sky of May,
They wandered once; clear as the dew on flowers:
But they fed not on the advancing hours:
Their hearts held cravings for the buried day.
Then each applied to each that fatal knife,
Deep questioning, which probes to endless dole.
Ah, what a dusty answer gets the soul
When hot for certainties in this our life! –
In tragic hints here see what evermore
Moves dark as yonder midnight ocean's force,
Thundering like ramping hosts of warrior horse,
To throw that faint thin line upon the shore!

Dante Gabriel Rossetti

414   *On Refusal of Aid between Nations*

Not that the earth is changing, O my God!
    Nor that the seasons totter in their walk, –
    Not that the virulent ill of act and talk
Seethes ever as a winepress ever trod, –
Not therefore are we certain that the rod
    Weighs in thine hand to smite thy world; though now
    Beneath thine hand so many nations bow,
So many kings: – not therefore, O my God! –

But because Man is parcelled out in men
    Even thus; because, for any wrongful blow,
        No man not stricken asks, 'I would be told
Why thou dost strike'; but his heart whispers then,
    'He is he, I am I.' By this we know
        That the earth falls asunder, being old.

415   From *Sonnets for Pictures*

'Our Lady of the Rocks'
By Leonardo da Vinci

Mother, is this the darkness of the end,
    The Shadow of Death? and is that outer sea
    Infinite imminent Eternity?
And does the death-pang by man's seed sustain'd
In Time's each instant cause thy face to bend
    Its silent prayer upon the Son, while he
    Blesses the dead with his hand silently
To his long day which hours no more offend?

Mother of grace, the pass is difficult,
    Keen as these rocks, and the bewildered souls
        Throng it like echoes, blindly shuddering through.
    Thy name, O Lord, each spirit's voice extols,
        Whose peace abides in the dark avenue
Amid the bitterness of things occult.

416   *The Woodspurge*

The wind flapped loose, the wind was still,
Shaken out dead from tree and hill:
I had walked on at the wind's will, –
I sat now, for the wind was still.

Between my knees my forehead was, –
My lips, drawn in, said not Alas!
My hair was over in the grass,
My naked ears heard the day pass.

My eyes, wide open, had the run
Of some ten weeds to fix upon;
Among those few, out of the sun,
The woodspurge flowered, three cups in one.

From perfect grief there need not be
Wisdom or even memory:
One thing then learnt remains to me, –
The woodspurge has a cup of three.

Christina Rossetti

417   *Song*

When I am dead, my dearest,
  Sing no sad songs for me;
Plant thou no roses at my head,
  Nor shady cypress tree:
Be the green grass above me
  With showers and dewdrops wet:
And if thou wilt, remember,
  And if thou wilt, forget.

I shall not see the shadows,
  I shall not feel the rain;
I shall not hear the nightingale
  Sing on as if in pain:
And dreaming through the twilight
  That doth not rise nor set,
Haply I may remember,
  And haply may forget.

418   *Goblin Market*

Morning and evening
Maids heard the goblins cry:
'Come buy our orchard fruits,
Come buy, come buy:
Apples and quinces,
Lemons and oranges,
Plump unpecked cherries,
Melons and raspberries,
Bloom-down-cheeked peaches,
Swart-headed mulberries,
Wild free-born cranberries,
Crab-apples, dewberries,
Pine-apples, blackberries,
Apricots, strawberries; –
All ripe together
In summer weather, –
Morns that pass by,
Fair eves that fly;
Come buy, come buy:
Our grapes fresh from the vine,
Pomegranates full and fine,

Dates and sharp bullaces,
Rare pears and greengages,
Damsons and bilberries,
Taste them and try:
Currants and gooseberries,
Bright-fire-like barberries,
Figs to fill your mouth,
Citrons from the South,
Sweet to tongue and sound to eye;
Come buy, come buy.'

    Evening by evening
Among the brookside rushes,
Laura bowed her head to hear,
Lizzie veiled her blushes:
Crouching close together
In the cooling weather,
With clasping arms and cautioning lips,
With tingling cheeks and finger tips.
'Lie close,' Laura said,
Pricking up her golden head:
'We must not look at goblin men,
We must not buy their fruits:
Who knows upon what soil they fed
Their hungry thirsty roots?'
'Come buy,' call the goblins
Hobbling down the glen.
'Oh,' cried Lizzie, 'Laura, Laura,
You should not peep at goblin men.'
Lizzie covered up her eyes,
Covered close lest they should look;
Laura reared her glossy head,
And whispered like the restless brook:
'Look Lizzie, look Lizzie,
Down the glen tramp little men.
One hauls a basket,
One bears a plate,
One lugs a golden dish
Of many pounds weight.
How fair the vine must grow
Whose grapes are so luscious;
How warm the wind must blow
Through those fruit bushes.'
'No,' said Lizzie; 'No, no, no;
Their offers should not charm us,
Their evil gifts would harm us.'
She thrust a dimpled finger
In each ear, shut eyes and ran:
Curious Laura chose to linger
Wondering at each merchant man.

One had a cat's face,
One whisked a tail,
One tramped at a rat's pace,
One crawled like a snail,
One like a wombat prowled obtuse and furry,
One like a ratel tumbled hurry skurry.
She heard a voice like voice of doves
Cooing all together:
They sounded kind and full of loves
In the pleasant weather.

    Laura stretched her gleaming neck
Like a rush-embedded swan,
Like a lily from the beck,
Like a moonlit poplar branch,
Like a vessel at the launch
When its last restraint is gone.

    Backwards up the mossy glen
Turned and trooped the goblin men,
With their shrill repeated cry,
'Come buy, come buy.'
When they reached where Laura was
They stood stock still upon the moss,
Leering at each other,
Brother with queer brother;
Signalling each other,
Brother with sly brother.
One set his basket down,
One reared his plate;
One began to weave a crown,
Of tendrils, leaves and rough nuts brown
(Men sell not such in any town);
One heaved the golden weight
Of dish and fruit to offer her:
'Come buy, come buy,' was still their cry.
Laura stared but did not stir,
Longed but had no money:
The whisk-tailed merchant bade her taste
In tones as smooth as honey,
The cat-faced purred,
The rat-paced spoke a word
Of welcome, and the snail-paced even was heard;
One parrot-voiced and jolly
Cried 'Pretty Goblin' still for 'Pretty Polly'; —
One whistled like a bird.

    But sweet-tooth Laura spoke in haste:
'Good folk, I have no coin;
To take were to purloin:

I have no copper in my purse,
I have no silver either,
And all my gold is on the furze
That shakes in windy weather
Above the rusty heather.'
'You have much gold upon your head,'
They answered all together:
'Buy from us with a golden curl.'
She clipped a precious golden lock,
She dropped a tear more rare than pearl,
Then sucked their fruit globes fair or red:
Sweeter than honey from the rock,
Stronger than man-rejoicing wine,
Clearer than water flowed that juice;
She never tasted such before,
How could it cloy with length of use?
She sucked and sucked and sucked the more
Fruits which that unknown orchard bore;
She sucked until her lips were sore;
Then flung the empty rinds away
But gathered up one kernel-stone,
And knew not was it night or day
And she turned home alone.

　　Lizzie met her at the gate
Full of wise upbraidings:
'Dear, you should not stay so late,
Twilight is not good for maidens;
Should not loiter in the glen
　In the haunts of goblin men.
Do you not remember Jeanie,
How she met them in the moonlight,
Took their gifts both choice and many,
Ate their fruits and wore their flowers
Plucked from bowers
Where summer ripens at all hours?
But ever in the noonlight
She pined and pined away;
Sought them by night and day,
Found them no more but dwindled and grew grey;
Then fell with the first snow,
While to this day no grass will grow
Where she lies low:
I planted daisies there a year ago
That never blow.
You should not loiter so.'
'Nay, hush,' said Laura:
'Nay, hush, my sister:
I ate and ate my fill,
Yet my mouth waters still;

To-morrow night I will buy more': and kissed her:
'Have done with sorrow;
I'll bring you plums to-morrow
Fresh on their mother twigs,
Cherries worth getting;
You cannot think what figs
My teeth have met in,
What melons icy-cold
Piled on a dish of gold
Too huge for me to hold,
What peaches with a velvet nap,
Pellucid grapes without one seed:
Odorous indeed must be the mead
Whereon they grow, and pure the wave they drink
With lilies at the brink,
And sugar-sweet their sap.'

   Golden head by golden head,
Like two pigeons in one nest
Folded in each other's wings,
They lay down in their curtained bed:
Like two blossoms on one stem,
Like two flakes of new-fall'n snow,
Like two wands of ivory
Tipped with gold for awful kings.
Moon and stars gazed in at them,
Wind sang to them lullaby,
Lumbering owls forbore to fly,
Not a bat flapped to and fro
Round their rest:
Cheek to cheek and breast to breast
Locked together in one nest.

   Early in the morning
When the first cock crowed his warning,
Neat like bees, as sweet and busy,
Laura rose with Lizzie:
Fetched in honey, milked the cows,
Aired and set to rights the house,
Kneaded cakes of whitest wheat,
Cakes for dainty mouths to eat,
Next churned butter, whipped up cream,
Fed their poultry, sat and sewed;
Talked as modest maidens should:
Lizzie with an open heart,
Laura in an absent dream,
One content, one sick in part;
One warbling for the mere bright day's delight,
One longing for the night.

At length slow evening came:
They went with pitchers to the reedy brook;
Lizzie most placid in her look,
Laura most like a leaping flame.
They drew the gurgling water from its deep;
Lizzie plucked purple and rich golden flags,
Then turning homewards said: 'The sunset flushes
Those furthest loftiest crags;
Come, Laura, not another maiden lags,
No wilful squirrel wags,
The beasts and birds are fast asleep.'
But Laura loitered still among the rushes
And said the bank was steep.

And said the hour was early still,
The dew not fall'n, the wind not chill:
Listening ever, but not catching
The customary cry,
'Come buy, come buy,'
With its iterated jingle
Of sugar-baited words:
Not for all her watching
Once discerning even one goblin
Raving, whisking, tumbling, hobbling;
Let alone the herds
That used to tramp along the glen,
In groups or single,
Of brisk fruit-merchant men.

Till Lizzie urged, 'O Laura, come;
I hear the fruit-call but I dare not look:
You should not loiter longer at this brook:
Come with me home.
The stars rise, the moon bends her arc,
Each glowworm winks her spark,
Let us get home before the night grows dark:
For clouds may gather
Though this is summer weather,
Put out the lights and drench us through;
Then if we lost our way what should we do?'

Laura turned cold as stone
To find her sister heard that cry alone,
That goblin cry,
'Come buy our fruits, come buy.'
Must she then buy no more such dainty fruits?
Must she no more that succous pasture find,
Gone deaf and blind?
Her tree of life drooped from the root:

She said not one word in her heart's sore ache;
But peering through the dimness, nought discerning,
Trudged home, her pitcher dripping all the way;
So crept to bed, and lay
Silent till Lizzie slept;
Then sat up in a passionate yearning,
And gnashed her teeth for baulked desire, and wept
As if her heart would break.

   Day after day, night after night,
Laura kept watch in vain
In sullen silence of exceeding pain.
She never caught again the goblin cry:
'Come buy, come buy'; —
She never spied the goblin men
Hawking their fruits along the glen:
But when the moon waxed bright
Her hair grew thin and grey;
She dwindled, as the fair full moon doth turn
To swift decay and burn
Her fire away.

   One day remembering her kernel-stone
She set it by a wall that faced the south;
Dewed it with tears, hoped for a root,
Watched for a waxing shoot,
But there came none;
It never saw the sun,
It never felt the trickling moisture run:
While with sunk eyes and faded mouth
She dreamed of melons, as a traveller sees
False waves in desert drouth
With shade of leaf-crowned trees,
And burns the thirstier in the sandful breeze.

   She no more swept the house,
Tended the fowls or cows,
Fetched honey, kneaded cakes of wheat,
Brought water from the brook:
But sat down listless in the chimney-nook
And would not eat.

   Tender Lizzie could not bear
To watch her sister's cankerous care
Yet not to share.
She night and morning
Caught the goblins' cry:
'Come buy our orchard fruits,
Come buy, come buy': —

Beside the brook, along the glen,
She heard the tramp of goblin men,
The voice and stir
Poor Laura could not hear;
Longed to buy fruit to comfort her,
But feared to pay too dear.
She thought of Jeanie in her grave,
Who should have been a bride;
But who for joys brides hope to have
Fell sick and died
In her gay prime,
In earliest Winter time,
With the first glazing rime,
With the first snow-fall of crisp Winter time.

   Till Laura dwindling
Seemed knocking at Death's door:
Then Lizzie weighed no more
Better and worse;
But put a silver penny in her purse,
Kissed Laura, crossed the heath with clumps of furze
At twilight, halted by the brook:
And for the first time in her life
Began to listen and look.

   Laughed every goblin
When they spied her peeping:
Come towards her hobbling,
Flying, running, leaping,
Puffing and blowing,
Chuckling, clapping, crowing,
Clucking and gobbling,
Mopping and mowing,
Full of airs and graces,
Pulling wry faces,
Demure grimaces,
Cat-like and rat-like,
Ratel- and wombat-like,
Snail-paced in a hurry,
Parrot-voiced and whistler,
Helter skelter, hurry skurry,
Chattering like magpies,
Fluttering like pigeons,
Gliding like fishes, –
Hugged her and kissed her,
Squeezed and caressed her:
Stretched up their dishes,
Panniers and plates:
'Look at our apples
Russet and dun,

Bob at our cherries,
Bite at our peaches,
Citrons and dates,
Grapes for the asking,
Pears red with basking
Out in the sun,
Plums on their twigs;
Pluck them and suck them,
Pomegranates, figs.' —

 'Good folk,' said Lizzie,
Mindful of Jeanie:
'Give me much and many': —
Held out her apron,
Tossed them her penny.
'Nay, take a seat with us,
Honour and eat with us';
They answered grinning:
'Our feast is but beginning.
Night is yet early,
Warm and dew-pearly,
Wakeful and starry:
Such fruits as these
No man can carry;
Half their bloom would fly,
Half their dew would dry,
Half their flavour would pass by.
Sit down and feast with us,
Be welcome guest with us,
Cheer you and rest with us.' —
'Thank you,' said Lizzie: 'But one waits
At home alone for me:
So without further parleying,
If you will not sell me any
Of your fruits though much and many,
Give me back my silver penny
I tossed you for a fee.' —
They began to scratch their pates,
No longer wagging, purring,
But visibly demurring,
Grunting and snarling.
One called her proud,
Cross-grained, uncivil;
Their tones waxed loud,
Their looks were evil.
Lashing their tails
They trod and hustled her,
Elbowed and jostled her,
Clawed with their nails,

Barking, mewing, hissing, mocking,
Tore her gown and soiled her stockings,
Twitched her hair out by the roots,
Stamped upon her tender feet,
Held her hands and squeezed their fruits
Against her mouth to make her eat.

   White and golden Lizzie stood,
Like a lily in a flood, –
Like a rock of blue-veined stone
Lashed by tides obstreperously, –
Like a beacon left alone
In a hoary roaring sea,
Sending up a golden fire, –
Like a fruit-crowned orange-tree
White with blossoms honey-sweet
Sore beset by wasp and bee, –
Like a royal virgin town
Topped with gilded dome and spire
Close beleaguered by a fleet
Mad to tug her standard down.

   One may lead a horse to water,
Twenty cannot make him drink.
Though the goblins cuffed and caught her,
Coaxed and fought her,
Bullied and besought her,
Scratched her, pinched her black as ink,
Kicked and knocked her,
Mauled and mocked her,
Lizzie uttered not a word;
Would not open lip from lip
Lest they should cram a mouthful in:
But laughed in heart to feel the drip
Of juice that syrupped all her face,
And lodged in dimples of her chin,
And streaked her neck which quaked like curd.
At last the evil people
Worn out by her resistance
Flung back her penny, kicked their fruit
Along whichever road they took,
Not leaving root or stone or shoot;
Some writhed into the ground,
Some dived into the brook
With ring and ripple,
Some scudded on the gale without a sound,
Some vanished in the distance.

In a smart, ache, tingle,
Lizzie went her way:
Knew not was it night or day;
Sprang up the bank, tore through the furze,
Threaded copse and dingle,
And heard her penny jingle
Bouncing in her purse, —
Its bounce was music to her ear.
She ran and ran
As if she feared some goblin man
Dogged her with gibe or curse
Or something worse:
But not one goblin scurried after,
Nor was she pricked by fear;
The kind heart made her windy-paced
That urged her home quite out of breath with haste
And inward laughter.

She cried 'Laura,' up the garden,
'Did you miss me?
Come and kiss me.
Never mind my bruises,
Hug me, kiss me, suck my juices
Squeezed from goblin fruits for you,
Goblin pulp and goblin dew.
Eat me, drink me, love me;
Laura, make much of me:
For your sake I have braved the glen
And had to do with goblin merchant men.'

Laura started from her chair,
Flung her arms up in the air,
Clutched her hair:
'Lizzie, Lizzie, have you tasted
For my sake the fruit forbidden?
Must your light like mine be hidden,
Your young life like mine be wasted,
Undone in mine undoing
And ruined in my ruin,
Thirsty, cankered, goblin-ridden?' —
She clung about her sister,
Kissed and kissed and kissed her:
Tears once again
Refreshed her sunken eyes,
Dropping like rain
After long sultry drouth;
Shaking with aguish fear, and pain,
She kissed and kissed her with a hungry mouth.

Her lips began to scorch,
That juice was wormwood to her tongue,
She loathed the feast:
Writhing as one possessed she leaped and sung,
Rent all her robe, and wrung
Her hands in lamentable haste,
And beat her breast.
Her locks streamed like the torch
Borne by a racer at full speed,
Or like the mane of horses in their flight,
Or like an eagle when he stems the light
Straight toward the sun,
Or like a caged thing freed,
Or like a flying flag when armies run.

Swift fire spread through her veins, knocked at her heart,
Met the fire smouldering there
And overbore its lesser flame;
She gorged on bitterness without a name:
Ah! fool, to choose such part
Of soul-consuming care!
Sense failed in the mortal strife:
Like the watch-tower of a town
Which an earthquake shatters down,
Like a lightning-stricken mast,
Like a wind-uprooted tree
Spun about,
Like a foam-topped waterspout
Cast down headlong in the sea,
She fell at last;
Pleasure past and anguish past,
Is it death or is it life?

Life out of death.
That night long Lizzie watched by her,
Counted her pulse's flagging stir,
Felt for her breath,
Held water to her lips, and cooled her face
With tears and fanning leaves:
But when the first birds chirped about their eaves,
And early reapers plodded to the place
Of golden sheaves,
And dew-wet grass
Bowed in the morning winds so brisk to pass,
And new buds with new day
Opened of cup-like lilies on the stream,
Laura awoke as from a dream,
Laughed in the innocent old way,
Hugged Lizzie but not twice or thrice;

Her gleaming locks showed not one thread of grey,
Her breath was sweet as May
And light danced in her eyes.

   Days, weeks, months, years,
Afterwards, when both were wives
With children of their own;
Their mother-hearts beset with fears,
Their lives bound up in tender lives;
Laura would call the little ones
And tell them of her early prime,
Those pleasant days long gone
Of not-returning time:
Would talk about the haunted glen,
The wicked, quaint fruit-merchant men,
Their fruits like honey to the throat
But poison in the blood;
(Men sell not such in any town:)
Would tell them how her sister stood
In deadly peril to do her good,
And win the fiery antidote:
Then joining hands to little hands
Would bid them cling together,
'For there is no friend like a sister
In calm or stormy weather;
To cheer one on the tedious way,
To fetch one if one goes astray,
To lift one if one totters down,
To strengthen whilst one stands.'

Lewis Carroll

419   Untitled poem from *Through the Looking-Glass*

In winter, when the fields are white,
I sing this song for your delight –

In spring, when woods are getting green,
I'll try and tell you what I mean:

In summer, when the days are long,
Perhaps you'll understand the song:

In autumn, when the leaves are brown,
Take pen and ink, and write it down.

I sent a message to the fish:
I told them 'This is what I wish.'

The little fishes of the sea,
They sent an answer back to me.

The little fishes' answer was
'We cannot do it, Sir, because –'

I sent to them again to say
'It will be better to obey.'

The fishes answered, with a grin,
'Why, what a temper you are in!'

I told them once, I told them twice:
They would not listen to advice.

I took a kettle large and new,
Fit for the deed I had to do.

My heart went hop, my heart went thump:
I filled the kettle at the pump.

Then some one came to me and said
'The little fishes are in bed.'

I said to him, I said it plain,
'Then you must wake them up again.'

I said it very loud and clear:
I went and shouted in his ear.

But he was very stiff and proud:
He said, 'You needn't shout so loud!'

And he was very proud and stiff:
He said 'I'd go and wake them, if –'

I took a corkscrew from the shelf:
I went to wake them up myself.

And when I found the door was locked,
I pulled and pushed and kicked and knocked.

And when I found the door was shut,
I tried to turn the handle, but –

420   *Jabberwocky*

'Twas brillig, and the slithy toves
    Did gyre and gimble in the wabe:
All mimsy were the borogoves,
    And the mome raths outgrabe.

'Beware the Jabberwock, my son!
    The jaws that bite, the claws that catch!
Beware the Jubjub bird, and shun
    The frumious Bandersnatch!'

He took his vorpal sword in hand:
    Long time the manxome foe he sought –
So rested he by the Tumtum tree,
    And stood awhile in thought.

And, as in uffish thought he stood,
    The Jabberwock, with eyes of flame,
Came whiffling through the tulgey wood,
    And burbled as it came!

One, two! One, two! And through and through
    The vorpal blade went snicker-snack!
He left it dead, and with its head
    He went galumphing back.

'And hast thou slain the Jabberwock?
    Come to my arms, my beamish boy!
O frabjous day! Callooh! Callay!'
    He chortled in his joy.

'Twas brillig, and the slithy toves
    Did gyre and gimble in the wabe:
All mimsy were the borogoves,
    And the mome raths outgrabe.

From *The Hunting of the Snark*

421   *The Baker's Tale*

They roused him with muffins – they roused him with ice –
    They roused him with mustard and cress –
They roused him with jam and judicious advice –
    They set him conundrums to guess.

When at length he sat up and was able to speak,
　　His sad story he offered to tell;
And the Bellman cried 'Silence! Not even a shriek!'
　　And excitedly tingled his bell.

There was silence supreme! Not a shriek, not a scream,
　　Scarcely even a howl or a groan,
As the man they called 'Ho!' told his story of woe
　　In an antediluvian tone.

'My father and mother were honest, though poor –'
　　'Skip all that!' cried the Bellman in haste.
'If it once becomes dark, there's no chance of a Snark –
　　We have hardly a minute to waste!'

'I skip forty years,' said the Baker in tears,
　　'And proceed without further remark
To the day when you took me aboard of your ship
　　To help you in hunting the Snark.

A dear uncle of mine (after whom I was named)
　　Remarked, when I bade him farewell –'
'Oh, skip your dear uncle!' the Bellman exclaimed,
　　As he angrily tingled his bell.

'He remarked to me then,' said that mildest of men,
　　' "If your Snark be a Snark, that is right:
Fetch it home by all means – you may serve it with greens
　　And it's handy for striking a light.

You may seek it with thimbles – and seek it with care –
　　You may hunt it with forks and hope;
You may threaten its life with a railway-share;
　　You may charm it with smiles and soap –" '

('That's exactly the method,' the Bellman bold
　　In a hasty parenthesis cried,
'That's exactly the way I have always been told
　　That the capture of Snarks should be tried!')

' "But oh, beamish nephew, beware of the day,
　　If your Snark be a Boojum! For then
You will softly and suddenly vanish away,
　　And never be met with again!"

It is this, it is this that oppresses my soul,
　　When I think of my uncle's last words:
And my heart is like nothing so much as a bowl
　　Brimming over with quivering curds!

'It is this, it is this –' 'We have had that before!'
   The Bellman indignantly said.
And the Baker replied 'Let me say it once more.
   It is this, it is this that I dread!

I engage with the Snark – every night after dark –
   In a dreamy delirious fight:
I serve it with greens in those shadowy scenes,
   And I use it for striking a light:

But if ever I meet with a Boojum, that day,
   In a moment (of this I am sure),
I shall softly and suddenly vanish away –
   And the notion I cannot endure!'

Richard Watson Dixon

422   *Dream*

I

With camel's hair I clothed my skin,
   I fed my mouth with honey wild;
And set me scarlet wool to spin,
   And all my breast with hyssop filled;
Upon my brow and cheeks and chin
   A bird's blood spilled.

I took a broken reed to hold,
   I took a sponge of gall to press;
I took weak water-weeds to fold
   About my sacrificial dress.

I took the grasses of the field,
   The flax was bolled upon my crine;
And ivy thorn and wild grapes healed
   To make good wine.

I took my scrip of manna sweet,
   My cruse of water did I bless;
I took the white dove by the feet,
   And flew into the wilderness.

II

The tiger came and played;
Uprose the lion in his mane;
The jackal's tawny nose
And sanguine dripping tongue
Out of the desert rose
And plunged its sands among;
The bear came striding o'er the desert plain.

Uprose the horn and eyes
And quivering flank of the great unicorn,
And galloped round and round;
Uprose the gleaming claw
Of the leviathan, and wound
In steadfast march did draw
Its course away beyond the desert's bourn.

I stood within a maze
Woven round about me by a magic art,
And ordered circle-wise:
The bear more near did tread,
And with two fiery eyes,
And with a wolfish head,
Did close the circle round in every part.

III

With scarlet corded horn,
With frail wrecked knees and stumbling pace,
The scapegoat came:
His eyes took flesh and spirit dread in flame
At once, and he died looking towards my face.

James Thomson ('B.V.')

423   From *The City of Dreadful Night*

XIV

Large glooms were gathered in the mighty fane,
    With tinted moongleams slanting here and there;
And all was hush: no swelling organ-strain,
    No chant, no voice or murmuring of prayer;
No priests came forth, no tinkling censers fumed,
And the high altar space was unillumed.

Around the pillars and against the walls
   Leaned men and shadows; others seemed to brood
Bent or recumbent in secluded stalls.
   Perchance they were not a great multitude
Save in that city of so lonely streets
Where one may count up every face he meets.

All patiently awaited the event
   Without a stir or sound, as if no less
Self-occupied, doomstricken, while attent.
   And then we heard a voice of solemn stress
From the dark pulpit, and our gaze there met
Two eyes which burned as never eyes burned yet:

Two steadfast and intolerable eyes
   Burning beneath a broad and rugged brow;
The head behind it of enormous size,
   And as black fir-groves in a large wind bow,
Our rooted congregation, gloom-arrayed,
By that great sad voice deep and full were swayed: –

O melancholy Brothers, dark, dark, dark!
O battling in black floods without an ark!
   O spectral wanderers of unholy Night!
My soul hath bled for you these sunless years,
With bitter blood-drops running down like tears:
   Oh, dark, dark, dark, withdrawn from joy and light!

My heart is sick with anguish for your bale!
Your woe hath been my anguish; yea, I quail
   And perish in your perishing unblest.
And I have searched the heights and depths, the scope
Of all our universe, with desperate hope
   To find some solace for your wild unrest.

And now at last authentic word I bring,
Witnessed by every dead and living thing;
   Good tidings of great joy for you, for all:
There is no God; no Fiend with names divine
Made us and tortures us; if we must pine,
   It is to satiate no Being's gall.

It was the dark delusion of a dream,
That living Person conscious and supreme,
   Whom we must curse for cursing us with life;
Whom we must curse because the life He gave
Could not be buried in the quiet grave,
   Could not be killed by poison or by knife.

This little life is all we must endure,
The grave's most holy peace is ever sure,
    We fall asleep and never wake again;
Nothing is of us but the mouldering flesh,
Whose elements dissolve and merge afresh
    In earth, air, water, plants, and other men.

William Morris

424   *The Haystack in the Floods*

Had she come all the way for this,
To part at last without a kiss?
Yea, had she borne the dirt and rain
That her own eyes might see him slain
Beside the haystack in the floods?

Along the dripping leafless woods,
The stirrup touching either shoe,
She rode astride as troopers do;
With kirtle kilted to her knee,
To which the mud splashed wretchedly;
And the wet dripped from every tree
Upon her head and heavy hair,
And on her eyelids broad and fair;
The tears and rain ran down her face.
By fits and starts they rode apace,
And very often was his place
Far off from her; he had to ride
Ahead, to see what might betide
When the roads crossed; and sometimes, when
There rose a murmuring from his men,
Had to turn back with promises;
Ah me! she had but little ease;
And often for pure doubt and dread
She sobbed, made giddy in the head
By the swift riding; while, for cold,
Her slender fingers scarce could hold
The wet reins; yea, and scarcely, too,
She felt the foot within her shoe
Against the stirrup: all for this,
To part at last without a kiss
Beside the haystack in the floods.

For when they neared that old soaked hay,
They saw across the only way
That Judas, Godmar, and the three
Red running lions dismally
Grinned from his pennon, under which,
In one straight line along the ditch,
They counted thirty heads.

                    So then,
While Robert turned round to his men,
She saw at once the wretched end,
And, stooping down, tried hard to rend
Her coif the wrong way from her head,
And hid her eyes; while Robert said:
'Nay, love, 'tis scarcely two to one,
At Poictiers where we made them run
So fast – why, sweet my love, good cheer.
The Gascon frontier is so near,
Nought after this.'

                But, 'O,' she said,
'My God! my God! I have to tread
The long way back without you; then
The court at Paris; those six men;
The gratings of the Chatelet;
The swift Seine on some rainy day
Like this, and people standing by,
And laughing, while my weak hands try
To recollect how strong men swim.
All this, or else a life with him,
For which I should be damned at last,
Would God that this next hour were past!'

He answered not, but cried his cry,
'St George for Marny!' cheerily;
And laid his hand upon her rein.
Alas! no man of all his train
Gave back that cheery cry again;
And, while for rage his thumb beat fast
Upon his sword-hilts, some one cast
About his neck a kerchief long,
And bound him.

             Then they went along
To Godmar; who said: 'Now, Jehane,
Your lover's life is on the wane
So fast, that, if this very hour
You yield not as my paramour,

He will not see the rain leave off –
Nay, keep your tongue from gibe and scoff,
Sir Robert, or I slay you now.'

She laid her hand upon her brow,
Then gazed upon the palm, as though
She thought her forehead bled, and – 'No.'
She said, and turned her head away,
As there were nothing else to say,
And everything were settled: red
Grew Godmar's face from chin to head:
'Jehane, on yonder hill there stands
My castle, guarding well my lands:
What hinders me from taking you,
And doing that I list to do
To your fair wilful body, while
Your knight lies dead?

                A wicked smile
Wrinkled her face, her lips grew thin,
A long way out she thrust her chin:
'You know that I should strangle you
While you were sleeping; or bite through
Your throat, by God's help – ah!' she said,
'Lord Jesus, pity your poor maid!
For in such wise they hem me in,
I cannot choose but sin and sin,
Whatever happens: yet I think
They could not make me eat or drink,
And so should I just reach my rest.'
'Nay, if you do not my behest,
O Jehane! though I love you well,'
Said Godmar, 'would I fail to tell
All that I know.' 'Foul lies,' she said.
'Eh? lies my Jehane? by God's head,
At Paris folks would deem them true!
Do you know, Jehane, they cry for you,
"Jehane the brown! Jehane the brown!
Give us Jehane to burn or drown!" –
Eh – gag me Robert! – sweet my friend,
This were indeed a piteous end
For those long fingers, and long feet,
And long neck, and smooth shoulders sweet;
An end that few men would forget
That saw it – So, an hour yet:
Consider, Jehane, which to take
Of life or death!'

                              So, scarce awake,
Dismounting, did she leave that place,
And totter some yards: with her face
Turned upward to the sky she lay,
Her head on a wet heap of hay,
And fell asleep: and while she slept,
And did not dream, the minutes crept
Round to the twelve again; but she,
Being waked at last, sighed quietly,
And strangely childlike came, and said:
'I will not.' Straightway Godmar's head,
As though it hung on strong wires, turned
Most sharply round, and his face burned.

For Robert – both his eyes were dry,
He could not weep, but gloomily
He seemed to watch the rain; yea, too,
His lips were firm; he tried once more
To touch her lips; she reached out, sore
And vain desire so tortured them,
The poor grey lips, and now the hem
Of his sleeve brushed them.

                              With a start
Up Godmar rose, thrust them apart;
From Robert's throat he loosed the bands
Of silk and mail; the empty hands
Held out, she stood and gazed, and saw,
The long bright blade without a flaw
Glide out from Godmar's sheath, his hand
In Robert's hair; she saw him bend
Back Robert's head; she saw him send
The thin steel down; the blow told well,
Right backward the knight Robert fell,
And moaned as dogs do, being half dead,
Unwitting, as I deem: so then
Godmar turned grinning to his men,
Who ran, some five or six, and beat
His head to pieces at their feet.

Then Godmar turned again and said:
'So, Jehane, the first fitte is read!
Take note, my lady, that your way
Lies backward to the Chatelet!'
She shook her head and gazed awhile
At her cold hands with a rueful smile,
As though this thing had made her mad.

This was the parting that they had
Beside the haystack in the floods.

Algernon Charles Swinburne

425   *A Forsaken Garden*

In a coign of the cliff between lowland and highland,
    At the sea-down's edge between windward and lee,
Walled round with rocks as an inland island,
    The ghost of a garden fronts the sea.
A girdle of brushwood and thorn encloses
    The steep square slope of the blossomless bed
Where the weeds that grew green from the graves of its roses
        Now lie dead.

The fields fall southward, abrupt and broken,
    To the low last edge of the long lone land.
If a step should sound or a word be spoken,
    Would a ghost not rise at the strange guest's hand?
So long have the grey bare walks lain guestless,
    Through branches and briars if a man make way,
He shall find no life but the sea-wind's, restless
        Night and day.

The dense hard passage is blind and stifled
    That crawls by a track none turn to climb
To the strait waste place that the years have rifled
    Of all but the thorns that are touched not of time.
The thorns he spares when the rose is taken;
    The rocks are left when he wastes the plain.
The wind that wanders, the weeds wind-shaken,
        These remain.

Not a flower to be pressed of the foot that falls not;
    As the heart of a dead man the seed-plots are dry;
From the thicket of thorns whence the nightingale calls not,
    Could she call, there were never a rose to reply.
Over the meadows that blossom and wither
    Rings but the note of a sea-bird's song;
Only the sun and the rain come hither
        All year long.

The sun burns sere and the rain dishevels
    One gaunt bleak blossom of scentless breath.
Only the wind here hovers and revels
    In a round where life seems barren as death.
Here there was laughing of old, there was weeping,
    Haply, of lovers none ever will know,
Whose eyes went seaward a hundred sleeping
        Years ago.

Heart handfast in heart as they stood, 'Look thither,'
   Did he whisper? 'look forth from the flowers to the sea;
For the foam-flowers endure when the rose-blossoms wither,
   And men that love lightly may die – but we?'
And the same wind sang and the same waves whitened,
   And or ever the garden's last petals were shed,
In the lips that had whispered, the eyes that had lightened,
    Love was dead.

Or they loved their life through, and then went whither?
   And were one to the end – but what end who knows?
Love deep as the sea as a rose must wither,
   As the rose-red seaweed that mocks the rose.
Shall the dead take thought for the dead to love them?
   What love was ever as deep as a grave?
They are loveless now as the grass above them
    Or the wave.

All are at one now, roses and lovers,
   Not known of the cliffs and the fields and the sea.
Not a breath of the time that has been hovers
   In the air now soft with a summer to be.
Not a breath shall there sweeten the seasons hereafter
   Of the flowers or the lovers that laugh now or weep,
When as they that are free now of weeping and laughter
    We shall sleep.

Here death may deal not again for ever;
   Here change may come not till all change end.
From the graves they have made they shall rise up never,
   Who have left nought living to ravage and rend.
Earth, stones, and thorns of the wild ground growing,
   While the sun and the rain live, these shall be;
Till a last wind's breath upon all these blowing
    Roll the sea.

Till the slow sea rise and the sheer cliff crumble,
   Till terrace and meadow the deep gulfs drink,
Till the strength of the waves of the high tides humble
   The fields that lessen, the rocks that shrink,
Here now in his triumph where all things falter,
   Stretched out on the spoils that his own hand spread,
As a god self-slain on his own strange altar,
    Death lies dead.

Thomas Hardy

426   *I Look into My Glass*

I look into my glass,
And view my wasting skin,
And say, 'Would God it came to pass
My heart had shrunk as thin!'

For then, I, undistrest
By hearts grown cold to me,
Could lonely wait my endless rest
With equanimity.

But Time, to make me grieve,
Part steals, lets part abide;
And shakes this fragile frame at eve
With throbbings of noontide.

427   *Drummer Hodge*

They throw in Drummer Hodge, to rest
    Uncoffined – just as found:
His landmark is a kopje-crest
    That breaks the veldt around;
And foreign constellations west
    Each night above his mound.

Young Hodge the Drummer never knew –
    Fresh from his Wessex home –
The meaning of the broad Karoo,
    The Bush, the dusty loam,
And why uprose to nightly view
    Strange stars amid the gloam.

Yet portion of that unknown plain
    Will Hodge for ever be;
His homely Northern breast and brain
    Grow to some Southern tree,
And strange-eyed constellations reign
    His stars eternally.

428   *The Self-Unseeing*

Here is the ancient floor,
Footworn and hollowed and thin,
Here was the former door
Where the dead feet walked in.

She sat here in her chair,
Smiling into the fire;
He who played stood there,
Bowing it higher and higher.

Childlike, I danced in a dream;
Blessings emblazoned that day;
Everything glowed with a gleam;
Yet we were looking away!

429   *Channel Firing*

That night your great guns, unawares,
Shook all our coffins as we lay,
And broke the chancel window-squares,
We thought it was the Judgment-day

And sat upright. While drearisome
Arose the howl of wakened hounds:
The mouse let fall the altar-crumb,
The worms drew back into the mounds,

The glebe cow drooled. Till God called, 'No;
It's gunnery practice out at sea
Just as before you went below;
The world is as it used to be:

All nations striving strong to make
Red war yet redder. Mad as hatters
They do no more for Christés sake
Than you who are helpless in such matters.

That this is not the judgment-hour
For some of them's a blessed thing,
For if it were they'd have to scour
Hell's floor for so much threatening. . . .

Ha, ha. It will be warmer when
I blow the trumpet (if indeed
I ever do; for you are men,
And rest eternal sorely need).'

So down we lay again. 'I wonder,
Will the world ever saner be,'
Said one, 'than when He sent us under
In our indifferent century!'

And many a skeleton shook his head.
'Instead of preaching forty year,'
My neighbour Parson Thirdly said,
'I wish I had stuck to pipes and beer.'

Again the guns disturbed the hour,
Roaring their readiness to avenge,
As far inland as Stourton Tower,
And Camelot, and starlit Stonehenge.

430   *The Going*

Why did you give no hint that night
That quickly after the morrow's dawn,
And calmly, as if indifferent quite,
You would close your term here, up and be gone
    Where I could not follow
    With wing of swallow
To gain one glimpse of you ever anon!

    Never to bid good-bye,
    Or lip me the softest call,
Or utter a wish for a word, while I
Saw morning harden upon the wall,
    Unmoved, unknowing
    That your great going
Had place that moment, and altered all.

Why do you make me leave the house
And think for a breath it is you I see
At the end of the alley of bending boughs
Where so often at dusk you used to be;
    Till in darkening dankness
    The yawning blankness
Of the perspective sickens me!

    You were she who abode
    By those red-veined rocks far West,
You were the swan-necked one who rode
Along the beetling Beeny Crest,
    And, reining nigh me,
    Would muse and eye me,
While Life unrolled us its very best.

Why, then, latterly did we not speak,
Did we not think of those days long dead,
And ere your vanishing strive to seek
That time's renewal? We might have said,
   'In this bright spring weather
   We'll visit together
Those places that once we visited.'

   Well, well! All's past amend,
   Unchangeable. It must go.
I seem but a dead man held on end
To sink down soon. . . . O you could not know
   That such swift fleeing
   No soul foreseeing –
Not even I – would undo me so!

431   *After a Journey*

Hereto I come to view a voiceless ghost;
   Whither, O whither will its whim now draw me?
Up the cliff, down, till I'm lonely, lost,
   And the unseen waters' ejaculations awe me.
Where you will next be there's no knowing,
   Facing round about me everywhere,
     With your nut-coloured hair,
And gray eyes, and rose-flush coming and going.

Yes: I have re-entered your olden haunts at last;
   Through the years, through the dead scenes I have tracked you;
What have you now found to say of our past –
   Scanned across the dark space wherein I have lacked you?
Summer gave us sweets, but autumn wrought division?
   Things were not lastly as firstly well
     With us twain, you tell?
But all's closed now, despite Time's derision.

I see what you are doing: you are leading me on
   To the spots we knew when we haunted here together,
The waterfall, above which the mist-bow shone
   At the then fair hour in the then fair weather,
And the cave just under, with a voice still so hollow
   That it seems to call out to me from forty years ago,
     When you were all aglow,
And not the thin ghost that I now frailly follow!

Ignorant of what there is flitting here to see,
  The waked birds preen and the seals flop lazily;
Soon you will have, Dear, to vanish from me,
  For the stars close their shutters and the dawn whitens hazily.
Trust me, I mind not, though Life lours,
  The bringing me here; nay, bring me here again!
    I am just the same as when
Our days were a joy, and our paths through flowers.

Pentargan Bay

432   *At Castle Boterel*

As I drive to the junction of lane and highway,
  And the drizzle bedrenches the waggonette,
I look behind at the fading byway,
  And see on its slope, now glistening wet,
      Distinctly yet

Myself and a girlish form benighted
  In dry March weather. We climb the road
Beside a chaise. We had just alighted
  To ease the sturdy pony's load
      When he sighed and slowed.

What we did as we climbed, and what we talked of
  Matters not much, nor to what it led, –
Something that life will not be balked of
  Without rude reason till hope is dead,
      And feeling fled.

It filled but a minute. But was there ever
  A time of such quality, since or before,
In that hill's story? To one mind never,
  Though it has been climbed, foot-swift, foot-sore,
      By thousands more.

Primaeval rocks form the road's steep border,
  And much have they faced there, first and last,
Of the transitory in Earth's long order;
  But what they record in colour and cast
      Is – that we two passed.

And to me, though Time's unflinching rigour,
  In mindless rote, has ruled from sight
The substance now, one phantom figure
  Remains on the slope, as when that night
      Saw us alight.

I look and see it there, shrinking, shrinking,
   I look back at it amid the rain
For the very last time; for my sand is sinking,
   And I shall traverse old love's domain
     Never again.

433   *Heredity*

    I am the family face;
    Flesh perishes, I live on,
    Projecting trait and trace
    Through time to times anon,
    And leaping from place to place
    Over oblivion.

    The years-heired feature that can
    In curve and voice and eye
    Despise the human span
    Of durance – that is I;
    The eternal thing in man,
    That heeds no call to die.

434   *The Oxen*

Christmas Eve, and twelve of the clock.
   'Now they are all on their knees,'
An elder said as we sat in a flock
   By the embers in hearthside ease.

We pictured the meek mild creatures where
   They dwelt in their strawy pen,
Nor did it occur to one of us there
   To doubt they were kneeling then.

So fair a fancy few would weave
   In these years! Yet, I feel,
If someone said on Christmas Eve,
   'Come; see the oxen kneel

In the lonely barton by yonder coomb
   Our childhood used to know,'
I should go with him in the gloom,
   Hoping it might be so.

435   *In Time of 'The Breaking of Nations'*

> Only a man harrowing clods
>   In a slow silent walk
> With an old horse that stumbles and nods
>   Half asleep as they stalk.
>
> Only thin smoke without flame
>   From the heaps of couch-grass;
> Yet this will go onward the same
>   Though Dynasties pass.
>
> Yonder a maid and her wight
>   Come whispering by:
> War's annals will cloud into night
>   Ere their story die.

436   *Afterwards*

When the Present has latched its postern behind my tremulous stay,
    And the May month flaps its glad green leaves like wings,
Delicate-filmed as new-spun silk, will the neighbours say,
    'He was a man who used to notice such things'?

If it be in the dusk when, like an eyelid's soundless blink,
    The dewfall-hawk comes crossing the shades to alight
Upon the wind-warped upland thorn, a gazer may think,
    'To him this must have been a familiar sight.'

If I pass during some nocturnal blackness, mothy and warm,
    When the hedgehog travels furtively over the lawn,
One may say, 'He strove that such innocent creatures should come to
        no harm,
    But he could do little for them; and now he is gone.'

If, when hearing that I have been stilled at last, they stand at
        the door,
    Watching the full-starred heavens that winter sees,
Will this thought rise on those who will meet my face no more,
    'He was one who had an eye for such mysteries'?

And will any say when my bell of quittance is heard in the gloom,
    And a crossing breeze cuts a pause in its outrollings,
Till they rise again, as they were a new bell's boom,
    'He hears it not now, but used to notice such things'?

Gerard Manley Hopkins

437   *Duns Scotus's Oxford*

Towery city and branchy between towers;
Cuckoo-echoing, bell-swarmèd, lark-charmèd, rook-racked,
    river-rounded;
The dapple-eared lily below thee; that country and town did
Once encounter in, here coped and poisèd powers;

Thou hast a base and brickish skirt there, sours
That neighbour-nature thy grey beauty is grounded
Best in; graceless growth, thou hast confounded
Rural rural keeping – folk, flocks, and flowers.

Yet ah! this air I gather and I release
He lived on; these weeds and waters, these walls are what
He haunted who of all men most sways my spirits to peace;

Of realty the rarest-veinèd unraveller; a not
Rivalled insight, be rival Italy or Greece;
Who fired France for Mary without spot.

438   *Andromeda*

Now Time's Andromeda on this rock rude,
With not her either beauty's equal or
Her injury's, looks off by both horns of shore,
Her flower, her piece of being, doomed dragon's food.
    Time past she has been attempted and pursued
By many blows and banes; but now hears roar
A wilder beast from West than all were, more
Rife in her wrongs, more lawless, and more lewd.

    Her Perseus linger and leave her tó her extremes? –
Pillowy air he treads a time and hangs
His thoughts on her, forsaken that she seems,
    All while her patience, morselled into pangs,
Mounts, then to alight disarming, no one dreams,
With Gorgon's gear and barebill, thongs and fangs.

439   *Felix Randal*

Felix Randal the farrier, O he is dead then? my duty all ended,
Who have watched his mould of man, big-boned and hardy-handsome
Pining, pining, till time when reason rambled in it and some
Fatal four disorders, fleshed there, all contended?

Sickness broke him. Impatient he cursed at first, but mended
Being anointed and all; though a heavenlier heart began some
Months earlier, since I had our sweet reprieve and ransom
Tendered to him. Ah well, God rest him all road ever he offended!

This seeing the sick endears them to us, us too it endears.
My tongue had taught thee comfort, touch had quenched thy tears,
Thy tears that touched my heart, child, Felix, poor Felix Randal;

How far from then forethought of, all thy more boisterous years,
When thou at the random grim forge, powerful amidst peers,
Didst fettle for the great grey drayhorse his bright and battering sandal!

440   *Spring and Fall:*

                    to a young child

                Márgarét, are you gríeving
                Over Goldengrove unleaving?
                Leáves, líke the things of man, you
                With your fresh thoughts care for, can you?
                Áh! ás the heart grows older
                It will come to such sights colder
                By and by, nor spare a sigh
                Though worlds of wanwood leafmeal lie;
                And yet you wíll weep and know why,
                Now no matter, child, the name:
                Sórrow's spríngs áre the same.
                Nor mouth had, no nor mind, expressed
                What heart heard of, ghost guessed:
                It ís the blight man was born for,
                It is Margaret you mourn for.

441   As kingfishers catch fire, dragonflies dráw fláme;
                As tumbled over rim in roundy wells
                Stones ring; like each tucked string tells, each hung bell's
                Bow swung finds tongue to fling out broad its name;

Each mortal thing does one thing and the same:
Deals out that being indoors each one dwells;
Selves — goes itself; *myself* it speaks and spells,
Crying *Whát I dó is me: for that I came.*

I say móre: the just man justices;
Kéeps gráce: thát keeps all his goings graces;
Acts in God's eye what in God's eye he is —
Chríst — for Christ plays in ten thousand places,
Lovely in limbs, and lovely in eyes not his
To the Father through the features of men's faces.

442

In honour of
St Alphonsus Rodriguez
Laybrother of the Society of Jesus

Honour is flashed off exploit, so we say;
And those strokes once that gashed flesh or galled shield
Should tongue that time now, trumpet now that field,
And, on the fighter, forge his glorious day.
On Christ they do and on the martyr may;
But be the war within, the brand we wield
Unseen, the heroic breast not outward-steeled,
Earth hears no hurtle then from fiercest fray.

Yet God (that hews mountain and continent,
Earth, all, out; who, with trickling increment,
Veins violets and tall trees makes more and more)
Could crowd career with conquest while there went
Those years and years by of world without event
That in Majorca Alfonso watched the door.

443 *Justus quidem tu es, Domine, si disputem tecum: verumtamen
justa loquar ad te: Quare via impiorum prosperatur? etc.*

Thou art indeed just, Lord, if I contend
With thee; but, sir, so what I plead is just.
Why do sinners' ways prosper? and why must
Disappointment all I endeavour end?
Wert thou my enemy, O thou my friend,
How wouldst thou worse, I wonder, than thou dost
Defeat, thwart me? Oh, the sots and thralls of lust
Do in spare hours more thrive than I that spend,

Sir, life upon thy cause. See, banks and brakes
Now, leavèd how thick! lacèd they are again
With fretty chervil, look, and fresh wind shakes
Them; birds build – but not I build; no, but strain,
Time's eunuch, and not breed one work that wakes.
Mine, O thou lord of life, send my roots rain.

Robert Bridges

444

   I love all beauteous things,
     I seek and adore them;
   God hath no better praise,
   And man in his hasty days
     Is honoured for them.

   I too will something make
     And joy in the making;
   Altho' to-morrow it seem
   Like the empty words of a dream
     Remembered on waking.

445 *Poor Poll*

I saw it all, Polly, how when you had call'd for sop
and your good friend the cook came & fill'd up your pan
you yerk'd it out deftly by beakfuls scattering it
away far as you might upon the sunny lawn
then summon'd with loud cry the little garden birds
to take their feast. Quickly came they flustering around
Ruddock & Merle & Finch squabbling among themselves
nor gave you thanks nor heed while you sat silently
watching, and I beside you in perplexity
lost in the maze of all mystery and all knowledge
felt how deep lieth the fount of man's benevolence
if a bird can share it & take pleasure in it.
  If you, my bird, I thought, had a philosophy
it might be a sounder scheme than what our moralists
propound: because thou, Poll, livest in the darkness
which human Reason searching from outside would pierce,
but, being of so feeble a candle-power, can only
show up to view the cloud that it illuminates.

Thus reason'd I: then marvell'd how you can adapt
your wild bird-mood to endure your tame environment
the domesticities of English household life
and your small brass-wire cabin, who sh^{dst} live on wing
harrying the tropical branch-flowering wilderness:
Yet Nature gave you a gift of easy mimicry
whereby you have come to win uncanny sympathies
and morsell'd utterance of our Germanic talk
as schoolmasters in Greek will flaunt their hackney'd tags
φωνᾶντα συνετοῖσιν and κτῆμα ἐς ἀεί,
ἡ γλῶσσ' ὁμώμοχ', ἡ δὲ φρὴν ἀνώμοτος
tho' you with a better ear copy ús more perfectly
nor without connotation as when you call'd for sop
all with that stumpy wooden tongue & vicious beak
that dry whistling shrieking tearing cutting pincer
now eagerly subservient to your cautious claws
exploring all varieties of attitude
in irrepressible blind groping for escape
– a very figure & image of man's soul on earth
the almighty cosmic Will fidgeting in a trap –
in your quenchless unknown desire for the unknown life
of which some homely British sailor robb'd you, alas!
'Tis all that doth your silly thoughts so busy keep
the while you sit moping like Patience on a perch
— *Wie viele Tag' und Nächte bist du geblieben!*
La possa delle gambe posta in tregue –
the impeccable spruceness of your grey-feather'd pôll
a model in hairdressing for the dandiest old Duke
enough to qualify you for the House of Lords
or the Athenaeum Club, to poke among the nobs
great intellectual nobs and literary nobs
scientific nobs and Bishops *ex officio*:
nor lack you simulation of profoundest wisdom
such as men's features oft acquire in very old age
by mere cooling of passion & decay of muscle
by faint renunciation even of untold regrets;
who seeing themselves a picture of that wh: man should-be
learn almost what it were to be what they are-not.
But you can never have cherish'd a determined hope
consciously to renounce or lose it, you will live
your threescore years & ten idle and puzzle-headed
as any mumping monk in his unfurnish'd cell
in peace that, poor Polly, passeth Understanding –
merely because you lack what we men understand
by Understanding. Well! well! that's the difference
C'est la seule différence, mais c'est important.
Ah! your pale sedentary life! but would you change?
exchange it for one crowded hour of glorious life,

one blind furious tussle with a madden'd monkey
who would throttle you and throw your crude fragments away
shreds unintelligible of an unmeaning act
dans la profonde horreur de l'éternelle nuit?
Why ask? You cannot know. 'Twas by no choice of yours
that you mischanged for monkeys' man's society,
'twas that British sailor drove you from Paradise –
Εἴθ' ὤφελ' Ἀργοῦς μὴ διαπτάσθαι σκάφος!
I'd hold embargoes on such a ghastly traffic.

    I am writing verses to you & grieve that you shd be
absolument incapable de les comprendre,
Tu, Polle, nescis ista nec potes scire: –
Alas! Iambic, scazon and alexandrine,
spondee or choriamb, all is alike to you –
my well-continued fanciful experiment
wherein so many strange verses amalgamate
on the secure bedrock of Milton's prosody:
not but that when I speak you will incline an ear
in critical attention lest by chánce I míght
póssibly say sómething that was worth repeating:
I am adding (do you think?) pages to literature
that gouty excrement of human intellect
accumulating slowly & everlastingly
depositing, like guano on the Peruvian shore,
to be perhaps exhumed in some remotest age
(*piis secunda, vate me, detur fuga*)
to fertilize the scanty dwarf'd intelligence
of a new race of beings the unhallow'd offspring
of them who shall have quite dismember'd & destroy'd
our temple of Christian faith & fair Hellenic art
just as that monkey would, poor Polly, have done for you.

446   *London Snow*

    When men were all asleep the snow came flying,
  In large white flakes falling on the city brown,
Stealthily and perpetually settling and loosely lying,
    Hushing the latest traffic of the drowsy town;
Deadening, muffling, stifling its murmurs failing;
Lazily and incessantly floating down and down:
    Silently sifting and veiling road, roof and railing;
Hiding difference, making unevenness even,
  Into angles and crevices softly drifting and sailing.
    All night it fell, and when full inches seven
It lay in the depth of its uncompacted lightness,
The clouds blew off from a high and frosty heaven;

And all woke earlier for the unaccustomed brightness
Of the winter dawning, the strange unheavenly glare:
The eye marvelled – marvelled at the dazzling whiteness;
   The ear hearkened to the stillness of the solemn air;
No sound of wheel rumbling nor of foot falling,
And the busy morning cries came thin and spare.
   Then boys I heard, as they went to school, calling,
They gathered up the crystal manna to freeze
Their tongues with tasting, their hands with snowballing;
   Or rioted in a drift, plunging up to the knees;
Or peering up from under the white-mossed wonder,
'O look at the trees!' they cried, 'O look at the trees!'
   With lessened load a few carts creak and blunder,
Following along the white deserted way,
A country company long dispersed asunder:
   When now already the sun, in pale display
Standing by Paul's high dome, spread forth below
His sparkling beams, and awoke the stir of the day.
   For now doors open, and war is waged with the snow;
And trains of sombre men, past tale of number,
Tread long brown paths, as toward their toil they go:
   But even for them awhile no cares encumber
Their minds diverted; the daily word is unspoken,
The daily thoughts of labour and sorrow slumber
At the sight of the beauty that greets them, for the charm
   they have broken.

447   *On a Dead Child*

Perfect little body, without fault or stain on thee,
   With promise of strength and manhood full and fair!
      Though cold and stark and bare,
The bloom and the charm of life doth awhile remain on thee.

Thy mother's treasure wert thou; – alas! no longer
   To visit her heart with wondrous joy; to be
      Thy father's pride; – ah, he
Must gather his faith together, and his strength make stronger.

To me, as I move thee now in the last duty,
   Dost thou with a turn or gesture anon respond;
      Startling my fancy fond
With a chance attitude of the head, a freak of beauty.

Thy hand clasps, as 'twas wont, my finger, and holds it:
  But the grasp is the clasp of Death, heartbreaking and stiff;
    Yet feels to my hand as if
'Twas still thy will, thy pleasure and trust that enfolds it.

So I lay thee there, thy sunken eyelids closing, –
  Go lie thou there in thy coffin, thy last little bed! –
    Propping thy wise, sad head,
Thy firm, pale hands across thy chest disposing.

So quiet! doth the change content thee? – Death, whither hath he taken
    thee?
  To a world, do I think, that rights the disaster of this?
    The vision of which I miss,
Who weep for the body, and wish but to warm thee and awaken thee?

Ah! little at best can all our hopes avail us
  To lift this sorrow, or cheer us, when in the dark,
    Unwilling, alone we embark,
And the things we have seen and have known and have heard of, fail us.

448   From *The Testament of Beauty*

The sky's unresting cloudland, that with varying play
sifteth the sunlight thru' its figured shades, that now
stand in massiv range, cumulated stupendous
mountainous snowbillowy up-piled in dazzling sheen,
Now like sailing ships on a calm ocean drifting,
Now scatter'd wispy waifs, that neath the eager blaze
disperse in air; Or now parcelling the icy inane
highspredd in fine diaper of silver and mother-of-pearl
freaking the intense azure; Now scurrying close o'erhead,
wild ink-hued random racers that fling sheeted rain
gustily, and with garish bows laughing o'erarch the land:
Or, if the spirit of storm be abroad, huge molten glooms
mount on the horizon stealthily, and gathering as they climb
deep-freighted with live lightning, thunder and drenching flood
rebuff the winds, and with black-purpling terror impend
til they be driven away, when grave Night peacefully
clearing her heav'nly rondure of its turbid veils
laỳeth bare the playthings of Creation's babyhood;
and the immortal fireballs of her uttermost space
twinkle like friendly rushlights on the countryside.

Them soon the jealous Day o'errideth to display
Earth's green robe, which the sun fostereth for shelter and shower
The dance of young trees that in a wild birch-spinney
toss to and fro the cluster of their flickering crests,
as rye curtseying in array to the breeze of May;
The ancestral trunks that mightily in the forest choirs
rear stedfast colonnade, or imperceptibly
    sway in tall pinewoods to their whispering spires;
The woodland's alternating hues, the vaporous bloom
of the first blushings and tender flushings of spring;
The slumbrous foliage of high midsummer's wealth;
Rich Autumn's golden quittance, to the bankruptcy
of the black shapely skeletons standing in snow:
Or, in gay months of swelling pomp, the luxury
of leisur'd gardens teeming with affection'd thought;
the heartfelt secrecy of rustic nooks, and valleys
vocal with angelic rilling of rocky streams,
by rambling country-lanes, with hazel and thorn embower'd
woodbine, bryony and wild roses; the landscape lure
of rural England, that held glory in native art
untill our painters took their new fashion from France.

    This spiritual elation and response to Nature
is Man's generic mark. A wolf that all his life
had hunted after nightfall neath the starlit skies
should he suddenly attain the first inklings of thought
would feel this Wonder: and by some kindred stir of mind
the ruminants can plead approach – the look of it
is born already of fear and gentleness in the eyes
of the wild antelope, and hence by fable assign'd
to the unseen unicorn reposed in burning lair –
a symbol of majestic sadness and lonely pride:
but the true intellectual wonder is first reveal'd
in children and savages and 'tis there the footing
of all our temples and of all science and art.
    Thus Rafaël once venturing to show God in Man
gave a child's eyes of wonder to the baby Christ;
and his Mantuan brother coud he hav seen that picture
would more truly hav foreshadow'd the incarnation of God.
'Tis the divinest childhood's incomparable bloom,
the loss whereof leaveth the man's face shabby and dull.

Digby Mackworth Dolben

449   *He Would Have His Lady Sing*

Sing me the men ere this
Who, to the gate that is
A cloven pearl uprapt,
The big white bars between
With dying eyes have seen
The sea of jasper, lapt
About with crystal sheen;

And all the far pleasance
Where linkèd Angels dance,
With scarlet wings that fall
Magnifical, or spread
Most sweetly over-head,
In fashion musical,
Of cadenced lutes instead.

Sing me the town they saw
Withouten fleck or flaw,
Aflame, more fine than glass
Of fair Abbayes the boast,
More glad than wax of cost
Doth make at Candlemas
The Lifting of the Host:

Where many Knights and Dames,
With new and wondrous names,
One great Laudaté Psalm
Go singing down the street; –
Tis peace upon their feet,
In hand 'tis pilgrim palm
Of Goddes Land so sweet: –

Where Mother Mary walks
In silver lily stalks,
Star-tirèd, moon-bedight;
Where Cecily is seen,
With Dorothy in green,
And Magdalen all white,
The maidens of the Queen.

Sing on – the Steps untrod,
The Temple that is God,
Where incense doth ascend,
Where mount the cries and tears
Of all the dolorous years,
With moan that ladies send
Of durance and sore fears: –

And Him who sitteth there,
The Christ of purple hair,
And great eyes deep with ruth,
Who is of all things fair
That shall be, or that were,
The sum, and very truth.
Then add a little prayer,

That since all these be so,
Our Liege, who doth us know,
Would fend from Sathanas,
And bring us, of His grace,
To that His joyous place:
So we the Doom may pass,
And see Him in the Face.

Robert Louis Stevenson

450   *To the Muse*

Resign the rhapsody, the dream,
　　To men of larger reach;
Be ours the quest of a plain theme,
　　The piety of speech.

As monkish scribes from morning break
　　Toiled till the close of light,
Nor thought a day too long to make
　　One line or letter bright:

We also with an ardent mind,
　　Time, wealth, and fame forgot,
Our glory in our patience find
　　And skim, and skim the pot:

Till last, when round the house we hear
　　The evensong of birds,
One corner of blue heaven appear
　　In our clear well of words.

Leave, leave it then, muse of my heart!
　　Sans finish and sans frame,
Leave unadorned by needless art
　　The picture as it came.

451   *The Land of Counterpane*

When I was sick and lay a-bed,
I had two pillows at my head,
And all my toys beside me lay
To keep me happy all the day.

And sometimes for an hour or so
I watched my leaden soldiers go,
With different uniforms and drills,
Among the bed-clothes, through the hills;

And sometimes sent my ships in fleets
All up and down among the sheets;
Or brought my trees and houses out,
And planted cities all about.

I was the giant great and still
That sits upon the pillow-hill,
And sees before him, dale and plain,
The pleasant land of counterpane.

John Davidson

452   *Thirty Bob a Week*

I couldn't touch a stop and turn a screw,
    And set the blooming world a-work for me,
Like such as cut their teeth – I hope, like you –
    On the handle of a skeleton gold key;
I cut mine on a leek, which I eat it every week:
    I'm a clerk at thirty bob as you can see.

But I don't allow it's luck and all a toss;
    There's no such thing as being starred and crossed;
It's just the power of some to be a boss,
    And the bally power of others to be bossed:
I face the music, sir; you bet I ain't a cur;
    Strike me lucky if I don't believe I'm lost!

For like a mole I journey in the dark,
    A-travelling along the underground
From my Pillar'd Halls and broad Suburbean Park,
    To come the daily dull official round;
And home again at night with my pipe all alight,
    A-scheming how to count ten bob a pound.

And it's often very cold and very wet,
  And my missis stitches towels for a hunks;
And the Pillar'd Halls is half of it to let –
  Three rooms about the size of travelling trunks.
And we cough, my wife and I, to dislocate a sigh,
  When the noisy little kids are in their bunks.

But you never hear her do a growl or whine,
  For she's made of flint and roses, very odd;
And I've got to cut my meaning rather fine,
  Or I'd blubber, for I'm made of greens and sod:
So p'r'aps we are in Hell for all that I can tell,
  And lost and damn'd and served up hot to God.

I ain't blaspheming, Mr Silver-tongue;
  I'm saying things a bit beyond your art;
Of all the rummy starts you ever sprung,
  Thirty bob a week's the rummiest start!
With your science and your books and your the'ries
      about spooks,
  Did you ever hear of looking in your heart?

I didn't mean your pocket, Mr, no:
  I mean that having children and a wife,
With thirty bob on which to come and go,
  Isn't dancing to the tabor and the fife:
When it doesn't make you drink, by Heaven! it makes
      you think
  And notice curious items about life.

I step into my heart and there I meet
  A god-almighty devil singing small,
Who would like to shout and whistle in the street,
  And squelch the passers flat against the wall;
If the whole world was a cake he had the power to take,
  He would take it, ask for more, and eat them all.

And I meet a sort of simpleton beside,
  The kind that life is always giving beans;
With thirty bob a week to keep a bride
  He fell in love and married in his teens:
At thirty bob he stuck; but he knows it isn't luck:
  He knows the seas are deeper than tureens.

And the god-almighty devil and the fool
  That meet me in the High Street on the strike,
When I walk about my heart a-gathering wool,
  Are my good and evil angels if you like.
And both of them together in every kind of weather
  Ride me like a double-seated bike.

That's rough a bit and needs its meaning curled.
   But I have a high old hot un in my mind –
A most engrugious notion of the world,
   That leaves your lightning 'rithmetic behind:
I give it at a glance when I say 'There ain't no chance,
   Nor nothing of the lucky-lottery kind.'

And it's this way that I make it out to be:
   No fathers, mothers, countries, climates – none;
Not Adam was responsible for me,
   Nor society, nor systems, nary one:
A little sleeping seed, I woke – I did, indeed –
   A million years before the blooming sun.

I woke because I thought the time had come;
   Beyond my will there was no other cause;
And everywhere I found myself at home,
   Because I chose to be the thing I was;
And in whatever shape of mollusc or of ape
   I always went according to the laws.

I was the love that chose my mother out;
   I joined two lives and from the union burst;
My weakness and my strength without a doubt
   Are mine alone for ever from the first:
It's just the very same with a difference in the name
   As 'Thy will be done.' You say it if you durst!

They say it daily up and down the land
   As easy as you take a drink, it's true;
But the difficultest go to understand,
   And the difficultest job a man can do,
Is to come it brave and meek with thirty bob a week,
   And feel that that's the proper thing for you.

It's a naked child against a hungry wolf;
   It's playing bowls upon a splitting wreck;
It's walking on a string across a gulf
   With millstones fore-and-aft about your neck;
But the thing is daily done by many and many a one;
   And we fall, face forward, fighting, on the deck.

A. E. Housman

453

    Into my heart an air that kills
      From yon far country blows:
    What are those blue remembered hills,
      What spires, what farms are those?

    That is the land of lost content,
      I see it shining plain,
    The happy highways where I went
      And cannot come again.

454

The stars have not dealt me the worst they could do:
My pleasures are plenty, my troubles are two.
But oh, my two troubles they reave me of rest,
The brains in my head and the heart in my breast.

Oh grant me the ease that is granted so free,
The birthright of multitudes, give it to me,
That relish their victuals and rest on their bed
With flint in the bosom and guts in the head.

455

Easter Hymn

    If in that Syrian garden, ages slain,
    You sleep, and know not you are dead in vain,
    Nor even in dreams behold how dark and bright
    Ascends in smoke and fire by day and night
    The hate you died to quench and could but fan,
    Sleep well and see no morning, son of man.

    But if, the grave rent and the stone rolled by,
    At the right hand of majesty on high
    You sit, and sitting so remember yet
    Your tears, your agony and bloody sweat,
    Your cross and passion and the life you gave,
    Bow hither out of heaven and see and save.

Arthur Symons

456   *White Heliotrope*

The feverish room and that white bed,
The tumbled skirts upon a chair,
The novel flung half-open, where
Hat, hair-pins, puffs, and paints, are spread;

The mirror that has sucked your face
Into its secret deep of deeps,
And there mysteriously keeps
Forgotten memories of grace;

And you, half dressed and half awake,
Your slant eyes strangely watching me,
And I, who watch you drowsily,
With eyes that, having slept not, ache;

This (need one dread? nay, dare one hope?)
Will rise, a ghost of memory, if
Ever again my handkerchief
Is scented with White Heliotrope.

Rudyard Kipling

457   *Tommy*

I went into a public-'ouse to get a pint o' beer,
The publican 'e up an' sez, 'We serve no red-coats here.'
The girls be'ind the bar they laughed an' giggled fit to die,
I outs into the street again an' to myself sez I:
    O it's Tommy this, an' Tommy that, an' 'Tommy, go away';
    But it's 'Thank you, Mister Atkins,' when the band begins to play —
    The band begins to play, my boys, the band begins to play,
    O it's 'Thank you, Mister Atkins,' when the band begins to play.

I went into a theatre as sober as could be,
They gave a drunk civilian room, but 'adn't none for me;
They sent me to the gallery or round the music-'alls,
But when it comes to fightin', Lord! they'll shove me in the stalls!
    For it's Tommy this, an' Tommy that, an' 'Tommy, wait outside';
    But it's 'Special train for Atkins' when the trooper's on the tide —
    The troopship's on the tide, my boys, the troopship's on the tide,
    O it's 'Special train for Atkins' when the trooper's on the tide.

Yes, makin' mock o' uniforms that guard you while you sleep
Is cheaper than them uniforms, an' they're starvation cheap;
An' hustlin' drunken soldiers when they're goin' large a bit
Is five times better business than paradin' in full kit.
    Then it's Tommy this, an' Tommy that, an' 'Tommy, 'ow's yer
       soul?'
    But it's 'Thin red line of 'eroes' when the drums begin to roll –
    The drums begin to roll, my boys, the drums begin to roll,
    O it's 'Thin red line of 'eroes' when the drums begin to roll.

We aren't no thin red 'eroes, nor we aren't no blackguards too,
But single men in barricks, most remarkable like you;
An' if sometimes our conduck isn't all your fancy paints,
Why, single men in barricks don't grow into plaster saints;
    While it's Tommy this, an' Tommy that, an' 'Tommy, fall be'ind,'
    But it's 'Please to walk in front, sir,' when there's trouble in the
      wind –
    There's trouble in the wind, my boys, there's trouble in the wind,
    O it's 'Please to walk in front, sir,' when there's trouble in the
      wind.

You talk o' better food for us, an' schools, an' fires, an' all:
We'll wait for extry rations if you treat us rational.
Don't mess about the cook-room slops, but prove it to our face
The Widow's Uniform is not the soldier-man's disgrace.
    For it's Tommy this, an' Tommy that, an' 'Chuck him out, the
      brute!'
    But it's 'Saviour of 'is country' when the guns begin to shoot;
    An' it's Tommy this, an' Tommy that, an' anything you please;
    An' Tommy ain't a bloomin' fool – you bet that Tommy sees!

458   *A St Helena Lullaby*

('A Priest in spite of Himself.' *Rewards and Fairies*)

'How far is St Helena from a little child at play?'
What makes you want to wander there with all the world between?
Oh, Mother, call your son again or else he'll run away.
(*No one thinks of winter when the grass is green!*)

'How far is St Helena from a fight in Paris Street?'
I haven't time to answer now – the men are falling fast.
The guns begin to thunder, and the drums begin to beat.
(*If you take the first step, you will take the last!*)

'How far is St Helena from the field of Austerlitz?'
You couldn't hear me if I told – so loud the cannon roar.
But not so far for people who are living by their wits.
(*'Gay go up' means 'Gay go down' the wide world o'er!*)

'How far is St Helena from an Emperor of France?'
I cannot see – I cannot tell – the Crowns they dazzle so.
The Kings sit down to dinner, and the Queens stand up to dance.
(*After open weather you may look for snow!*)

'How far is St Helena from the Capes of Trafalgar?'
A longish way – a longish way – with ten year more to run.
It's South across the water underneath a falling star.
(*What you cannot finish you must leave undone!*)

'How far is St Helena from the Beresina ice?'
An ill way – a chill way – the ice begins to crack.
But not so far for gentlemen who never took advice.
(*When you can't go forward you must e'en come back!*)

'How far is St Helena from the field of Waterloo?'
A near way – a clear way – the ship will take you soon.
A pleasant place for gentlemen with little left to do.
(*Morning never tries you till the afternoon!*)

'How far from St Helena to the Gate of Heaven's Grace?'
That no one knows – that no one knows – and no one ever will.
But fold your hands across your heart and cover up your face,
And after all your trapesings, child, lie still!

W. B. Yeats

459   *In Memory of Major Robert Gregory*

Now that we're almost settled in our house
I'll name the friends that cannot sup with us
Beside a fire of turf in th' ancient tower,
And having talked to some late hour
Climb up the narrow winding stair to bed:
Discoverers of forgotten truth
Or mere companions of my youth,
All, all are in my thoughts to-night being dead.

Always we'd have the new friend meet the old
And we are hurt if either friend seem cold,
And there is salt to lengthen out the smart
In the affections of our heart,

And quarrels are blown up upon that head;
But not a friend that I would bring
This night can set us quarrelling,
For all that come into my mind are dead.

Lionel Johnson comes the first to mind,
That loved his learning better than mankind,
Though courteous to the worst; much falling he
Brooded upon sanctity
Till all his Greek and Latin learning seemed
A long blast upon the horn that brought
A little nearer to his thought
A measureless consummation that he dreamed.

And that enquiring man John Synge comes next,
That dying chose the living world for text
And never could have rested in the tomb
But that, long travelling, he had come
Towards nightfall upon certain set apart
In a most desolate stony place,
Towards nightfall upon a race
Passionate and simple like his heart.

And then I think of old George Pollexfen,
In muscular youth well known to Mayo men
For horsemanship at meets or at racecourses,
That could have shown how pure-bred horses
And solid men, for all their passion, live
But as the outrageous stars incline
By opposition, square and trine;
Having grown sluggish and contemplative.

They were my close companions many a year,
A portion of my mind and life, as it were,
And now their breathless faces seem to look
Out of some old picture-book;
I am accustomed to their lack of breath,
But not that my dear friend's dear son,
Our Sidney and our perfect man,
Could share in that discourtesy of death.

For all things the delighted eye now sees
Were loved by him: the old storm-broken trees
That cast their shadows upon road and bridge;
The tower set on the stream's edge;
The ford where drinking cattle make a stir
Nightly, and startled by that sound
The water-hen must change her ground;
He might have been your heartiest welcomer.

When with the Galway foxhounds he would ride
From Castle Taylor to the Roxborough side
Or Esserkelly plain, few kept his pace;
At Mooneen he had leaped a place
So perilous that half the astonished meet
Had shut their eyes; and where was it
He rode a race without a bit?
And yet his mind outran the horses' feet.

We dreamed that a great painter had been born
To cold Clare rock and Galway rock and thorn,
To that stern colour and that delicate line
That are our secret discipline
Wherein the gazing heart doubles her might.
Soldier, scholar, horseman, he,
And yet he had the intensity
To have published all to be a world's delight.

What other could so well have counselled us
In all lovely intricacies of a house
As he that practised or that understood
All work in metal or in wood,
In moulded plaster or in carven stone?
Soldier, scholar, horseman, he,
And all he did done perfectly
As though he had but that one trade alone.

Some burn damp faggots, others may consume
The entire combustible world in one small room
As though dried straw, and if we turn about
The bare chimney is gone black out
Because the work had finished in that flare.
Soldier, scholar, horseman, he,
As 'twere all life's epitome.
What made us dream that he could comb grey hair?

I had thought, seeing how bitter is that wind
That shakes the shutter, to have brought to mind
All those that manhood tried, or childhood loved
Or boyish intellect approved,
With some appropriate commentary on each;
Until imagination brought
A fitter welcome; but a thought
Of that late death took all my heart for speech.

460   *To a Young Girl*

My dear, my dear, I know
More than another
What makes your heart beat so;
Not even your own mother
Can know it as I know,
Who broke my heart for her
When the wild thought,
That she denies
And has forgot,
Set all her blood astir
And glittered in her eyes.

461   *The Leaders of the Crowd*

They must to keep their certainty accuse
All that are different of a base intent;
Pull down established honour; hawk for news
Whatever their loose fantasy invent
And murmur it with bated breath, as though
The abounding gutter had been Helicon
Or calumny a song. How can they know
Truth flourishes where the student's lamp has shone,
And there alone, that have no solitude?
So the crowd come they care not what may come.
They have loud music, hope every day renewed
And heartier loves; that lamp is from the tomb.

462   *A Prayer for My Son*

Bid a strong ghost stand at the head
That my Michael may sleep sound,
Nor cry, nor turn in the bed
Till his morning meal come round;
And may departing twilight keep
All dread afar till morning's back,
That his mother may not lack
Her fill of sleep.

Bid the ghost have sword in fist:
Some there are, for I avow
Such devilish things exist,
Who have planned his murder, for they know
Of some most haughty deed or thought
That waits upon his future days,
And would through hatred of the bays
Bring that to nought.

Though You can fashion everything
From nothing every day, and teach
The morning stars to sing,
You have lacked articulate speech
To tell Your simplest want, and known,
Wailing upon a woman's knee,
All of that worst ignominy
Of flesh and bone;

And when through all the town there ran
The servants of Your enemy,
A woman and a man,
Unless the Holy Writings lie,
Hurried through the smooth and rough
And through the fertile and waste,
Protecting, till the danger past,
With human love.

463   *Leda and the Swan*

A sudden blow: the great wings beating still
Above the staggering girl, her thighs caressed
By the dark webs, her nape caught in his bill,
He holds her helpless breast upon his breast.

How can those terrified vague fingers push
The feathered glory from her loosening thighs?
And how can body, laid in that white rush,
But feel the strange heart beating where it lies?

A shudder in the loins engenders there
The broken wall, the burning roof and tower
And Agamemnon dead.
                 Being so caught up,
So mastered by the brute blood of the air,
Did she put on his knowledge with his power
Before the indifferent beak could let her drop?

464 *Byzantium*

The unpurged images of day recede;
The Emperor's drunken soldiery are abed;
Night resonance recedes, night-walkers' song
After great cathedral gong;
A starlit or a moonlit dome disdains
All that man is,
All mere complexities,
The fury and the mire of human veins.

Before me floats an image, man or shade,
Shade more than man, more image than a shade;
For Hades' bobbin bound in mummy-cloth
May unwind the winding path;
A mouth that has no moisture and no breath
Breathless mouths may summon;
I hail the superhuman;
I call it death-in-life and life-in-death.

Miracle, bird or golden handiwork,
More miracle than bird or handiwork,
Planted on the star-lit golden bough,
Can like the cocks of Hades crow,
Or, by the moon embittered, scorn aloud
In glory of changeless metal
Common bird or petal
And all complexities of mire or blood.

At midnight on the Emperor's pavement flit
Flames that no faggot feeds, nor steel has lit,
Nor storm disturbs, flames begotten of flame,
Where blood-begotten spirits come
And all complexities of fury leave,
Dying into a dance,
An agony of trance,
An agony of flame that cannot singe a sleeve.

Astraddle on the dolphin's mire and blood,
Spirit after spirit! The smithies break the flood,
The golden smithies of the Emperor!
Marbles of the dancing floor
Break bitter furies of complexity,
Those images that yet
Fresh images beget,
That dolphin-torn, that gong-tormented sea.

465   *Crazy Jane Talks with the Bishop*

I met the Bishop on the road
And much said he and I.
'Those breasts are flat and fallen now,
Those veins must soon be dry;
Live in a heavenly mansion,
Not in some foul sty.'

'Fair and foul are near of kin,
And fair needs foul,' I cried.
'My friends are gone, but that's a truth
Nor grave nor bed denied,
Learned in bodily lowliness
And in the heart's pride.

A woman can be proud and stiff
When on love intent;
But Love has pitched his mansion in
The place of excrement;
For nothing can be sole or whole
That has not been rent.'

466   *Crazy Jane on God*

That lover of a night
Came when he would,
Went in the dawning light
Whether I would or no;
Men come, men go;
All things remain in God.

Banners choke the sky;
Men-at-arms tread;
Armoured horses neigh
Where the great battle was
In the narrow pass:
All things remain in God.

Before their eyes a house
That from childhood stood
Uninhabited, ruinous,
Suddenly lit up
From door to top:
All things remain in God.

I had wild Jack for a lover;
Though like a road
That men pass over
My body makes no moan
But sings on:
All things remain in God.

467   *Crazy Jane Grown Old Looks at the Dancers*

I found that ivory image there
Dancing with her chosen youth,
But when he wound her coal-black hair
As though to strangle her, no scream
Or bodily movement did I dare,
Eyes under eyelids did so gleam;
Love is like the lion's tooth.

When she, and though some said she played
I said that she had danced heart's truth,
Drew a knife to strike him dead,
I could but leave him to his fate;
For no matter what is said
They had all that had their hate;
Love is like the lion's tooth.

Did he die or did she die?
Seemed to die or died they both?
God be with the times when I
Cared not a thraneen for what chanced
So that I had the limbs to try
Such a dance as there was danced –
Love is like the lion's tooth.

Charlotte Mew

468   *The Quiet House*

When we were children old Nurse used to say,
The house was like an auction or a fair
Until the lot of us were safe in bed.
It has been quiet as the country-side
Since Ted and Janey and then Mother died
And Tom crossed Father and was sent away.
After the lawsuit he could not hold up his head,
    Poor Father, and he does not care
    For people here, or to go anywhere.

To get away to Aunt's for that week-end
    Was hard enough; (since then, a year ago,
    He scarcely lets me slip out of his sight –)
At first I did not like my cousin's friend,
    I did not think I should remember him:
    His voice has gone, his face is growing dim
And if I like him now I do not know.
    He frightened me before he smiled –
    He did not ask me if he might –
    He said that he would come one Sunday night,
    He spoke to me as if I were a child.

No year has been like this that has just gone by;
    It may be that what Father says is true,
If things are so it does not matter why:
    But everything has burned, and not quite through.
    The colours of the world have turned
    To flame, the blue, the gold has burned
In what used to be such a leaden sky.
When you are burned quite through you die.

    Red is the strangest pain to bear;
In Spring the leaves on the budding trees;
In Summer the roses are worse than these,
    More terrible than they are sweet:
    A rose can stab you across the street
        Deeper than any knife:
    And the crimson haunts you everywhere –
Thin shafts of sunlight, like the ghosts of reddened swords
        have struck our stair
As if, coming down, you had spilt your life.

    I think that my soul is red
Like the soul of a sword or a scarlet flower:
    But when these are dead
    They have had their hour.

I shall have had mine, too,
   For from head to feet
I am burned and stabbed half through,
   And the pain is deadly sweet.

The things that kill us seem
   Blind to the death they give:
It is only in our dream
   The things that kill us live.

The room is shut where Mother died,
  The other rooms are as they were,
The world goes on the same outside,
  The sparrows fly across the Square,
  The children play as we four did there,
  The trees grow green and brown and bare,
The sun shines on the dead Church spire,
  And nothing lives here but the fire.
While Father watches from his chair
     Day follows day
The same, or now and then a different grey,
    Till, like his hair,
Which Mother said was wavy once and bright,
    They will all turn white.

   To-night I heard a bell again –
Outside it was just the same mist of fine rain,
The lamps just lighted down the long, dim street,
     No one for me –
   I think it is myself I go to meet:
I do not care; some day I *shall* not think; I shall not *be*.

Hilaire Belloc

469   *Dedication on the Gift of a Book to a Child*

Child! Do not throw this book about!
  Refrain from the unholy pleasure
Of cutting all the pictures out!
  Preserve it as your chiefest treasure.

Child, have you never heard it said
  That you are heir to all the ages?
Why then, your hands were never made
  To tear these beautiful thick pages!

Your little hands were made to take
    The better things and leave the worse ones:
They also may be used to shake
    The Massive Paws of Elder Persons.

And when your prayers complete the day,
    Darling, your little tiny hands
Were also made, I think, to pray
    For men that lose their fairylands.

Walter de la Mare

470   *A Hare*

Eyes that glass fear, though fear on furtive foot
    Track thee, in slumber bound;
Ears that whist danger, though the wind sigh not,
    Nor Echo list a sound;
Heart – oh, what hazard must thy wild life be,
With sapient Man for thy cold enemy!

Fleet Scatterbrains, thou hast thine hours of peace
    In pastures April-green,
Where the shrill skylark's raptures never cease,
And the clear dew englobes the white moon's beam.
All happiness God gave thee, albeit thy foe
Roves Eden, as did Satan, long ago.

471   *Song of the Mad Prince*

Who said, 'Peacock Pie'?
    The old king to the sparrow:
Who said, 'Crops are ripe'?
    Rust to the harrow:
Who said, 'Where sleeps she now?
    Where rests she now her head,
Bathed in earth's loveliness'? –
    That's what I said.

Who said, 'Ay, mum's the word'?
    Sexton to willow:
Who said 'Green dusk for dreams,
    Moss for a pillow'?

Who said, 'All time's delight
Hath she for narrow bed;
Life's troubled bubble broken'? –
That's what I said.

Edward Thomas

472

The Owl

Downhill I came, hungry, and yet not starved;
Cold, yet had heat within me that was proof
Against the North wind; tired, yet so that rest
Had seemed the sweetest thing under a roof.

Then at the inn I had food, fire, and rest,
Knowing how hungry, cold, and tired was I.
All of the night was quite barred out except
An owl's cry, a most melancholy cry

Shaken out long and clear upon the hill,
No merry note, nor cause of merriment,
But one telling me plain what I escaped
And others could not, that night, as in I went.

And salted was my food, and my repose,
Salted and sobered, too, by the bird's voice
Speaking for all who lay under the stars,
Soldiers and poor, unable to rejoice.

473

Thaw

Over the land freckled with snow half-thawed
The speculating rooks at their nests cawed
And saw from elm-tops, delicate as flower of grass,
What we below could not see, Winter pass.

474   *The New House*

Now first, as I shut the door,
    I was alone
In the new house; and the wind
    Began to moan.

Old at once was the house,
    And I was old;
My ears were teased with the dread
    Of what was foretold,

Nights of storm, days of mist, without end;
    Sad days when the sun
Shone in vain: old griefs and griefs
    Not yet begun.

All was foretold me; naught
    Could I foresee;
But I learned how the wind would sound
    After these things should be.

John Masefield

475   *The Waggon-Maker*

I have made tales in verse, but this man made
Waggons of elm to last a hundred years;
The blacksmith forged the rims and iron gears,
His was the magic that the wood obeyed.

Each deft device that country wisdom bade,
Or farmers' practice needed, he preserved.
He wrought the subtle contours, straight and curved,
Only by eye, and instinct of the trade.

No weakness, no offence in any part,
It stood the strain in mired fields and roads
In all a century's struggle for its bread;
Bearing, perhaps, eight thousand heavy loads.
Beautiful always as a work of art,
Homing the bride, and harvest, and men dead.

476   *Sonnet*

There, on the darkened deathbed, dies the brain
That flared three several times in seventy years.
It cannot lift the silly hand again,
Nor speak, nor sing, it neither sees nor hears;
And muffled mourners put it in the ground
And then go home, and in the earth it lies
Too dark for vision and too deep for sound,
The million cells that made a good man wise.
Yet for a few short years an influence stirs,
A sense or wraith or essence of him dead,
Which makes insensate things its ministers
To those beloved, his spirit's daily bread;
Then that, too, fades; in book or deed a spark
Lingers, then that, too, fades; then all is dark.

James Stephens

477   *Egan O Rahilly*

Here in a distant place I hold my tongue;
I am O Rahilly!

When I was young,
Who now am young no more,
I did not eat things picked up from the shore:
The periwinkle, and the tough dog-fish
At even-tide have got into my dish!

The great, where are they now! the great had said –
This is not seemly! Bring to him instead
That which serves his and serves our dignity –
And that was done.

I am O Rahilly!
Here in a distant place he holds his tongue,
Who once said all his say, when he was young!

                                        (*From the Irish*)

James Joyce

478

Thou leanest to the shell of night,
  Dear lady, a divining ear.
In that soft choiring of delight
  What sound hath made thy heart to fear?
Seemed it of rivers rushing forth
From the grey deserts of the north?

That mood of thine, O timorous,
  Is his, if thou but scan it well,
Who a mad tale bequeaths to us
  At ghosting hour conjurable –
And all for some strange name he read
In Purchas or in Holinshed.

479

Ecce Puer

Of the dark past
A child is born
With joy and grief
My heart is torn.

Calm in his cradle
The living lies.
May love and mercy
Unclose his eyes!

Young life is breathed
On the glass;
The world that was not
Comes to pass.

A child is sleeping:
An old man gone.
O, father forsaken,
Forgive your son!

T. E. Hulme

480   *The Embankment*

(The fantasia of a fallen gentleman on a cold, bitter night)

Once, in finesse of fiddles found I ecstasy,
In the flash of gold heels on the hard pavement.
Now see I
That warmth's the very stuff of poesy.
Oh, God, make small
The old star-eaten blanket of the sky,
That I may fold it round me and in comfort lie.

D. H. Lawrence

481   *End of Another Home Holiday*

When shall I see the half-moon sink again
Behind the black sycamore at the end of the garden?
When will the scent of the dim white phlox
Creep up the wall to me, and in at my open window?

Why is it, the long, slow stroke of the midnight bell
        (Will it never finish the twelve?)
Falls again and again on my heart with a heavy reproach?

The moon-mist is over the village, out of the mist speaks the bell,
And all the little roofs of the village bow low, pitiful, beseeching,
            resigned.
– Speak, you my home! what is it I don't do well?

Ah home, suddenly I love you
As I hear the sharp clean trot of a pony down the road,
Succeeding sharp little sounds dropping into silence
Clear upon the long-drawn hoarseness of a train across the valley.

            .   .   .   .   .

The light has gone out, from under my mother's door.
        That she should love me so! –
        She, so lonely, greying now!
        And I leaving her,
        Bent on my pursuits!

Love is the great Asker.
The sun and the rain do not ask the secret
Of the time when the grain struggles down in the dark.
The moon walks her lonely way without anguish,
Because no-one grieves over her departure.

Forever, ever by my shoulder pitiful love will linger,
Crouching as little houses crouch under the mist when I turn.
Forever, out of the mist, the church lifts up a reproachful finger,
Pointing my eyes in wretched defiance where love hides her face
   to mourn.

Oh! but the rain creeps down to wet the grain
That struggles alone in the dark,
And asking nothing, patiently steals back again!
The moon sets forth o' nights
To walk the lonely, dusky heights
Serenely, with steps unswerving;
Pursued by no sigh of bereavement,
No tears of love unnerving
Her constant tread:
While ever at my side,
Frail and sad, with grey, bowed head,
The beggar-woman, the yearning-eyed
Inexorable love goes lagging.

The wild young heifer, glancing distraught,
With a strange new knocking of life at her side
   Runs seeking a loneliness.
The little grain draws down the earth, to hide.
Nay, even the slumberous egg, as it labours under the shell
   Patiently to divide and self-divide,
Asks to be hidden, and wishes nothing to tell.

But when I draw the scanty cloak of silence over my eyes
Piteous love comes peering under the hood;
Touches the clasp with trembling fingers, and tries
To put her ear to the painful sob of my blood;
While her tears soak through to my breast,
   Where they burn and cauterise.

     .   .   .   .   .

The moon lies back and reddens.
In the valley a corncrake calls
   Monotonously,
With a plaintive, unalterable voice, that deadens
   My confident activity;
With a hoarse, insistent request that falls
   Unweariedly, unweariedly,
   Asking something more of me,
     Yet more of me.

482   *Kangaroo*

In the northern hemisphere
Life seems to leap at the air, or skim under the wind
Like stags on rocky ground, or pawing horses, or springy scut-tailed rabbits.

Or else rush horizontal to charge at the sky's horizon,
Like bulls or bisons or wild pigs.

Or slip like water slippery towards its ends,
As foxes, stoats, and wolves, and prairie dogs.

Only mice, and moles, and rats, and badgers, and beavers, and perhaps bears
Seem belly-plumbed to the earth's mid-navel.
Or frogs that when they leap come flop, and flop to the centre of the earth.

But the yellow antipodal Kangaroo, when she sits up,
Who can unseat her, like a liquid drop that is heavy, and just touches earth.

The downward drip
The down-urge.
So much denser than cold-blooded frogs.

Delicate mother Kangaroo
Sitting up there rabbit-wise, but huge, plumb-weighted,
And lifting her beautiful slender face, oh! so much more gently and finely
    lined than a rabbit's, or than a hare's,
Lifting her face to nibble at a round white peppermint drop, which she
    loves, sensitive mother Kangaroo.

Her sensitive, long, pure-bred face.
Her full antipodal eyes, so dark,
So big and quiet and remote, having watched so many empty dawns in silent
    Australia.

Her little loose hands, and drooping Victorian shoulders.
And then her great weight below the waist, her vast pale belly
With a thin young yellow little paw hanging out, and straggle of a long thin
    ear, like ribbon,
Like a funny trimming to the middle of her belly, thin little dangle of an
    immature paw, and one thin ear.

Her belly, her big haunches
And, in addition, the great muscular python-stretch of her tail.

There, she shan't have any more peppermint drops.
So she wistfully, sensitively sniffs the air, and then turns, goes off in slow sad
    leaps

On the long flat skis of her legs,
Steered and propelled by that steel-strong snake of a tail.

Stops again, half turns, inquisitive to look back.
While something stirs quickly in her belly, and a lean little face comes out, as
    from a window,
Peaked and a bit dismayed,
Only to disappear again quickly away from the sight of the world, to snuggle
    down in the warmth,
Leaving the trail of a different paw hanging out.

Still she watches with eternal, cocked wistfulness!
How full her eyes are, like the full, fathomless, shining eyes of an Australian
    black-boy
Who has been lost so many centuries on the margins of existence!
She watches with insatiable wistfulness.
Untold centuries of watching for something to come,
For a new signal from life, in that silent lost land of the South.

Where nothing bites but insects and snakes and the sun, small life.
Where no bull roared, no cow ever lowed, no stag cried, no leopard
    screeched, no lion coughed, no dog barked,
But all was silent save for parrots occasionally, in the haunted blue bush.

Wistfully watching, with wonderful liquid eyes.
And all her weight, all her blood, dripping sack-wise down towards the
    earth's centre,
And the live little-one taking in its paw at the door of her belly.

Leap then, and come down on the line that draws to the earth's deep, heavy
    centre.

Sydney.

Andrew Young

483   *Man and Cows*

I stood aside to let the cows
Swing past me with their wrinkled brows,
Bowing their heads as they went by
As to a woodland deity
To whom they turned mute eyes
To save them from the plaguing god of flies.

And I too cursed Beelzebub,
Watching them stop to rub
A bulging side or bony haunch
Against a trunk or pointing branch
And lift a tufted tail
To thresh the air with its soft flail.

They stumbled heavily down the slope,
As Hethor led them or the hope
Of the lush meadow-grass,
While I remained, thinking it was
Strange that we both were held divine,
In Egypt these, man once in Palestine.

Rupert Brooke

484   *Heaven*

Fish (fly-replete, in depth of June,
Dawdling away their wat'ry noon)
Ponder deep wisdom, dark or clear,
Each secret fishy hope or fear.
Fish say, they have their Stream and Pond;
But is there anything Beyond?
This life cannot be All, they swear,
For how unpleasant, if it were!
One may not doubt that, somehow, Good
Shall come of Water and of Mud;
And, sure, the reverent eye must see
A Purpose in Liquidity.
We darkly know, by Faith we cry,
The future is not Wholly Dry.
Mud unto mud! – Death eddies near –
Not here the appointed End, not here!
But somewhere, beyond Space and Time,
Is wetter water, slimier slime!
And there (they trust) there swimmeth One
Who swam ere rivers were begun,
Immense, of fishy form and mind,
Squamous, omnipotent, and kind;
And under that Almighty Fin,
The littlest fish may enter in.
Oh! never fly conceals a hook,
Fish say, in the Eternal Brook,
But more than mundane weeds are there,
And mud, celestially fair;
Fat caterpillars drift around,
And Paradisal grubs are found;
Unfading moths, immortal flies,
And the worm that never dies.
And in that Heaven of all their wish,
There shall be no more land, say fish.

Edwin Muir

485   *The Animals*

They do not live in the world,
Are not in time and space.
From birth to death hurled
No word do they have, not one
To plant a foot upon,
Were never in any place.
For with names the world was called
Out of the empty air,
With names was built and walled,
Line and circle and square,
Dust and emerald;
Snatched from deceiving death
By the articulate breath.

But these have never trod
Twice the familiar track,
Never never turned back
Into the memoried day.
All is new and near
In the unchanging Here
Of the fifth great day of God,
That shall remain the same,
Never shall pass away.

On the sixth day we came.

T. S. Eliot

486   *The Love Song of J. Alfred Prufrock*

S'io credessi che mia risposta fosse
a persona che mai tornasse al mondo,
questa fiamma staria senza più scosse.
Ma per ciò che giammai di questo fondo
non tornò vivo alcun, s'i' odo il vero,
senza tema d'infamia ti rispondo.

Let us go then, you and I,
When the evening is spread out against the sky
Like a patient etherised upon a table;
Let us go, through certain half-deserted streets,

The muttering retreats
Of restless nights in one-night cheap hotels
And sawdust restaurants with oyster-shells:
Streets that follow like a tedious argument
Of insidious intent
To lead you to an overwhelming question. . .
Oh, do not ask, 'What is it?'
Let us go and make our visit.

In the room the women come and go
Talking of Michelangelo.

The yellow fog that rubs its back upon the window-panes,
The yellow smoke that rubs its muzzle on the window-panes,
Licked its tongue into the corners of the evening,
Lingered upon the pools that stand in drains,
Let fall upon its back the soot that falls from chimneys,
Slipped by the terrace, made a sudden leap,
And seeing that it was a soft October night,
Curled once about the house, and fell asleep.

And indeed there will be time
For the yellow smoke that slides along the street
Rubbing its back upon the window-panes;
There will be time, there will be time
To prepare a face to meet the faces that you meet;
There will be time to murder and create,
And time for all the works and days of hands
That lift and drop a question on your plate;
Time for you and time for me,
And time yet for a hundred indecisions,
And for a hundred visions and revisions,
Before the taking of a toast and tea.

In the room the women come and go
Talking of Michelangelo.

And indeed there will be time
To wonder, 'Do I dare?' and, 'Do I dare?'
Time to turn back and descend the stair,
With a bald spot in the middle of my hair –
(They will say: 'How his hair is growing thin!')
My morning coat, my collar mounting firmly to the chin,
My necktie rich and modest, but asserted by a simple pin –
(They will say: 'But how his arms and legs are thin!')
Do I dare
Disturb the universe?
In a minute there is time
For decisions and revisions which a minute will reverse.

For I have known them all already, known them all —
Have known the evenings, mornings, afternoons,
I have measured out my life with coffee spoons;
I know the voices dying with a dying fall
Beneath the music from a farther room.
　　So how should I presume?

And I have known the eyes already, known them all —
The eyes that fix you in a formulated phrase,
And when I am formulated, sprawling on a pin,
When I am pinned and wriggling on the wall,
Then how should I begin
To spit out all the butt-ends of my days and ways?
　　And how should I presume?

And I have known the arms already, known them all —
Arms that are braceleted and white and bare
(But in the lamplight, downed with light brown hair!)
Is it perfume from a dress
That makes me so digress?
Arms that lie along a table, or wrap about a shawl.
　　And should I then presume?
　　And how should I begin?

　　　　·　　·　　·　　·　　·

Shall I say, I have gone at dusk through narrow streets
And watched the smoke that rises from the pipes
Of lonely men in shirt-sleeves, leaning out of windows? . . .

I should have been a pair of ragged claws
Scuttling across the floors of silent seas.

　　　　·　　·　　·　　·　　·

And the afternoon, the evening, sleeps so peacefully!
Smoothed by long fingers,
Asleep . . . tired . . . or it malingers,
Stretched on the floor, here beside you and me.
Should I, after tea and cakes and ices,
Have the strength to force the moment to its crisis?
But though I have wept and fasted, wept and prayed,
Though I have seen my head (grown slightly bald) brought in
　　upon a platter,
I am no prophet — and here's no great matter;
I have seen the moment of my greatness flicker,
And I have seen the eternal Footman hold my coat, and
　　snicker,
And in short, I was afraid.

And would it have been worth it, after all,
After the cups, the marmalade, the tea,
Among the porcelain, among some talk of you and me,

Would it have been worth while,
To have bitten off the matter with a smile,
To have squeezed the universe into a ball
To roll it towards some overwhelming question,
To say: 'I am Lazarus, come from the dead,
Come back to tell you all, I shall tell you all' –
If one, settling a pillow by her head,
    Should say: 'That is not what I meant at all.
    That is not it, at all.'

    And would it have been worth it, after all,
Would it have been worth while,
After the sunsets and the dooryards and the sprinkled streets,
After the novels, after the teacups, after the skirts that trail
    along the floor –
And this, and so much more? –
It is impossible to say just what I mean!
But as if a magic lantern threw the nerves in patterns on a
    screen:
Would it have been worth while
If one, settling a pillow or throwing off a shawl,
And turning toward the window, should say:
    'That is not it at all,
    That is not what I meant, at all.'

       .   .   .   .   .

    No! I am not Prince Hamlet, nor was meant to be;
Am an attendant lord, one that will do
To swell a progress, start a scene or two,
Advise the prince; no doubt, an easy tool,
Deferential, glad to be of use,
Politic, cautious, and meticulous;
Full of high sentence, but a bit obtuse;
At times, indeed, almost ridiculous –
Almost, at times, the Fool.

    I grow old . . . I grow old . . .
I shall wear the bottoms of my trousers rolled.

    Shall I part my hair behind? Do I dare to eat a peach?
I shall wear white flannel trousers, and walk upon the beach.
I have heard the mermaids singing, each to each.

I do not think that they will sing to me.

I have seen them riding seaward on the waves
Combing the white hair of the waves blown back
When the wind blows the water white and black.

We have lingered in the chambers of the sea
By sea-girls wreathed with seaweed red and brown
Till human voices wake us, and we drown.

487   *Gerontion*

> *Thou hast nor youth nor age*
> *But as it were an after dinner sleep*
> *Dreaming of both.*

Here I am, an old man in a dry month,
Being read to by a boy, waiting for rain.
I was neither at the hot gates
Nor fought in the warm rain
Nor knee deep in the salt marsh, heaving a cutlass,
Bitten by flies, fought.
My house is a decayed house,
And the jew squats on the window sill, the owner,
Spawned in some estaminet of Antwerp,
Blistered in Brussels, patched and peeled in London.
The goat coughs at night in the field overhead;
Rocks, moss, stonecrop, iron, merds.
The woman keeps the kitchen, makes tea,
Sneezes at evening, poking the peevish gutter.

                    I an old man,
A dull head among windy spaces.

Signs are taken for wonders. 'We would see a sign!'
The word within a word, unable to speak a word,
Swaddled with darkness. In the juvescence of the year
Came Christ the tiger

In depraved May, dogwood and chestnut, flowering judas,
To be eaten, to be divided, to be drunk
Among whispers; by Mr Silvero
With caressing hands, at Limoges
Who walked all night in the next room;

By Hakagawa, bowing among the Titians;
By Madame de Tornquist, in the dark room
Shifting the candles; Fraülein von Kulp
Who turned in the hall, one hand on the door.
    Vacant shuttles
Weave the wind. I have no ghosts,
An old man in a draughty house
Under a windy knob.

After such knowledge, what forgiveness? Think now
History has many cunning passages, contrived corridors
And issues, deceives with whispering ambitions,
Guides us by vanities. Think now
She gives when our attention is distracted
And what she gives, gives with such supple confusions

That the giving famishes the craving. Gives too late
What's not believed in, or if still believed,
In memory only, reconsidered passion. Gives too soon
Into weak hands, what's thought can be dispensed with
Till the refusal propagates a fear. Think
Neither fear nor courage saves us. Unnatural vices
Are fathered by our heroism. Virtues
Are forced upon us by our impudent crimes.
These tears are shaken from the wrath-bearing tree.

The tiger springs in the new year. Us he devours.
   Think at last
We have not reached conclusion, when I
Stiffen in a rented house. Think at last
I have not made this show purposelessly
And it is not by any concitation
Of the backward devils.
I would meet you upon this honestly.
I that was near your heart was removed therefrom
To lose beauty in terror, terror in inquisition.
I have lost my passion: why should I need to keep it
Since what is kept must be adulterated?
I have lost my sight, smell, hearing, taste and touch:
How should I use it for your closer contact?

These with a thousand small deliberations
Protract the profit of their chilled delirium,
Excite the membrane, when the sense has cooled,
With pungent sauces, multiply variety
In a wilderness of mirrors. What will the spider do,
Suspend its operations, will the weevil
Delay? De Bailhache, Fresca, Mrs Cammel, whirled
Beyond the circuit of the shuddering Bear
In fractured atoms. Gull against the wind, in the windy
   straits
Of Belle Isle, or running on the Horn,
White feathers in the snow, the Gulf claims,
And an old man driven by the Trades
To a sleepy corner.

                Tenants of the house,
Thoughts of a dry brain in a dry season.

Isaac Rosenberg

488   *August 1914*

What in our lives is burnt
In the fire of this?
The heart's dear granary?
The much we shall miss?

Three lives hath one life —
Iron, honey, gold.
The gold, the honey gone —
Left is the hard and cold.

Iron are our lives
Molten right through our youth.
A burnt space through ripe fields
A fair mouth's broken tooth.

489   *Louse Hunting*

Nudes — stark and glistening,
Yelling in lurid glee. Grinning faces
And raging limbs
Whirl over the floor one fire.
For a shirt verminously busy
Yon soldier tore from his throat, with oaths
Godhead might shrink at, but not the lice.
And soon the shirt was aflare
Over the candle he'd lit while we lay.

Then we all sprang up and stript
To hunt the verminous brood.
Soon like a demons' pantomime
The place was raging.
See the silhouettes agape,
See the gibbering shadows
Mixed with the battled arms on the wall.
See gargantuan hooked fingers
Pluck in supreme flesh
To smutch supreme littleness.
See the merry limbs in hot Highland fling
Because some wizard vermin
Charmed from the quiet this revel
When our ears were half lulled
By the dark music
Blown from Sleep's trumpet.

Hugh MacDiarmid

490   *The Innumerable Christ*

'Other stars may have their Bethlehem, and their Calvary too.'
(Professor J. Y. Simpson)

Wha kens on whatna Bethlehems   *knows*
Earth twinkles like a star the nicht,
An' whatna shepherds lift their heids
    In its unearthly licht?

'Yont a' the stars oor een can see   *beyond*
An' farther than their lichts can fly,
I' mony an unco warl' the nicht   *strange*
    The fatefu' bairnies cry,

I' mony an unco warl' the nicht
The lift gaes black as pitch at noon,   *sky*
An' sideways on their chests the heids
    O' endless Christs roll doon.

An' when the earth's as cauld's the mune
An' a' its folk are lang syne deid,   *long since*
On coontless stars the Babe maun cry
    An' the Crucified maun bleed.

491   From *A Drunk Man Looks at the Thistle*

Dae what ye wull ye canna parry
This skeleton-at-the-feast that through the starry
Maze o' the warld's intoxicatin' soiree
Claughts ye, as micht at an affrontit quean   *clutches*
A bastard wean!

Prood mune, ye needna thring your shouder there,   *shrug*
And at your puir get like a snawstorm stare?   *poor offspring*
It's yours – there's nae denyin't – and I'm shair
You'd no' enjoy the evenin' much the less
Gin you'd but openly confess!

Dod! It's an eaten and a spewed-like thing,
Fell like a little-bodie's changeling,   *fairy's*
And it's nae credit t'ye that you s'ud bring
The like to life – yet, gi'en a mither's love,
– Hee, hee! – wha kens hoo't micht improve? . . .

Or is this Heaven, this yalla licht,
And I the aft'rins o' the Earth,   *off-scourings*
Or sic's in this wanchancy time   *unfortunate*
May weel fin' sudden birth?

The roots that wi' the worms compete
Hauf-publish me upon the air.
The struggle that divides me still
Is seen fu' plainly there.

The thistle's shank scarce holes the grun',
My grave'll spare nae mair I doot.
– The crack's fu' wide; the shank's fu' strang;
A' that I was is oot.

My knots o' nerves that struggled sair
Are weel reflected in the herb;
My crookit instincts were like this,
As sterile and acerb.

My self-tormented spirit took
The shape repeated in the thistle;
Sma' beauty jouked my rawny banes   *avoided; prominent*
And maze o' gristle.

I seek nae peety, Paraclete,
And, fegs, I think the joke is rich
– Pairt soul, pairt skeleton's come up;
They kentna which was which! . . .   *did not know*

Thou Daith in which my life
Sae vain a thing can seem,
Frae whatna source d'ye borrow
Your devastatin' gleam?

Nae doot that hidden sun
'Ud look fu' wae ana',   *extremely sad as well*
Gin I could see it in the licht
That frae the Earth you draw! . . .

Shudderin' thistle, gi'e owre, gi'e owre!
A'body's gi'en in to the facts o' life;
The impossible truth'll triumph at last,
And mock your strife.

Your sallow leafs can never thraw,
Wi' a' their oorie shakin',   *weird*
Ae doot into the hert o' life
That it may be mistak'n . . .

O Scotland is
THE barren fig.
Up, carles, up   *fellows*
And roond it jig.

Auld Moses took
A dry stick and
Instantly it
Floo'ered in his hand.

Pu' Scotland up,
And wha can say
It winna bud
And blossom tae.

A miracle's
Oor only chance.
Up, carles, up
And let us dance!

492   *By Wauchopeside*

Thrawn water? Aye, owre thrawn to be aye thrawn!
I ha'e my wagtails like the Wauchope tae,
Birds fu' o' fechtin' spirit, and o' fun,
That whiles jig in the air in lichtsome play
Like glass-ba's on a fountain, syne stand still
Save for a quiver, shoot up an inch or twa, fa' back
Like a swarm o' winter-gnats, or are tost aside,
         By their inclination's kittle loup,
         To balance efter hauf a coup.

There's mair in birds than men ha'e faddomed yet.
Tho' maist churn oot the stock sangs o' their kind
There's aiblins genius here and there; and aince
'Mang whitebeams, hollies, siller birks –
         The tree o' licht –
         I mind
I used to hear a blackie mony a nicht
Singin' awa' t'an unconscionable 'oor
Wi' nocht but the water keepin't company
(Or nocht that ony human ear could hear)
– And wondered if the blackie heard it either
Or cared whether it was singin' tae or no'!

O there's nae sayin' what my verses awn
To memories like these. Ha'e I come back
To find oot? Or to borrow mair? Or see
Their helpless puirness to what gar'd them be?
      Late sang the blackie but it stopt at last.
      The river still ga'ed singin' past.

O there's nae sayin' what my verses awn
To memories, or my memories to me.
But a'e thing's certain; ev'n as things stand
I could vary them in coontless ways and gi'e
Wauchope a new course in the minds o' men,
The blackie gowden feathers, and the like,
An yet no' cease to be dependent on
The things o' Nature, and create insteid
      Oot o' my ain heid
      Or get ootside the range
          O' trivial change
Into that cataclysmic country which
Natheless a' men inhabit – and enrich.

For civilization in its struggle up
Has mair than seasonal changes o' ideas,
Glidin' through periods o' flooers and fruit,
Winter and Spring again; to cope wi' these
Is difficult eneuch to tax the patience
O' Methuselah himsel' – but transformations,
Yont physical and mental habits, symbols, rites,
That mak' sic changes nane, are aye gaen on,
Revolutions in the dynasty o' live ideals
– The stuff wi' which alane true poetry deals.
Wagtail or water winna help me here,
(That's clearer than Wauchope at its clearest's clear!)
Where the life o' a million years is seen
Like a louch look in a lass's een.

493   *Prayer for a Second Flood*

There'd ha'e to be nae warnin'. Times ha'e changed
And Noahs are owre numerous nooadays,
(And them the vera folk to benefit maist!)
Knock the feet frae under them, O Lord, wha praise
Your unsearchable ways sae muckle and yet hope
      To keep within knowledgeable scope!

Ding a' their trumpery show to blauds again.
Their measure is the thimblefu' o' Esk in spate.
Like whisky the tittlin' craturs mete oot your poo'ers
Aince a week for bawbees in the kirk-door plate,
— And pit their umbrellas up when they come oot
     If mair than a pulpitfu' o' You's aboot!

O arselins wi' them! Whummle them again!
Coup them heels-owre-gowdy in a storm sae gundy
That mony a lang fog-theekit face I ken
'll be sooked richt doon under through a cundy
In the High Street, afore you get weel-sterted
     And are still hauf-herted!

Then flush the world in earnest. Let yoursel' gang,
Scour't to the bones, and mak' its marrow holes
Toom as a whistle as they used to be
In days I mind ere men fidged wi' souls,
But naething had forgotten you as yet,
     Nor you forgotten it.

Up then and at them, ye Gairds o' Heaven.
The Divine Retreat is owre. Like a tidal bore
Boil in among them; let the lang lugs nourished
On the milk o' the word at last hear the roar
O' human shingle; and replenish the salt o' the earth
     In the place o' their birth.

Wilfred Owen

494   *Anthem for Doomed Youth*

What passing-bells for these who die as cattle?
   Only the monstrous anger of the guns.
   Only the stuttering rifles' rapid rattle
Can patter out their hasty orisons.
No mockeries now for them; no prayers nor bells,
   Nor any voice of mourning save the choirs, —
The shrill, demented choirs of wailing shells;
   And bugles calling for them from sad shires.

What candles may be held to speed them all?
   Not in the hands of boys, but in their eyes
Shall shine the holy glimmers of good-byes.
   The pallor of girls' brows shall be their pall;
Their flowers the tenderness of patient minds,
And each slow dusk of drawing-down of blinds.

495   *The Roads Also*

> The roads also have their wistful rest,
> When the weathercocks perch still and roost,
> And the town is quite like a candle-lit room –
> The streets also dream their dream.
>
> The old houses muse of the old days
> And their fond trees leaning on them doze,
> On their steps chatter and clatter stops,
> On their doors a strange hand taps.
>
> Men remember alien ardours
> As the dusk unearths old mournful odours.
> In the garden unborn child souls wail
> And the dead scribble on walls.
>
> Though their own child cry for them in tears,
> Women weep but hear no sound upstairs.
> They believe in loves they had not lived
> And in passion past the reach of the stairs
>   To the world's towers or stars.

Aldous Huxley

496   *September*

> Spring is past and over these many days,
> Spring and summer. The leaves of September droop,
> Yellowing and all but dead on the patient trees.
> Nor is there any hope in me. I walk
> Slowly homewards. Night is empty and dark
> Behind my eyes as it is dark without
> And empty round about me and over me.
> Spring is past and over these many days,
> But, looking up, suddenly I see
> Leaves in the upthrown light of a street lamp shining,
> Clear and luminous, young and so transparent,
> They seem but the coloured foam of air, green fire,
> No more than the scarce-embodied thoughts of leaves.
> And it is spring within that circle of light.
> Oh, magical brightness! The old leaves are made new.
> In the mind, too, some coloured accident
> Of beauty revives and makes all young again,
> A chance light shines and suddenly it is spring.

David Jones

497   From *The Anathemata*

From *The Lady of the Pool*

Did he meet Lud at the Fleet Gate? did he count the top.
Trees in the anchored forest of Llefelys
                              under the White Mount?

Did ever he walk the twenty-six wards of the city, within
and extra, did he cast his nautic eye on her
                              clere and lusty under kell
in the troia'd lanes of the city?
And was it but a month and less from the septimal month,
and did he hear, seemly intuned in *East-Seaxna*-nasal
        (whose nestle-cock *polis* but theirs knows the sweet
gag and in what *urbs* would he hear it if not in Belin's
oppidum, the greatest *burh* in nordlands?)

   Who'll try my sweet prime lavendula
   I cry my introit in a Dirige-*time*
   Come buy for summer's weeds, threnodic stalks
   For in Jane's ditch Jack soon shall white his earliest rime
        Come, come buy
                good for a ditty-box, my fish-eye
        good to sweeten y'r poop-bower, cap'n.
        Come buy
                or else y'r duck'ill cry.
        Come buy my sweet lavender
                that bodes the fall-gale westerlies
        and ice on slow old Baldpate
        when the Nore gulls fly this way that tell to Lear's
        river a long winter's tale.
   Was already rawish crost the Lower Pool afore four o'
the clock this fine summer mornin' – it might 've been
Lemon's Day. An' cuckoo seeming but bare flown and
Ember Ides not yet by a long way come, in pontiff Juliuses
'versal colander and them not yet sung their Crouchmasses
by tax-chandler's Black Exchecky Book nor yet thumbed
Archie's piscopal *Ordo* to figure out the moon of it.
        From the Two Sticks an' a' Apple to Bride o'
the Shandies' Well over the Fleet; from Hallows-on-Wall to
the keel-haws; from the ditch without the Vicinal Gate to
Lud's hill; within and extra the fending circuit, both banks
the wide and demarking middle-brook that waters, from the
midst of the street of it, our twin-hilled Urbs. At Martin
miles in the Pomarary (where the Roman pippins grow) at

winged Marmor *miles*, gilt-lorica'd on his wheat-hill, stick-
ing the Laidly Worm as threats to coil us all.
           At the Lady-at-Hill
above Romeland's wharf-lanes
at the Great Mother's newer *chapelle*
at New Heva's Old Crepel.
           (Chthonic *matres* under the croft:
springan a Maye's *Aves* to clerestories.
           Delphi in sub-crypt:
luce flowers to steeple.)
           At Paul's
and faiths under Paul
where
           so Iuppiter me succour!
they do garland them with Roman roses and do have stitched
on their zoomorphic apparels and vest 'em gay for Artemis.
           When is brought in her stag to be pierced,
when is bowed his meek head between the porch and the
altar, when is blowed his sweet death at the great door, on the
day before the calends o' Quintilis.
           At the tunicled martyr's
from where prills the seeding under-stream.
           At Mary of the Birth
by her long bourn of sweet water.
           In where she mothers
her painters an' limners.
           In Pellipar's
where she's *virgo inter virgines*
for the skinner's boys an' budge-dressers.
           In all the memorials
of her buxom will
           (what brought us ransom, captain!)
as do renown our city.
She's as she of Aulis, master:
not a puff of wind without her!
her fiat is our fortune, sir: like Helen's face
t'was that as launched the ship.
           Or may I never
keep company more with a dunce of a maudlin inceptor –
though he were a seraph for sub-distinctions.
           . . . did black deth
have him young? Or does he sit degreed an' silked in oriel'd
halls, in a cure o' Christ and shorn to sign it, warming their
disputations till frigid syllogism pulses like mother nature
– by a most exact art?
           Oh! do the budged owls pluck where their forelocks
were, as did remunerated errand boys – when manners was
– for proper admiration to see divine science by the muse so
fired?

Is their chilly curia a very thalamos: is Lady Verity
with Poesy now wed, and at that bed, by Prudentia cur-
tained close, does the Trivium curtsy and does each take
hand and to the Quadrivium call: Music! for a saraband?

And does serene Astronomy carry the tonic *Ave* to the
created spheres, does old Averroes show a leg? – for what's
the song b' Seine and Isis determines toons in caelian consis-
tories – or so this cock-clerk once said.

                Do all in *aula* rise
and cede him his hypothesis:
                Mother is requisite to son?
Or would they have none
                of his *theosis*?
He were a one for what's due her, captain.
Being ever a one for what's due *us*, captain.
He knew his Austin!
                                But he were ever

at his distinctions, captain.
They come – and they go, captain.

Robert Graves

498   *Sick Love*

O Love, be fed with apples while you may,
And feel the sun and go in royal array,
A smiling innocent on the heavenly causeway,

Though in what listening horror for the cry
That soars in outer blackness dismally,
The dumb blind beast, the paranoiac fury:

Be warm, enjoy the season, lift your head,
Exquisite in the pulse of tainted blood,
That shivering glory not to be despised.

Take your delight in momentariness,
Walk between dark and dark – a shining space
With the grave's narrowness, though not its peace.

499   *End of Play*

We have reached the end of pastime, for always,
Ourselves and everyone, though few confess it
Or see the sky other than, as of old,
A foolish smiling Mary-mantle blue;

Though life may still seem to dawdle golden
In some June landscape among giant flowers,
The grass to shine as cruelly green as ever,
Faith to descend in a chariot from the sky —

May seem only: a mirror and an echo
Mediate henceforth with vision and sound.
The cry of faith, no longer mettlesome,
Sounds as a blind man's pitiful plea of 'blind'.

We have at last ceased idling, which to regret
Were as shallow as to ask our milk-teeth back;
As many forthwith do, and on their knees
Call lugubriously upon chaste Christ.

We tell no lies now, at last cannot be
The rogues we were — so evilly linked in sense
With what we scrutinized that lion or tiger
Could leap from every copse, strike and devour us.

No more shall love in hypocritic pomp
Conduct its innocents through a dance of shame,
From timid touching of gloved fingers
To frantic laceration of naked breasts.

Yet love survives, the word carved on a sill
Under antique dread of the headsman's axe;
It is the echoing mind, as in the mirror
We stare on our dazed trunks at the block kneeling.

500   *She Tells Her Love while Half Asleep*

She tells her love while half asleep,
In the dark hours,
With half-words whispered low:
As Earth stirs in her winter sleep
And puts out grass and flowers
Despite the snow,
Despite the falling snow.

501   *To Juan at the Winter Solstice*

There is one story and one story only
That will prove worth your telling,
Whether as learned bard or gifted child;
To it all lines or lesser gauds belong
That startle with their shining
Such common stories as they stray into.

Is it of trees you tell, their months and virtues,
Of strange beasts that beset you,
Of birds that croak at you the Triple will?
Or of the Zodiac and how slow it turns
Below the Boreal Crown,
Prison of all true kings that ever reigned?

Water to water, ark again to ark,
From woman back to woman:
So each new victim treads unfalteringly
The never altered circuit of his fate,
Bringing twelve peers as witness
Both to his starry rise and starry fall.

Or is it of the Virgin's silver beauty,
All fish below the thighs?
She in her left hand bears a leafy quince;
When, with her right she crooks a finger smiling,
How may the King hold back?
Royally then he barters life for love.

Or of the undying snake from chaos hatched,
Whose coils contain the ocean,
Into whose chops with naked sword he springs,
Then in black water, tangled by the reeds,
Battles three days and nights,
To be spewed up beside her scalloped shore?

Much snow is falling, winds roar hollowly,
The owl hoots from the elder,
Fear in your heart cries to the loving-cup:
Sorrow to sorrow as the sparks fly upward.
The log groans and confesses
There is one story and one story only.

Dwell on her graciousness, dwell on her smiling,
Do not forget what flowers
The great boar trampled down in ivy time.
Her brow was creamy as the crested wave,
Her sea-blue eyes were wild
But nothing promised that is not performed.

Charles Sorley

502   *'All the Hills and Vales Along'*

All the hills and vales along
Earth is bursting into song,
And the singers are the chaps
Who are going to die perhaps.
    O sing, marching men,
    Till the valleys ring again.
    Give your gladness to earth's keeping,
    So be glad, when you are sleeping.

Cast away regret and rue,
Think what you are marching to.
Little live, great pass.
Jesus Christ and Barabbas
Were found the same day.
This died, that went his way.
    So sing with joyful breath,
    For why, you are going to death.
    Teeming earth will surely store
    All the gladness that you pour.

Earth that never doubts nor fears,
Earth that knows of death, not tears,
Earth that bore with joyful ease
Hemlock for Socrates,
Earth that blossomed and was glad
'Neath the cross that Christ had,
Shall rejoice and blossom too
When the bullet reaches you.
    Wherefore, men marching
    On the road to death, sing!
    Pour your gladness on earth's head,
    So be merry, so be dead.

From the hills and valleys earth
Shouts back the sound of mirth,
Tramp of feet and lilt of song
Ringing all the road along.
All the music of their going,
Ringing swinging glad song-throwing,
Earth will echo still, when foot
Lies numb and voice mute.
    On, marching men, on
    To the gates of death with song.

Sow your gladness for earth's reaping,
So you may be glad, though sleeping.
Strew your gladness on earth's bed,
So be merry, so be dead.

William Soutar

503   *The Tryst*

O luely, luely, cam she in
And luely she lay doun:
I kent her be her caller lips
And her breists sae sma' and roun'.

A' thru the nicht we spak nae word
Nor sinder'd bane frae bane:
A' thru the nicht I heard her hert
Gang soundin' wi' my ain.

It was about the waukrife hour
Whan cocks begin to craw
That she smool'd saftly thru the mirk
Afore the day wud daw.

Sae luely, luely, cam she in
Sae luely was she gaen;
And wi' her a' my simmer days
Like they had never been.

504   *The Room*

Into the quiet of this room
Words from the clamorous world come:
The shadows of the gesturing year
Quicken upon the stillness here.

The wandering waters do not mock
The pool within its wall of rock
But turn their healing tides and come
Even as the day into this room.

C. S. Lewis

505   *Scazons*

Walking to-day by a cottage I shed tears
When I remembered how once I had walked there
With my friends who are mortal and dead. Years
Little had healed the wound that was laid bare.

Out, little spear that stabs! I, fool, believed
I had outgrown the local unique sting.
I had transmuted wholly (I was deceived)
Into Love universal the lov'd thing.

But Thou, Lord, surely knewest thine own plan
When the angelic indifferencies with no bar
Universally loved, but Thou gav'st man
The tether and pang of the particular,

Which, like a chemic drop, infinitesimal,
Plashed into pure water, changing the whole,
Embodies and embitters and turns all
Spirit's sweet water to astringent soul,

That we, though small, might quiver with Fire's same
Substantial form as Thou — not reflect merely
Like lunar angels back to Thee cold flame.
Gods are we, Thou hast said; and we pay dearly.

506   From *Epigrams and Epitaphs, 6*

Save yourself. Run and leave me. I must go back.
Though we have escaped the sentry and are past the wall,
Though returning means mockery and the whip and the rack,
Yet their sending is too strong; I must turn at their call.
Save yourself. Leave me. I must go back.

Stevie Smith

507   *Scorpion*

'This night shall thy soul be required of thee'
My soul is never required of *me*
It always has to be somebody else of course
Will my soul be required of me tonight perhaps?

(I often wonder what it will be like
To have one's soul required of one
But all I can think of is the Out-Patients' Department –
'Are you Mrs Briggs, dear?'
No, I am Scorpion.)

I should like my soul to be required of me, so as
To waft over grass till it comes to the blue sea
I am very fond of grass, I always have been, but there must
Be no cow, person or house to be seen.

Sea and *grass* must be quite empty
Other souls can find somewhere *else*.

O Lord God please come
And require the soul of thy Scorpion

Scorpion so wishes to be gone.

George Orwell

508   A dressed man and a naked man
Stood by the kip-house fire,
Watching the sooty cooking-pots
That bubble on the wire;

And bidding tanners up and down,
Bargaining for a deal,
Naked skin for empty skin,
Clothes against a meal.

'Ten bob it is,' the dressed man said,
'These boots cost near a pound,
This coat's a blanket of itself
When you kip on the frosty ground.'

'One dollar,' said the naked man,
'And that's a hog too dear;
I've seen a man strip off his shirt
For a fag and a pot of beer.'

'Eight and a tanner,' the dressed man said,
'And my life-work is yours,
All I've earned at the end of a life
Knocking at farmers' doors;

Turnips, apples, hops and peas,
And the spike when times are slack,
Fifty years I've tobied it
For these clothes upon my back.'

'Take seven,' said the naked man,
'It's cold and the spikes are shut;
Better be naked here in kip
Than dressed in Lambeth Cut.'

'One tanner more,' the dressed man said,
'One tanner says the word,
Off comes my coat of ratcatcher
And my breeches of velvet cord;

Now pull my shirt over my head,
I'm naked sole to crown,
And that's the end of fifty years
Tobying up and down.'.

A minute and they had changed about,
And each had his desire;
A dressed man and a naked man
Stood by the kip-house fire.

William Empson

509   *This Last Pain*

This last pain for the damned the Fathers found:
'They knew the bliss with which they were not crowned.'
    Such, but on earth, let me foretell,
    Is all, of heaven or of hell.

Man, as the prying housemaid of the soul,
May know her happiness by eye to hole:
    He's safe; the key is lost; he knows
    Door will not open, nor hole close.

'What is conceivable can happen too,'
Said Wittgenstein, who had not dreamt of you;
   But wisely; if we worked it long
   We should forget where it was wrong.

Those thorns are crowns which, woven into knots,
Crackle under and soon boil fool's pots;
   And no man's watching, wise and long,
   Would ever stare them into song.

Thorns burn to a consistent ash, like man;
A splendid cleanser for the frying-pan:
   And those who leap from pan to fire
   Should this brave opposite admire.

All those large dreams by which men long live well
Are magic-lanterned on the smoke of hell;
   This then is real, I have implied,
   A painted, small, transparent slide.

These the inventive can hand-paint at leisure,
Or most emporia would stock our measure;
   And feasting in their dappled shade
   We should forget how they were made.

Feign then what's by a decent tact believed
And act that state is only so conceived,
   And build an edifice of form
   For house where phantoms may keep warm.

Imagine, then, by miracle, with me,
(Ambiguous gifts, as what gods give must be)
   What could not possibly be there,
   And learn a style from a despair.

510   *Note on Local Flora*

There is a tree native in Turkestan,
Or further east towards the Tree of Heaven,
Whose hard cold cones, not being wards to time,
Will leave their mother only for good cause;
Will ripen only in a forest fire;
Wait, to be fathered as was Bacchus once,
Through men's long lives, that image of time's end.
I knew the Phoenix was a vegetable.
So Semele desired her deity
As this in Kew thirsts for the Red Dawn.

John Betjeman

511   *The Arrest of Oscar Wilde at the Cadogan Hotel*

He sipped at a weak hock and seltzer
As he gazed at the London skies
Through the Nottingham lace of the curtains
Or was it his bees-winged eyes?

To the right and before him Pont Street
Did tower in her new built red,
As hard as the morning gaslight
That shone on his unmade bed,

'I want some more hock in my seltzer,
And Robbie, please give me your hand –
Is this the end or beginning?
How can I understand?

So you've brought me the latest *Yellow Book*:
And Buchan has got in it now:
Approval of what is approved of
Is as false as a well-kept vow.

More hock, Robbie – where is the seltzer?
Dear boy, pull again at the bell!
They are all little better than *cretins*,
Though this *is* the Cadogan Hotel.

One astrakhan coat is at Willis's –
Another one's at the Savoy:
Do fetch my morocco portmanteau,
And bring them on later, dear boy.'

A thump, and a murmur of voices –
('Oh why must they make such a din?')
As the door of the bedroom swung open
And TWO PLAIN CLOTHES POLICEMEN came in:

'Mr Woilde, we 'ave come for tew take yew
Where felons and criminals dwell:
We must ask yew tew leave with us quoietly
For this *is* the Cadogan Hotel.'

He rose, and he put down *The Yellow Book*.
He staggered – and, terrible-eyed,
He brushed past the palms on the staircase
And was helped to a hansom outside.

512   *The Metropolitan Railway*
              Baker Street Station Buffet

Early Electric! With what radiant hope
    Men formed this many-branched electrolier,
Twisted the flex around the iron rope
    And let the dazzling vacuum globes hang clear,
And then with hearts the rich contrivance fill'd
Of copper, beaten by the Bromsgrove Guild.

Early Electric! Sit you down and see,
    'Mid this fine woodwork and a smell of dinner,
A stained-glass windmill and a pot of tea,
    And sepia views of leafy lanes in PINNER, –
Then visualize, far down the shining lines,
Your parents' homestead set in murmuring pines.

Smoothly from HARROW, passing PRESTON ROAD,
    They saw the last green fields and misty sky,
At NEASDEN watched a workmen's train unload,
    And, with the morning villas sliding by,
They felt so sure on their electric trip
That Youth and Progress were in partnership.

And all that day in murky London Wall
    The thought of RUISLIP kept him warm inside;
At FARRINGDON that lunch hour at a stall
    He bought a dozen plants of London Pride;
While she, in arc-lit Oxford Street adrift,
Soared through the sales by safe hydraulic lift.

Early Electric! Maybe even here
    They met that evening at six-fifteen
Beneath the hearts of this electrolier
    And caught the first non-stop to WILLESDEN GREEN,
Then out and on, through rural RAYNER'S LANE
To autumn-scented Middlesex again.

Cancer has killed him. Heart is killing her.
    The trees are down. An Odeon flashes fire
Where stood their villa by the murmuring fir
    When 'they would for their children's good conspire.'
Of all their loves and hopes on hurrying feet
Thou art the worn memorial, Baker Street.

W. H. Auden

Prologue

O love, the interest itself in thoughtless Heaven,
Make simpler daily the beating of man's heart; within,
There in the ring where name and image meet,

Inspire them with such a longing as will make his thought
Alive like patterns a murmuration of starlings
Rising in joy over wolds unwittingly weave;

Here too on our little reef display your power,
This fortress perched on the edge of the Atlantic scarp,
The mole between all Europe and the exile-crowded sea;

And make us as Newton was, who in his garden watching
The apple falling towards England, became aware
Between himself and her of an eternal tie.

For now that dream which so long has contented our will,
I mean, of uniting the dead into a splendid empire,
Under whose fertilising flood the Lancashire moss

Sprouted up chimneys, and Glamorgan hid a life
Grim as a tidal rock-pool's in its glove-shaped valleys,
Is already retreating into her maternal shadow;

Leaving the furnaces gasping in the impossible air,
The flotsam at which Dumbarton gapes and hungers;
While upon wind-loved Rowley no hammer shakes

The cluster of mounds like a midget golf course, graves
Of some who created these intelligible dangerous marvels;
Affectionate people, but crude their sense of glory.

Far-sighted as falcons, they looked down another future;
For the seed in their loins were hostile, though afraid of their pride,
And, tall with a shadow now, inertly wait.

In bar, in netted chicken-farm, in lighthouse,
Standing on these impoverished constricting acres,
The ladies and gentlemen apart, too much alone,

Consider the years of the measured world begun,
The barren spiritual marriage of stone and watér.
Yet, O, at this very moment of our hopeless sigh

When inland they are thinking their thoughts but are watching
    these islands,
As children in Chester look to Moel Fammau to decide
On picnics by the clearness or withdrawal of her treeless crown,

Some possible dream, long coiled in the ammonite's slumber
Is uncurling, prepared to lay on our talk and kindness
Its military silence, its surgeon's idea of pain;

And out of the Future into actual History,
As when Merlin, tamer of horses, and his lords to whom
Stonehenge was still a thought, the Pillars passed

And into the undared ocean swung north their prow,
Drives through the night and star-concealing dawn
For the virgin roadsteads of our hearts an unwavering keel.

514

May with its light behaving
Stirs vessel, eye, and limb;
The singular and sad
Are willing to recover,
And to the swan-delighting river
The careless picnics come,
The living white and red.

The dead remote and hooded
In their enclosures rest; but we
From the vague woods have broken,
Forests where children meet
And the white angel-vampires flit;
We stand with shaded eye,
The dangerous apple taken.

The real world lies before us;
Animal motions of the young,
The common wish for death,
The pleasured and the haunted;
The dying master sinks tormented
In the admirers' ring,
The unjust walk the earth.

And love that makes impatient
The tortoise and the roe, and lays
The blonde beside the dark,
Urges upon our blood,
Before the evil and the good
How insufficient is
The endearment and the look.

515

Fish in the unruffled lakes
The swarming colours wear,
Swans in the winter air
A white perfection have,
And the great lion walks
Through his innocent grove;
Lion, fish, and swan
Act, and are gone
Upon Time's toppling wave.

We till shadowed days are done,
We must weep and sing
Duty's conscious wrong,
The Devil in the clock,
The Goodness carefully worn
For atonement or for luck;
We must lose our loves,
On each beast and bird that moves
Turn an envious look.

Sighs for folly said and done
Twist our narrow days;
But I must bless, I must praise
That you, my swan, who have
All gifts that to the swan
Impulsive Nature gave,
The majesty and pride,
Last night should add
Your voluntary love.

516   *The Shield of Achilles*

She looked over his shoulder
  For vines and olive trees,
Marble well-governed cities
  And ships upon untamed seas,
But there on the shining metal
  His hands had put instead
An artificial wilderness
  And a sky like lead.

A plain without a feature, bare and brown,
  No blade of grass, no sign of neighbourhood,
Nothing to eat and nowhere to sit down,
  Yet, congregated on its blankness, stood
  An unintelligible multitude.
A million eyes, a million boots in line,
Without expression, waiting for a sign.

Out of the air a voice without a face
   Proved by statistics that some cause was just
In tones as dry and level as the place:
   No one was cheered and nothing was discussed;
   Column by column in a cloud of dust
They marched away enduring a belief
Whose logic brought them, somewhere else, to grief.

     She looked over his shoulder
       For ritual pieties,
     White flower-garlanded heifers,
       Libation and sacrifice,
     But there on the shining metal
       Where the altar should have been,
     She saw by his flickering forge-light
       Quite another scene.

Barbed wire enclosed an arbitrary spot
   Where bored officials lounged (one cracked a joke)
And sentries sweated for the day was hot:
   A crowd of ordinary decent folk
   Watched from without and neither moved nor spoke
As three pale figures were led forth and bound
To three posts driven upright in the ground.

The mass and majesty of this world, all
   That carries weight and always weighs the same
Lay in the hands of others; they were small
   And could not hope for help and no help came:
   What their foes liked to do was done, their shame
Was all the worst could wish; they lost their pride
And died as men before their bodies died.

     She looked over his shoulder
       For athletes at their games,
     Men and women in a dance
       Moving their sweet limbs
     Quick, quick, to music,
       But there on the shining shield
     His hands had set no dancing-floor
       But a weed-choked field.

A ragged urchin, aimless and alone,
   Loitered about that vacancy, a bird
Flew up to safety from his well-aimed stone:
   That girls are raped, that two boys knife a third,
   Were axioms to him, who'd never heard
Of any world where promises were kept.
Or one could weep because another wept.

The thin-lipped armourer,
  Hephaestos hobbled away,
Thetis of the shining breasts
  Cried out in dismay
At what the god had wrought
  To please her son, the strong
Iron-hearted man-slaying Achilles
  Who would not live long.

Louis MacNeice

517   *The Sunlight on the Garden*

The sunlight on the garden
Hardens and grows cold,
We cannot cage the minute
Within its nets of gold,
When all is told
We cannot beg for pardon.

Our freedom as free lances
Advances towards its end;
The earth compels, upon it
Sonnets and birds descend;
And soon, my friend,
We shall have no time for dances.

The sky was good for flying
Defying the church bells
And every evil iron
Siren and what it tells:
The earth compels,
We are dying, Egypt, dying

And not expecting pardon,
Hardened in heart anew,
But glad to have sat under
Thunder and rain with you,
And grateful too
For sunlight on the garden.

518   *Leaving Barra*

The dazzle on the sea, my darling,
Leads from the western channel,
A carpet of brilliance taking
My leave for ever of the island.

I never shall visit that island
Again with its easy tempo –
The seal sunbathing, the circuit
Of gulls on the wing for garbage.

I go to a different garbage
And scuffle for scraps of notice,
Pretend to ignore the stigma
That stains my life and my leisure.

For fretful even in leisure
I fidget for different values,
Restless as a gull and haunted
By a hankering after Atlantis.

I do not know that Atlantis
Unseen and uncomprehended,
Dimly divined but keenly
Felt with a phantom hunger.

If only I could crush the hunger
If only I could lay the phantom
Then I should no doubt be happy
Like a fool or a dog or a buddha.

O the self-abnegation of Buddha
The belief that is disbelieving
The denial of chiaroscuro
Not giving a damn for existence!

But I would cherish existence
Loving the beast and the bubble
Loving the rain and the rainbow,
Considering philosophy alien.

For all the religions are alien
That allege that life is a fiction,
And when we agree in denial
The cock crows in the morning.

If only I could wake in the morning
And find I had learned the solution,
Wake with the knack of knowledge
Who as yet have only an inkling.

Though some facts foster the inkling —
The beauty of the moon and music,
The routine courage of the worker,
The gay endurance of women,

And you who to me among women
Stand for so much that I wish for,
I thank you, my dear, for the example
Of living like a fugue and moving.

For few are able to keep moving,
They drag and flag in the traffic;
While you are alive beyond question
Like the dazzle on the sea, my darling.

Lawrence Durrell

519   *Lesbos*

The Pleiades are sinking calm as paint,
And earth's huge camber follows out,
Turning in sleep, the oceanic curve,

Defined in concave like a human eye
Or cheek pressed warm on the dark's cheek,
Like dancers to a music they deserve.

This balcony, a moon-anointed shelf
Above a silent garden holds my bed.
I slept. But the dispiriting autumn moon,

In her slow expurgation of the sky
Needs company: is brooding on the dead,
And so am I now, so am I.

520   *Seferis*

Time quietly compiling us like sheaves
Turns round one day, beckons the special few,
With one bird singing somewhere in the leaves,
Someone like K. or somebody like you,
Free-falling target for the envious thrust,
So tilting into darkness go we must.

Thus the fading writer signing off
Sees in the vast perspectives of dispersal
His words float off like tiny seeds,
Wind-borne or bird-distributed notes,
To the very end of loves without rehearsal,
The stinging image riper than his deeds.

Yours must have set out like ancient
Colonists, from Delos or from Rhodes,
To dare the sun-gods, found great entrepôts,
Naples or Rio, far from man's known abodes,
To confer the quaint Grecian script on other men;
A new Greek fire ignited by your pen.

How marvellous to have done it and then left
It in the lost property office of the loving mind,
The secret whisper those who listen find.
You show us all the way the great ones went,
In silences becalmed, so well they knew
That even to die is somehow to invent.

George Barker

521   *Memorial Couplets for the Dying Ego*

1. I clasp in the hot pit and bed
    My living body and my spirit dead.

2. At quiet pools beside twisted trees
    Fall the cold tears of the Eumenides.

3. The voice of the sun cries out in despair:
    'Nowhere is everywhere! Everywhere is nowhere!'

4. On the far shore of his long dream, in
    Peace I sleep within my father's semen.

5. Where the dog barks no ghost goes by
    Only a man invisible to the eye.

6. The kingdom of love extends across the vast
    Four inch desert of the human heart.

7. Out of the blind beggar's cup
    Psyche in gold rises up.

8. Over the mountains and the morning lakes
    The sun rises like a heart, and breaks.

9. I have seen the Gates of Hell
    And run when I pressed the bell.

10. The daughterless and sonless seem
    Born to haunt the salmon stream.

11. Up from the dead mind and dead heart
    The roses of Golgotha start.

12. I burn like St Catherine's wheel
    Spun on fires I cannot feel.

Dylan Thomas

522

The force that through the green fuse drives the flower
Drives my green age; that blasts the roots of trees
Is my destroyer.
And I am dumb to tell the crooked rose
My youth is bent by the same wintry fever.

The force that drives the water through the rocks
Drives my red blood; that dries the mouthing streams
Turns mine to wax.
And I am dumb to mouth unto my veins
How at the mountain spring the same mouth sucks.

The hand that whirls the water in the pool
Stirs the quicksand; that ropes the blowing wind
Hauls my shroud sail.
And I am dumb to tell the hanging man
How of my clay is made the hangman's lime.

The lips of time leech to the fountain head;
Love drips and gathers, but the fallen blood
Shall calm her sores.
And I am dumb to tell a weather's wind
How time has ticked a heaven round the stars.

And I am dumb to tell the lover's tomb
How at my sheet goes the same crooked worm.

523   *The Conversation of Prayer*

The conversation of prayers about to be said
By the child going to bed and the man on the stairs
Who climbs to his dying love in her high room,
The one not caring to whom in his sleep he will move
And the other full of tears that she will be dead,

Turns in the dark on the sound they know will arise
Into the answering skies from the green ground,
From the man on the stairs and the child by his bed.
The sound about to be said in the two prayers
For the sleep in a safe land and the love who dies

Will be the same grief flying. Whom shall they calm?
Shall the child sleep unharmed or the man be crying?
The conversation of prayers about to be said
Turns on the quick and the dead, and the man on the stairs
To-night shall find no dying but alive and warm

In the fire of his care his love in the high room.
And the child not caring to whom he climbs his prayer
Shall drown in a grief as deep as his true grave,
And mark the dark eyed wave, through the eyes of sleep,
Dragging him up the stairs to one who lies dead.

524   *A Refusal to Mourn the Death, by Fire,*
                  of a Child in London

Never until the mankind making
Bird beast and flower
Fathering and all humbling darkness
Tells with silence the last light breaking
And the still hour
Is come of the sea tumbling in harness

And I must enter again the round
Zion of the water bead
And the synagogue of the ear of corn
Shall I let pray the shadow of a sound
Or sow my salt seed
In the least valley of sackcloth to mourn

The majesty and burning of the child's death.
I shall not murder
The mankind of her going with a grave truth
Nor blaspheme down the stations of the breath
With any further
Elegy of innocence and youth.

Deep with the first dead lies London's daughter,
Robed in the long friends,
The grains beyond age, the dark veins of her mother,
Secret by the unmourning water
Of the riding Thames.
After the first death, there is no other.

525   *The Hunchback in the Park*

The hunchback in the park
A solitary mister
Propped between trees and water
From the opening of the garden lock
That lets the trees and water enter
Until the Sunday sombre bell at dark

Eating bread from a newspaper
Drinking water from the chained cup
That the children filled with gravel
In the fountain basin where I sailed my ship
Slept at night in a dog kennel
But nobody chained him up.

Like the park birds he came early
Like the water he sat down
And Mister they called Hey mister
The truant boys from the town
Running when he had heard them clearly
On out of sound

Past lake and rockery
Laughing when he shook his paper
Hunchbacked in mockery
Through the loud zoo of the willow groves
Dodging the park keeper
With his stick that picked up leaves.

And the old dog sleeper
Alone between nurses and swans
While the boys among willows

Made the tigers jump out of their eyes
To roar on the rockery stones
And the groves were blue with sailors

Made all day until bell time
A woman figure without fault
Straight as a young elm
Straight and tall from his crooked bones
That she might stand in the night
After the locks and chains

All night in the unmade park
After the railings and shrubberies
The birds the grass the trees the lake
And the wild boys innocent as strawberries
Had followed the hunchback
To his kennel in the dark.

John Heath-Stubbs

526   *Mozart*

Mozart walking in the garden,
Tormented beside cool waters,
Remembered the empty-headed girl,
And the surly porters,

The singing-bird in the snuff-box,
And the clown's comic nose;
And scattered the thin blue petals
Of a steel rose.

From *Artorius*

527   [1]

The Age of Bronze awoke now in brutality:
Barbarian warriors blustered out of the wastelands,
And wars were waged with more effective weapons.
The handsome heroes exhibited their hardihood
In wild tumult, by windy Troys,
Fighting in chariots, fiercely cheered on
To plunder and pillage, by Homeric poets.

The Age of Iron, out of Asia, extended
A worse development of destruction – war
Become less human, more horrible and more hideous;
The wheel is in motion, willy-nilly we march on
To the uses of artillery, and atomic overkill.
Each technical gain entails the giving up
Of a spiritual good, of certainty and security.
This puts paid, we presume, to that specious puerility
Which professes to hail, in History, a progress.
Mutability masters us – no myth of improvement
Is the law of life; laugh it off, if you will –
Anangke is the arbitress, and enjoins us: 'Adapt!'
    The Saturnalia was celebrated at the Winter Solstice
In remembrance, by the Romans, of the reign of Saturn:
By ritualised ribaldry, and licensed riot –
The posts are decked, the porticoes and the doorways,
With gaiety and greenery, and gifts exchanged;
The slaves sit down and are served by their masters,
Reconstructing a far-off and irrecoverable freedom
Nostalgically lost in the long-ago of legend,
When the world was governed by wiser gods.
But at this season of mid-winter mirth, the Saviour,
Christ, was born in the cavern at Bethlehem,
To oust from Olympus the etiolated eidola;
Jove and his fellows fell under the judgement
Of old age also, and entered that emptiness
Where man's lost dreams dwindle in darkness.
The stable, for once, was the centre of the world;
Not the dialectical dragons, but the dumb ox
And the ass in humility, hung their heads
By a manger of straw, where Mary the Mother
Looked at her Love and hushed Him with a lullaby.
From the Solstice of Capricorn the Cross stems up,
The ends of the transom transfixing the equinoxes,
The summit at Cancer – Christ in the circle
Of the stars of fatality, to ensure our freedom,
Slain for our salvation, in the celestial wheel,
From the foundation of the world; He was found worthy.
    At this Feast it is the kindly custom of Christians
To honour in each other the Divine Image
By the giving of gifts; as with incense and gold,
And with myrrh, the Magi from the marches of the world
Were beckoned to Bethlehem by a bright comet.
Feasting and frolic and jollity are found here –
Not the mirth of Saturn's mythical magisterium,
But the felt prescience of a possible freedom
Eschatologically offered at the end of the ages,
Whose shoots are burgeoning, and begin now to show.

But the Prince of Darkness delights to pervert this:
The affluent honour Gluttony and Avarice,
In spewing drunkenness and a spending spree,
Guzzling their guts and giving for advantage,
Disdaining the Lazaruses who languish at their doors.
In Gehenna these gourmets will get their reward –
Trussed up and transformed into battery turkeys,
With sprigs of holly stuck in their holes;
In the form of a foolish and florid Santa Claus,
With cottonwool whiskers, as a witty contrivance,
Beelzebub bastes them with their own butter.

They kept the feast at the castle of Cadbury;
While solid snow silvered the landscape,
And hungrily the wolves howled to the wind.
Artorius and his army were abroad – in Armorica,
Some said. They slogged through sombre forests;
There were rumours that he reared at the authority of Rome,
As Carausius and Constantine and Maximus had claimed to.
No certainty was divulged; despatches were sparse;
A dreary and disappointing campaign dragged on.

The governance of his realm was given to Guanhumara –
The Queen ruling, with a Council of Regency;
The sons of his sister had seemed the most fitting:
The courteous Gwalchmai kept at the court,
Arranging all things in the absence of Artorius;
With his younger brother, black-haired and beloved
Of the popular party – for plainly men saw
In Modred the most charming and mannerly of mortals;
Nor guessed, under the guise of that graciousness, his heart
Inwardly consumed, cankered and calloused.
The ferocious passion of a frustrated poet,
Self-regarding romanticism, ravaged his soul.

Resinous pine torches perfumed the palace,
Casting through the gloom a guttering glare.
The hall was gay and garnished with greenery –
The bright holly, with bloody berries,
Decked it, and the ivy dedicate to Dionysus:
Rubicund and pugnacious, the robin red-breast,
Who murders, they say, each midsummer his sire,
Harbours in the holly, and the ivy holds
The King of the ramage, the cutty wren,
A trilling troglodyte. From the topmost rafter
Was suspended a sprig of the sacral mistletoe,
A Golden Bough, from the great boles
Of ancient oaks and Avalonian apple-trees
Darkly with incantations by the Druids castrated –
Mysterious, as the flower of the midsummer fern:
It hung there for lovers lightly to hallow.

The boards were loaded with baked boars' heads,
Venison, and various seasonable viands;
Barrels were broached, of beer and mead.
The dinner being done, they called for diversions
Of mirth and pastime, for the promoting of merriment.
Bards and buffoons and minstrels were brought in.
Dwarfish jesters, and jugglers disported;
Self-pitying songs of amatory suffering,
By acclaimed artists were executed for the auditors.
    Popular plaudits hailed this performance;
But somewhat sadly smiling, the Queen,
Guanhumara, gravely gave her opinion:
'This jejune jangling jars on our nerves;
Nor charms nor cheers us, but the revolutions of chance
Brings into mind, and the bitter memory
Of Artorius, absent oversea in Armorica:
News of his campaign comes niggard to our knowledge.
This occasion asks entertainment more aulic –
Gwion, our poet, is pensioned for this purpose;
Let him touch the high tones of his harp,
And bring forth some lay or legend – of Bronwen,
White-bosomed sister of Bran the Blessed;
Of her sorrow, the victim of a vicious slander;
Of her heart's breaking for the brave men, the heroes
Laid in the cold clay for her cause,
Two islands destroyed – her tragic destiny.'

528   [2]

[The ending: the hero's body is given to the sea]

It was the virgin Zennora, who dwelt
In a cranny of the cliff, among the scooped-out holes
Of shearwater and puffin. None could remember
A time when she did not dwell there, even the oldest;
Nor knew for a certainty what manner of woman she was.
Some said a Christian votaress, and some
A Druid lady of the standing stones;
And some said Myrddyn's sister.
Her food was the bulbs of the wild garlic
That flourished all about, and fish
Which her three seals brought her
Out of the deep waters –
Silkie, Sæhund and Slippa.
And these attended her now,
Clumsily lolloping along behind her.

When the men saw those creatures,
With their great liquid eyes, they crossed themselves.
They thought them human souls who, for some unknown sin,
Did penance in those bodies. They were wrong,
Construing thus those harmless beasts.

They saw that she held in her hands a great crowd,
Or a lyre, formed from the shell of a green sea-turtle,
Strung with dolphin's sinews. She greeted them
In a gruff deep voice: 'Men, what do you here,
In your beauty, strength, and hideousness,
Carrying a corpse?' And Glewlwyd: 'This body is
Artorius, erstwhile Emperor in this island;
And we consign it to the sea. It is our wyrd.'
And she: 'You do well:
Not wise the thought, a grave for Arthur.'
Then Morvran: 'There is no one here
To hallow this parting, or to sing
The praises of the dead. Lady, if you have any skill
In music, sing for us.' And she: 'I have such skill,
And I will sing.'

Then, while they pushed the raft of boughs and the coffin
Into the outgoing tide, she took her crowd,
Preluding among the strings – they awoke
Sea-echoes of deep caves, and the moan of breakers
On grinding shingle. Enchanted by the sound,
Silkie, Sæhund and Slippa
Were still and listened, their eyes wide,
Forgetting their fear of man. The raft drifted
Further and further from the shore,
Over the darkening waves. Then she began to sing,
Her voice booming over the waters:

       'We send you, body of a notable man,
       By the waste paths of the sea,
       The salt, unharvested element,

       'To the polity of the fish,
       To the furtiveness of the crab,
       To the tentacle of the squid,

       'To the red ruler of the tornado,
       To the green ruler of the undersea,
       To the black ruler of the dead,

       'To the three-headed dog,
       To the sharp-toothed Scylla –
       Cuttle-fish, and sea-bitch.

'O Lord, who said to the deep:
"So far, and no further!"
Deliver Thy darling from the tooth of the shark.

'O Christ, descending
To the profound, redeem him
From the belly of the fish.

'O Spirit, brooding on tohu-bohu, save
From the embrace of the sea-morgan,
From Tiamat, the formless –

'Dove, bearing your olive leaf
Through the rains of the new year,
Breathe into the nostrils of the drowned.

'Star of the Sea,
In intercession gleam
Over the black waters.

'And our vows follow him,
Like petrels flittering
Over the crests and troughs of the waves.

'To the verdict and oblivion of the sea,
Artorius, we consign
Your actions, your defeat.'

She ceased; and Silkie and his two brothers
Shook themselves out of their trance, and saw
The strangers standing by.
Then Sæhund gave a soft and sudden 'Bao!'
They slid into the sea, following the raft
Far out from shore. They bobbed and plunged,
Joyfully, in the rolling waves.
The unfallen creatures danced in the salt element:
The source and origin of all life.

Philip Larkin

529   *No Road*

Since we agreed to let the road between us
Fall to disuse,
And bricked our gates up, planted trees to screen us,
And turned all time's eroding agents loose,
Silence, and space, and strangers – our neglect
Has not had much effect.

Leaves drift unswept, perhaps; grass creeps unmown;
No other change.
So clear it stands, so little overgrown,
Walking that way tonight would not seem strange,
And still would be allowed. A little longer,
And time will be the stronger,

Drafting a world where no such road will run
From you to me;
To watch that world come up like a cold sun,
Rewarding others, is my liberty.
Not to prevent it is my will's fulfilment.
Willing it, my ailment.

530   *If, My Darling*

If my darling were once to decide
Not to stop at my eyes,
But to jump, like Alice, with floating skirt into my head,

She would find no tables and chairs,
No mahogany claw-footed sideboards,
No undisturbed embers;

The tantalus would not be filled, nor the fender-seat cosy,
Nor the shelves stuffed with small-printed books for the Sabbath,
Nor the butler bibulous, the housemaids lazy:

She would find herself looped with the creep of varying light,
Monkey-brown, fish-grey, a string of infected circles
Loitering like bullies, about to coagulate;

Delusions that shrink to the size of a woman's glove
Then sicken inclusively outwards. She would also remark
The unwholesome floor, as it might be the skin of a grave,

From which ascends an adhesive sense of betrayal,
A Grecian statue kicked in the privates, money,
A swill-tub of finer feelings. But most of all

She'd be stopping her ears against the incessant recital
Intoned by reality, larded with technical terms,
Each one double-yolked with meaning and meaning's rebuttal:

For the skirl of that bulletin unpicks the world like a knot,
And to hear how the past is past and the future neuter
Might knock my darling off her unpriceable pivot.

531   *Days*

What are days for?
Days are where we live.
They come, they wake us
Time and time over.
They are to be happy in:
Where can we live but days?

Ah, solving that question
Brings the priest and the doctor
In their long coats
Running over the fields.

532   *MCMXIV*

Those long uneven lines
Standing as patiently
As if they were stretched outside
The Oval or Villa Park,
The crowns of hats, the sun
On moustached archaic faces
Grinning as if it were all
An August Bank Holiday lark;

And the shut shops, the bleached
Established names on the sunblinds,
The farthings and sovereigns,
And dark-clothed children at play
Called after kings and queens,
The tin advertisements
For cocoa and twist, and the pubs
Wide open all day;

And the countryside not caring:
The place-names all hazed over
With flowering grasses, and fields
Shadowing Domesday lines
Under wheat's restless silence;
The differently-dressed servants
With tiny rooms in huge houses,
The dust behind limousines;

Never such innocence,
Never before or since,
As changed itself to past
Without a word – the men
Leaving the gardens tidy,
The thousands of marriages
Lasting a little while longer:
Never such innocence again.

533   *Homage to a Government*

Next year we are to bring the soldiers home
For lack of money, and it is all right.
Places they guarded, or kept orderly,
Must guard themselves, and keep themselves orderly.
We want the money for ourselves at home
Instead of working. And this is all right.

It's hard to say who wanted it to happen,
But now it's been decided nobody minds.
The places are a long way off, not here,
Which is all right, and from what we hear
The soldiers there only made trouble happen.
Next year we shall be easier in our minds.

Next year we shall be living in a country
That brought its soldiers home for lack of money.
The statues will be standing in the same
Tree-muffled squares, and look nearly the same.
Our children will not know it's a different country.
All we can hope to leave them now is money.

1969

534   *The Explosion*

On the day of the explosion
Shadows pointed towards the pithead:
In the sun the slagheap slept.

Down the lane came men in pitboots
Coughing oath-edged talk and pipe-smoke,
Shouldering off the freshened silence.

One chased after rabbits; lost them;
Came back with a nest of lark's eggs;
Showed them; lodged them in the grasses.

So they passed in beards and moleskins,
Fathers, brothers, nicknames, laughter,
Through the tall gates standing open.

At noon, there came a tremor; cows
Stopped chewing for a second; sun,
Scarfed as in a heat-haze, dimmed.

The dead go on before us, they
Are sitting in God's house in comfort,
We shall see them face to face —

Plain as lettering in the chapels
It was said, and for a second
Wives saw men of the explosion

Larger than in life they managed —
Gold as on a coin, or walking
Somehow from the sun towards them,

One showing the eggs unbroken.

Laurence Lerner

535   *Raspberries*

Once, as a child, I ate raspberries. And forgot.
And then, years later,
A raspberry flowered on my palate, and the past
Burst in unfolding layers within me.
It tasted of grass and honey.
You were there, watching and smiling.
Our love unfolded in the taste of raspberries.

More years have passed; and you are far, and ill;
And I, unable to reach you, eating raspberries.
Their dark damp red, their cool and fragile fur
On the always edge of decay, on the edge of bitter,
Bring a hush of taste to the mouth

Tasting of earth and of crushed leaves,
Tasting of summer's insecurity,
Tasting of crimson, dark with the smell of honey,

Tasting of childhood and of remembered childhood,
And now, now first, the darker taste of dread.

Sap and imprisoned sunlight and crushed grass
Lie on my tongue like a shadow,
Burst like impending news on my aching palate

Tasting not only of death (I could bear that)
But of death and of you together,
The folded layers of love and the sudden future,
Tasting of earth and the thought of you as earth

As I go on eating, waiting for the news.

John Wain

536   *Arrival*

Rich blood disturbed my thought
I knew no shape nor size
I wondered, and was not.

Cradled in salt, I had
no tears to dim my eyes
my coupled veins were glad.

love held me cradled there
but still I dreamed of air.

Love held me soft and coiled
O but the mind, the mind!
that tenderness was foiled:

I fed on love alone
yet in its tender rind
my brain cried out for bone.

I writhed in my own heat
I willed my heart to beat.

I shouldered love aside
the cold air spoke my name
I clutched the air: I cried:

my mother's flesh lay spent
cool ashes after flame
she sighed: she gave consent:

caressed by light, I lay
small, in the human day.

Elizabeth Jennings

537   *Song for a Birth or a Death*

Last night I saw the savage world
And heard the blood beat up the stair;
The fox's bark, the owl's shrewd pounce,
The crying creatures – all were there,
And men in bed with love and fear.

The slit moon only emphasised
How blood must flow and teeth must grip.
What does the calm light understand,
The light which draws the tide and ship
And drags the owl upon its prey
And human creatures lip to lip?

Last night I watched how pleasure must
Leap from disaster with its will:
The fox's fear, the watch-dog's lust
Know that all matings mean a kill:
And human creatures kissed in trust
Feel the blood throb to death until

The seed is struck, the pleasure's done,
The birds are thronging in the air;
The moon gives way to widespread sun.
Yes but the pain still crouches where
The young fox and the child are trapped
And cries of love are cries of fear.

John Montague

538   *Like Dolmens round My Childhood,*
              the Old People

Like dolmens round my childhood, the old people.

Jamie MacCrystal sang to himself,
A broken song without tune, without words;
He tipped me a penny every pension day,
Fed kindly crusts to winter birds.
When he died, his cottage was robbed,
Mattress and money box torn and searched.
Only the corpse they didn't disturb.

Maggie Owens was surrounded by animals,
A mongrel bitch and shivering pups,
Even in her bedroom a she-goat cried.
She was a well of gossip defiled,
Fanged chronicler of a whole countryside;
Reputed a witch, all I could find
Was her lonely need to deride.

The Nialls lived along a mountain lane
Where heather bells bloomed, clumps of foxglove.
All were blind, with Blind Pension and Wireless,
Dead eyes serpent-flicked as one entered
To shelter from a downpour of mountain rain.
Crickets chirped under the rocking hearthstone
Until the muddy sun shone out again.

Ted Hughes

539   *Cleopatra to the Asp*

The bright mirror I braved: the devil in it
Loved me like my soul, my soul:
Now that I seek myself in a serpent
My smile is fatal.

Nile moves in me; my thighs splay
Into the squalled Mediterranean;
My brain hides in that Abyssinia
Lost armies foundered towards.

Desert and river unwrinkle again.
Seeming to bring them the waters that make drunk
Caesar, Pompey, Antony I drank.
Now let the snake reign.

A half-deity out of Capricorn,
This rigid Augustus mounts
With his sword virginal indeed; and has shorn
Summarily the moon-horned river

From my bed. May the moon
Ruin him with virginity! Drink me, now, whole
With coiled Egypt's past; then from my delta
Swim like a fish toward Rome.

540   *Urn Burial*

Born to these gentle stones and grass,
The whole of himself to himself:
Cheek by jowl in with the weasel;
Caesar no ghost but his passion.

An improvement on the eagle's hook,
The witty spider competitor,
Sets his word's strength against the rock,
No foot wrong in the dance figure –

So by manners, by music, to abash
The wretch of death that stands in his shoes:
The aping shape of earth – sure
Of its weight now as in future.

Peter Levi

541   In stone settlements when the moon is stone
and gardens have died back to the bare bone
the stars consume to frost, they have their wish,
they wither and flourish.

A wrinkled ocean washes out star-frost,
nothing survives in it, nothing is lost,
far deeper than the cold shadows of fish
I wither and flourish.

As the wild rose in winter is not seen,
the weak scent and the prickle and the green,
but hedges live, the sun is dragonish,
we wither and flourish.

Seamus Heaney

542   *The Tollund Man*

I

Some day I will go to Aarhus
To see his peat-brown head,
The mild pods of his eye-lids,
His pointed skin cap.

In the flat country nearby
Where they dug him out,
His last gruel of winter seeds
Caked in his stomach,

Naked except for
The cap, noose and girdle,
I will stand a long time.
Bridegroom to the goddess,

She tightened her torc on him
And opened her fen,
Those dark juices working
Him to a saint's kept body,

Trove of the turfcutters'
Honeycombed workings.
Now his stained face
Reposes at Aarhus.

II

I could risk blasphemy,
Consecrate the cauldron bog
Our holy ground and pray
Him to make germinate

The scattered, ambushed
Flesh of labourers,
Stockinged corpses
Laid out in the farmyards,

Tell-tale skin and teeth
Flecking the sleepers
Of four young brothers, trailed
For miles along the lines.

III

Something of his sad freedom
As he rode the tumbril
Should come to me, driving,
Saying the names

Tollund, Grabaulle, Nebelgard,
Watching the pointing hands
Of country people,
Not knowing their tongue.

Out there in Jutland
In the old man-killing parishes
I will feel lost,
Unhappy and at home.

543   *The Singer's House*

When they said *Carrickfergus* I could hear
the frosty echo of saltminers' picks.
I imagined it, chambered and glinting,
a township built of light.

What do we say any more
to conjure the salt of our earth?
So much comes and is gone
that should be crystal and kept

and amicable weathers
that bring up the grain of things,
their tang of season and store,
are all the packing we'll get.

So I say to myself *Gweebarra*
and its music hits off the place
like water hitting off granite.
I see the glittering sound

framed in your window,
knives and forks set on oilcloth,
and the seals' heads, suddenly outlined,
scanning everything.

People here used to believe
that drowned souls lived in the seals.
At spring tides they might change shape.
They loved music and swam in for a singer

who might stand at the end of summer
in the mouth of a whitewashed turf-shed,
his shoulder to the jamb, his song
a rowboat far out in evening.

When I came here first you were always singing,
a hint of the clip of the pick
in your winnowing climb and attack.
Raise it again, man. We still believe what we hear.

Brian Patten

544   *After Frost*

It's hard to tell what bird it is
Singing in the misty wood,
Or the reason for its song
So late after evening's come.

When all else has dropped its name
Down into the scented dark
Its song grown cool and clear says
Nothing much to anyone,

But catches hold a whisper in my brain
That only now is understood.
It says, rest your life against this song,
It's rest enough for anyone.

Acknowledgments and References

Introduction (p. 27). Extract from the essay 'The Three Voices of Poetry' reprinted from *On Poetry and Poets* by T. S. Eliot by permission of Faber and Faber Ltd, and of Farrar, Straus and Giroux, Inc. Copyright © 1943, 1945, 1951, 1956, 1957 by T. S. Eliot.

1. Reprinted by kind permission of Sally Purcell.

2. Copyright © John Wain, 1979. First published in *Argo*, 1979.

3. Reprinted by permission of Oxford University Press from *Anglo-Saxon Poetry*, 1943, by Gavin Bone.

4. Reprinted by kind permission of Sally Purcell.

5. Copyright © John Wain, 1981.

6. Reprinted by permission of Oxford University Press from *Anglo-Saxon Poetry*, 1943, by Gavin Bone.

9, 11–23. Reprinted by permission of Oxford University Press from *The Oxford Book of Medieval English Verse*, chosen and edited by Celia and Kenneth Sisam, © Oxford University Press, 1970.

25. Reprinted by permission of Oxford University Press from *Definition of a Waterfall* by John Ormond, © Oxford University Press, 1973.

26–27. Reprinted by permission of J. M. Dent and Sons Ltd from *Pearl, Cleanness, Patience and Sir Gawain and the Green Knight*, edited by A. C. Cawley and J. J. Anderson (Everyman's Library Series). **26** *Pearl*, I, 1–24; **27** *Sir Gawain and the Green Knight*, 1178–207.

28–30. Reprinted by permission of J. M Dent & Sons Ltd from *The Vision of Piers Plowman* by William Langland, edited by A. V. C. Schmidt (Everyman's Library Series). **28** Prologue, 1–19; **29** II, 1–28; **30** XVIII, 110–409.

33. *Troilus and Criseyde*, III, clxx-clxxxix.

34–6. Reprinted by permission of J. M. Dent and Sons Ltd from *Canterbury Tales* by Geoffrey Chaucer, edited by A. C. Cawley (Everyman's Library Series). **34** Prologue, 445–76; **35** The Miller's Tale, 3233–70; **36** The Pardoner's Tale, 918–68.

37–38. Reprinted by permission of Oxford University Press from *The Oxford Book of Medieval English Verse*, chosen and edited by Celia and Kenneth Sisam, © Oxford University Press, 1970.

39. *The Testament of Cresseid*, 36–98.

43. *The Tretis of the Tua Mariit Wemen and the Wedo*, 385–496.

44. *Ane Ballat of Our Lady*, 61–83.

53. *The Tunning of Elinor Rumming*, Fit the Fifth, 37–85.

80–1. *The Faerie Queene*, **80** I, 1, i–xx; **81** II, 12, lviii–lxxx.

110. *Venus and Adonis*, 259–366.

111–12. *Henry V*, **111** Act III, Prologue; **112** *from* Act IV, Prologue.

113–14. *Hamlet*, **113** *from* I, iv; **114** *from* V, i.

115–16. *Othello*, **115** *from* I, iii; **116** *from* V, ii.

117–18. *Macbeth*, **117** *from* II, ii; **118** *from* V, v.

119. *King Lear, from* IV, vii.

120–1. *Antony and Cleopatra*, **120** *from* IV, xiv; **121** *from* IV, xv.

122. *Timon of Athens, from* IV, iii.

123. *Pericles, from* III, i.

124–5. *Cymbeline, from* IV, ii.

126. *The Tempest, from* V, i.

135–7. Reprinted by permission of J. M. Dent & Sons Ltd from *Complete Plays and Poems* by Christopher Marlowe, edited by J. C. Maxwell and E. D. Pendry (Everyman's Library Series). **135** *Tamburlaine the Great, Part I, from* V, i; **136** *Doctor Faustus, from* [V, i]; **137** *Hero and Leander*, II, 227–334.

138. *Hero and Leander*, IV, 1–75.

163. From *Summer's Last Will and Testament*.

192. *The Alchemist, from* II, i.

198. *The White Devil, from* V, iv.

205–9. Reprinted by permission of J. M. Dent and Sons Ltd from *The English Poems of George Herbert*, edited by C. A. Patrides (Everyman's Library Series).

218–24. *Paradise Lost*, **218** I, 1–270; **219** I, 457–89; **220** II, 629–734; **221** II, 871–1055; **222** III, 416–515; **223** IV, 689–775; **224** VII, 1–39.

225. *Paradise Regain'd*, II, 260–389.

226–9. *Samson Agonistes*, **226** 326–67; **227** 577–98; **228** 909–96; **229** 1612–758.

231–2. *Hudibras*, **231** I, i, 1–230; **232** III, ii, 267–350.

252. *Annus Mirabilis*, ccx–cclxxxvi.

253. 'To My Honour'd Kinsman, John Driden', 36–134.

256–7. *Absalom and Achitophel*, **256** 543–659; **257** 933–1031.

261–3. Reprinted from *Complete Poems* by John Wilmot, Earl of Rochester, 1968, edited by David Vieth and published by Yale University Press.

266. 'Verses on the Death of Dr Swift', 73–280.

268. 'Epistle to Augustus', 201–301.

269. 'Epistle to Dr Arbuthnot', 125–214.

270. *The Rape of the Lock*, Canto II.

272. *The Dunciad*, IV, 627–56.

275–6. *The Seasons*, **275** II, 432–537; **276** IV, 223–321.

288. 'A Song to David', i–xxvii.

290–1. Reprinted by permission of J. M. Dent and Sons Ltd from *Poems and Plays* by Oliver Goldsmith, edited by Tom Davis (Everyman's Library Series). *The Deserted Village*, **290** 75–264; **291** 395–430.

296. 'Phoebe Dawson', 59–116.

300. *Milton*, Book the First, Plate xxix, 8–29.

313–14. *The Prelude* (1805), **313** IV, 316–45; **314** XIII, 1–119.

331. *Childe Harold's Pilgrimage*, xxi–xxviii.

333. *Don Juan*, x–xxviii.

335–9. Reprinted by permission of J. M. Dent and Sons Ltd from *Selected Poems* by Percy Bysshe Shelley, edited by Timothy Webb (Everyman's Library Series). **336** 'Letter to Maria Gisborne', 193–323.

340–1. Reprinted by permission of J. M. Dent & Sons Ltd from *Selected Poems* by John Clare, edited by John William and Anne Tibble (Everyman's Library Series).

355. Reprinted by permission of Lawrence and Wishart from *Come All Ye Bold Miners*, 1952, edited by A. L. Lloyd.

358–9. *The Rubáiyát of Omar Khayyám* (first version), **358** xvii–xxviii; **359** lxvii–lxxv.

361. *The Passing of Arthur*, 301–60.

405. *Amours de Voyage*, Canto II to end of Letter IV.

426–36. Reprinted from *Collected Poems* by Thomas Hardy, published by Macmillan, New York, 1953.

448. *The Testament of Beauty*, I, 277–336.

453. Reprinted by permission of the Society of Authors as the literary representative of the Estate of A. E. Housman and Jonathan Cape Ltd, publishers of A. E. Housman's *Collected Poems*; and of Holt, Rinehart and Winston, Publishers, from

'A Shropshire Lad' (Authorized Edition) from *The Collected Poems of A. E. Housman*. Copyright 1939, 1940, © 1965 by Holt, Rinehart and Winston. Copyright © 1967, 1968 by Robert E. Symons.

454–5. Reprinted by permission of the Society of Authors as the literary representative of the Estate of A. E. Housman and Jonathan Cape Ltd, publishers of A. E. Housman's *Collected Poems*; and of Holt, Rinehart and Winston, Publishers, from *The Collected Poems of A. E. Housman*. Copyright 1936 by Barclay's Bank Ltd. Copyright © 1964 by Robert E. Symons.

456. Reprinted by permission of William Heinemann Ltd, London.

457. Reprinted by permission of The National Trust and Macmillan London Ltd, and of Doubleday and Company, Inc. from *The Definitive Edition of Rudyard Kipling's Verse*.

458. Reprinted by permission of The National Trust and Methuen and Co. Ltd from *The Definitive Edition of Rudyard Kipling's Verse*.

459–67. Reprinted by permission of Michael and Anne Yeats and the Macmillan Company of London Ltd, and of Macmillan Publishing Company Inc., from *Collected Poems* by William Butler Yeats. **459–60** 'In Memory of Major Robert Gregory' and 'To a Young Girl' copyright 1919 by Macmillan Publishing Company Inc., renewed 1947 by Bertha Georgie Yeats; **461** 'The Leaders of the Crowd', copyright 1924 by Macmillan Publishing Company Inc., renewed 1952 by Bertha Georgie Yeats; **462–3** 'A Prayer for My Son' and 'Leda and the Swan', copyright 1928 by Macmillan Publishing Company Inc., renewed 1956 by Bertha Georgie Yeats; **464–7** 'Byzantium', 'Crazy Jane Talks with the Bishop', 'Crazy Jane on God' and 'Crazy Jane Grown Old Looks at the Dancers', copyright 1933 by Macmillan Publishing Company Inc., renewed 1961 by Bertha Georgie Yeats.

469. Reprinted by permission of A. D. Peters Ltd.

470–1. Reprinted by permission of the Literary Trustees of Walter de la Mare and the Society of Authors as their representative.

475. Reprinted by permission of the Society of Authors as the literary representative of the Estate of John Masefield; and of Macmillan Publishing Company Inc. from *A Letter from Pontus* by John Masefield. Copyright 1936 by John Masefield, renewed 1964 by John Masefield.

476. Reprinted by permission of the Society of Authors as the literary representative of the Estate of John Masefield; and of Macmillan Publishing Company Inc. from *Poems* by John Masefield. Copyright 1916 by John Masefield, renewed 1944 by John Masefield.

477. Reprinted by permission of Mrs Iris Wise and Macmillan, London and Basingstoke, and of Macmillan Publishing Company Inc., from *Collected Poems* by James Stephens.

478–9. Reprinted by permission of the Society of Authors as the literary representative of the Estate of James Joyce; and of Viking Penguin Inc. from *Collected Poems* by James Joyce. Copyright 1918 by B. W. Huebsch, 1946 by Nora Joyce.

481–2. Reprinted by permission of Laurence Pollinger Ltd and the Estate of the late Mrs Frieda Lawrence Ravagli from *The Collected Poems of D. H. Lawrence*, published by Martin Secker, 1928; and of Viking Penguin Inc. from *The Portable D. H. Lawrence*. **481** 'End of Another Home Holiday' copyright 1929 by Jonathan Cape and H. Smith, © renewed 1957 by Frieda Lawrence; **482** 'Kangaroo' copyright 1923 by Thomas Seltzer, Inc., copyright renewed 1951 by Frieda Lawrence.

483. Reprinted by permission of Martin Secker and Warburg Ltd from *Complete Poems* by Andrew Young, edited by Leonard Clark.

485. Reprinted by permission of Faber and Faber Ltd from *The Collected Poems of Edwin Muir*.

486–7. Reprinted by permission of Faber and Faber Ltd and of Harcourt Brace Jovanovich, Inc. from *Collected Poems 1909–1962* by T. S. Eliot. Copyright 1936 by Harcourt Brace Jovanovich, Inc; copyright © 1963, 1964 by T. S. Eliot.

488–9. Reprinted by permission of the Author's Literary Estate and Chatto and Windus; and of Oxford University Press, Inc., from *The Collected Works of Isaac Rosenberg*, edited by Ian Parsons. Copyright © The Literary Executors of Mrs A. Wynick, 1937 and 1979.

490–1. Reprinted by permission of Routledge and Kegan Paul Ltd, London, from *The Hugh MacDiarmid Anthology 1972*, edited by Michael Grieve and Alexander Scott.

492–3. Reprinted by permission of Granada Publishing Ltd from *Lap of Honour* by Hugh MacDiarmid.

496. Reprinted by permission of Harper and Row, Publishers, Inc. from *The Collected Poetry of Aldous Huxley*, edited by Donald Watt. Copyright 1929, 1931 by Aldous Huxley.

497. Reprinted by permission of Faber and Faber Ltd from *The Anathemata* by David Jones.

498–501. Reprinted by kind permission of Robert Graves.

503–4. Reprinted by permission of the Trustees of the National Gallery of Scotland. (William Soutar was bedridden for the last thirteen years of his life.)

505. Reprinted by permission of Collins Publishers from *Poems* by C. S. Lewis, edited by Walter Hooper.

506. Reprinted by permission of Collins Publishers and of Harcourt Brace Jovanovich, Inc. from *Poems* by C. S. Lewis, edited by Walter Hooper, copyright © 1964 by the Executors of the Estate of C. S. Lewis.

507. Reprinted by permission of James MacGibbon, executor of the Stevie Smith Estate, from *The Collected Poems of Stevie Smith*, Allen Lane, 1975.

508. Reprinted by permission of Mrs Sonia Brownell Orwell and Martin Secker and Warburg Ltd from *George Orwell: Collected Journalism and Letters*.

509–10. Reprinted by permission of Chatto and Windus and of Harcourt Brace Jovanovich, Inc. from *Collected Poems* by William Empson. Copyright 1949, 1977 by William Empson.

511–12. Reprinted by permission of John Murray (Publishers) Ltd and of Houghton Mifflin Company from *Collected Poems* by John Betjeman.

513. Reprinted by permission of Faber and Faber Ltd and of Random House Inc., New York, from *The English Auden*, by W. H. Auden.

514–16. Reprinted by permission of Faber and Faber Ltd and of Random House Inc., New York, from *Collected Poems* by W. H. Auden.

517–18. Reprinted by permission of Faber and Faber Ltd from *The Collected Poems of Louis MacNeice*.

519. Reprinted by permission of Faber and Faber Ltd and of Curtis Brown Ltd, Authors' Agents, from *Collected Poems* by Lawrence Durrell.

520. Reprinted by permission of Faber and Faber Ltd and of The Overlook Press, New York, from *Vega* by Lawrence Durrell.

521. Reprinted by permission of Faber and Faber Ltd and of John Johnson, Authors' Agents, from *Poems of Places and People* by George Barker.

522–5. Reprinted by permission of the Trustees for the Copyrights of the late Dylan Thomas, and of New Directions, New York from *The Poems* of Dylan Thomas published by J. M. Dent and Sons Ltd and New Directions. Copyright 1939, 1943, 1946 by New Directions Publishing Corporation.

526. Reprinted by permission of Oxford University Press from *Selected Poems* by John Heath-Stubbs, 1965.

527–8. Reprinted by permission of the Enitharmon Press from *Artorius* by John Heath-Stubbs.

529–30. Reprinted by permission of The Marvell Press, England, from *The Less Deceived* by Philip Larkin.

531–2. Reprinted by permission of Faber and Faber Ltd from *The Whitsun Weddings* by Philip Larkin.

533–4. Reprinted by permission of Faber and Faber Ltd and of Farrar, Straus and Giroux, Inc. from *High Windows* by Philip Larkin. Copyright © 1974 by Philip Larkin.

535. Reprinted by permission of Martin Secker and Warburg Ltd, Publishers, from *The Man I Killed* by Laurence Lerner.

536. Reprinted by permission of Macmillan, London and Basingstoke, and of Viking Penguin Inc. from *Wildtrack* by John Wain. Copyright © 1965 by John Wain.

537. Reprinted by permission of Carcanet Press from *Selected Poems* by Elizabeth Jennings.

538. Reprinted by permission of A. D. Peters and Company Ltd.

539. Reprinted by permission of Faber and Faber Ltd from *Lupercal* by Ted Hughes; and of Harper and Row, Publishers, Inc. from *Selected Poems* by Ted Hughes. Copyright © 1960 by Ted Hughes.

540. Reprinted by permission of Faber and Faber Ltd, and of Harper and Row, Publishers, Inc. from *Lupercal* by Ted Hughes. Copyright © 1960 by Ted Hughes.

541. Reprinted from *Five Ages*, © Peter Levi, 1978. Published by Anvil Press Poetry.

542. Reprinted by permission of Faber and Faber Ltd, and of Oxford University Press, Inc. from *Wintering Out* by Seamus Heaney. Copyright © 1972 by Seamus Heaney.

543. Reprinted by permission of Faber and Faber Ltd, and of Farrar, Straus and Giroux, Inc. from *Fieldwork* by Seamus Heaney. Copyright © 1976, 1979 by Seamus Heaney.

544. Reprinted by permission of George Allen and Unwin from *Vanishing Trick* by Brian Patten.

Index of Authors

References are to page numbers

Index of Titles and First Lines

Titles are printed in italics; references are to page numbers